Fundamentals of
Management 10e

Ricky W. Griffin
Texas A&M University

CENGAGE

Australia • Brazil • Canada • Mexico • Singapore • United Kingdom • United States

Fundamentals of Management, Tenth Edition

Ricky W. Griffin

Senior Vice President, Higher Education & Skills Product: Erin Joyner

Product Director: Joe Sabatino

Senior Product Manager: Heather Mooney

Learning Designer: Courtney Wolstoncroft

Content Manager: Kate Begley Reed

Product Assistant: Nick Perez

Marketing Manager: Audrey Wyrick

Marketing Coordinator: Alexis Cortez

Intellectual Property Analyst: Diane Garrity

Intellectual Property Project Manager: Kelli Besse

Production Service: SPi Global

Art Director: Bethany Bourgeois

Text Designer: Tippy McIntosh/ Bethany Bourgeois

Cover Designer: Foo Toon Check

Cover Image:
© iStock.com/Olemedia

For product information and technology assistance, contact us at
Cengage Learning Asia Customer Service, 65-6410-1200

We reserve the right to refuse any product and/or technology assistance if this book is used outside Asia

For permission to use material from this text or product, submit all requests online at **www.cengage.com/permissions**

Further permissions questions can be e-mailed to
asia.permissionrequest@cengage.com

ISBN: 978-981-49-8623-6

Cengage Learning Asia Pte Ltd
151 Lorong Chuan
#02-08 New Tech Park
Singapore 556741

Cengage is a leading provider of customized learning solutions with office locations around the globe. In Asia, we have offices in 11 territories including Singapore, China, Japan, Korea, Malaysia and more. To locate your nearest local office or sales representative, kindly visit **www.cengageasia.com/office-address**

To learn more about Cengage digital solutions, e-learning options or titles, please visit **www.cengageasia.com**

Printed in Singapore
Print Number: 01   Print Year: 2021

For Andrew Preston Griffin
My first grandson and bearer of important family names—I love you, Drew

Brief Contents

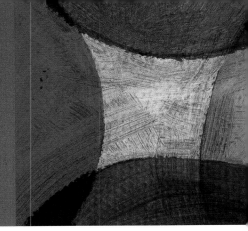

Contents

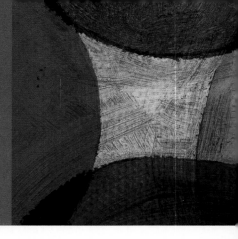

PART 2   Planning

PART 3   Organizing

PART 4   Leading

CHAPTER 9
Basic Elements of Individual Behavior in Organizations   235

PART 5   Controlling

Preface

Hundreds of books have been written for introductory management courses. As the theory, research, and practice of management has grown and expanded, authors have continued to mirror this expansion of material in their books. Writers have understood the importance of adding new material about traditional topics, such as planning and organizing, while simultaneously adding coverage of emerging newer topics, such as sustainability, ethics, and social media. As a by-product of this trend, our traditional textbooks have grown longer and longer but also more difficult to cover in one course.

Another trend in management education is a focus on teaching in a broader context. That is, introductory management courses are increasingly being taught with less emphasis on theory alone and more emphasis on the application of concepts. Teaching students how to apply management concepts successfully often involves focusing more on skills development and the human side of the organization. This trend requires that books cover theoretical concepts within a flexible framework that enables instructors to make use of interactive tools such as case studies, exercises, and projects. It also dictates that a text be as relevant to students as possible. Hence, while this book draws examples and cases from older large businesses like Ford, IBM, and General Electric, it also makes extensive use of newer firms such as Google, Tesla, Netflix, Facebook, Starbucks, Urban Outfitters, and others.

Indeed, this book represents a synthesis of these trends toward a more manageable and practical approach. By combining concise text discussion, proven pedagogical tools, lively and current content, an emphasis on organizational behavior, and exciting skills development material, *Fundamentals of Management* answers the need for a new approach to management education. This book provides almost limitless flexibility, a solid foundation of knowledge-based material, and an action-oriented learning dimension unique in the field. Indeed, over half a million students were introduced to the field of management using the first nine editions of this book. This tenth edition builds solidly on the successes of the earlier editions.

ORGANIZATION OF THE BOOK

Most management instructors today organize their course around the traditional management functions of planning, organizing, leading, and controlling. *Fundamentals of Management* uses these functions as its organizing framework. The book consists of five parts, with fifteen chapters.

Part One introduces management through two chapters. Chapter 1 provides a basic overview of the management process in organizations, and Chapter 2 introduces students to the environment of management. Part Two covers the first basic management function, planning. Chapter 3 introduces the fundamental concepts of planning and discusses strategic management. Managerial decision making is the topic of Chapter 4. Finally, Chapter 5 covers entrepreneurship and the management of new ventures.

The second basic management function, organizing, is the subject of Part Three. In Chapter 6, the fundamental concepts of organization structure and design are introduced and discussed. Chapter 7 explores organization change and organizational innovation. Chapter 8 is devoted to the management of human resources.

Many instructors and managers believe that the third basic management function, leading, is especially important in contemporary organizations. Thus, Part Four consists of five chapters devoted to this management function. Basic concepts and processes associated with individual behavior are introduced and discussed in Chapter 9. Employee motivation is the subject of Chapter 10. Chapter 11 examines leadership and influence processes in organizations. Communication in organizations is the topic of Chapter 12. The management of groups and teams is covered in Chapter 13.

The fourth management function, controlling, is the subject of Part Five. Chapter 14 introduces the fundamental concepts and issues associated with management of the control process. A special area of control today, managing for total quality, is discussed in Chapter 15.

SKILLS-FOCUSED PEDAGOGICAL FEATURES

Both the overarching framework and streamlined topical coverage make it possible to address new dimensions of management education without creating a book so long that it is unwieldy. Specifically, each chapter is followed by a proven, applied set of skills-based exercises and related activities. These resources have been created to bring an active and a behavioral orientation to management education by inviting students to solve problems, make decisions, respond to situations, and work in teams. In short, these materials simulate many of the day-to-day challenges and opportunities that real managers face.

The Summary of Learning Objectives and Key Points ties content and student learning back to the objectives introduced at the beginning of the chapter and three kinds of Discussion Questions (Review, Analysis, and Application) help transition from content mastery to skills applications. Among the true skills-based exercises are two different *Building Effective Skills* features organized around the set of basic management skills introduced in Chapter 1. A *Skills Self-Assessment Instrument* exercise also helps readers learn something about their own approach to management.

New to the tenth edition, each chapter also contains interesting boxed features, two per chapter, centered around **sustainability**, **leadership**, **technology**, **diversity**, and **nontraditional settings**. These features depart briefly from the flow of the chapter to highlight or extend especially interesting or emerging points and issues related to boxed feature titles.

In addition to the end-of-chapter exercises, every chapter includes important time-tested and proven pedagogy: learning objectives, a chapter outline, an opening case, key terms, photographs with captions, tables, figures, an end-of-chapter case with questions, and questions tied back to the opening case.

CHANGES TO THE TENTH EDITION

The tenth edition of *Fundamentals of Management* retains the same basic structure and format as the previous edition. However, within that framework the content of the book has been thoroughly revised and updated. The following changes are illustrative of the new material that has been added:

(1) New topical coverage related to both domestic and global economic conditions is included. The book also places greater emphasis on the services sector of the economy. Coverage of managerial and organizational implications of the 2020 COVID-19 pandemic, the resulting economic impact of the pandemic on businesses, and other topical issues has also been added. Moreover, all data regarding international business activity, entrepreneurship and small businesses, and workforce diversity have been updated to the most current figures available.

(2) Several of the newest management techniques are also included in this edition. Examples include prospect theory and evidence-based management. These and other new techniques are discussed in several places in the book.

(3) The latest research findings regarding globalization, strategic management, organizing, motivation, leadership, and control have been incorporated into the text and referenced at the end of the book. Over 150 new articles and books are cited.

(4) Virtually all of the cases and boxed inserts are new to this edition of *Fundamentals of Management*, while the few retained from earlier editions have been updated as needed. They reflect a wide variety of organizations and illustrate both successful and less successful practices and decisions.

(5) As noted earlier, this book features a rich and diverse array of end-of-chapter materials to facilitate both learning and skill development. For this edition, a substantial portion of this material has been replaced or substantially revised.

SUPPLEMENTS

Instructor Support Materials

- Instructor Companion Website: Instructors can find course support materials, including Instructor's Resource Manual, Test Bank files, and PowerPoint® slides.

- Instructor's Manual: Designed to provide support for instructors new to the course, as well as innovative materials for experienced professors, the Instructor's Manual includes activities and assessments for each chapter and their correlation to specific learning objectives, an outline, key terms with definitions, a chapter summary, and ideas for engaging with students–such as discussion questions, ice breakers, case studies, and social learning activities that may be conducted in an on-ground, hybrid, or online modality.

- Cengage Learning Testing Powered by Cognero: Cognero is a flexible online system that allows you to author, edit, and manage test bank content from multiple Cengage Learning solutions; create multiple test versions in an instant; and deliver tests from your LMS, your classroom, or wherever you want.

- PowerPoint Lecture Presentation: The PowerPoint Lecture Presentations are closely tied to the Instructor Manual, providing ample opportunities for generating classroom discussion and interaction. They offer ready-to-use, visual outlines of each chapter, which may be easily customized for your lectures.

- Guide to Teaching Online: This guide presents technological and pedagogical considerations and suggestions for teaching the Management course when you can't be in the same room with students.

- Transition Guide: This guide highlights all of the changes in the text and in the digital offerings from the previous edition to this edition.

Student Support Materials

- MindTap brings together quality learning and convenience through seamless, LMS integrated access to a curated set learning tools designed intentionally for the Principles of Management learner. Each MindTap follows a "Learn It, Apply It, Study It" structure that guides students through bite sized learning exercises, followed by authentic scenario-based application opportunities and then gives them the necessary tools to prepare for quizzes and exams.

- WHY DOES THIS TOPIC MATTER TO ME? Each major part of the course is introduced in MindTap with a "Why Does [This Topic] Matter to Me?" to help showcase relevance and applicability of the material students are about to learn–in an engaging, fun format.

- LEARN IT ACTIVITIES: New "Learn It" modules are designed to help students learn the basics of theories and concepts presented in a chapter through digestible summaries and randomized questions that help check their comprehension of the chapter material.

- APPLY IT CHAPTER ASSIGNMENTS & CASE ACTIVITIES: "Apply It" Chapter Assignments and Case Activities bridge the understanding of concepts with their real-world applications in the practice of management.

- STUDY IT: The "Study It" module for each chapter includes Practice Tests powered by A+ Test Prep, a student-powered practice exam tool that allows them to tailor practice tests to fit their needs, and receive immediate feedback and links back to the material they need to review. The "Study It" module also contains digital flashcards to help students practice key terminology and a student-facing version of the PowerPoint slides that accompany the text.

- YOU MAKE THE DECISION: You Make the Decision mini-simulation activities build critical thinking and decision-making skills by challenging students to use what they know about concepts and theories in the context of a scenario as it unfolds. Throughout the scenario, the student would be provided with information and subsequently faced with decisions. The scenario can change dynamically based on the decisions the students make throughout the short simulation, resulting in different end points that showcase the consequences of the decisions made along the way.

Acknowledgments

I would like to acknowledge the many contributions that others have made to this book. My faculty colleagues at Texas A&M University have contributed enormously both to this book and to my thinking about management education. The contributions of Erin Hoelscher, my student assistant, and Phyllis Washburn, my staff assistant, have been invaluable to this revision. My colleague Brad Wesner also handled the revision of the communications chapter. The fine team of professionals at Cengage Learning has been instrumental in the success of this book. Joe Sabatino, Heather Mooney, Allie Janneck, Courtney Wolstoncroft, Kate Begley Reed, Carol Moore, Chandrasekar Subramani, and Mohanarengan Dilli all contributed in myriad ways to this edition. Their attention to detail, student and learning focus, and emphasis on quality have been uniformly impressive.

Many reviewers have played a critical role in the continuous evolution and improvement of this project. They examined my work in detail and with a critical eye. I would like to tip my hat to the following reviewers, whose imprint can be found throughout this text:

Joseph Adamo (Cazenovia College), Sally Alkazin (Linfield College), Robert Ash (Santiago Canyon College), Sherryl Berg-Ridenour (DeVry College–Pomona), Alain Broder (Touro College), Murray Brunton (Central Ohio Tech), Sam Chapman (Diablo Valley College), Elizabeth Anne Christo-Baker (Terra Community College), Gary Corona (Florida Community College–Jacksonville), Dr. Anne Cowden (California State University), Suzanne Crampton (Grand Valley State University), Thomas DeLaughter (University of Florida), Anita Dickson (Northampton Community College), Joe Dobson (Western Illinois University), Michael Dutch (University of Houston), Dale Eesley (University of Nebraska–Omaha), Norb Elbert (Eastern Kentucky University), Teri Elkins (University of Houston), Jan Feldbauer (Schoolcraft College), Tamela D. Ferguson (University of Louisiana at Lafayette), Anne Fiedler (Barry University), Eugene Garaventa (College of Staten Island), Phillip Gonsher (Johnson Community College), Patricia Green (Nassau Community College), John Guess (Delgado Community College), Joseph S. Hooker, Jr. (North Greenville College), David Hudson (Spalding University), George W. Jacobs (Middle Tennessee State University), Tim McCabe (Tompkins Cortland Community College), Garry McDaniel (Franklin University), Lauryn Migenes (University of Central Florida), Christopher Neck (Arizona State University), Judy Nixon (University of Tennessee–Chattanooga), Ranjna Patel (Bethune–Cookman College), Lisa Reed (University of Portland), Virginia Rich (Caldwell College), Dr. Joan Rivera (Angelo State University), Roberta B. Slater (Pennsylvania College of Technology), Bob Smoot (Hazard Community College), Howard Stanger (Canisius College), Sheryl A. Stanley (Newman University), Roy Strickland (Ozarks Technical Community College), Mike L. Stutzman (Mt. Mercy College and Kirkwood College), Abe Tawil (Baruch University), Lynn Turner (California Polytech University–Pomona), Barry Van Hook (Arizona State University), Ruth Weatherly (Simpson College), and Mary Williams (Community College of Nevada).

My wife, Glenda, and our children, Dustin, Ashley, Matt, and Lura, are of course due the greatest thanks. Their love, care, interest, and enthusiasm help sustain me in all that I do. And my grandchildren, Griffin, Sutton, Drew, and Ben, bring joy to my heart and a smile to my face every time I think about them.

I enthusiastically invite your feedback on this book. If you have any questions, suggestions, or issues to discuss, please feel free to contact me. The most efficient way to reach me is through email at rgriffin@tamu.edu.

R.W.G.

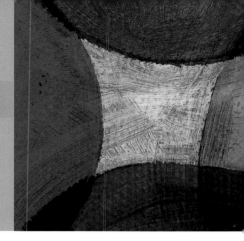

CHAPTER 1

Understanding the Manager's Job

Learning Outcomes

After studying this chapter, you should be able to:

1-1 Describe *management* and the kinds of managers found in organizations.

1-2 Explain the four basic management functions.

1-3 Describe the fundamental management skills and the concept of management as both science and art.

1-4 Explain the importance of history and theory to managers.

1-5 Explain the evolution of management thought through the classical, behavioral, and quantitative perspectives.

1-6 Discuss the key contemporary management perspectives represented by the systems and contingency perspectives.

1-7 Identify the major challenges and opportunities faced by managers today.

In this chapter, we examine the general nature of management, its dimensions, and its challenges. We explain the basic concepts of management and managers, discuss the management process, and summarize the origins of contemporary management thought. We conclude this chapter by introducing critical challenges and issues that managers are facing now and will continue to encounter in the future. First, however, let's examine the work of one successful manager, Reed Hastings.

Reed Hastings Creates Chaos with Netflix

"Don't be afraid to change the model."

—Netflix CEO Reed Hastings

Several years ago, Reed Hastings, a California entrepreneur, incurred a $40 late fee at Blockbuster. "It was six weeks late," he admits. "I had misplaced the cassette [and] I didn't want to tell my wife. . . . I was embarrassed about it." The next day he dropped off the VHS cassette and paid the late fee on his way to the local gym. As it turns out, his itinerary for the day was quite opportune: In the middle of his workout, he recalls, "I realized [the gym] had a much better business model. You could pay $30 or $40 a month and work out as little or as much as you wanted."

Thus was born the idea for Netflix—paying a monthly fee for unlimited video rentals. But Hastings knew he needed to start slowly. So, when Netflix was launched in 1997, its only real innovation involved the convenience of ordering

karen roach/Shutterstock.com

movies online and receiving and returning them by mail; Netflix merely rented movies for $4 apiece plus $2 for postage (and, yes, it charged late fees). Basically, the customer base consisted of people who wanted to watch movies without having to leave their home. But Hastings and cofounder Marc Randolph then quickly moved to test the subscription-based model, unlimited rentals by mail for a flat fee, and, perhaps more important, no due dates (and thus no late fees). Current customers were first offered the opportunity to shift from their pay-per-rental plans to subscription plans on a free, trial basis and then given the chance to renew the subscription plan on a paid basis. "We knew it wouldn't be terrible," says Hastings, "but we didn't know if it would be great." In the first month, however, 80 percent of Netflix users who'd tried the no-cost subscription plan had renewed on a paid basis.

"Having unlimited due dates and no late fees," said Hastings back in 2003, "has worked in a powerful way and now seems obvious, but at that time, we had no idea if customers would even build and use an online queue." The "queue," as any long-time Netflix user will tell you, was the list of movies that the customer wanted to watch. Netflix maintained your queue, followed your online directions in keeping it up to date, and automatically sent you the next movie you wanted each time you sent one back.

The essence of queuing—and of the original Netflix business model—is clearly convenience. Today, with most users streaming content rather than using DVDs, Netflix has replaced traditional queuing with menus that keep track of what shows you have been watching and suggesting new ones related to your viewing habits. Although the ability to enhance customer convenience, even when combined with cost savings, often gives a company a competitive advantage in its industry, it doesn't always have the industrywide effect that it has had in the case of Netflix. Not only did the Netflix subscriber model improve the service provided by the industry in an unexpected way, but ultimately it also weakened the competitive positions of companies already doing business in the industry—notably, Blockbuster. Blockbuster eventually declared bankruptcy and its few remaining assets are now owned by Dish Network. Netflix, meanwhile, has seen its market cap soar above the $50 billion mark by mid-2016 with more than 61 million subscribers in 57 countries.

How had Hastings's upstart company managed to put itself in such an enviable position? For one thing, it got off to a fast start. In 1997, when DVDs were just being test-marketed in the United States, Hastings and Randolph gambled that the new medium would eventually overtake videocassettes as the format of choice for both the home-movie industry and the home-movie renter. They were right, of course— by 2002, one in four U.S. households owned a DVD player, but the number today is more than nine in ten. (In any case, it would have cost about $4 to mail a videocassette both ways compared to the $0.78 that it costs to ship a DVD back and forth.)

More important, as the first company to rent movies by mail, Netflix was the first to establish a rental-by-mail customer base. At first, says Hastings, "people thought the idea was crazy. But it was precisely because it was a contrarian idea that [it] enabled us to get ahead of our competitors." As Netflix has continued to expand and nurture its subscriber base, it has also generated both brand recognition and brand loyalty. "Netflix has customer loyalty. It's a passion brand," explains Hastings, who hastens to add that keeping customers happy is crucial "because the more someone uses Netflix, the more likely they are to stay with us."

Netflix also puts a premium on hiring the very best people. Hastings hires bright people, pays them above-market wages, and provides innovative and interesting benefits. For instance, Netflix employees can take as much vacation time as they

organization
A group of people working together in a structured and coordinated fashion to achieve a set of goals

management
A set of activities (including planning and decision making, organizing, leading, and controlling) directed at an organization's resources (human, financial, physical, and information) with the aim of achieving organizational goals in an efficient and effective manner

want so long as they perform their jobs at a high level. But at the same time, the firm has very high performance standards and employees sometimes complain about too much pressure. As Hastings says, "We treat our top performers very well. We provide average employees with reasonable severance package[s]."

Today Netflix continues to be at the forefront of innovation and has established a strong position in the growing video-on-demand market. In 2013, the company obtained exclusive rights to distribute the original series *The House of Cards*, *Hemlock Grove*, *Orange Is the New Black*, and the revival of *Arrested Development*. Netflix soon began to expand its list of original offerings such as *Russian Doll* and *Unbelievable* and by 2020 was showing more original series and movies than any other media outlet. All told, Netflix's 61 million subscribers watch about 4 billion hours of programs every quarter on more than 1,000 different devices—indeed, on a normal evening, Netflix accounts for over a third of all internet usage in North America! And viewership surged even further during the 2020 COVID-19 pandemic.

Never one to stand still, Reed Hastings continues to look for the "next big thing." Unlike most traditional managers, Hastings doesn't have an office. He simply wanders around headquarters, talking to people about their work and their ideas, and occasionally grabbing an empty chair or desk to check his email. When he needs solitude to think and ponder major decisions, he retreats to a rooftop "cube" with four glass walls overlooking the Santa Cruz Mountains. And from that cube, Hastings will continue to ponder his next set of moves.[1]

1-1 AN INTRODUCTION TO MANAGEMENT

An organization is a group of people working together in a structured and coordinated fashion to achieve a set of goals, which may include profit (Netflix, Starbucks, and Facebook), the discovery of knowledge (the University of Nebraska or the National Science Foundation), national defense (the U.S. Navy or Marines), the coordination of various local charities (the United Way of America), or social satisfaction (a fraternity or sorority).

manager
Someone whose primary responsibility is to carry out the management process

efficient
Using resources wisely in a cost-effective way

effective
Making the right decisions and successfully implementing them

Managers are responsible for using the organization's resources to help achieve its goals. More precisely, management can be defined as a set of activities (including planning and decision making, organizing, leading, and controlling) directed at an organization's resources (human, financial, physical, and information) with the aim of achieving organizational goals in an efficient and effective manner. A manager, then, is someone whose primary responsibility is to carry out the management process. By efficient, we mean using resources wisely in a cost-effective way. By effective, we mean making the right decisions and successfully implementing them. In general, successful organizations are both efficient and effective.[2]

To be effective, businesses must produce products that consumers are willing to buy. A company like Sony could very efficiently produce portable cassette tape players like this one but will not be successful.

Today's managers face myriad interesting and challenging situations. The average executive works at least 62.5 hours a week; has enormous demands placed on his or her time; and faces increased complexities posed by globalization, domestic competition, government regulation, shareholder pressure, emerging technologies, the growing impact of social media, and other technology-driven uncertainties. Their job is complicated even more by rapid changes, unexpected disruptions (such as the COVID-19 pandemic in 2020), and both minor and major crises. The manager's job is unpredictable and fraught with challenges, but it is also filled with opportunities to make a difference. Good managers can propel an organization into unprecedented realms of success, whereas poor managers can devastate even the strongest of organizations.[3]

Axel Bueckert/Shutterstock.com

1-1a Kinds of Managers

Many different kinds of managers work in organizations today. Figure 1.1 shows how various kinds of managers within an organization can be differentiated by level and by area.

Levels of Management   One way to classify managers is in terms of their level in the organization. *Top managers* make up the relatively small group of executives who manage the overall organization. Titles found in this group include president, vice president (VP), and chief executive officer (CEO). Top managers create the organization's goals, overall strategy, and operating policies. They also officially represent the organization to the external environment by meeting with government officials, executives of other organizations, and so forth.

Reed Hastings is a top manager. Kevin Johnson, CEO of Starbucks, is also a top manager, as is Matthew Ryan, the firm's global chief marketing executive. Likewise, Mark Zuckerberg (Facebook's founder and top executive), Tim Cook (CEO of Apple), and Mary Barra (CEO of General Motors) are also top managers. The job of a top manager is likely to be complex and varied. Top managers make decisions about activities such as acquiring other companies, investing in R&D, entering or abandoning various markets, and building new plants and office facilities. They often work long hours and spend much of their time in meetings or on their phones. In most cases, top managers are also very well paid. In fact, the elite top managers of very large firms sometimes make several million dollars a year in salary, bonuses, and stock.[4] In 2019, Starbucks' Kevin Johnson received total compensation of $13.4 million. This total included a base salary, a bonus, stock and option awards, and other forms of compensation.

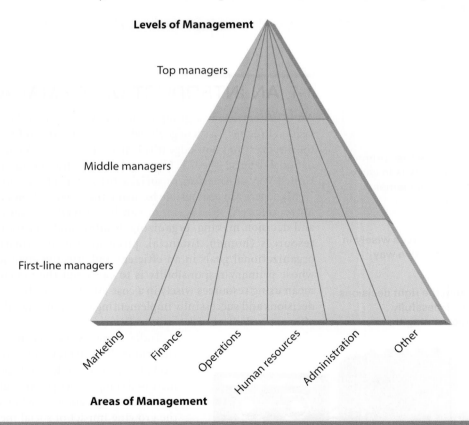

FIGURE 1.1

Kinds of Managers by Level and Area

Organizations generally have three levels of management, represented by top managers, middle managers, and first-line managers. Regardless of level, managers are also usually associated with a specific area within the organization, such as marketing, finance, operations, human resources, administration, or some other area.

Mary Barra, CEO of General Motors, is a top manager. She makes major decisions about the firm's competitive strategies, organizational structure, research-and-development investments, new facilities, other senior leaders, and strategic alliances.

Middle management is probably the largest group of managers in most organizations. Common middle-management titles include plant manager, operations manager, and division head. *Middle managers* are primarily responsible for implementing the policies and plans developed by top managers and for supervising and coordinating the activities of lower-level managers. Jason Hernandez, a regional manager at Starbucks responsible for the firm's operations in three eastern states, is a middle manager.

First-line managers supervise and coordinate the activities of operating employees. Common titles for first-line managers are supervisor, coordinator, and office manager. Positions like these are often the first held by employees who enter management from the ranks of operating personnel. John Koch and Nita Garcia, managers of Starbucks coffee shops in Texas, are first-line managers. They oversee the day-to-day operations of their respective stores, hire operating employees to staff them, and handle other routine administrative duties required of them by the parent corporation. In contrast to top and middle managers, first-line managers typically spend a large proportion of their time supervising the work of their subordinates.

1-1b Managing in Different Areas of the Organization

Regardless of their level, managers may work in various areas within an organization. In any given firm, for example, these areas may include marketing, financial, operations, human resources, administrative, and others.

Marketing managers work in areas related to the marketing function—getting consumers and clients to buy the organization's products or services (be they Samsung smartphones, Subaru automobiles, *Entertainment Weekly* magazines, Associated Press news reports, streaming video rentals from Netflix or Disney+, or lattes at Starbucks). These areas include new product development, promotion, and distribution. Given the importance of marketing for virtually all organizations, developing good managers in this area is critical.

Financial managers deal primarily with an organization's financial resources. They are responsible for activities such as accounting, cash management, and investments. In some businesses, especially banking and insurance, financial managers are found in large numbers.

Operations managers are concerned with creating and managing the systems that create an organization's products and services. Typical responsibilities of operations managers include production control, inventory control, quality control, plant layout, and site selection.

Human resources managers are responsible for hiring and developing employees. They are typically involved in human resource planning, recruiting and selecting employees, training and development, designing compensation and benefit systems, formulating performance appraisal systems, and discharging low-performing and problem employees.

Administrative, or general, managers are not associated with any particular management specialty. Probably the best example of an administrative management position is that of a hospital or clinic administrator. Administrative managers tend to be generalists; they have some basic familiarity with all functional areas of management rather than specialized training in any one area.[5]

Many organizations have specialized management positions in addition to those already described. Public relations managers, for example, deal with the public and media for firms such as Facebook, Instagram, and Unilever to protect and enhance the image of their organizations. R&D managers coordinate the activities of scientists and engineers working on scientific projects in organizations such as Google, Shell Oil, and NASA. Internal consultants are used in organizations such as Prudential Insurance to provide specialized expert advice to operating managers. International operations are often coordinated by specialized managers in organizations like Walmart and General Electric. The number, nature, and importance of these specialized managers vary tremendously from one organization to another. As contemporary organizations continue to grow in complexity and size, the number and importance of such managers are also likely to increase. Our *Tech Watch* feature highlights one newly emerging management position, the social media manager.

Manager's Checklist

☐ Managers use a mix of resources—human, financial, physical, and information—to promote efficiency and effectiveness.

☐ Organizations need managers at multiple levels. The most common classifications by level are top, middle, and first-line managers. Large organizations usually have multiple levels within each of these broad categories.

☐ Organizations also need managers within different areas, such as marketing, finance, operations, human resources, general administration, and other areas.

☐ While it may seem like common sense, you should always have an understanding of the level and area of both your current job and the next job you aspire to have.

1-2 BASIC MANAGEMENT FUNCTIONS

Regardless of level or area, management involves the four basic functions of planning and decision making, organizing, leading, and controlling. This book is organized around these basic functions, as shown in Figure 1.2.

FIGURE 1.2

The Management Process

Management involves four basic activities—planning and decision making, organizing, leading, and controlling. Although there is a basic logic for describing these activities in this sequence (as indicated by the solid arrows), most managers engage in more than one activity at a time and often move back and forth between the activities in unpredictable ways (as shown by the dotted arrows).

1-2a **Planning and Decision Making**

planning
Setting an organization's goals and deciding how best to achieve them

decision making
Part of the planning process that involves selecting a course of action from a set of alternatives

organizing
Determining how activities and resources are to be grouped

In its simplest form, planning means setting an organization's goals and deciding how best to achieve them. Decision making, a part of the planning process, involves selecting a course of action from a set of alternatives. Planning and decision making help managers maintain their effectiveness by serving as guides for their future activities. In other words, the organization's goals and plans clearly help managers know how to allocate their time and resources. Part 2 of this book is devoted to planning and decision-making activities and concepts.

1-2b **Organizing**

Once a manager has set goals and developed a workable plan, his or her next management function is to organize people and the other resources necessary to carry out the plan. Specifically, organizing involves determining how activities and resources are to be grouped. Although some people equate this function with the creation of an organization chart, we will see in Part 3 that it is actually much more.

TECH WATCH

". . . But What Is a Social Media Manager?"

While operations, marketing, and financial managers have been common in organizations for several decades, recent years have seen the emergence of a new kind of manager—social media managers. According to Ashley Coombe, social media strategy consultant, "2013 was the year social media managers earned legitimacy. . . . Business owners began to realize that they could no longer hire their friend's daughter to do their social media just because she had a lot of friends on Facebook." (2013 was the year that Twitter went public and Facebook acquired Instagram.)

Just what do *social media managers* do? Why is your friend's daughter likely to be in over her head? It's a pretty new position, so job descriptions understandably vary. Here, however, is a generic description crafted by a veteran social media executive:

> The Social Media Manager will implement the Company's Social Media Strategy, developing brand awareness, generating inbound traffic, and encouraging product adoption. This role coordinates with the internal marketing and PR teams to support their respective missions, ensuring consistency in voice and cultivating a social media referral network.

Primarily, social media managers handle information and communications through social media outlets—tracking trends and determining posting rates, creating positive communications, and maintaining a congenial media relationship with a company's community of customers. As you can also see from the job description, a key function of the position is *coordination*. Typically, social media managers work out of marketing departments and perform a variety of marketing-related tasks—replying to customer inquiries (sales), responding to customer complaints (customer service), and handling external communications (public relations). At the same time, however, because they often manage the use of social media among all of a company's employees and communicate information about all of its activities, the scope of responsibilities is companywide.

Even with all of this newfound responsibility, some social media managers aren't quite sure how much "legitimacy" they've earned. "At the last place I was a social media manager," reports one brand specialist at a large corporation, "high-level VPs would come over and say I was messing around on the internet too much." According to another veteran of corporate media management, "the biggest misconception is that, compared to other marketers, we don't understand analytics or don't have the education or background when it comes to the technical side." Old-school executives, charges a third social media strategist, "see [social media] as the warm and fuzzy side of marketing. In reality," he says, "it's a powerful revenue driver when it's given proper funding and attention. . . . When you show them the ROI, people start changing their minds."

References: Erik Sass, "Marketers Plan to Spend More on Social Media in 2020," *The Social Graf*, www.mediapost.com on February 2, 2020; Blaise Grimes-Viort, "Social Media Manager Job Description," *Online Communities and Social Media*, http://blaisegv.com on December 5, 2019; Julian Rio, "Social Media Manager: What Role Does He Really Have?" *JulianRio.com Marketing Solutions*, www.julianrio.com on January 2, 2020; "Confessions of Big Brand Social Media Managers," *Digiday*, http://digiday.com on January 2, 2020.

1-2c Leading

leading
The set of processes used to get members of the organization to work together to further the interests of the organization

The third basic managerial function is leading. Some people consider leading to be both the most important and the most challenging of all managerial activities. Leading is the set of processes used to get members of the organization to work together to further the interests of the organization. We cover the leading function in detail in Part 4.

"We have good people. They just need a leader who can guide and inspire them."

—William Clay Ford, Chairman of Ford[6]

1-2d Controlling

controlling
Monitoring organizational progress toward goal attainment

The final phase of the management process is controlling, or monitoring the organization's progress toward its goals. As the organization moves toward its goals, managers must monitor progress to ensure that it is performing in such a way as to arrive at its "destination" at the appointed time. Part 5 explores the control function.

Manager's Checklist

- ☐ The management process involves a variety of functions. The primary management functions are planning and decision making, organizing, leading, and controlling.

- ☐ Remember, though, that as a manager your activities will typically not follow a predictable and logical sequence and that the resources you manage may vary in unexpected ways.

1-3 FUNDAMENTAL MANAGEMENT SKILLS

To carry out these management functions most effectively, managers rely on a number of different fundamental management skills and apply them through a mix of science and art. While literally hundreds of skills have been proposed for managers, the most important are technical, interpersonal, conceptual, diagnostic, communication, decision-making, and time management skills.[7] Our *Leading the Way* feature also illustrates how one successful manager has relied on both basic management functions and fundamental management skills to propel herself to the top of a successful corporation.

technical skills
The skills necessary to accomplish or understand the specific kind of work done in an organization

Technical Skills   Technical skills are necessary to accomplish or understand the specific kind of work done in an organization. Technical skills are especially important for first-line managers. These managers spend much of their time training their subordinates and answering questions about work-related problems. If they are to be effective managers, they must know how to perform the tasks assigned to those they supervise. While Reed Hastings now spends most of his time dealing with strategic and management issues, he also keeps abreast of new and emerging technologies and trends that may affect Netflix.

interpersonal skills
The ability to communicate with, understand, and motivate both individuals and groups

Interpersonal Skills   Managers spend considerable time interacting with people both inside and outside the organization. For obvious reasons, then, they also need interpersonal skills—the ability to communicate with, understand, and motivate both individuals and groups. As a manager climbs the organizational ladder, he or she must be able to get along with subordinates, peers, and those at higher levels of the organization. Because of the multitude of roles that managers must fulfill, a manager must also be able to work with suppliers, customers, investors, and others outside the organization.

conceptual skills
The manager's ability to think in the abstract

Conceptual Skills   Conceptual skills depend on the manager's ability to think in the abstract. Managers need the mental capacity to understand the overall workings of the organization and its environment, to grasp how all the parts of the organization fit together, and to view the organization in a holistic manner. This ability allows them to think strategically, to see the "big picture," and to make broad-based decisions that serve the overall organization. Reed Hastings's idea to extend the payment model used by health clubs to the video rental market came from his strong conceptual skills.

diagnostic skills
The manager's ability to visualize the most appropriate response to a situation

Diagnostic Skills   Successful managers also possess diagnostic skills that enable them to visualize the most appropriate response to a situation. A physician diagnoses a patient's illness by analyzing symptoms and determining their probable cause. Similarly, a manager can diagnose and analyze a problem in the organization by studying its symptoms and then developing a solution.[8]

communication skills
The manager's abilities both to effectively convey ideas and information to others and to effectively receive ideas and information from others

Communication Skills   Communication skills refer to the manager's abilities to both effectively convey ideas and information to others and effectively receive ideas and information from others. These skills enable a manager to transmit ideas to subordinates so that they know what is expected, to coordinate work with peers and colleagues so that they work well together, and to keep higher-level managers informed about what is going on. In addition, communication skills help the manager listen to what others say and to understand the real meaning behind emails, texts, letters, reports, and other written communication.

decision-making skills
The manager's ability to correctly recognize and define problems and opportunities and to then select an appropriate course of action to solve problems and capitalize on opportunities

Decision-Making Skills   Effective managers also have good decision-making skills. Decision-making skills refer to the manager's ability to correctly recognize and define problems and opportunities and to then select an appropriate course of action to solve problems and capitalize on opportunities. No manager makes the right decision all the time. However, effective managers make good decisions most of the time. And, when they do make a bad decision, they usually recognize their mistake quickly and then make good decisions to recover with as little cost or damage to their organization as possible. Managers at Netflix made a poor decision when they decided to split their mail delivery and streaming services into two businesses, but they quickly reversed themselves before things got too bad.

"The important thing, besides getting up early, is to have a system by which you manage your tasks."

—Chad Dickerson, CEO of ETSY[9]

time management skills
The manager's ability to prioritize work, to work efficiently, and to delegate appropriately

Time Management Skills   Finally, effective managers usually have good time management skills. Time management skills refer to the manager's ability to prioritize work, to work efficiently, and to delegate work appropriately. As already noted, managers face many different pressures and challenges. It is too easy for a manager to get bogged down doing work that can easily be postponed or delegated to others.[10] When this happens, unfortunately, more pressing and higher-priority work may get neglected.[11]

The Egyptians used basic management functions to construct the pyramids.

Dan Breckwoldt/Shutterstock.com

1-3a **The Science and the Art of Management**

Given the complexity inherent in the manager's job, a reasonable question relates to whether management is a science or an art. In fact, effective management is a blend of both science and art. And successful executives recognize the importance of combining both the science and art of management as they practice their craft.[12]

The Science of Management   Many management problems and issues can be approached in ways that are rational, logical, objective, and systematic. Managers can gather data, facts, and objective information. They can use quantitative models and decision-making techniques to arrive at "correct" decisions. And they need to take such a scientific approach to solving problems whenever possible, especially when they are dealing with relatively routine and straightforward issues. When

Starbucks considers entering a new market, its managers look closely at a wide variety of objective details as they formulate their plans. Technical, diagnostic, and decision-making skills are especially important when approaching a management task or problem from a scientific perspective.

LEADING THE WAY

On the Fast Track

Kat Cole started her climb up the corporate ladder in orange shorts. At 16, she took a part-time job serving chicken wings and beer at Hooters, and 19 years later—at the relatively young age of 35—she was president of Cinnabon, a franchise that sells cinnamon-laced concoctions out of 1,100 locations in 56 countries. In 2015 Cole was promoted to head up Focus Brands, the firm that owns Cinnabon, as well as Moe's and Auntie Anne's, and now leads a team of employees that ranges over four generations in age and includes many men who are much older than she is.

Obviously, it was a fast climb, but Cole didn't skip any rungs (except getting a college degree—she dropped out but eventually earned an MBA). She got started by taking advantage of opportunities that opened up in the Hooters outlet where she was waiting tables. "When the cook quit," Cole reports, "I learned how to run the kitchen, and when the manager quit, I learned how to run a shift." By the time she was 18, her responsibilities included training new employees. "My general manager saw the potential in me," she recalls, "and my role as a trainer expanded to other stores."

A year later, while still in college, Cole was asked to join the company's international expansion team, which was headed to Australia. She spent 40 days with the team in Sydney, and within ten days of her return to the United States, Cole was on her way to open the first Hooters in Central America, "then ones in South America, Asia, Africa, and Canada. By the time I was 20, I'd opened up the first Hooters on most continents outside the U.S. and was failing school. So I quit to become head of Hooters corporate training."

It was worth a 50 percent pay cut, because Cole rose quickly through the ranks, becoming an executive VP at age 26. When she was 29, mentors urged her to go back to school, and so she entered the MBA program at Georgia State. Companies like Cinnabon were already calling, but in 2010, Cole decided to stay at Hooters long enough to take advantage of one more opportunity—helping to manage the sale of the company. She found herself "dealing with analysts, brokers, investors, and the internal team. . . . I would go to class one day and learn about transactions, and I would go to work on Monday and be in the middle of the transaction, and I'd think, 'Thank God I went to class that day.'"

Later in 2010, at age 32, Cole took the job as chief operating officer (COO) of Cinnabon, and two months later, she finished her MBA. She was appointed president of the company in 2011. Under Cole's leadership, Cinnabon opened 200 new outlets (called "bakeries") and entered licensing programs with such franchises as Burger King and Taco Bell. Cole also launched a host of branded products, including a cinnamon-scented air freshener, a cinnamon-flavored vodka, and a cinnamon-spiced Keurig coffee blend (although she vetoed a cinnamon-flavored mouthwash). She has also partnered with international packaged-goods companies such as Pillsbury and Kellogg's and such big-box retailers as Costco, Walmart, and Target. Under Cole's leadership Cinnabon accumulated around 50,000 points of distribution around the world and has more than $1 billion in annual sales. "My management style," she says, "is fast and direct. . . . We totally celebrate fast failure," adds Cole, who's perfectly willing to launch a product that's only 75 percent ready for market. "We move as fast as something feels good."

Clearly, speed to market isn't a strategy for the risk averse. Taking risks means making tough calls, but Cole figures that if she has to make a tough call, it's better to make it too soon rather than too late: "If you don't take a risk," she advises, "your competition will." Ironically, Cole regards moving fast and taking risks as good reasons for pausing to get other people's opinions. Her thinking? By the time you get around to making a decision, "there are usually lots of people around you who've known that it's the right thing to do for a long time. The key, in business and in leadership, is staying really close to the other people who kind of know what's going on so that it doesn't take you too long to figure it out."

References: Catherine Clifford, "How Kat Cole Went from Hooters Girl to President of Cinnabon by Age 32," *Entrepreneur*, www.entrepreneur.com on February 6, 2020; Jenna Goudreau, "From Hooters to Hot Buns: How Kat Cole Turned Cinnabon into a $1 Billion Brand," *Forbes*, November 27, 2012, www.forbes.com on February 6, 2020; Barbara Babbit Kaufman, "Kat Cole: From Hooters Girl to CEO, by Age 35," *Atlanta Business Chronicle*, August 23, 2013, www.bizjournals.com on February 6, 2020; Laura Dunn, "Women in Business: Q&A with Kat Cole, President of Cinnabon," *Huffington Post*, August 8, 2013, www.huffingtonpost.com on April 28, 2017; Lydia Dishman, "How Kat Cole Operates Cinnabon Like a Tech Startup," *Fast Company*, April 9, 2014, www.fastcompany.com on April 28, 2017; and Blair Chancey, "Leadership: Kat Cole Style," *QSR Magazine*, September 2011, www.qsrmagazine.com on June April 28, 2017.

The Art of Management   Even though managers may try to be scientific as often as possible, they must frequently make decisions and solve problems on the basis of intuition, experience, instinct, and personal insights. Relying heavily on conceptual, communication, interpersonal, and time management skills, for example, a manager may have to decide among multiple courses of action that look equally attractive. And even "objective facts" may prove to be wrong. When Starbucks was planning its first store in New York City, market research clearly showed that New Yorkers strongly preferred drip coffee to more exotic espresso-style coffees. After first installing more drip coffee makers and fewer espresso makers than in their other stores, managers had to backtrack when the New Yorkers lined up clamoring for espresso. Starbucks now introduces a standard menu and layout in all its stores, regardless of presumed market differences, and makes necessary adjustments later.[13] Thus, managers must blend an element of intuition and personal insight with hard data and objective facts.

Manager's Checklist

☐   Managers rely on a mix of key skills as they perform their jobs.

☐   You should strive to understand your relative strengths and weaknesses across the key management skills and how those strengths and weaknesses affect your job and job performance.

1-4 THE IMPORTANCE OF THEORY AND HISTORY

Some people question the value of history and theory. Their arguments are usually based on the assumptions that history is not relevant to contemporary society and that theory is abstract and of no practical use. In reality, however, both theory and history are important to all managers today.

1-4a Why Theory?

theory
A conceptual framework for organizing knowledge and providing a blueprint for action

A **theory** is simply a conceptual framework for organizing knowledge and providing a blueprint for action.[14] Although some theories seem abstract and irrelevant, others appear very simple and practical. Management theories, which are used to build organizations and guide them toward their goals, are grounded in reality.[15] Practically any organization that uses assembly lines (such as Toyota and Whirlpool) is drawing on what we describe later in this chapter as *scientific management*. Many organizations, including Nucor and Google, use the behavioral perspective (also introduced later in this chapter) to improve employee satisfaction and motivation. And naming a large company that does not use one or more techniques from the quantitative management perspective would be difficult. For example, retailers such as Kroger, Walmart, and Target routinely use operations management to determine how many checkout lines they need to have open at any given time. In addition, most managers develop and refine their own theories of how they should run their organizations and manage the behavior of their employees. James Sinegal, founder and former CEO of Costco Wholesale, always argued that paying his employees above-market wages while focusing cost-cutting measures elsewhere were the key ingredients in the early success of his business. This belief was essentially based on his personal theory of competition in the warehouse retailing industry.

1-4b Why History?

Awareness and understanding of important historical developments are also important to contemporary managers.[16] Understanding the historical context of management provides a sense of heritage and can help managers avoid the mistakes of others. Most courses in U.S. history devote time to business and economic developments in this country, including the Industrial Revolution, the early labor movement, and the Great Depression, and to captains of

U.S. industry such as Cornelius Vanderbilt (railroads), John D. Rockefeller (oil), and Andrew Carnegie (steel). The contributions of those and other industrialists left a profound imprint on contemporary culture.[17]

Many managers are also realizing that they can benefit from a greater understanding of history in general. For example, Ian M. Ross of AT&T's Bell Laboratories cites *The Second World War* by Winston Churchill as a major influence on his approach to leadership. Other books often mentioned by managers for their relevance to today's business problems include such classics as Plato's *Republic*, Homer's *Iliad*, Sun Tzu's *The Art of War*, and Machiavelli's *The Prince*.[18] And recent business history books have also been directed at women managers and the lessons they can learn from the past.[19]

Managers at Wells Fargo clearly recognize the value of history. For example, the company maintains an extensive archival library of its old banking documents and records, and even employs a full-time corporate historian. As part of their orientation and training, new managers at Wells Fargo take courses to become acquainted with the bank's history.[20] Similarly, Shell Oil, Levi Strauss, Walmart, Lloyd's of London, Disney, Honda, and Unilever all maintain significant archives about their pasts and frequently evoke images from those pasts in their orientation and training programs, advertising campaigns, and other public relations activities.

 **Manager's Checklist**

☐ Don't dismiss theory as something that is too abstract to be relevant—a theory can often be a useful conceptual framework for organizing knowledge and serving as a blueprint for action.

☐ History, too, can serve as a useful tool in today's business world by reminding us of what has and has not worked in the past.

1-5 THE EVOLUTION OF MANAGEMENT

For all of the reasons described previously, most managers today recognize the importance of history and theory in their work. For instance, knowing the origins of their organization and the kinds of practices that have led to success—or failure—can be an indispensable tool in managing the contemporary organization. Thus, in our next section, we briefly trace the history of management thought. Then we move forward to the present day by introducing contemporary management issues and challenges.

1-5a The Historical Context of Management

The practice of management can be traced back thousands of years. The Egyptians used the management functions of planning, organizing, and controlling when they constructed the pyramids. Alexander the Great employed a staff organization to coordinate activities during his military campaigns. The Roman Empire developed a well-defined organizational structure that greatly facilitated communication and control. Socrates discussed management practices and concepts in 400 B.C., Plato described job specialization in 350 B.C., and the Persian scientist and philosopher Al-Farabi listed several leadership traits in A.D. 900.[21]

In spite of this history, the serious study of management did not begin until the nineteenth century. Two of its pioneers were Robert Owen and Charles Babbage. Owen (1771–1858), a British industrialist and reformer, was one of the first managers to recognize the importance of an organization's human resources and to express concern for the personal welfare of his workers. Babbage (1792–1871), an English mathematician, focused his attention on efficiencies of production. He placed great faith in the division of labor and advocated the application of mathematics to such problems as the efficient use of facilities and materials.

1-5b The Classical Management Perspective

Early in the twentieth century, the preliminary ideas and writings of these and other managers and theorists converged with the emergence and evolution of large-scale businesses and management practices. This created interest and focused attention on how businesses should be operated. The first important ideas to emerge are now called the classical management perspective, which actually includes two different viewpoints: scientific management and administrative management.

classical management perspective
Consists of two distinct branches— scientific management and administrative management

Scientific Management   Productivity emerged as a serious business problem during the early years of the twentieth century. Business was expanding and capital was readily available, but labor was in short supply. Hence, managers began to search for ways to use existing labor more efficiently. In response to this need, experts began to focus on ways to improve the performance of individual workers. Their work led to the development of scientific management. Some of the earliest advocates of scientific management included Frederick W. Taylor (1856–1915), Frank Gilbreth (1868–1924), Lillian Gilbreth (1878–1972), and Henry Gantt (1861–1919).[22]

scientific management
Concerned with improving the performance of individual workers

Taylor was the best-known contributor. One of Taylor's first jobs was as a foreman at the Midvale Steel Company in Philadelphia. There he observed a phenomenon he called soldiering—employees deliberately working at a pace slower than their capabilities. Taylor studied and timed each element of the steelworkers' jobs. He determined what each worker should be producing, and then he designed the most efficient way of doing each part of the overall task. Next, Taylor implemented a piecework pay system. Rather than paying all employees the same wage, he began increasing the pay of each worker who met and exceeded the target level of output set for his or her job.

soldiering
Employees deliberately working at a slow pace

After Taylor left Midvale, he worked as a consultant for several companies, including Simonds Rolling Machine Company and Bethlehem Steel. At Simonds he studied and redesigned jobs, introduced rest periods to reduce fatigue, and implemented a piecework pay system. The results were higher quality and quantity of output and improved morale. At Bethlehem Steel, Taylor studied efficient ways of loading and unloading railcars and applied his conclusions with equally impressive results. During these experiences, he formulated the basic ideas that he called *scientific management*. Figure 1.3 illustrates the basic steps Taylor suggested. He believed that managers who followed his guidelines would improve the efficiency of their workers.[23]

Taylor's work had a significant impact on U.S. industry. By applying his principles, many organizations achieved major gains in efficiency. Taylor was not without his detractors, however. Labor argued that scientific management was just a device to get more work from each employee and to reduce the total number of workers needed by a firm. There was a congressional investigation into Taylor's ideas, and some evidence suggests that he may have falsified some of his findings.[24] Nevertheless, Taylor's work left a lasting imprint on business.[25]

Frederick W. Taylor was one of the first management consultants and helped create scientific management. Time-and-motion studies and performance-based pay systems were among the innovations Taylor and his associates introduced. Mass-production assembly-line technologies also benefited from Taylor's ideas and insights.

Bettmann/Getty Images

"Hardly a competent workman can be found who does not devote a considerable amount of time to studying just how slowly he can work and still convince his employer that he is going at a good pace."
—Frederick W. Taylor, Early Management Pioneer[26]

Frank and Lillian Gilbreth, contemporaries of Taylor, were a husband-and-wife team of industrial engineers. One of Frank Gilbreth's most interesting contributions was to the craft of bricklaying. After studying bricklayers at work, he developed several procedures for doing the job more efficiently. For example, he specified standard materials and techniques, including the

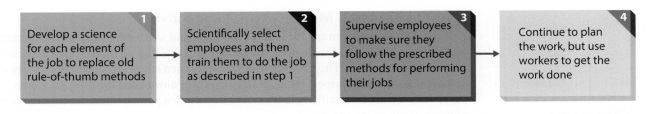

1	2	3	4
Develop a science for each element of the job to replace old rule-of-thumb methods	Scientifically select employees and then train them to do the job as described in step 1	Supervise employees to make sure they follow the prescribed methods for performing their jobs	Continue to plan the work, but use workers to get the work done

FIGURE 1.3

Steps in Scientific Management

Frederick Taylor developed this system of scientific management, which he believed would lead to a more efficient and productive workforce. Bethlehem Steel was among the first organizations to profit from scientific management. Many companies still use elements of scientific management today.

positioning of the bricklayer, the bricks, and the mortar at different levels. The results of these changes were a reduction from 18 separate physical movements to five and an increase in the output of about 200 percent. Lillian Gilbreth made equally important contributions to several different areas of work, helped shape the field of industrial psychology, and made substantive contributions to the field of personnel management. Working individually and together, the Gilbreths developed numerous techniques and strategies for eliminating inefficiency. They applied many of their ideas to their family and documented their experiences raising 12 children in the book and original 1950 movie *Cheaper by the Dozen*.

administrative management
Focuses on managing the total organization

Administrative Management   Whereas scientific management deals with the jobs of individual employees, **administrative management** focuses on managing the total organization. The primary contributors to administrative management were Henri Fayol (1841–1925), Lyndall Urwick (1891–1983), and Max Weber (1864–1920).

Henri Fayol was administrative management's most articulate spokesperson. A French industrialist, Fayol was unknown to U.S. managers and scholars until his most important work, *General and Industrial Management*, was translated into English in 1930.[27] Drawing on his own managerial experience, he attempted to systematize management practice to provide guidance and direction to other managers. Fayol was also the first to identify the specific managerial functions of planning, organizing, leading, and controlling. He believed that these functions accurately reflect the core of the management process. Most contemporary management books (including this one) still use this framework, and practicing managers agree that these functions are critical parts of their jobs.

After a career as a British army officer, Lyndall Urwick became a noted management theorist and consultant. He integrated scientific management with the work of Fayol and other administrative management theorists. Urwick also advanced modern thinking about the functions of planning, organizing, and controlling. Like Fayol, he developed a list of guidelines for improving managerial effectiveness. Urwick is noted not so much for his own contributions as for his synthesis and integration of the work of others.

Although Max Weber lived and worked at the same time as Fayol and Taylor, his contributions were not recognized until some years had passed. Weber was a German sociologist, and his most important work was not translated into English until 1947.[28] Weber's work on bureaucracy laid the foundation for contemporary organization theory, which is discussed in detail in Chapter 6. The concept of bureaucracy, as we discuss later in this book, is based on a rational set of guidelines for structuring organizations in the most efficient manner.

The Classical Management Perspective Today   The classical management perspective provides many management techniques and approaches that are still relevant today. For example, many of the job specialization techniques and scientific methods espoused by Taylor and his contemporaries are still reflected in how many manufacturing jobs are designed today.[29] Moreover, many contemporary organizations still use some of the bureaucratic procedures suggested by Weber. Also, these early theorists were the first to focus attention on management as a meaningful field of study. Several aspects of the classical perspective are also relevant to our later discussions of planning, organizing, and controlling. And recent advances in areas such as business-to-business (B2B) digital commerce and supply chain management also have efficiency as their primary goal. On the other hand, the classical perspective focused on stable, simple organizations; many organizations today, in contrast, are changing and complex. They also proposed universal guidelines that we now recognize do not fit every organization. A third limitation of the classical management perspective is that it slighted the role of the individual in organizations. This role was much more fully developed by advocates of the behavioral management perspective.

1-5c The Behavioral Management Perspective

Early advocates of the classical management perspective viewed organizations and jobs from an essentially mechanistic point of view; that is, they essentially sought to conceptualize organizations as machines and workers as cogs within those machines. Even though many early writers recognized the role of individuals, their focus tended to be on how managers could control and standardize the behavior of their employees. In contrast, the behavioral management perspective placed much more emphasis on individual attitudes, behaviors, and group processes and recognized the importance of behavioral processes in the workplace.

> **behavioral management perspective**
> Emphasizes individual attitudes, behaviors, and group processes

The behavioral management perspective was stimulated by many writers and theoretical movements. One of those movements was industrial psychology, the practice of applying psychological concepts to industrial settings. Hugo Münsterberg (1863–1916), a noted German psychologist, is recognized as the father of industrial psychology. He established a psychological laboratory at Harvard University in 1892, and his pioneering book, *Psychology and Industrial Efficiency*, was translated into English in 1913.[30] Münsterberg suggested that psychologists could make valuable contributions to managers in the areas of employee selection, training, and motivation. Industrial psychology is still a major course of study at many colleges and universities. Another early advocate of the behavioral approach to management was Mary Parker Follett (1868–1933).[31] Follett worked during the scientific management era but quickly came to recognize the human element in the workplace. Indeed, her work clearly anticipated the behavioral management perspective, and she appreciated the need to understand the role of behavior in organizations.

The Hawthorne Studies   Although Münsterberg and Follett made major contributions to the development of the behavioral approach to management, its primary catalyst was a series of studies conducted near Chicago at Western Electric's Hawthorne plant between 1927 and 1932. The research, originally sponsored by General Electric, was conducted by Elton Mayo and his associates.[32] Mayo was a faculty member and consultant at Harvard. The first study at Hawthorne involved manipulating illumination for one group of workers and comparing their subsequent productivity with the productivity of another group whose illumination was not changed. Surprisingly, when illumination was increased for the experimental group, productivity went up in both groups. Productivity continued to increase in both groups, even when the lighting for the experimental group was decreased. Not until the lighting was reduced to the level of moonlight did productivity begin to decline (and General Electric withdrew its sponsorship).

Another experiment at Hawthorne established a piecework incentive pay plan for a group of nine men assembling terminal banks for telephone exchanges. Scientific management would have predicted that each man would try to maximize his pay by producing as many units as possible. Mayo and his associates, however, found that the group itself informally established an acceptable level of output for its members. Workers who overproduced were branded *rate busters*, and underproducers were labeled *chiselers*. To be accepted by the group, workers produced at the accepted level. As they approached this acceptable level of output, workers slacked off to avoid overproducing.

Other studies, including an interview program involving several thousand workers, led Mayo and his associates to conclude that human behavior was much more important in the workplace than had been previously believed. In the lighting experiment, for example,

Courtesy of AT&T Archives and History Center

The Hawthorne studies were a series of early experiments that focused on behavior in the workplace. In one experiment involving this group of workers, for example, researchers monitored how productivity changed as a result of changes in working conditions. The Hawthorne studies and subsequent experiments led scientists to the conclusion that the human element is very important in the workplace.

the results were attributed to the fact that both groups received special attention and sympathetic supervision for perhaps the first time. The incentive pay plans did not work because wage incentives were less important to the individual workers than was social acceptance in determining output. In short, individual and social processes played major roles in shaping worker attitudes and behavior.

The Human Relations Movement   The human relations movement, which grew from the Hawthorne studies and was a popular approach to management for many years, proposed that workers respond primarily to the social context of the workplace, including social conditioning, group norms, and interpersonal dynamics. A basic assumption of the human relations movement was that the manager's concern for workers would lead to increased satisfaction, which would in turn result in improved performance. Two writers who helped advance the human relations movement were Abraham Maslow (1908–1970) and Douglas McGregor (1906–1964).

In 1943, Maslow advanced a theory suggesting that people are motivated by a hierarchy of needs, including monetary incentives and social acceptance.[33] Maslow's hierarchy, perhaps the best-known human relations theory, is described in detail in Chapter 10. Meanwhile, Douglas McGregor's Theory X and Theory Y model best represents the essence of the human relations movement (see Table 1.1).[34] According to McGregor, Theory X and Theory Y reflect two extreme belief sets that different managers have about their workers. Theory X is a relatively pessimistic and negative view of workers and is consistent with the views of scientific management. Theory Y is more positive and represents the assumptions made by human relations advocates. In McGregor's view, Theory Y was a more appropriate philosophy for managers to adhere to. Both Maslow and McGregor notably influenced the thinking of many practicing managers.

human relations movement
Proposed that workers respond primarily to the social context of the workplace, including social conditioning, group norms, and interpersonal dynamics

theory X
A pessimistic and negative view of workers, consistent with the views of scientific management

theory Y
A positive view of workers; it represents the assumptions that human relations advocates make

Table 1.1	Theory X and Theory Y
Theory X Assumptions	1. People do not like work and try to avoid it. 2. People do not like work, so managers have to control, direct, coerce, and threaten employees to get them to work toward organizational goals. 3. People prefer to be directed, to avoid responsibility, and to want security; they have little ambition.
Theory Y Assumptions	1. People do not naturally dislike work; work is a natural part of their lives. 2. People are internally motivated to reach objectives to which they are committed. 3. People are committed to goals to the degree that they receive personal rewards when they reach their objectives. 4. People will both seek and accept responsibility under favorable conditions. 5. People have the capacity to be innovative in solving organizational problems. 6. People are bright, but under most organizational conditions, their potential is underutilized.

Douglas McGregor developed Theory X and Theory Y. He argued that Theory X best represented the views of scientific management and Theory Y represented the human relations approach. McGregor believed that Theory Y was the best philosophy for all managers.

Source: D. McGregor and W. Bennis. (1960). The human side of enterprise: 25th anniversary printing. New York: McGraw Hill.

Contemporary Behavioral Science in Management   Münsterberg, Mayo, Maslow, McGregor, and others have made valuable contributions to management. Contemporary theorists, however, have noted that many of the human relationists' assertions were simplistic and provided inadequate descriptions of work behavior. Current behavioral perspectives on management, known as **organizational behavior**, acknowledge that human behavior in organizations is much more complex than the human relationists realized. The field of organizational behavior draws from a broad, interdisciplinary base of psychology, sociology, anthropology, economics, and medicine. Organizational behavior takes a holistic view of behavior and addresses individual, group, and organization processes. These processes are major elements in contemporary management theory.[35] Important topics in this field include job satisfaction, stress, motivation, leadership, group dynamics, organizational politics, interpersonal conflict, and the structure and design of organizations.[36] A contingency orientation also characterizes the field (discussed more fully later in this chapter). Our discussions of organizing (Chapters 6–8) and leading (Chapters 9–13) are heavily influenced by organizational behavior. And, finally, managers need a solid understanding of human behavior as they address diversity-related issues such as ethnicity and religion in the workplace. Indeed, all these topics are useful in helping managers better deal with the consequences of layoffs and job cuts and to motivate today's workers.

organizational behavior
Contemporary field focusing on behavioral perspectives on management

The Behavioral Management Perspective Today   The primary contributions of this approach relate to how it has changed managerial thinking. Managers are now more likely to recognize the importance of behavioral processes and to view employees as valuable resources instead of mere tools. However, organizational behavior is still relatively imprecise in its ability to predict behavior, especially the behavior of a specific individual. It is not always accepted or understood by practicing managers. Hence the contributions of the behavioral school are just beginning to be fully realized.

1-5d The Quantitative Management Perspective

The third major school of management thought began to emerge during World War II. During the war, government officials, statisticians, and scientists in England and the United States worked to help the military deploy its resources more efficiently and effectively. These groups

Automobile manufacturers around the world today use crash-test dummies like this one to test safety features in their cars. Statistical techniques and methods derived from management science help engineers and managers assess the effectiveness of various safety features. The results include safer vehicles and lower costs for manufacturers.

took some of the mathematical approaches to management developed decades earlier by Taylor and Gantt and applied these approaches to logistical problems during the war.[37] They learned that challenges regarding troop, equipment, and submarine deployment, for example, could all be solved through mathematical analysis. After the war, companies such as DuPont, General Motors, and General Electric began to use the same techniques for deploying employees, choosing plant locations, and planning warehouses. Basically, then, this perspective is concerned with applying quantitative techniques to management. More specifically, the **quantitative management perspective** focuses on decision making, cost-effectiveness, mathematical models, and the use of computers. There are two branches of the quantitative approach: management science and operations management.

Management Science   Unfortunately, the term *management science* appears to be related to scientific management, the approach developed by Taylor and others early in the twentieth century. But the two have little in common and should not be confused. **Management science** focuses specifically on the development of mathematical models. A mathematical model is a simplified representation of a system, process, or relationship.

At its most basic level, management science focuses on models, equations, and similar representations of reality. For example, managers at Detroit Edison use mathematical models to determine how best to route repair crews during blackouts. Citizens Bank of New England uses models to figure out how many tellers need to be on duty at each location at various times throughout the day. In recent years, paralleling the advent of the personal computer, management science techniques have become increasingly sophisticated. For example, automobile manufacturers Daimler AG and General Motors use realistic computer simulations to study collision damage to cars. These simulations help them lower costs by crashing actual test cars only after multiple simulations have refined the most important areas to test.

Operations Management   Operations management is somewhat less mathematical and statistically sophisticated than management science, and it can be applied more directly to managerial situations. Indeed, we can think of **operations management** as a form of applied management science. Operations management techniques are generally concerned with helping the organization produce its products or services more efficiently and can be applied to a wide range of problems.

For example, Unilever and Home Depot each uses operations management techniques to manage its inventories. (Inventory management is concerned with specific inventory problems, such as balancing carrying costs and ordering costs and determining the optimal order quantity.) Linear programming (which involves computing simultaneous solutions to a set of linear equations) helps United Airlines plan its flight schedules, Consolidated Freightways develop its shipping routes, and General Instrument Corporation plan what devices to produce at various times. Other operations management techniques include queuing theory, break-even analysis, and simulation. All these techniques and procedures apply directly to operations, but they are also helpful in areas such as finance, marketing, and human resource management.[38]

The Quantitative Management Perspective Today   Like the other management perspectives, the quantitative management perspective has made important contributions and has certain limitations. It has provided managers with an abundance of decision-making tools and techniques and has increased understanding of overall organizational processes. This perspective has been particularly useful in the areas of planning and

quantitative management perspective
Applies quantitative techniques to management

management science
Focuses specifically on the development of mathematical models

operations management
Concerned with helping the organization produce its products or services more efficiently

controlling. Relatively new management concepts such as supply chain management and new techniques such as enterprise resource planning, both discussed later in this book, also evolved from the quantitative management perspective. Mathematicians are also using tools and techniques from the quantitative perspective to develop models that might be helpful in the war against terrorism.[39] More recently these models were also used to track and predict the spread of COVID-19 during the 2020 pandemic. However, mathematical models cannot fully account for individual behaviors and attitudes. Some believe that the time needed to develop competence in quantitative techniques retards the development of other managerial skills. Finally, mathematical models typically require a set of assumptions that may not be realistic.

 **Manager's Checklist**

☐ The lessons learned from scientific and administrative management thinking can still play a role in promoting productivity and efficiency today. However, remember that focusing too much on productivity and efficiency can have a negative impact on other factors that promote overall effectiveness.

☐ Never overlook the importance of the human element in organizations but avoid making simplistic assumptions about how to affect employee behavior.

☐ Quantitative perspectives such as management science and operations management are important management tools. When possible, it is useful to quantify problems and opportunities; however, this is often not possible, and so managers need to also consider other perspectives and approaches.

1-6 CONTEMPORARY MANAGEMENT PERSPECTIVES

It is important to recognize that the classical, behavioral, and quantitative approaches to management are not necessarily contradictory or mutually exclusive. Even though each of the three perspectives makes very different assumptions and predictions and focuses on different things, each can also complement the others. Indeed, a complete understanding of management requires an appreciation of all three perspectives. The systems and contingency perspectives can help us integrate these earlier approaches and enlarge our understanding of all three.

1-6a The Systems Perspective

system
An interrelated set of elements functioning as a whole

open system
A system that interacts with its environment

closed system
A system that does not interact with its environment

subsystem
A system within a broader system

The systems perspective is one important contemporary management perspective. A system is an interrelated set of elements functioning as a whole.[40] As shown in Figure 1.4, by viewing an organization as a system, we can identify four basic elements: inputs, transformation processes, outputs, and feedback. First, inputs are the material, human, financial, and information resources that an organization gets from its environment. Next, through technological and managerial processes, inputs are transformed into outputs. Outputs include products, services, or both (tangible and intangible); profits, losses, or both (even not-for-profit organizations must operate within their budgets); employee behaviors; and information. Finally, the environment reacts to these outputs and provides feedback to the system.

Thinking of organizations as systems provides us with a variety of important viewpoints on organizations, such as the concepts of open systems, subsystems, synergy, and entropy. Open systems are systems that interact with their environment, whereas closed systems do not interact with their environment. Although organizations are open systems, some make the mistake of ignoring their environment and behaving as though it is not important.

The systems perspective also stresses the importance of subsystems—systems within a broader system. For example, the marketing, production, and finance functions within

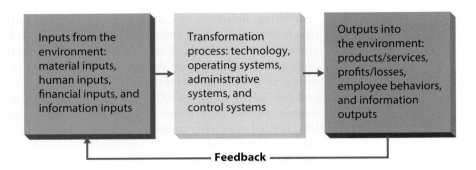

| Inputs from the environment: material inputs, human inputs, financial inputs, and information inputs | → | Transformation process: technology, operating systems, administrative systems, and control systems | → | Outputs into the environment: products/services, profits/losses, employee behaviors, and information outputs |

Feedback

FIGURE 1.4

The Systems Perspective of Organizations

By viewing organizations as systems, managers can better understand the importance of their environment and the level of interdependence among their organization's subsystems. Managers must also understand how their decisions affect and are affected by the organization's other subsystems.

Disney is a master of synergy. The company's movies, theme-park attractions, and merchandise, for example, are all linked together so that each enhances the others. For instance, the Disney movie *Frozen II* was widely promoted at Disney World and Disneyland before the movie even opened. And long after the movie left theaters, people could still buy *Frozen II* merchandise throughout all Disney retail outlets.

Sarunyu L/Shutterstock.com

Hasbro are systems in their own right but are also subsystems within the overall organization. Because they are interdependent, a change in one subsystem can affect other subsystems as well. If the production department at Hasbro lowers the quality of the toys being made (by buying lower-quality materials, for example), the effects are felt in finance (improved cash flow in the short run owing to lower costs) and marketing (decreased sales in the long run because of customer dissatisfaction). Managers must therefore remember that although organizational subsystems can be managed with some degree of autonomy, their interdependence should not be overlooked. For instance, recent research has underscored the interdependence of strategy and operations in businesses.[41]

Synergy suggests that organizational units (or subsystems) may often be more successful working together than working alone. The Walt Disney Company, for example, benefits greatly from synergy. The company's movies, theme parks, television programs, and merchandise-licensing programs all benefit one another. Children who enjoy Disney movies like *Moana* and *Frozen II* want to go to Disney World to see the attractions and shows based on the movies and their favorite characters; and when they shop at Target, they see and want to buy stuffed toys and action figures of the same characters. Music from the films generates additional revenues for the firm, as do computer games and other licensing arrangements for lunchboxes, clothing, and so forth. Synergy is an important concept for managers because it emphasizes the importance of working together in a cooperative and coordinated fashion.[42]

Finally, **entropy** is a normal process that leads to system decline. When an organization does not monitor feedback from its environment and make appropriate adjustments, it may fail. For example, witness the problems and eventual demise of Blockbuster and Circuit City. Each of these organizations went bankrupt because it failed to revitalize itself and keep pace with changes in its environment. A primary objective of management, from a systems perspective, is to continually reenergize the organization to avoid entropy.

synergy
Two or more subsystems working together to produce more than the total of what they might produce working alone

"The whole is greater than the sum of its parts"

—Aristotle

entropy
A normal process leading to system decline

1-6b The Contingency Perspective

universal perspective
An attempt to identify the one best way to do something

contingency perspective
Suggests that appropriate managerial behavior in a given situation depends on, or is contingent on, unique elements in a given situation

Another noteworthy recent addition to management thinking is the contingency perspective. The classical, behavioral, and quantitative approaches are considered universal perspectives because they try to identify the "one best way" to manage organizations. The contingency perspective, in contrast, suggests that universal theories cannot be applied to organizations because each organization is unique. Instead, the contingency perspective suggests that appropriate managerial behavior in a given situation depends on, or is contingent on, unique elements in that situation.[43]

Stated differently, effective managerial behavior in one situation cannot always be generalized to other situations. Recall, for example, that Frederick Taylor assumed that all workers would generate the highest possible level of output to maximize their own personal economic gain. We can imagine some people being motivated primarily by money—but we can just as easily imagine other people being motivated by the desire for leisure time, status, social acceptance, or any combination of these (as Mayo found at the Hawthorne plant). When Reed Hastings launched Netflix, he was intimately involved with virtually every small decision made to get the company up and running. But as the firm grew into a major international business he has stepped back and taken on a more strategic role. Hence, his management style and approach have changed because the situation in which he manages has changed.

Manager's Checklist

- ☐ The systems perspective is useful for reminding managers of both the interconnectedness within organizations and the organization and its environment.

- ☐ Managers need to remember that universal approaches are seldom effective; instead, they should focus on contingencies and the situation.

- ☐ You should understand that all of the various techniques and perspectives are really tools that managers can draw on to carry out their responsibilities. Just as a carpenter uses different tools for different tasks, the manager's tools will also vary based on the situation.

1-7 CONTEMPORARY MANAGEMENT ISSUES AND CHALLENGES

Interest in management theory and practice has heightened in recent years as new issues and challenges have emerged. No new paradigm has been formulated that replaces the traditional views, but managers continue to strive toward a better understanding of how they can better compete and lead their organizations toward improved effectiveness.

1-7a Contemporary Applied Perspectives

Several applied authors have significant influence on modern management theory and practice. Among the most popular applied authors today are Peter Senge, Stephen Covey, Tom Peters, Jim Collins, Michael Porter, John Kotter, and Gary Hamel.[44] Their books highlight the management practices of successful firms such as Shell Oil, Ford, and IBM, or they outline conceptual or theoretical models or frameworks to guide managers as they formulate strategies or motivate their employees. Malcolm Gladwell's books *The Tipping Point, Blink, Outliers*, and *Talking to Strangers* have all caught the attention of many contemporary managers. Scott Adams, creator of the popular comic strip *Dilbert*, also remains popular today. Adams is a former communications industry worker who developed his strip to illustrate some of the absurdities that occasionally afflict contemporary organizational life. The daily strip is routinely emailed and posted outside office doors, above copy machines, and beside water coolers in hundreds of offices.

1-7b Contemporary Management Challenges

Managers today also face an imposing set of challenges as they guide and direct the fortunes of their companies. Coverage of each of these challenges is thoroughly integrated throughout this book. In addition, many of them are highlighted or given focused coverage in one or more special ways.

One significant challenge (and opportunity) is globalization. Managing in a global economy poses many different challenges and opportunities. For example, at a macro level, business ownership arrangements vary widely. So does the availability of natural resources and infrastructure components, as well as government's role in business. Moreover, behavioral processes vary widely across cultural and national boundaries. For example, values, symbols, and beliefs differ sharply among cultures. Different work norms and the role that work plays in a person's life, for example, influence patterns of both work-related behavior and attitudes toward work. They also affect the nature of supervisory relationships, decision-making styles and processes, and organizational configurations. Group and intergroup processes, responses to stress, and the nature of political behaviors in organizations also differ from culture to culture.

Another management challenge that has taken on renewed importance is ethics and social responsibility and their relationship to corporate governance. Unfortunately, business scandals involving unethical conduct have become almost commonplace today. For example, in the wake of serious problems associated with Boeing's 737 Max airplanes and subsequent evidence of how the firm had tried to hide key information, the company's CEO was fired. From a social responsibility perspective, increasing attention has been focused on pollution and business's obligation to help clean up our environment, the issue of climate change, business contributions to social causes, and so forth. The proper framework for corporate governance is often at the center of these debates and discussions.[45]

Quality also continues to pose an important management challenge today. Quality is an important issue for several reasons. First, more and more organizations are using quality as a basis for competition. Lexus, for example, stresses its high rankings in the J. D. Power survey of customer satisfaction in its print advertising. Second, improving quality tends to increase productivity because making higher-quality products generally results in less waste and rework. Third, enhancing quality lowers costs. Managers at Whistler Corporation once came to realize that the firm was using 100 of its 250 employees to repair defective radar detectors that had been built incorrectly in the first place.

The shift toward a service economy also continues to be important. Traditionally, most U.S. businesses were manufacturers—using tangible resources like raw materials and machinery to create tangible products like automobiles and steel. And manufacturing is indeed still important in the U.S. economy. In the last few decades, however, the service sector of the economy has become much more important. Although there are obviously many similarities between managing in a manufacturing organization and managing in a service organization, there are also many fundamental differences.

The economic recession of 2008–2010 and slow recovery in 2011–2017 have also created myriad challenges, as well as some opportunities, for managers. Most businesses struggled, and some failed to survive. But some managers also used this period as a framework for reducing their costs, streamlining their operating systems and procedures, and fine-tuning their business strategies. As the economy slowly began to rebound in 2015, firms like Apple, Target, and Delia were all well positioned for new growth and began hiring new employees. By 2019 unemployment was so low that many businesses had trouble finding new workers. But as is often the case history repeated itself in 2020 largely due to the COVID-19 pandemic. Companies reduced or closed operations, workers lost their jobs, and business revenues and profits plunged.

A related challenge for managers is the rapidly changing workplace.[46] Indeed, this new workplace is accompanied by both dramatic challenges and amazing opportunities. Among other things, workplace changes relate in part to both workforce reductions and expansion. For example, many firms hired large numbers of new workers during the economic expansion that was taking place between 2002 and early 2008. But as the recession of

2008–2010 took hold, many of those same firms had to reduce their workforces, while others cut hours and pay and suspended all hiring until conditions showed signs of improvement. But even more central to the idea of workplace change are developments such as workforce diversity and the characteristics of new workers themselves. Likewise, while many firms allowed some levels of remote work for some jobs the COVID-19 pandemic led to dramatic increases in remote work as the need for social distancing became more and more important.

The management of diversity continues to be an important organizational opportunity—and challenge—today. The term *diversity* refers to differences among people. Diversity may be reflected along numerous dimensions, but most managers tend to focus on age, gender, ethnicity, and physical abilities and disabilities.[47] For example, the average age of workers in the United States is gradually increasing. An increasing number of women have also entered the U.S. workforce. In the early 1960s only about one-third of U.S. women worked outside their homes; in 2019, around 60 percent of women aged 16 and older are in the workforce. The ethnic composition of the workplace is also changing. Further, the social unrest that swept the country in mid-2020 caused many businesses to reassess their brands, their images, and how they interacted with their employees.

Aside from its demographic composition, the workforce today is changing in other ways. During the 1980s, many people entering the workforce came to be called yuppies, slang for *young urban professionals*. These individuals were highly motivated by career prospects, sought employment with big corporations, and often were willing to make work their highest priority. Thus, they put in long hours and could be expected to remain loyal to the company, regardless of what happened.

But younger people entering the workforce over the past 20–30 years are frequently quite different from their parents and other older workers. Generation X, Generation Y, Generation Z, and Millennials, as these groups are called, tend to be less devoted to long-term career prospects and less willing to adapt to a corporate mindset that stresses conformity and uniformity. Instead, they often seek work in smaller, more entrepreneurial firms that allow flexibility and individuality. They also place a premium on lifestyle preferences, often putting location high on their list of priorities when selecting an employer.

Thus, managers are increasingly faced with the challenge of, first, creating an environment that will be attractive to today's worker and, second, addressing the challenge of providing new and different incentives to keep people motivated and interested in their work. They must build enough flexibility into the organization to accommodate an ever-changing set of lifestyles and preferences. And, of course, as these generations eventually move into top spots of major corporations, there may even be entirely new paradigms for managing that cannot be foreseen today.[48]

Managers must also be prepared to address organization change.[49] This has always been a concern, but the rapid, constant environmental change faced by businesses today has made change management even more critical. Simply put, an organization that fails to monitor its environment and to change to keep pace with that environment is doomed to failure. But more and more managers are seeing change as an opportunity, not a cause for alarm. Indeed, some managers think that if things get too calm in an organization and people start to become complacent, they should shake things up to get everyone energized.

The role and impact of social media in business also pose unique challenges for business. Few large businesses have grasped how to use social media to compete more effectively, but most would also agree that social media can have a major impact on business. Unfortunately, this impact is often negative. For example, a customer who has a bad experience in a restaurant can use social media to spread the word about that experience, and the story can then get passed along over and over again. Since it seems that many people are more prone to read and react to negative experiences than to positive ones, the ripple effects of poor service (as one example) can be quite damaging. In a similar vein, online sites such as glassdoor.com offer a platform to both current and former employees on which to post anonymous feedback about employers. While no organization is perfect, a pattern of negative comments about a firm can make it much harder for that company to attract new employees.

Manager's Checklist

- ☐ Many managers remain current by reading leading business books.
- ☐ All managers need to be aware of how globalization, ethics and social responsibility, quality, the service economy, and social media can affect their work both now and in the future.
- ☐ You should also remain alert for new and emerging management challenges and opportunities.

SUMMARY OF LEARNING OUTCOMES AND KEY POINTS

1-1. Describe *management* and the kinds of managers found in organizations.

- Management is a set of activities (planning and decision making, organizing, leading, and controlling) directed at using an organization's resources (human, financial, physical, and information) to achieve organizational goals in an efficient and effective manner.

- A manager is someone whose primary responsibility is to carry out the management process within an organization.

- Managers can be classified by level: top managers, middle managers, and first-line managers.

- Managers can also be classified by area: marketing, finances, operations, human resources, administration, and specialized.

1-2. Explain the four basic management functions.

- The basic activities of the management process include:

- Planning and decision making (determining courses of action)

- Organizing (coordinating activities and resources)

- Leading (motivating and managing people)

- Controlling (monitoring and evaluating activities)

1-3. Describe the fundamental management skills and the concept of management as both science and art.

- Effective managers have the following skills: technical, interpersonal, conceptual, diagnostic, communication, decision making, and time management.

- The effective practice of management requires a synthesis of science and art, a blend of rational objectivity and intuitive insight.

1-4. Explain the importance of history and theory to managers.

- Understanding the historical context can help managers avoid repeating the mistakes of others.

- Theory helps managers develop and apply useful frameworks and new ways of thinking.

1-5. Explain the evolution of management thought through the classical, behavioral, and quantitative perspectives.

- The classical management perspective, which paid little attention to the role of workers, had two major branches: scientific management (concerned with improving efficiency and work methods for individual workers) and administrative management (concerned with how organizations themselves should be structured and arranged for efficient operations).

- The behavioral management perspective, characterized by a concern for individual and group behavior, emerged primarily as a result of the Hawthorne studies. The human relations movement recognized the importance and potential of behavioral processes in organizations but made many overly simplistic assumptions about those processes. Organizational behavior, a more realistic outgrowth of the behavioral perspective, is of interest to many contemporary managers.

- The quantitative management perspective, which attempts to apply quantitative techniques to decision making and problem solving, has two components: management science and operations management. These areas are also of considerable importance to contemporary managers. Their contributions have been facilitated by the tremendous increase in the use of personal computers and integrated information networks.

1-6. Discuss the key contemporary management perspectives represented by the systems and contingency perspectives.

- There are two relatively recent additions to management theory that can serve as frameworks for integrating the other perspectives: the systems perspective and the contingency perspective.

1-7. Identify the major challenges and opportunities faced by managers today.

- A variety of popular applied perspectives influence management practice today.

- Important issues and challenges facing managers include employee retention, diversity, the new workforce, organization change, ethics and social responsibility, the importance of quality, and the continued shift toward a service economy.

DISCUSSION QUESTIONS

Questions for Review

1. What are the three basic levels of management that can be identified in most organizations? How precise are the lines differentiating these levels? In which of the basic areas do managers work?
2. What are the four basic functions that make up the management process? How are they related to one another?
3. Identify several of the important skills that help managers succeed. Give an example of each. How might the importance of different skills vary by level and area within an organization?
4. Briefly describe the principles of scientific management and administrative management. What assumptions do these perspectives make about workers? To what extent are these assumptions still valid today?

Questions for Analysis

1. Why is a business organization considered an open system?
2. Recall a recent group project or task in which you have participated. Explain how members of the group displayed each of the managerial skills.
3. The text notes that management is both a science and an art. Recall an interaction you have had with someone at a higher level in an organization (manager, teacher, group leader, or the like). In that interaction, how did the individual use science? If he or she did not use science, what could have been done to use science? In that interaction, how did the individual use art? If she or he did not use art, what could have been done to use art?

Questions for Application

1. Watch a movie that involves an organization of some type. *The Secret Life of Walter Mitty*, *The Avengers*, and *Up in the Air* would all be good choices. Identify as many management activities and skills as you can.
2. Young, innovative, or high-tech firms often adopt the strategy of ignoring history or attempting to do something radically new. In what ways might this strategy help them? In what ways might this strategy hinder their efforts?
3. Can a manager use tools and techniques from several different perspectives at the same time? For example, can a manager use both classical and behavioral perspectives? Give an example of a time when a manager did this and explain how it enabled him or her to be effective.

BUILDING EFFECTIVE INTERPERSONAL SKILLS

Johari Window

Purpose: This exercise has two purposes: to encourage you to analyze yourself more accurately and to start you working on small-group cohesiveness. This exercise encourages you to share data about yourself and then to assimilate and process feedback. Small groups are typically more trusting and work better together, as you will be able to see after this exercise has been completed. The Johari Window is a particularly good model for understanding the perceptual process in interpersonal relationships and building interpersonal skills.

Introduction: Each individual has four sets of personality characteristics. One set, which includes such characteristics as working hard, is well known to the individual and to others. A second set is unknown to the individual but obvious to others. For example, in a working situation, a peer group might observe that your jumping in to move the group off dead center is appropriate. At other times,

you jump in when the group is not really finished, and you seem to interrupt. A third set of personality characteristics is known to the individual but not to others. These are situations that you have elected not to share, perhaps because of a lack of trust. Finally, there is a fourth set, which is not known to the individual or to others, such as why you are uncomfortable at office parties.

Instructions: Refer to the Johari Window. In quadrant 1, list three things that you know about yourself and that you think others know. List three things in quadrant 3 that others do not know about you. Finally, in quadrant 2, list three things that you did not know about yourself last semester that you learned from others.

Source: Adapted from Joseph Luft, *Group Processes: An Introduction to Group Dynamics* (Palo Alto, CA: Mayfield, 1970), pp. 10–11; and William C. Morris and Marshall Sashkin, *Organizational Behavior in Action* (St. Paul, MN: West, 1976), p. 56.

	My Own Perceptions	
	Things I Know About Myself	**Things I Do Not Know About Myself**
Things Others Know About Me	**Quadrant 1** **"The Open Self"** Characteristics apparent to me and to others _____ _____ _____	**Quadrant 2** **"The Blind Self"** Characteristics not apparent to me _____ _____ _____
Things Others Do Not Know About Me	**Quadrant 3** **"The Concealed Self"** Characteristics known to me but kept hidden from others _____ _____ _____	**Quadrant 4** **"The Unknown Self"** The Blind Area

Other Persons' Perceptions

BUILDING EFFECTIVE TIME MANAGEMENT SKILLS

Exercise Overview

Time management skills refer to the ability to prioritize tasks, to work efficiently, and to delegate appropriately. This exercise allows you to assess your own current time management skills and to gather some suggestions for how you can improve in this area.

Exercise Background

As we saw in this chapter, effective managers must be prepared to switch back and forth among the four basic activities in the management process. They must also be able to fulfill a number of different roles in their organizations, and they must exercise a variety of managerial skills in doing so. On top of everything else, their schedules are busy and full of tasks—personal and job-related activities that require them to "switch gears" frequently throughout the workday.

Stephen Covey, a management consultant and author of *The 7 Habits of Highly Effective People*, has developed a system for prioritizing tasks. First, he divides them into two categories—urgent and *critical*. *Urgent* tasks, such as those with approaching deadlines, must be performed right away. *Critical* tasks are tasks of high importance—say, those that will affect significant areas of one's life or work. Next, Covey plots both types of tasks on a grid with four quadrants: A task may be *urgent, critical, urgent and critical*, or *not urgent and not critical*.

Most managers, says Covey, spend too much time on tasks that are urgent when in fact they should be focused on tasks that are *critical*. He observes, for example, that managers who concentrate on urgent tasks meet their deadlines but tend to neglect such critical areas as long-term planning.

In short, effective managers must learn to balance the demands of urgent tasks with those of critical tasks by redistributing the amount of time devoted to each type.

Exercise Task

1. First, make a list of your current activities, projects, and so forth. Think of this as your "to-do" list. Identify at least ten things. Try to include a variety of things both job or school related and also personal in nature. Number them in the order in which you are currently planning to do them.
2. Next, label each of these as being urgent, critical, both, or neither. For example, if "go grocery shopping" is on your list and you have no food at home it may be both urgent and critical. But, if you have plenty of food at home but want to shop for a special dinner you plan to cook next week, this might be critical but not urgent.
3. Examine how your numbered list from step one matches your labels in step two. That is, are you planning to tackle activities and projects that are both urgent and critical first? Based on your labeling in step two, how might you more efficiently change the order in which you plan to do things?
4. Think of a task that you regularly perform and which, if you were being perfectly honest, you could label *not urgent and not critical*. How much time do you spend on this task? What might be a more appropriate amount of time? To what other tasks could you give some of the time that you spend on this *not-urgent-not-critical* task?
5. What one thing can you do today to make better use of your time? Try it to see if your time management improves.

SKILL-BUILDING PERSONAL ASSESSMENT

How Do I Rate as a Manager?

This self-assessment will help you understand your current understanding of the practice of management and your own approach to management. This assessment outlines four important functions of management: planning, organizing, leading, and controlling. You should respond to this in one of three ways:

(a) Respond based on your own managerial experience if you have any;
(b) Respond about effective (or ineffective) managers you have observed in your work experience; or
(c) Respond in terms of how you think an ideal manager should behave.

Instructions: Recall a situation in which you were a member of a group or team that had a specific task or project to complete. This may have been at work, in a class, or in a church, club, or civic organization. Now assess your behavior in each of the functions. For each question, rate yourself according to the following scale.

Rating scale: Insert your score from one of the following five options for each of the statements that follow:

- 5 *Definitely true of me*
- 4 *Probably true of me*
- 3 *Neither true nor not true, or undecided*
- 2 *Probably not true of me*
- 1 *Definitely not true of me*

I. Planning

_____ 1. I prepare an agenda for meetings.

_____ 2. I try to anticipate what will happen in the future as a result of my current actions and decisions.

_____ 3. I establish clear goals for myself and others.

_____ 4. I carefully analyze the pros and cons involved in situations before reaching decisions.

_____ 5. I am quite willing to try new things, to experiment.

_____ 6. I have a clear vision for accomplishing the task at hand.

_____ 7. I put plans in writing so that others can know exactly what they are.

_____ 8. I try to remain flexible so that I can adapt to changing conditions.

_____ 9. I try to anticipate barriers to goal accomplishment and how to overcome them.

_____ 10. I discuss plans and involve others in arriving at those plans.

_____ Section I Total

II. Organizing

_____ 1. I try to follow the plan while working on the task.

_____ 2. I try to develop any understanding of the different steps or parts needed to accomplish the task at hand.

_____ 3. I evaluate different ways of working on the task before deciding on which course of action to follow.

_____ 4. I have a clear sense of the priorities necessary to accomplish the task.

_____ 5. I arrange for others to be informed about the degree of progress in accomplishing the task.

_____ 6. I am open to alternative, even novel ways of working on the task.

_____ 7. I adapt the sequence of activities involved if circumstances change.

_____ 8. I have a clear sense of how the steps involved in accomplishing the task should be structured.

_____ 9. I lead or follow where appropriate to see to it that progress is made toward accomplishing the task.

_____ 10. I coordinate with others to assure steady progress on the task.

_____ Section II Total

III. Leading

_____ 1. I set an example for others to follow.

_____ 2. I am effective at motivating others.

_____ 3. I try to keep a balance between getting the work done and keeping a spirit of teamwork.

_____ 4. I try to handle conflict in nonthreatening, constructive ways.

_____ 5. I help others in the group and provide them with guidance and training to better perform their roles.

_____ 6. I am open to suggestions from others.

_____ 7. I keep everyone informed about the group's activities and progress.

_____ 8. I show a genuine interest in the work of others.

_____ 9. I am considerate when providing constructive suggestions to others.

_____ 10. I understand the needs of others and encourage their initiative in meeting those needs.

_____ Section III Total

IV. Controlling

_____ 1. I regularly assess the quantity and quality of progress on the task at hand.

_____ 2. I try to ensure that the information I have is timely, accurate, complete, and relevant.

_____ 3. I routinely share information with others to help them accomplish their tasks.

_____ 4. I compare progress with plans and take corrective action as warranted.

_____ 5. I manage my time and help others to manage theirs.

_____ 6. I have good sources of information or methods for obtaining information.

_____ 7. I use technology (computers, tablets, smartphones, etc.) to aid in monitoring progress and communicating with others.

_____ 8. I anticipate possible negative reactions and take action to minimize them.

_____ 9. I recognize that fixing problems *before* they occur is better than fixing problems *after* they occur.

_____ 10. I try to balance my attention on the many different steps needed to accomplish the task at hand.

_____ Section IV Total

Overall Scoring: Total the values you assigned to each statement in each Section. Your score for each Section should be between 50 (if you gave yourself a 5 for each statement) and 10 (if you gave yourself a 1 for each statement). A score between 41 and 50 is considered to be very high, so this suggests that you have strong skills related to that function. A score between 31 and 40 is somewhat high, a score between 21 and 30 is somewhat low, and a score between 10 and 20 is low. Where you fall on each management function can be used as one indicator of where you might want to concentrate your future skill development efforts.

Source: Adapted from D. D. Van Fleet, E. W. Van Fleet, and G. J. Seperich, *Principles of Management for Agribusiness* (Clifton Park, NY: Cengage Learning, 2013); R. W. Griffin, *Management* (Mason, OH: Cengage Learning, 2017); and D. D. Van Fleet, *Behavior in Organizations* (Boston: Houghton Mifflin, 1991) in collaboration with G. Moorhead and R. W. Griffin.

MANAGEMENT AT WORK
Some Keys to Making a Steinway

Everybody knows what a grand piano looks like, although it's hard to describe its contour as anything other than "piano shaped." From a bird's-eye view, you might recognize something like a great big holster. The *case*—the curved lateral surface that runs around the whole instrument—appears to be a single continuous piece of wood, but it isn't really. If you look carefully at the case of a piano built by Steinway & Sons, you'll see that you're actually looking at a remarkable composite of raw material, craftsmanship, and technology. The process by which this component is made—like most of the processes for making a Steinway grand—is a prime example of a *technical*, or *task*, *subsystem* at work in a highly specialized factory.

The *case* starts out as a *rim*, which is constructed out of separate slats of wood, mostly maple (eastern rock maple, to be precise). Once raw boards have been cut and planed, they're glued along their lengthwise edges to the width of 12½ inches. These composite pieces are then jointed and glued end to end to form slats 22 feet long—the measure of the piano's perimeter. Next, a total of 18 separate slats—14 layers of maple and four layers of other types of wood—are glued and stacked together to form a *book*—one (seemingly) continuous "board" 3¼ inches thick. Then comes the process that's a favorite of visitors on the Steinway factory tour—bending this rim into the shape of a piano. Steinway does it pretty much the same way that it has for more than a century—by hand and all at once. Because the special glue is in the process of drying, a crew of six has just 20 minutes to wrestle the book, with block and tackle and wooden levers and mallets, into a *rim-bending press*—"a giant piano-shaped vise," as Steinway describes it—which will force the wood to "forget" its natural inclination to be straight and assume the familiar contour of a grand piano.

Visitors report the sound of splintering wood, but Steinway artisans assure them that the specially cured wood isn't likely to break or the specially mixed glue to lose its grip. It's a good thing, too, both because the wood is expensive and because the precision Steinway process can't afford much wasted effort. The company needs 12 months, 12,000 parts, 450 craftspeople, and countless hours of skilled labor to produce a grand piano. Today, the New York factory turns out about 10 pianos in a day or 2,500 a year. (A mass producer might build 2,000 pianos a week.) The result of this painstaking task system, according to one business journalist with a good ear, is "both impossibly perfect instruments and a scarcity," and that's why Steinways are so expensive—currently, somewhere between $45,000 and $110,000.

But Steinway pianos, the company reminds potential buyers, have always been "built to a standard, not to a price." "It's a product," says company executive Leo F. Spellman, "that in some sense speaks to people and will have a legacy long after we're gone. What [Steinway] craftsmen work on today will be here for another 50 or 100 years." Approximately 90 percent of all concert pianists prefer the sound of a Steinway, and the company's attention to manufacturing detail reflects the fact that when a piano is being played, the entire instrument vibrates—and thus affects its sound. In other words—and not surprisingly—the better the raw materials, design, and construction, the better the sound.

That's one of the reasons Steinway craftsmen put so much care into the construction of the piano's case: It's a major factor in the way the body of the instrument resonates. The maple wood for the case, for example, arrives at the factory with a water content of 80 percent. It's then dried, both in the open air and in kilns, until the water content is reduced to about 10 percent—suitable for both strength and pliability. To ensure that strength and pliability remain stable, the slats must be cut so that they're horizontally grained and arranged, with the "inside" of one slat—the side that grew toward the center of the tree—facing the "outside" of the next one in the book. The case is removed from the press after one day and then stored for ten weeks in a humidity-controlled *rim-bending room*. Afterward, it's ready to be sawed, planed, and sanded to specification—a process called *frazing*. A black lacquer finish is added, and only then is the case ready to be installed as a component of a grand piano in progress.

The Steinway process also puts a premium on skilled workers. Steinway has always been an employer of immigrant labor, beginning with the German craftsmen and laborers hired by founder Henry Steinway in the 1860s and 1870s. Today, Steinway employees come from much different places—Haitians and Dominicans in the 1980s, exiles from war-torn Yugoslavia in the 1990s—and it still takes time to train them. It takes about a year, for instance, to train a case maker, and "when you lose one of them for a long period of time," says Gino Romano, a senior supervisor hired in 1964, "it has a serious effect on our output." Romano recalls one year in mid-June when a case maker was injured in a car accident and was out for several weeks. His department fell behind schedule, and it was September before Romano could find a suitable replacement (an experienced case maker in Florida who happened to be a relative of another Steinway worker).

The company's employees don't necessarily share Spellman's sense of the company's legacy, but many of them are well aware of the brand recognition commanded by the products they craft, according to Romano:

> *The payback is not in [the factory]. The payback is outside, when you get the celebrity treatment for building a Steinway, when you meet somebody for the first time and they* ooh *and* ahh: *"You build Steinways? Wow."* You're automatically put on a higher level, and you go, "I didn't realize I was that notable."50

Case Questions

1. Explain the process by which a Steinway grand piano is constructed as a *subsystem* of a larger *system*. From what the text tells you, give some examples of how the production subsystem is affected by the management, financial, and marketing subsystems.

2. Discuss the Steinway process in terms of the *systems perspective* of organizations summarized in Figure 1.4. Explain the role of each of the three elements highlighted by the figure—*inputs from the environment*, the *transformation process*, and *outputs into the environment*.

3. Discuss some of the ways the principles of *behavioral management* and *operations management* can throw light on the Steinway process. How about the *contingency perspective*? In what ways does the Steinway process reflect a *universal perspective*, and in what ways does it reflect a *contingency perspective*?

You Make the Call

Reed Hastings Doesn't Like Standing Still

1. You're a Netflix employee, and Reed Hastings has just stopped by your desk. "I'd like to know," he says, "what do you like most and least about working here?" How do you think you might respond?

2. You're a major Netflix stockholder attending the firm's annual board meeting. When you bump into Reed Hastings at a reception, he asks you, "How do you think we're doing with this company?" How would you respond?

3. You're the founder and owner of a small media company, and Netflix has indicated an interest in buying your business. Reed Hastings wants you to stay on and run the business as a unit of Netflix. In addition to price, what other factors (if any) are important to you?

4. You've been contacted by a marketing research company doing work for Netflix. The researcher asks if you use Netflix and, if not, why? If you do use Netflix, the researcher asks what you like and dislike most about it. What would you say?

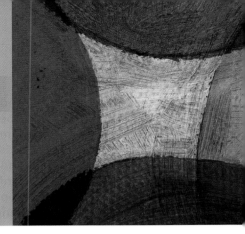

CHAPTER 2

The Environments of Organizations and Managers

Learning Outcomes

After studying this chapter, you should be able to:

2-1 Discuss the nature of an organization's environments and the components of its general, task, and internal environments.

2-2 Describe managerial ethics and the ethical environment of management.

2-3 Discuss the concept of social responsibility.

2-4 Discuss the international environment of management.

2-5 Describe the importance and determinants of an organization's culture.

Organizations exist for a variety of reasons. Some pursue profits. Others exist to serve the public good. But regardless of its purpose or mission, any organization must be properly aligned with its environment if it is to be effective. Of course, there are disparate views on how this alignment should be achieved and how an organization can legitimately pursue and then use revenues or profits. Some companies aggressively seek to maximize their profits, grow at any cost, and focus on nothing but what is best for the company. Others take a much different approach to business and actively work for the betterment of society, even when it means less profit for the owners. Clearly, then, the environmental context of business today is changing in unprecedented—and often unpredictable—ways.

Management in Action

Turbulence In the Air

"This airplane is designed by clowns who in turn are supervised by monkeys."

—Unnamed Boeing employee in company email

Boeing is among the world's largest aerospace companies and the largest defense contractor in the world. The firm designs and manufactures airplanes, rotocraft (helicopter-type aircraft), rockets, satellites, telecommunications equipment, and missiles worldwide. Boeing is also the largest U.S. exporter based on dollar value. Most members of the general public, though, know Boeing primarily and simply as a large manufacturer of commercial airplanes. In a good year Boeing generates over $95 billion in revenue and $9–10 billion in profits.

Boeing planes that are popular today include the 737, 767, 777, and 787. These planes are sold to airlines around the world and are used by dozens of major airlines. Boeing is also known for the iconic 747, once the world's largest passenger plane. Today, though, the 747 has been taken out of service by most passenger airlines and is primarily used for cargo. The 737 is the firm's best-selling plane and among the top-selling commercial jets in aviation history. In 2010, however, Boeing's primary competitor, Airbus, announced a major new product, the A320 family of planes, designed to be much more fuel and operationally efficient than existing planes. Boeing quickly realized that the A320 posed a significant threat and felt a strong competitive urgency to follow suit. And indeed, it was with great fanfare that Boeing announced the latest (fourth) version of the 737 in 2011. The appeal of the new generation of 737s was to be a combination of increased passenger capacity and much lower fuel costs. The firm initially budgeted $3 billion for research and development costs.

Dubbed the 737 MAX, the new plane took its maiden voyage in 2016 and received final Federal Aviation Administration (FAA) certification in 2017. Interestingly, during the plane's development Boeing had pushed the FAA for quick approvals and the government regulatory agency actually delegated some of the review processes to Boeing itself, effectively allowing the firm to review its own products. The plane was an instant hit and Boeing quickly secured orders for almost 5,000 of the new planes. The first two planes were delivered to overseas airlines and then the next batch was delivered to Southwest Airlines in 2017. After one year Boeing had delivered 137 737 MAXs to 28 airlines in several countries. (In keeping with standard practice, the 737 MAX is available in three configurations, the 7, 8, and 9, each with different seating capacities.)

Unfortunately, though, disaster soon struck. A MAX 8 crashed in October 2018 and another crashed in March 2019, resulting in 346 deaths. Aviation authorities around the world quickly grounded all 737 MAXs while investigations were conducted into the cause(s) of these two crashes.

The initial problem was soon discovered. The new 737 series planes were built with a new enhanced navigation system. One part of this system was programmed to take control of the plane and force it into a nosedive under certain emergency conditions. However, details about this part of the enhanced navigation system were omitted from both technical flight manuals and flight crew training programs. Complicating things even more, the system could be unnecessarily activated if a single sensor failed and pilots were not informed of how to override it if it was activated. As Boeing and the FAA investigated more fully, however, it was also learned that there were other technical, mechanical, and electronic problems with the 737 MAX series and production of new planes was halted until these problems could be fixed. In December 2019 Boeing fired its CEO because of his handling of the crisis and estimated that it would incur costs of nearly $20 billion for litigation and compensation for the crashes, reworking the planes, and penalty payments to airlines for not being able to meet delivery schedules. Boeing also announced that no new 737s would be produced until at least late 2020.

As all of these events unfolded, other problems began to surface. For one thing, there seemed to be some evidence that Boeing was aware of the problems with the new planes for at least a year before the first crash. Boeing's board of directors was also criticized for lack of oversight and ineffective corporate governance. Further compounding the problem, Boeing was forced to release documents that showed numerous derogatory emails sent between Boeing employees about the design of the MAX series, about the FAA, and about poor training being provided to pilots. All things considered, these events have painted Boeing in a very poor light and public relations experts suggest it may take the firm years to improve its image and reputation.

History, unfortunately, provides an unflattering view of Boeing and its ethical context. Over the past few decades the firm has pled guilty to numerous instances of questionable conduct. These include:

- 1989: pled guilty and paid a fine for corporate espionage
- 1994: paid a fine to settle charges for overcharging the government

- 2000: paid a fine to settle two whistleblower complaints about using defective components in helicopters
- 2003: paid a fine for corporate espionage
- 2004–2020: paid several fines for overcharging the government

Boeing has also been fined numerous times for environmental damages, for improper labor practices, and for violating numerous export rules and laws.

Looking ahead, as noted earlier, Boeing fired its CEO in December 2019. His departure package included around $62 million in compensation and pension benefits. The new CEO, David Calhoun, received a $10 million signing bonus, a base salary of $1.4 million, another $2.5 million in bonuses tied to various financial targets, and additional potential bonuses tied to getting the 737 MAX back on track and fixing other problems. One industry expert said, "Putting in place a world-class leader like Dave at the helm of Boeing is good for the company and important to the country." Not everyone was impressed, though. Another industry expert noted, "He seems like a capable manager, but he was on the board when all the decisions [about the 737 MAX] were made." To state the obvious, going forward many people will be paying close attention to what happens next at Boeing.[1]

2-1 THE ORGANIZATION'S ENVIRONMENTS

As we noted in Chapter 1, managers must have a deep understanding and appreciation of the environments in which they and their organizations function. Without this understanding, they are like rudderless ships—moving along, but with no way of maneuvering or changing direction. The external environment is everything outside an organization's boundaries that might affect it. It is actually most helpful, though, to talk about two separate external environments: the general environment and the task environment. An organization's internal environment consists of conditions and forces within the organization.

2-1a The General Environment

Each of the following dimensions embodies conditions and events that have the potential to influence the organization in significant ways.

The Economic Dimension   The economic dimension of an organization's general environment is the overall health and vitality of the economic system in which the organization operates.[2] Particularly important economic factors for business are general economic growth, inflation, interest rates, and unemployment. After several strong years of growth, the U.S. economy fell into recession during 2008 and only began to recover from it in 2012. During this period, energy and related prices jumped, business and economic growth slowed dramatically, and unemployment mushroomed as one struggling business after another made workforce cuts. As the economy began to recover in 2013, though, prices stabilized, businesses began to grow again, and unemployment began to decline as companies again started to hire new employees. By 2019 unemployment was approaching record lows and some businesses had trouble finding new employees. However, during the COVID-19 pandemic in 2020 many businesses laid off thousands of workers due to the overall economic slowdown. As a result, unemployment surged.

Consider how these factors affect an organization like McDonald's. When unemployment is low, McDonald's may have difficulty hiring new employees because higher-paying full-time jobs are available elsewhere. But at the same time more people may be eating at McDonald's because of its low prices. Similarly, low inflation means that the prices McDonald's must pay for its supplies remain relatively constant, but it also is somewhat constrained from increasing the prices it charges consumers for a hamburger or milkshake. The economic dimension is

---

external environment
Everything outside an organization's boundaries that might affect it

general environment
The set of broad dimensions and forces in an organization's surroundings that determines its overall context

task environment
Specific organizations or groups that affect the organization

internal environment
The conditions and forces within an organization

economic dimension
The overall health and vitality of the economic system in which the organization operates

also important to nonbusiness organizations. For example, during weak economic conditions, funding for state universities may drop, and charitable organizations such as the Salvation Army are asked to provide greater assistance at the same time that their incoming contributions dwindle. Similarly, hospitals are affected by the number of uninsured patients who come to their emergency rooms for treatment.

> "If you manage the business well throughout the good times, then the bad times are not quite as pronounced or profound. But it's actually more difficult to manage during the good times."
>
> —William Weldon, Former Ceo of Johnson & Johnson[3]

technological dimension
The methods available for converting resources into products or services

political–legal dimension
The government regulation of business and the relationship between business and government

The Technological Dimension The technological dimension of the general environment is made up of the methods available for converting resources into products or services. Although technology is applied within the organization, the forms and availability of that technology come from the general environment. Computer-assisted manufacturing and design techniques, for example, allow Airbus to simulate the more than three miles of hydraulic tubing that runs through its new A320 aircraft. The results include decreased warehouse needs, higher-quality tube fittings, lower labor costs, and major time savings. Although some people associate technology with manufacturing firms, it is also relevant in the service sector. For example, just as an automobile follows a predetermined path along an assembly line as it is built, a hamburger at McDonald's follows a predefined path as the meat is cooked, the burger assembled, and the finished product wrapped and bagged for a customer. And the company has installed kiosks in many of its stores so that customers can place orders on a touch screen and pay without having to stand in line. The rapid infusion of web-based technologies into all areas of business also reflects the technological dimension. Another recent advancement is the rapid growth of integrated business software systems. Relatively new approaches to communication, ranging from social media to hardware, are also influencing businesses in many different ways.

The Political–Legal Dimension The political–legal dimension of the general environment consists of government regulation of business and the relationship between business and government. This dimension is important for three basic reasons. First, the legal system partially defines what an organization can and cannot do. Although the United States is basically a free-market economy, major regulation of business activity still exits. McDonald's, for example, is subject to a variety of political and legal forces, including food preparation standards and local zoning requirements.

Second, pro- or anti-business sentiment in government influences business activity. For example, during periods of pro-business sentiment, firms find it easier to compete and have fewer concerns about antitrust issues. On the other hand, during a period of anti-business sentiment, firms may find their competitive strategies more restricted and have fewer opportunities for mergers and acquisitions because of antitrust concerns. During the prolonged period of economic growth that ended in 2008, the U.S. government adopted a very "hands-off" approach to business, letting market forces determine business successes and failures. However, as the economy ground

Most people associate the word *technology* with *tangible* products such as airplanes, smartphones, and so forth. But technology also applies to service organizations as well. Take this food service operation, for instance. Workers are preparing and serving food using assembly-line technology pioneered in the manufacturing sector.

iStock.com/andresr

to a halt in 2008 and first one and then another industry began to stumble, critics began to point to lack of regulation and oversight as contributing factors. As a result, lawmakers began to take a much more pronounced interest in adopting new and stricter regulations for business.[4] During the administration of President Donald Trump, though, regulations were again rolled back, especially those that had been imposed for purposes related to environmental protection.

monticello/Shutterstock.com

McDonald's has historically competed with other hamburger chains such as Burger King and Wendy's. Recently, though, it has also taken on Starbucks with its line of McCafe premium coffee products and its more casual and comfortable in-store seating areas.

Finally, political stability has ramifications for planning. No business wants to set up shop in another country unless trade relationships with that country are relatively well defined and stable. Hence, U.S. firms are more likely to do business in Germany, Mexico, and Canada than in Syria and Afghanistan. Similar issues are relevant to assessments of local and state governments. A new city council or governor can affect many organizations, especially small firms that do business in only one location and are susceptible to deed and zoning restrictions, property and school taxes, and the like.

2-1b The Task Environment

Because the general environment's impact is often vague, imprecise, and long term, most organizations tend to focus attention on their task environment, which includes competitors, customers, suppliers, strategic partners, and regulators. Although the task environment is also quite complex, it provides useful information more readily than the general environment because the manager can identify environmental factors of specific interest to the organization, rather than deal with the more abstract dimensions of the general environment.[5] Figure 2.1 illustrates the task environment of McDonald's.

competitor
An organization that competes with other organizations for resources

Competitors   An organization's competitors are other organizations that compete with it for resources. The most obvious resources that competitors vie for are customer dollars. Nike and Under Armour are competitors, as are Albertson's, Wegmans, Safeway, and Kroger. McDonald's competes with other fast-food operations, such as Burger King, Wendy's, Subway, and Dairy Queen; it has also taken on Starbucks with its McCafe line of premium coffee products. But competition also occurs between substitute products. Thus, Ford competes with Yamaha (motorcycles), Schwinn (bicycles), and various public transportation systems for your transportation dollars; and Walt Disney World, Carnival Cruise Lines, and the National Park system compete for your vacation dollars. Nor is competition limited to business firms. Universities compete with trade schools, the military, other universities, and the external labor market to attract good students; and art galleries compete with one another to attract the best collections and exhibits.

customer
Whoever pays money to acquire an organization's products or services

Customers   A second dimension of the task environment is customers or whoever pays money to acquire an organization's products or services. Most McDonald's customers are individuals who buy food. But customers need not be individuals. Schools, hospitals, government agencies, wholesalers, retailers, and manufacturers are just a few of the many kinds of organizations that may be major customers of other organizations. Some institutional customers, such as schools, prisons, and hospitals, also buy food in bulk from restaurants such as McDonald's.

supplier
An organization that provides resources for other organizations

Supplier   Suppliers are organizations that provide resources for other organizations. McDonald's buys soft-drink products from Coca-Cola; individually packaged servings of

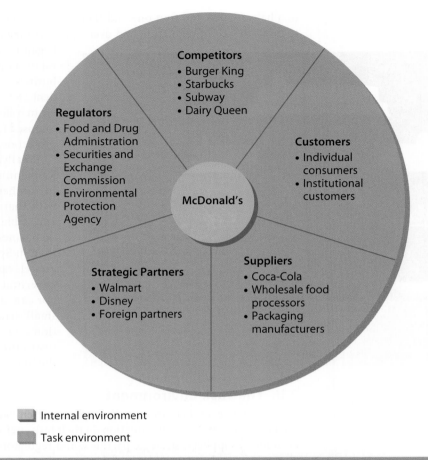

Internal environment

Task environment

FIGURE 2.1

McDonald's Task Environment

An organization's task environment includes its competitors, customers, suppliers, strategic partners, and regulators. This figure clearly highlights how managers at McDonald's can use this framework to identify and understand their key constituents.

regulator
A body that has the potential to control, legislate, or otherwise influence the organization's policies and practices

regulatory agencies
An agency created by the government to regulate business activities

Organizations can serve a variety of different kinds of customers. For example, customers can be individuals, the government, or other businesses. This pizza delivery person, for example, is dropping off pizzas for the staff of a hospital emergency room.

salt, pepper, and ketchup from various suppliers; Big Mac ingredients from wholesale food processors; and napkins, sacks, and sandwich wrappers from packaging manufacturers. Besides material resources such as these, businesses also rely on suppliers for information (such as economic statistics), labor (in the form of employment agencies), and capital (from lenders such as banks). Some businesses strive to avoid depending exclusively on particular suppliers. Others, however, find it beneficial to create strong relationships with single suppliers. One of the most significant economic "ripple" effects of the COVID-19 virus pandemic in 2020 was its impact on global supply chains.

Regulators   Regulators are elements of the task environment that have the potential to control, legislate, or otherwise influence an organization's policies and practices. There are two important kinds of regulators. Regulatory agencies are created by the government to protect the public from certain business practices or to protect organizations from one another. Powerful federal regulatory agencies include the Environmental Protection Agency, the Securities and Exchange Commission (SEC), the Food and Drug Administration

(FDA), and the Equal Employment Opportunity Commission. Many of these agencies play important roles in protecting the rights of individuals. The FDA, for example, helps ensure that the food is free from contaminants; thus, it is an important regulator for McDonald's and Starbucks. There are also numerous state, regional, and local regulatory agencies that also affect businesses. Perhaps not surprisingly, some managers complain that there is too much government regulation. Most large companies must dedicate thousands of labor hours and hundreds of thousands of dollars a year to comply with government regulations. To complicate managers' lives even more, different regulatory agencies sometimes provide inconsistent—and even contradictory—mandates.

interest group
A group organized by its members to attempt to influence organizations

The other basic form of regulator is the interest group. Prominent interest groups include Mothers Against Drunk Driving (MADD), the National Rifle Association (NRA), the League of Women Voters, the Sierra Club, Ralph Nader's Center for the Study of Responsive Law, Consumers Union, and industry self-regulation groups such as the Council of Better Business Bureaus. Although interest groups lack the official power of government agencies, they can exert considerable influence by using the media to call attention to their positions. MADD, for example, puts considerable pressure on alcoholic-beverage producers (to put warning labels on their products), automobile companies (to make it more difficult for intoxicated people to start their cars), local governments (to stiffen drinking ordinances), and bars and restaurants (to refuse to sell alcohol to people who are drinking too much).

strategic partner
(also called *strategic ally*)
An organization working together with one or more other organizations in a joint venture or similar arrangement

Strategic Partners   Another dimension of the task environment is strategic partners (also called *strategic allies*)—two or more companies that work together in joint ventures or other partnerships.[6] As shown in Figure 2.1, McDonald's has several strategic partners. For example, it has one arrangement with Walmart whereby small McDonald's restaurants are built inside some Walmart stores. The firm also has a long-term deal with Disney: McDonald's promotes Disney movies in its stores, and Disney has allowed McDonald's to open restaurants near its resorts. And many of the firm's foreign stores are built in collaboration with local investors. Strategic partnerships help companies get from other companies the expertise they lack. The partnerships also help spread risk and open new market opportunities. Indeed, most strategic partnerships are actually among international firms. For example, Nestlé (a Swiss company) and General Mills (a U.S. company) have a global alliance called Cereal Partners Worldwide, or CPW. When the new venture was launched in 1991 General Mills provided brand recognition and propriety cereal-processing techniques, while Nestlé provided global distribution channels and marketing expertise. Today CPW markets cereals and other breakfast foods in over 130 countries.

McDonald's and Walmart have a strategic partnership. Under the terms of this partnership McDonald's owns and operates restaurants inside many Walmart stores. This "Golden Arches" restaurant, for example, is inside a Walmart store.

2-1c The Internal Environment

Organizations also have an internal environment that consists of their owners, boards of directors, employees, and physical work environment. (Another especially important part of the internal environment is the organization's culture, discussed separately later in this chapter.)

owner
Whoever can claim property rights to an organization

Owners   The owners of a business are, of course, the people who have legal property rights to that business. Owners can be a single individual who establishes and runs a small business, partners who jointly own the business, individual investors who buy stock in a corporation, or other organizations. McDonald's has 764 million shares of stock, each of which represents one unit of ownership in the firm. The family of McDonald's founder Ray Kroc stills owns a large block of this stock, as do several large institutional investors. In addition, there are thousands of individuals who own just a few shares each. McDonald's, in turn, owns other businesses. For example, it owns several large regional bakeries that supply its restaurants with buns. Each of these is incorporated as a separate legal entity and managed as a wholly owned subsidiary by the parent company. McDonald's is also a partner in some Russian farms that grow potatoes to supply regional restaurants with french fries.

board of directors
Governing body that is elected by a corporation's stockholders and charged with overseeing the general management of the firm to ensure that it is being run in a way that best serves the stockholders' interests

Board of Directors   A corporate board of directors is a governing body that is elected by the stockholders and charged with overseeing a firm's general management to ensure that it is run to best serve the stockholders' interests. Some boards are relatively passive: They perform a general oversight function but seldom get actively involved in how the company is really run. But this trend is changing, as more and more boards are carefully scrutinizing the firms they oversee and exerting more influence over how they are being managed. This trend has been accelerated by numerous recent business scandals. In some cases, board members have been accused of wrongdoing. In other cases, boards have been found negligent for failing to monitor the actions of the firm's executives. At issue is the concept of corporate governance—who is responsible for governing the actions of a business? McDonald's has a board of directors composed of 13 members. This board includes three inside members (full-time executives of the firm) and ten outside members (individuals who do not work directly for the firm). This presumably allows decisions to be made in ways that protect the interests of diverse stakeholders.

Employees   An organization's employees are also a major element of its internal environment. Of particular interest to managers today is the changing nature of the workforce, which is becoming increasingly more diverse in terms of gender, ethnicity, age, and other dimensions. Workers are also calling for more job ownership—either partial ownership in the company or at least more say in how they perform their jobs.[7] Another trend in many firms is increased reliance on temporary workers—individuals hired for short periods of time with no expectation of permanent employment. Employers often prefer to use "temps" because they provide greater flexibility, earn lower wages, and often do not participate in benefits programs. In 2019 the United Auto Workers went on strike against General Motors, demanding more job security and a clearer path to permanent employment for temporary workers. But these managers also have to deal with what often amounts to a two-class workforce and with a growing number of employees who have no loyalty to the organization where they work because they may be working for a different one tomorrow.[8] Our *Doing Business on Planet Earth* feature highlights an interesting twist on how one company is succeeding by providing its employees with some unusual perks.

Physical Work Environment   A final part of the internal environment is the organization's actual physical environment and the work that people do. Some firms have their facilities in downtown skyscrapers, usually spread across several floors. Others locate in suburban or rural settings and may have facilities more closely resembling a college campus. Some facilities have long halls lined with traditional offices. Others have modular cubicles with partial walls and no doors. Pitney Bowes Credit Corporation remodeled its offices to create something like an indoor theme park with cobblestone-like carpet, a town square clock, a café, and a diner.

DOING BUSINESS ON PLANET EARTH

Raising the CSR Bar

To celebrate a recent company anniversary, Clif Bar & Co., a maker of organic nutrition foods and beverages, gave all of its employees—more than 250 of them— new bicycles. It may not be the workplace perk for everyone, but it caught the eye of Leon Kaye, a consultant specializing in corporate social responsibility (CSR). Kaye put the company's bicycle giveaway on his list of the year's "Top 10 Employee Engagement Strategies."

As a matter of fact, bicycles figure prominently in Clif Bar's "Cool Commute" program: Employees can take advantage of financial incentives for riding their bicycles to work, and those who missed out on a free bike can still get a $500 stipend toward the purchase of one. Other programs provide incentives for buying fuel-efficient cars and making eco-friendly home improvements. In turn, the "Cool Commute" program reflects two of Clif Bar's five core values—"Sustaining Our Planet" and "Sustaining Our People." The company is also committed to sustaining its community, business, and brands and, taken together, these five values constitute its "Five Aspirations."

Kit Crawford, who co-owns Clif Bar with husband Gary Erickson, stresses "the interconnectivity of the Five Aspirations," which, as she's also quick to point out, serve as the company's "five bottom lines." "Gary and I," she says, "use these bottom lines … as a measurement of our return on investment," and all five are "of equal importance" in determining how well the company is using its resources to achieve its goals. In addition, says Crawford, the five commitments ensure that "our people have a clear understanding of Clif Bar's values." By providing a clear "decision-making framework," they also guide employees in "exploring, creating, and launching ideas that are in tune with the company's priorities." Finally, they figure into each employee's annual review: "Our people," explains Crawford, "receive specific feedback on their contributions to each of the Five Aspirations.... These assessments determine each employee's bonus for the year."

The company itself works out of a state-of-the-art solar-powered facility in Emeryville, California, where 80 percent of the waste is reused or recycled. There's even a staff ecologist on the payroll. For founder Gary Erickson, the goals of sustaining the planet and sustaining his company's people are inseparable threads in a single fabric of socially responsible leadership: "We want to sustain a business," he says, "where people can live, not just make a living. We believe that if we provide meaningful work as well as something beyond work, people will do their jobs well and lead healthier, more balanced lives."

Clif Bar thus maintains an elaborate wellness program that encourages employees to get out and enjoy the natural environment that they're working to sustain. Employees who've been with the company for seven years, for instance, can take six to eight weeks of paid sabbatical, and the Emeryville facility boasts an in-house fitness center where employees can get paid time off to work out under the guidance of full-time personal trainers.

How has all of this socially responsible conduct affected the bottom line—that is, the bottom line that is typically defined as how much money a company makes? In 1992, its first year of business, Clif Bar had $700,000 in sales. That figure doubled every year up to 1997, when sales hit $20 million. Since then, the company has continued to grow rapidly ("stratospherically," as Kaye would have it), achieving a remarkable compounded annual growth rate of 23 percent in the 10 years from 2002 until 2011, when sales reached $340 million. A year later, sales topped $500 million and by 2019 topped $6.2 billion.

References: Leon Kaye, "Top 10 Employment Engagement Strategies," *TriplePundit*, April 15, 2013, www.triplepundit.com on January 15, 2020; Susan McPherson, "The Most Dynamic Social Innovation Initiatives of 2012," *Forbes.com*, December 17, 2012, www.forbes.com on January 15, 2020; Bob Vanourek and Gregg Vanourek, "Sustainable Leadership': Interview with Kit Crawford," *Triple Crown Leadership*, October 18, 2012, www.triplecrown-leadership.com on January 15, 2020; Robert Girling, "Good Companies Like Clif Bar: How They Do It," *TriplePundit*, July 17, 2012, www.triplepundit.com on January 15, 2020; Great Place to Work, "Clif Bar & Company," *Great Rated*, 2014, http://us.greatrated.com on January 15, 2020; Lauren Drell, "Six Companies with Awesome Employee Perks," *Mashable*, August 7, 2011, http://mashable.com on January 15, 2020.

Increasingly, newer facilities have an even more open arrangement, where people work in large rooms, moving among different tables to interact with different people on different projects. Freestanding computer workstations are available for those who need them, and a few small rooms might be off to the side for private business.

Employee safety and health regulations have caused many organizations to pay more attention to their internal environment. This concern, in turn, has also fostered new business opportunities. Rebecca Boenigk, founder and CEO of Neutral Posture, turned a small operation in her garage into an international company selling neutral body posture chairs designed by her father, Dr. Jerome Congleton.

Manager's Checklist

- ☐ Managers need to understand the general environment and the core elements of the task environment and how elements of their environment affect their business.

- ☐ If managers can not only understand their general and task environments but also be able to anticipate changes, they can use their insights for competitive advantage.

- ☐ Managers need to understand the main parts of their organization's internal environment, as well as how it affects the organization's success.

- ☐ Regardless of their level, managers should have a clear knowledge of their organization's governance structure.

2-2 THE ETHICAL AND SOCIAL ENVIRONMENT OF MANAGEMENT

The ethical and social environment has become an especially important area for managers in the last few years. In this section, we first explore the concept of individual ethics and then describe social responsibility.

2-2a Individual Ethics in Organizations

ethics
An individual's personal beliefs about whether a behavior, action, or decision is right or wrong

ethical behavior
Behavior that conforms to generally accepted social norms

unethical behavior
Behavior that does not conform to generally accepted social norms

managerial ethics
Standards of behavior that guide individual managers in their work

We define **ethics** as an individual's personal beliefs about whether a behavior, action, or decision is right or wrong.[9] Note that we define *ethics* in the context of the individual—people have ethics, whereas organizations do not. Likewise, what constitutes ethical behavior varies from one person to another. For example, one person who finds a $20 bill on the floor of an empty room may believe that it is okay to keep it, whereas another may feel compelled to turn it in to the lost-and-found department. Furthermore, although **ethical behavior** is in the eye of the beholder, the term usually refers to behavior that conforms to generally accepted social norms. **Unethical behavior**, then, is behavior that does not conform to generally accepted social norms.

Managerial Ethics   **Managerial ethics** consists of the standards of behavior that guide individual managers in their work.[10] One important area of managerial ethics is the treatment of employees by the organization. It includes, for example, hiring and firing, wages and working conditions, and employee privacy and respect. An example of how different managers might approach this area involves minimum wages. While the U.S. government sets a minimum hourly wage, this amount is often not enough to live above the poverty level in high-cost areas such as New York and San Francisco. Some managers might say that paying only the legal minimum is the right business practice, while others might be inclined to pay a wage more attuned to local conditions (sometimes called a *living wage*).

Numerous ethical issues stem from how employees treat the organization, especially in regard to conflicts of interest, secrecy and confidentiality, and honesty. A *conflict of interest* occurs when an employee's decision potentially benefits the individual to the possible detriment of the organization. To guard against such practices, most companies have

Corporate expense accounts are sometimes the subject of ethical lapses. For instance, these two colleagues are having lunch together and discussing business. In theory, it may be easy for one of them to "pad" the lunch expense so as to be reimbursed for more money than was actually spent.

TORWAISTUDIO/Shutterstock.com

policies that forbid their buyers from accepting gifts from suppliers. Divulging company secrets is also clearly unethical. A few employees who work for businesses in highly competitive industries—electronics, software, and fashion apparel, for example—have been caught selling information about their companies' plans to competitors. Another area of concern is honesty in general. Relatively common problems in this area include activities such as using business assets for personal activities, using social media during work hours, stealing supplies, and padding expense accounts. Although most employees are inherently honest, organizations must nevertheless be vigilant to avoid problems with such behaviors.

> **"I must stand with anybody that stands right, and stand with him while he is right, and part with him when he is wrong."**
>
> —Abraham Lincoln[11]

Managerial ethics also comes into play in the relationship between the firm and its employees with other economic agents. The primary agents of interest include customers, competitors, stockholders, suppliers, dealers, and unions. The behaviors between the organization and these agents that may be subject to ethical ambiguity include advertising and promotions, financial disclosures, ordering and purchasing, shipping and solicitations, bargaining and negotiation, and other business relationships.

For example, state pharmacy boards are charged with overseeing prescription drug safety in the United States. All told, almost 300 pharmacists serve on such boards. One study found that 72 of these pharmacists were actually employees of major drugstore chains and supermarket pharmacies. These arrangements, while legal, could create the potential for conflicts of interest because they might give the pharmacist's employers influence over the regulatory system designed to monitor their own business practices.[12]

James Lauritz/Digital Vision/Getty Images

Unethical behavior refers to behavior that does not conform to generally accepted social norms. Bribery is one form of behavior that is both illegal and unethical. This individual, for example, might be paying off a building inspector to get a favorable inspection or a customer to get a big order.

Another recent area of concern involves financial reporting by various e-commerce firms. Because of the complexities inherent in valuing the assets and revenues of these firms, some of them have been very aggressive in presenting their financial position in a highly positive light. And at least a few firms have substantially overstated their earnings projections to entice more investment. Moreover, some of today's accounting scandals in traditional firms have stemmed from similarly questionable practices. For example, Diamond Foods, a distributor of nuts and popcorn snacks, had to restate its earnings twice because it had improperly accounted for $80 million in payments to almond growers.[13]

Managing Ethical Behavior   Spurred partially by increased awareness of ethics scandals in business and partially by a sense of enhanced corporate consciousness about the distinction between ethical and unethical behaviors, many organizations have reemphasized ethical behavior on the part of employees. This emphasis takes many forms, but any effort to enhance ethical behavior must begin with top management. It is top managers, for example, who establish the organization's culture and define what will and what will not be acceptable behavior. Some companies have also started offering employees training in how to cope with ethical dilemmas. At Boeing, for example, line managers lead training sessions for other employees, and the company has an ethics committee that reports directly to the board of directors. The training sessions involve discussions of different ethical dilemmas that employees might face and how managers might handle those dilemmas. Chemical Bank,

Halliburton, and Xerox also have ethics training programs for their managers. Still, issues continue to arise. For instance, one recent study found an increase in the number of employees who called in sick when they were not, in fact, ill but just wanted to have a day off.[14]

Organizations are also making greater efforts to formalize their ethical standards. Some, such as General Mills and Johnson & Johnson, have prepared guidelines that detail how employees are to treat suppliers, customers, competitors, and other constituents. Others, such as Whirlpool, Texas Instruments, and HP, have developed a formal code of ethics—written statements of the values and ethical standards that guide the firms' actions. Of course, firms must adhere to such codes if they are to be of value. In one now-infamous case, Enron's board of directors voted to set aside the firm's code of ethics to implement a business plan that was in violation of that code.[15]

Of course, no code, guideline, or training program can truly substitute for the quality of an individual's personal judgment about what is right behavior and what is wrong behavior in a particular situation. Such devices may prescribe what people should do, but they often fail to help people understand and live with the consequences of their choices. Making ethical choices may lead to very unpleasant outcomes—firing, rejection by colleagues, and the forfeiture of monetary gain, to name a few. Thus, managers must be prepared to confront their own conscience and weigh the options available when making difficult ethical decisions.

code of ethics
A formal, written statement of the values and ethical standards that guide a firm's action

2-2b Emerging Ethical Issues

Ethical scandals have become almost commonplace in today's world. Ranging from business and sports to politics and the entertainment industry, these scandals have rocked stakeholder confidence and called into question the moral integrity of our society. At the same time, most women and men today conduct themselves and their affairs in accordance with high ethical standards. Hence, as we summarize several emerging ethical issues in organizations, it is important to remember that one cannot judge everyone by the transgressions of a few.

How businesses interact with the natural environment plays a complex role in social responsibility. This scene alone, for example, shows a wind farm set near an industrial site spewing black smoke into the environment.

AniphaeS/Getty Images

Ethical Leadership   In recent years, the media have been rife with stories about unscrupulous corporate leaders. For every unethical senior manager, of course, there are many highly ethical ones. But the actions of such high-profile deposed executives as Martin Shkreli (Turing Pharmaceuticals), Carlos Ghosn (Nissan), Roger Ailes (Fox News), and Les Moonves (ViacomCBS) have substantially increased the scrutiny directed at all executives. As a direct result, executives everywhere are expected to exhibit nothing but the strongest ethical conduct. This leadership, in turn, is expected to help set the tone for the rest of the organization and to establish both norms and a culture that reinforce the importance of ethical behavior.

Sarbanes–Oxley Act of 2002
A law that requires CEOs and CFOs to vouch personally for the truthfulness and fairness of their firms' financial disclosures and imposes tough new measures to deter and punish corporate and accounting fraud and corruption

The basic premise behind ethical leadership is that because leaders serve as role models for others, their every action is subject to scrutiny. If a senior executive exercises questionable judgment, this sends a signal to others that such actions are acceptable. This signal may, in turn, be remembered by others when they face similar situations. As a result, CEOs like General Motors' Mary Barra and Costco's W. Craig Jelinek are sometimes held up as the standard against which others should be measured. The basic premise is that CEOs must set their company's moral tone by being honest and straightforward and by taking responsibility for any shortcomings that are identified. To support this view, Congress passed the Sarbanes–Oxley Act of 2002, requiring CEOs and CFOs to vouch personally for the truthfulness and fairness of their firms' financial disclosures. The law also imposes tough new measures to deter and punish corporate and accounting fraud and corruption.

Corporate Governance   A related area of emerging concern is ethical issues in corporate governance. As discussed earlier in this chapter, the board of directors of a public corporation is expected to ensure that the business is being properly managed and that the decisions made by its senior management are in the best interests of shareholders and other stakeholders. But many of the recent ethical scandals discussed here actually started with a breakdown in the corporate governance structure. For instance, World-Com's board once approved a personal loan to the firm's then-CEO, Bernard Ebbers, for $366 million, even though there was little evidence that he could repay it. And as we noted in our opening case Boeing's board was criticized for its poor oversight during the development of the 737 MAX. Boards of directors are also criticized when they are seen as not being sufficiently independent from senior management.[16] Only three of the 13 directors at McDonald's are also members of the firm's top management team.

Ethics and Information Technology   A final set of issues that has emerged in recent times involves information technology. Among the specific focal points in this area are individual rights to privacy and individuals' potential abuse of information technology. Indeed, online privacy has become a hot topic as companies sort out the related ethical and management issues. Both Facebook and Google have come under fire in recent years when it was discovered that these firms were looking into ways to track people's movement as individuals logged into the sites. Regulatory agencies continue to look into how to both protect privacy while also not overly restraining free trade.

One way in which management can address these concerns is to post a privacy policy on the company website. The policy should explain exactly what data the company collects and who gets to see the data. It should also allow people a choice about having their information shared with others and indicate how people can opt out of data collection. Disney, IBM, and other companies support this position by refusing to advertise on websites that have no posted privacy policies.

In addition, companies can offer web surfers the opportunity to review and correct information that has been collected, especially medical and financial data. In the offline world, consumers are legally allowed to inspect their own credit and medical records. In the online world, this kind of access can be costly and cumbersome because data are often spread across several computer systems. Despite the technical difficulties, government agencies are already working on online privacy guidelines, which means that companies will need internal guidelines, training, and leadership to ensure that they are in compliance.

Manager's Checklist

☐ When assessing the ethical context of decisions, be sure to consider everyone who might be affected.

☐ Remember that while you think you will make ethical decisions, until you face hard choices you may not know for sure.

2-3 SOCIAL RESPONSIBILITY IN ORGANIZATIONS

As we have seen in this chapter, ethics are associated with individuals and their decisions and behaviors. Organizations themselves do not have ethics, but they relate to their environments in ways that often involve ethical dilemmas and decisions. These situations are generally referred to within the context of the organization's social responsibility. Specifically, social responsibility is the set of obligations an organization has to protect and enhance the societal context in which it functions. Some of the more salient arguments on both sides of this contemporary debate are summarized in Figure 2.2 and are further explained in the following sections.

social responsibility
The set of obligations that an organization has to protect and enhance the societal context in which it functions

2-3a Arguments for and Against Social Responsibility

People who argue in favor of social responsibility claim that—because organizations create many of the problems that need to be addressed, such as air and water pollution and resource depletion—organizations should play a major role in solving them. They also argue that, because corporations are legally defined entities with most of the same privileges as private

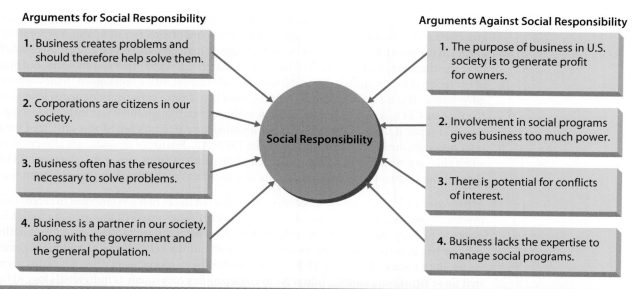

Arguments for Social Responsibility

1. Business creates problems and should therefore help solve them.

2. Corporations are citizens in our society.

3. Business often has the resources necessary to solve problems.

4. Business is a partner in our society, along with the government and the general population.

Social Responsibility

Arguments Against Social Responsibility

1. The purpose of business in U.S. society is to generate profit for owners.

2. Involvement in social programs gives business too much power.

3. There is potential for conflicts of interest.

4. Business lacks the expertise to manage social programs.

FIGURE 2.2

Arguments for and Against Social Responsibility

Although many people want everyone to see social responsibility as a desirable aim, there are in fact several strong arguments that can be advanced both for and against social responsibility. Hence organizations and their managers should carefully assess their own values, beliefs, and priorities when deciding which stance and approach to take regarding social responsibility.

citizens, businesses should not try to avoid their obligations as citizens. Advocates of social responsibility point out that, whereas governmental organizations have stretched their budgets to the limit, many large businesses often have surplus revenues that could be used to help solve social problems. For example, Dell donates surplus computers to schools, and many restaurants give leftover food to homeless shelters.

Some people, however, including famous economist Milton Friedman, argue that widening the interpretation of social responsibility will undermine the U.S. economy by detracting from the basic mission of business: to earn profits for owners. For example, money that Chevron or General Electric contributes to social causes or charities is money that could otherwise be distributed to owners in the form of dividends. Shareholders of Ben & Jerry's Homemade Holdings once expressed outrage when the firm refused to accept a lucrative exporting deal to Japan simply because the Japanese distributor did not have a strong social agenda.

Another objection to increasing the social responsibility of businesses reflects the position that corporations already wield enormous power and that involvement in social programs gives them even more power. Still another argument against social responsibility focuses on the potential for conflicts of interest. Suppose, for example, that one manager is in charge of deciding which local social program or charity will receive a large grant from her business. The local civic opera company (a not-for-profit organization that relies on contributions for its existence) might offer her front-row tickets for the upcoming season in exchange for her support. If opera is her favorite form of music, she may be tempted to direct the money toward the local company when it might actually be needed more in other areas.

Finally, critics argue that organizations lack the expertise to understand how to assess and make decisions about worthy social programs. How can a company truly know, they ask, which cause or program is most deserving of its support or how money might best be spent?

2-3b Managing Social Responsibility

The demands for social responsibility placed on contemporary organizations by an increasingly sophisticated and educated public are probably stronger than ever. As we have seen, there are pitfalls for managers who fail to adhere to high ethical standards and for companies that try to circumvent their legal obligations. Organizations therefore need to fashion an approach to social responsibility in the same way that they develop any other business strategy. In other words, they should view social responsibility as a major challenge that requires careful planning, decision making, consideration, and evaluation. They may accomplish this through both formal and informal dimensions of managing social responsibility.

Formal Organizational Dimensions   Some dimensions of managing social responsibility are formal and planned activities on the part of the organization. The formal organizational dimensions through which businesses can manage social responsibility include legal compliance, ethical compliance, and philanthropic giving.

legal compliance
The extent to which an organization complies with local, state, federal, and international laws

Legal compliance is the extent to which the organization conforms to local, state, federal, and international laws. The task of managing legal compliance is generally assigned to the appropriate functional managers. For example, the organization's top human resource executive is responsible for ensuring compliance with regulations concerning hiring, pay, and workplace safety and health. Likewise, the top finance executive generally oversees compliance with securities and banking regulations. The organization's legal department is likely to contribute to this effort by providing general oversight and answering queries from managers about the appropriate interpretation of laws and regulations. Unfortunately, though, legal compliance may not be enough—in some cases, for instance, perfectly legal accounting practices have still resulted in deception and other problems.

ethical compliance
The extent to which an organization and its members follow basic ethical standards of behavior

Ethical compliance is the extent to which the organization's members follow basic ethical (and legal) standards of behavior. We noted earlier that organizations have increased their efforts in this area—providing training in ethics and developing guidelines and codes of conduct, for example. These activities serve as vehicles for enhancing ethical compliance. Many organizations also establish formal ethics committees, which may be asked to review proposals for new projects, to help evaluate new hiring strategies, or to assess a new environmental protection plan. They might also serve as a peer-review panel to evaluate alleged ethical misconduct by an employee.

philanthropic giving
Awarding funds or gifts to charities or other worthy causes

Finally, **philanthropic giving** is the awarding of funds or gifts to charities or other worthy causes. Target routinely gives a share pretax income to charity and social programs. Omaha Steaks gives more than $100,000 per year to support the arts. Giving across national boundaries is also becoming more common. For example, Alcoa gave $112,000 to a small town in Brazil to build a sewage treatment plant. And Japanese firms such as Sony and Mitsubishi make contributions to many social programs in the United States. Many firms that make contributions are increasingly targeting them to programs or areas where the firm will get something in return. For example, firms today are more likely than they were a few years ago to give money to job-training programs rather than to the arts. The logic is that they get a more direct payoff from the former type of contribution—in this instance, a better-trained workforce from which to hire new employees.[17]

Informal Organizational Dimensions   In addition to these formal dimensions of managing social responsibility, there are also informal ones. Leadership, organizational culture, and how the organization responds to whistle-blowers all help shape and define people's perceptions of the organization's stance on social responsibility.

Leadership practices and organizational culture can go a long way toward defining the social responsibility stance an organization and its members will adopt.[18] As described earlier in this chapter, for example, ethical leadership often sets the tone for the entire organization. Our opening case notes how senior managers at Boeing may have contributed to ethical lapses at the firm. From a similar perspective, Walmart was charged with bribing officials in other countries in order to sidestep local regulations and expedite building permits for new stores. Investigators alleged that top managers, including the CEO at the time, knew about these practices but did nothing to stop them.[19]

whistle-blowing
The disclosure, by an employee, of illegal or unethical conduct on the part of others within the organization

Whistle-blowing is an employee's disclosure of illegal or unethical conduct by others within the organization.[20] How an organization responds to this practice often indicates its values as they relate to social responsibility. Whistle-blowers may have to proceed through a number of channels to be heard, and they may even get fired for their efforts. Many organizations, however, welcome their contributions. A person who observes questionable behavior typically first reports the incident to his or her boss. If nothing is done, the whistle-blower may then inform higher-level managers or an ethics committee, if one exists. Eventually, the person may have to go to a regulatory agency or even the media to be heard. Harry Markopolos, a portfolio manager at Rampart Investments, spent nine years trying to convince the SEC that a money management firm run by Bernard Madoff was falsifying the results it was reporting to investors. Only when the U.S. economy went into recession in 2008 did the truth about Madoff come out.[21] In response, the SEC announced plans to overhaul its whistle-blowing system.[22] More recently, Bradley Birkenfeld provided evidence proving that Swiss banking giant UBS was evading corporate taxes. UBS eventually was fined $780 million for its transgressions.[23]

 **Manager's Checklist**

☐ Remember that the views of others about social responsibility may not necessarily be the same as your views.

☐ Understand how the government affects social responsibility as it relates to an organization and how organizations influence (or try to influence) the government in terms of social responsibility.

2-4 THE INTERNATIONAL ENVIRONMENT OF MANAGEMENT

Another important competitive issue for managers today is the international environment. After describing recent trends in international business, we examine levels of internationalization and the international context of business.

> "... This world is changing enormously. In any position in a company you need to work very hard on learning new skills every day, but you also need to unlearn some of the old skills from the past ..."
>
> —Alan Jope, CEO of Unilever

2-4a Trends in International Business

The stage for today's international business environment was set at the end of World War II. Businesses in war-torn countries such as Germany and Japan had no choice but to rebuild from scratch. Consequently, they had to rethink every facet of their operations, including technology, production, finance, and marketing. Although these countries took many years to recover, they eventually did so, and their economic systems were subsequently poised for growth. During the same era, many U.S. companies grew somewhat complacent. Their customer base was growing rapidly. Increased population, spurred by the baby boom, and increased affluence resulting from the postwar economic boom greatly raised the average person's standard of living and expectations. The U.S. public continually wanted newer and better products and services. Many U.S. companies profited greatly from this pattern, but most were also guilty of taking it for granted.

U.S. firms are no longer isolated from global competition or the global market. A few simple numbers help tell the full story of international trade and industry. First of all, the volume of international trade increased more than 3,000 percent between 1960 and 2015. Furthermore, although 121 of the world's largest corporations are headquartered in the United States, there are also 119 in China, 52 in Japan, 31 in France, 29 in Germany, and 18 in Britain.[24] Within certain industries, the preeminence of non-U.S. firms is even more striking. For example, only one of the world's 10 largest banks and none of the largest electronics companies are based in the United States. Only three of the 10 largest chemical companies are U.S. firms. On the other hand, U.S. firms comprise seven of the 10 largest aerospace companies, three of the six largest airlines, and three of the nine largest computer companies.[25]

U.S. firms are also finding that international operations are an increasingly important element of their sales and profits. For example, in 2019 ExxonMobil realized 64 percent of its revenues and 55 percent of its profits abroad.[26] Hollywood is also getting in on the act. The highest

Importing and exporting are common forms of international business. Exporters load their products into cargo containers such as these. The containers are shipped to foreign markets and unloaded for distribution and sale there.

grossing movie of all time, 2019's *Avengers: Endgame*, earned $2.79 billion in revenues, with around 65 percent of that total coming from foreign markets. From any perspective, then, it is clear that we live in a truly global economy. Virtually all businesses today must be concerned with the competitive situations they face in lands far from home and with how companies from distant lands are competing in their homelands.

2-4b Levels of International Business Activity

Firms can choose various levels of international business activity as they seek to gain a competitive advantage in other countries. The general levels are exporting and importing, licensing, strategic alliances, and direct investment. Table 2.1 summarizes the advantages and disadvantages of each approach.

exporting
Making a product in the firm's domestic marketplace and selling it in another country

importing
Bringing a good, service, or capital into the home country from abroad

Exporting and Importing   Importing or exporting (or both) is usually the first type of international business in which a firm gets involved. Exporting, or making a product in the firm's domestic marketplace and selling it in another country, can involve both merchandise and services. Importing is bringing a good, service, or capital into the home country from abroad. For example, automobiles (Mazda, Ford, Volkswagen, Mercedes-Benz, and Ferrari) and stereo equipment (Sony, Bang & Olufsen, and Sanyo) are routinely exported by their manufacturers to other countries. Likewise, many wine distributors buy products from vineyards in France, Italy, or the United States and import them into their own country for resale. U.S. sports brands, such as team jerseys and logo caps, have become one of the latest hot exports.

When organizations decide to increase their level of internationalization, they can adopt several strategies. Each strategy is a matter of degree, as opposed to being a discrete and mutually exclusive category. And each has unique advantages that must be considered.

Table 2.1	Advantages and Disadvantages of Different Approaches to Internationalization	
Approach to Internationalization	**Advantages**	**Disadvantages**
Importing or exporting	1. Small cash outlay 2. Little risk 3. No adaptation necessary	1. Tariffs and taxes 2. High transportation costs 3. Government restrictions
Licensing	1. Increased profitability 2. Extended profitability	1. Inflexibility 2. Competition
Strategic alliances or joint ventures	1. Quick market entry 2. Access to materials and technology	1. Shared ownership (limits control and profits)
Direct investment	1. Enhanced control 2. Existing infrastructure	1. Complexity 2. Greater economic and political risk 3. Greater uncertainty

licensing
An arrangement whereby one company allows another company to use its brand name, trademark, technology, patent, copyright, or other assets in exchange for a royalty based on sales

strategic alliance
A cooperative arrangement between two or more firms for mutual gain

joint venture
A special type of strategic alliance in which the partners share in the ownership of an operation on an equity basis

direct investment
When a firm builds or purchases operating facilities or subsidiaries in a different country from the one where it has its headquarters

maquiladoras
Light assembly plants that are built in northern Mexico close to the U.S. border and are given special tax breaks by the Mexican government

Licensing   A company may prefer to arrange for a foreign company to manufacture or market its products under a licensing agreement. Factors leading to this decision may include excessive transportation costs, government regulations, and home production costs. Licensing is an arrangement whereby a firm allows another company to use its brand name, trademark, technology, patent, copyright, or other assets. In return, the licensee pays a royalty, usually based on sales. Franchising, a special form of licensing, is also widely used in international business. Kirin Brewery, Japan's largest producer of beer, wanted to expand its international operations but feared that the time involved in shipping it from Japan would cause the beer to lose its freshness. Thus, it has entered into a number of licensing arrangements with breweries in other markets. These brewers make beer according to strict guidelines provided by the Japanese firm and then package and market it as Kirin beer. They pay a royalty to Kirin for each case sold. Molson produces Kirin in Canada under such an agreement, and the Charles Wells Brewery does the same in England.[27]

Strategic Alliances   In a strategic alliance, two or more firms jointly cooperate for mutual gain.[28] For example, Unisys and Oracle have a strategic alliance that provides customers with the service and technology of Unisys and the enterprise software of Oracle. A joint venture is special type of strategic alliance in which the partners actually share ownership of a new enterprise. Strategic alliances have enjoyed a tremendous upsurge in the past few years.

Direct Investment   Another level of commitment to internationalization is direct investment. Direct investment occurs when a firm headquartered in one country builds or purchases operating facilities or subsidiaries in a foreign country. The foreign operations then become wholly owned subsidiaries of the firm. Examples are BP's acquisition of Amoco, Dell Computer's massive factory in China, and the newest Disney theme park in Shanghai. Coca-Cola invested $150 million to build a new bottling and distribution network in India. Similarly, PepsiCo paid $4.2 billion for a Russian yogurt company. Many U.S. firms use *maquiladoras* for the same purpose. Maquiladoras are light assembly plants built in northern Mexico close to the U.S. border. The plants are given special tax breaks by the Mexican government, and the area is populated with workers willing to work for low wages.

Licensing can allow a company to extend the life of its technology. For instance, older versions of computer hardware and software that have limited markets in industrialized countries may still be widely used in less-developed parts of the world. This Egyptian library, for example, uses computers that have little market value in the United States.

travelpix/Alamy Stock Photo

2-4c The Context of International Business

Managers involved in international business should also be aware of the cultural environment, controls on international trade, the importance of economic communities, and the role of the GATT and WTO.

The Cultural Environment   One significant contextual challenge for the international manager is the cultural environment and how it affects business. A country's culture includes all the values, symbols, beliefs, and language that guide behavior. Cultural values and beliefs are often unspoken; they may even be taken for granted by those who live in a particular country. Cultural factors do not necessarily cause problems for managers when the cultures of two countries are similar. Difficulties can arise, however, when there is little overlap between a manager's home culture and the culture of the country in which business is to be conducted. For example, most U.S. managers find the culture and traditions of England relatively familiar. The people of both countries speak the same language and share strong historical roots, and there is a history of strong commerce between the two countries. When U.S. managers begin operations in Vietnam, the People's Republic of China, or the Middle East, however, many of those commonalities disappear.

Cultural differences between countries can have a direct impact on business practice. For example, the religion of Islam teaches that people should not make a living by exploiting the misfortune of others; as a result, charging interest is seen as immoral. This means that in Saudi Arabia, few businesses provide towing services to transport stalled cars to a repair shop (because doing so would be capitalizing on misfortune), and in the Sudan, banks cannot pay or charge interest. Given these cultural and religious constraints, those two businesses—automobile towing and banking—seem to hold little promise for international managers in those particular countries!

Some cultural differences between countries can be even more subtle and yet have a major impact on business activities. For example, in the United States most managers clearly agree about the value of time. Most U.S. managers schedule their activities very tightly and then try hard to adhere to their schedules. Other cultures do not put such a premium on time. In the Middle East, managers do not like to set appointments, and they rarely keep appointments set too far into the future. U.S. managers interacting with managers from the Middle East might misinterpret the late arrival of a potential business partner as a negotiation ploy or an insult, when it is merely a simple reflection of different views of time and its value.[29]

Language itself can be an important factor. Beyond the obvious and clear barriers posed when people speak different languages, subtle differences in meaning can also play a major role. For example, Imperial Oil of Canada markets gasoline under the brand name Esso. When the firm tried to sell its gasoline in Japan, it learned that *esso* means "stalled car" in Japanese. Likewise, when Chevrolet first introduced a U.S. model called the Nova in Latin America, General Motors executives could not understand why the car sold poorly. They eventually learned, though, that, in Spanish, *no va* means "it doesn't go." The color green is used extensively in Muslim countries, but it signifies death in some other lands. The color associated with femininity in the United States is pink, but in many other countries yellow is the most feminine color. And when Disney was initially promoting one of its theme parks in Hong Kong, its print ads featured a family consisting of two parents and two children, failing to consider that the Chinese government limits most families to a single child. As a result, people who saw the ad were confused until Disney relaunched the campaign to show parents and a single child visiting the park.[30]

Controls on International Trade   Another element of the international context that managers need to consider is the extent to which there are controls on international trade. These controls include tariffs, quotas, export restraint agreements, and "buy national" laws. A tariff is a tax collected on goods shipped across national boundaries. Tariffs can be collected by the exporting country, by countries through which goods pass, or by the importing country. Import tariffs, which are the most common, can be levied to protect domestic companies by increasing the cost of foreign goods. Japan charges U.S. tobacco producers a tariff on cigarettes imported into Japan as a way to keep their prices higher than the prices charged by domestic firms. Tariffs can also be levied, usually by less-developed countries, to raise money for the government.

Quotas are the most common form of trade restriction. A quota is a limit on the number or value of goods that can be traded. The quota amount is typically designed to ensure that domestic competitors will be able to maintain a certain market share. Honda is allowed to import 425,000 autos each year into the United States. This quota is one reason why Honda opened manufacturing facilities here. The quota applies to cars imported into the United States, but the company can produce as many other cars within U.S. borders as it wants; such cars are not considered imports. Export restraint agreements are designed to convince other governments to limit voluntarily the volume or value of goods exported to or imported from a particular country. They are, in effect, export quotas. Japanese steel producers voluntarily limit the amount of steel they send to the United States each year.

---

tariff
A tax collected on goods shipped across national boundaries

quota
A limit on the number or value of goods that can be traded

export restraint agreements
Accords reached by governments in which countries voluntarily limit the volume or value of goods they export to or import from one another

Most countries impose controls on international trade. This Russian Customs Inspector in Moscow is inspecting a shipment from Japan to make sure that proper tariffs have been paid.

Free Wind 2014/Shutterstock.com

"Buy national" legislation gives preference to domestic producers through content or price restrictions. Several countries have this type of legislation. Brazil requires that Brazilian companies purchase only Brazilian-made computers. The United States requires that the Department of Defense purchase military uniforms manufactured only in the United States, even though the price of foreign uniforms would be only half as much. Mexico requires that 50 percent of the parts of cars sold in Mexico be manufactured inside its own borders.

Economic Communities Just as government policies can either increase or decrease the political risk that international managers face, trade relations between countries can either help or hinder international business. Relations dictated by quotas, tariffs, and so forth can hurt international trade. There is currently a strong movement around the world to reduce many of these barriers. This movement takes its most obvious form in international economic communities.

economic community
A set of countries that agrees to markedly reduce or eliminate trade barriers among member nations (a formalized market system)

An international economic community is a set of countries that agrees to markedly reduce or eliminate trade barriers among member nations. The first (and in many ways still the most important) of these economic communities is the European Union. The European Union (or EU, as it is often called) can be traced to 1957 when Belgium, France, Luxembourg, Germany, Italy, and the Netherlands signed the Treaty of Rome to promote economic integration. Between 1973 and 1986 these countries were joined by Denmark, Ireland, the United Kingdom, Greece, Spain, and Portugal, and the group became known first as the European Committee and then as the European Union. Austria, Finland, and Sweden joined the EU in 1995; 12 additional countries (mostly from the formerly communist-controlled eastern European region) joined between 2004 and 2007, bringing the EU's membership to 27 countries. For years these countries have followed a basic plan that led to the systematic elimination of most trade barriers. The new market system achieved significantly more potential when most of the EU members eliminated their home currencies (such as French francs and Italian lira) beginning on January 1, 2002, and adopted a new common currency called the *euro*. The EU was dealt a setback in 2016, however, when the citizens of Great Britain voted to withdraw from the EU. This withdrawal was finalized in 2019 but it will take some time to fully implement, however, and its effects will be complex and potentially far reaching.

European Union (EU)
The first and most important international market system

"In China today, Bill Gates is Britney Spears. In America today, Britney Spears is Britney Spears—and that is our problem."
—Thomas L. Friedman, *New York Times* Journalist and Three-Time Pulitzer Prize Winner[31]

North American Free Trade Agreement (NAFTA)
An agreement between the United States, Canada, and Mexico to promote trade with one another

Another important economic community encompasses the United States, Canada, and Mexico. These countries have long been major trading partners with one another; more than 80 percent of Mexico's exports go to the United States, and more than 50 percent of Mexico's imports come from the United States. During the last several years, these countries have negotiated a variety of agreements to make trade even easier. The North American Free Trade Agreement (NAFTA) eliminated many of the trade barriers—such as quotas and tariffs—that

United States–Mexico–Canada Agreement (USMCA)
Revised and amended NAFTA to provide greater incentives for Mexico to increase its imports from the United States

existed previously.[32] President Trump, however, felt that NAFTA did not do enough to help the United States. As a result, he pushed for a revised agreement called the United States–Mexico–Canada Agreement (USMCA), which was signed by the three partner countries in 2018. From the standpoint of the United States, a primary goal of the renegotiated treaty is to increase exports from the United States to Mexico (primarily) and Canada. The USMCA will eventually replace NAFTA but this process will take at least a few years to fully complete.

The Role of the GATT and WTO The context of international business is also increasingly being influenced by the General Agreement on Tariffs and Trade (GATT) and the World Trade Organization (WTO). The GATT was first negotiated following World War II in an effort to avoid trade wars that would benefit rich nations and harm poorer ones. Essentially, the GATT is a trade agreement intended to promote international trade by reducing trade barriers and making it easier for all nations to compete in international markets. The GATT was a major stimulus to international trade after it was first ratified in 1948 by 23 countries; by 1994, a total of 117 countries had signed the agreement.

General Agreement on Tariffs and Trade (GATT)
A trade agreement intended to promote international trade by reducing trade barriers and making it easier for all nations to compete in international markets

One key component of the GATT was the identification of the so-called *most favored national* (MFN) principle. This provision stipulates that if a country extends preferential treatment to any other nation that has signed the agreement, then that preferential treatment must be extended to all signatories to the agreement. Members can extend such treatment to nonsignatories as well, but they are not required to do so.

World Trade Organization (WTO)
An organization, which currently includes 164 member nations and 23 observer countries, that requires members to open their markets to international trade and to follow WTO rules

The World Trade Organization (WTO) came into existence on January 1, 1995. The WTO replaced the GATT and absorbed its mission. The WTO is headquartered in Geneva, Switzerland, and currently includes 164 member nations and 23 observer countries. Members are required to open their markets to international trade and to follow WTO rules. The WTO has three basic goals:

1. To promote trade flows by encouraging nations to adopt nondiscriminatory and predictable trade policies
2. To reduce remaining trade barriers through multilateral negotiations
3. To establish impartial procedures for resolving trade disputes among its members

The WTO is certain to continue to play a major role in the evolution of the global economy. At the same time, it has also become a lightning rod for protesters and other activists, who argue that the WTO focuses too narrowly on globalization issues to the detriment of human rights and the environment.

 **Manager's Checklist**

☐ Managers should know the current and forecasted economic conditions in all relevant marketplaces.

☐ You should have a clear understanding of possible international assignments your firm may have in mind for you and the role of those assignments in your career progression.

☐ Managers need to know how the four elements of the political–legal environment affect their organization and their own jobs.

☐ You should also develop an appreciation for cultural differences and how those differences affect you, your colleagues and employees, and your business.

organizational culture
The set of values, beliefs, behaviors, customs, and attitudes that helps the organization's members understand what it stands for, how it does things, and what it considers important

2-5 THE ORGANIZATION'S CULTURE

As we noted earlier in this chapter, an especially important part of an organization's internal environment is its culture. Organizational culture is the set of values, beliefs, behaviors, customs, and attitudes that helps the organization's members understand what it stands for, how it does things, and what it considers important.[33] The importance of organizational culture is introduced in our *Leading the Way* feature.

2-5a The Importance of Organizational Culture

Culture determines the organization's "feel." A strong and clear culture can play an important role in the competitiveness of a business. At the same time, though, there is no universal culture that will help all organizations. The stereotypic image of Microsoft, for example, is that of a workplace where people dress very casually and work very long hours. In contrast, the image of Bank of America for some observers is that of a formal setting with rigid work rules and people dressed in conservative business attire. And Texas Instruments likes to talk about its "shirtsleeve" culture, in which ties are avoided and few managers even wear jackets. Southwest Airlines maintains a culture that stresses fun and excitement.

Of course, the same culture is not necessarily found throughout an entire organization. For example, the sales and marketing department may have a culture quite different from that of the operations and manufacturing department. Regardless of its nature, however, culture is a powerful force in organizations, one that can shape the firm's overall effectiveness and long-term success. Companies that can develop and maintain a strong culture, such as Starbucks and Procter & Gamble, tend to be more effective than companies that have trouble developing and maintaining a strong culture, such as Kmart.[34]

> **"It's creating a sense [in your employees] that 'If I want to make a difference, I can make a difference.' Freedom is only one part of the Netflix culture; the other is responsibility. [Netflix] has created a culture of high performance. 'Adequate performance gets a generous severance package.'"**
> —Reed Hastings, Co-Founder, Chairman, and CEO of Netflix[35]

2-5b Determinants of Organizational Culture

Where does an organization's culture come from? Typically, it develops and blossoms over a long period of time. Its starting point is often the organization's founder. For example, James Cash Penney believed in treating employees and customers with respect and dignity. Employees at JC Penney are still called *associates* rather than *employees* (to reflect partnership), and customer satisfaction is of paramount importance. The impact of Sam Walton, Ross Perot, and Walt Disney is still felt in the organizations they founded.[36] As an organization grows, its culture is modified, shaped, and refined by symbols, stories, heroes, slogans, and ceremonies. And many decisions at Walt Disney Company today are still framed by asking, "What would Walt have done?"

Corporate success and shared experiences also shape culture. For example, Hallmark Cards has a strong culture derived from its years of success in the greeting card industry. Employees speak of "the Hallmark family" and care deeply about the company; many have worked there for years. At Kmart, in contrast, the culture has been quite weak, the management team has changed rapidly, and few people sense any direction or purpose in the company. Indeed, some observers predict that Kmart will not survive much longer. The differences in culture at Hallmark and Kmart are in part attributable to past successes and shared experiences.

2-5c Managing Organizational Culture

How can managers deal with culture, given its clear importance but intangible nature? Essentially, the manager must understand the current culture and then decide whether it should be maintained or changed. By understanding the organization's current culture, managers can take appropriate actions. Culture can also be maintained by rewarding and promoting people whose behaviors are consistent with the existing culture and by articulating the culture through slogans, ceremonies, and so forth.

But managers must walk a fine line between maintaining a culture that still works effectively and changing a culture that has become dysfunctional. For example, many of the firms already noted, as well as numerous others, take pride in perpetuating their culture. Shell

LEADING THE WAY

Happy Fit

Tony Hsieh (pronounced "Shay"), the son of Taiwanese immigrants, started his first company in 1996, just after he graduated from Harvard. LinkExchange was an ingenious Internet advertising network that permitted members to exchange ad space on their own sites for space on other members' sites. Two-and-a-half years later, Hsieh and his partner sold their company to Microsoft for $265 million. It wasn't the money, says Hsieh; LinkExchange just wasn't a fun place to work at anymore.

"It worked great," he recalls, "until we got to about 15 or 20 people, and then we ran out of friends to hire. So then we started hiring people who had all the right skill sets but weren't necessarily great for the company culture. By the time we got to 100 people, I myself dreaded getting out of bed in the morning." He knew it was time to move on, recalls Hsieh, when "the culture just went completely downhill."

What does Hsieh want in a company culture? "For me," he says, "the initial motivation was what would make me happy. . . . If I was going to go to an office, I wanted it to be with people I would choose to be around even if we didn't have to work together." Fortunately, Hsieh had a choice of the office he worked in and the people he worked with. He originally joined an online shoe retailer as an investor and advisor but soon became co-CEO, and the company, now known as Zappos, reached two of his chief goals by 2008: It topped $1 billion in sales (two years early) and made *Fortune* magazine's list (at #23) of the "Top 100 Companies to Work For."

In November 2009, Hsieh and his partners sold Zappos to Amazon for $1.2 billion. Amazon agreed to let its new acquisition operate independently, and Hsieh agreed to stay on as CEO—for a salary of only $36,000. "That's my way of making sure that I'm actually there for my own happiness," explains Hsieh, "not for the money." This time, he was determined to foster the kind of company culture that he deemed optimum for both personal satisfaction and business success: "I didn't want to repeat the same mistake I'd made at [LinkExchange, where]," he admits, "[we hadn't] paid any attention to company culture [because] we just didn't know any better."

As far as Hsieh is concerned, "Company culture is all about making employees happy," and Zappos is certainly an employee-friendly workplace: Cafeteria food is free, for instance, and the company covers all medical benefits. In 2014, Hsieh unveiled plans to take his concept of "company culture" a giant step further by announcing Zappos would move toward becoming a full-fledged *holacracy.* It's one of the latest concepts in radical management, and, basically, it calls for two things that should make employees happy: (1) bosses quit being bosses and (2) all employees are authorized to do whatever they want (especially to experiment with innovative ideas) until they screw up entirely. The CEO gives up his centralized authority, and the whole company is reorganized into decentralized teams, usually called "circles," that choose their own goals and assign their own roles in order to perform whatever organizational task needs to be done.

According to Hsieh, holacracy holds out the possibility of turning the bureaucratic model of organization into one that reflects the model of a city. He points out that when cities double in size, innovation and productivity per citizen go up by 15 percent, whereas corporations that double in size typically decline on both measures. Why? "In a city," says Hsieh, "people are self-organizing." He wants Zappos to "function more like a city and less like an organization" because self-organized employees "actually increase the innovation and productivity of an organization." In theory, everyone should be happier. And so far, the grand experiment at Zappos seems to be working well.

References: Rob Wallace and Marc Dorian, "More Than Money: Surprising Stories of the Superrich and How They Gave Back," ABC News, October 28, 2011, http://abcnews.go.com on January 15, 2020; Peter Hopkins, "*Big Think* Interview with Tony Hsieh," http://bigthink.com on July 22, 2014; Gregory Ferenstein, "Zappos Just Abolished Bosses: Inside Tech's Latest Management Craze," *Vox,* July 11, 2014, www.vox.com on January 15, 2020; Nicole Leinbach-Reyhle, "Shedding Hierarchy: Could Zappos Be Setting an Innovative Trend?" *Forbes,* July 15, 2014, forbes.com on January 15, 2020; Cameron Albert Deitch, "Zappos Tony Hsieh's Biggest Management Experiment Is Evolving Again (in a Very Intriguing Way)," *Inc.,* January 30, 2020, www.inc.com on March 16, 2020.

Oil, for example, has an elaborate display in the lobby of its Houston headquarters that tells the story of the firm's past. But other companies may face situations in which their culture is no longer a strength. For example, some critics feel that Ford's culture places too much emphasis on product development and internal competition among divisions and not enough on marketing and competition with other firms.

Culture problems sometimes arise from mergers or the growth of rival factions within an organization. For example, Delta merged with Northwest Airlines. Combining the two companies led to numerous cases of conflict and operational difficulties because the cultures of the two firms were so different.[37] To change culture, managers must have a clear idea of what they want to create. When United and Continental Airlines merged, top managers stressed that they wanted the new firm to personify Continental's employee-friendly culture and avoid the old United culture that was fraught with hostility and mistrust between management and labor.[38] However, things did not go well because managers underestimated how long it would take to blend two disparate cultures.

 **Manager's Checklist**

☐ All members of an organization should understand its culture.

☐ Managers need to help create, communicate, and sustain a strong organization culture.

SUMMARY OF LEARNING OUTCOMES AND KEY POINTS

2-1. Discuss the nature of an organization's environments and the components of its general, task, and internal environments.

- Managers need to have a thorough understanding of the environment in which they operate and compete. The general environment consists of the economy, technology, and the political–legal climate. The task environment consists of competitors, customers, suppliers, strategic partners, and regulators.

- The internal environment consists of the organization's owners, board of directors, employees, physical environment, and culture. Owners are those who have claims on the property rights of the organization. The board of directors, elected by stockholders, is responsible for overseeing a firm's top managers. Individual employees are other important parts of the internal environment. The physical environment, yet another part of the internal environment, varies greatly across organizations.

2-2. Describe managerial ethics and the ethical environment of management.

- The ethical and social environment of management is also quite important. Understanding the differences between ethical and unethical behavior, as well as appreciating the special nature of managerial ethics, can help guide effective decision making.

2-3. Discuss the concept of social responsibility.

- Understanding the meaning of and arguments for and against social responsibility can help a manager effectively address both the formal and informal dimensions of social responsibility.

2-4. Discuss the international environment of management.

- The international environment of management can be a crucial one. Current trends have resulted in the increasing globalization of markets, industries, and businesses. Organizations seeking to become more international can rely on importing, exporting, licensing (including franchising), strategic alliances, and direct investment to do so. National culture, controls on international trade, economic communities, and the WTO combine to determine the context of international business.

2-5. Describe the importance and determinants of an organization's culture.

- Organizational culture is the set of values, beliefs, behaviors, customs, and attitudes that helps the organization's members understand what it stands for, how it does things, and what it considers important. Organizational culture is an important environmental concern for managers. Managers must understand that culture is a key determinant of how well their organization will perform. Culture can be assessed and managed in a number of different ways.

DISCUSSION QUESTIONS

Questions for Review

1. Identify and discuss each major dimension of the general environment and the task environment.
2. What are the arguments for and against social responsibility on the part of businesses? In your opinion, which set of arguments is more compelling?
3. Describe the basic levels of international business involvement. Why might a firm use more than one level at the same time?
4. Describe various barriers to international trade. Why do such barriers exist?

Questions for Analysis

1. Can you think of dimensions of the task environment that are not discussed in this chapter? Indicate their linkages to those that are discussed.
2. What is the relationship between the law and ethical behavior? Can a behavior be ethical but illegal at the same time?

3. What is the culture of your college, university, or place of employment? How clear is it? What are its most positive and most negative characteristics?

Questions for Application

1. Identify a situation where a firm competes with another firm but the two firms also have a strategic alliance or joint venture. Explain why situations such as this exist.
2. Use online resources to find Codes of Ethics for three different businesses. Assess each one in terms of its strengths and weaknesses.
3. What industries do you think will feel the greatest impact of international business in the future? Will some industries remain relatively unaffected by globalization? If so, which ones? If not, explain why not.

BUILDING EFFECTIVE CONCEPTUAL SKILLS

Assessing Organizational Culture

Purpose: While organizational culture is intangible, it is not difficult to observe. This activity will help you improve your conceptual skills by observing and interpreting organizational culture, which can help to make you a more effective participant and leader in organizations.

Introduction: Clues to organizational culture may be found by observing details that relate to member behavior, traditions or customs, stories, attitudes, values, communication patterns, organizational structure, employee dress and appearance, and even office space arrangements. Do members address each other by first names? Are office doors left open or closed? What do members wear? How are achievements recognized? Does the workplace feel energized or laid-back? Do members smile and laugh often? Does seniority or expertise earn more respect?

Instructions: First, observe clues to organizational behavior at your school, college, or university. To the extent possible, observe a diversity of members including students, teaching

faculty, and nonteaching staff. Write down specific examples. For example, students typically wear blue jeans while instructors may dress more "formally." In the cafeteria, freshmen sit mainly with other freshmen. A professor may be referred to as "Doctor" by staff, while he or she may refer to staff by their first name.

Second, interpret the facts. Use your observations to describe the organization's core values. What does it value most? How did you come to that conclusion?

Third, with the class or in small groups, discuss your facts and interpretations. Focus especially on areas of disagreement. Where individuals disagree about the culture, try to understand why the disagreement occurs. If the facts differ, perhaps the individuals observed two different groups. For example, students majoring in business may be different from students in engineering or education. Or perhaps the organizational culture tolerates or encourages lots of differences. If there is agreement on facts but interpretations differ, then perhaps the individuals making the interpretations can explore their differing perceptions.

BUILDING EFFECTIVE COMMUNICATION SKILLS

Exercise Overview

Communication skills consist of a manager's ability to effectively receive information and ideas from others and to effectively convey information and ideas to others. This exercise will help you develop your communication skills while also helping you understand the importance of knowing the customer segments in an organization's task environment.

Exercise Background

Assume that you are a newly hired middle manager in the marketing department of a large food manufacturer. You have just completed your formal study of management and are excited about the opportunity to apply some of those theories to the real-life problems of your firm. One problem in particular intrigues you. Your boss, the marketing VP, recently developed a consumer survey to solicit feedback about products from customers. The feedback the firm has received varies considerably, ranging from 2 to 5 on a scale from 1 to 5, which gives your firm no helpful data. In addition, sales of your company's products have been slowly but steadily declining over time, and the marketing department is under some pressure from upper management to determine why. You have an idea that the survey is not an accurate reflection of consumer preferences, so you make a suggestion to your boss: "Why don't we gather some information about our customers, in order to understand their needs better? For example, our products are purchased by individual consumers, schools, restaurants, and other organizations. Maybe each type of consumer wants something different from our product." Your boss's response is to stare at you, perplexed, and say, "No. We're not changing anything about the survey." When you ask, "Why?" the boss responds that the product has been a best-seller for years, that "good quality is good quality," and thus that all customers must want the same thing. He then says, "I'll spare you the embarrassment of failure by refusing your request."

Exercise Task

1. With this background in mind, compose a written proposal for your boss, outlining your position. Be sure to emphasize your fundamental concern—that the marketing department must understand the needs of each customer segment better in order to provide products that meet those needs. Consider ways to persuade your boss to change his mind. (*Hint*: Telling him bluntly that he is wrong is unlikely to be effective.)

2. On the basis of what you wrote in response to Exercise Task 1, do you think your boss will change his mind? If yes, exactly what will persuade him to change his mind? If no, what other actions could you take in a further effort to have your ideas adopted by the firm?

SKILL-BUILDING PERSONAL ASSESSMENT

Refining Your Sense of Culture

This exercise is designed to help you assess what you now know about organization culture. The ten statements in the following table reflect certain opinions about the nature of work performed in the context of organization culture. Indicate the extent to which you agree or disagree with each opinion by circling the number in the appropriate column.

Statement of Opinion	Strongly Agree				Strongly Disagree
1. If a person can do well in one organization, he or she can do well in any organization.	1	2	3	4	5
2. Skills and experience are all that really matter; how a job candidate will "fit in" is not an important factor in hiring.	1	2	3	4	5
3. Members of an organization explicitly tell people how to adhere to its culture.	1	2	3	4	5

Statement of Opinion	Strongly Agree				Strongly Disagree
4. After appropriate study, astute managers can fairly quickly change a corporate culture.	1	2	3	4	5
5. A common culture is important for unifying employees but does not necessarily affect the firm's financial health.	1	2	3	4	5
6. Conscientious workers are not really influenced by an organization's culture.	1	2	3	4	5
7. Strong organization cultures are not necessarily associated with high organization performance.	1	2	3	4	5
8. Members of a subculture share the common values of the subculture but not those of the dominant organization culture.	1	2	3	4	5
9. Job candidates seeking to understand a prospective employer's culture can do so by just asking the people who interview them.	1	2	3	4	5
10. Culture can be assessed by observing the behaviors of people in an organization.	1	2	3	4	5

How to Score: To get your total score, add up the values of the numbers that you have circled. You can then interpret your score as follows:

40–50	You have excellent instincts about organization cultures and how people respond to them.
30–39	You show average or above-average awareness of the principles of organization culture.
20–29	You have some sense of how cultures affect workers, but you need to improve your knowledge.
10–19	You definitely need to bolster your knowledge before thinking further about assessing or modifying an organization culture.

Source: Hunsaker, P. L. (2005). Management: A skills approach. Upper Saddle River, NJ: Prentice Hall.

MANAGEMENT AT WORK
Is Doing Good Always What It Seems to Be?

"Often fair trade is sold at a premium, but the entire premium goes to the middlemen."

—Researcher Lawrence Solomon

More than 70 percent of the world's supply of cacao beans comes from small family farms scattered throughout several small West African nations, including Ivory Coast and Ghana. These farmers, their families, and hired hands toil long hours to produce the magical beans that are used to produce cocoa. In the past two decades, however, advocacy groups and consumers have become increasingly aware of a particularly disturbing business practice prevalent on some of these farms—the use of child slave labor.

In countries such as Ivory Coast, one-half of the country's exports are cocoa. Cocoa farmers often earn less than the poverty level, even with the use of child and slave labor.

Cocoa is an extremely unstable commodity—global prices fluctuate significantly. Along with price instability, profitability depends on factors over which farmers have no control, such as drought and crop disease. To improve their chances of making a profit, cocoa farmers look for ways to cut costs, and the use of slave and child labor is one of the most effective money-saving measures.

This is where the idea of "fair trade" comes in. *Fair trade* refers to programs designed to ensure that export-dependent farmers in developing countries receive fair prices for their crops. Organizations such as TransFair USA monitor and certify that farmers supplying cocoa products are paid fair prices, while paying their employees reasonable wages and providing a safe and environmentally friendly workplace. While many fair-trade products are also organic this is not a requirement for certification by Transfair USA. However, the organization does ban the use of genetically modified organisms (GMOs) and encourages farmers to limit their use of pesticides and fertilizers.

A 3.5-ounce candy bar labeled *fair trade* may sell for $3.49, compared to about $1.84 for one that's not. Why so much? Because the fair-trade candy bar, says TransFair USA spokesperson Nicole Chettero, occupies a niche market. She predicts, however, that, "as the demand and volume of Fair Trade–certified products increase, the market will work itself out. ... [R]etailers will naturally start to drop prices to remain competitive." Ultimately, she concludes, "there is no reason why fair-trade [products] should cost astronomically more than traditional products."

Some critics of fair-trade practices and prices agree in principle but contend that consumers don't need to pay such excessive prices, even under *current* market conditions. They point out that, according to TransFair's own data, cocoa farmers get only 3 cents of the $3.49 that a socially conscious consumer pays for a Fair Trade–certified candy bar. "Farmers often receive very little," reports consumer researcher Lawrence Solomon. "Often fair trade is sold at a premium," he charges, "but the entire premium goes to the middlemen."

Critics like Solomon suggest that sellers of fair-trade products are taking advantage of consumers who are socially but not particularly price conscious. They point out that if sellers priced that $3.49 candy bar at $2.49, farmers would still be entitled to 3 cents. The price, they contend, is inflated to $3.49 simply because there's a small segment of the market willing to pay it. Fair-trade programs, advises English economist Tim Harford, "make a promise that the producers will get a good deal. They do not promise that the consumer will get a good deal. That's up to you as a savvy shopper."

Divine Chocolate is a company that is taking fair-trade cocoa to the next level. Unlike other companies selling fair-trade chocolates, Divine returns a share of their profits to the farmers in their supply chain. Divine's largest shareholder group is Kuapa Kokoo, a fair-trade cocoa cooperative. Cocoa farmers who belong to this group not only receive a fair-trade price for their cocoa but also receive dividends from the profits of Divine Chocolate.[39]

Case Questions

1. While Divine Chocolate has embraced the concept of fair trade, their products are not organic. On their website, they argue that purely organic production methods could result in greater instability in production because cocoa is very disease-prone. Do you think that Divine has an ethical obligation to require farmers to become organic? Why or why not?

2. How would you describe Divine Chocolate's approach to social responsibility? How do they balance their responsibilities to their stakeholders?

3. Do you pay attention to fair-trade products in your own purchasing behavior? For what kinds of products might you be willing to pay a premium price to help those who produce the ingredients?

4. Under what circumstances might fair trade actually cause harm? To whom? At what point would fair-trade trade-offs no longer be acceptable?

You Make the Call

Turbulence in the Air

1. Identify the major stakeholders that have a vested interest in Boeing. What does the opening case say about each one?

2. How would you assess the CEO compensation for both the departed and the new Boeing CEO?

3. In your opinion, how do the ethical practices and social responsibility portrayed by Boeing compare to those of most other large businesses?

4. Boeing and the Boeing Foundation donate upward of a quarter billion dollars each year to social and community causes. How do you reconcile this with the behaviors described previously?

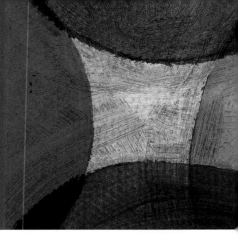

CHAPTER **3**

Planning and Strategic Management

Learning Outcomes

After studying this chapter, you should be able to:

3-1 Summarize the planning process and organizational goals.

3-2 Discuss the components of strategy and the types of strategic alternatives.

3-3 Describe how to use SWOT analysis in formulating strategy.

3-4 Discuss various alternative approaches to business-level strategy formulation.

3-5 Describe various alternative approaches to corporate-level strategy formulation.

3-6 Discuss how tactical plans are developed and implemented.

3-7 Describe the basic types of operational plans used by organizations.

This chapter discusses how organizations manage planning and strategy and how managers engage in strategic planning. As we noted in Chapter 1, planning and decision making comprise the first managerial functions that organizations must address. This chapter is the first of three that explore planning and decision making.

Management in Action

The Lap of Luxury

"Money is just a consequence. I always say to my team, don't worry too much about profitability. If you do your job well, the profitability will come."

—Bernard Arnault, Chairman and CEO of LVMH

When people think about luxury products, they often come up with names like Givenchy, Fendi, Christian Dior, Dom Perignon, and Louis Vuitton. But what many people don't realize is that all of these brands—plus dozens of other luxury brands—are all owned by the same French company, LVMH.

Although some LVMH brands are literally centuries old (the oldest, wine producer Chateau d'Yquem, dates back to 1593), the origin of LVMH per se started in 1971 when champagne producer Moet & Chandon merged with Hennessy, a prestigious cognac maker, and branded itself as Moet Hennessey. A few years later, in 1987, this firm merged with luxury luggage company Louis Vuitton to become (officially) LVMH Moet Hennessey-Louis Vuitton SE, or LVMH for short.

poludziber/Shutterstock.com

LVMH has thrived by using related diversification. Its portfolio of high-end luxury products all appeal to similar kinds of consumers and are generally marketed and managed in similar ways. These LVMH stores, for instance, are all in a Singapore shopping complex. This makes it easier for shoppers to move from store-to-store.

Enter Bernard Arnault. Arnault is CEO and the majority shareholder of fashion icon Christian Dior. Arnault had acquired Dior in 1984 and slowly but surely built it into a global powerhouse. As his wealth and the firm's resources grew, so too did his vision and aspirations. Specifically, he began to see that there could be significant economies of scale if he could gain control of other luxury goods companies. His first acquisition, he decided, would be LVMH and he initiated efforts to gain control of that company in 1988. At first, LVMH tried to avoid being taken over through various financial maneuvers but Arnault eventually succeeded in the summer of 1989.

Arnault structured his new firm as a holding company. Specifically, his original firm, Christian Dior SE, owns around 41 percent of the shares of LVMH but controls 59 percent of its voting rights. Apart from LVMH, Christian Dior itself continues to function as an autonomous business but under the same corporate ownership umbrella. Publicly, though, the firm continues to use the LVMH "brand" name. And because this model worked well from the beginning Arnault decided that future brand acquisitions would also continue to function as separate businesses but also be organized by product or customer group.

Over the next several years the company began to expand by buying one luxury brand after another. Among the more significant acquisitions have been Celine (1988), Guerlain (1994), Marc Jacobs and Sephora (1997), Emilio Pucci (2000), Fendi and DKNY (2001), and Bulgari (2011). LVMH's latest major acquisition was Tiffany & Co. in 2019. Also, in 2019 LVMH launched an all-new fashion house, Fenty, in partnership with singer Rihanna.

To help manage its portfolio of businesses, LVMH has structured itself into six distinct divisions:

- The Wines and Spirits division, with 22 distinct brands
- The Fashion and Leather Goods division, with 18 brands
- The Perfumes and Cosmetics division, with 14 brands
- The Watches and Jewelry division, with seven brands
- The Selective Retailing division, with five brands
- An unnamed "miscellaneous" division that includes two small hotel brands, a bicycle manufacturer, a small chain of upscale coffee houses, and three luxury yacht leasing companies

While the roots of LVMH are firmly planted in Europe, the firm has enjoyed considerable success with international expansion. Ten percent of its revenues are generated in France and another 19 percent from other European countries. The United States generates 25 percent of the firm's revenues and Japan another 7 percent. Most recent growth, though, has come from other Asian countries, most notably China. LVMH has also successfully entered the world of online retailing without noticeably harming its reputation for luxury products and impeccable service. Indeed, it looks as though LVMH can do little wrong as it continues its strategic efforts to control the world's leading luxury brands and businesses.[1]

3-1 PLANNING AND ORGANIZATIONAL GOALS

"No plan survives first contact with the enemy"—historians are not sure who said this first—Dwight Eisenhower, Napoleon, Patton, or (most likely) a nineteenth-century Prussian field marshal named Helmuth Von Moltke. The sentiment, however, is undeniable. No matter how effectively leaders make decisions, plan, and strategize, it is impossible to predict with certainty exactly how well those decisions, plans, and strategies will work once they are set in motion. Unexpected responses by other businesses, faulty assumptions, human error, or simple luck can all cause business plans to fail or to succeed far better than expected. Nevertheless, when leaders do work to make good decisions and develop effective plans and strategies, like those at LVMH, they substantially increase their chances of success. Similarly, though, if leaders make bad decisions, develop ineffective strategies, and execute plans poorly when things do go wrong, they will likely make matters far worse.

All organizations engage in planning activities, but no two organizations plan in exactly the same fashion. Figure 3.1 is a general representation of the planning process that many organizations attempt to follow. But although most firms follow this general framework, each also has its own nuances and variations.[2]

As Figure 3.1 shows, all planning occurs within an environmental context. If managers do not understand this context, they are unable to develop effective plans. Thus, understanding the environment is essentially the first step in planning. Chapter 2 covered many of the basic environmental issues that affect organizations and how they plan. With this understanding as

FIGURE 3.1

The Planning Process

The planning process takes place within an environmental context. Managers must develop a complete and thorough understanding of this context to determine the organization's mission and to develop its strategic, tactical, and operational goals and plans.

a foundation, managers must then establish the organization's mission. The mission outlines the organization's purpose, premises, values, and directions. Flowing from the mission are parallel streams of goals and plans. Directly following the mission are strategic goals. These goals and the mission help determine strategic plans. Strategic goals and plans are primary inputs for developing tactical goals. Tactical goals and the original strategic plans help shape tactical plans. Tactical plans, in turn, combine with the tactical goals to shape operational goals. These goals and the appropriate tactical plans determine operational plans. Finally, goals and plans at each level can also be used as inputs for future activities at all levels.

3-1a Organizational Goals

Goals are critical to organizational effectiveness, and they serve a number of purposes. Organizations can also have several different kinds of goals, all of which must be appropriately managed. And a number of different kinds of managers must be involved in setting goals.

> **"Policy making could go on and on endlessly, and there are always resources to be allocated. 'Decision' implies the end of deliberation and the beginning of action."**
> —William Starbuck, Leading Management Theorist[4]

General Motors has announced a goal that by 2030 50 percent of the materials in their vehicles will be sustainable. One of GM's newer domestic competitors, Tesla, has a goal of delivering 400,000 vehicles per year by 2025 and doubling the storage capacity of its batteries by an unspecified date. And when Disney launched its online streaming service Disney+ in 2019, the firm announced a goal of having "at least" 60 million global subscribers by the year 2025.[3]

Purposes of Goals   Goals serve four important purposes. First, they provide guidance and a unified direction for people in the organization. Goals can help everyone understand where the organization is going and why getting there is important.[5] General Motors' goal communicates the firm's commitment to sustainability, and Disney's goal demonstrates its emphasis on streaming services as a future growth opportunity.

Second, goal-setting practices strongly affect other aspects of planning. Effective goal setting promotes good planning, and good planning facilitates future goal setting. For example, one competitive advantage that Disney has for its streaming service is a large library of content—Disney, Pixar, Marvel, Lucas Films, and Fox movies and television programs. At the same time, though, the firm doesn't want to release all of this content at one time. For example, going forward, when Disney releases its next major blockbuster movie, it will first target traditional theatergoers. Then, at a later date, it will release that movie in other formats such as DVD and streaming. The timing of these decisions is important—the second wave of releases can't come too quickly because it would reduce traditional theater box-office revenue, but it also cannot come too late or the film's "momentum" may have slowed.

Third, goals can serve as a source of motivation for an organization's employees. Goals that are specific and moderately difficult can motivate people to work harder, especially if attaining the goal is likely to result in rewards.[6] Italian furniture manufacturer Industrie Natuzzi SpA uses goals to motivate its workers. Each craftsperson has a goal for how long it should take to perform his or her job, such as sewing leather sheets together to make a sofa cushion or building wooden frames for chair arms. At the completion of assigned tasks, workers enter their ID numbers and job numbers into the firm's computer system. If they get a job done faster than their goal, a bonus is automatically added to their paycheck.[7] Firms that take a strong—and public—position on sustainability may help motivate employees who are concerned with environmental issues to be more motivated and to feel more engagement with the firm.

Finally, goals provide an effective mechanism for evaluation and control. This means that performance can be assessed in the future in terms of how successfully today's goals are accomplished. For example, Disney attracted more Disney+ subscribers in its first six months of availability than was expected. As a result, it raised its subscriber goal from 60 million to between 60 and 90 million. On the other hand, firms also may need to revise their goals downward. It's common, for instance, for publicly traded businesses to provide investors and financial analysts with goals for revenues and profits on a yearly basis. Due to the economic turmoil created by the COVID-19 virus in 2020, though, most businesses realized that they were not going to meet their goals and so revised them to lower levels. Others announced that they were abandoning their short-term goals due to so much uncertainty. Target, for instance, experienced extreme volatility due to a spike in sales on some products (such as toilet paper and cleaning products) but a drop in sales of apparel and other staples.[8]

Kinds of Goals   Goals are set for and by different levels within an organization. An organization's **mission** is a statement of its "fundamental, unique purpose that sets a business apart from other firms of its type and identifies the scope of the business's operations in product and market terms."[9] For instance, Starbucks' mission statement is to be "the premier purveyor of the finest coffee in the world while maintaining our uncompromising principles while we grow." The principles referred to in the mission help managers at Starbucks make decisions and direct resources in clear and specific ways.

mission
A statement of an organization's fundamental purpose

Strategic goals are set by and for an organization's top management. They focus on broad, general issues. For example, Starbucks has a strategic goal of increasing the profitability of each of its coffee stores by 20 percent over the next five years. Tactical goals are set by and for middle managers. Their focus is on how to operationalize actions necessary to achieve the strategic goals. To achieve Starbucks' goal of increasing its per-store profitability, managers are working on tactical goals related to company-owned versus licensed stores and the global distribution of stores in different countries. Operational goals are set by and for lower-level managers. Their concern is with shorter-term issues associated with the tactical goals. An operational goal for Starbucks might be to boost the profitability of a certain number of stores in each of the next five years. (Some managers use the words *objective* and *goal* interchangeably. When they are differentiated, however, the term *objective* is usually used instead of *operational goal*.)

strategic goals
A goal set by and for an organization's top management

tactical goals
A goal set by and for an organization's middle managers

operational goals
A goal set by and for an organization's lower-level managers

"If you're bored with life—you don't get up every morning with a burning desire to do things—you don't have enough goals."
—Lou Holtz, Former Football Coach[10]

3-1b Kinds of Organizational Plans

Organizations establish many different kinds of plans. At a general level, these include strategic, tactical, and operational plans.

Strategic Plan   Strategic plans are developed to achieve strategic goals. More precisely, a **strategic plan** is a general plan outlining decisions about resource allocation, priorities, and action steps necessary to reach strategic goals. These plans are set by the board of directors and top management, generally have an extended time horizon, and address questions of scope, resource deployment, competitive advantage, and synergy. We discuss strategic planning further in the next major section of this chapter.

strategic plan
A general plan outlining decisions about the resource allocation, priorities, and action steps necessary to reach strategic goals

Tactical Plans   A tactical plan, aimed at achieving tactical goals, is developed to implement specific parts of a strategic plan. Tactical plans typically involve upper and middle management and, compared with strategic plans, have a somewhat shorter time horizon and a more specific and concrete focus. Thus, tactical plans are concerned more with actually getting things done than with deciding what to do. Tactical planning is covered in detail later in this chapter.

Operational Plans   An **operational plan** focuses on carrying out tactical plans to achieve operational goals. Developed by middle- and lower-level managers, operational plans have a short-term focus and are relatively narrow in scope. Each one deals with a fairly small set of activities. We also cover operational planning in more detail later in this chapter.

operational plan
A plan that focuses on carrying out tactical plans to achieve operational goals

---

Manager's Checklist

- ☐ Remember that goals and goal setting are a major part of a manager's job.

- ☐ It's also important to remember that goals are targets, not necessarily absolute objectives that must be attained.

- ☐ Managers need to also keep in mind that they will often need to optimize among and across multiple goals.

- ☐ Be aware of the different kinds of plans that exist for your organization.

3-2 THE NATURE OF STRATEGIC MANAGEMENT

strategy
A comprehensive plan for accomplishing an organization's goals

strategic management
A comprehensive and ongoing management process aimed at formulating and implementing effective strategies; a way of approaching business opportunities and challenges

effective strategies
A strategy that promotes a superior alignment between the organization and its environment and the achievement of strategic goals

distinctive competence
An organizational strength possessed by only a small number of competing firms

scope
When applied to strategy, it specifies the range of markets in which an organization will compete

resource deployment
How an organization distributes its resources across the areas in which it competes

A **strategy** is a comprehensive plan for accomplishing an organization's goals. **Strategic management**, in turn, is a way of approaching business opportunities and challenges—it is a comprehensive and ongoing management process aimed at formulating and implementing effective strategies. Finally, **effective strategies** are those that promote a superior alignment between the organization and its environment and the achievement of strategic goals.[11]

"People in any organization are always attached to the obsolete—the things that should have worked but did not, the things that once were productive and no longer are."
—Peter Drucker, Management Pioneer and Consultant[12]

3-2a The Components of Strategy

In general, a well-conceived strategy addresses three areas: distinctive competence, scope, and resource deployment. A **distinctive competence** is something the organization does exceptionally well. (We discuss distinctive competencies more fully later.) A distinctive competence of Zara is its ability to manage its supply chain more effectively than most of its competitors. It tracks consumer preferences daily with real-time point-of-sale data, digitally transmitting orders to suppliers in Hong Kong and other manufacturing centers, and can have products in stores in a day or two. Because most other retailers generally need weeks to accomplish the same things, Zara has used this distinctive competence to grow. One of Zara's competitors, Abercrombie & Fitch, is pursuing a similar strategy. It recently implemented what it calls Management Dynamics' Supply Chain Visibility to streamline its supply chain process and provide real-time visibility. The system provides one detailed view of shipments to track, display any in-transit delays, and respond to potential crises across A&F's 34 trading partners and international business units. A&F has found that the new system further decreases cycle time and increases availability through improvements in stores' inventory allocations.[13]

The **scope** of a strategy specifies the range of markets in which an organization will compete. Hershey Foods has essentially restricted its scope to the confectionery business, with a few related activities in other food-processing areas. In contrast, its biggest competitor, Mars, has adopted a broader scope by competing in the pet food business and the electronics industry, among others. Some organizations, called *conglomerates*, compete in dozens or even hundreds of markets.

A strategy should also include an outline of the organization's projected **resource deployment**—how it will distribute its resources across the areas in which it competes. For years, GE, for example, used profits from its highly successful U.S. operations to invest heavily in new businesses in Europe and Asia. Alternatively, the firm might have chosen to invest in different industries in its domestic market or to invest more heavily in Latin America. The choices it makes as to where and how much to invest reflect decisions about resource deployment. Disney used profits from its existing theme parks and movie businesses to generate the funds needed to buy Marvel Comics and Lucas Films. And then, profits from those businesses were used to buy Fox and launch Disney+. Alternatively, Disney could have instead chosen to build new theme parks in places like South America and Australia.

"Strategy is a pattern in a stream of decisions."
—Henry Mintzberg, Leading Management Scholar[14]

business-level strategy
The set of strategic alternatives from which an organization chooses as it conducts business in a particular industry or market

3-2b Types of Strategic Alternatives

Most businesses today develop strategies at two distinct levels: the business level and corporate level. These levels provide a rich combination of strategic alternatives for organizations. **Business-level strategy** is the set of strategic alternatives from which an organization chooses as it conducts business in a particular industry or market. Such alternatives help the organization focus its competitive efforts for each industry or market in a targeted and focused manner.

Abercrombie and Fitch's Management Dynamics' Supply Chain Visibility makes it possible to manage their 34 trading partners and international business units, including off-shore factories like this one.

corporate-level strategy
The set of strategic alternatives from which an organization chooses as it manages its operations simultaneously across several industries and several markets

Corporate-level strategy is the set of strategic alternatives from which an organization chooses as it manages its operations simultaneously across several industries and several markets. As we discuss later in this chapter, most large companies today compete in various industries and markets. Thus, although they develop business-level strategies for each industry or market, they also develop an overall strategy that helps define the mix of industries and markets that are of interest to the firm.

Resource deployment is an essential element of strategic planning. Microsoft, for example, has used profits from its U.S. operations to invest in new business opportunities in Europe and Asia.

strategy formulation
The set of processes involved in creating or determining an organization's strategies; it focuses on the content of strategies

Drawing a distinction between strategy formulation and strategy implementation is also instructive. Strategy formulation is the set of processes involved in creating or determining the organization's strategies, whereas strategy implementation is the methods by which those strategies are operationalized or executed. The primary distinction is along the lines of content versus process: The formulation stage determines what the strategy is, and the implementation stage focuses on how the strategy is achieved.

"However beautiful the strategy, you should occasionally look at the results."

—Sir Winston Churchill[15]

Manager's Checklist

☐ Managers need to understand the differences between corporate and business strategies.

☐ Managers need to also remember the distinctions between strategy formulation and strategy implementation. Strategy formulation is the set of processes involved in creating or determining the strategies of the organization, whereas strategy implementation is the methods by which strategies are operationalized or executed within the organization.

strategy implementation
The methods by which strategies are operationalized or executed within the organization; it focuses on the processes through which strategies are achieved

SWOT
An acronym that stands for strengths, weaknesses, opportunities, and threats

organizational strengths
A skill or capability that enables an organization to create and implement its strategies

3-3 USING SWOT ANALYSIS TO FORMULATE STRATEGY

The starting point in formulating strategy is usually SWOT (strengths, weaknesses, opportunities, and threats) analysis. As shown in Figure 3.2, SWOT analysis is a careful evaluation of an organization's internal strengths and weaknesses as well as its environmental opportunities and threats. In SWOT analysis, the best strategies accomplish an organization's mission by (1) exploiting an organization's opportunities and strengths while (2) neutralizing its threats and (3) avoiding (or correcting) its weaknesses.

3-3a Evaluating an Organization's Strengths

Organizational strengths are skills and capabilities that enable an organization to create and implement its strategies. Strengths may include things like a deep pool of managerial talent, surplus capital, a unique reputation and/or brand name, and well-established distribution channels.[16] Amazon, for example, has been successful in part due to its strengths in supply chain management. The firm started out by selling books with an online store front. Once the fledgling business achieved high levels of efficiency, its founder and CEO, Jeff Bezos, realized that the same supply chain methods used to sell and distribute books could also be used to sell and distribute other products as well. Different strategies call on different skills and capabilities. For example, while Amazon has demonstrated strengths in distribution, this expertise does not guarantee success if the company decided to expand into insurance, swimming pool manufacturing, or fast food. Different strategies like these require different organizational strengths. SWOT analysis divides organizational strengths into two categories: common strengths and distinctive competencies.

A *distinctive competence*, introduced earlier in this chapter, is a strength possessed by only a small number of competing firms. Distinctive competencies are rare among a set of competitors. When George Lucas founded Industrial Light & Magic (ILM), for example, the new venture brought the cinematic art of special effects to new heights. Some of ILM's special effects can be produced by no other organization; these rare special effects are thus ILM's distinctive competencies. Indeed, ILM (now owned by Disney) had no real competitor until Peter Jackson formed Weta Digital Effects to help bring *Lord of the Rings* to the screen. But even so, although ILM and Weta have some of the same competences, each also has proprietary

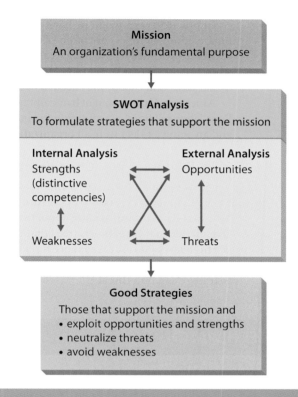

Mission
An organization's fundamental purpose

SWOT Analysis
To formulate strategies that support the mission

Internal Analysis
Strengths
(distinctive
competencies)

Weaknesses

External Analysis
Opportunities

Threats

Good Strategies
Those that support the mission and
• exploit opportunities and strengths
• neutralize threats
• avoid weaknesses

FIGURE 3.2

SWOT Analysis

SWOT analysis is one of the most important steps in formulating strategy. Using the organization's mission as a context, managers assess internal strengths (distinctive competencies) and weaknesses as well as external opportunities and threats. The goal is then to develop good strategies that exploit opportunities and strengths, neutralize threats, and avoid weaknesses.

organizational weaknesses
A skill or capability that does not enable an organization to choose and implement strategies that support its mission

A distinctive competence is a strength possessed by only a small number of competing firms. Industrial Light & Magic, founded by George Lucas in 1975, remains a leading provider of special visual effects for major movies due to its patented technologies. In addition to all of the *Star Wars* and Marvel movies, IL&M has also contributed to such recent films as *Us*, *Black Panther*, *Captain Marvel*, *Avengers: Endgame*, and *Jurassic World*.

technology that gives it certain unique advantages. Organizations that exploit their distinctive competencies often obtain a competitive advantage and attain above-normal economic performance.[17] Indeed, a main purpose of SWOT analysis is to discover an organization's distinctive competencies so that the organization can choose and implement strategies that exploit its unique organizational strengths.

3-3b Evaluating an Organization's Weaknesses

Organizational weaknesses are skills and capabilities that do not enable an organization to choose and implement strategies that support its mission. An organization has essentially two ways of addressing weaknesses. First, it may need to make investments to obtain the strengths required to implement strategies that support its mission. Second, it may need to modify its mission so that it can be accomplished with the skills and capabilities that the organization already possesses.

In practice, organizations have a difficult time focusing on weaknesses, in part because organization members are often reluctant to admit that they do not possess all the skills and capabilities needed. Evaluating weaknesses also calls into question the judgment of managers who chose the organization's mission and strategy in the first place and who failed to invest in the skills and capabilities needed to accomplish it.

American Airlines sought bankruptcy protection a few years ago in order to restructure itself. Poor labor relations, a reputation for indifferent customer service, insufficient cash reserves, and an aging jet fleet were all organizational weaknesses that led to the firm's problems.

organizational opportunities
An area in the environment that, if exploited, may generate higher performance

organizational threats
An area that increases the difficulty of an organization performing at a high level

3-3c Evaluating an Organization's Opportunities and Threats

Whereas evaluating strengths and weaknesses focuses attention on the internal workings of an organization, evaluating opportunities and threats requires analyzing an organization's environment. Organizational opportunities are areas that may generate higher performance. Organizational threats are areas that increase the difficulty of an organization performing at a high level. As discussed more fully in our *Tech Watch* feature, managers are beginning to realize that a strong social media strategy can be an opportunity whereas the absence of such a strategy can be a threat.

TECH WATCH

Starting Conversations

If you run a business and are aware of the fact that most American adults have a social media account, then you have undoubtedly arrived at an inescapable conclusion: *Your business needs a social media strategy.* What you need, in other words, is a set of goals and objectives for your social media marketing efforts, as well as a set of marketing tools and a set of metrics to figure out if those tools are getting the job done.

Fortunately, there's no shortage of specialized consultancies out there ready to help you maximize your social media strategy. Many of them have even prepared step-by-step procedures for developing or massaging strategies. The plan of one agency, for example, promises that you can develop a "Social Media Strategy in 8 Steps." Here are a few highlights:

- *Build an Ark.* "Your social media strategy should be more like air (everywhere) than like water (you have to go get it)."
- *What's Your One Thing?* "How will your company appeal to the heart of your audience rather than the head?"
- *How Will You Be Human?* "Your company has to act like a person, not an entity."

To be fair, some of the plan's recommendations make common sense and have obvious practical value. For example: *Analyze Your Audiences:* "What are the characteristics of your current or prospective customers? How does the answer to that question affect what you can and should attempt in social media?" Jess Collins, of

Type Communications, a full-service ad agency in Britain, offers an increasingly common answer to these questions: "It's not quantity," she says. "It's quality. It's about attracting fans/followers that are your target market, and so you need to make sure you're speaking to real fans rather than looking popular but not being seen by the people who matter most."

"Fans and follower counts are over," adds Jan Rezab, former CEO of the social media metrics company Social-bakers. "Now it's about what is social doing for you and your real business objectives." Take, for example, the Ritz-Carlton Hotel Co., which operates luxury hotels and resorts in 26 countries. A few years ago, the company bought a series of Facebook ads to promote its brand page. The ads attracted a large number of fans—too many, as far as Ritz-Carlton was concerned. "We were fearful that our engagement and connection with our community was dropping," explains VP of global public relations Allison Sitch. Rather than amassing fans and followers, Ritz-Carlton's strategy calls for analyzing its social media *conversations*—the networks of connections built and sustained by the most "passionate" users of a company's social media—in order to determine what real customers really do and don't like about the company's products.

Today, even social networking services admit that companies should start rethinking their social media strategies. Not surprisingly, for example, Twitter maintains that it's a good thing for companies to have big followings, but director of brand strategy Ross Hoffman hastens to add that "engagement is the key and ... can in turn further

(Continued)

TECH WATCH (CONTINUED)

grow your audience." A spokesman for Facebook agrees: "Fans," he says, "should be a means to positive business outcomes, not the end in themselves."

References: Lisa Parkin, "Why Businesses Don't Need a Social Media Strategy," *Huffington Post*, June 6, 2014, www .huffingtonpost.com on March 14, 2020; Jay Baer, "Social Media Strategy in Eight Steps," Convince & Convert LLC, www

.convinceandconvert.com on March 14, 2020; Jess Collins, "Social Media Strategy: Seven Lessons for Engaging Your Fanbase," *The Guardian*, August 8, 2014, www.theguardian .com on March 14, 2020; "Social Media Fail to Live Up to Early Marketing Hype," *Wall Street Journal*, June 23, 2014, http:// online.wsj.com on March 14, 2020; John Rampton, "Why Most Social Media Strategies Fail," *Forbes*, April 22, 2014, www .forbes.com on March 14, 2020.

✓ **Manager's Checklist**

☐ Managers need a clear understanding of SWOT analysis as they go about formulating strategy.

☐ At the same time, managers should also recognize that SWOT analysis is partially based on perceptions and subjective assessment and may, therefore, not lead to expected options.

differentiation strategy
A strategy in which an organization seeks to distinguish itself from competitors through the quality of its products or services

3-4 FORMULATING BUSINESS-LEVEL STRATEGIES

A number of frameworks have been developed for identifying the major strategic alternatives that organizations should consider when choosing their business-level strategies. Two of the most important ones are Porter's generic strategies and strategies based on the product life cycle.

Rolex has been very successful in using a differentiation strategy based on product quality. Its differentiated image, in turn, allows Rolex to charge premium prices for its watches. Rolex also maintains its differentiated image through exclusive partnerships with high-end retailers, celebrity endorsements, and not offering discounted prices.

Bloomberg/Getty Images

3-4a Generic Strategies

According to Harvard's Michael Porter, organizations may pursue a differentiation, overall cost leadership, or focus strategy at the business level.[18] An organization that pursues a **differentiation strategy** seeks to distinguish itself from competitors through the quality (broadly defined) of its products or services. Firms that successfully implement a differentiation strategy are able to charge more than competitors because customers are willing to pay more to obtain the extra value they perceive.[19] Rolex pursues a differentiation strategy. Rolex watches are handmade of stainless steel and precious metals such as gold or platinum, and they are subjected to strenuous tests of quality and reliability. The firm's reputation enables it to charge thousands of dollars for its watches. Coca-Cola and Pepsi compete in the market for bottled water on the basis of differentiation. Coke touts its Dasani brand on the basis of its fresh taste, whereas Pepsi promotes its Aquafina brand on the basis of its purity. Other firms that use differentiation strategies are Lexus, Godiva, Nikon, Mont Blanc, Apple, and Ralph Lauren, as well as each of the businesses owned by LVMH. Retailers such as American Eagle Outfitters, Quiksilver, and

Aéropostale attempt to differentiate on the basis of style. Similarly, other firms tried to provide strong differentiation on the basis of outstanding customer service.[20]

overall cost leadership strategy

A strategy in which an organization attempts to gain a competitive advantage by reducing its costs below the costs of competing firms

An organization implementing an **overall cost leadership strategy** attempts to gain a competitive advantage by reducing its costs below the costs of competing firms. By keeping costs low, the organization is able to sell its products at low prices and still make a profit. Timex uses an overall cost leadership strategy. For decades, this firm has specialized in manufacturing relatively simple, low-cost watches for the mass market. The price of Timex watches, starting around $39.95, is low because of the company's efficient high-volume manufacturing capacity. Poland Springs and Crystal Geyser bottled waters are promoted on the basis of their low cost. Other firms that implement overall cost leadership strategies are Kia, BIC, Old Navy, and Hershey. When the economy slumps, as it did during the 2020 COVID-19 pandemic, Hershey usually experiences a jump in sales—during hard times, consumers may cut back on high-end chocolate products from Godiva but aren't willing to forgo chocolate altogether. Likewise, other low-cost producers also benefit as consumers avoid higher-priced brand-name products (i.e., those with a differentiation strategy) in favor of lower-priced goods. For instance, both P&G and Colgate may see sales of products such as Tide, Pampers, and Colgate toothpaste decline, whereas sales of lower-priced private-label products increase.

focus strategy

A strategy in which an organization concentrates on a specific regional market, product line, or group of buyers

A firm pursuing a **focus strategy** concentrates on a specific regional market, product line, or group of buyers. This strategy may have either a differentiation focus, whereby the firm differentiates its products in the focus market, or an overall cost leadership focus, whereby the firm manufactures and sells its products at low cost in the focus market. In the watch industry, Tag Heuer follows a focus differentiation strategy by selling only rugged waterproof watches to active consumers. Tata Motors follows a focus cost leadership strategy by selling its inexpensive automobiles only in India. Alfa Romeo uses focus differentiation to sell its high-performance cars only in markets where customers can pay over $100,000 for a car. Fisher-Price uses focus differentiation to sell electronic calculators with large, brightly colored buttons to the parents of preschoolers; stockbroker Edward Jones focuses on small-town settings. General Mills focuses one part of its new-

27063

Red Robin GOURMET BURGERS AND BREWS

Red Robin OPEN FOR TO-GO AND DELIVERY

LUNCH MEETINGS JUST GOT LEGIT

Red Robin CATERING

Robert V Schwemmer/Shutterstock.com

Before the COVID-19 pandemic, many restaurants focused on dine-in services for people looking for particular types of cuisine such as seafood, burgers, and so forth. During the various forms of "shelter-in-place" initiatives, though, many of these same restaurants shifted their focus to pick-up and/or delivery.

product development on consumers who eat meals while driving—its watchword is "Can we make it 'one-handed'?" so that drivers can safely eat or drink it. Two investors realized that most Las Vegas casinos were targeting either high-end big spenders or the young hip market. So, they bought the venerable old Tropicana casino, renovated it, and began marketing it to so-called Middle America—middle-aged or older gamblers who aren't into big-dollar wagering. Their occupancy rates have soared, as did their profits.[21] Likewise, prior to the COVID-19 pandemic most higher-priced restaurants kept their focus on dine-in services for people looking for particular types of cuisine. During the various forms of "shelter-in-place" initiatives, though, many of these same restaurants shifted their focus to pick-up and/or delivery.

> **"The important thing is not being afraid to take a chance. Remember, the greatest failure is to not try. Once you find something you love to do, be the best at doing it."**
> —Debbi Fields, Founder of Mrs. Fields Cookies[22]

3-4b **Strategies Based on the Product Life Cycle**

product life cycle
A model that portrays how sales volume for products changes over the life of products

The product life cycle is a model that shows how sales volume changes over the life of products. Understanding the four stages in the product life cycle helps managers recognize that strategies need to evolve over time. As Figure 3.3 shows, the cycle begins when a new product or technology is first introduced. In this introduction stage, demand may be very high and sometimes outpaces the firm's ability to supply the product. At this stage, managers need to focus their efforts on "getting product out the door" without sacrificing quality. Managing growth by hiring new employees and managing inventories and cash flow are also concerns during this stage.

Hershey uses an overall cost leadership strategy to promote its candy bars. By keeping its costs as low as possible, the firm can provide good-quality snacks at competitive prices. This strategy benefited the firm during the most recent recession as customers cut back on higher-priced candy, allowing Hershey to gain new market share.

During the growth stage, more firms begin producing the product, and sales continue to grow. Important management issues include ensuring quality and delivery and beginning to differentiate an organization's product from competitors' products. Entry into the industry during the growth stage may threaten an organization's competitive advantage; thus, strategies to slow the entry of competitors are important.

After a period of growth, products enter a third phase. During this maturity stage, overall demand growth for a product begins to slow down, and the number of new firms producing the product begins to decline. The number of established firms producing the product may also begin to decline. This period of maturity is essential if an organization is going to survive in the long run. Product differentiation concerns are still important during this stage, but also keeping costs low and beginning the search for new products or services are important strategic considerations.

In the *decline stage*, demand for the product or technology decreases, the number of organizations producing the product drops, and total sales drop. Demand often declines because all those who were interested in purchasing a particular product have already done so. Organizations that fail to anticipate the decline stage in earlier stages of the life cycle may go out of business. Those that differentiate their product, keep their costs low, or develop new products or services may do well during this stage.

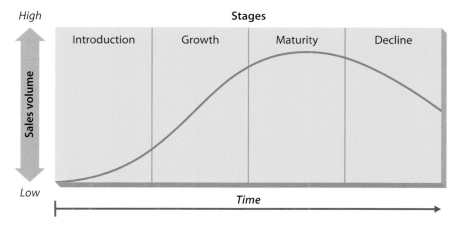

FIGURE 3.3

The Product Life Cycle

Managers can use the framework of the product life cycle—introduction, growth, maturity, and decline—to plot strategy. For example, management may decide on a differentiation strategy for a product in the introduction stage and a prospector approach for a product in the growth stage. By understanding this cycle and where a particular product falls within it, managers can develop more effective strategies for extending product life.

☐ Regardless of the business-level strategy being pursued, managers need to be sure their decisions are consistent with that strategy.

☐ Managers should strive to develop a logical business-level strategy based on their SWOT analysis.

3-5 FORMULATING CORPORATE-LEVEL STRATEGIES

Most large organizations are engaged in several businesses, industries, and markets. Each business or set of businesses within such an organization is frequently referred to as a *strategic business unit (SBU)*. An organization such as LVMH operates dozens of different businesses. As noted in our opening case, the firm groups these businesses into six SBUs. Even organizations that sell only one product may operate in several distinct markets.

Decisions about which businesses, industries, and markets an organization will enter, and how to manage these different businesses, are based on an organization's corporate strategy. The most important strategic issue at the corporate level concerns the extent and nature of organizational diversification. Diversification describes the number of different businesses that an organization is engaged in and the extent to which these businesses are related to one another. There are three types of diversification strategies: single-product strategy, related diversification, and unrelated diversification.[23]

diversification
The number of different businesses that an organization is engaged in and the extent to which these businesses are related to one another

3-5a Single-Product Strategy

An organization that pursues a single-product strategy manufactures just one product or service and sells it in a single geographic market. The WD-40 Company, for example, basically manufactures one product, WD-40 spray lubricant, and for years sold it just in North America. WD-40 has started selling its lubricant in Europe and Asia, but it continues to center all manufacturing, sales, and marketing efforts on one product. Similarly, Michelin has remained faithful to the cause of strictly manufacturing quality tires.

The single-product strategy has one major strength and one major weakness. By concentrating its efforts so completely on one product and market, a firm is likely to be very successful in manufacturing and marketing that product. Because it has staked its survival on a single product, the organization works very hard to make sure that the product is a success. Of course, if the product is not accepted by the market or is replaced by a new one, the firm will suffer. Typewriters essentially became obsolete when personal computers and word-processing software were introduced.

single-product strategy
A strategy in which an organization manufactures just one product or service and sells it in a single geographic market

3-5b Related Diversification

Given the disadvantage of the single-product strategy, most large businesses today operate in several different businesses, industries, or markets.[24] If the businesses are somehow linked, that organization is implementing a strategy of related diversification. Virtually all larger businesses in the United States use related diversification.

Pursuing a strategy of related diversification has three primary advantages. First, it reduces an organization's dependence on any one of its business activities and thus reduces economic risk. Even if one or two of a firm's businesses lose money, the organization as a whole may still survive because the healthy businesses will generate enough cash to support the others.[25] For instance, Disney closed its theme parks and resorts during the 2020 COVID-19 pandemic. Part of the lost revenue from these closures, though, was offset by a surge in new subscriptions for the Disney+ streaming service. Similarly, Uber lost revenue at its ride-sharing businesses during this same period as many people "sheltered in place," but Uber Eats, its food and grocery delivery operations, saw an increase in revenue as more people ordered food for home delivery.

related diversification
A strategy in which an organization operates in several businesses that are somehow linked with one another

Second, by managing several businesses at the same time, an organization can reduce the overhead costs associated with managing any one business. In other words, if the normal administrative costs required to operate any business, such as legal services and accounting, can be spread over a large number of businesses, then the overhead costs per business will be lower than they would be if each business had to absorb all costs itself. LVMH, for example, secures advertising contracts for several of its businesses at the same time. By contracting with an ad agency to develop advertising campaigns for, say, 20 businesses, the ad costs for each business will be lower than if that business had contracted for a single campaign. Thus, the overhead costs of businesses in a firm that pursues related diversification are usually lower than those of similar businesses that are not part of a larger corporation.[26]

Third, related diversification allows an organization to exploit its strengths and capabilities in more than one business. When organizations do this successfully, they capitalize on synergies, which are complementary effects that exist among their businesses. Synergy exists among a set of businesses when the businesses' economic value together is greater than their economic value separately. McDonald's has used synergy as it diversified into other restaurant and food businesses. For example, its McCafé premium coffee stands in some McDonald's restaurants allow the firm to create new revenue opportunities while using the firm's existing strengths in food-product purchasing and distribution. Similarly, Starbucks has experimented with an evening menu featuring wine and cheese in a select number of stores. The *Leading the Way* feature provides another example of effective related diversification.

3-5c **Unrelated Diversification**

unrelated diversification
A strategy in which an organization operates multiple businesses that are not logically associated with one another

Firms that implement a strategy of unrelated diversification operate multiple businesses that are not logically associated with one another. At one time, for example, Quaker Oats owned clothing chains, toy companies, and a restaurant business. Unrelated diversification was once a very popular strategy. During that time, several conglomerates such as ITT and Transamerica grew by acquiring literally hundreds of other organizations and then running these numerous businesses as independent entities. Today TRT Holdings is a Dallas-based company that owns Omni Hotels, Gold's Gym, Tana Exploration (an oil and gas exploration company), and Waldo's Dollar Mart, a Mexican discount chain. Even if there are potential synergies among their different businesses, organizations implementing a strategy of unrelated diversification do not attempt to exploit them.

In theory, unrelated diversification has two advantages. First, a business that uses this strategy should be able to achieve relatively stable performance over time. During any given period, some businesses owned by the organization are in a cycle of decline, whereas others

A few businesses adopt a corporate strategy of unrelated diversification. This means that various businesses owned by the corporation are not related to one another. For instance, TRT Holdings owns Gold's Gym, the Omni hotel chain, Tana Exploration (an oil and gas exploration firm), and Waldo's Dollar Mart, a Mexican discount chain. These businesses obviously have little in common.

LEADING THE WAY

The Beauty of Differentiation

One day back in the late 1990s, an urbane Englishman stopped two Chinese women on a street in Shanghai. He wanted to know if they used L'Oréal products to color their hair. No, they replied, they had it done in a salon. The gentleman promptly escorted them to the nearest department store, where a couple of models in shimmering Lycra were dancing in front of a huge backdrop of the New York City skyline. "This brand comes from America," intoned a Chinese saleswoman. "It's very trendy." The Englishman offered the two women that he'd brought with him free hair-color kits.

The L'Oréal front man was actually the company's CEO at the time, Lindsay Owen-Jones, and the hair color was from Maybelline, which L'Oréal had acquired a few years earlier. "We have made a conscious effort to diversify the cultural origins of our brands," said Owen-Jones at the time. The giant French cosmetics and beauty company had given Maybelline a radical makeover, promoting it as "urban American chic" to underscore both its bold new product line and its U.S. origins.

When he took over L'Oréal in 1988, Owen-Jones (who stepped down in 2006) was faced with a problem confronting many global companies—how to resolve the tension between "global integration" and "local responsiveness." Owen-Jones saw the issue as a question of how far to optimize the mass-market appeal of L'Oréal's product lines or how far to diversify them in an effort to appeal to a range of multicultural markets. He chose multiculturalism, especially in light of emerging markets in the Asia Pacific region, Africa, and the Middle East.

The strategy is called "global branding," and Owen-Jones's version called for a two-pronged approach: diversifying L'Oréal's brands according to countries of origin (which include France, Britain, Germany, Italy, and Japan) and then calling upon the company's marketing expertise to cultivate the allure of different cultures and exotic brand offerings in markets from China to Mexico. "We like to try stuff," explains Stéphane Bérubé, chief marketing officer

of L'Oréal Western Europe, "and we're not afraid to go first into testing and new adventures." When it expanded in India, for example, L'Oréal was the first company to offer any hair-color alternatives to black.

Bérubé reports that the company has recently done a lot of research into three global-market segments: "the South Asian consumer, the Chinese consumer, and the baby boomers, which are three booming markets in terms of both growth and buying power. . . . We have products from most of our brands," he adds, "that are targeted to these three segments," but he admits that the company can still do better in two areas that reflect Owen-Jones's original two-pronged marketing strategy: "One, to have more offerings and, two, to better target" selected consumers.

"The name of the game right now," says Bérubé, "is to have the right product at the right time in front of the consumer. And that," he states, "can be done through digital or in-store." To help facilitate this transition, L'Oréal entered into a partnership with Sitecore, a marketing-technology firm whose platform can be used to connect across media and electronic consumer touch points with thousands of stores and millions of customers, potentially on a one-to-one basis. "The goal," said Sitecore's chief strategy officer at the time, "is understanding the person behind the keyboard and then delivering experiences that matter."

References: Hae-Jung Hong and Yves Doz, "L'Oréal Masters Multiculturalism," *Harvard Business Review*, June 2013), http://hbr.org on March 15, 2020; Gail Edmondson et al., "L'Oréal: The Beauty of Global Branding," *Bloomberg Businessweek*, June 28, 1999), www.businessweek.com on March 15, 2020; Tanya Kostiw, "L'Oréal Homes In On a One-on-One Approach with Shoppers," *Strategy*, May 28, 2014, http://strategyonline.ca on March 15, 2020; John Koetsier, "One-to-One Marketing, Global Scale: Sitecore Lands L'Oréal to Personalize Beauty," *Venture Beat*, April 16, 2014, http://venturebeat.com on March 15, 2020.

may be in a cycle of growth. Second, unrelated diversification is also thought to have resource allocation advantages. Every year, when a corporation allocates capital, people, and other resources among its various businesses, it must evaluate information about the future of those businesses so that it can place its resources where they have the highest potential for return. Given that it owns the businesses in question and thus has full access to information about the future of those businesses, a firm implementing unrelated diversification should be able to allocate capital to maximize corporate performance.

Despite these presumed advantages, research suggests that unrelated diversification usually does not lead to high performance. First, corporate-level managers in such a company usually do not know enough about the unrelated businesses to provide helpful strategic guidance or to allocate capital appropriately. To make strategic decisions, managers must have complete and subtle understanding of a business and its environment. Because corporate managers often have difficulty fully evaluating the economic importance of investments for all the businesses under their wing, they tend to concentrate only on a business's current performance. This narrow attention at the expense of broader planning eventually hobbles the entire organization.

Second, because organizations that implement unrelated diversification fail to exploit important synergies, they may be at a competitive disadvantage compared to organizations that use related diversification. Universal Studios has been at a competitive disadvantage relative to Disney because its theme parks, movie studios, and licensing divisions are less integrated and therefore achieve less synergy.

For these reasons, most companies have abandoned unrelated diversification as a corporate-level strategy. Transamerica, for instance, sold off numerous unrelated businesses and now concentrates on a core set of related businesses and markets. Large corporations that have not concentrated on a core set of businesses have eventually been acquired by other companies and then broken up. Research suggests that these organizations are often worth more when broken up into smaller pieces than when joined.[27]

"Hope is not a strategy."
—Vince Lombardi, Famed Football Coach[28]

3-5d Managing Diversification

However, when an organization implements diversification—whether through internal development, vertical integration, or mergers and acquisitions—it must monitor and manage its strategy. Portfolio management techniques are methods that diversified organizations use to determine which businesses to engage in and how to manage these businesses to maximize corporate performance. Two important portfolio management techniques are the BCG matrix and the GE Business Screen.

BCG Matrix   The BCG (Boston Consulting Group) matrix provides a framework for evaluating the relative performance of businesses in which a diversified organization operates. It also prescribes the preferred distribution of cash and other resources among these businesses.[29] The BCG matrix uses two factors to evaluate an organization's set of businesses: the growth rate of a particular market and the organization's share of that market. The matrix suggests that fast-growing markets in which an organization has the highest market share are more attractive business opportunities than slow-growing markets in which an organization has small market share. Dividing market growth and market share into two categories (low and high) creates the simple matrix shown in Figure 3.4.

The matrix classifies the types of businesses in which a diversified organization can engage as dogs, cash cows, question marks, and stars. *Dogs* are businesses that have a very small share of a market that is not expected to grow. Because these businesses do not hold much economic promise, the BCG matrix suggests that organizations either should not invest in them or should consider selling them as soon as possible. *Cash cows* are businesses that have a large share of a market that is not expected to grow substantially. These businesses characteristically generate high profits that the organization should use to support question marks and stars. (Cash cows are "milked" for cash to support businesses in markets that have greater growth potential.)

Question marks are businesses that have only a small share of a fast-growing market. The future performance of these businesses is uncertain. A question mark that is able to capture increasing amounts of this growing market may be very profitable. On the other hand, a question mark unable to keep up with market growth is likely to have low profits. The BCG matrix suggests that organizations should invest carefully in question marks. If their performance does not live up to expectations, question marks should be reclassified as dogs and divested. *Stars* are businesses that have the largest share of a rapidly growing market. Cash generated by cash cows should be invested in stars to ensure their preeminent position. For example, BMW bought Rover several years ago, thinking that its products would help the German automaker reach new consumers. But the company was not able to capitalize on this opportunity, so it ended up selling Rover's car business to a British firm and Land Rover to Ford. Ford couldn't get leverage out of Rover either and ended up selling it (along with Jaguar) to India's Tata Motors.

portfolio management techniques
Methods that diversified organizations use to determine which businesses to engage in and how to manage these businesses to maximize corporate performance

BCG matrix
A framework for evaluating businesses relative to the growth rate of their market and the organization's share of the market

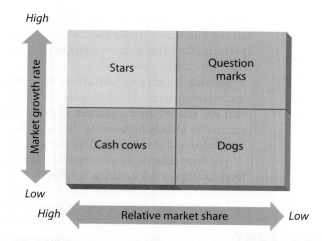

FIGURE 3.4

The BCG Matrix

The BCG matrix helps managers develop a better understanding of how different SBUs contribute to the overall organization. By assessing each SBU on the basis of its market growth rate and relative market share, managers can make decisions about whether to commit further financial resources to the SBU or to sell or liquidate it.

Source: *Perspectives*, No. 66, "The Product Portfolio." Adapted by permission from The Boston Consulting Group, Inc., 1970.

GE business screen
A method of evaluating businesses along two dimensions: (1) industry attractiveness and (2) competitive position; in general, the more attractive the industry and the more competitive the position, the more an organization should invest in a business

GE Business Screen   Because the BCG matrix is relatively narrow and overly simplistic, GE developed the GE Business Screen, a more sophisticated approach to managing diversified business units. The GE Business Screen is a portfolio management technique that can also be represented in the form of a matrix. Rather than focusing solely on market growth and market share, however, the GE Business Screen considers industry attractiveness and competitive position. These two factors are divided into three categories to make the nine-cell matrix shown in Figure 3.5.[30] These cells, in turn, classify business units as winners, losers, question marks, average businesses, or profit producers.

As Figure 3.5 shows, both market growth and market share appear in a broad list of factors that determine the overall attractiveness of an industry and the overall quality of a firm's competitive position. Other determinants of an industry's attractiveness (in addition to market growth) include market size, capital requirements, and competitive intensity. In general, the greater the market growth, the larger the market, the smaller the capital requirements, and the less the competitive intensity, the more attractive an industry will be. Other determinants of an organization's competitive position in an industry (besides market share) include technological know-how, product quality, service network, price competitiveness, and operating costs. In general, businesses with large market share, technological know-how, high product quality, a quality service network, competitive prices, and low operating costs are in a favorable competitive position.

Think of the GE Business Screen as a way of applying SWOT analysis to the implementation and management of a diversification strategy. The determinants of industry attractiveness are similar to the environmental opportunities and threats in SWOT analysis, and the determinants of competitive position are similar to organizational strengths and weaknesses. By conducting this type of SWOT analysis across several businesses, a diversified organization can decide how to invest its resources to maximize corporate performance. In general, organizations should invest in winners and question marks (where industry attractiveness and competitive position are both favorable), should maintain the market position of average businesses and profit producers (where industry attractiveness and competitive position are average), and should sell losers.

<table>
<tr><td rowspan="3">Industry attractiveness</td><td>High</td><td>Winner</td><td>Winner</td><td>Question mark</td></tr>
<tr><td>Medium</td><td>Winner</td><td>Average business</td><td>Loser</td></tr>
<tr><td>Low</td><td>Profit producer</td><td>Loser</td><td>Loser</td></tr>
<tr><td></td><td>Good</td><td>Medium</td><td>Poor</td></tr>
</table>

Competitive position

Competitive position	Industry attractiveness
1. Market share	1. Market growth
2. Technological know-how	2. Market size
3. Product quality	3. Capital requirements
4. Service network	4. Competitive intensity
5. Price competitiveness	
6. Operating costs	

FIGURE 3.5

The GE Business Screen

The GE Business Screen is a more sophisticated approach to portfolio management than the BCG matrix. As shown here, several factors combine to determine a business's competitive position and the attractiveness of its industry. These two dimensions, in turn, can be used to classify businesses as winners, question marks, average businesses, losers, or profit producers. Such a classification enables managers to allocate the organization's resources more effectively across various business opportunities.

Source: From *Strategy Formulation: Analytical Concepts*, 1st ed., by Charles W. Hofer and Dan Schendel. Copyright © 1978. Reprinted with permission of South-Western, a division of Thomson Learning, www.thomsonrights.com.

For example, Unilever recently assessed its business portfolio using a similar framework and, as a result, decided to sell off several specialty chemical units that were not contributing to the firm's profitability as much as other businesses. The firm then used the revenues from these divestitures and bought more related businesses such as the Dollar Shave Club. During the recent economic recession, many diversified businesses took an especially aggressive approach to selling or closing underperforming businesses. For instance, Japan's Pioneer electronics business sold its television business, Home Depot shut down its Expo home-design stores, and Textron closed a business unit that financed real-estate deals.[31]

 **Manager's Checklist**

☐ Managers should be aware of the different ways to formulate corporate-level strategies and know the advantages and disadvantages of each.

☐ Managers who pursue a single-product strategy need to be aware that potential threats can affect them very dramatically.

☐ If managers pursue a diversification strategy, they need to clearly understand what they hope to achieve and make sure their decisions support these goals.

☐ Before acquiring other businesses, managers need to have a clear understanding of how the acquisitions fit its corporate-level strategy.

3-6 TACTICAL PLANNING

tactical plans
A plan aimed at achieving tactical goals and developed to implement parts of a strategic plan; an organized sequence of steps designed to execute strategic plans

As we noted earlier in the chapter, tactical plans are developed to implement specific parts of a strategic plan. You have probably heard the saying about winning the battle but losing the war. Tactical plans are to battles what strategy is to a war: an organized sequence of steps designed to execute strategic plans. Strategy focuses on resources, environment, and mission, whereas tactics focus primarily on people and action.[32]

3-6a Developing Tactical Plans

Although effective tactical planning depends on many factors, which vary from one situation to another, we can identify some basic guidelines. First, the manager needs to recognize that tactical planning must address a number of tactical goals derived from a broader strategic goal.[33] An occasional situation may call for a stand-alone tactical plan, but most of the time tactical plans flow from and must be consistent with a strategic plan.

For example, a few years ago Disney developed a strategy calling for growth through the acquisition of new intellectual properties. Over the next several years the firm acquired the Muppets, Pixar, Marvel, and Lucasfilm. After acquiring each of these properties Disney next needed to create various tactical plans for developing new sources of revenue for each property. These tactical plans involved television programs, movies, theme-park attractions, merchandising, and so forth.

Second, although strategies are often stated in general terms, tactics must specify resources and time frames. A strategy can call for being number one in a particular market or industry, but a tactical plan must specify precisely what activities will be undertaken to achieve that goal. Consider the Disney example again. Due to a preexisting licensing agreement with Universal, Disney cannot use Marvel characters in its theme parks in Orlando. However, it is building major new theme-park attractions in its Hollywood Studios theme park at Disney World. Each attraction is part of a tactical plan with its own time frame, budget, and so forth.

Finally, tactical planning requires the use of human resources. Managers involved in tactical planning spend a great deal of time working with other people. They must be in a position to receive information from others within and outside the organization, process that information most effectively, and then pass it on to others who might use it. Disney has designated teams assigned to each of its new intellectual properties. Each team, in turn, is tasked with looking for ways to best capitalize on that property.

3-6b Executing Tactical Plans

Regardless of how well a tactical plan is formulated, its ultimate success depends on the way it is carried out. Successful implementation, in turn, depends on the astute use of resources, effective decision making, and insightful steps to ensure that the right things are done at the right times and in the right ways. A manager can see an absolutely brilliant idea fail because of improper execution.

Proper execution depends on a number of important factors. First, the manager needs to evaluate every possible course of action in light of the goal it is intended to reach. Next, he or she needs to make sure that each decision-maker has the information and resources necessary to get the job done. Vertical and horizontal communication and integration of activities must be present to minimize conflict and inconsistent activities. And, finally, the manager must monitor ongoing activities derived from the plan to make sure they are achieving the desired results. This monitoring typically takes place within the context of the organization's ongoing control systems.

Manager's Checklist

☐ You need to clearly understand how to both develop and then execute tactical plans.

☐ Remember that tactical plans need to be consistent with overarching strategic plans.

3-7 OPERATIONAL PLANNING

Another critical element in effective organizational planning is the development and implementation of operational plans. Operational plans are derived from tactical plans and are aimed at achieving operational goals. Thus, operational plans tend to be narrowly focused, have relatively short time horizons, and involve lower-level managers. The two most basic forms of operational plans and specific types of each are summarized in Table 3.1.

Organizations develop various operational plans to help achieve operational goals. In general, there are two types of single-use plans and three types of standing plans.

3-7a Single-Use Plans

single-use plan
Developed to carry out a course of action that is not likely to be repeated in the future

A single-use plan is developed to carry out a course of action that is not likely to be repeated in the future. As Disney plans a new restaurant for one of its theme parks, and if managers know that unique elements of the restaurant will not allow it to be replicated in other theme parks, it will develop a single-use plan for that restaurant. The two most common forms of single-use plans are programs and projects.

program
A single-use plan for a large set of activities

Programs A program is a single-use plan for a large set of activities. It might consist of identifying procedures for introducing a new product line, opening a new facility, or changing the organization's mission. When United and Continental Airlines merged, a program was needed to integrate every facet of the two firms' operations. The overall program required the integration of 1,400 technology systems (600 at Continental and 800 at United) and took three years to complete.[34]

project
A single-use plan of less scope and complexity than a program

Projects A project is similar to a program but is generally of less scope and complexity. A project may be a part of a broader program or it may be a self-contained single-use plan. During the United–Continental merger, one project that was handled by the beverage committee involved deciding what coffee to use on the new airline. What might seem like a simple decision required thousands of taste tests and changes in both coffee suppliers and coffee-making equipment and took over a year. Projects are also used to introduce a new product within an existing product line or to add a new benefit option to an existing salary package.

3-7b Standing Plans

standing plan
Developed for activities that recur regularly over a period of time

Whereas single-use plans are developed for nonrecurring situations, a standing plan is used for activities that recur regularly over a period of time. Standing plans can greatly enhance efficiency by making decision making routine. Policies, standard operating procedures (SOPs), and rules and regulations are three kinds of standing plans.

Table 3.1	Types of Operational Plans
Plan	**Description**
Single-use plan	Developed to carry out a course of action not likely to be repeated in the future
Program	Single-use plan for a large set of activities
Project	Single-use plan of less scope and complexity than a program
Standing plan	Developed for activities that recur regularly over a period of time
Policy	Standing plan specifying the organization's general response to a designated problem or situation
Standard operating procedure	Standing plan outlining steps to be followed in particular circumstances
Rules and regulations	Standing plans describing exactly how specific activities are to be carried out

policy
A standing plan that specifies the organization's general response to a designated problem or situation

Policies   As a general guide for action, a **policy** is the most general form of standing plan that specifies the organization's general response to a designated problem or situation. For example, McDonald's has a policy that it will not grant a franchise to an individual who already owns a competing fast-food restaurant. Similarly, Starbucks has a policy that it will not franchise to individuals at all, instead retaining ownership of all Starbucks coffee shops. Likewise, a university admissions office might establish a policy that admission will be granted only to applicants with a minimum SAT score of 1,200 and a ranking in the top quarter of their high school class. Admissions officers may routinely deny admission to applicants who fail to reach these minimums. A policy is also likely to describe how exceptions are to be handled. The university's policy statement, for example, might create an admissions appeals committee to evaluate applicants who do not meet minimum requirements but may warrant special consideration.

SOP
A standard plan that outlines the steps to be followed in particular circumstances

Standard Operating Procedures   Another type of standing plan is the **SOP**. An SOP is more specific than a policy, in that it outlines the steps to be followed in particular circumstances. For instance, Quicken Loans has SOPs that guide loan decisions. An application that exceeds all minimum requirements for credit scores, applicant income, and so forth will be automatically routed to approval offices who will check various elements of the application for accuracy and then initiate a loan approval process. Likewise, an application that fails to meet minimum requirements will be routed to different offices for a final review and then initiate the loan denial process. Finally, a loan application that comes very close to meeting minimum requirements but not quite meet them may be routed to a still different office. In this case the applicant might be offered the opportunity to correct certain things in order to meet minimum requirements. For example, the applicant might be advised to pay off a debt or to increase the amount of the proposed down payment in order to meet requirements. Gallo Vineyards in California has a 300-page manual of SOPs. This planning manual is credited with making Gallo one of the most efficient winemaking operations in the United States. McDonald's has SOPs explaining exactly how Big Macs are to be cooked, how long they can stay in the warming rack, and so forth.

rules and regulations
Describe exactly how specific activities are to be carried out

Rules and Regulations   The narrowest of the standing plans, **rules and regulations**, describe exactly how specific activities are to be carried out. Rather than guiding decision making, rules and regulations actually take the place of decision making in various situations. Each McDonald's restaurant has a rule prohibiting customers from using its telephones, for example. A university admissions office might have a rule stipulating that if an applicant's online file is not complete two months before the beginning of a semester, the student cannot be admitted until the next semester. Of course, in most organizations a manager at a higher level can suspend or bend the rules. If the high school transcript of the child of a prominent university alumnus and donor arrives a few days late, the director of admissions might waive the two-month rule. Indeed, rules and regulations can become problematic if they are excessive or enforced too rigidly.

Rules and regulations and SOPs are similar in many ways. They are both relatively narrow in scope, and each can serve as a substitute for decision making. An SOP typically describes a sequence of activities, whereas rules and regulations focus on one activity. Recall our examples: The admissions SOP consisted of three activities, whereas the two-month rule related to only one activity. For example, a business with an SOP for onboarding a new employee could involve enrolling the person in various benefit options, introducing him or her to coworkers and supervisors, and providing a tour of the facilities. A pertinent rule for the new employee might involve when to come to work each day.

contingency planning
The determination of alternative courses of action to be taken if an intended plan is unexpectedly disrupted or rendered inappropriate

crisis management
The set of procedures the organization uses in the event of a disaster or other unexpected calamity

3-7c Contingency Planning and Crisis Management

Another important type of planning is **contingency planning**, or the determination of alternative courses of action to be taken if an intended plan of action is unexpectedly disrupted or rendered inappropriate.[35] **Crisis management**, a related concept, is the set of procedures the organization uses in the event of a disaster or other unexpected calamity. Some elements of crisis management may be orderly and systematic, whereas others may be more ad hoc and develop as events unfold. Disney does a reasonably good job of contingency planning. Its theme park operations in central Florida, for example, have occasionally been forced to shut down temporarily in anticipation of hurricanes. When the COVID-19 pandemic hit in 2020, Disney was able to utilize many components of its existing weather-based contingency plans to systematically first close its theme parks and then its adjacent resorts. Similarly, Disney was also able to then begin to plan for how and under what circumstances its resorts and theme parks would reopen.[36] Other firms have contingency plans in place to deal with events such as terrorism, online security breaches, and so forth. However, given the uncertainty of when and how crises may unfold, it is actually very difficult to know in advance how to respond.[37]

Natural disasters like hurricanes and earthquakes can have a devastating impact on business. Large companies often have crisis management plans in place to provide at least partial direction and support for those affected by such a disaster. But smaller businesses like this one are likely to suffer long-term financial consequences and many do not survive. This Austin bar was forced to close during the COVID-19 pandemic in 2020.

Seeing the consequences of poor crisis management after the terrorist attacks of September 11, 2001, and the 2005 hurricanes, many firms today have actively tried to create new and better crisis management plans and procedures. For example, both Reliant Energy and Duke Energy rely on computer trading centers where trading managers actively buy and sell energy-related commodities. If a terrorist attack or natural disaster were to strike their trading centers, they would essentially be out of business. Consequently, Reliant and Duke have created secondary trading centers at other locations. In the event of a shutdown at their main trading centers, these firms can quickly transfer virtually all their core trading activities to their secondary centers within 30 minutes or less.[38] However, many firms still do not have comprehensive crisis management strategies. For example, as the COVID-19 pandemic swept around the world in 2020, a survey found that only about 57 percent of U.S. businesses had plans in place to deal with such a viral or bacterial pandemic. As a result, many businesses had to make decisions "on the fly" and respond to events with a much greater sense of urgency than might have been the case had they had better plans in place.

"This fight [against terrorism] will not be decided on the battlefield, but in the classrooms, workplaces, and places of worship of the world."

—John Kerry, Former U.S. Secretary of State[39]

The mechanics of contingency planning are shown in Figure 3.6. In relation to an organization's other plans, contingency planning comes into play at four action points. At action point 1, management develops the organization's basic plans. These may include strategic, tactical, and operational plans. As part of this development process, managers usually consider various contingency events. Some management groups even assign someone the role of devil's advocate, who asks "But what if . . .?" about each course of action. A variety of contingencies is usually considered.

Never Settle Media/Shutterstock.com

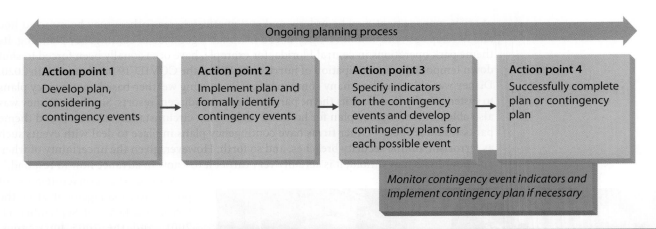

FIGURE 3.6

Contingency Planning

Most organizations develop contingency plans. These plans specify alternative courses of action to be taken if an intended plan is unexpectedly disrupted or rendered inappropriate.

At action point 2, the plan that management chooses is put into effect. The most important contingency events are also defined. Only the events that are likely to occur and whose effects will have a substantial impact on the organization are used in the contingency-planning process. Next, at action point 3, the company specifies certain indicators or signs that suggest that a contingency event is about to take place. A bank might decide that a 2 percent drop in interest rates should be considered a contingency event. An indicator might be two consecutive months with a drop of 0.5 percent in each. As indicators of contingency events are being defined, the contingency plans themselves should also be developed. Examples of contingency plans for various situations are delaying plant construction, developing a new manufacturing process, and cutting prices.

After this stage, the organization's managers monitor the indicators identified at action point 3. If the situation dictates, a contingency plan is implemented. Otherwise, the primary plan of action continues in force. Finally, action point 4 marks the successful completion of either the original or a contingency plan.

Contingency planning is becoming increasingly important for most organizations, especially for those operating in particularly complex or dynamic environments. Few managers have such an accurate view of the future that they can anticipate and plan for everything. Contingency planning is a useful technique for helping managers cope with uncertainty and change. However, crisis management, by its very nature, is more difficult to anticipate. But organizations that have a strong culture, strong leadership, and a capacity to deal with the unexpected stand a better chance of successfully weathering a crisis than other organizations.[40]

Manager's Checklist

☐ As a manager, keep in mind that single-use and standing plans are a common and necessary part of doing business.

☐ At the same time, though, it can become dysfunctional to fall back on rules, SOPs, and so forth without understanding their intended purpose.

☐ Managers should also be familiar with their organization's crisis and contingency plans.

SUMMARY OF LEARNING OUTCOMES AND KEY POINTS

3-1. Summarize the planning process and organizational goals.

- The planning process includes understanding the environment, formulating a mission, and creating goals and plans.

- Goals serve four basic purposes: They provide guidance and direction, facilitate planning, inspire motivation and commitment, and promote evaluation and control.

- With an understanding of the environmental context, managers develop a number of different types of goals and plans, including strategic, tactical, and operational plans.

3-2. Discuss the components of strategy and the types of strategic alternatives.

- A strategy is a comprehensive plan for accomplishing the organization's goals.

- Effective strategies address three organizational issues: distinctive competence, scope, and resource deployment.

3-3. Describe how to use SWOT analysis in formulating strategy.

- SWOT analysis considers an organization's strengths, weaknesses, opportunities, and threats.

- Using SWOT analysis, an organization chooses strategies that support its mission, exploit its opportunities and strengths, neutralize its threats, and avoid its weaknesses.

3-4. Discuss various alternative approaches to business-level strategy formulation.

- A business-level strategy is the plan an organization uses to conduct business in a particular industry or market.

- Porter suggests that businesses may formulate a differentiation strategy, an overall cost leadership strategy, or a focus strategy.

- Business-level strategies may also take into account the stages in its products' life cycles.

3-5. Describe various alternative approaches to corporate-level strategy formulation.

- A corporate-level strategy is the plan an organization uses to manage its operations across several businesses.

- A firm that does not diversify is implementing a single-product strategy.

- An organization pursues a strategy of related diversification when it operates a set of businesses that are somehow linked.

- An organization pursues a strategy of unrelated diversification when it operates a set of businesses that are not logically associated with one another.

- Organizations manage diversification through the organization structure that they adopt and through portfolio management techniques. The BCG matrix classifies an organization's diversified businesses as dogs, cash cows, question marks, or stars according to market share and market growth rate. The GE Business Screen classifies businesses as winners, losers, question marks, average businesses, or profit producers according to industry attractiveness and competitive position.

3-6. Discuss how tactical plans are developed and implemented.

- Tactical plans are at the middle of the organization, have an intermediate time horizon, and are moderate in scope.

- Tactical plans are developed to implement specific parts of a strategic plan.

- Tactical plans must flow from strategy, specify resource and time issues, and commit human resources.

3-7. Describe the basic types of operational plans used by organizations.

- Operational plans are at the lower level of the organization, have a shorter time horizon, and are narrower in scope. They are derived from a tactical plan and are aimed at achieving one or more operational goals.

- Two major types of operational plans are single-use and standing plans. Single-use plans are designed to carry out a course of action that is not likely to be repeated in the future. Programs and projects are examples of single-use plans. Standing plans are designed to carry out a course of action that is likely to be repeated several times. Policies, SOPs, and rules and regulations are all standing plans.

- Contingency planning and crisis management are also emerging as very important forms of operational planning.

DISCUSSION QUESTIONS

Questions for Review

1. Describe the nature of organizational goals. Be certain to include both the purposes and the kinds of goals.
2. Identify and describe Porter's generic strategies.
3. What are the basic differences among a single-product strategy, a strategy based on related diversification, and one based on unrelated diversification?
4. What is tactical planning? What is operational planning? What are the similarities and differences between them?

Questions for Analysis

1. Managers are sometimes criticized for focusing too much attention on the achievement of short-term goals. In your opinion, how much attention should be given to long-term versus short-term goals? In the event of a conflict, which should be given priority? Explain your answers.
2. Which strategy—business or corporate level—should a firm develop first? Describe the relationship between a firm's business- and corporate-level strategies.

3. Cite examples of operational plans that you use or encounter (now or in the past) at work, at school, or in your personal life.

Questions for Application

1. Interview the head or director of the department in which you are majoring. What kinds of goals exist for the department and for the members of the department? Share your findings with the rest of the class.
2. Interview a manager and categorize the business- and corporate-level strategies of his or her organization according to Porter's generic strategies and extent of diversification.
3. Use online resources to find one example each of businesses following a single-product strategy, a related diversification strategy, and an unrelated diversification strategy. What level of performance would you expect from each firm, based on its strategy? Examine the firm's profitability to see whether your expectations were accurate.

BUILDING EFFECTIVE TIME-MANAGEMENT SKILLS

Exercise Overview

Time-management skills refer to the ability to prioritize tasks, to work efficiently, and to delegate appropriately. This exercise asks you to apply your time-management skills to the process of goal optimization.

Exercise Background

All managers face a variety of goals, challenges, opportunities, and, of course, demands on their time. Juggling all these demands successfully requires a clear understanding of priorities, scheduling, and a number of related factors. You're about to learn just how difficult this task is because you're about to open your own business: a retail store in a local shopping mall. You're starting from scratch, with no prior business connections, but you do have a strong business plan and you're sure that it will work.

In getting ready to open your business, you know that you need to meet and draw up plans with each of the following parties:

1. The mall manager, to negotiate a lease
2. A local banker, to arrange partial financing

3. An attorney, to incorporate your business
4. An accountant, to set up a bookkeeping system
5. Suppliers, to arrange credit terms and delivery schedules
6. An advertising agency, to start promoting your business
7. A staffing agency, to hire employees
8. A design firm, to plan the physical layout of the store

Exercise Task

Review all the preceding information and then do the following:

1. Develop a schedule listing the sequence in which you need to meet with the eight parties that you've listed. Do the best that you can to minimize backtracking (seeing one party and then having to see him again after seeing someone else).
2. Compare your schedule with that of a classmate and discuss the differences. Do you find that it's possible to draw up different schedules that are nevertheless equally valid? If so, why? If not, why not?

BUILDING EFFECTIVE DECISION-MAKING SKILLS

Exercise Overview

Decision-making skills refer to the ability to recognize and define problems and opportunities correctly and then to select an appropriate course of action for solving problems or capitalizing on opportunities. As we noted in this chapter, many organizations use SWOT analysis as part of the strategy-formulation process. This exercise will help you better understand both how managers obtain the information they need to perform such an analysis and how they use it as a framework for making decisions.

Exercise Background

SWOT is an acronym for *strengths, weaknesses, opportunities, and threats.* The idea behind SWOT is that a good strategy exploits an organization's opportunities and strengths while neutralizing threats and avoiding or correcting weaknesses.

You've just been hired to run a medium-size company that manufactures electric motors, circuit breakers, and similar electronic components for industrial use. In recent years, the firm's financial performance has gradually eroded, and your job is to turn things around.

At one time, the firm was successful in part because it was able to charge premium prices for top-quality products. In recent years, however, management has tried cutting costs as a means of bringing prices in line with those of new competitors in the market. Unfortunately, the strategy hasn't worked very well, with the effect of cost cutting being primarily a fall-off in product quality. Convinced that a new strategy is called for, you've decided to begin with a SWOT analysis.

Exercise Task

Reviewing the situation, you take the following steps:

1. List the sources that you'll use to gather information about the firm's strengths, weaknesses, opportunities, and threats.
2. Then ask yourself: For what types of information are data readily available online? What categories of data are difficult or impossible to find online?
   (*Note:* When using online resources, be sure to provide specific websites or URLs.)
3. Next, rate each source that you consult in terms of probable reliability. Finally, ask yourself how confident you'd be in basing decisions on the information that you've obtained.

SKILL-BUILDING PERSONAL ASSESSMENT

Effective strategic management requires strong conceptual skills. Effective conceptual skills, in turn, often rely on our abilities to solve problems. This personal assessment will give you insights into your preferred problem-solving style.

For each of the following questions, indicate the response that usually describes your concerns and behaviors. There are no right or wrong answers to the questions. For each question, indicate which of the two alternative statements is more characteristic of you. Some statements may seem to be equally characteristic or uncharacteristic of you. While that may be true, try to choose the statement that is relatively more characteristic of what you do or feel in your everyday life. You will be working with pairs of statements and will have 5 points to distribute among the statements. Points may be divided between each A and B statement in any of the following combination pairs.

- If A is completely characteristic of you and B is completely uncharacteristic,

$$\frac{A \mid B}{5 \mid 0}$$

write a 5 on your answer sheet under A and a 0 under B.
- If A is considerably more characteristic of you and B is somewhat characteristic,

$$\frac{A \mid B}{4 \mid 1}$$

write a 4 on your answer sheet under A and a 1 under B.
- If A is only slightly more characteristic of you than B, write a 3 on your answer

$$\frac{A \mid B}{3 \mid 2}$$

sheet under A and a 2 under B.
- Each of the above three combinations may be used in reverse order. For example,

$$\frac{A \mid B}{2 \mid 3}$$

should you feel that B is slightly more characteristic of you than A, write a 2 on your answer sheet under A and a 3 under B (and so on, for A = 1 and B = 4 or A = 0 and B = 5).

Be sure that the numbers you assign to each pair sum to 5 points. Relate each question in the index to your own behavior. Remember, there is no right or wrong answer. Attempts to give a "correct" response merely distort the meaning of your answers and render the inventory's results valueless.

Questions	Score

1. Are you more
   (A) pragmatic
   (B) idealistic
	$\frac{A \mid B}{\mid}$

2. Are you more impressed by
   (A) standards
   (B) sentiments
	$\frac{A \mid B}{\mid}$

3. Are you more interested in that which
   (A) convinces you by facts
   (B) emotionally moves you
	$\frac{A \mid B}{\mid}$

Questions	Score

4. It is worse to
    (A) be practical
    (B) have a boring routine

    A | B
    ‾‾‾|‾

5. Are you more attracted to
    (A) a person with common sense
    (B) a creative person

    A | B
    ‾‾‾|‾

6. In judging others, are you more swayed by
    (A) the rules
    (B) the situation

    A | B
    ‾‾‾|‾

7. Are you more interested in
    (A) what has happened
    (B) what can happen

    A | B
    ‾‾‾|‾

8. Do you more often have
    (A) presence of mind
    (B) warm emotions

    A | B
    ‾‾‾|‾

9. Are you more frequently
    (A) a realistic sort of person
    (B) an imaginative sort of person

    A | B
    ‾‾‾|‾

10. Are you more
    (A) faithful
    (B) logical

    A | B
    ‾‾‾|‾

11. Are you more
    (A) action oriented
    (B) creation oriented

    A | B
    ‾‾‾|‾

12. Which guides you more,
    (A) your brain
    (B) your heart

    A | B
    ‾‾‾|‾

13. Do you take pride in your
    (A) realistic outlook
    (B) imaginative ability

    A | B
    ‾‾‾|‾

14. Which is more of a personal compliment:
    (A) you are consistent in reasoning
    (B) you are considerate of others

    A | B
    ‾‾‾|‾

15. Are you more drawn to
    (A) basics
    (B) implications

    A | B
    ‾‾‾|‾

16. It is better to be
    (A) fair
    (B) sentimental

    A | B
    ‾‾‾|‾

17. Would you rather spend time with
    (A) realistic people
    (B) idealistic people

    A | B
    ‾‾‾|‾

18. Would you describe yourself as
    (A) hard
    (B) soft

    A | B
    ‾‾‾|‾

19. Would your friends say that you are
    (A) someone who is filled by new ideas
    (B) someone who is a realist

    A | B
    ‾‾‾|‾

20. It is better to be called a person who shows
    (A) feelings
    (B) reasonable consistency

    A | B
    ‾‾‾|‾

Scoring: The letter "S" under column I-A refers to sensation. The letter "N" under column II-B refers to intuitive. The letter "I" under column III-A refers to thinking, and the letter "F" under column IV-B refers to feeling.

The first two columns identify your sensation-intuitive scores. Generally, people have preferred one of these two styles for gathering information. The following table presents a summary of characteristics about these two styles.

Comparisons of Sensation and Intuitive Types of People

Characteristic	Sensation Type	Intuitive Type
Focus	Details, practical, action, gets things done quickly	Patterns, innovation, ideas, long-range planning
Time orientation	Present, lives life as it is	Future achievement, change, rearrange
Work environment	Pays attention to detail, patient with details and does not make factual errors, not risk-takers	Looks at the "big picture," patient with complexity, risk-takers
Strengths	Pragmatic, results-oriented, objective, competitive	Original, imaginative, creative, idealistic
Possible weaknesses	Impatient when projects get delayed, decides issues too quickly, lacks long-range perspective, can oversimplify a complex task	Lacks follow-through, makes errors of fact, impractical, takes people's contributions for granted

The next two columns represent the thinking–feeling scores. People generally prefer to evaluate information based on one of these two styles. The table below summarizes the characteristics about these two styles.

Comparisons of Thinking and Feeling Types of People

Characteristic	Thinking Type	Feeling Type
Focus	Logic of situation, truth, organization principles	Human values and needs, harmony, feelings, emotions
Time orientation	Past, present, future	Past
Work environment	Businesslike, impersonal, treats others fairly, well organized	Naturally friendly, personal, harmony, care and concern for others
Strengths	Good at putting things in logical order, tends to be firm and tough-minded, rational, objective, predicts logical results	Enjoys pleasing people, sympathetic, loyal, draws out feelings in others, takes interest in person behind the job or idea
Possible weaknesses	Overly analytical, unemotional, too serious, rigid, verbose	Sentimental, postpones unpleasant tasks, avoids conflict

MANAGEMENT AT WORK
Alphabet Soup

"We don't talk about our strategy . . . because it's strategic. I would rather have people think we're confused than let our competitors know what we're going to do."

—Larry page, Google co-founder

For the past several years Sergey Brin and Larry Page have been running one of the world's largest technology companies. They have named their enterprise Alphabet because they felt that it held a dual meaning, both as a collection of letters that represent language and as a reference to the investment term *alpha* (returns above a benchmark). The two met at Stanford University in 1995, where they were graduate students in computer science. At the time, Page was working on a software-development project designed to create an index of websites by scouring sites for key words and other linkages. Brin joined him on the project, and when they were satisfied that they'd developed something with commercial value, they tried to license the technology to other companies like Yahoo! and Microsoft that had developed and were promoting search engines. As luck would have it, though, they couldn't find a buyer and settled instead for procuring enough investment capital to keep refining and testing their product.

In 2000, Brin and Page ran across the description of a marketing-based business model that relied on the concept of selling advertising in the form of sponsored links and search-specific ads. They adapted it to work with their own technologies and launched a new business they named Google. Google grew rapidly and after a short time became the world's most popular search engine. But their ambitions and innovations didn't stop there. As their revenues grew they next went on an aggressive buying spree and in short order they had purchased more than 200 companies. Among the most notable were businesses such as Android, YouTube, and DoubleClick. One thing they were committed to, though, was that all of their acquisitions had to be consistent with their original mission: to organize the world's information and make it universally accessible and useful.

At first, Brin and Page tried to integrate their various acquisitions into the Google organization itself. They soon realized, though, that each acquisition and attempted integration just made the existing structure more and more unwieldy. It also made it hard to measure the success of each individual enterprise. So, in late 2015 they decided they needed to figure out a new way of doing things and soon came up with a solution. They formed a new company called Alphabet and made Google the largest business within the new corporate structure. Each of the other major enterprises were set up as their own stand-alone businesses within the Alphabet umbrella, while smaller ones were grouped together. The plan, though, was that as these smaller enterprises grew, they might also be pulled out as a stand-alone Alphabet division.

The two co-founders redirected their own efforts to running Alphabet and turned the helm of Google itself over to an up-and-coming star manager named Sundar Pichai. By the end of 2019, the company was generating more than $160 billion in revenues and that year posted profits of $34 billion. Alphabet also employed 119,000 employees. Google, its major subsidiary, provided over 80 percent of the world's search market. In December 2019 Brin and Page announced that at the end of 2020 they would step down and simply become "employees" while remaining on the board and retaining their majority ownership of the firm. They also announced that Pichai would be elevated to serve as CEO of Alphabet.

How did two young computer scientists build this astoundingly successful company, and where will they take it in the future? Brin and Page have been remarkably successful in attracting talented and creative employees, like Pichai, and providing them with a work environment and culture that foster the kind of productivity and innovation for which they were hired. They've also remained in the forefront of Alphabet's search for technological innovations, but nobody knows for sure what Brin and Page have on the drawing board. In fact, outsiders—notably potential investors—often criticized Alphabet, in general, and Google, in particular, for being a "black box" when they want a few more details on the company's long-range strategy. "We don't talk about our strategy," explains Page, "… because it's strategic. I would rather have people think we're confused than let our competitors know what we're going to do."

Indeed, the lack of transparency was also a catalyst for creating Alphabet. But critics argue that if this was a goal, they missed the mark. Alphabet's semi-secret research facility "X," also known as the "moonshot factory," has its own website and is currently working on self-driving cars and trucks, fuel from seawater, and other long-shot, innovative projects that may or may not pan out. If there is a long-term strategic vision, it may be simply to provide the resources and freedom to some of the best and brightest dreamers in the world, and then to let their ideas develop into the reality of the future.[41]

Case Questions

1. In your judgement, why has Google (and Alphabet) been so successful? Discuss their activities most clearly related to strategy formulation and strategy implementation.

2. Describe the corporate and business strategies illustrated in this case. Do these companies seem to be relying more on deliberate or emergent strategies?

3. Develop a SWOT analysis for Alphabet, being as specific as possible.

4. During the 2020 COVID-19 pandemic many businesses like restaurants, hotels, and movie theater chains suffered significant economic costs because they either closed or significantly reduced their operations. However, Alphabet (and Google) were not as adversely impacted. To what kinds of environmental upheavals, though, would Alphabet and Google be more susceptible? What kinds of contingency/crisis plans might be most effective to address these?

You Make the Call

The Lap of Luxury

1. In your judgment, why has LVMH been so successful?

2. How have changing customer demographics affected LVMH? How well positioned is the firm to address these changes?

3. Two other luxury good companies, Swiss luxury giant Richemont and French-based Kering, have come to recognize the effectiveness of Arnault's strategy and have started trying to imitate it. What risks, if any, does this pose for LVMH?

4. The Great Recession did surprisingly little damage to LVMH. While the firm's revenues were essentially flat during this period it remained profitable. Use online resources to look into how the COVID-19 pandemic of 2020 affected LVMH.

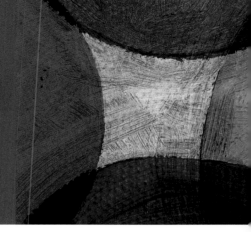

CHAPTER 4

Managing Decision Making

Learning Outcomes

After studying this chapter, you should be able to:

4-1   Discuss the meaning of decision making, types of decisions, and decision-making conditions.

4-2   Discuss rational perspectives on decision making, including the steps in rational decision making.

4-3   Describe the behavioral aspects of decision making.

4-4   Discuss group and team decision making, including its advantages and disadvantages and how it can be more effectively managed.

Regardless of their industry—banking, retailing, manufacturing, transportation, health care, or professional sports—all managers have to make decisions about resource allocations, goals, options, and strategies. Indeed, making effective decisions, as well as recognizing when bad decisions have been made and responding quickly to mistakes, is a key ingredient in organizational effectiveness. Indeed, some experts believe that decision making is the most basic and fundamental of all managerial activities. Thus, we discuss it here in the context of the first management function: planning. Keep in mind, however, that although decision making is perhaps most closely linked to the planning function, it is also part of organizing, leading, and controlling. We begin our discussion by exploring the nature of decision making. We then describe rational perspectives on decision making. Behavioral aspects of decision making are then introduced and described. We conclude with a discussion of group and team decision making. Let's begin, though, by looking at the role of decision making at Viking Cruises.

Management in Action

Sailing the Seas

"Obviously, to be on a bus is not nice. And to be on a 3,000-passenger ship is not nice. It's not nice under the best of circumstances, and under the worst, bad."

—Torstein Hagen, Founder and CEO of Viking Cruises

If you've ever watched *Masterpiece Theatre* on PBS you are no doubt familiar with Viking Cruises. The scenic views of Viking River Boats sailing along European rivers and entering Budapest have become almost iconic images of how travel should be done (at least for some people). The company behind these images is Viking Cruises, a company that has become one of the world's largest and most successful cruise lines as a result of numerous effective decisions made over three decades.

Viking was started and is still run by Torstein Hagen, a native of Norway, in 1997. In the early years of his career, and after getting an MBA from Harvard, Hagen worked as a consultant for McKinsey & Company in Europe. One of his biggest assignments there was helping to save Holland America, a large cruise line, from bankruptcy in 1974. This work enabled him to learn the intricacies of maritime business in general and the cruise business in particular, skills that would later pay off handsomely. Hagen subsequently left McKinsey and became CEO of Bergen Steamship Company in Norway in 1976 and four years later was recruited to head up the Royal Viking Line. Royal Viking was subsequently bought by Norwegian Cruise Lines and its ships rebranded as part of the company's fleet.

In the mid-1990s a group of Russian investors hired Hagen to help them arrange the purchase and financing for a shipping company. At the time these investors owned four river cruise ships. Hagen learned that after the investors bought the shipping company they wanted to sell the river ships, and so he offered to buy them. The boats, constructed to operate on various rivers in Russia, became the first Viking fleet. Hagen soon recognized that the river cruise industry had a lot of potential for growth and in 2000 he purchased KD River Cruises of Europe, bringing the Viking fleet total to 26 and making it the largest river cruise fleet in the world.

Under Hagen's direction Viking renovated all of its ships to meet certain business requirements. For one thing, they got rid of "frills" such as gyms, pools, and specialty restaurants. They also standardized their ships in order to improve operational efficiency (in the same way that Southwest Airlines only flies Boeing 737 planes). In addition, Hagen clearly defined his target market: older and affluent English-speaking couples from the United States and Western Europe. (Viking has been criticized for this approach by some observers because it suggests that some people are not welcome. Viking does indicate that it will accept bookings from anyone over the age of 18 but no accommodation will be made for non-English speakers.)

Over the next few years Viking expanded its fleet to include vessels especially built for cruising rivers in China and opened sales offices in the United Kingdom, Canada, and the United States. The firm also started to renovate its ships to use hybrid diesel engines, saving fuel costs and boosting profits. In 2011 Viking also made two major decisions that really accelerated its growth. First, it launched its sponsorship of *Masterpiece Theater*, a move that dramatically elevated its visibility among its target audience. In addition, Viking announced a new phase of growth using a new boat design called "longships," placing orders for 40 ships with this new design. The longship boosted capacity on each boat while also creating larger public spaces.

Hagen's next major decision was made public in 2013 when the company announced its intentions to enter the ocean cruise business with the launch of several small-scale ocean cruise vessels. The first Viking ocean-going ship, the *Viking Star*, set sail in 2015 and was followed in short order by several more over the next few years. Most other ocean cruise lines try to make each of their ships distinctive to provide repeat passengers with a variety of experiences. Following its success with its standardized river cruise vessels, however, Viking again standardized its ocean ships, making only minor refinements as each new ship was launched.

In 2019 Viking announced it would be entering a third cruise market, this one centered on so-called expedition cruises. Expedition cruises focus on exotic and hard-to-reach destinations, often requiring custom-made vessels with special kinds of equipment. The initial plan called for two small specialty ships, each capable of carrying 389 passengers, to travel to such destinations as Antarctica, the Arctic Circle, North America's Great Lakes, and the Galapagos Islands. The projected launch date for these cruises was announced as 2022. Viking also has plans to begin river cruises in the United States, primarily on the Mississippi River, but no launch date has been announced.

Like many businesses, Viking was hit hard by the 2020 COVID-19 pandemic. Indeed, cruise ships have an unfortunate history when it comes to contagious diseases—when a viral or bacterial infection hits passengers on a cruise ship, it often travels quickly, impacting many people onboard. Compounding the problem is that people have no escape—they are "trapped" on the boat and the boat itself may not be able to dock. To Viking's credit, it reacted quickly and decisively when it became apparent that COVID-19 was going to become a global health concern. Viking became the first major cruise line to suspend operations when on March 12, 2020, it announced that it was immediately suspending all operations through the end of June 2020. Viking later extended its suspension of services through the end of 2020. In its press release, Hagen said "Since we started Viking nearly 23 years ago, we have always cared first and foremost about our guests and our employees. As a private company with strong finances, we do not have to worry about quarterly profit expectations—and that flexibility allows us the ability to do what is best for our guests and our employees, as we have always done."[1]

4-1 THE NATURE OF DECISION MAKING

Managers at Morgan Stanley recently made the decision to buy E*Trade for $13 billion. At about the same time, the general manager of the Ford dealership in College Station, Texas, made a decision to sponsor a local youth soccer team for $300. Each of these examples reflects a decision, but the decisions differ in many ways. Thus, as a starting point in understanding decision making, we must first explore the meaning of decision making as well as types of decisions and conditions under which decisions are made.[2]

4-1a Decision Making Defined

decision making
The act of choosing one alternative from among a set of alternatives

decision-making process
Recognizing and defining the nature of a decision situation, identifying alternatives, choosing the "best" alternative, and putting it into practice

Decision making can refer to either a specific act or a general process. Decision making *per se* is the act of choosing one alternative from among a set of alternatives. The decision-making process, however, is much more than this. One step of the process, for example, is that the person making the decision must both recognize that a decision is necessary and identify the set of feasible alternatives before selecting one.[3] Hence, the decision-making process includes recognizing and defining the nature of a decision situation, identifying alternatives, choosing the "best" alternative, and putting it into practice.[4]

The word *best*, of course, implies effectiveness. Effective decision making requires that the decision maker understand the situation driving the decision. Most people would consider an effective decision to be one that optimizes some set of factors, such as profits, sales, employee welfare, and market share. In some situations, though, an effective decision may be one that minimizes losses, expenses, or employee turnover. It may even mean selecting the best method for going out of business, laying off employees, or terminating a strategic alliance.

"Too many think inaction is the least risky path. Sometimes action is the most conservative and safest path. Not doing anything is exceedingly dangerous."

—Frederick Smith, Founder and CEO of Fedex[5]

We should also note that managers make decisions about both problems and opportunities. For example, making decisions about how to cut costs by 10 percent reflects a problem—an undesirable situation that requires a solution. But decisions are also necessary in

A great deal of information was gathered and discussed at high levels of Morgan Stanley before the brokerage firm decided to acquire E*Trade in a recent merger.

Ascannio/Shutterstock.com

situations of opportunity. Learning that the firm is earning higher-than-projected profits, for example, requires a subsequent decision. Should the extra funds be used to increase shareholder dividends, reinvest in current operations, or expand into new markets?

Of course, it may take a long time before a manager can know if the right decision was made. For example, in 2020 government leaders made decisions to invest billions of dollars in businesses impacted by the COVID-19 pandemic and grant billions more to individual citizens impact by the virus. It will be years—or perhaps decades—before leaders, economists, and other experts will know if those were sound decisions and if the funds were allocated in the most effective way.

4-1b Types of Decisions

programmed decision
A decision that is fairly structured or recurs with some frequency (or both)

Managers must make many different types of decisions. In general, however, most decisions fall into one of two categories: programmed and nonprogrammed.[6] A **programmed decision** is one that is relatively structured or recurs with some frequency (or both). Each Starbucks coffee shop uses programmed decisions to order new supplies of coffee beans, cups, and napkins, and Starbucks employees are trained in exact procedures for brewing coffee. Likewise, the College Station Ford dealer made a decision that he will sponsor a youth soccer team each year. Thus, when the soccer club president calls, the dealer already knows what he will do. Many decisions about basic operating systems and procedures and standard organizational transactions are of this variety and can therefore be programmed.[7]

nonprogrammed decision
A decision that is relatively unstructured and occurs much less often than a programmed decision

Nonprogrammed decisions, on the other hand, are relatively unstructured and occur much less often. Disney's decision to buy Fox was a nonprogrammed decision. Managers faced with such decisions must treat each one as unique, investing enormous amounts of time, energy, and resources into exploring the situation from all perspectives. Intuition and experience are major factors in nonprogrammed decisions. Most of the decisions made by top managers involving strategy (including mergers, acquisitions, and takeovers) and organization design are nonprogrammed. So are decisions about new facilities, new products, labor contracts, and legal issues.

4-1c Decision-Making Conditions

Just as there are different kinds of decisions, there are also different conditions in which decisions must be made. Managers sometimes have a very clear understanding of conditions surrounding a decision, but at other times they have much less information about those conditions. In general, as shown in Figure 4.1, the circumstances that exist for the decision maker are conditions of certainty, risk, or uncertainty.[8]

When the general manager of the Ford dealership in Bryan, Texas, made a decision to sponsor a local youth soccer team for $300, he was making a programmed decision. Each year he will make this same contribution.

Monkey Business Images/Shutterstock.com

Decision Making under Certainty   When the decision maker knows with reasonable certainty what the alternatives are and what conditions are associated with each alternative, a **state of certainty** exists. Suppose, for example, that managers at Singapore Airlines make a decision to buy five new jumbo jets. Their next decision is from whom to buy them. Because there are only two companies in the world that make jumbo jets, Boeing and Airbus, Singapore Airlines knows its options with relative certainty. Each manufacturer has proven products and will guarantee prices and delivery dates. The airline thus knows the alternative conditions associated with each. There is little ambiguity and relatively little chance of making a bad decision. (Of course, this changes if the purchase is for a new airplane that has not yet undergone final testing, as happened during the launch of Boeing's 737 MAX series.)

state of certainty
A condition in which the decision maker knows with reasonable certainty what the alternatives are and what conditions are associated with each alternative

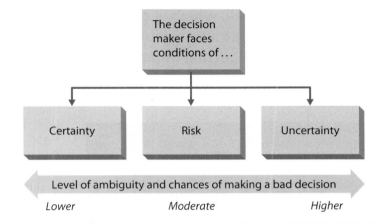

FIGURE 4.1

Decision-Making Conditions

Most major decisions in organizations today are made under a state of uncertainty. Managers making decisions in these circumstances must be sure to learn as much as possible about the situation and approach the decision from a logical and rational perspective.

Ianc66/Shutterstock.com

Singapore Airlines engages in decision making under certainty when deciding from whom to purchase jumbo jets. Only two manufacturers make them, Boeing and Airbus, thus reducing the risk of Singapore Airlines making a bad decision.

state of risk

A condition in which the availability of each alternative and its potential payoffs and costs are all associated with probability estimates

Few organizational decisions, however, are made under conditions of true certainty. The complexity and turbulence of the contemporary business world make such situations rare. Even the airplane purchase decision we just considered has less certainty than it appears. The aircraft companies may not be able to really guarantee delivery dates, so they may write cost-increase or inflation clauses into contracts. Thus, the airline may be only partially certain of the conditions surrounding each alternative.

Decision Making under Risk A more common decision-making condition is a state of risk. Under a state of risk, the availability of each alternative and its potential payoffs and costs are all associated with probability estimates.[9] Suppose, for example, that a labor contract negotiator for a company receives a "final" offer from the union right before a strike deadline. The negotiator has two alternatives: to accept or to reject the offer. The risk centers on whether the union representatives are bluffing. If the company negotiator accepts the offer, she avoids a strike but commits to a relatively costly labor contract. If she rejects the contract, she may get a more favorable contract if the union is bluffing, but she may provoke a strike if it is not.

On the basis of past experience, relevant information, the advice of others, and her own judgment, she may assess that there is about a 75 percent chance that union representatives are bluffing and about a 25 percent chance that they will back up their threats. Thus, she can base a calculated decision on the two alternatives (accept or reject the contract demands) and the probable consequences of each. When making decisions under a state of risk, managers must reasonably estimate the probabilities associated with each alternative. For example, if the union negotiators are committed to a strike if their demands are not met, and the company negotiator rejects their demands because she guesses they will not strike, her miscalculation may prove costly.

"What's served me very well, which is easy to say for me now that I'm as successful as I am, is being patient, is not getting impatient and making stupid career decisions."
—Robert Iger, Former CEO of Disney[10]

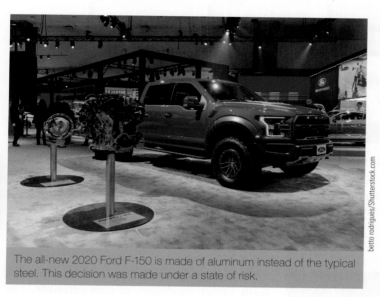

The all-new 2020 Ford F-150 is made of aluminum instead of the typical steel. This decision was made under a state of risk.

betto rodrigues/Shutterstock.com

state of uncertainty
A condition in which the decision maker does not know all the alternatives, the risks associated with each, or the consequences each alternative is likely to have

As indicated in Figure 4.1, decision making under conditions of risk is accompanied by moderate ambiguity and chances of a bad decision. For instance, Ford made the decision to redesign its F-150 pickup, the firm's best-selling and most profitable vehicle. The key element in the new design was to replace the typical steel pickup bed with one made from aluminum. The firm's logic was that aluminum is much lighter than steel, so the F-150 could get better gas mileage with no loss of functionality. The risk was that if buyers rejected the concept of an aluminum pickup, or if the vehicle's quality was compromised by the redesign, then Ford would have done perhaps irreparable harm to the image and reputation of its most important vehicle. Thus far, Ford's risk has paid off, as the F-150 has actually gained market share over its rivals.

Decision Making under Uncertainty Most of the major decision making in contemporary organizations is done under a state of uncertainty. The decision maker does not know all the alternatives, the risks associated with each, or the likely consequences of each alternative. This uncertainty stems from the complexity and dynamism of contemporary organizations and their environments. The emergence of various forms of online commerce as a significant force in today's competitive environment has served to increase both revenue potential and uncertainty for most managers. Most major decisions made during the early stages of the 2020 COVID-19 pandemic were of this nature because managers were unsure of how quickly and how far the virus would spread, how long the pandemic would last, and how to most effectively respond to it. Similarly, as decision-makers cautiously started to move back to normal in early Fall 2020 they were again faced with uncertainty regarding when to re-open businesses, what changes to make in how businesses operate, and so forth.

"The absence of paid time off has been shown to exacerbate some infectious disease outbreaks. It can also prevent people from getting preventative care."
—Trust for America's Health, A Nonpartisan Public Health Policy Organization[11]

To make effective decisions in these circumstances, managers must acquire as much relevant information as possible and approach the situation from a logical and rational perspective. Intuition, judgment, and experience always play major roles in the decision-making process under conditions of uncertainty. Even so, uncertainty is the most ambiguous condition for managers and the one most prone to error.[12] Lorraine Brennan O'Neil is the founder and former CEO of 10 Minute Manicure, a quick-service salon located in airports. The company found quick success and experienced rapid growth from its start in 2006, but the economic downturn in 2008 required O'Neil to rethink her plans in an attempt to stay afloat through a rocky and unknown future. Knowing that the company no longer had the time to wait and monitor new stores' success, she opted to focus solely on existing stores with profits, shutting down those with losses. Aside from this, O'Neil restructured her business plan, seeking nontraditional locations, reducing corporate overhead, cutting products, and developing an online product line as a second source of income.[13] The firm maintained its market position and profits for the next several years but, like most businesses, was hit hard by the 2020 COVID-19 pandemic.

 **Manager's Checklist**

☐ Managers should seek to program routine decisions but to also recognize when decisions are not programmable.

☐ Managers also need to understand the conditions under which they make decisions.

4-2 RATIONAL PERSPECTIVES ON DECISION MAKING

Most managers like to think of themselves as rational decision makers. And, indeed, many experts argue that managers should try to be as rational as possible in making decisions.[14] This section highlights the fundamental and rational perspectives on decision making.

> "Nothing is more difficult, and therefore more precious, than to be able to decide."
>
> —Napoleon Bonaparte[15]

4-2a The Classical Model of Decision Making

classical decision model
A prescriptive approach to decision making that tells managers how they should make decisions; assumes that managers are logical and rational and that their decisions will be in the best interests of the organization

The **classical decision model** is a prescriptive approach that tells managers how they should make decisions. It rests on the assumptions that managers are logical and rational and that they make decisions that are in the best interests of the organization. Figure 4.2 shows how the classical model views the decision-making process.

1. Decision makers have complete information about the decision situation and possible alternatives.
2. They can effectively eliminate uncertainty to achieve a decision condition of certainty.
3. They evaluate all aspects of the decision situation logically and rationally.

As we will see later, these conditions rarely, if ever, actually exist.

4-2b Steps in Rational Decision Making

steps in rational decision making
Recognize and define the decision situation; identify appropriate alternatives; evaluate each alternative in terms of its feasibility, satisfactoriness, and consequences; select the best alternative; implement the chosen alternative; follow up and evaluate the results of the chosen alternative

A manager who really wants to approach a decision rationally and logically should try to follow the **steps in rational decision making**, listed in Table 4.1. These steps help keep the decision maker focused on facts and logic and help guard against inappropriate assumptions and pitfalls.

> "You can't make decisions based on fear and the possibility of what might happen."
>
> —Michelle Obama, Former First Lady[16]

Recognizing and Defining the Decision Situation   The first step in rational decision making is recognizing that a decision is necessary—that is, there must be some stimulus or spark to initiate the process. For many decisions and problem situations, the stimulus may

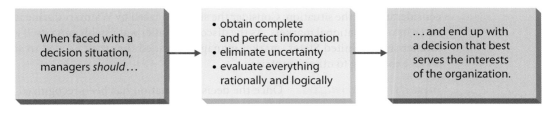

FIGURE 4.2

The Classical Model of Decision Making

The classical model of decision making assumes that managers are rational and logical. It tries to prescribe how managers should approach decision situations.

Table 4.1	Steps in the Rational Decision-Making Process	
Step	**Detail**	**Example**
1. Recognizing and defining the decision situation	Some stimulus indicates that a decision must be made. The stimulus may be positive or negative.	A plant manager sees that employee turnover has increased by 5 percent.
2. Identifying alternatives	Both obvious and creative alternatives are desired. In general, the more important the decision, the more alternatives should be generated.	The plant manager can increase wages, increase benefits, or change hiring standards.
3. Evaluating alternatives	Each alternative is evaluated to determine its feasibility, its satisfactoriness, and its consequences.	Increasing benefits may not be feasible. Increasing wages and changing hiring standards may satisfy all conditions.
4. Selecting the best alternative	Consider all situational factors and choose the alternative that best fits the manager's situation.	Changing hiring standards will take an extended period of time to cut turnover, so increase wages.
5. Implementing the chosen alternative	The chosen alternative is implemented into the organizational system.	The plant manager may need permission from corporate headquarters. The human resource department establishes a new wage structure.
6. Following up and evaluating the results	At some time in the future, the manager should ascertain the extent to which the alternative chosen in step 4 and implemented in step 5 has worked.	The plant manager notes that, six months later, turnover dropped to its previous level.

Although the presumptions of the classical decision model rarely exist, managers can still approach decision making with rationality. By following the steps of rational decision making, managers ensure that they are learning as much as possible about the decision situation and its alternatives.

occur without any prior warning. When equipment malfunctions, the manager must decide whether to repair or replace it. Or, when a major crisis erupts, as described in Chapter 3, the manager must quickly decide how to deal with it. As we already noted, the stimulus for a decision may be either positive or negative. A manager who must decide how to invest surplus funds, for example, faces a positive decision situation. A negative financial stimulus could involve having to trim budgets because of cost overruns.

Inherent in problem recognition is the need to define precisely what the problem is. The manager must develop a complete understanding of the problem, its causes, and its relationship to other factors. This understanding comes from careful analysis and thoughtful consideration of the situation. Consider the situation faced by Walmart during its growth and entry into international markets. As the discount retailer was establishing itself as a dominant retailer in the United States, market managers decided that they needed to start thinking about expanding to other countries.

Identifying Alternatives   Once the decision situation has been recognized and defined, the second step is to identify alternative courses of effective action. Developing both obvious, standard alternatives and creative, innovative alternatives is generally useful.[17] In general, the more important the decision, the more attention is directed to developing alternatives.[18] If the decision involves a multimillion-dollar relocation, a great deal of time and expertise will be devoted to identifying the best locations. Pinterest moved its corporate headquarters from Palo Alto to downtown San Francisco. Similarly, General Electric moved its headquarters from rural Connecticut to Boston.[19] If the problem is to choose a color for the company softball

Moving a firm's corporate headquarters is a significant and costly decision. Pinterest recently made the decision to move its corporate offices from Palo Alto to downtown San Francisco in this office tower. The firm spent a great deal of time considering the move and identifying potential locations before selecting this one.

As Walmart has expanded into foreign markets, it has had to carefully evaluate each alternative in a rational and logical manner. The retail giant has had success in Asia with stores like this one, primarily through joint ventures with local partners.

team uniforms, much less time and expertise will be brought to bear.

Although managers should seek creative solutions, they must also recognize that various constraints often limit their alternatives. Common constraints include legal restrictions, moral and ethical norms, those imposed by power and authority, available technology, economic considerations, and unofficial social norms. Argentina, Mexico, China, and Russia were among the various international markets Walmart considered entering.

Evaluating Alternatives   The third step in the decision-making process is evaluating each of the alternatives. Figure 4.3 presents a decision tree that can be used to judge different alternatives. The figure suggests that each alternative be evaluated in terms of its *feasibility*, its *satisfactoriness*, and its *consequences*. The first question to ask is whether an alternative is feasible. Is it within the realm of probability and practicality? For a small, struggling firm, an alternative requiring a huge financial outlay is probably out of the question. Other alternatives may not be feasible because of legal barriers. And limited human, material, and information resources may make other alternatives impractical.

When an alternative has passed the test of feasibility, it must next be examined to see how well it satisfies the conditions of the decision situation. For example, a manager searching for ways to double production capacity might initially consider purchasing an existing plant from another company. If more detailed analysis reveals that the new plant would increase production capacity by only 35 percent, this alternative may not be satisfactory. Finally, when an alternative has proven both feasible and satisfactory, its probable consequences must still be assessed. To what extent will a particular alternative influence other parts of the organization? What financial and nonfinancial costs will be associated with such influences? For example, a plan to boost sales by cutting prices may disrupt cash flows, require a new advertising program, and alter the behavior of sales representatives because it requires a different commission structure. The manager, then, must put "price tags" on the consequences of each alternative. Even an alternative that is both feasible and satisfactory must be eliminated if its consequences are too expensive for the total system.

Selecting an Alternative   Even though many alternatives fail to pass the triple tests of feasibility, satisfactoriness, and affordable consequences, two or more alternatives may remain. Choosing the best of these is the real crux of decision making. One approach is to choose the alternative with the optimal combination of feasibility, satisfactoriness, and affordable consequences. Even though most situations do not lend themselves to objective, mathematical analysis, the manager can often develop subjective estimates and weights for choosing an alternative.

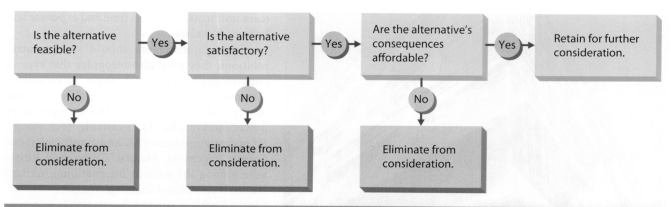

Evaluating Alternatives in the Decision-Making Process

Managers must thoroughly evaluate all the alternatives, which increases the chances that the alternative finally chosen will be successful. Failure to evaluate an alternative's feasibility, satisfactoriness, and consequences can lead to a wrong decision.

Optimization is also a frequent goal. Because a decision is likely to affect several individuals or units, any feasible alternative will probably not maximize all of the relevant goals. Suppose that the manager of the Kansas City Royals needs to select a new outfielder for the upcoming baseball season. Bill hits .350 but has difficulty catching fly balls; Joe hits only .175 but is outstanding in the field; and Sam hits .290 and is a solid but not outstanding fielder. The manager probably would select Sam because of the optimal balance of hitting and fielding. Decision makers should also remember that finding multiple acceptable alternatives may be possible; selecting just one alternative and rejecting all the others might not be necessary. For example, the Royals' manager might decide that Sam will start each game, Bill will be retained as a pinch hitter, and Joe will be retained as a defensive substitute. In many hiring decisions, the candidates remaining after evaluation are ranked. If the top candidate rejects the offer, it may be automatically extended to the number-two candidate and, if necessary, to the remaining candidates in order. Walmart eliminated several potential foreign markets, including Pakistan, but kept several others under active consideration.

Implementing the Chosen Alternative   After an alternative has been selected, the manager must put it into effect. In some decision situations, implementation is fairly easy; in others, it is more difficult. In the case of an acquisition, for example, managers must decide how to integrate all the activities of the new business, including purchasing, human resource practices, and distribution, into an ongoing organizational framework. Operational plans, which we discussed in Chapter 6, are useful in implementing alternatives. Managers must also consider people's resistance to change when implementing decisions. The reasons for such resistance include insecurity, inconvenience, and fear of the unknown. (Resistance to change is covered in Chapter 12.) Managers should also recognize that even when all alternatives have been evaluated as precisely as possible and the consequences of each alternative weighed, unanticipated consequences are still likely. Any number of factors—unexpected cost increases, a less-than-perfect fit with existing organizational subsystems, or unpredicted effects on cash flow or operating expenses, for example—could develop after implementation has begun. Walmart opened offices in each country it wanted to enter. Managers in those offices, in turn, began learning about local market details, governmental requirements for market entry, potential supplies, and so forth.

Following Up and Evaluating the Results   The final step in the decision-making process requires that managers evaluate the effectiveness of their decision—that is, they should make sure that the chosen alternative has served its original purpose. If an implemented alternative appears not to be working, the manager can respond in several ways. Another previously identified alternative (the original second or third choice, for instance) could be adopted. Or the manager might recognize that the situation was not correctly defined to begin with and start the process all over again. Finally, the manager might decide that the original alternative is in fact appropriate but has not yet had time to work or should be implemented in a different way.[20]

Walmart managers determined that entry into Mexico and Argentina, among others, would be relatively easy and that the company would be allowed to set up a wholly owned subsidiary to operate there. Entry into China would be more difficult but could be done through joint ventures with local partners. This was also the case for several other countries. Russia, though, looked to be more challenging. Walmart concluded that the only viable way to enter the market there would be to buy one or more existing retailers. Eventually, after several potential deals fell through, Walmart abandoned its plans to enter Russia and closed its office in that country.

4-2c Evidence-Based Management

Attempting to make rational decisions may seem like a no-brainer, but some researchers worry that managers tend all too often to slip into bad decision-making habits. As a result, some experts have recently reminded managers of the need to use rationality and evidence when making decisions. This reminder has been called *evidence-based management*, or *EBM*.[21] "Management decisions," they argue, "[should] be based on the best evidence, managers [should] systematically learn from experience, and organizational practices [should] reflect sound principles of thought and analysis." Experts define evidence-based management as "a commitment to finding and using the best theory and data available at the time to make decisions," but their "Five Principles of Evidence-Based Management" make it clear that EBM means more than just sifting through data and crunching numbers. Here's what the experts recommend:

1. Face the hard facts and build a culture in which people are encouraged to tell the truth, even if it's unpleasant.
2. Be committed to "fact-based" decision making—which means being committed to getting the best evidence and using it to guide actions.
3. Treat your organization as an unfinished prototype—encourage experimentation and learning by doing.
4. Look for the risks and drawbacks in what people recommend (even the best medicine has side effects).
5. Avoid basing decisions on untested but strongly held beliefs, what you have done in the past, or on uncritical "benchmarking" of what winners do.

This perspective is particularly persuasive when EBM is used to question the outcomes of decisions based on "untested but strongly held beliefs" or on "uncritical benchmarking." For instance, consider the popular policy of paying high performers significantly more than low performers. EBM research shows that pay-for-performance policies get good results when employees work solo or independently. But it's another matter altogether when it comes to collaborative teams—the kind of team that makes so many organizational decisions today. Under these circumstances, the greater the gap between highest- and lowest-paid executives, the weaker the firm's financial performance. Why? According to the experts, wide disparities in pay often weaken both trust among team members and the social connectivity that contributes to strong team-based decision making.[22]

Or consider another once-common method for evaluating and rewarding talent. Pioneered at General Electric by the legendary Jack Welch, the practice of "forced ranking" divides employees into three groups based on performance—the top 20 percent, middle 70 percent, and bottom 10 percent—and terminates those at the bottom. EBM research suggests that, according to many HR managers, forced ranking impaired morale and collaboration and ultimately reduced productivity. The researchers also concluded that automatically firing the bottom 10 percent resulted too often in the unnecessary disruption of otherwise effective teamwork. That's how they found out that 73 percent of the errors committed by commercial airline pilots occur on the first day that reconfigured crews work together.

 **Manager's Checklist**

☐ Whenever possible, managers should engage in rational decision making, applying logic and evidence to the decision-making process.

☐ At the same time, you should understand that some decisions do not lend themselves to rational analysis, and some do not allow time to follow all of the rational steps.

4-3 BEHAVIORAL ELEMENTS IN DECISION MAKING

If all decision situations were approached as logically as described in the previous section, more decisions might prove to be successful. Yet decisions are often made with little consideration for logic and rationality. Some experts have estimated that U.S. companies approach decisions rationally less than 20 percent of the time.[23] And even when organizations try to be logical, they sometimes fail. For example, when Starbucks opened its first coffee shops in New York, it relied on rigorous scientific marketing research, taste tests, and rational deliberation in making a decision to emphasize drip over espresso coffee. However, that decision still proved wrong, as New Yorkers strongly preferred the same espresso-style coffees that were Starbucks mainstays in the West. Hence, the firm had to hastily reconfigure its stores to better meet customer preferences.

". . . I'm a bit of a maverick. I listen, but I've got the final say. Then it's up to me to make it work so I don't lose my credibility."
—Richard Branson, Founder and Majority Owner of Virgin Group[25]

On the other hand, sometimes when a decision is made with little regard for logic, it can still turn out to be correct.[24] An important ingredient in how these forces work is the behavioral aspect of decision making. The administrative model better reflects these subjective considerations. Other behavioral aspects include political forces, intuition and escalation of commitment, risk propensity, and ethics.

administrative model
A decision-making model that argues that decision makers (1) use incomplete and imperfect information, (2) are constrained by bounded rationality, and (3) tend to "satisfice" when making decisions

4-3a The Administrative Model

Herbert A. Simon was one of the first experts to recognize that decisions are not always made with rationality and logic.[26] Simon was subsequently awarded the Nobel Prize in economics. Rather than prescribing how decisions should be made, his view of decision making, now called the administrative model, describes how decisions often are actually made. As illustrated in Figure 4.4, the model holds that managers (1) use incomplete and imperfect information, (2) are constrained by bounded rationality, and (3) tend to "satisfice" when making decisions.

bounded rationality
A concept suggesting that decision makers are limited by their values and unconscious reflexes, skills, and habits

Bounded rationality suggests that decision makers are limited by their values and unconscious reflexes, skills, and habits. They are also limited by less-than-complete information and knowledge. Bounded rationality partially explains how U.S. auto executives allowed Japanese automakers to get such a strong foothold in the U.S. domestic market. For

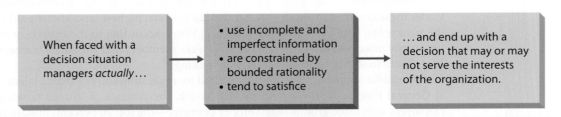

FIGURE 4.4

The Administrative Model of Decision Making

The administrative model is based on behavioral processes that affect how managers make decisions. Rather than prescribing how decisions should be made, it focuses more on describing how they are made.

years, executives at GM, Ford, and Chrysler compared their companies' performance only to one another's and ignored foreign imports. The foreign "threat" was not acknowledged until the domestic auto market had been changed forever. If managers had gathered complete information from the beginning, they might have been better able to thwart foreign competitors. These same companies face similar issues today as they struggle to figure out how to compete with firms like Tesla, Google, and Uber. Essentially, then, the concept of bounded rationality suggests that although people try to be rational decision makers, their rationality can be interpreted in different ways. This point is illustrated in our A *World of Difference* feature.

satisficing
The tendency to search for alternatives only until one is found that meets some minimum standard of sufficiency

Another important part of the administrative model is satisficing. This concept suggests that rather than conducting an exhaustive search for the best possible alternative, decision makers tend to search only until they identify an alternative that meets some minimum standard of sufficiency. A manager looking for a site for a new plant, for example, may select the first site she finds that meets basic requirements for transportation, utilities, and price, even though a further search might yield a better location. People satisfice for a variety of reasons. Managers may simply be unwilling to ignore their own motives (such as reluctance to spend time making a decision) and therefore may not be able to continue searching after a minimally acceptable alternative is identified. The decision maker may be unable to weigh and evaluate large numbers of alternatives and criteria. Also, subjective and personal considerations often intervene in decision situations.

Because of the inherent imperfection of information, bounded rationality, and satisficing, the decisions made by a manager may or may not actually be in the best interests of the organization. A manager may choose a particular location for the new plant because it offers the lowest price and best availability of utilities and transportation. Or she may choose the site because it is located in a community where she wants to live.

In summary, then, the classical and administrative models paint quite different pictures of decision making. Which is more correct? Actually, each can be used to better understand how managers make decisions. The classical model is prescriptive: It explains how managers can at least try to be more rational and logical in their approaches to decisions. The administrative model can be used by managers to develop a better understanding of their inherent biases and limitations.[27] In the following sections, we describe more fully other behavioral forces that can influence decisions.

4-3b Political Forces in Decision Making

Political forces are another major element that contributes to the behavioral nature of decision making. Organizational politics is covered in Chapter 16, but one major element of politics, coalitions, is especially relevant to decision making. A coalition is an informal alliance of individuals or groups formed to achieve a common goal. This common goal is often a preferred decision alternative. For example, coalitions of stockholders often band together to force a board of directors to make a certain decision.

coalition
An informal alliance of individuals or groups formed to achieve a common goal

The impact of coalitions can be either positive or negative. They can help astute managers get the organization on a path toward effectiveness and profitability, or they can strangle well-conceived strategies and decisions. Managers must recognize when to use coalitions, how to assess whether coalitions are acting in the best interests of the organization, and how to constrain their dysfunctional effects.[28]

4-3c Intuition and Escalation of Commitment

Two other important decision processes that go beyond logic and rationality are intuition and escalation of commitment to a chosen course of action.

intuition
An innate belief about something, without conscious consideration

Intuition Intuition is an innate belief about something, without conscious consideration. Managers sometimes decide to do something because it "feels right" or they have a "hunch." This feeling is usually not arbitrary, however. Rather, it is based on years of experience and practice in making decisions in similar situations.[29] An inner sense may help managers make

A WORLD OF DIFFERENCE

Sometimes Doing the "Right Thing" Can Be Confusing

Beatrice Dixon's multimillion-dollar company, Honey Pot, manufactures and distributes affordable, plant-based feminine care products. She is one of the first 40 women of color to raise over $1 million in venture capital. On February 4, 2020, in honor of Black History Month and as part of a series of ads titled "Founders We Believe In," Target featured Bea Dixon and her company. The captioning for the ad reads: "For Bea Dixon . . . it's all about opening doors and inspiring the next generation of entrepreneurs. She's just one of the many diverse business leaders Target is committed to empowering and investing in to strengthen the communities we call home."

Bea says at one point in the 30-second spot, "The reason why it's so important for Honey Pot to do well is so the next black girl that comes up with a great idea—she can have a better opportunity. That means a lot to me." But taking a personal stand for a socially responsible position doesn't always mean accolades. Within weeks of the video's release, Honey Pot's five-star rating on Trustpilot took a nose-dive as an unusually high number of reviews poured in, most of them posting one-star reviews not about the product but about Bea's statement, accusing her of racism.

This kind of trolling isn't uncommon. When a gun rights advocate discovered that the sponsor of a bill that would restrict "large-capacity" ammunition magazines in New Hampshire was the general manager of Lucky's Coffee Garage in the little town of Lebanon, he launched a smear campaign by recruiting his social media followers to post negative reviews on Yelp, TripAdvisor, and other similar sites. The owner of Lucky's tried to get some help from local officials, but the police determined that although the reviews seemed to be fake, the content of the messages did not violate New Hampshire law. Up until the trolling, Lucky's had a five-star rating and, in addition to good food and atmosphere, the little shop had received a Preservation Achievement Award in 2018 for bringing their historic building back to life.

Despite the negative trolling, Lucky's has recovered, and Dixon's company continues to do well. In fact, in a happy twist of fate and an affirmation of the old adage that "any publicity is good publicity," Honey Pot actually saw an increase in sales after her plight made national news. Both of these companies diverted time, energy, and money into rebutting false claims. When a business owner decides to take a stand of social responsibility, it can have unintended consequences that require additional planning and management, both short and long term.

References: "Founders We Believe In: The Honey Pot," YouTube, February 4, 2020, https://www.youtube.com on March 31, 2020; John Lippman, "Lebanon Coffee Shop Targeted on Social Media Over Lawmaker Employee's Gun Bill," *Valley News*, February 15, 2020, https://www.vnews.com on March 31; 2020; Shalwah Evans, "Target Responds to the Honey Pot Backlash," *Essence*, March 4, 2020, https://www.essence.com on March 31, 2020; Sonia Thompson, "The Real Reason People Called Target's Ad For Honey Pot Racist and How It Impacts Your Brand," *Forbes*, March 5, 2020, https://www.forbes.com on March 31, 2020.

---

an occasional decision without going through a full-blown rational sequence of steps. For example, Kip Tindell, CEO of The Container Store, emphasizes the use of intuition throughout his company and urges employees to believe that it is critical in the workplace. He is quoted as saying, "Intuition is only the sum total of your life experiences. So why would you want to leave it at home when you come to work in the morning?"[30] Of course, all managers, but most especially inexperienced ones, should be careful not to rely too heavily on intuition. If rationality and logic are continually flouted in favor of "what feels right," the odds are that disaster will strike one day.

> **"Intuition is a very powerful thing—more powerful than intellect, in my opinion."**
> —Steve Jobs, Cofounder and Longtime CEO of Apple[31]

escalation of commitment
A decision maker's staying with a decision even when it appears to be wrong

Escalation of Commitment Another important behavioral process that influences decision making is escalation of commitment to a chosen course of action. In particular, decision makers sometimes make decisions and then become so committed to the courses of action suggested by those decisions that they stay with them even when the decisions appear to have been wrong.[32] For example, when people buy stock in a company, they are often reluctant to sell it even after repeated drops in price. They choose a course of action—buying the stock in anticipation of making a profit—and then stay with it even in the face of increasing losses. Moreover, after the value drops, they rationalize that they can't sell now because they will lose money.

For years Sears and Kmart were dominant forces in the U.S. retailing sector. Sears was an anchor for most shopping centers and was the nation's largest retailer. Its Christmas catalogs

This coalition appears to have two co-conspirators. Their secretive stance and body language do not appear to be beneficial to group decision making.

Few business decisions are made under a condition of certainty. Sears has made many decisions over the years under conditions of uncertainty but has generally continued to follow old strategies with ineffective execution. As a result, the once-great retailer has been losing market share and closing stores and is not expected to survive much longer.

risk propensity
The extent to which a decision maker is willing to gamble when making a decision

were widely anticipated each year and its stores were known for "one-stop-shopping" destinations that carried everything from tools to toys. Kmart, meanwhile, was the country's largest discount retailer and was known as *the* place to shop for low prices. However, Sears essentially didn't see the growth of such competitive threats as online shopping and specialized "big-box" stores like Home Depot, Best Buy, and similar stores. Kmart, for its part, didn't see Walmart as a threat and was slow to adopt leading-edge technologies. Consequently, both businesses have struggled and lost most of their market share.

In contrast, a group of investors licensed the use of Hard Rock logos and trademarks for a theme park—Hard Rock Park—to be built in South Carolina. After six years of planning and construction and an investment of over $400 million, the park opened in Myrtle Beach to dismal reviews and poor attendance. Rather than increasing their investment and trying to increase attendance, owners decided after only nine months to shut the park down and sell off its assets.[33] Thus, decision makers must walk a fine line. On the one hand, they must guard against sticking too long with an incorrect decision. To do so can bring about financial decline. On the other hand, managers should not bail out of a seemingly incorrect decision too soon.

4-3d Risk Propensity and Decision Making

Risk propensity, another important behavioral element, is the extent to which a decision maker is willing to gamble when making a decision. Some managers are cautious about every decision they make. They try to adhere to the rational model and are extremely conservative in what they do. Such managers are more likely to avoid mistakes, and they infrequently make decisions that lead to big losses. Other managers are extremely aggressive in making decisions and are willing to take risks.[34] They rely heavily on intuition, reach decisions quickly, and often risk big investments on their decisions. As in gambling, these managers are more likely than their conservative counterparts to achieve big successes with their decisions—but they are also more likely to incur greater losses.[35] The organization's culture is a prime ingredient in fostering different levels of risk propensity.

4-3e Ethics and Decision Making

As we introduced in Chapter 4, individual ethics are personal beliefs about right and wrong behavior. Ethics are clearly related to decision making in a number of ways. For example, suppose that, after careful analysis, a manager realizes that his company could save money by closing his own department and subcontracting with a supplier for the same services. But to recommend this course of action would result in the loss of several jobs, including his own.

DOING BUSINESS ON PLANET EARTH

Lighting the Stove

Unsafe drinking water and household air pollution are major causes of illness and death around the world. In Rwanda, where most people living in rural areas cook their meals on open stoves, smoke and fumes from wood and charcoal have been linked to pneumonia, low birth weight, and impaired development in children. The Rwandan government has tried for years to address this issue, along with the lack of safe drinking water, but the efforts lacked financial support.

As a general rule, we expect business decision makers to react to consumer needs, but that doesn't always happen. Business seeks profit, and not all consumer needs are profitable, such as clean-burning stoves for Rwandan families. Nonprofit organizations like the Red Cross work to serve the public good or solve social problems, but those organizations can't supply every demand. Enter the B corporation.

B corps are for-profit businesses that volunteer to be graded by the nonprofit B Lab each year to ensure they're meeting the highest standards of social and environmental performance, public transparency, and legal accountability. Corporate performance is measured not only by profits or growth in stock price but also by the organization's impact on society and the environment. One example of a successful B corp is EcoZoom.

After a successful career in the transportation industry, EcoZoom founder Ben West went back to school to earn an MBA. One of his professors was on the board of directors of Aprovecho, a nonprofit that designed cookstoves for use in developing countries. Although Aprovecho had developed great technology, they didn't know how to get the product to the market. West decided he could do something, and so he made

the decision to start a company to do just that. Now, EcoZoom manufactures stoves in China and, although it sells them in the United States for camping and other outdoor uses, its primary market is developing countries. Rwanda, where women and children are being exposed to toxic smoke from inefficient stoves that make them more susceptible to acute illnesses such as pneumonia, lung cancer, and heart disease, is one such market.

In addition to reducing the air pollution inside and around the home, EcoZoom's low-emission, energy-efficient cookstoves reduce fuel use and cooking time, giving women more time to spend with their families and on other tasks, such as maintaining their gardens. The stoves can burn traditional biomass fuels, such as corn cobs and cow dung, as well as wood and charcoal. Since fuel costs can run up to 30 percent of a family's monthly income, the simple addition of an efficient stove makes a huge difference.

EcoZoom is providing stoves to a host of other African countries and is expanding distribution globally to wherever it is most needed. As their mission states: "We believe that household products should be healthy, efficient and eco-friendly for everyone, regardless of socio-economic status. A global social enterprise, our products are changing lives in 23 countries worldwide."

References: Micha Dhanjal, "EocZoom Global Announces Strategic Partnership with Bilite to Serve Kenya Market," EocZoom, July 22, 2019, https://ecozoom.com on March 31, 2020; "EcoZoom," Wikipedia, https://en.wikipedia.org/wiki/EcoZoom on March 31, 2020; "BioLite and EcoZoom Form Strategic Stove Partnership," BioLite, March 14, 2020, https://blog.bioliteenergy.com on March 31, 2020.

His own ethical standards will clearly shape how he proceeds.[36] Indeed, each component of managerial ethics (relationships of the firm to its employees, of employees to the firm, and of the firm to other economic agents) involves a wide variety of decisions, all of which are likely to have an ethical component. A manager must remember, then, that, just as behavioral processes such as politics and risk propensity affect the decisions he makes, so, too, do his ethical beliefs.[37] The *Doing Business on Planet Earth* feature provides a detailed example of how social responsibility and decision making are intertwined.

Manager's Checklist

☐ Managers should remember that even though they think they are rational and logical, in fact several different behavioral forces might influence their decisions.

☐ You should also understand, though, that deviating from rationality will not necessarily lead to bad decisions. Intuition, for example, can often help improve decision-making effectiveness.

4-4 GROUP AND TEAM DECISION MAKING IN ORGANIZATIONS

In many organizations today, important decisions are made by groups and teams rather than by individuals. Examples include the executive committee of The Walt Disney Company, product design teams at Texas Instruments, and marketing planning groups at Olive Garden. Managers can typically choose whether to have individuals or groups and teams make a particular decision. Thus, knowing about forms of group and team decision making and their advantages and disadvantages is important.[38]

4-4a Forms of Group and Team Decision Making

The most common methods of group and team decision making are interacting groups, Delphi groups, and nominal groups. Increasingly, these methods of group decision making are being conducted online. Moreover, online group decision making became even more widespread during the 2020 COVID-19 pandemic when many people were required to work from home to facilitate social distancing. Popular apps such as Zoom and FaceTime can be useful for online group decision making.

interacting groups and team
A decision-making group or team in which members openly discuss, argue about, and agree on the best alternative

Interacting Groups and Teams   Interacting groups and teams are the most common form of decision-making group. The format is simple—either an existing or a newly designated group or team is asked to make a decision. Existing groups or teams might be functional departments, regular work teams, or standing committees. Newly designated groups or teams can be ad hoc committees, task forces, or newly constituted work teams. The group or team members talk among themselves, argue, agree, argue some more, form internal coalitions, and so forth. Finally, after some period of deliberation, the group or team makes its decision. An advantage of this method is that the interaction among people often sparks new ideas and promotes understanding. A major disadvantage, though, is that political processes can play too big a role.

Delphi group
A form of group decision making in which a group is used to achieve a consensus of expert opinion

Delphi Groups   A Delphi group is sometimes used to develop a consensus of expert opinion. Developed by the Rand Corporation, the Delphi procedure solicits input from a panel of experts who contribute individually. Their opinions are combined and, in effect, averaged. Assume, for example, that the problem is to establish an expected date for a major technological breakthrough in converting coal into usable energy. The first step in using the Delphi procedure is to obtain the cooperation of a panel of experts. For this situation, experts might include various research scientists, university researchers, and executives in a relevant energy industry. At first, the experts are asked to anonymously predict a time frame for the expected breakthrough. The persons coordinating the Delphi group collect the responses, average them, and ask the experts for another prediction. In this round, the experts who provided unusual or extreme predictions may be asked to justify them. These explanations may then be relayed to the other experts. When the predictions stabilize, the average prediction is taken to represent the decision of the group of experts.

The time, expense, and logistics of the Delphi technique rule out its use for routine, everyday decisions, but it has been successfully used for forecasting technological breakthroughs at Boeing, market potential for new products at General Motors, research and development patterns at Eli Lilly, and future economic conditions by the U.S. government. Moreover, the Delphi method originally relied on paper-and-pencil responses obtained and shared through the mail; modern communication technologies based on various online platforms have enabled Delphi users to get answers much more quickly than in the past. (It is also worth noting that a technique called *crowdsourcing* is similar to Delphi. However, not everyone who contributes to crowdsourcing data is an expert. To offset this, most crowdsourcing methods use very large sets of responses.)

nominal group
A structured technique used to generate creative and innovative alternatives or ideas

Nominal Groups   Another useful group and team decision-making technique that is occasionally used is the **nominal group**. Unlike the Delphi method, in which group members do not see one another, nominal group members are in a face-to-face setting, either together or online. The members represent a group in name only, however; they do not talk to one another freely like the members of interacting groups. Nominal groups are used most often to generate creative and innovative alternatives or ideas. To begin, the manager assembles a group of knowledgeable experts and outlines the problem to them. The group members are then asked to individually write down as many alternatives as they can think of. The members then take turns stating their ideas, which are recorded on a flip chart or board at the front of the room. Discussion is limited to simple clarification. After all alternatives have been listed, more open discussion takes place. Group members then vote, usually by rank-ordering the various alternatives. The highest-ranking alternative represents the decision of the group. Of course, the manager in charge may retain the authority to accept or reject the group decision.[39]

4-4b Advantages of Group and Team Decision Making

The advantages and disadvantages of group and team decision making relative to individual decision making are summarized in Table 4.2. One advantage is simply that more information is available in a group or team setting—as suggested by the old axiom, "Two heads are better than one." A group or team represents a variety of education, experience, and perspective. Partly as a result of this increased information, groups and teams typically can identify and evaluate more alternatives than can one person.[40] The people involved in a group or team decision understand the logic and rationale behind it, are more likely to accept it, and are equipped to communicate the decision to their work group or department.[41]

Group decision making has several advantages (as well as disadvantages). This group, for instance, is carefully reviewing possible alternatives for an important decision. The members bring more experience and different perspectives to the decision than might any one of them working alone. At the same time, though, this process will take longer and be more expensive.

4-4c Disadvantages of Group and Team Decision Making

Perhaps the biggest drawback of group and team decision making is the additional time and hence the greater expense entailed. The increased time stems from interaction and discussion among group or team members. If a given manager's time is worth $50 an hour, and if the manager spends two hours making a decision, the decision "costs" the organization $100. For the same decision, a group of five managers might require three hours of time. At the same $50-an-hour rate, the decision "costs" the organization $750. Assuming the group or team decision is better, the additional expense may be justified, but the fact remains that group and team decision making is more costly.

Group or team decisions may also represent undesirable compromises.[42] For example, hiring a top manager on a compromise may be a bad decision in the long run because he or she may not be able to respond adequately to various subunits in the organization nor have everyone's complete support. Sometimes one person dominates the group process to the point where others cannot make a full contribution. This dominance may stem from a desire for power or from a naturally dominant personality. The problem is that what appears to emerge as a group decision may actually be the decision of one person.

Table 4.2	Advantages and Disadvantages of Group and Team Decision Making	
Advantages	**Disadvantages**	
More information and knowledge are available.	The process takes longer than individual decision making, so it is costlier.	
More alternatives are likely to be generated.	Compromise decisions resulting from indecisiveness may emerge.	
More acceptance of the final decision is likely.	One person may dominate the group.	
Enhanced communication of the decision may result.	Groupthink may occur.	
Better decisions generally emerge.		

To increase the chances that a group or team decision will be successful, managers must learn how to manage the process of group and team decision making. FedEx, IBM, and many other organizations often use groups and teams in the decision-making process.

groupthink
A situation that occurs when a group or team's desire for consensus and cohesiveness overwhelms its desire to reach the best possible decision

Finally, a group or team may succumb to a phenomenon known as "groupthink." Groupthink occurs when the desire for consensus and cohesiveness overwhelms the goal of reaching the best possible decision.[43] Under the influence of groupthink, the group may arrive at decisions that are made not in the best interests of either the group or the organization, but rather to avoid conflict among group members. One of the most clearly documented examples of groupthink involved the space shuttle *Challenger* disaster. As NASA was preparing to launch the shuttle, many problems and questions arose. At each step of the way, however, decision makers argued that there was no reason to delay and that everything would be fine. Shortly after its launch, the shuttle exploded, killing all seven crew members.

4-4d Managing Group and Team Decision-Making Processes

Managers can do several things to help promote the effectiveness of group and team decision making. One is simply being aware of the pros and cons of having a group or team make a decision to start with. Time and cost can be managed by setting a deadline by which the decision must be made final. Dominance can be at least partially avoided if a special group is formed just to make the decision. An astute manager, for example, should know who in the organization may try to dominate and can either avoid putting that person in the group or put several strong-willed people together.

To avoid groupthink, each member of the group or team should critically evaluate all alternatives. So that members present divergent viewpoints, the leader should not make his or her own position known too early. At least one member of the group or team might be assigned the role of devil's advocate. And after reaching a preliminary decision, the group or team should hold a follow-up meeting wherein divergent viewpoints can be raised again if any group members wish to do so.[44] Gould Paper Corporation used these methods by assigning managers to two different teams. The teams then spent an entire day in a structured debate, presenting the pros and cons of each side of an issue to ensure the best possible decision.

 **Manager's Checklist**

☐ Managers should be familiar with the advantages and disadvantages of group versus individual decision making and try to use the best approach for each situation.

☐ You should also be aware of the different formats for group decision making.

SUMMARY OF LEARNING OUTCOMES AND KEY POINTS

4-1. Discuss the meaning of decision making, types of decisions, and decision-making conditions.

- Decision making is the act of choosing one alternative from among a set of alternatives.
- The decision-making process includes recognizing and defining the nature of a decision situation, identifying alternatives, choosing the "best" alternative, and putting it into practice.
- Two common types of decisions are programmed and nonprogrammed.
- Decisions may be made under states of certainty, risk, or uncertainty.

4-2. Discuss rational perspectives on decision making, including the steps in rational decision making.

- Rational perspectives on decision making rest on the classical model.
- This model assumes that managers have complete information and that they will behave rationally. The primary steps in rational decision making are:
  - Recognizing and defining the situation
  - Identifying alternatives
  - Evaluating alternatives
  - Selecting the best alternative
  - Implementing the chosen alternative
  - Following up and evaluating the effectiveness of the alternative after it is implemented.

4-3. Describe the behavioral aspects of decision making.

- Behavioral aspects of decision making rely on the administrative model.
- This model recognizes that managers use incomplete information and that they do not always behave rationally.
- The administrative model also recognizes the concepts of bounded rationality and satisficing.
- Political activities by coalitions, managerial intuition, and the tendency to become increasingly committed to a chosen course of action are all important.
- Risk propensity is also an important behavioral perspective on decision making.
- Ethics also affect how managers make decisions.

4-4. Discuss group and team decision making, including its advantages and disadvantages and how it can be more effectively managed.

- To help enhance decision-making effectiveness, managers often use interacting, Delphi, or nominal groups or teams.
- Group and team decision making in general has both advantages and disadvantages compared to individual decision making.
- Managers can adopt a number of strategies to help groups and teams make better decisions.

DISCUSSION QUESTIONS

Questions for Review

1. Describe the differences between programmed and nonprogrammed decisions. What are the implications of these differences for decision makers?
2. Describe the behavioral nature of decision making. Be certain to provide some detail about political forces, risk propensity, ethics, and commitment in your description.
3. What is meant by the term *escalation of commitment*? In your opinion, under what conditions is escalation of commitment likely to occur?
4. Explain the differences between three common methods of group decision making—interacting groups, Delphi groups, and nominal groups.

Questions for Analysis

1. Was your decision about what college or university to attend a rational decision? Did you go through each step in rational decision making? If not, why not?
2. Most business decisions are made under conditions of either risk or uncertainty. In your opinion, is it easier to

make a decision under a condition of risk or a condition of uncertainty? Why?

3. Consider the following list of business decisions. Which decisions would be handled most effectively by group or team decision making? Which would be handled most effectively by individual decision making? Explain your answers.

   - A decision about switching pencil suppliers
   - A decision about hiring a new CEO
   - A decision about firing an employee for stealing
   - A decision about calling 911 to report a fire in the warehouse
   - A decision about introducing a brand-new product

Questions for Application

1. Much business activity in the United States was shut down in Spring 2020 to help combat the spread of COVID-19. In April and May some businesses started to re-open, although often under different circumstances. For example, in some locations restaurants that re-opened had to limit their capacity to 50 percent of their normal capacity in order to facilitate social distancing. Using online resources identify 5 business-related decisions related to re-opening in late spring 2020. Describe each in terms of its associated conditions and if, in your judgement, decision making was handled effectively.

2. Describe a recent decision you made that relied on intuition. In your opinion, what experiences formed the source of your intuition? Did the decision lead to attainment of the desired outcomes? Did your intuition play a positive or negative role in goal attainment? Explain.

3. Interview a department head at your college or university to determine whether group or team decision making is used. If it is, how does the head try to overcome the disadvantages of group decision making? Are the attempts successful? Why or why not?

BUILDING EFFECTIVE CONCEPTUAL SKILLS

Exercise Overview

Conceptual skills require you to think in the abstract—an area that's fraught with the risk of error (or at least mistakes in judgment). This exercise is designed to show you how certain pitfalls in abstract thinking—namely, nonrational biases and risk propensity—can lead to faulty decision making.

Exercise Background

Psychologists Amos Tversky and Daniel Kahneman conducted much of the research contributing to the current state of our knowledge about decision-making biases. Tversky and Kahneman tested tendencies in people's real-life choices by presenting experimental subjects with laboratory-simulated decision-making situations. From the results they developed a set of principles called *prospect theory* to explain why people tend to be nonrational in making economic decisions.

Tversky and Kahneman's most important finding was that an individual's *perception* of gain or loss in a situation is more important than an objective measure of gain or loss. In this respect, they're being *nonrational*—that is, they aren't making decisions based purely on rational criteria. Similarly, they found that different people think differently about gains and losses—a phenomenon they call *framing*. Not surprisingly, people also tend to allow their perceptions to be skewed (positively or negatively) by the information they receive about a situation. Unfortunately, when new information later becomes available, they have a hard time letting go of their initial perceptions, even if the new information contradicts their original impressions. Tversky and Kahneman refer to this process as *anchoring and adjustment*.

In this exercise, we're going to ask you to answer a few questions. To answer them, however, you must know how to calculate an *expected value*. To do this, you multiply each possible outcome value of a situation by the probability of its occurrence and then sum all the results. Here's a simple example: Let's say you have a 50 percent chance of earning 80 points on an exam and a 50 percent chance of earning 70 points. You can calculate the expected value as

$$(.5*80) + (.5*70) = 75$$

In other words, a .5 chance of 80 points equals 40 points and a .5 chance of 70 points equals 35 points. Therefore, the expected value of your exam is 40 + 35 = 75 points.

Exercise Task

1. Respond to the list of brief questions that your professor provides to you. *Remember*: No answer is correct or incorrect; simply choose *your most likely response*. Then, when your instructor tells you to, share your answers with the class.

2. Discuss the answers given by the class. Why do students' answers differ?

3. What have you learned from this exercise about decision-making biases and risk propensity?

BUILDING EFFECTIVE DECISION-MAKING SKILLS

Exercise Overview

Decision-making skills refer to the ability to recognize and define problems and opportunities correctly and then to select an appropriate course of action for solving problems or capitalizing on opportunities. This exercise allows you to compare the results of individual decision making with the results of decision making conducted by nominal groups.

Exercise Background

Individual decision making, of course, has its advantages—speed, simplicity, lack of conflict. At times, however, these advantages are outweighed by other considerations. In particular, solitary decision making isn't conducive to innovation. Groups are better at innovating because they benefit from the input of diverse individuals, which, in turn, generates greater variety in alternative courses of action.

Nominal groups—so called because they exist *in name only*—are especially well suited for fostering creativity. They provide the freedom to develop as many creative options as possible without risk of criticism or political pressure. Nominal groups also pool input from many individuals and encourage creative responses to the pooled input. In short, nominal groups foster creativity because they combine techniques for improving both individual and group creativity.

Exercise Task

Listen as your professor describes a problem situation and then do the following:

1. Write down as many creative responses to the problem as you can. Don't worry about whether or not they're practical. In fact, try to come up with as many unexpected—even "far-out"—responses as you can.
2. When your instructor calls on you, share your list with the class.
3. Query other students about their suggestions for clarification only. *Do not, under any circumstances, reveal whether you think any idea is "good" or "bad."*
4. After all individual ideas have been listed and clarified, add to the list any other ideas that you've developed while participating in the in-class part of the exercise.
5. Vote on the list, focusing on the "creativity" of individual items: Which suggestion does the class regard as the "best" solution to the problem at hand?
6. Did the nominal-group technique generate more creative alternatives than those that you generated on your own?
7. In your opinion, is the alternative voted "best" by the class a "better" solution than anything you thought of on your own? Explain your answer.
8. Give some suggestions about the types of organizational decisions that could be more effective if made by nominal groups. When should nominal groups *not* be used?

SKILL-BUILDING PERSONAL ASSESSMENT

Decision-Making Styles

Decision making is clearly important. However, individuals differ in their decision-making styles, or the way they approach decisions. The following assessment is designed to help you understand your decision-making style. Respond to the following statements by indicating the extent to which they describe you. Circle the response that best represents your self-evaluation.

1. Overall, I'm _____ to act.
   1. quick   2. moderately fast   3. slow
2. I spend _____ amount of time making important decisions as/than I do making less important ones.
   1. about the same   2. a greater   3. a much greater
3. When making decisions, I _____ go with my first thought.
   1. usually   2. occasionally   3. rarely
4. When making decisions, I'm _____ concerned about making errors.
   1. rarely   2. occasionally   3. often

5. When making decisions, I _____ check my work more than once.
   1. rarely   2. occasionally   3. usually
6. When making decisions, I gather _____ information.
   1. little   2. some   3. lots of
7. When making decisions, I consider _____ alternatives.
   1. few   2. some   3. lots of
8. I usually make decisions _____ before the deadline.
   1. way   2. somewhat   3. just
9. After making a decision, I _____ look for other alternatives, wishing I had waited.
   1. rarely   2. occasionally   3. usually
10. I _____ regret having made a decision.
    1. rarely   2. occasionally   3. often

Source: Lussier, R. N. (1994). Supervision: A skill-building approach. Irwin.

Scoring: Generally, there are three decision-making styles: reflexive, consistent, and reflective. To determine your style, add up your score by totaling the numbers assigned to each response. The total will be between 10 and 30. A score from 10 to 16 indicates a reflexive style, a score from 17 to 23 indicates a consistent style, and a score from 24 to 30 indicates a reflective style.

Reflexive style: A reflexive decision maker likes to make quick decisions (to shoot from the hip) without taking the time to get all the information that may be needed and without considering all alternatives. On the positive side, reflexive decision makers are decisive; they do not procrastinate. On the negative side, making quick decisions can lead to waste and duplication when the best possible alternative is overlooked. Employees may see a reflexive decision maker as a poor supervisor if he or she consistently makes bad decisions. If you use a reflexive style, you may want to slow down and spend more time gathering information and analyzing alternatives.

Reflective style: A reflective decision maker likes to take plenty of time to make decisions, gathering considerable information and analyzing several alternatives. On the positive side, the reflective type does not make hasty decisions. On the negative side, he or she may procrastinate and waste valuable time and other resources. The reflective decision maker may be viewed as wishy-washy and indecisive. If you use a reflective style, you may want to speed up your decision making. As Andrew Jackson once said, "Take time to deliberate; but when the time for action arrives, stop thinking and go on."

Consistent style: Consistent decision makers tend to make decisions without either rushing or wasting time. They know when they have enough information and alternatives to make a sound decision. Consistent decision makers tend to have the best record for making good decisions.

MANAGEMENT AT WORK

The Not-So-Smart Phone Company

"We would say, 'We know better, and they'll eventually figure it out.'"
—Former Blackberry Executive on Customer Relations at RIM

During the runup to his first inauguration, in 2009, President-elect Barack Obama was informed by security advisors that his beloved BlackBerry smartphone was a potential security risk. Hackers and spy agencies, they warned him, might figure out how to get into his email. "They're going to pry it out of my hands," joked Obama, but he was adamant about his phone privileges, and security officials ultimately gave in. For one thing, BlackBerry was already known for such features as Secure Work Space and was the phone of choice for business leaders in security-sensitive positions. In addition, it was possible to modify the BlackBerry with enhanced encryption, and Obama soon became the first president to be connected by email.

In 2014, however, the White House Communications Agency announced that it was testing smartphones from Samsung and LG for future use by administration officials. President Obama would be holding onto his BlackBerry, but the announcement was bad news for the Canadian maker of BlackBerrys, especially coming on the heels of a $423 million loss for the quarter ending on March 1. The company's U.S. market share had also plunged to 3 percent—down from 43 percent just four years earlier. What had happened to the corporate inventor of the smartphone and one of the world's most influential technology companies?

Arguably, bad decision making.

In 1999, Research in Motion (RIM), as the company was originally known, released the first version of its mobile email device. The RIM 5810, with a tactile keyboard and preinstalled app for email, became an instant hit—indeed, a cultural icon—and in the next decade, RIM would become the global leader in mobile email communications. The BlackBerry was designed for and marketed to business customers—the executives who ran corporate IT programs and selected devices for use by all of the company's employees who needed to stay in constant touch. RIM management assumed that mobile email adoption would follow the same pattern as so much previous technology: Like the typewriter and the computer, the BlackBerry would win over business users and then extend its reach to individual consumers.

Unfortunately, the world was on the verge of a revolution in technological diffusion: It's commonly called the *consumerization of IT*, and it means that the adoption process started to flow in the opposite direction—from consumers to corporate buyers. New products like the iPhone (which was introduced in 2007) and the Android (2008) caught on with consumers, and although they came with a lot of extraneous apps, businesses began to consider them because employees were so attached to them.

When it was first introduced, RIM co-CEOs Mike Lazaridis and Jim Balsillie publicly dismissed the iPhone as a potential threat to their product line. Said Balsillie: "It's kind of one more entrant into an already busy space with lots of choice for consumers. . . . But in terms of a sea-change for BlackBerry, I think that's overstating it." According to some insiders, BlackBerry management suspected that iPhone technology was superior, but Lazaridis and Balsillie continued to express confidence in the BlackBerry's security features and, especially, its tactile QWERTY keyboard: "Try typing a web key on an iPhone touchscreen," suggested Lazaridis. "It's a real challenge—you can't see what you type." As late as 2012, Lazaridis would hold up a BlackBerry for his board to see: "I get this," he'd say. "It's clearly differentiated." Then he'd hold up a touchscreen phone: "I *don't* get *this*," he would declare. Lazaridis saw no reason to abandon RIM's core corporate customers in order to cater to the perceived needs of consumers in a rapidly crowding market.

It's important to point out that the Apple iPhone had been developed in collaboration with the internet provider AT&T. Its touchscreen was more responsive, its browser was faster, and it was loaded with more apps, and it wasn't long before it was being touted as a "BlackBerry killer." As early as July 2007, RIM had been approached by AT&T competitor Verizon with a plan to develop an "iPhone killer" (which would feature a touchscreen and no keyboard). When the BlackBerry Storm was released in November 2008, however, customers didn't like it. The touchscreen was awkward and the processor was slow. "The technology," admitted one RIM executive, "was cobbled together quickly and wasn't quite ready." RIM abandoned the Storm, and Verizon turned to Motorola, which succeeded in adapting Google's new Android operating system to its Droid phone, which came out in 2009 with a user-friendly interface.

Not only was the Droid itself immensely successful, but Android quickly became the most popular mobile OS, with Android devices now outselling those with Windows, iOS, and Mac OS combined. Within 14 months, Android's market share had climbed from 5.2 percent to 23.5 percent, while RIM's share dropped 10 points, to 31.6 percent. A year later, Android commanded a 47.3 percent share and RIM a mere 16 percent.

Back in 2007, when he first opened up an iPhone to have a look inside, Lazaridis, an engineer who'd founded RIM in 1984, was surprised to find that the device broke most of the rules that he'd helped to write. For one thing, the iPhone had a fully internet-capable browser —one of two—and its Android OS took up 700 megabytes. RIM's OS,

which had been designed in the 1990s, ran on one processor and used 32 megabytes. "I said, 'How did they get AT&T to allow that?'" Lazaridis later recalled. He was certain that the iPhone would overstrain the network of its wireless partner. AT&T, however, was preparing to ride the consumerization wave. "There was a time," says former RIM executive VP Patrick Spence, "when wireless carriers tried to keep data usage predictable. Then, when the iPhone became compelling, they shifted to . . . trying to drive much more usage in different packages."

BlackBerry users told RIM that they wanted features like those on the iPhone, but RIM held onto the business rationale that it had pioneered—the one that operated on the assumption that the value of a smartphone lay in its hardware rather than in its software applications. Says a former company insider:

> We believed we knew better what customers needed long term than they did. Consumers would say, "I want a faster browser." We might say, "You might think you want a faster browser, but you don't want to pay overage on your bill." "Well, I want a super-big, very responsive touchscreen." "Well, you might think you want that, but you don't want your phone to die at 2:00 p.m." We would say, "We know better, and they'll eventually figure it out."[45]

Case Questions

1. Once the iPhone and Androids penetrated the market, RIM faced a serious challenge: It had two distinct groups of customers to which it had to market its products. What were those two groups, and why were their needs and wants incompatible? Explain how this situation put RIM in a *state of uncertainty*. What *risks* did it face in making decisions to respond to this situation?

2. When RIM decided to incorporate personal apps into the BlackBerry, developers were required to use the company's Java-based operating system, which had been created in the 1990s. In addition, they were required to submit apps for prior approval. Several apps—including Instagram and Tumblr—went elsewhere. Explain this problem as one of *bounded rationality*. Judging from what you know about RIM from the case, in what other ways would you say that RIM decision makers were hampered by bounded rationality?

3. Hersh Schefrin, a pioneer in the behavioral aspects of financial decision making, studies how a specific set of psychological traps snare decision makers, causing them to make inferior decisions. Two of the most common are excessive optimism and overconfidence. People learn to be excessively optimistic and overconfident. This means that successful people overestimate their past successes, which

feeds these biases. Judging from the details of the case, explain how these two forms of "bias" affected decision making at RIM. How might RIM's "inferior decisions" have been avoided if executives like Lazaridis and Balsillie had applied the *steps in rational decision making*?

4. The barrier between work and home is becoming increasingly blurred. Several years ago the standard was that businesses would provide phones for employees to use for business purposes and individuals would have their own phones for personal use. Now, though, most people have a single phone. Can employers take advantage of the fact that you're "plugged in all day long"? Is it a problem if people use their phone for personal business when they're at work?

You Make the Call

Sailing the Seas

1. In your opinion, which one decision has made the greatest impact on Viking's success? Why?
2. Select any one of the decisions made by Hagen as described in the case. Trace through the steps that he may have followed using the rational decision-making process as a framework.
3. Which of the major decisions noted in the case were made under conditions of certainty, risk, and uncertainty?
4. Using online resources, find out when Viking was able to resume operations following the COVID-19 pandemic and how the health crisis affected Viking.

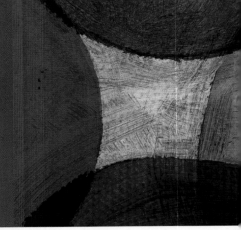

CHAPTER 5

Entrepreneurship and New Venture Management

Learning Outcomes

After studying this chapter, you should be able to:

5-1 Discuss the meaning of entrepreneurship, start-ups, and new ventures.

5-2 Describe the role of entrepreneurships, start-ups, and new ventures in society.

5-3 Identify the major issues involved in choosing strategies for small businesses and the role of international management in start-ups and new ventures.

5-4 Discuss the structural challenges unique to start-ups and new ventures.

5-5 Summarize the determinants of the performance of entrepreneurs, start-ups, and new ventures.

The process of starting a new business or business venture, sometimes failing and sometimes succeeding, is part of what is called "entrepreneurship," the subject of this chapter. The new businesses themselves are often referred to as start-ups or new ventures. First, we look more closely at entrepreneurship, the underlying ingredient of all new businesses. We then explore the nature of start-ups and new ventures. Next, we examine the role of start-ups and new ventures in the business world and discuss strategies for start-ups and new ventures organizations. Finally, we describe the structure and performance of start-ups and new ventures. First, though, let's look at one wildly successful entrepreneur and the business he launched.

Management in Action

Putting the Greek into Yogurt

"We had the right product. And we had it in the right place. And I think we used the right approach, which was making a delicious, nutritious, natural and accessible product."

—Hamdi Ulukaya, Founder of Chobani Yogurt

Hamdi Ulukaya was born and raised in Turkey. He helped in the family dairy and loved eating the thick, tangy yogurt that his mother prepared from an old family recipe. As he traveled through Europe as a young man, he found similar kinds of yogurt all along the way and became a real aficionado. He later learned that European yogurt has generally always been made using the so-called "Greek process" that removes the whey from the final product (whey is the water left after the milk has been cultured), resulting in a thick, creamy yogurt.

Hamdi Ulukaya is the founder and CEO of Chobani yogurt. His entrepreneurial vision has transformed Chobani into a multibillion-dollar corporation.

Ulukaya moved to the United States in 1994 to study English. While he loved his new country, he quickly grew to detest the yogurt varieties marketed in this country by Dannon, Yoplait, and other companies. These manufacturers produced yogurt using a different process that left the whey in the yogurt—harmless, but resulting in a thinner, less creamy product. He thought it tasted poorly in comparison to the yogurt he grew up with. Meanwhile, Ulukaya started a small business producing feta cheese for restaurants called Euphrates, built it into a successful operation, and accumulated some savings from his new enterprise.

One day in 2004 Ulukaya read an article about an old yogurt plant that Kraft Foods was closing. As he thought about the old yogurt factory being shuttered and his own disdain for local yogurt products, an idea began to take shape. The next day he drove to upstate New York, inspected the plant, and quickly decided to buy it. He used a combination of personal savings and a loan from the U.S. Small Business Association to buy the plant at an undisclosed but bargain price. He also hired four of the former Kraft employees who had worked at the plant plus a skilled yogurt maker he knew by reputation from Turkey.

Next, he needed to set up equipment and develop a production system. The old Kraft plant had all of the basic yogurt-making equipment he needed. However, since he wanted to extract the whey as it was done in Europe, he also needed some additional machinery. After a brief search he found a used machine called a separator in Wisconsin and bought it for $50,000. In addition, he bought a few other pieces of specialized equipment—mostly used—and was ready to start testing recipes and production processes.

He also wanted to create some unique packaging for his new line of yogurt. Ulukaya didn't feel that he could afford traditional advertising for his start-up operation but concluded that he could attract consumer attention with packaging. He created a model of his yogurt containers that was squatter and fatter than other manufacturers were using. This would both attract attention and make the containers look a bit larger. In addition, he decided that he wanted the labels to be shrunken-on plastic sleeves instead of being printed directly on the yogurt containers, which would result in sharper and brighter colors, further differentiating his packaging and attracting the consumer's attention.

But these decisions resulted in some temporary roadblocks for Ulukaya. The first step in making the yogurt containers would be to create a mold. The lowest bid he could get from a U.S. supplier for this job was $250,000—half of his working capital. Eventually, though, he found a company in Colombia that would do the job for half that amount. So, now he had a plant, equipment, workers, and packaging. But he still needed a product.

Finally, after a couple of years of trying and testing recipes and getting his business plan finalized, Ulukaya launched his new yogurt in 2007. He named it *Chobani*—Turkish for "shepherd." To keep control over the product, as well as its pricing and placement, Ulukaya and his first marketing representative approached retailers directly rather than going through existing distributors. It was important to Ulukaya, for example, that his yogurt be sold with all of the other yogurts rather than in the organic section. Their first order was 300 cases for a grocer on Long Island. A week later the grocer called Ulukaya, told him the product was flying off the shelf, and ordered another 300 cases.

And to say Chobani has been successful would be an understatement. For example, Ulukaya's business plan called for achieving a sell rate of 20,000 cases of Chobani a week within 36 months. If the new start-up could not reach that level, Ulukaya knew he would need to close the operation. As it turned out, though, his target was way too low—by a year and a zero. By mid-2009, 200,000 cases a week were going out the door. When Chobani was first launched, Greek yogurt accounted for less than 1 percent of U.S. yogurt sales. Now, that figure has increased to 50 percent.

As growth continued to skyrocket, the firm opened a second plant in Twin Falls, Idaho. This facility, the largest yogurt plant in the world, employs around 7,000 people. The firm has also expanded to foreign markets, including Europe, the United Kingdom, Australia, Canada, Mexico, and parts of Asia. In 2017 Chobani passed Yoplait to become the second largest yogurt company in the world (trailing only Danone). Chobani has also branched out into other product lines, including plant-based beverages made from organic oats, Chobani Coffee Creamer, and Chobani Savor, a yogurt-based condiment.

Hamdi Ulukaya is now a billionaire. But he also believes in sharing the wealth. For example, in 2016 he gave 10 percent of the company to its employees, making millionaires out of some of those with the longest tenure. That same year he also announced that Chobani would grant six weeks of paid time off for new parents. Not bad for a Turkish immigrant just looking to learn a foreign language![1]

Just like Hamdi Ulukaya, thousands of people all over the world start new businesses each year. Some of them succeed but many, unfortunately, fail. Some of the people who fail in a new business try again, and sometimes it takes two or more failures before a successful business gets underway. Henry Ford, for example, went bankrupt twice before succeeding with Ford Motor Company. On the other hand, of course, there are the Hamdi Ulukayas who succeed once (with Euphrates, in his case), try again, and succeed a second time.

5-1 THE MEANING OF ENTREPRENEURSHIP

entrepreneurship
The process of planning, organizing, operating, and assuming the risk of a start-up or new venture

entrepreneur
Someone who engages in entrepreneurship

small business
A business that is privately owned by one individual or a small group of individuals and has revenues and assets that are not large enough to influence its environment

start-up or **new venture**
A relatively new small business

Entrepreneurship is the process of planning, organizing, operating, and assuming the risk of a start-up or new venture. An entrepreneur, in turn, is someone who engages in entrepreneurship. Hamdi Ulukaya, who launched and still runs Chobani, is an entrepreneur. He put his own resources on the line and took a personal stake in the success or failure of Chobani. On the other hand, business owners who hire professional managers to run their businesses and then turn their attention to other interests are not true entrepreneurs. Although they are assuming the risk of the venture, they are not actively involved in organizing or operating it. Likewise, professional managers whose job is running someone else's business are not entrepreneurs because they assume less than total personal risk for the success or failure of the business.

Entrepreneurs start new businesses, usually small ones. We define a small business as one that is privately owned by one individual or a small group of individuals and has revenues and assets that are not large enough to influence its environment. A small, two-person software development company with annual sales of $100,000 would clearly be a small business, whereas Microsoft Corporation is just as clearly a large business. But the boundaries are not always this clear-cut. For example, a regional retail chain with 20 stores and annual revenues of $30 million may sound large but is really very small when compared to such giants as Walmart and Target. We also define a start-up or new venture as a relatively new small business. Any start-up or new venture may succeed and grow to become a large business, succeed but remain small, fail and shut down, or be bought by an existing business.

5-2 THE ROLE OF ENTREPRENEURS, START-UPS, AND NEW VENTURES IN SOCIETY

The history of entrepreneurship and of the development of new businesses is in many ways the history of great wealth and of great failure. Some entrepreneurs have been very successful and have accumulated vast fortunes from their entrepreneurial efforts. For example, when Microsoft Corporation first sold its stock to the public in 1986, Bill Gates, then just 30 years old, received $350 million for his share of Microsoft.[2] Today his holdings—valued at almost $100 billion—make him one of the richest persons not only in the United States but also in the entire world. Many more entrepreneurs, however, have lost a great deal of money. Research suggests that the majority of new businesses fail within the first few years after founding.[3] Many that last longer do so only because the entrepreneurs themselves work long hours for very little income.

A small business is one that is privately owned and whose assets and revenues are not large enough to influence its environment. This flower grower, a small business, is checking a shipment destined for a local garden center.

Figure 5.1a shows that 85.43 percent of all businesses employ 20 or fewer people. Another 12.13 percent employ between 20 and 99 people, and 2.18 percent employ between 100 and 499 people. Only about 0.5 percent employ 500 or more people. Figure 5.1b shows that 23.52 percent of all workers are employed by firms with fewer than 20 people, and 29.62 percent are employed by firms with between 20 and 99 people. Another 25.29 percent are employed by firms with between 100 and 499 people.[4]

On the basis of numbers alone, then, small business is a strong presence in the economy, which is also true in virtually all of the world's mature economies. In Germany, for example, companies with fewer than 500 employees generate over 99 percent of the country's sales tax revenue and two-thirds of the nation's gross national product, train nine of 10 apprentices, and employ four of every five workers. Small businesses also play major roles in the economies of Italy, France, Ireland, and Brazil. In addition, experts agree that small businesses will be quite important in the emerging economies of countries such as Russia and Vietnam. The contribution of start-ups and new ventures can be measured in terms of their effects on key aspects of an economic system. In the United States, these aspects include job creation, innovation, and importance to big business.

A start-up or new venture refers to a relatively new small business. This computer retailer, for example, has just opened its doors. The firm may one day grow into a giant international chain, may remain small and focused on its local market, or eventually fail.

5-2a Job Creation

Small businesses—especially in certain industries—are an important source of new (and often well-paid) jobs. In recent years, for instance, small businesses have accounted for around 35–45 percent of all new jobs in high-technology sectors of the economy and many of these jobs pay above-average wages.[5] However, relative job growth among businesses of different sizes is not easy to determine. For one thing, when a successful small business starts adding employees at a rapid clip, it may quickly cease being small. For example, Dell Computer had exactly one employee in 1984 (Michael Dell himself). However, the payroll grew to around 100 employees in 1986; over 2,000 in 1992; more than 39,000 in 2004; 94,300 in 2010; and over 157,000 in 2020. Although there was no precise point at which Dell turned from "small" into "large," some of the jobs it created would have been counted in the small-business sector and some in the large. Table 5.1 lists job creation numbers for recent start-up businesses you probably recognize.

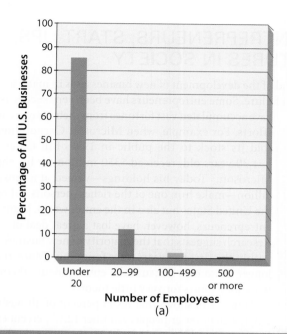
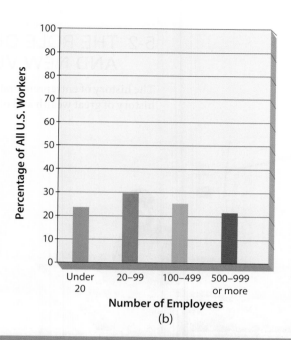

FIGURE 5.1

The Importance of Small Business in the United States

(a) Percentage of all U.S. businesses. (b) Percentages of all U.S. workers.

Source: https://www.naics.com/business-lists/counts-by-company-size/, accessed on March 1, 2020.

It is important to note, though, that tracking job gains and losses is very complicated and somewhat imprecise. For instance, suppose a business eliminates one full-time job but later replaces it with two part-time jobs. Some statistics would count this as a loss of one job followed by a gain of two jobs. Similarly, the job numbers attributed to a company can

Table 5.1	Job Creation by Recent Successful Start-Ups and New Ventures	
Firm	**Year Started**	**Number of Jobs in 2020**
Alphabet	1997	103,550
Amazon	1994	750,000
Buffalo Wild Wings	1982	44,000
Cinemark	1985	19,915
Dell Computer	1984	157,000
eBay	1997	14,000
Facebook	2004	44,900
GameStop	1994	61,000
JetBlue	2000	22,000
LinkedIn	2003	16,000
NetFlix	1997	6,700
Starbucks	1971	291,000
Tesla	2003	45,000
Twitter	2007	3,920
Whole Foods	1978	91,000

All businesses create and eliminate jobs. Because of their size, the magnitude of job creation and elimination is especially pronounced in bigger businesses. But successful start-ups and new ventures add jobs, sometimes slowly and sometimes very rapidly.

fluctuate when it acquires or sells a business unit. For instance, media outlets once reported that Halliburton had "cut" 53,000 jobs in the previous year. But in reality, those "losses" actually came when the firm sold its largest subsidiary, KBR. Only a handful of jobs were actually eliminated; instead, over 50,000 jobs were simply moved to a new firm.

At least one message is clear: Entrepreneurial business success, more than business size, accounts for most new job creation. Whereas successful retailers like Walmart and Best Buy have been growing and adding thousands of new jobs, struggling chains like Kmart have been eliminating thousands. Hence, most firms, especially those in complex and dynamic environments, go through periods of growth when they add new jobs but also have periods when they cut jobs.

Some start-ups and new ventures grow and expand, some remain the same size, and others fail. The business on the left is growing and needs to hire new employees. However, the one on the right is shutting down and its workers are losing their jobs.

The reality, then, is that jobs are created by entrepreneurial companies of all sizes, all of which hire workers and all of which lay them off. Although small firms often hire at a faster rate than large ones, they are also likely to eliminate jobs at a far higher rate. Small firms are also usually the first to hire in times of economic recovery, whereas large firms are generally the last. Conversely, however, big companies are also the last to lay off workers during economic downswings.

5-2b Innovation

History has shown that major innovations are as likely to come from start-ups and new ventures as from big businesses. For example, small firms and individuals invented the personal computer and the stainless-steel razor blade, the transistor radio and the photocopying machine, the jet engine and the self-developing photograph. They also gave us the helicopter and power steering, automatic transmissions and air conditioning, cellophane and the disposable ballpoint pen. Today, says the Small Business Administration (SBA), start-ups and new ventures consistently supply over half of all "innovations" introduced into the U.S. marketplace each year. In particular, of all businesses that produce 15 or more patents during the most recent four-year period, start-ups and new ventures produce 16 times more patents per employee than large firms.[6]

Not surprisingly, history is repeating itself with increasing rapidity in the age of high-tech communication and social media. For example, much of today's most innovative software is being written at relatively new start-up companies. Yahoo! and Netscape (now distant memories) brought the Internet into the average U.S. living room, and online companies such as Amazon, eBay, and Google have used it to redefine our shopping habits. Instagram, Facebook, and Twitter have changed how we interact with one another.[7] Each of these firms started out as a small business.

Of course, not all successful new start-ups are leading-edge dot-com enterprises. Take Sacha White, for example. He moved to Oregon a few years ago and got a job as a bicycle messenger. He began to tinker with his bike, and eventually built himself a custom one from

"[Twitter's founders] created a new way for people to communicate publicly and instantaneously."

—Fred Wilson, Venture Capitalist[8]

Many small businesses provide valuable services to larger businesses. This FreshDirect delivery van, for example, is bringing fresh fruit shipped in from citrus farms in other parts of the country to a regional wholesaler. The wholesaler, in turn, will then sell the fruit to grocery outlets like Kroger and Walmart.

scratch. Other riders took note and started wanting him to build bikes for them as well. White eventually started his own business called Vanilla Bicycles. He handcrafts each one and has a waiting list of five years. All told, he makes around 50 bikes per year; about 40 percent of these bikes are sold domestically, the rest to international customers. The custom bikes range in price from $5,000 to $12,000. Entrepreneurs have also achieved success in such diverse fields as specialized dog training, hand-crafted musical instruments, and finely balanced fly-fishing equipment.

5-2c Importance to Big Business

Most of the products made by big manufacturers are sold to consumers by small businesses. For example, the majority of dealerships selling Fords, Chevrolets, Toyotas, and Kias are independently owned and operated. Moreover, small businesses provide big businesses with many of the services, supplies, and raw materials they need. Likewise, Microsoft (once a start-up business) relies heavily on small businesses in the course of its routine business operations. For example, the software giant outsources much of its routine code-writing function to hundreds of sole proprietorships and other small firms. It also outsources much of its packaging, delivery, and distribution to smaller companies. Dell Computer (also a former new venture) uses this same strategy, buying most of the parts and components used in its computers from small suppliers around the world.

Manager's Checklist

☐ Managers should understand the complexities of assessing and comparing job creation and job elimination.

☐ You should also remember the key role that start-ups and new ventures play in both innovation and their contributions to big business.

5-3 STRATEGY FOR START-UPS AND NEW VENTURES

One of the most basic challenges facing a start-up operation is choosing a strategy. The three strategic challenges facing small firms are choosing an industry in which to compete, emphasizing distinctive competencies, and writing a business plan.[9]

5-3a Choosing an Industry

Not surprisingly, start-ups and new ventures are more common in some industries than in others. The major industry groups that include successful new ventures and small businesses are services, retailing, construction, financial and insurance, wholesaling, transportation, and manufacturing. Obviously, each group differs in its requirements for employees, money, materials, and machines. In general, the more resources an industry requires, the harder it is to start a business and the less likely that the industry is dominated by small firms. Remember, too, that *small* is a relative term: The criteria (number of employees and total annual sales)

"Entrepreneurship is certainly not the exclusive province of business. It can mushroom anywhere."

—Barron Harvey, Dean of Howard University's School of Business[10]

differ from industry to industry and are often meaningful only when compared with businesses that are truly large. Figure 5.2 shows the distribution of all U.S. businesses employing fewer than 20 people across industry groups.

Services   Primarily because they require few resources, service businesses are the fastest-growing segment of small-business enterprise. In addition, no other industry group offers a higher return on time invested for start-ups and new ventures. Finally, services appeal to the talent for innovation typified by many new enterprises. As Figure 5.2 shows, around 56.2 percent of all businesses with fewer than 20 employees are services.

Small-business services range from shoeshine parlors to car rental agencies, from marriage counseling to computer software, from accounting and management consulting to professional dog walking. In Dallas, for example, Jani-King has prospered by selling commercial cleaning services to local companies. In Virginia Beach, Virginia, Jackson Hewitt Tax Services has found a profitable niche in providing computerized tax preparation and electronic tax-filing services. Great Clips, Inc. is a fast-growing family-run chain of hair salons headquartered in Minneapolis. During the COVID-19 pandemic in 2020 some entrepreneurs started new businesses to assist with home-delivery of food and other necessities.

Retailing   A retail business sells directly to consumers products manufactured by other firms. There are hundreds of different kinds of retailers, ranging from wig shops and frozen yogurt stands to automobile dealerships and department stores. Usually, however, people who start small businesses favor specialty shops—for example, big-men's clothing or gourmet coffee—which let them focus limited resources on narrow market segments. Retailing accounts for around 13.69 percent of all businesses with fewer than 20 employees. John Mackey, for example, launched Whole Foods out of his own frustration at being unable to find a full range of natural

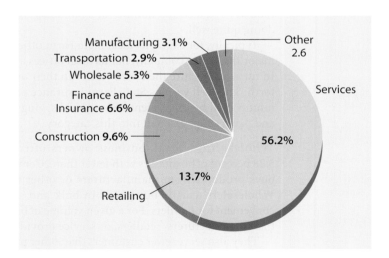

FIGURE 5.2

Small Businesses (Businesses with Fewer than 20 Employees) by Industry

Small businesses are especially strong in certain industries, such as retailing and services. On the other hand, there are relatively fewer small businesses in industries such as transportation and manufacturing. The differences are affected primarily by factors such as the investment costs necessary to enter markets in these industries. For example, starting a new airline would require the purchase of large passenger aircraft and airport gates, as well as hiring an expensive cadre of employees.

Source: https://www.census.gov/library/publications/2011/compendia/statab/131ed/labor-force-employment-earnings.html, accessed on March 20, 2020.

Retailing is a common industry for start-ups and new ventures. About 13.69 percent of all businesses with fewer than 20 employers compete in the retail industry. Many college towns have small apparel retailers.

foods at other stores. He soon found, however, that he had tapped a lucrative market and started an ambitious expansion program. Today, with more than 500 outlets scattered across the United States, Canada, and the United Kingdom, Whole Foods is the world's leader in natural and organic foods supermarkets.[11]

Construction   About 9.57 percent of businesses with fewer than 20 employees are involved in construction. Because many construction jobs are relatively small local projects, local construction firms are often ideally suited as contractors. Many such firms are begun by skilled craftspeople who start out working for someone else and subsequently decide to work for themselves. Common examples of small construction firms include home builders, wood finishers, roofers, painters, and plumbing, electrical, and roofing contractors.

For example, Marek Brothers Construction in College Station, Texas, was started by two brothers, Pat and Joe Marek. They originally worked for other contractors but then started their own partnership several years ago. Their only employee is a receptionist. They manage various construction projects, including new-home construction and remodeling, subcontracting out the actual work to other businesses or to individual craftspeople. Marek Brothers has an annual gross income of about $6.5 million.

Finance and Insurance   Financial and insurance businesses comprise about 6.6 percent of all firms with fewer than 20 employees. In most cases, these businesses are either affiliates of or sell products provided by larger national firms. Although the deregulation of the banking industry reduced the number of small local banks, other businesses in this sector are still doing quite well.

Typically, for example, local State Farm offices are small businesses. State Farm itself is a major insurance company, but its local offices are run by around 19,000 independent agents. In turn, agents hire their own staff, run their own offices as independent businesses, and so forth. They sell various State Farm insurance products and earn commissions from the premiums paid by their clients. Some local savings-and-loan operations, mortgage companies, and pawn shops also fall into this category.

Wholesaling   Small-business owners often do very well in wholesaling, too; about 5.28 percent of businesses with fewer than 20 employees are wholesalers. A wholesale business buys products from manufacturers or other producers and then sells them to retailers. Wholesalers usually buy goods in bulk and store them in quantity at locations that are convenient for retailers. For a given volume of business, therefore, they need fewer employees than manufacturers, retailers, or service providers.

They also serve fewer customers than other providers—usually those who repeatedly order large volumes of goods. Wholesalers in the grocery industry, for instance, buy packaged food in bulk from companies like Del Monte and Campbell and then sell it to both large grocery chains and smaller independent grocers. Luis Espinoza found a promising niche for Inca Quality Foods, a midwestern wholesaler that imports and distributes Latino foods for consumers from Mexico, the Caribbean, and Central America. Partnered with the large grocery-store chain Kroger, Inca became a profitable business and was eventually bought by a larger wholesaler.

Transportation   Some small firms—about 2.91 percent of all companies with fewer than 20 employees—do well in transportation and transportation-related businesses. Such firms include local taxi and limousine companies in smaller markets, charter airplane services, and tour operators. In addition, in many smaller markets, bus companies and regional airlines subcontract local equipment maintenance to small businesses.

Consider, for example, some of the transportation-related small businesses at the Steamboat Springs ski resort in Colorado. Most visitors fly to the town of Hayden, about 15 miles from Steamboat Springs. Although some visitors rent vehicles, many others use the services of Alpine Taxi, a small local operation, to transport them to their destinations in Steamboat Springs. While on vacation, they also rely on the local bus service, which is subcontracted by the town to another small business, to get to and from the ski slopes each day. Other small businesses offer van tours of the region, hot-air balloon rides, and helicopter lifts to remote areas for extreme skiers. Still others provide maintenance support at Hayden for the American and United aircraft that serve the area during ski season.

Manufacturing   More than any other industry, manufacturing lends itself more to big businesses than smaller businesses—and for good reason. Because of the investment normally required in equipment, energy, and raw materials, a good deal of money is usually needed to start a manufacturing business. Automobile manufacturing, for example, calls for millions of dollars of investment money and thousands of workers before the first automobile rolls off the assembly line. Obviously, such requirements shut out most individuals. Although Henry Ford began with $28,000, it would take a much larger sum today to create a new car company from scratch. Tesla, the newest automaker, raised over $100 million before it was able to start production.

Research has shown that manufacturing costs often fall as the number of units produced by an organization increases. This relationship between cost and production is called an *economy of scale*.[12] Small organizations usually cannot compete effectively on the basis of economies of scale. As depicted in Figure 5.3(a), organizations with higher levels of production have a major cost advantage over those with lower levels of production. Given the cost positions of small and large firms when there are strong economies of scale in manufacturing, it is not surprising that small manufacturing organizations generally do not do as well as large ones.

Manufacturing tends to be a more favorable industry for larger businesses rather than smaller ones. This is due in large part to large initial investment required to build and outfit a factory or other production facility. Still, some start-ups and new ventures manage to succeed in manufacturing.

Interestingly, when technology in an industry changes, it often shifts the economies-of-scale curve, thereby creating opportunities for smaller organizations. For example, steel manufacturing was historically dominated by a few large companies, which owned several huge facilities. With the development of mini-mill technology, however, extracting economies of scale at a much smaller level of production became possible. This type of shift is depicted in Figure 5.3b. Point A in this panel is the low-cost point with the original economies of scale. Point B is the low-cost point with the economies of scale brought on by the new technology. Notice that the number of units needed for low costs is considerably lower for the new technology. This has allowed the entry of many smaller firms into the steel industry. Such entry would not have been possible with the older technology.

This is not to say that there are no small-business owners who do well in manufacturing— about 3.05 percent of businesses with fewer than 20 employees are involved in some aspect of manufacturing. Indeed, it is not uncommon for small manufacturers to outperform big business in such innovation-driven industries as chemistry, electronics, toys, and computer software. Some small manufacturers prosper by serving as suppliers to large manufacturers. Our *Leading the Way* feature highlights a high-profile start-up manufacturer that, so far at least, seems to be doing very well.

5-3b Emphasizing Distinctive Competencies

As we defined in Chapter 7, an organization's distinctive competencies are the aspects of business that the firm performs better than its competitors. The distinctive competencies of

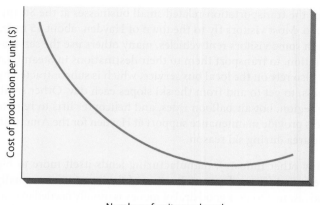

(a) Standard economies-of-scale curve

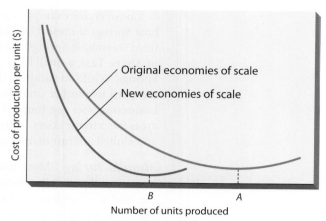

(b) Change in technology that shifts economies of scale and may make small-business manufacturing possible

FIGURE 5.3

Economies of Scale in Small-Business Organizations

Small businesses sometimes find it difficult to compete in manufacturing-related industries because of the economies of scale associated with plant, equipment, and technology. As shown in (a), firms that produce a large number of units (i.e., larger businesses) can do so at a lower per-unit cost. At the same time, however, new forms of technology occasionally cause the economies-of-scale curve to shift, as illustrated in (b). In this case, smaller firms may be able to compete more effectively with larger ones because of the drop in per-unit manufacturing cost.

small business usually fall into three areas: the ability to identify new niches in established markets, the ability to identify new markets, and the ability to move quickly to take advantage of new opportunities.

established market
A market in which several large firms compete according to relatively well-defined criteria

Identifying Niches in Established Markets   An **established market** is one in which several large firms compete according to relatively well-defined criteria. For example, for years the cellular telephone market was dominated by firms like Nokia and Motorola. These firms competed on the bases of size, design, and price. Meanwhile, so-called personal digital assistants like the BlackBerry prospered by providing remote email service. But then Apple introduced the iPhone and everything changed. The iPhone served as a telephone, an email device, a camera, and also provided web-browsing service.

Apple's approach to competition has actually long been to identify a new niche in an established market. The first Apple computers, for example, used parts from other computer manufacturers. It was user-friendliness that separated Apple from the rest of the pack. A

niche
A segment of a market not currently being exploited

niche is simply a segment of a market that is not currently being exploited. In general, start-ups and new ventures are better at discovering these niches than are larger organizations. Large organizations usually have so many resources committed to older, established business practices that they are less vigilant about new opportunities. Entrepreneurs can see these opportunities and move quickly to take advantage of them.[13]

Dave Gilboa and Neil Blumenthal founded Warby Parker, a business that sells prescription eyewear through the mail. The entrepreneurs determined that most consumers disliked the experience of going to an optical shop to try on glasses and then were irritated at the price of those glasses. So, Warby Parker offers lower-priced glasses with fashionable designs and a money-back guarantee. Astute marketing then allowed them to get a quick start with their niche business, selling over 50,000 pairs of glasses and generating profits after only a single year of operation.[14] Warby Parker continues to grow and is currently selling hundreds of thousands of pairs of glasses each year.

Identifying New Markets   Successful entrepreneurs also excel at discovering whole new markets. Discovery can happen in at least two ways. First, an entrepreneur can transfer a product or service that is well established in one geographic market to a second market. This is what Marcel Bich did with ballpoint pens, which occupied a well-established market in Europe before Bich introduced them to this country. Bich's company, Société Bic, eventually came to dominate the U.S. market for low-priced pens.

Second, entrepreneurs can sometimes create entire industries. Entrepreneurial inventions of the dry paper copying process and the semiconductor have created vast new industries. Not only have the first companies into these markets been very successful (Xerox and National Semiconductor, respectively), but their entrepreneurial activity has spawned the development

 **LEADING THE WAY**

Current Affairs in the Electric Vehicle Business

On June 12, 2014, Tesla Motors CEO Elon Musk informed the high-tech world that "Tesla will not initiate patent lawsuits against anyone who, in good faith, wants to use our technology." Musk's unexpected open-source initiative was no mere token of technological outreach: Tesla holds more than 375 valuable patents—with many more pending—on the technology behind mass-produced fully electric cars.

Even so, Musk says that his patent-sharing overture is "a modest thing." In order to reach the kind of goals that he's set for Tesla, Musk feels that he can't be satisfied with the usual pace of technological advancement, whether in his own company or among other organizations that share his goals. If there's a certain sense of urgency in Musk's gambit, it's because his ultimate goal isn't merely to sell more electric cars than anybody else. What he really wants to do is to disrupt the global automotive infrastructure in order to make the planet safe for automotive transportation. "I don't think people quite appreciate the gravity of what's going on [with regard to global warming]," says Musk. "We really need to do something. It would be shortsighted if we try to hold these things close to the vest."

As drastic as it may seem, Musk's strategy isn't unheard of in Silicon Valley, where firms that rely heavily on innovative technology must often be more concerned with developing a market for innovative ideas than with protecting them. Musk has done the math. There are about 2 billion cars on the road worldwide, with new-vehicle production approaching 100 million units per year. Unfortunately, zero-emission vehicles like Tesla's latest Model S account for less than 1 percent of those 100 million vehicles, and neither Musk nor anyone else can do much for the planet at that rate. At the same time, however, there are potential customers for electric cars—literally billions, in fact—and Tesla sees his biggest challenge as persuading a significant number of them to switch from gasoline-powered vehicles. He reasons that if competitors share Tesla's vested interest in electric-car technology, then they'll contribute not only to the technology but to the effort to develop a market for it. In short, Musk is convinced that "Tesla, other companies

making electric cars, and the world would all benefit from a common, rapidly evolving technological platform. . . .

"It's the velocity of innovation that matters," says Musk. "You want to be innovating so fast that you invalidate your prior patents, in terms of what really matters." Musk, for whom staying ahead of the competition and leading the way to the car of the future are the same thing, isn't worried about either the pace at which other companies can make use of Tesla technology or about Tesla's ability to pick up its own pace in improving in-house technology. Right now, Tesla has a comfortable lead in the all-important areas of battery-pack and power-management technology, including the circuitry in its large battery pack, the process by which it cools the batteries in the pack, and the software that regulates the power flow between battery pack and motor.

Tesla has already cut the cost of the battery back—a flat slab of densely packed lithium-ion cells tucked inconspicuously between the rear wheels of the Model S—from half the car's total cost to less than a fourth. It also gives the Model S a range of 285 miles between charges—about triple that of Nissan's Leaf and Chevy's Volt—and it's supported by a (currently modest) network of "supercharger" stations that deliver a 200-mile charge in 30 minutes, compared to several hours at ordinary stations. Finally, Tesla has built a massive $5 billion "Gigafactory" to manufacture both cars and batteries.

References: Ashlee Vance, "Why Elon Musk Just Opened Tesla's Patents to His Biggest Rivals," *BusinessWeek*, June 12, 2014, www.businessweek.com on March 5, 2020; William J. Watkins, Jr., "Rethinking Patent Enforcement: Tesla Did What?" *Forbes*, June 17, 2014, www.forbes.com on March 5, 2020; Elmira Mateva, "Tesla Motors Inc. Share Price Down, Musk Opens Patents Vault to Speed Up Electric Car Development," *Trading Pedia*, June 13, 2014, www.tradingpedia.com on March 5, 2020; Kevin Bullis, "How Tesla Is Driving Electric Car Innovation," *MIT Technology Review*, August 7, 2013, www.technologyreview.com on March 5, 2020; John Gertner, "Why Tesla Motors Is Betting on the Model S," *Fast Company*, March 19, 2012, www.fastcompany.com on March 5, 2020; Kyle Stock, "With Big Obstacles Ahead, Tesla Still Isn't Checking Its Rear View Mirror," *BusinessWeek*, May 8, 2014, www.businessweek.com on March 5, 2020.

of hundreds of other companies and hundreds of thousands of jobs. Again, because entrepreneurs are not encumbered with a history of doing business in a particular way, they are usually better at discovering new markets than are larger, more mature organizations.

first-mover advantage
Any advantage that comes to a firm because it exploits an opportunity before any other firm does

First-Mover Advantages   A **first-mover advantage** is any advantage that comes to a firm because it exploits an opportunity before any other firm does. Many of the "app" developers for smartphones exploit first-mover advantage. Sometimes large firms discover niches within existing markets or new markets at just about the same time as start-ups or new ventures, but they cannot move as quickly as these smaller companies to take advantage of these opportunities.

There are many reasons for this difference. For example, many large organizations make decisions slowly because each of their many layers of hierarchy has to approve an action before it can be implemented. Also, large organizations may sometimes put a great deal of their assets at risk when they take advantage of new opportunities. Every time Airbus decides to build a new model of a commercial jet, it is making a decision that could cost the company hundreds of millions of dollars. The size of the risk may make large organizations cautious. The dollar value of the assets at risk in a small organization, in contrast, is quite small. Managers may be willing to "bet the company" when the value of the company is only $100,000. They might be unwilling to "bet the company" when the value of the company is $1 billion.

5-3c Writing a Business Plan

business plan
A document that summarizes the business strategy and structure

Once an entrepreneur has chosen an industry to compete in and determined which distinctive competencies to emphasize, these choices are usually included in a document called a **business plan**. In a business plan the entrepreneur summarizes the business strategy and how that strategy is to be implemented. The very act of preparing a business plan forces prospective entrepreneurs to crystallize their thinking about what they must do to launch their business successfully and obliges them to develop their business on paper before investing time and money in it. The idea of a business plan is not new. What is new is the growing use of specialized business plans by entrepreneurs, mostly because creditors and investors demand them for use in deciding whether to help finance a small business.[15]

The plan should describe the match between the entrepreneur's abilities and the requirements for producing and marketing a particular product or service. It should define strategies for production and marketing, legal aspects and organization, and accounting and finance. In particular, it should answer three questions: (1) What are the entrepreneur's goals and objectives? (2) What strategies will the entrepreneur use to obtain these goals and objectives? and (3) How will the entrepreneur implement these strategies?

Business plans should also account for the sequential nature of much strategic decision making in start-ups and new ventures. For example, entrepreneurs cannot forecast sales revenues without first researching markets. The sales forecast itself is one of the most important elements in the business plan. Without such forecasts, it is all but impossible to estimate intelligently the size of a plant, store, or office or to determine how much inventory to carry or how many employees to hire.

Another important component of the overall business plan is financial planning, which translates all other activities into dollars. Generally, the financial plan is made up of a cash budget, an income statement, balance sheets, and a breakeven chart. The most important of these statements is the cash budget because it tells entrepreneurs how much money they need before they open for business and how much money they need to keep the business operating.

California-based Gold's Gym has enjoyed considerable success in international markets, including Russia, Australia, Spain, and Japan.

Jerome LABOUYRIE/Shutterstock.com

5-3d Entrepreneurship and International Markets

Finally, although many people associate international management with big business, many smaller companies are also finding expansion and growth opportunities in foreign countries. For example, California-based Gold's Gym has expanded into other countries and has been especially successful in Russia, Australia, Japan, and Spain. And Markel Corporation, a small Philadelphia-based firm that manufactures tubing and insulated wiring, derives around 40 percent of its annual revenues (currently around $78 million) from international sales. Although such ventures are accompanied by considerable risks, they also give entrepreneurs new opportunities and can be a real catalyst for success.

 **Manager's Checklist**

☐ Would-be entrepreneurs need to carefully assess industries and be fully aware of distinctive competencies when launching a start-up or new venture.

☐ Entrepreneurs should also not underestimate the importance of a well-constructed business plan.

5-4 STRUCTURE OF START-UPS AND NEW VENTURES

With a strategy in place and a business plan in hand, the entrepreneur can then proceed to devise a structure that turns the vision of the business plan into a reality. Many of the same concerns in structuring any business, which are described in the next five chapters of this book, are also relevant to small businesses. For example, entrepreneurs need to consider organization design and develop job descriptions, organization charts, and management control systems.

Getting into business today is easier and faster than ever before, there are many more potential opportunities than at any other time in history, and the ability to gather and assimilate information is at an all-time high. Even so, would-be entrepreneurs must still make the right decisions when they start. They must decide, for example, precisely how to get into business. Should they buy an existing business or build from the ground up? In addition, would-be entrepreneurs must find appropriate sources of financing and decide when and how to seek the advice of experts.

5-4a Starting the New Business

The first step in launching a start-up or new venture is the individual's commitment to becoming a business owner. Next comes choosing the goods or services to be offered—a process that means investigating one's chosen industry and market. Making this choice also requires would-be entrepreneurs to assess not only industry trends but also their own skills. Like the managers of existing businesses, new business owners must also be sure that they understand the true nature of the enterprise in which they are engaged.

Buying an Existing Business   After choosing a product and making sure that the choice fits their own skills and interests, entrepreneurs must decide whether to buy an existing business or to start from scratch. Consultants often recommend the first approach. Quite simply, the odds are better: If successful, an existing business has already proved its ability to draw customers at a profit. It has also established working relationships with lenders, suppliers, and the community. Moreover, the track record of an existing business gives potential buyers a much clearer picture of what to expect than any estimate of a new business's prospects. Around 30 percent of the new businesses started each year are bought from someone else. The McDonald's empire, for example, was started when Ray

"It never really feels like, 'I have arrived,' or we are where we want to be. I am never surprised. I am happy, I am pleased, but we have so much to do."
—Susan Peterson, Founder of Herbalife[16]

Kroc bought an existing hamburger business and then turned it into a global phenomenon. Likewise, Starbucks was a struggling mail-order business when Howard Schultz bought it and turned his attention to retail expansion.

Starting from Scratch   Some people, however, prefer the satisfaction that comes from planting an idea, nurturing it, and making it grow into a strong and sturdy business. There are also practical reasons to start a business from scratch. A new business does not suffer the ill effects of a prior owner's errors. The start-up owner is also free to choose lenders, equipment, inventories, locations, suppliers, and workers, unbound by a predecessor's commitments and policies. Between 60 and 70 percent of the start-ups and new ventures launched each year are started from scratch.

Not surprisingly, though, the risks of starting a business from scratch are greater than those of buying an existing firm. Founders of start-ups and new ventures can only make predictions and projections about their prospects. Success or failure thus depends heavily on identifying a genuine business opportunity—a product for which many customers will pay well but which is currently unavailable to them. To find openings, entrepreneurs must study markets and answer the following questions: (1) Who are my customers? (2) Where are they? (3) At what price will they buy my product? (4) In what quantities will they buy? (5) Who are my competitors? and (6) How will my product differ from those of my competitors?

Finding answers to these questions is a difficult task even for large, well-established firms. But where can the new business owner get the necessary information? Other sources of assistance are discussed later in this chapter, but we briefly describe three of the most accessible here. For example, the best way to gain knowledge about a market is to work in it before going into business in it. If you once worked in a bookstore and now plan to open one of your own, you probably already have some idea about the kinds of books people request and buy. Second, a quick online scan will reveal many potential competitors, as will advertisements in trade journals. Personal visits to these establishments and websites can give you insights into their strengths and weaknesses. And, third, studying magazines, books, and websites aimed specifically at start-ups and new ventures can also be of help, as can hiring professionals to survey the market for you.

5-4b Financing the New Business

Although the choice of how to start is obviously important, it is meaningless unless a new business owner can obtain the money to set up shop. Among the more common sources for funding are family and friends, personal savings, banks and similar lending institutions, investors, and government agencies. Lending institutions are more likely to help finance the purchase of an existing business than a new business because the risks are better understood. Individuals launching a start-up or new venture are more likely to have to rely on their personal resources.

Personal Resources   According to research by the National Federation of Independent Business, an owner's personal resources, not loans, are the most important source of money. Including money borrowed from friends and relatives, personal resources account for over two-thirds of all money invested in start-ups and new ventures and one-half of that invested in the purchase of existing businesses. Hamdi Ulukaya used personal savings and profits from his cheese business to launch Chobani; John Mackey started Whole Foods with a $10,000

Fred Smith, founder of FedEx, saw a need for efficient and fast delivery of goods. He used a $4 million inheritance to realize his entrepreneurial dream.

Northfoto/Shutterstock.com

loan from his father; Fred Smith used $4 million he had inherited from his father to launch FedEx. And Rebecca Boenigk started Neutral Posture, an ergonomic chair company, with personal savings and loans from several family members.

Strategic Alliances   Strategic alliances are also becoming a popular method for financing business growth. For instance, commercial real estate developers occasionally develop alliances with regional restaurant chains. The restaurant chain may commit to opening new dining establishments in different new developments. The developer benefits from this by having some early tenants and businesses that attract visitors. In return, the developer may give the restaurants priority preferences for locations, assistance with construction costs, and lower rent. Midway, a Texas developer, has this sort of arrangement with three different restaurant chains, including Zoes Kitchen, Grub Burger, and Hopdoddy.

Traditional Lenders   Although banks, independent investors, and government loans all provide much smaller portions of start-up funds than the personal resources of owners, they are important in many cases. Getting money from these sources, however, requires some extra effort. Banks and private investors usually want to see and evaluate formal business plans—detailed outlines of proposed businesses and markets, owners' backgrounds, and other sources of funding. Government loans have strict eligibility guidelines.

venture capital company
A group of small investors seeking to make profits on companies with rapid growth potential

Venture Capital Companies   Venture capital companies are groups of investors seeking to make profits on companies with rapid growth potential. Most of these firms do not lend money: They invest it, supplying capital in return for stock. The venture capital company may also demand a representative on the board of directors. In some cases, managers may even need approval from the venture capital company before making major decisions. Of all venture capital currently committed in the United States, around 25 percent comes from pure venture capital firms. In 2018 venture capital firms invested $130.9 billion in new start-ups in the United States.[17]

As noted earlier, Fred Smith used his inheritance to launch FedEx. Once he got his business plan developed and started service, though, he needed an infusion of substantial additional capital. All told, he raised about $80 million in venture capital to buy his first small fleet of planes. Venture capital was also important in the launch of both Facebook and Twitter.

Small-Business Investment Companies   Taking a more balanced approach in their choices than venture capital companies, *small-business investment companies (SBICs)* seek profits by investing in companies with potential for rapid growth. Created by the Small Business Investment Act of 1958, SBICs are federally licensed to borrow money from the SBA and to invest it in or lend it to start-ups and new ventures. They are themselves investments for their shareholders. Past beneficiaries of SBIC capital include Apple, Intel, and FedEx. In addition, the government has recently begun to sponsor *minority enterprise small-business investment companies (MESBICs)* under a separate program. As the name suggests, MESBICs specialize in financing businesses that are owned and operated by minorities.

SBA Financial Programs   Since its founding in 1953, the SBA has offered more than 20 financing programs to small businesses (both new and ongoing) that meet certain standards of size and independence. Eligible firms must also be unable to get private financing at reasonable terms. Because of these and other restrictions, SBA loans have never been a major source of small-business financing. In addition, budget cutbacks at the SBA have reduced the number of firms benefiting from loans. Nevertheless, several SBA programs currently offer funds to qualified applicants.

For example, under the SBA's guaranteed loans program, small businesses can borrow from commercial lenders. The SBA guarantees to repay 75–85 percent of the loan amount, not to exceed $5 million. Under a related program, small companies engaged in international trade can also borrow up to $5 million. Such loans may be made for as long as 15 years for machinery and equipment and up to 25 years for real estate. Most SBA lending activity flows through this program.

Sometimes, however, both desired bank and SBA-guaranteed loans are unavailable (perhaps because the business cannot meet stringent requirements). In such cases, the SBA may help finance the entrepreneur through its immediate participation loan program. Under this arrangement, the SBA and the bank each puts up a share of the money, with the SBA's share not to exceed $150,000. Under the local development companies (LDCs) program, the SBA works with a corporation (either for-profit or nonprofit) founded by local citizens who want to boost the local economy. The SBA can lend up to $500,000 for each small business to be helped by an LDC.

Crowdfunding   In the last few years new sources of funding for start-ups and new ventures have also emerged. The most common ones are a form of crowdfunding. This is done through several different online services. Essentially, entrepreneurs post details of their ideas for a start-up or new venture, along with other key information. Would-be investors then peruse the ideas that are posted and decide if they want to help fund the start-up or new venture. Some services limit investments to ownership stakes (i.e., invest a certain number of dollars for a certain percentage of ownership in the business). Other services focus more on loans with agreed-upon repayment terms.

5-4c **Sources of Management Advice**

Financing is not the only area in which start-ups and new ventures may need help. Until World War II, for example, the business world involved few regulations, few taxes, few records, few big competitors, and no computers. Since then, simplicity has given way to complexity. Today, few entrepreneurs are equipped with all the business skills they need to survive. New business owners can no longer be their own troubleshooters, lawyers, bookkeepers, financiers, and tax experts. For these jobs, they rely on professional help. To survive and grow, however, start-ups and new ventures may also need advice about management. This advice is usually available from four sources: advisory boards, management consultants, the SBA, and the process of networking.

Advisory Boards   All companies, even those that do not legally need boards of directors, can benefit from the problem-solving abilities of advisory boards. Thus, some start-ups and new ventures create boards to provide advice and assistance. For example, an advisory board might help an entrepreneur determine the best way to finance a plant expansion or to start selling and exporting products to foreign markets.

Management Consultants   Opinions vary widely about the value of management consultants—experts who charge fees to help managers solve problems. They often specialize in one area, such as international business, start-ups and new ventures, ongoing small businesses, or manufacturing. Thus, they can bring an objective and trained outlook to problems and provide logical recommendations. They can be quite expensive, however, as some consultants charge $3,000 or more for a day of assistance.

Like other professionals, consultants should be chosen with care. They can be found through major corporations that have used their services and can provide references and reports on their work. Not surprisingly, they are most effective when the client helps (e.g., by providing schedules and written proposals for work to be done).

The Small Business Administration   Even more important than its financing role is the SBA's role in helping new business owners improve their management skills. It is easy for entrepreneurs to spend money; SBA programs are designed to show them how to spend it wisely. The SBA offers small businesses a variety of advisory programs at little or no cost.

An entrepreneur who needs help in starting a new business can get it free through the Service Corps of Retired Executives (SCORE). All SCORE members are retired executives, and all are volunteers. Under this program, the SBA tries to match the expert to the need. For example,

Thomas M. Sullivan

Bloomberg/Getty Images

The Small Business Administration plays an important role in the success of many new businesses. This speaker, for example, is sharing advice and information with small business owners at an SBA-sponsored conference.

if a new business owner needs help putting together a marketing plan, the SBA will link the business owner with a SCORE counselor with marketing expertise. SCORE currently includes more than 13,000 counselors.[18]

The talents and skills of students and instructors at colleges and universities are fundamental to the Small Business Institute. Under the guidance of seasoned professors of business administration, students seeking advanced degrees work closely with small-business owners to help solve specific problems, such as sagging sales or rising costs. Students earn credit toward their degree, with their grades depending on how well they handle a client's problems. Several hundred colleges and universities counsel thousands of small-business owners through this program every year.

Finally, another SBA management counseling project is its Small Business Development Center (SBDC) program. SBDCs are designed to consolidate information from various disciplines and institutions, including technical and professional schools. Then they make this knowledge available to new and existing small businesses. Currently, universities in 36 states take part in the program.

Networking   More and more, entrepreneurs and new business owners are discovering the value of networking—meeting regularly with one another to discuss common problems and opportunities and, perhaps most important, to pool resources. Businesspeople have long joined organizations such as the local chamber of commerce and the National Federation of Independent Businesses to make such contacts.

Today, organizations are springing up all over the United States to facilitate small-business networking. One such organization, the Council of Smaller Enterprises of Cleveland, boasts a total membership of nearly 14,000 small-business owners, the largest number in the country. This organization offers its members not only networking possibilities but also educational programs and services tailored to their needs. In a typical year, its 85 educational programs draw more than 8,500 small-business owners.

In particular, women and minorities have found networking to be an effective problem-solving tool. The National Association of Women Business Owners (NAWBO), for example, provides a variety of networking forums. The NAWBO also has chapters in most major cities, where its members can meet regularly. Increasingly, women are relying more on other women to help locate venture capital, establish relationships with customers, and provide such essential services as accounting and legal advice. According to Patty Abramson of the Women's Growth Capital Fund, all of these tasks have traditionally been harder for women because, until now, they have never had friends in the right places. "I wouldn't say this is about discrimination," adds Abramson. "It's about not having the relationships, and business is about relationships."

franchising agreement
A contract between an entrepreneur (the franchisee) and a parent company (the franchiser); the entrepreneur pays the parent company for the use of its trademarks, products, formulas, and business plans

5-4d Franchising

The next time you drive or walk around town, be on the alert for a McDonald's, Taco Bell, Subway, Denny's, or KFC restaurant; a 7-Eleven or Circle K convenience store; a RE/MAX or Coldwell Banker real-estate office; a Holiday Inn or Ramada Inn motel; a Sylvan Learning Center or Mathnasium educational center; an Express Oil Change or Precision Auto Wash service center; or a Supercuts hair salon. What do these businesses have in common? In most cases, they are franchised operations, operating under licenses issued by parent companies to local entrepreneurs who own and manage them.

As many would-be business owners have discovered, **franchising agreements** are a common and accessible doorway to entrepreneurship.

Networking is playing an increasingly important role in new ventures and start-ups. These people, for example, either own a new business or are in the process of launching one. This networking event will help them make important contacts and share advice.

Hero Images/Getty Images

A franchise is an arrangement that permits the *franchisee* (buyer) to sell the product of the *franchiser* (seller, or parent company). Franchisees can thus benefit from the selling corporation's experience and expertise. They can also consult the franchiser for managerial and financial help.[19]

For example, the franchiser may supply financing. It may pick the store location, negotiate the lease, design the store, and purchase necessary equipment. It may train the first set of employees and managers and provide standardized policies and procedures. Once the business is open, the franchiser may offer franchisees savings by allowing them to purchase from a central location. Marketing strategy (especially advertising) may also be handled by the franchiser. Finally, franchisees may benefit from continued management counseling. In short, franchisees receive—that is, invest in—not only their own ready-made business but also expert help in running it.

Franchises offer many advantages to both sellers and buyers. For example, franchisers benefit from the ability to grow rapidly by using the investment money provided by franchisees. This strategy has enabled giant franchisers such as McDonald's and Subway to mushroom into billion-dollar concerns in a brief time.

For the franchisee, the arrangement combines the incentive of owning a business with the advantage of access to big-business management skills. Unlike the person who starts from scratch, the franchisee does not have to build a business step by step. Instead, the business is established virtually overnight. Moreover, because each franchise outlet is probably a carbon copy of every other outlet, the chances of failure are reduced. McDonald's, for example, is a model of consistency—Big Macs taste the same everywhere.

Of course, owning a franchise also involves certain disadvantages. Perhaps the most significant is the start-up cost. Franchise prices vary widely. Fantastic Sams hair salon franchise costs are $185,000. Extremely profitable or hard-to-get franchises are much more expensive, though. A McDonald's franchise only costs $45,000, but the franchisee must have $750,000 in liquid assets and also cover the costs of construction and outfitting the restaurant.

BEYOND TRADITIONAL BUSINESS

Taxi Dancing around the Question of Regulation

One day, Larry Downes, project director at the Georgetown University Center for Business and Public Policy, had to catch a cab from a San Francisco train station:

> As the law requires, I could only choose the first cab in line, which was filthy. The driver begrudgingly popped the trunk, which was full of garbage, so I had to stow my own suitcase inside. Throughout the ride, he never stopped talking on a headset connected to his cell phone, blasting the radio in the back seat so I couldn't overhear his private conversation.
>
> The driver had no idea where he was going . . . and asked me repeatedly to tell him how to get there—directions he ignored, nearly missing every turn. He said nothing when I paid him and sped off before I'd made it to the curb.

According to Downes, the incident is typical of "the bizarro world of licensed taxicabs and limousines." What the industry needed, said Downes, coauthor of *Big Bang Disruption: Strategy in the Age of Devastating Innovation*, was "the sudden arrival of disruptive technologies that could vastly improve quality, efficiency, and profitability while also introducing new competitors."

As Downes well knew, the taxi and limousine industry was already experiencing *disruption*—the displacement of an existing market, industry, or technology by something new and more efficient. It had arrived in 2009 in the form of Uber, a San Francisco–based ridesharing service that matches people who need rides with privately owned vehicles that can take them where they want to go. It's sort of the eBay of taxi services, and Benchmark, a venture capitalist firm that invested in both start-ups, points out that Uber has grown even faster than eBay did. By the end of 2019, Uber, with operations in 785 metropolitan areas worldwide, was valued at $120 billion. "Uber is probably the fastest-growing company that we've ever had," says Benchmark partner Bill Gurley.

How does Uber go about the business of disruption? The so-called "e-hail" process begins when you create an account by logging in with your credit card information.

(Continued)

BEYOND TRADITIONAL BUSINESS (CONTINUED)

Then you can download an app to your smartphone. When you need a ride, you fire up your app, and between your phone's GPS and Uber's ultra-sophisticated traffic-modeling technology, you'll find out how long it will be until the nearest car can reach you (usually within 10 minutes). If you're satisfied with the ETA, you push a button and wait (from whatever comfy location you happen to be in) for a text message telling you when your ride is waiting. Then you get in and go. Billing (including tip) is automatic.

"It's an elegant use of technology to hack the legal system," says journalist Matthew Yglesias. "Through the magic of computer power, a sedan becomes a cab without changing its legal status." Yet Yglesias also admits that Uber "arguably shouldn't exist at all. It's [nothing more] than a solution to a ridiculous problem created by [taxi] cartels and overregulation." Downes agrees: "There's nothing especially novel or proprietary about the platform Uber has built—at least nothing that couldn't or shouldn't have already been implemented by existing taxi and limo services." Downes, however, is not surprised by the way that the industry has reacted to the advent of Uber: "Instead of responding to a new kind of virtual competitor with better products and services," charges Downes, "highly regulated taxi and limousine companies have instead gone the route of trying to ban Uber."

Uber hasn't always been welcomed. For example, it was initially forbidden from operating in some cities, including Miami, Las Vegas, and Brussels. In most cities, however, Uber has successfully battled regulatory resistance. For instance, a transportation bill in Washington, D.C., proposed a floor under car-service prices that would have made Uber five times more expensive than a taxi ride. Uber reached out to its clientele, who responded with 50,000 emails and 37,000 tweets to local policymakers. Before the year was out, the proposed bill had been turned on its head: When finally passed, it had not only lost its minimum-price provisions, but also provided a legal framework for the concept of "digital dispatch" at the heart of Uber's business model. Uber riders, says co-founder Travis Kalanick, "are the most affluent, influential people in their cities. When we get to critical mass, it's impossible to shut us down."

Fortified by $50 million in venture capital, Uber may be reconciled to the short-term necessity of combating regulatory resistance, but that doesn't mean that executives are resigned to what Kalanick once called "corruption and cronyism and *regulatory capture*"—the process whereby regulators and regulated industries eventually develop a mutually vested interest in maintaining the regulatory system. In the taxi and limousine industry, regulation covers such factors as insurance, fare structure, vehicle condition, and background screening for drivers, and such regulations could interfere with the Uber business model.

The company's opponents, however, scoff at Uber's claim that it can't be regulated like a taxi or limo provider because it doesn't own any cars or directly employ any drivers. Kalanick also asserted that Uber hasn't introduced anything other than the software that enables its transactions, but opponents reply that there's a big difference between Uber and other innovative ventures in the tech-facilitated "sharing economy." "Uber," said Trevor Johnson of the San Francisco Cab Drivers Association, "may be the next Amazon, but Amazon doesn't have the same potential to leave a trail of bodies in the street."

Larry Downes agrees that such "public-interest goals" as safety can be served only by regulation. "Watch what happens," he wrote in early 2013, "the first time a shared-ride vehicle gets into a serious accident." He didn't have long to wait. On New Year's Eve, an Uber driver ran into a San Francisco family, killing 6-year-old Sofia Liu. Syed Muzafar was charged with vehicular manslaughter. "We have deactivated his Uber account," said a company statement, and when the family filed suit against the company for wrongful death, Uber defended itself by arguing that Muzafar "was not transporting a rider who requested transportation services through the Uber app. He was not en route to pick up a rider who requested transportation services through the Uber app. He was not receiving a request for transportation services through the Uber app."

A month earlier, an Uber driver had allegedly assaulted a passenger when they got into an argument. Although Uber claims a zero-tolerance policy on drug-related offenses, the driver had two felony convictions for selling drugs and was on probation for a charge of battery. He had, however, received good reviews from other passengers, and in challenging the ruling of the California Public Utilities Commission that it should be regulated as a taxi company, Uber had argued that its system of gathering customer feedback meant that it was self-regulating. Eventually, Uber came under so much criticism for these kinds of problems that it fired its CEO and hired Dara Khosrowshahi to come in and clean things up.

References: Larry Downes, "Lessons from Uber: Why Innovation and Regulation Don't Mix," *Forbes*, February 6, 2013, www.forbes.com on March 5, 2020; Matthew Yglesias, "When Is a Taxi Not a Taxi?" *Slate*, December 15, 2011, www.slate.com, on March 5, 2020; Romain Dillet, "Benchmark's Bill Gurley: 'Uber Is Growing Faster Than eBay Did,'" *TechCrunch*, April 29, 2013, http://techcrunch.com on October 29, 2014; Katie Lobosco, "Uber Cheaper Than New York City Taxi—For Now," *CNN*, July 7, 2014, http://money.cnn.com on March 5, 2020; L. Gordon Crovitz, "Uber Shocks the Regulators," *Wall Street Journal*, June 15, 2014, http://wsj.com on March 5, 2020; Christine Lagorio-Chafkin, "Resistance Is Futile," *Inc.*, July/August 2013, www.inc.com on March 5, 2020.

Franchisees may also have continued obligations to contribute percentages of sales to the parent corporation. McDonald's franchisees, for example, must pay the parent company 5 percent of their annual revenue and buy most of their ingredients (buns, meat patties, etc.) from McDonald's or McDonald'sowned businesses.

Buying a franchise also entails less-tangible costs. For one thing, the small-business owner sacrifices some independence. A McDonald's franchisee cannot change the way its hamburgers or milkshakes are made. Nor can franchisees create an individual identity in their community; for all practical purposes, the McDonald's owner is anonymous. In addition, many franchise agreements are difficult to terminate.

Finally, although franchises minimize risks, they do not guarantee success. Many franchisees have seen their investments—and their dreams—disappear because of poor location, rising costs, or lack of continued franchiser commitment. Moreover, figures on failure rates are artificially low because they do not include failing franchisees bought out by their franchising parent companies. An additional risk is that the chain itself could collapse. In any given year, dozens—sometimes hundreds—of franchisers close shop or stop selling franchises.

Manager's Checklist

☐ Would-be new business owners need a clear understanding of the pros and cons of starting a new business versus buying an existing one.

☐ Entrepreneurs need a clear financial plan in order to finance their start-up or new venture in the most effective manner possible. What are the pros and cons of starting a new business from scratch versus buying an existing business?

☐ Regardless of the size of their enterprise, managers should be aware of the various sources to which they may turn for advice and information.

5-5 THE PERFORMANCE OF START-UPS AND NEW VENTURES

The formulation and implementation of an effective strategy plays a major role in determining the overall performance of a start-up or new venture. This section examines how start-ups and new ventures evolve over time and the attributes of these firms that enhance their chances of success. For every Henry Ford, Elon Musk, Walt Disney, Mary Kay Ash, Steve Jobs, or Bill Gates—people who transformed fledgling small businesses into major corporations—there are many small-business owners and entrepreneurs who fail.

Exact numbers of start-ups and failures are surprisingly difficult to determine, however. For instance, a business may shut down because it is out of money (a failure) or simply because the owner decides to do something else; or the business may be sold to another business and cease to exist as an independent entity. Likewise, an ongoing sole proprietorship that becomes a partnership or corporation is not really a new business but may be counted as such in some statistics; similarly, a large corporation might launch a new enterprise as a new wholly owned but separately incorporated enterprise.

In general, though, experts believe that new business start-ups generally run between 400,000 and 450,000 per year and that business failures generally run between 425,000 and 475,000 per year. In this section, we look first at a few key trends in small-business start-ups. Then we examine some of the main reasons for success and failure in small-business undertakings.

> "I consider your rejection a lucky charm, because everything that ever happened in my life came on the heels of failure."
> —Barbara Corcoran, *Shark Tank* Investor/Real Estate Mogul/Serial Entrepreneur[20]

5-5a Trends in Start-Ups and New Ventures

Thousands of new businesses are started in the United States every year. Several factors account for this trend, and in this section we focus on four of them.

Emergence of E-Commerce   Clearly, one of the most significant recent trends in start-ups and new ventures is the rapid emergence of online electronic commerce. Because online platforms have provided fundamentally new ways of doing business, savvy entrepreneurs have been able to create and expand new businesses faster and more easily than ever before. Such leading-edge firms as Google, Amazon, eBay, and Facebook, for example, owe their very existence to the internet. At the same time, however, many would-be internet entrepreneurs have also gone under. Still, in 2019, online retail sales approached $600 billion.[21]

Crossovers from Big Business   It is interesting to note that increasing numbers of businesses are being started by people who have opted to leave big corporations and put their experience and know-how to work for themselves. In some cases, these individuals see great new ideas they want to develop. Often, they get burned out working for a big corporation. Sometimes they have lost their jobs, only to discover that working for themselves was a better idea anyway.

Cisco Systems founder and former long-time CEO John Chambers is acknowledged as one of the best entrepreneurs around. But he spent several years working first at IBM and then at Wang Laboratories before he set out on his own. Under his leadership, Cisco became one of the most important technology companies in the world. In a more unusual case, Gilman Louie left an executive position at Hasbro toy company's online group to help lead a CIA-backed venture capital firm called In-Q-Tel (IQT). The firm's mission is to help nurture high-tech companies making products of interest to the nation's intelligence community.

Opportunities for Minorities and Women   In addition to big-business expatriates, minorities and women are starting more small businesses. For example, the number of African American–owned businesses totals about 2.6 million, an increase of 34.5 percent since 2007. These businesses account for around 9.3 percent of all U.S. businesses, generate $176.5 billion in revenue, and employ almost 1 million people. Latino-owned businesses have grown at a rate of 41.4 percent and now number about 4.4 million. Other ethnic groups are also making their presence felt among U.S. business owners. Business ownership among Asians and Pacific Islanders has increased 30.8 percent, to over 1.9 million. Although the number of businesses owned by American Indians and Alaska Natives is still somewhat small, at slightly over 247,000, the total nevertheless represents a five-year increase of 17.6 percent.[22]

The number of women entrepreneurs is also growing rapidly. There are now around 11.6 million businesses owned by women—about 29 percent of all businesses in the United States and an increase of 29.7 percent since 2010. Combined, they generate around $1.2 trillion in revenue a year and employ 8.5 million people. Anne Beiler bought a small Amish-owned pretzel stand to support her family when her husband decided to become a no-fee marriage counselor. She worked long hours and continued to tinker with both her menu and pretzel recipes until things began to take off. She grew her business into a national chain called Auntie Anne's Soft Pretzels before selling to another company. Beatrice Dixon's multimillion-dollar company, Honey Pot, manufactures and distributes affordable, plant-based feminine care products, and she is one of the first 40 women of color to raise over $1 million in venture capital.

"Attitudes about women in the workplace, period, have changed, let alone women running their own businesses."
—Erin Fuller, Former Director of the National Association of Women Business Owners[23]

Better Survival Rates   Finally, more people are encouraged to test their skills as entrepreneurs because the failure rate among small businesses has been declining in recent years. About half of start-ups and new ventures survive at least five years today. About a third survive at least 10 years, and over a quarter are still in operation after 15 years. For reasons discussed in the next section, start-ups and new ventures do suffer a higher mortality rate than larger concerns. Even so, however, survival rates are better now than at any time in the last 50 years.

5-5b Reasons for Failure

Why do some businesses succeed and others fail? Although no set pattern has been established, four general factors contribute to new business failure. The first factor is managerial incompetence or inexperience. Some would-be entrepreneurs assume that they can succeed through common sense, overestimate their own managerial acumen, or think that hard work alone will lead to success. But if managers do not know how to make basic business decisions or understand the basic concepts and principles of management, they are unlikely to be successful in the long run.

Second, neglect can also contribute to failure. Some entrepreneurs try either to launch their ventures in their spare time or to devote only a limited amount of time to a new business. But starting a new business requires an overwhelming time commitment. Entrepreneurs who are not willing to put in the time and effort that a business requires are unlikely to survive.

Third, weak control systems can lead to serious problems. Effective control systems are needed to keep a business on track and to help alert entrepreneurs to potential trouble. If control systems do not signal impending problems, managers may be in serious trouble before more visible difficulties alert them.

Finally, insufficient capital can contribute to new business failure. Some entrepreneurs are overly optimistic about how soon they will start earning profits. In most cases, however, it takes months or years before a business is likely to start turning a profit. Amazon.com, for example, has only recently started to generate profits. Most experts say that a new business should have enough capital to operate for at least six months without earning a profit; some recommend enough to last a year.[24] Many small business owners struggled or closed altogether in 2020 because they lacked sufficient capital to survive the effects of the COVID-19 virus pandemic.

> **"Like many small businesses . . . across the country, we did not anticipate this sort of shutdown. Most small businesses operate on a month or two of cash and beyond that, we'll really struggle."**
>
> —Jonathan Goldstein, Small Business Owner[25]

5-5c Reasons for Success

Similarly, four basic factors are typically cited to explain new business success. The first factor is hard work, drive, and dedication. New business owners must be committed to succeeding and be willing to put in the time and effort to make it happen. Having positive feelings and a good outlook on life may also play an important role.[26] Kendra Scott started making unique jewelry with $500 in her pocket. Hard work, long hours, drive, and an innate sense of optimism kept her going. Today her jewelry is sold in Nordstrom, Bloomingdales, Neiman-Marcus, and many small fashion boutiques.

Second, careful analysis of market conditions can help new business owners assess the probable reception of their products in the marketplace. This will provide insights about market demand for proposed products and services. Whereas attempts to expand local restaurants specializing in baked potatoes, muffins, and gelato have been largely unsuccessful, hamburger and pizza chains continue to have an easier time expanding into new markets. When Reed Hastings was planning to launch Netflix, he gambled on certain market conditions. For example, VHS tapes were still the most common form of video rentals, but their size and weight would have made mail delivery and return cost-prohibitive. Hastings saw the market transitioning to DVDs, a format much more amenable to mail service.

Third, managerial competence also contributes to success. Successful new business owners may acquire competence through training or experience or by using the expertise of others. Few successful entrepreneurs succeed alone or straight out of college. Most spend time working in successful companies or partner with others in order to bring more expertise to a new business.

Finally, luck also plays a role in the success of some firms. For example, after Alan McKim started Clean Harbors, an environmental cleanup firm based in New England, he struggled to keep his business afloat. Then the U.S. government committed $1.6 billion to toxic waste cleanup—McKim's specialty. He was soon able to get several large government contracts and put his business on solid financial footing. Had the government fund not been created at just the right time, McKim may well have failed.[27]

Manager's Checklist

☐ Any would-be entrepreneur needs to understand important trends that may affect his or her business.

☐ Managers of start-ups and new ventures should also candidly assess the factors that may lead to failure or success for their business.

SUMMARY OF LEARNING OUTCOMES AND KEY POINTS

5-1. Discuss the meaning of entrepreneurship, start-ups, and new ventures.

- Entrepreneurship is the process of planning, organizing, operating, and assuming the risk of a business venture.

- An entrepreneur is someone who engages in entrepreneurship. In general, entrepreneurs start new businesses.

5-2. Describe the role of entrepreneurships, start-ups, and new ventures in society.

- Start-ups and new ventures are an important source of innovation.

- Start-ups and new ventures create many jobs.

- Start-ups and new ventures contribute to the success of large businesses.

5-3. Identify the major issues involved in choosing strategies for small businesses and the role of international management in start-ups and new ventures.

- In choosing strategies, entrepreneurs have to consider the characteristics of the industry in which they are going to conduct business.

- Start-ups and new ventures generally have several distinctive competencies that they should exploit in choosing their strategy. Start-ups and new ventures are usually skilled at identifying niches in established markets, identifying new markets, and acting quickly to obtain first-mover advantages.

- Start-ups and new ventures are usually not skilled at exploiting economies of scale.

- Once an entrepreneur has chosen a strategy, the strategy is normally written down in a business plan. Writing a business plan forces an entrepreneur to plan thoroughly and to anticipate problems that might occur.

5-4. Discuss the structural challenges unique to start-ups and new ventures.

- With a strategy and business plan in place, entrepreneurs must choose a structure to implement them. All of the structural issues summarized in the next five chapters of this book are relevant to the entrepreneur.

- In addition, the entrepreneur has some unique structural choices to make. For example, the entrepreneur can buy an existing business or start a new one.

- In determining financial structure, an entrepreneur has to decide how much personal capital to invest in an organization, how much bank and government support to obtain, and whether to encourage venture capital firms to invest.

- Entrepreneurs can also rely on various sources of advice.

5-5. Summarize the determinants of the performance of entrepreneurs, start-ups, and new ventures.

- Several interesting trends characterize new business start-ups today.

- There are several reasons why some new businesses fail and others succeed.

DISCUSSION QUESTIONS

Questions for Review

1. Describe the similarities and differences between entrepreneurial firms and large firms in terms of their job creation and innovation.
2. What characteristics make an industry attractive to entrepreneurs? Based on these characteristics, which industries are most attractive to entrepreneurs?
3. Describe recent trends in new business start-ups.
4. What are the different sources of advice for entrepreneurs? What type of information would an entrepreneur be likely to get from each source? What are the drawbacks or limitations of each source?

Questions for Analysis

1. Entrepreneurs and start-ups and new ventures play a variety of important roles in society. If these roles are so important, do you think that the government should do more to encourage the development of start-ups and new ventures? Why or why not?
2. Consider the four major reasons for new business failure. What actions can entrepreneurs take to minimize or avoid each cause of failure?

3. The U.S. automotive industry is well established, with several large and many small competitors. Describe the unexploited niches in the U.S. auto industry and tell how entrepreneurs could offer products that fill those niches.

Questions for Application

1. Assume that you are opening a new business in your town. What are your financing options? Which option or options are you likely to choose, and why?
2. List five entrepreneur-owned businesses in your community. In which industry does each business compete? Based on the industry, how do you rate each business's long-term chances for success? Explain your answers.
3. Using the information about managing start-ups and new ventures presented in this chapter, analyze whether you would like to work in a start-up or new venture, either as an employee or as a founder. Given your personality, background, and experience, does working in or starting a new business appeal to you? What are the reasons for your opinion?

BUILDING EFFECTIVE INTERPERSONAL SKILLS

Exercise Overview

Interpersonal skills refer to your ability to communicate with, understand, and motivate both individuals and groups. Needless to say, such skills are extremely important to the manager of a new or small business who wants to improve his or her chances of survival and success through the process of *networking*—getting together with other managers to discuss common problems and opportunities. This exercise asks you to take stock of your networking skills, whether well developed already or likely to be developed as you embark on your work life.

Exercise Task

Consider each of the following statements. How accurately does each describe your current attitudes or behavior? Rate each item on a scale of 1–5 according to how well it describes you: If it describes you very well, give it a 5; if it doesn't describe you, rate it a 1.

1. _____ When I start something (e.g., taking on a new project, making a major purchase, making a career move), I seek help from people whom I know and look for new contacts who may be helpful.

2. _____ I view networking as a way to create win–win situations.
3. _____ I like meeting new people; I don't have trouble striking up conversations with people whom I don't know.
4. _____ I can quickly explain two or three of my most significant accomplishments.
5. _____ Before contacting businesspeople who may be of help to me in my career (say, by providing me with career information), I set goals that I want to achieve through the interaction.
6. _____ Before contacting businesspeople who may be of help to me, I plan out a short opening statement.
7. _____ Before contacting businesspeople who may be of help to me, I draw up a set of questions to ask.
8. _____ When I contact businesspeople who may be of help to me, I make sure to praise their accomplishments.
9. _____ I have contact information for at least 10 people who may be of help to me.
10. _____ I maintain a file or database of people who may be of help to me; I keep it updated and continually add new names.

11. _____ During communications with people who may be of help to me, I ask them for the names of other people whom I can contact for further information.

12. _____ When seeking help from other people, I ask them how I might be of help to them.

13. _____ When people help me, I thank them at the time, and when someone does me an especially important favor, I follow up with thanks.

14. _____ I keep in touch with people who have helped me or may help me at least once a year and update them on my career progress.

15. _____ I maintain regular communications with people who work in other organizations related to my line of business, such as members of trade or professional organizations.

16. _____ I attend trade, professional, and career meetings in order to maintain relationships and make new contacts.

Now add up your total score and place it on the following continuum:

Effective networking 80–70–60–50–40–30–16 Ineffective networking

Adapted from Robert N. Lussier and Christopher F. Achua, *Leadership: Theory, Application, and Skill Development*, 4th ed. (Mason, OH: Cengage Learning, 2010), pp. 127–128.

BUILDING EFFECTIVE CONCEPTUAL SKILLS

Exercise Overview

Conceptual skills require you to think in the abstract. This exercise helps you apply your conceptual skills to an analysis of certain criteria for successful entrepreneurship.

Exercise Background

Now that you're about to graduate, you've decided to open a new business in the local community where you've been attending college. We won't ask where you got them, but we'll assume that you have enough funds to start a business without having to worry about finding investors.

Based solely on your personal interests, list five businesses that you might want to open and operate. For the moment, forget about such technicalities as market potential or profitability. If, for example, you like riding your bicycle, think about opening a shop that caters to cyclists.

Next, *without regard to any personal interest you might have in them*, list five businesses that you might want to open and operate. In this case, your only criteria are market opportunity and profitability. What types of businesses might be profitable in your chosen community? Use the internet to gather information on such factors as population, local economic conditions, local competition, franchising opportunities, and so on.

Finally, evaluate the prospects for success of each of the 10 businesses that you've listed and jot down some notes to summarize your conclusions.

Exercise Task

Reviewing your lists, the information that you've gathered, and the conclusions that you've drawn, do the following:

1. Form a small group of four or five classmates and discuss your respective lists. Look for instances in which the same type of business appears either on (1) both of your lists or (2) on one of your lists and one of a classmate's lists. Also look for cases in which the same business appears on more than one list with either similar or dissimilar prospects for success.

2. At this point, how important do you regard personal interest as a factor in small-business success?

3. How important do you regard market potential as a factor in small-business success?

SKILL-BUILDING PERSONAL ASSESSMENT

An Entrepreneurial Quiz

Introduction: Entrepreneurs are starting ventures all the time. These new businesses are vital to the economy. The following assessment is designed to help you understand your readiness to start your own business—to be an entrepreneur.

Instructions: Place a checkmark or an X in the box next to the response that best represents your self-evaluation.

1. Are you a self-starter?

   ☐ I do things on my own. Nobody has to tell me to get going.

   ☐ If someone gets me started, I keep going all right.

   ☐ Easy does it. I don't push myself until I have to.

2. How do you feel about other people?

   ☐ I like people. I can get along with just about anybody.
   ☐ I have plenty of friends—I don't need anybody else.
   ☐ Most people irritate me.

3. Can you lead others?

   ☐ I can get most people to go along when I start something.
   ☐ I can give orders if someone tells me what we should do.
   ☐ I let someone else get things moving. Then I go along if I feel like it.

4. Can you take responsibility?

   ☐ I like to take charge of things and see them through.
   ☐ I'll take over if I have to, but I'd rather let someone else be responsible.
   ☐ There are always eager-beavers around wanting to show how smart they are. I let them.

5. How good an organizer are you?

   ☐ I like to have a plan before I start. I'm usually the one to get things lined up when the group wants to do something.
   ☐ I do all right unless things get too confused. Then I quit.
   ☐ You get all set and then something comes along and presents too many problems. So I just take things as they come.

6. How good a worker are you?

   ☐ I can keep going as long as I need to. I don't mind working hard for something I want.
   ☐ I'll work hard for a while, but when I've had enough, that's it.
   ☐ I can't see that hard work gets you anywhere.

7. Can you make decisions?

   ☐ I can make up my mind in a hurry if I have to. It usually turns out OK, too.
   ☐ I can if I have plenty of time. If I have to make up my mind fast, I think later I should have decided the other way.
   ☐ I don't like to be the one who has to decide things.

8. Can people trust what you say?

   ☐ You bet they can. I don't say things I don't mean.
   ☐ I try to be on the level most of the time, but sometimes I just say what's easiest.
   ☐ Why bother if the other person doesn't know the difference?

9. Can you stick with it?

   ☐ If I make up my mind to do something, I don't let anything stop me.
   ☐ I usually finish what I start—if it goes well.
   ☐ If it doesn't go well right away, I quit. Why beat your brains out?

10. How good is your health?

    ☐ I never run down!
    ☐ I have enough energy for most things I want to do.
    ☐ I run out of energy sooner than most of my friends.

    Total the checks or Xs in each column here _____.

Scoring: If most of your marks are for the first choice, you probably have what it takes to run a business. If most of your marks are for the second choice, you are likely to have more trouble than you can handle by yourself. You should look for a partner who is strong on the points on which you are weak. If most of your marks are for the third choice, not even a good partner will be able to shore you up. Now go back and answer the first question on the self-assessment.

Source: Dible, D. M. (1978). Business startup basics. Reston, VA: Reston Publishing Company.

MANAGEMENT AT WORK

Leaping to Constructions

How much does it cost to build a school? As a rule, between $280 and $310 per square foot. Ash Notaney, however, told officials in Santa Ana, California, that he could build one for $200–$210 per square foot, and Santa Ana's El Sol Academy gave him a chance to make good on his sales pitch in the summer of 2013. As of May, demolition of the old El Sol structure hadn't yet begun, and work on the new building couldn't begin until July, but Notaney was undeterred by the daunting schedule: He promised to finish construction by December. The two-story, 12-classroom building was finished when Notaney said it would be, and on top of everything else, it was 40–50 percent more energy-efficient than buildings erected by conventional means. When a second phase of construction was completed, the total price tag totalled $15 million—about 20–25 percent cheaper per square foot than that of traditional permanent structures.

Ash Notaney was VP of product and innovation at Project Frog at the time, a San Francisco–based builder of component structures designed for onsite assembly. "We design a common chassis or platform for different types of buildings that people can reprogram according to their needs," explains CEO Drew Buechley, who thinks of his company as more of a tech firm than a construction company. Project Frog (which stands for *Flexible Response to Ongoing Growth*) was founded in 2006 and started to really take off after RockPort Capital had invested $8 million in the company in 2009.

RockPort thought of Project Frog as a "smart building start-up," and Ann Hand, CEO at the time, realized that its industry "space" was located in the vicinity of the construction industry, if not necessarily within its traditional perimeters. "You would look at construction," she recalled, "and say that nothing much had changed in a thousand years. It was an industry just waiting to be disrupted." Hand thus benchmarked companies like Toyota and Boeing—manufacturers noted for process efficiency—and from the beginning, her approach to industry-wide disruption has involved both product and process. Like Boeing, she insisted, "we are a product manufacturer, but if Boeing can assemble a 747 in eight days, why does it take 24 months to design and construct a building?" According to Project Frog President Adam Tibbs, "We focus on smart manufacturing techniques rather than merely shifting construction from onsite to offsite. By doing this, we can bring the same efficiencies as really smart, highly efficient industries. . . . This is about being smarter and building a process that can be replicated easily in order to both stay efficient and maintain quality."

How does "smart manufacturing" work at Project Frog? The company manufactures building components, ships them in flat packs to the construction site, and partners with local contractors to assemble the finished building. The process begins at the design stage, which, as Notaney put it, "we see as an opportunity to rethink everything." In a traditional building, for example, one contractor will put up the ceiling, another will add insulation, and then an electrician will come in to install the wiring and the lighting. A Project Frog ceiling, on the other hand, already includes insulation and energy-efficient LED light fixtures. Likewise, other components include such features as motorized blinds and temperature-control systems—items that might get engineered out of a conventional building when the architect estimates the cost of heating, ventilating, and air conditioning. Thus, a Project Frog building is not merely "prefab" or "modular"; the company prefers the term *componentized* in order to underscore the fact that its buildings are highly customizable. El Sol Academy, for example, features plasma-TV-screen "learning" walls.

In designing a componentized building, says Notaney, "you have to get all the details right up front, as it's all about sequencing and assembly." The process thus begins with a detailed 3D software rendering. "It's complicated and time-consuming to develop a 3D model," admits Tibbs, but he hastens to add that Project Frog developed "a proprietary 3D design tool" in 2008. In fact, that's just about the only thing that the company did in 2008: "We spent a lot of 2008 taking the time to learn from initial prototypes and to lock in a solution that we really feel delivers value," explains Tibbs.

The company's software, for example, creates models of all the pieces of steel needed for a particular building. According to Tibbs, "The program then applies special algorithms to determine the most efficient way to cut as little steel as possible from a sheet. . . . Then we look at all the pieces of steel we need and the order in which we'll need to assemble them. . . . By spending 2008 building our software, we've been able to drastically cut the cost of steel per project and also to speed up the amount of time it takes to build a Project Frog building."

Equally important, adds Tibbs, its software program allows Project Frog to incorporate component features that make its buildings "greener—50 percent more energy efficient than code. . . . When you buy a Project Frog structure, you get performance-monitoring software and embedded sensors that automatically monitor energy performance and maintenance." Combined with designs that maximize the use of daylight, componentized LED lighting-control systems can cut lighting demand by 85 percent. Some Project Frog buildings use zero energy, and some even export energy to the electrical power grid.

Then there's the matter of waste. Tibbs points out that "more than one-fifth of all materials brought to [a conventional] building site are thrown away. . . . If you can get to a near zero-waste facility, that's a huge savings . . . from using less material and eliminating the need for waste removal." Besides, waste is a special item on Hand's disruption agenda: "I won't rest," she says, "until we shake up the industry and attach some guilt to wasteful construction."

Hand's number-one goal, however, reflected the sort of aspiration that you more often hear from CEOs: She was working toward "a sales volume north of nine digits." How did she plan to get there? "With a few school districts alone," she said, "we can be a $100 million company." That's why Project Frog's current focus is on small- to medium-sized commercial buildings like the 19,000-square-foot El Sol Academy building.

The competition, says Tibbs, comes mostly from "portables" (think double-wide trailers), which "do not have to pass code. They're very energy inefficient and not made to last, and the biggest problem is mold." Back in 2009, Hand admitted that "we can't compete with portables on price" because the "only objective in the school world is to hit a cost number when there's no spec for quality or energy efficiency." Four years later, however, she was able to announce that "we now have a price point affordable to the masses." Project Frog's mission, says Education VP Marijke Smit, "is to democratize school buildings that work to service the kids that inhabit them. By making them affordable, we've now created access to a whole new market."

Project Frog bet that, in addition to being eco-friendly, its innovative classroom designs would improve student performance. More and more school systems think it's a good bet. Project Frog recently filled its largest contract to date: more than 250,000 square feet of educational facilities for the South San Francisco United School District. All of the buildings were designed to perform 40 percent better than California's strict energy-code standards.[28]

Case Questions

1. What are Project Frog's distinctive competencies? In what ways has it succeeded in emphasizing them?
2. Now that it has a foothold in school construction, Project Frog has set its sights on an even more promising sector—healthcare construction. Why is the construction of healthcare facilities consistent with Project Frog's *distinctive competencies*? Why does the company see this sector as such a promising area of growth?
3. The Center for Green Schools reports that students' ability to learn can be enhanced by improvements in indoor air, acoustics, thermal comfort, and daylighting. Former president Bill Clinton says that "we should

be right now engaged in retrofitting every school in America for sustainability." What about you? Judging from your own experience—whether positive, negative, or somewhere in between—do you think that the environmental quality of school facilities is an important factor in helping students to learn? How did the schools that you attended measure up on environmental support for learning? How about the classroom that you're sitting in now?

4. As the case informs us, RockPort Capital played a crucial role in providing Project Frog with financing at an early stage of its development ($8 million in 2008). In 2011, GE Energy Financial Services led a second round of funding totaling $22 million. A third round, in 2013, netted $20 million, mostly from Convergent Capital Management (CCM), bringing the total to $50 million. All three investment firms are *venture capital companies*. Check out each of these companies online (you probably don't have to go much further than the home page). You'll find that each company has different investment criteria. It should also be clear that Project Frog was a good investment match for each one. Why?

You Make the Call

Putting the Greek into Yogurt

1. What ingredients (no pun intended!) led to Hamdi Ulukaya's success with Chobani?
2. What are the distinctive competencies illustrated by Ulukaya?
3. Comment on the role that globalization has played in Chobani's success.
4. If Ulukaya were to ask you what strategy he should adopt going forward, what advice would you give him?

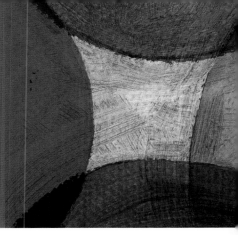

CHAPTER 6

Organization Structure and Design

Learning Outcomes

After studying this chapter, you should be able to:

6-1 Identify the basic elements of organizations.

6-2 Describe the bureaucratic perspective on organization design.

6-3 Explain key situational influences on organization design.

6-4 Describe the basic forms of organization design that characterize many organizations.

6-5 Identify emerging issues in organization design.

This chapter, the first of three devoted to organizing, discusses many of the critical elements of organization structure and design that managers can control. We first identify and describe the various elements of organizing. Next, we explore how those elements can be combined to create an overall design for the organization. Then we introduce situational factors and how they impact organization design. We conclude by describing three emerging issues in organization design.

Management in Action

The Stress of Screening

"You have to have courtesy, patience, politeness, and an attention to personal appearance. . . . Even though we're on a team, the work itself can be fairly solitary since we have little time to socialize among each other."

—**Unidentified Transportation Security Officer**

The Transportation Security Administration, or TSA, was created in the aftermath of the September 11, 2001, terror attacks. Its primary purpose is to maintain security for air travel. The TSA was originally designated as part of the U.S. Department of Transportation but was later moved to be a part of the Department of Homeland Security. The TSA is funded primarily by a $2.50 fee that is a part of every airline ticket sold. During the period between February and December 2002 more than 1.7 million people applied for 55,000 screening jobs.

Prior to the creation of the TSA, airport security was handled by dozens of private security businesses. Each airport was free to hire its own security firm, and there was considerable variation in screening procedures between airports. Airports can actually still opt out of using the TSA and hire their own contractors to provide security. However, these private contractors must meet rigorous standards and must follow all TSA procedures.

The hierarchy of the TSA consists of several levels. The senior leadership level has 35 executive positions arranged across five levels. Within the Aviation Security department of the TSA (its largest division, by far) there are an additional eight levels, with four of these levels residing in each of over 450 individual airports across the country. (The other units of the TSA are Transportation Security Support and Intelligence, Federal Air Marshalls, Transportations Threat Assessment and Credentialing, and Surface Transportation Security.) The TSA's total annual budget is almost $8 billion. In total, the TSA employs around 54,200 people, with the majority of those individuals, over 47,000, working as TSOs, or Transportation Security Officers. Most travelers know the TSOs as the security screeners at airports.

TSOs are required to be U.S. citizens or nationals, be at least 18 years old, and pass drug screening and medical evaluation tests and are subject to both credit and criminal background checks. The base starting pay for TSOs is around $29,000 per year with some additional allowances for airports located in high cost-of-living areas such as New York City and the state of Hawaii. In addition, airports that experience high turnover rates also offer annual retention bonuses.

At any individual airport TSOs are responsible for controlling terminal entry and exit points; verifying passenger credentials at the beginning of the security screening process; directing passengers as they approach security screening; monitoring various screening equipment such as body scanners, x-ray machines, and so forth; and performing follow-up screening and searches, including pat-downs and checking the contents of passenger bags and personal items as warranted.

At each security station the TSOs are loosely organized into teams. However, because of the pace of the jobs and the need to keep focused, there is actually limited interaction among team members. Focus, in particular, can be an issue for TSOs. For example, sitting in front of an x-ray screen and paying close attention to images of backpacks, computer cases, briefcases, small suitcases, and so forth as they pass through on a moving belt requires intense concentration and can be mentally tiring.

Similarly, the agents directing passengers often have to deal with nervous inexperienced travelers, harried travelers concerned about missing their flight, passengers who may be hostile to the screening process, travelers distracted with helping small children, passengers who may not be familiar with all of the requirements relating to carry-on items, and international travelers who may not be proficient in English and so can't easily understand instructions being given in what to them is a foreign language.

To help combat the mental fatigue associated with some of these jobs (such as monitoring the x-ray screening) and the potential loss of patience with others (such as directing passengers), TSOs rotate across the various positions within each security station every 20 minutes. So, for example, a given agent might verify passenger credentials for 20 minutes, then direct passengers as they approach the actual screening line for 20 minutes, then watch the x-ray monitor for 20 minutes, then manage passengers as they proceed through the body scanners for 20 minutes, and then handle pat-downs and searches for 20 minutes before moving back to their initial task of verifying credentials. There are also other positions they may rotate through as well.

Each task within a TSO team is very tightly defined and agents have very little discretion in what standards they must apply, standard operating procedures, and so forth. For example, passengers are allowed liquids, gels, and aerosols in travel-size containers that are 3.4 ounces or less and all such items have to fit into a one-quart clear bag. TSO agents cannot allow a passenger to proceed with a liquid container that is 4 ounces or more or if a passenger has a one-quart bag plus other liquids that won't fit into the bag.

Perhaps not surprisingly, there is considerable turnover in the TSA. Agents complain that the pay is low, the job monotonous, and the stress associated with the job excessive. The jobs are also dangerous due to illegal articles that people may be trying to sneak onto a plane, potentially unruly passengers, and few opportunities for advancement. While turnover rates vary between different airports, one in five new screeners quits within the first five months of their employment; at some airports annual turnover has approached 80 percent.[1]

6-1 THE BASIC ELEMENTS OF ORGANIZING

Most organizations are structured into various positions or jobs. Some jobs are very complex or technical whereas others may be simple and straightforward. The working relationships between jobs and people in a team or organization are some of the most critical elements in managing an organization. As you will see in this chapter, addressing the basic frameworks that organizations use to get their work done—structure and design—is a fundamental part of the management process.

The term *organization structure and design* refers to the overall set of elements that can be used to configure an organization. This section introduces and describes these elements: job specialization, departmentalization, reporting relationships, distribution of authority, and coordination.

6-1a Job Specialization

job specialization
The degree to which the overall task of the organization is broken down and divided into smaller component parts

The first building block of organization structure is job specialization. **Job specialization** is the degree to which the overall task of the organization is broken down and divided into smaller component parts. For example, when Walt Disney started his company, he did everything himself—scripted cartoons, drew them, added the character voices, and then marketed them to theaters. As his business grew, though, he eventually hired others to perform many of these same functions. As growth continued, so, too, did specialization. For example, as animation artists work on Disney movies today, they may specialize in generating computer images of a single character or doing only background scenery. Others provide voices, and marketing specialists develop promotional campaigns. And today, the Walt Disney Company has literally thousands of different specialized jobs. Clearly, no one person could perform them all.

Benefits and Limitations of Specialization   Job specialization provides four basic benefits to organizations.[2] First, workers performing small, simple tasks will become very proficient at each task. Second, transfer time between tasks decreases. If employees perform several different tasks, some time is lost as they stop doing the first task and start doing the next. Third, the more narrowly defined a job is, the easier it is to develop specialized equipment to assist with that job. Fourth, when an employee who performs a highly specialized job is absent or resigns, the manager is able to train someone new at relatively low cost. Although specialization is generally thought of in terms of operating jobs, organizations have also extended the basic elements of specialization to managerial and professional levels.[3]

Job specialization is the basis for mass-production assembly lines such as this one. Tasks are broken down into small component elements. Partially assembled products move along the assembly line as each worker adds to the product by attaching or building new parts of the product.

BartlomiejMagierowski/Shutterstock.com

On the other hand, job specialization can have negative consequences. The foremost criticism is that workers who perform highly specialized jobs quickly become bored and dissatisfied. The job may be so specialized that it offers no challenge or stimulation. Boredom and monotony set in, absenteeism rises, and the quality of work may suffer. Furthermore, the anticipated benefits of specialization do not always occur. For example, a classic study conducted at Maytag found that the time spent moving work in process from one worker to another was greater than the time needed for the same individual to change from job to job.[4] Thus, although some degree of specialization is necessary, it should not be carried to extremes because of the possible negative consequences. Managers must be sensitive to situations in which extreme specialization should be avoided. And indeed, several alternative approaches to designing jobs have been developed.

"The best [Tour de France] teams have specialists to help position leaders for a win."
—Paul Hochman, Business Writer[5]

Alternatives to Specialization   To counter the problems associated with specialization, managers have sought other approaches to job design that achieve a better balance between organizational demands for efficiency and productivity and individual needs for creativity and autonomy. Five alternative approaches are job rotation, job enlargement, job enrichment, job characteristics approach, and work teams.[6]

Job rotation involves systematically moving employees from one job to another. A worker in a warehouse might unload trucks on Monday, carry incoming inventory to storage on Tuesday, verify invoices on Wednesday, pull outgoing inventory from storage on Thursday, and load trucks on Friday. Thus, the jobs do not change, but instead workers move from job to job. Unfortunately, for this very reason, job rotation has not been especially successful in enhancing employee motivation or satisfaction. Jobs that are amenable to rotation tend to be relatively standard and routine. Workers who are rotated to a "new" job may be more satisfied at first, but satisfaction soon wanes. Although many companies (among them Raytheon, Ford, and Prudential Insurance) have tried job rotation, it is most often used today as a training device to improve worker skills and flexibility. The TSA (Transportation Security Administration) also rotates security screeners at airports several times a day to offset problems of boredom that might set in if the same task were being performed all the time.

Wally Skalij/Los Angeles Times/Getty Images

By utilizing job rotation, the Transportation Security Administration can help security screeners avoid becoming too complacent and losing their focus on their tasks. The screener shown here, rotating jobs every 20 minutes, will head to the entryway checkpoint entrance next. Rotation also helps offset monotony and keeps screeners focused on their tasks.

job rotation
An alternative to job specialization that involves systematically moving employees from one job to another

job enlargement
An alternative to job specialization that increases the total number of tasks that workers perform

"[Rotating jobs] . . . makes the day go by. You don't get bored doing the same thing over and over."
—Rick Rush, General Motors Assembly-Line Worker[7]

Job enlargement was developed to increase the total number of tasks workers perform. As a result, all workers perform a wide variety of tasks, which presumably reduces the level of job dissatisfaction. Many organizations have used job enlargement, including IBM, Detroit Edison, AT&T, the U.S. Civil Service, and Maytag. At Maytag, for example, the assembly line for producing washing machine water pumps was systematically changed so that work that had originally been performed by six workers, who passed the work sequentially from one person to another, was performed by four workers, each of whom assembled a complete pump.[8] Unfortunately, although job enlargement does have some positive consequences, they are often offset by some disadvantages: (1) training costs usually increase, (2) unions argued that pay should increase because the worker is doing more tasks, and (3) in many cases the work tends to remain boring and routine even after job enlargement.

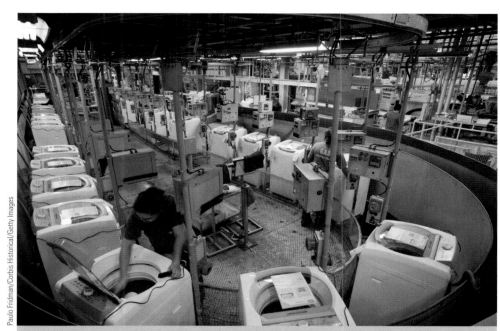

Many products like Maytag washers and dryers are manufactured using job specialization and assembly-line technology. While this approach promotes efficiency, it can also lead to monotony and worker boredom. To help counter these negative effects, Maytag has experimented with job enlargement and other alternatives to job specialization.

job enrichment
An alternative to job specialization that attempts to increase both the number of tasks a worker does and the control the worker has over the job

A more comprehensive alternative, job enrichment, assumes that increasing the range and variety of tasks is not sufficient by itself to improve employee motivation.[9] Thus, job enrichment attempts to increase both the number of tasks a worker does and the control the worker has over the job. To implement job enrichment, managers remove some controls from the job, delegate more authority to employees, and structure the work in complete, natural units. These changes increase subordinates' sense of responsibility. Another part of job enrichment is to continually assign new and challenging tasks, thereby increasing employees' opportunity for growth and advancement. AT&T, Texas Instruments, IBM, and General Foods are among the firms that have used job enrichment. This approach, however, also has disadvantages. For example, work systems need to be analyzed before enrichment, but this seldom happens, and managers rarely ask for employee preferences when enriching jobs.

job characteristics approach
An alternative to job specialization that suggests that jobs should be diagnosed and improved along five core dimensions, taking into account both the work system and employee preferences

The job characteristics approach is an alternative to job specialization that does take into account the work system and employee preferences.[10] As illustrated in Figure 6.1, the job characteristics approach suggests that jobs should be diagnosed and improved along five core dimensions:

1. *Skill variety*, the number of things a person does in a job
2. *Task identity*, the extent to which the worker does a complete or identifiable portion of the total job
3. *Task significance*, the perceived importance of the task
4. *Autonomy*, the degree of control the worker has over how the work is performed
5. *Feedback*, the extent to which the worker knows how well the job is being performed

Increasing the presence of these dimensions in a job presumably leads to higher motivation, higher-quality performance, higher satisfaction, and lower absenteeism and turnover. A large number of studies have been conducted to test the usefulness of the job characteristics approach. Prudential Insurance, for example, implemented this approach in its claims division. Results included moderate declines in turnover and a small but measurable improvement in work quality. A few studies, though, have not supported this approach as strongly. Thus,

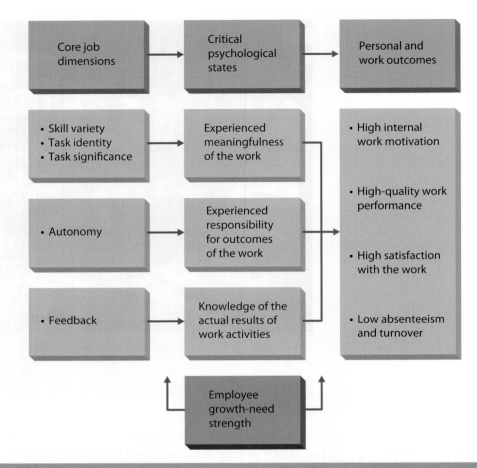

FIGURE 6.1

The Job Characteristics Approach

The job characteristics approach to job design provides a viable alternative to job specialization. Five core job dimensions may lead to critical psychological states that, in turn, may enhance motivation, performance, and satisfaction while also reducing absenteeism and turnover.

Source: J. R. Hackman and G. R. Oldham, "Motivation through the Design of Work: Test of a Theory," *Organizational Behavior and Human Performance*, 1976, Vol. 16, pp. 250–279.

although the job characteristics approach is one of the most promising alternatives to job specialization, it is probably not the final answer.

Another alternative to job specialization is work teams. Under this arrangement, a group is given responsibility for designing the work system to be used in performing an interrelated set of tasks. In the typical assembly-line system, the work flows from one worker to the next, and each worker has a specified job to perform. In a work team, however, the group itself decides how jobs will be allocated. For example, the work team assigns specific tasks to members, monitors and controls its own performance, and has autonomy over work scheduling.

6-1b Grouping Jobs: Departmentalization

The second element of organization structure is the grouping of jobs according to some logical arrangement. The process of grouping jobs is called departmentalization. When organizations are small and have few employees, the owner-manager can personally supervise and coordinate the jobs of everyone who works there. As an organization grows and adds more and more employees, however, this becomes increasingly difficult for the owner-manager.

work teams
An alternative to job specialization that allows an entire group to design the work system it will use to perform an interrelated set of tasks

departmentalization
The process of grouping jobs according to some logical arrangement

Departmentalization involves grouping jobs according to a logical arrangement. Individuals needing out-patient services at this hospital know to follow the directional markers on this sign, as do patients coming for x-ray services. The hospital will also have multiple other departments such as emergency, surgery, physical therapy, and so forth.

functional departmentalization
Grouping jobs involving the same or similar activities

product departmentalization
Grouping activities around products or product groups

customer departmentalization
Grouping activities to respond to and interact with specific customers or customer groups

Consequently, new managerial positions are created to supervise or coordinate the work of others. Employees are not assigned to particular managers randomly. Rather, jobs are grouped according to some plan. The logic embodied in such a plan is the basis for all departmentalization.[11]

Functional Departmentalization The most common base for departmentalization, especially among smaller organizations, is by function. Functional departmentalization groups together those jobs involving the same or similar activities. (The word *function* is used here to mean organizational functions such as finance and production, rather than the basic managerial functions, such as planning or controlling.) This approach, which is most common in smaller organizations, has three primary advantages. First, each department can be staffed by experts in that functional area. Marketing experts can be hired to run the marketing function, for example. Second, supervision is facilitated because an individual manager needs to be familiar with only a relatively narrow set of skills. And, third, coordinating activities inside each department is easier.

On the other hand, as an organization begins to grow in size, several disadvantages of this approach may emerge. For one, decision making tends to become slower and more bureaucratic. Employees may also begin to concentrate too narrowly on their own function and lose sight of the total organizational system. Finally, accountability and performance become increasingly difficult to monitor. For example, determining whether a new product fails because of production deficiencies or a poor marketing campaign may not be possible.

Product Departmentalization Product departmentalization, a second common approach, involves grouping and arranging activities around products or product groups. Most larger businesses adopt this form of departmentalization for grouping activities at the business or corporate level. Product departmentalization has three major advantages. First, all activities associated with one product or product group can be easily integrated and coordinated. Second, the speed and effectiveness of decision making are enhanced. Third, the performance of individual products or product groups can be assessed more easily and objectively, thereby improving the accountability of departments for the results of their activities.

Product departmentalization also has two major disadvantages. For one, managers in each department may focus on their own product or product group to the exclusion of the rest of the organization. For example, a marketing manager may see his or her primary duty as helping the group rather than helping the overall organization. For another, administrative costs rise because each department must have its own functional specialists for areas such as market research and financial analysis.

Customer Departmentalization Under customer departmentalization, the organization structures its activities to respond to and interact with specific customers or customer groups. The lending activities in most banks, for example, are usually tailored to meet the needs of different kinds of customers (business, consumer, mortgage, and agricultural loans, for instance). The basic advantage of this approach is that the organization is able to use skilled specialists to deal with unique customers or customer groups. It takes one set of skills to evaluate a business's balance sheet and lend $5 million for operating capital and a different set of skills to evaluate an individual's creditworthiness and lend $40,000 for a new car. However, a fairly large administrative staff is required to integrate the activities of the various departments. In banks, for example, coordination is necessary to make sure that the organization does not overcommit itself in any one area and to handle collections on delinquent accounts from a diverse set of customers.

Location Departmentalization   **Location departmentalization** groups jobs on the basis of defined geographic sites or areas. The defined sites or areas may range in size from a hemisphere to only a few blocks of a large city. Transportation companies, police departments (precincts represent geographic areas of a city), and the Federal Reserve Bank all use location departmentalization. The primary advantage of location departmentalization is that it enables the organization to respond easily to unique customer and environmental characteristics in the various regions. On the negative side, a larger administrative staff may be required if the organization must keep track of units in scattered locations.

location departmentalization
Grouping jobs on the basis of defined geographic sites or areas

6-1c Establishing Reporting Relationships

The third basic element of organizing is the establishment of reporting relationships among positions. The purpose of this activity is to clarify the chain of command and the span of management.

chain of command
A clear and distinct line of authority among the positions in an organization

This shift of factory workers is leaving the plant floor. They have just been relieved by the second-shift crew.

Sean Gallup/Getty Images

Chain of Command   Chain of command is an old concept, first popularized over 100 years ago. For example, early writers about the **chain of command** argued that clear and distinct lines of authority need to be established among all positions in an organization. The chain of command actually has two components. The first, called *unity of command*, suggests that each person within an organization must have a clear reporting relationship to one and only one boss (as we see later, newer models of organization design routinely—and successfully—violate this premise). The second, called the *scalar principle*, suggests that there must be a clear and unbroken line of authority that extends from the lowest to the highest position in the organization. The popular saying "The buck stops here" is derived from this idea—someone in the organization must ultimately be responsible for every decision.

Span of Management   Another part of establishing reporting relationships is determining how many people will report to each manager. This defines the **span of management** (sometimes called the *span of control*). For years, managers and researchers sought to determine the optimal span of management. Today we recognize that the span of management is a crucial factor in structuring organizations but that there are no universal, cut-and-dried prescriptions for an ideal or optimal span.[12]

Tall versus Flat Organizations   In recent years, managers have begun to focus attention on the optimal number of layers in their organizational hierarchy. Having more layers

span of management
The number of people who report to a particular manager

results in a taller organization, whereas having fewer layers results in a flatter organization. What difference does it make whether the organization is tall or flat? One early study at Sears, back when that organization was much larger than it is today, found that a flat structure led to higher levels of employee morale and productivity.[13] Researchers have also argued that a tall structure is more expensive (because of the larger number of managers involved) and that it fosters more communication problems (because of the increased number of people through whom information must pass). On the other hand, a wide span of management in a flat organization may result in a manager having more administrative responsibility (because there are fewer managers) and more supervisory responsibility (because there are more subordinates reporting to each manager). If these additional responsibilities become excessive, the flat organization may suffer.[14]

Many experts agree that businesses can function effectively with fewer layers of organization than they currently have. The Franklin Mint, for example, reduced its number of management layers from six to four. At the same time, the CEO increased his span of management from six to 12. The British firm Cadbury PLC, maker of Cadbury Dairy chocolates, Trident gum, and other confectionary products, eliminated a layer of management separating the CEO and the firm's operating units. The specific reasons for the change were to improve communication between the CEO and the operating unit heads and to speed up decision making.[15] One additional reason for this trend is that improved digital communication technologies allow managers to stay in touch with a larger number of subordinates than was possible even just a few years ago.

6-1d Distributing Authority

Another important building block in structuring organizations is the determination of how authority is to be distributed among positions. Authority is power that has been legitimized by the organization.[16] Two specific issues that managers must address when distributing authority are delegation and decentralization.

The Delegation Process Delegation is the establishment of a pattern of authority between a superior and one or more subordinates. Specifically, delegation is the process by which managers assign a portion of their total workload to others.[17] In concept, the delegation process involves three steps. First, the manager assigns responsibility or gives the subordinate a job to do. The assignment of responsibility might range from telling a subordinate to prepare a report to placing the person in charge of a task force. Along with the assignment, the individual is also given the authority to do the job. The manager may give the subordinate the power to requisition needed information from confidential files or to direct a group of other workers. Finally, the manager establishes the subordinate's accountability—that is, the subordinate accepts an obligation to carry out the task assigned by the manager. For instance, the CEO of AutoZone will sign off for the company on financial performance only when the individual manager responsible for each unit has certified his or her own results as being accurate. The firm believes that this high level of accountability will help it avoid the kind of accounting scandal that has hit many businesses in recent times.

Decentralization and Centralization Just as authority can be delegated from one individual to another, organizations also develop patterns of authority across a wide variety of positions and departments. Decentralization is the process of systematically delegating power and authority throughout the organization to middle- and lower-level managers. It is important to remember that decentralization is actually one end of a continuum anchored at the other end by centralization, the process of systematically retaining power and authority in the hands of higher-level managers. Hence, a decentralized organization is one in which decision-making power and authority are delegated as far down the chain of command as possible. Conversely, in a centralized organization, decision-making power and authority are retained at higher levels in the organization. Our *Leading the Way* feature illustrates how one fast-growing restaurant chain has prospered by moving from a centralized to a decentralized training model for its restaurants.

What factors determine an organization's position on the decentralization–centralization continuum? One common determinant is the organization's external environment. In general,

authority
Power that has been legitimized by the organization

delegation
The process by which a manager assigns a portion of his or her total workload to others

"We must build a corporate lattice, not a corporate ladder."
—Unnamed Partner, Deloitte LLP

decentralization
The process of systematically delegating power and authority throughout the organization to middle- and lower-level managers

centralization
The process of systematically retaining power and authority in the hands of higher-level managers

Authority is power that has been legitimized by the organization. This supply chain manager is using her authority to instruct one of her subordinates on how to complete a project at one of the firm's distribution centers.

wavebreakmedia/Shutterstock.com

the greater the complexity and uncertainty of the environment, the greater is the tendency to decentralize. Another crucial factor is the history of the organization. Firms have a tendency to do what they have done in the past, so there is likely to be some relationship between what an organization did in its early history and what it chooses to do today in terms of centralization or decentralization. The nature of the decisions being made is also considered. The costlier and riskier the decisions, the more pressure there is to centralize. In short, managers have no clear-cut guidelines for determining whether to centralize or decentralize. Many successful organizations, such as General Electric and Johnson & Johnson, are quite decentralized. But many equally successful firms, such as McDonald's and Walmart, have remained centralized.

 **LEADING THE WAY**

Feeding the Chicken

Jessica Webb started working at Zaxby's, a Georgia-based franchise chain of fast-casual restaurants, when she was still in high school. "I didn't like cleaning up after people," she admits, and when she was assigned to the kitchen, she found that she didn't like to cook either. "But," she hastens to add, "it was all a part of getting more on-the-job training." Today, she confesses that "nothing can replace the experience I got in the kitchen. . . . I kept trying to improve myself because I was young, and I needed to learn all I could as fast as I could." Now 25, Webb has been general manager of the outlet for six years. When it comes to training new managers (many of whom are older than she is), "I tell them that it doesn't make any difference how long any of us work, there will still be things to learn."

It's an ideal attitude for getting ahead at Zaxby's, which puts a premium on employee learning and companywide continuous improvement. "We want someone who wants to get better every day," says COO David Waters. "Success is the development of people." Zaxby's share of success—it's grown to 900 outlets in just over two decades—derives in large part from its conviction that employee training reduces turnover, improves standards of performance, and, in the process, helps it meet such business goals as maintaining brand consistency and preserving the company's Southern culture. "Our mission," explains Richard Fletcher, VP of Talent Management, "is to attract and retain a talented workforce and provide them with a supportive learning environment that enhances performance in alignment with the company's vision and values."

Much of Zaxby's learning and training program is designed for franchisees, who own 80 percent of those 900 restaurants. Originally, CEO Zach McLeroy believed that centralized training was essential to maintaining brand consistency, so a franchisee's management candidates traveled to corporate classrooms and certified training restaurants at the franchisee's expense (an average of $6,000 per student). Unfortunately, trainees were absent from their home restaurants for six weeks. Many quit during training, while others failed to attain certification and others were deemed unsuitable. As a result, certified managers were running only 25 percent of Zaxby's outlets, where turnover was a robust 100 percent.

As a matter of fact, those numbers were about par for the industry, but corporate leadership was unhappy, and so were franchisees, who wanted more control over training. "We had to find a way," recalls Fletcher, "to balance the need for consistent training with franchisee demand for control overtraining." So in 2018, Zaxby's unveiled its Licensee Managed Training Program. It begins with an online *licensed management system (LMS)* that allows trainees to customize their learning plans within a basic modular structure. The company also provides material pegged to such specific managerial roles as "front of the house," "back of the house," "manager," and even "owner." Franchisees are free to alter materials to suit their own needs. Finally, the program tracks progress through both conventional and hands-on tests that allow trainees to demonstrate the skills that they've learned.

A trainee's success is acknowledged by a program called "feeding the chicken." Each individual's learning plan features Zaxby's learning logo—a cartoon chicken sporting a mortarboard—and as he or she meets a customized goal, the chicken turns increasingly gold, culminating in a solid-gold image when training has been completed.

References: Dwight Dana, "Worker Sticks with Zaxby's for Nine Years," *SCNow*, January 2, 2013, www.scnow.com on April 10, 2020; Christine LaFave Grace, "Chasing Improvement, Not Trends," *Technomic*, http://blogs.technomic.com on April 10, 2020; Terry Mayhew, "Zaxby's Appoints a New VP of Talent Management," *QSR*, November 19, 2012, www.qsrmagazine .com on April 10, 2020; Lisa Goldstein, "Meet Richard Fletcher of Zaxby's Franchising," http://ldglobalevents.com on April 10, 2020; John Tabellione, "Zaxby's CEO McLeroy Drums Up Decades of Growth," http://savannahceo.com on April 10, 2020; Paul Harris, "'The Chicken' Rules Zaxby's Learning Roost," www.astd.org on April 10, 2020.

IBM has recently undergone a transformation from using a highly centralized approach to a much more decentralized approach to managing its operations. A great deal of decision-making authority was passed from the hands of a select group of top executives down to six product and marketing groups. The reason for the move was to speed up the company's ability to make decisions, introduce new products, and respond to customers. Similarly, Toyota recently announced its intent to provide more autonomy to country managers, especially those in the United States. This move came in part because of poor and slow decision making during a recent quality crisis involving Toyota products.[18] In contrast, Royal Dutch Shell, long operated in a highly decentralized manner, has recently gone through several major changes all intended to make the firm more centralized. The firm's CEO went so far as to note that "fewer people will make strategic decisions."[19] And indeed, during the COVID-19 pandemic in 2020, most organizations pulled decision-making authority to higher levels.

6-1e Coordinating Activities

The fifth major element of organizing is coordination. As we discussed earlier, job specialization and departmentalization involve breaking down jobs into small units and then combining those jobs into departments. Once this has been accomplished, the activities of the departments must be linked—systems must be put into place to keep the activities of each department focused on the attainment of organizational goals. This is accomplished by coordination—the process of linking the activities of the various departments of the organization.[20]

coordination
The process of linking the activities of the various departments of the organization

The Need for Coordination   The primary reason for coordination is that departments and work groups are interdependent—they depend on one another for information and resources to perform their respective activities. The greater the interdependence between departments, the more coordination the organization requires if departments are to be able to perform effectively. There are three major forms of interdependence: pooled, sequential, and reciprocal.[21]

Pooled interdependence represents the lowest level of interdependence. Units with pooled interdependence operate with little interaction—the output of the units is pooled at the organizational level. Old Navy clothing stores operate with pooled interdependence. Each store is considered a "department" by the parent corporation. Each has its own operating budget, staff, and so forth. The profits or losses from each store are simply "added together" at the organizational level. The stores are interdependent to the extent that the final success or failure of one store affects the others, but they do not generally interact on a day-to-day basis.

pooled interdependence
When units operate with little interaction; their output is pooled at the organizational level

In sequential interdependence, the output of one unit becomes the input for another in a sequential fashion. This creates a moderate level of interdependence. At Nissan, for example, one plant assembles engines and then ships them to a final assembly site at another plant, where the cars are completed. The plants are interdependent in that the final assembly plant must have the engines from engine assembly before it can perform its primary function of producing finished automobiles. But the level of interdependence is generally one way—the engine plant is not necessarily dependent on the final assembly plant.

sequential interdependence
When the output of one unit becomes the input for another in a sequential fashion

Reciprocal interdependence exists when activities flow both ways between units. This form is clearly the most complex. Within a Marriott hotel, for example, the reservations department, front-desk check-in, and housekeeping are all reciprocally interdependent. Reservations has to provide front-desk employees with information about how many guests to expect each day, and housekeeping needs to know which rooms require priority cleaning. If any of the three units does not do its job properly, all the others will be affected.

reciprocal interdependence
When activities flow both ways between units

Structural Coordination Techniques   Because of the obvious coordination requirements that characterize most organizations, many techniques for achieving coordination have been developed. Some of the most useful devices for maintaining coordination among interdependent units are the managerial hierarchy, rules and procedures, liaison roles, task forces, and integrating departments.[22]

Organizations that use the hierarchy to achieve coordination place one manager in charge of interdependent departments or units. In Walmart distribution centers, major activities include receiving and unloading bulk shipments from railroad cars and loading

A warehouse facility like this one often requires considerable coordination. At any given time shipments are coming in while other shipments are going out. Boxes and crates are also being moved from one location to another at the same time that merchandise is being packed for shipment.

other shipments onto trucks for distribution to retail outlets. The two groups (receiving and shipping) are interdependent in that they share the same loading docks and some equipment. To ensure coordination and minimize conflict, one manager is in charge of the whole operation.

Routine coordination activities can be handled through rules and standard procedures. In the Walmart distribution center, an outgoing truck shipment has priority over an incoming rail shipment. Thus, when trucks are to be loaded, the shipping unit is given access to all of the center's auxiliary forklifts. This priority is specifically stated in a rule. But, as useful as rules and procedures often are in routine situations, they are not particularly effective when coordination problems are complex or unusual.

As a device for coordination, a manager in a liaison role coordinates interdependent units by acting as a common point of contact. This individual may not have any formal authority over the groups but instead simply facilitates the flow of information between units. Two engineering groups working on component systems for a large project might interact through a liaison. The liaison maintains familiarity with each group as well as with the overall project. She can answer questions and otherwise serve to integrate the activities of all the groups.

A task force may be created when the need for coordination is acute. When interdependence is complex and several units are involved, a single liaison person may not be sufficient. Instead, a task force might be assembled by drawing one representative from each group. The coordination function is thus spread across several individuals, each of whom has special information about one of the groups involved. When the project is completed, task force members return to their original positions. For example, a college overhauling its degree requirements might establish a task force made up of representatives from each department affected by the change. Each person not only retains his or her regular departmental affiliation and duties but also serves on the special task force. After the new requirements are agreed on, the task force is dissolved. In 2020 the COVID-19 pandemic created the need for greater coordination within organizations, and the creation of task forces was a common approach to helping address these needs.

Integrating departments are occasionally used for high-level coordination. These are somewhat similar to task forces but are more permanent. An integrating department generally has some permanent members as well as members who are assigned temporarily from units that are particularly in need of coordination. One study found that successful firms in the plastics industry, which is characterized by complex and dynamic environments, used integrating departments to maintain internal integration and coordination.[23] An integrating department usually has more authority than a task force and may even be given some budgetary control by the organization.

Digital Coordination   Advances in electronic information technology are also providing useful mechanisms for coordination. Email and text messaging, for example, make it easier for people to communicate with one another. This communication, in turn, enhances coordination. Similarly, many people in organizations today use digital scheduling, at least some of which is accessible to others. Hence, if someone needs to set up a meeting with two colleagues, he can often check their virtual schedules to determine their availability, making it easier to coordinate their activities. During the COVID-19 pandemic there was a surge in the use of online meetings and conferences. A variety of digital tools were used to first schedule and then conduct the meetings and conferences.

Local networks, increasingly managed by digital devices, are also making it easier to coordinate activities. Bechtel, for example, now requires its contractors, subcontractors, and suppliers to use a common web-based communication system to improve coordination among their myriad activities. The firm estimates that this improved coordination technology routinely saves it thousands of dollars on every big construction project it undertakes. On Viking cruises, restaurant servers enter meal requests into handheld devices. The orders are transmitted to video screens in the kitchen where cooks and preparers assemble the meals. When each order is complete the server gets "pinged" and knows to return to the kitchen and collect the meals to serve to passengers.

 **Manager's Checklist**

☐ Managers need to understand the advantages and disadvantages of each approach to job design but also need to also realize that there is no one perfect way to design jobs.

☐ Managers should know the most common bases of departmentalization and the advantages and disadvantages of each.

☐ Managers need to have a clear understanding of the factors that should be considered when determining the appropriate span of management for a particular setting.

☐ Managers should understand their own tendencies, as well as the tendencies of their managers, if those tendencies relate to delegation and be aware of the extent to which their organization is relatively more centralized or relatively more decentralized.

☐ Managers need to be aware of the three kinds of interdependence that necessitate coordination and the primary coordination mechanisms used in their organization.

6-2 THE BUREAUCRATIC MODEL OF ORGANIZATION DESIGN

The various elements of organizing discussed in the previous section—job specialization, departmentalization, reporting relationships, distribution of authority, and coordination—are all parts of an overall organization design. We now turn our attention to the organization itself. As we will see, managers can combine these various elements in many different ways to create an overall organization design that best fits their needs. We start with a brief look back at some of the early thinking about organization design.

Max Weber, an influential German sociologist, was a pioneer in the study of organization design. At the core of Weber's writings was what he called the bureaucratic model of organizations.[24] The Weberian perspective suggests that a **bureaucracy** is a model of organization design based on a legitimate and formal system of authority. However, the concept of bureaucracy has come to conjure images of "red tape," rigidity, and passing the buck. For example, how many times have you heard people refer disparagingly to "the federal bureaucracy"? And in a similar vein, many U.S. managers believe that bureaucracy in the Chinese government is a major impediment to the ability of the United States to do business there.

But Weber originally viewed the bureaucratic form of organization as logical, rational, and efficient. He offered the model as a framework to which all organizations should aspire—the "one best way" of doing things. According to Weber, the ideal bureaucracy exhibits five basic characteristics:

1. The organization should adopt a distinct division of labor, and each position should be filled by an expert.
2. The organization should develop a consistent set of rules to ensure that task performance is uniform.

bureaucracy
A model of organization design based on a legitimate and formal system of authority

3. The organization should establish a hierarchy of positions or offices that creates a chain of command from the top of the organization to the bottom.

4. Managers should conduct business in an impersonal way and maintain an appropriate social distance between themselves and their subordinates.

5. Employment and advancement in the organization should be based on technical expertise, and employees should be protected from arbitrary dismissal.

Perhaps the best examples of bureaucracies today are government agencies and universities. Large labor unions are also usually organized as bureaucracies.[25] Consider, for example, the steps you must go through and the forms you must fill out to apply for admission to college, request housing, register each semester, change majors, submit a degree plan, substitute a course, and file for graduation. Even as paper has been replaced with digital media, the steps are often the same. The reason these procedures are necessary is that universities deal with large numbers of potential and accepted students who must be treated equally and fairly. Hence, rules, regulations, and standard operating procedures are needed. Some bureaucracies, such as the U.S. Postal Service, have been trying to portray themselves as less mechanistic and impersonal. The strategy of the Postal Service is to become more service oriented as a way to fight back against competitors such as FedEx and UPS.

A primary strength of the bureaucratic model is that several of its elements (such as reliance on rules and employment based on expertise) do, in fact, often improve efficiency. Bureaucracies also help minimize favoritism or bias (because everyone must follow the rules) and make procedures and practices very clear to everyone. Unfortunately, however, this approach also has several disadvantages. One major disadvantage is that the bureaucratic model results in inflexibility and rigidity. Once rules are created and put in place, making exceptions (even when warranted) or changing them (when circumstances change) is often difficult. In addition, the bureaucracy often results in the neglect of human and social processes within the organization.

This woman pulls a number while at the Department of Motor Vehicles. She is in line to renew her license. Many drivers often complain about the DMV's bureaucratic and archaic processes.

dlewis33/E+/Getty Images

✓ Manager's Checklist

☐ Managers should avoid the mistake of assuming there is one best way to design an organization.

☐ You should not automatically assume an organization that uses the bureaucratic model is ineffective.

6-3 SITUATIONAL INFLUENCES ON ORGANIZATION DESIGN

situational view of organization design
Based on the assumption that the optimal design for any given organization depends on a set of relevant situational factors

Weber argued that the bureaucratic model would always be ideal. Other experts subsequently began to offer different models that they argued could be used in any situation. It eventually became apparent, though, that no one universal model of organization design would ever be identified. Instead, experts now acknowledge that there is no one best form of organization design. That is, the **situational view of organization design** is based on the assumption that the optimal design for any given organization depends on a set of relevant situational factors. In other words, situational factors play a role in determining the best organization design for any particular circumstance.[26] Four basic situational factors—technology, environment, size, and organizational life cycle—are discussed here. The *World of Difference* feature also explores some of these ideas in more detail. Another factor, strategy, is described in the next section.

6-3a Core Technology

technology
Conversion process used to transform inputs into outputs

Technology consists of the conversion processes used to transform inputs (such as materials or information) into outputs (such as products or services). Most organizations use multiple technologies, but an organization's most important one is called its *core technology*. Although most people visualize assembly lines and machinery when they think of technology, the term can also be applied to service organizations. For example, an investment firm like Fidelity uses technology to transform investment dollars into income in much the same way that Union Carbide uses natural resources to manufacture chemical products.

The link between technology and organization design was first recognized by Joan Woodward.[27] Woodward studied 100 manufacturing firms in southern England. She collected information about things such as the history of each organization, its manufacturing processes, its forms and procedures, and its financial performance. Woodward expected to find a relationship between the size of an organization and its design, but no such relationship emerged. As a result, she began to seek other explanations for differences. Close scrutiny of the firms in her sample led her to recognize a potential relationship between technology and organization design. This follow-up analysis led Woodward to first classify the organizations according to their technology. Three basic forms of technology were identified by Woodward:

Fidelity Investments uses technology to transform investment dollars into growth and income for investors. This technology, in turn, plays a significant role in the kind of organization design that best serves Fidelity. Other firms that use different technologies, meanwhile, will likely use different forms of organization design.

1. *Unit or small-batch technology.* Products are custom-made to customer specifications or produced in small quantities. Organizations using this form of technology include a tailor shop specializing in custom suits, a software company that creates specialized software for a single company, a printing shop that produces business cards and company stationery, and a photography studio.

2. *Large-batch or mass-production technology.* Products are manufactured in assembly-line fashion by combining component parts into another part or finished product. Examples are automobile manufacturers like Subaru, plants that make apparel for large retailers like Old Navy, appliance makers like Whirlpool Corporation, and electronics firms like Philips.

3. *Continuous-process technology.* Raw materials are transformed to finished products by a series of machine or process transformations. The composition of the materials themselves

An organization's core technology can play an important role in organization design. This factory, for example, makes use of a lot of different kinds of equipment and machinery to create the firm's products. The core technology for the business, therefore, is reflected by this equipment and machinery.

is changed. Examples are petroleum refineries like ExxonMobil and Shell and chemical refineries like Dow Chemical and Hoechst AG.

These forms of technology are listed in order of their assumed levels of complexity. In other words, unit or small-batch technology is presumed to be the least complex and continuous-process technology the most complex. Woodward found that different configurations of organization design were associated with each technology.

Specifically, Woodward found that the two extremes (unit or small-batch and continuous-process) tended to have very little bureaucracy, whereas the middle-range organizations (large-batch or mass-production) were much more bureaucratic. The large-batch and mass-production organizations also had a higher level of specialization.[28] Finally, she found that organizational success was related to the extent to which organizations followed the typical pattern. For example, successful continuous-process organizations tended to have less bureaucracy, whereas less successful firms with the same technology tended to be more bureaucratic.

6-3b Environment

Environmental elements and organization design are specifically linked in a number of ways. The first widely recognized analysis of environment–organization design linkages was provided by Tom Burns and G. M. Stalker.[29] Like Woodward, Burns and Stalker worked in

A WORLD OF DIFFERENCE

Keeping the Organizational Tools Sharp

There's been quite a bit of news about the death of manufacturing jobs in the United States, but Illinois Tool Works (NYSE:ITW), headquartered in Glenview, Illinois, is out to prove the critics wrong. Established in 1912 to manufacture metal-cutting tools, the company has grown over the last century to more than 48,000 employees around the globe. Beginning in 1980, ITW grew through the acquisition of hundreds of smaller companies, acquiring their product lines and distinctive competencies. Today, the company is organized into seven segments or operating divisions: Automotive OEM; Test and Measurement and Electronics; Food Equipment; Polymers and Fluids; Welding; Construction Products; and Specialty Products. Its products and services are quite diverse—in its Automotive OEM division, it produces plastic and metal components for automobiles and light trucks, while its Polymers and Fluids division produces industrial adhesives, cleaning and lubrication fluids, and polymers and fillers for automotive repairs and maintenance.

ITW's structure is built around a highly decentralized philosophy. Each of the seven operating divisions is designed to operate as a smaller, more flexible and entrepreneurial organization, maintaining its own revenue and cost centers. Decision making is highly decentralized, with most decisions about strategy made within the divisions. The company believes that this ITW business model not only responds effectively to customer needs, but it also maximizes economic performance.

Another key to Illinois Tool Works' success is its 80/20 Business Process. This is an operating philosophy that states that 80 percent of its revenues and profits should come from just 20 percent of its customers. In a company where innovation is key, this philosophy has helped ITW to focus its energies on product lines that will create the most synergy. ITW also emphasizes *customer back innovation*, a term it uses to describe that innovation is customer centered and focuses on the key needs of its most important constituents.

Illinois Tool Works has a strong global presence, operating in 57 countries, with major operations in Australia, Belgium, Brazil, Canada, China, Czech Republic, Denmark, France, Germany, Ireland, Italy, the Netherlands, Spain, Switzerland, and the United Kingdom. Though the United States is its biggest market, more than one-quarter of its revenues are in Europe, and more than 10 percent in Asia. This geographic diversification helps to mitigate the risk associated with a downturn in any regional economy.

Despite the unpredictability of the economy, sticking with these winning strategies for over 30 years has paid off for Illinois Tool Works. Like most companies, it was hit hard by the 2008–2009 recession, dropping from an all-time high of $60 per share to $30, but by 2016 the per share price was up to $100 and had reached $190 in early 2020. So far, ITW's key organizational strategies have allowed it to weather tough times and in all likelihood will continue to serve the company well in the future.

References: https://finance.yahoo.com/quote/ITW/ on April 10, 2020; https://www.itw.com/ on April 10, 2020; https://www.bloomberg.com/profile/company/ITW:US on April 10, 2020; "Illinois Tool Works," Wikipedia, https://en.wikipedia.org/wiki/Illinois_Tool_Works on April 10, 2020.

England. Their first step was identifying two extreme forms of organizational environment: stable (one that remains relatively constant over time) and unstable (subject to uncertainty and rapid change). Next, they studied the designs of organizations in each type of environment. Not surprisingly, they found that organizations in stable environments tended to have a different kind of design than organizations in unstable environments. The two kinds of design that emerged were called mechanistic and organic organization.

mechanistic organization
Similar to the bureaucratic model, most frequently found in stable environments

A mechanistic organization, quite similar to the bureaucratic model, was most frequently found in stable environments. Free from uncertainty, organizations structured their activities in rather predictable ways by means of rules, specialized jobs, and centralized authority. Mechanistic organizations are also quite similar to bureaucracies. Although no environment is completely stable, Abercrombie & Fitch and Wendy's use mechanistic designs. Each A&F store, for example, has prescribed methods for store design and merchandise-ordering processes. Little or no deviation is allowed from these methods. An organic organization, on the other hand, was most often found in unstable and unpredictable environments, in which constant change and uncertainty usually dictate a much higher level of fluidity and flexibility. Verizon (facing rapid technological change) and Apple (facing both technological change and constant change in consumer tastes) both use organic designs. A manager at Verizon, for example, has considerable discretion over how work is performed and how problems can be solved.

organic organization
Very flexible and informal model of organization design, most often found in unstable and unpredictable environments

differentiation
Extent to which the organization is broken down into subunits

These ideas were extended in the United States by Paul R. Lawrence and Jay W. Lorsch.[30] They agreed that environmental factors influence organization design but believed that this influence varies between different units of the same organization. In fact, they predicted that each organizational unit has a unique environment and responds by developing unique attributes. Lawrence and Lorsch suggested that organizations could be characterized along two primary dimensions.

integration
Degree to which the various subunits must work together in a coordinated fashion

One of these dimensions, differentiation, is the extent to which the organization is broken down into subunits. A firm with many subunits is highly differentiated; one with few subunits has a low level of differentiation. The second dimension, integration, is the degree to which the various subunits must work together in a coordinated fashion. For example, if each unit competes in a different market and has its own production facilities, they may need little integration. Lawrence and Lorsch reasoned that the degree of differentiation and integration needed by an organization depends on the stability of the environments that its subunits face.

"Networks are becoming the locus for innovation. Firms . . . are more porous and decentralized."
—Walter Powell, Professor at Stanford University[31]

6-3c Organizational Size and Life Cycle

The size and life cycle of an organization may also affect its design.[32] Although several definitions of size exist, we define organizational size as the total number of full-time or full-time-equivalent employees. A team of researchers at the University of Aston in Birmingham, England, believed that Woodward had failed to find a size–structure relationship (which was her original expectation) because almost all the organizations she studied were relatively small (three-fourths had fewer than 500 employees).[33] Thus, they decided to undertake a study of a wider array of organizations to determine how size and technology both individually and jointly affect an organization's design.

organizational size
Total number of full-time or full-time-equivalent employees

"Managerial problems and practices are rooted in time. They do not last throughout the life of an organization."
—Larry Greiner, Organization Design Expert

Their primary finding was that technology did in fact influence structural variables in small firms, probably because all their activities tend to be centered on their core technologies. In large firms, however, the strong technology–design link broke down, most likely because technology is not as central to ongoing activities in large organizations. The Aston studies yielded a number of basic generalizations: When compared to small organizations, large organizations tend to be characterized by higher levels of job specialization, more standard operating procedures, more rules, more regulations, and a greater degree of decentralization. Walmart is a good case in point. The firm expects to continue to grow for the foreseeable future, adding several thousand new jobs in the next few years. But, as it grows, the firm acknowledges that it will have to become more decentralized for its first-line managers to stay in tune with

Organizational life cycle affects organization design. New and modern firms such as this one are often designed in ways that are very different from older, more traditional companies.

their customers. Of course, size is not constant. As we noted in Chapter 5, for example, some small businesses are formed but soon disappear. Others remain as small, independently operated enterprises as long as their owner-manager lives. A few, such as Facebook, JetBlue, and Starbucks, skyrocket to become organizational giants. And occasionally large organizations reduce their size through layoffs or divestitures. Marathon Oil, for instance, split into two independent businesses a few years ago. One business retained Marathon's core operations and name but became a much smaller entity.

Although no clear pattern explains changes in size, many organizations progress through a four-stage **organizational life cycle**.[34] The first stage is the birth of the organization. The second stage, youth, is characterized by growth and the expansion of organizational resources. Midlife is a period of gradual growth evolving eventually into stability. Finally, maturity is a

organizational life cycle
Progression through which organizations evolve as they grow and mature

period of stability, perhaps eventually evolving into decline. Firms like Netflix, Starbucks, and Amazon, for instance, are still in their youth stage; Halliburton, Walmart, and Chevron are in midlife; and Ford and Procter & Gamble are in maturity. (A key challenge for managers, of course, is to avoid allowing a mature organization to begin to decline. Hence, they must be alert for opportunities to reenergize the organization with new products and new markets.)

Managers must confront a number of organization design issues as the organization progresses through these stages. In general, as an organization passes from one stage to the next, it becomes bigger, more mechanistic, and more decentralized. It also becomes more specialized, devotes more attention to planning, and takes on an increasingly large staff component. Finally, coordination demands increase, formalization increases, organizational units become geographically more dispersed, and control systems become more extensive. Thus, an organization's size and design are clearly linked, and this link is dynamic because of the organizational life cycle.

Manager's Checklist

☐ Managers need to understand how technology, the environment, organization size, and organizational life cycle all affect organization design.

☐ You should also have a clear understanding of your own organization's technology, environment, size, and life cycle.

6-4 BASIC FORMS OF ORGANIZATION DESIGN

Because technology, environment, size, and life cycle can all influence organization design, it should come as no surprise that organizations adopt many different kinds of designs. Most designs, however, fall into one of four basic categories. Others are hybrids based on two or more of the basic forms.

6-4a Functional (U-Form) Design

functional design
Based on the functional approach to departmentalization

conglomerate design
Used by an organization made up of a set of unrelated businesses

The **functional design** is an arrangement based on the functional approach to departmentalization. This design has been termed the *U-form* (for unitary) approach.[35] Under the U-form arrangement, the members and units in the organization are grouped into functional departments such as marketing and production.

This employee of the McIlhenny Company, famous makers of TABASCO sauce, is part of the production team. Her company uses the U-form design, where members and units are grouped into functional departments.

For the organization to operate efficiently in this design, there must be considerable coordination across departments. This integration and coordination are most commonly the responsibility of the CEO and members of senior management. Figure 6.2 shows the U-form design applied to the corporate level of a small manufacturing company. In a U-form organization, none of the functional areas can survive without the others. Marketing, for example, needs products from operations to sell and funds from finance to pay for advertising. The WD-40 Company, which makes a popular lubricating oil, the McIlhenny Company, which makes TABASCO sauce, and Red Bull GmbH are all examples of firms that use the U-form design.

In general, this approach shares the basic advantages and disadvantages of functional departmentalization. Thus, it allows the organization to staff all important positions with functional experts and it facilitates coordination and integration. On the other hand, it also promotes a functional, rather than an organizational, focus and tends to promote centralization. Functionally based designs are most commonly used in small organizations because an individual CEO can easily oversee and coordinate the entire organization. As an organization grows, the CEO finds staying on top of all functional areas increasingly difficult.

6-4b Conglomerate (H-Form) Design

Another common form of organization design is the conglomerate, or *H-form* (for holding, as in holding company), approach.[36] The **conglomerate design** is used by an organization made up of a set of unrelated businesses. Thus, the H-form design is essentially a holding company that results from unrelated diversification.

This approach is based loosely on the product form of departmentalization. Each business or set of businesses is operated by a general manager who is responsible for its profits or losses, and each general manager functions

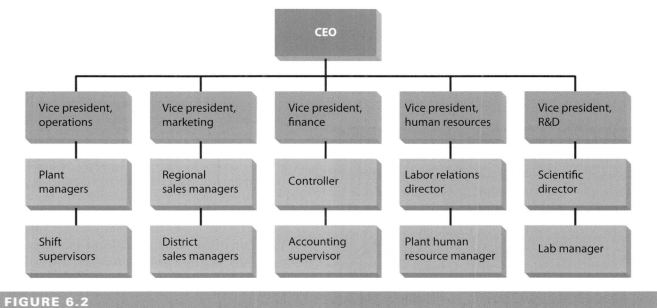

FIGURE 6.2

Functional (U-Form) Design for a Small Manufacturing Company

The U-form design is based on functional departmentalization. This small manufacturing firm uses managers at the vice-presidential level to coordinate activities within each functional area of the organization. Note that each functional area is dependent on the others.

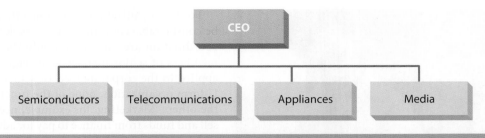

Conglomerate (H-Form) Design at Samsung

Samsung Electronics Company, a South Korean firm, uses the conglomerate form of organization design. This design, which results from a strategy of unrelated diversification, is a complex one to manage. Managers find that comparing and integrating activities among the dissimilar operations are difficult. Companies may abandon this design for another approach, such as the M-form design.

independently of the others. Samsung Electronics Company, a South Korean firm, uses the H-form design. As illustrated in Figure 6.3, Samsung consists of four basic business groups. Other firms that use the H-form design include General Electric (power and water, oil and gas, renewable energy, lighting, health care, transportation, and other unrelated businesses) and TRT Holdings (gyms, hotels, oil and gas exploration, and retailing).

In an H-form organization, a corporate staff usually evaluates the performance of each business, allocates corporate resources across companies, and shapes decisions about buying and selling businesses. The basic shortcoming of the H-form design is the complexity associated with holding diverse and unrelated businesses. Managers usually find comparing and integrating activities across a large number of diverse operations difficult. Research suggests that many organizations following this approach achieve only average-to-weak financial performance.[37] Thus, although some U.S. firms are still using the H-form design, many have abandoned it for other approaches.

6-4c **Divisional (M-Form) Design**

divisional design
Based on multiple businesses in related areas operating within a larger organizational framework

In the **divisional design**, which is becoming increasingly popular, a product form of organization is also used; in contrast to the H-form approach, however, the divisions are related. Thus, the divisional design, or *M-form* (for multidivisional) approach, is based on multiple businesses in related areas operating within a larger organizational framework. This design results from a strategy of related diversification.

Some activities are extremely decentralized down to the divisional level; others are centralized at the corporate level.[38] For example, as shown in Figure 6.4, Hilton Hotels uses this approach. Each of its divisions is headed by a president or executive VP and operates with reasonable autonomy, but the divisions also coordinate their activities as is appropriate. Other firms that use this approach are the Walt Disney Company (theme parks, movies, television, and merchandising units, all interrelated) and HP (computers, printers, scanners, electronic medical equipment, and other electronic instrumentation).

The opportunities for coordination and shared resources represent one of the biggest advantages of the M-form design. Hilton's market research and purchasing departments are centralized. Thus, a site selector can visit a city and look for possible locations for different Hilton brands, and a buyer can purchase bed linens for multiple

Hilton uses a divisional (M-form) organization design. Each of the hotel's brands, such as Garden Inn, Hampton Inn, DoubleTree, and Hilton, are run as separate divisions.

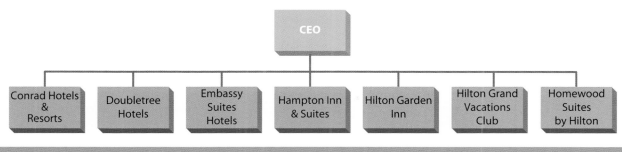

Multidivisional (M-Form) Design at Hilton Hotels

Hilton Hotels uses the multidivisional approach to organization design. Although each unit operates with relative autonomy, all units function in the same general market. This design resulted from a strategy of related diversification. Other firms that use M-form designs include PepsiCo and the Walt Disney Company.

Hilton brands from the same supplier. The M-form design's basic objective is to optimize internal competition and cooperation. Healthy competition for resources among divisions can enhance effectiveness, but cooperation should also be promoted. Research suggests that the M-form organization that can achieve and maintain this balance will outperform large U-form and all H-form organizations.[39]

6-4d Matrix Design

matrix design

Based on two overlapping bases of departmentalization

The **matrix design**, another common approach to organization design, is based on two overlapping bases of departmentalization.[40] The foundation of a matrix is a set of functional departments. A set of product groups, or temporary departments, is then superimposed across the functional departments. Employees in a matrix are simultaneously members of a functional department (such as engineering) and of a project team.

Figure 6.5 shows a basic matrix design. At the top of the organization are functional units headed by VPs of engineering, production, finance, and marketing. Each of these managers has several subordinates. Along the side of the organization are a number of positions called *project manager*. Each project manager heads a project group composed of representatives or workers from the functional departments. Note from the figure that a matrix reflects a *multiple-command structure*—any given individual reports to both a functional superior and one or more project managers.

The project groups, or teams, are assigned to designated projects or programs. For example, the company might be developing a new product. Representatives are chosen from each functional area to work as a team on the new product. They also retain membership in the original functional group. At any given time, a person may be a member of several teams as well as a member of a functional group. Ford uses this approach every time it redesigns such popular models as the Mustang automobile and F-150 pickup truck. For instance, in its most recent redesign of the Mustang, it formed a group called "Team Mustang" made up of designers, engineers, production specialists, marketing specialists, and other experts from different areas of the company. This group facilitated getting a very successful product to the market at least a year earlier than would have been possible using traditional product design methods.

Martha Stewart also uses a matrix organization for her lifestyle business. The company was first organized broadly into media and merchandising groups, each of which has specific product and product groups. Layered on top of this structure are teams of lifestyle experts organized into groups such as cooking, crafts, and weddings. Each of these groups is targeted toward specific customer needs, but they work as necessary across all of the product groups. For example, a wedding expert might contribute to an article on wedding planning for a *Martha Stewart Living* magazine, contribute a story idea for a cable TV program, and supply content for a Martha Stewart website. This same individual might also help select fabrics suitable for wedding gowns for retailing.

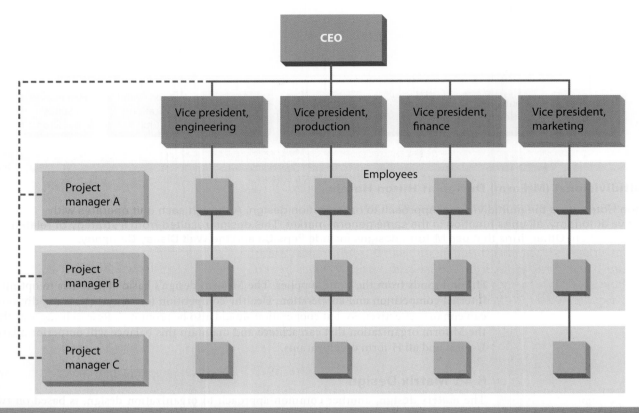

A Matrix Organization

A matrix organization design is created by superimposing a product form of departmentalization on an existing functional organization. Project managers coordinate teams of employees drawn from different functional departments. Thus, a matrix relies on a multiple-command structure.

The matrix form of organization design is most often used in one of three situations.[41] First, a matrix may work when there is strong pressure from the environment. For example, intense external competition may dictate the sort of strong marketing thrust that is best spearheaded by a functional department, but the diversity of a company's products may argue for product departments. Second, a matrix may be appropriate when large amounts of information need to be processed. For example, creating lateral relationships by means of a matrix is one effective way to increase the organization's capacity for processing information. Third, the matrix design may work when there is pressure for shared resources. For example, a company with ten product departments may have resources for only three marketing specialists. A matrix design would allow all the departments to share the company's scarce marketing resources.

Both advantages and disadvantages are associated with the matrix design. Researchers have observed six primary advantages of matrix designs. First, they enhance flexibility because teams can be created, redefined, and dissolved as needed. Second, because they assume a major role in decision making, team members are likely to be highly motivated and committed to the organization. Third, employees in a matrix organization have considerable opportunity to learn new skills. Fourth, the matrix design provides an efficient way for the organization to take full advantage of its human resources. Fifth, team members retain membership in their functional unit so that they can serve as a bridge between the functional unit and the team, enhancing cooperation. Sixth, the matrix design gives top management a useful vehicle for decentralization. Once the day-to-day operations have been delegated, top management can devote more attention to areas such as long-range planning. Several large companies, including Disney, Target, and AT&T, temporarily adopted a matrix design during the 2020 COVID-19 pandemic to help them better cope with the unfolding risks and uncertainties associated with turbulent environmental forces and pressures.

On the other hand, the matrix design also has some major disadvantages. Employees may be uncertain about reporting relationships, especially if they are simultaneously assigned to a functional manager and to several project managers. To complicate matters, some managers see the matrix as a form of anarchy in which they have unlimited freedom. Another set of problems is associated with the dynamics of group behavior. Groups take longer than individuals to make decisions, may be dominated by one individual, and may compromise too much. They may also get bogged down in discussion and not focus on their primary objectives. Finally, in a matrix, more time may also be required for coordinating task-related activities.[42]

6-4e Hybrid Designs

Some organizations use a design that represents a hybrid of two or more of the common forms of organization design.[43] For example, an organization may have five related divisions and one unrelated division, making its design a cross between an M form and an H form. Indeed, few companies use a single design in its pure form; most firms have one basic organization design as a foundation for managing the business but maintain sufficient flexibility so that temporary or permanent modifications can be made for strategic purposes. As noted earlier, for example, while Ford uses the matrix approach for some new model redesign programs, the company is basically a U-form organization showing signs of moving to an M-form design as it explores autonomous vehicles, electric vehicles, and other forms of transportation. As we noted earlier, any combination of factors may dictate the appropriate form of design for any particular company.

Manager's Checklist

☐ Managers need to understand the basic forms of organization design.

☐ They should also know the advantages and disadvantages of each and how most organizations use hybrid approaches.

6-5 EMERGING ISSUES IN ORGANIZATION DESIGN

In today's complex and ever-changing environment, it should come as no surprise that managers continue to explore and experiment with new forms of organization design. Many organizations are creating designs for themselves that maximize their ability to adapt to changing circumstances and to a changing environment. They try to accomplish this by not becoming too compartmentalized or too rigid. As we noted earlier, bureaucratic organizations are hard to change, slow, and inflexible. To avoid these problems, then, organizations can try to be as different from bureaucracies as possible—relatively few rules, general job descriptions, and so forth. This final section highlights some of the most important emerging issues.[44]

6-5a The Team Organization

team organization
An approach to organization design that relies almost exclusively on project-type teams, with little or no underlying hierarchy

Many organizations today are using the team organization, an approach to organization design that relies almost exclusively on project-type teams, with little or no underlying functional hierarchy. Within such an organization, people float from project to project as necessitated by their skills and the demands of those projects. At Cypress Semiconductor, top managers have long refused to allow the organization to grow so large that it could not function this way. Whenever a unit or group started getting too large, managers simply split it into smaller units. Consequently, all units within the organization are still relatively small.

This allows them to change direction, explore new ideas, and try new methods without dealing with a rigid bureaucratic organizational context. Apple, Xerox, and Amazon are among the more well-known firms that emphasize a team-based organization design. Even organizations that have not made widespread use of teams a part of their design quickly created new teams to help navigate during the COVID-19 pandemic and its aftermath.

6-5b The Virtual Organization

Closely related to the team organization is the virtual organization that has little or no formal structure. Such an organization typically has only a handful of permanent employees and a very small staff and administrative headquarters facility. As the needs of the organization change, its managers bring in temporary workers, lease facilities, and outsource basic support services to meet the demands of each unique situation. As the situation changes, the temporary workforce changes in parallel, with some people leaving the organization and others entering. Facilities and the services subcontracted to others change as well. Thus, the organization exists only in response to its needs. And, increasingly, virtual organizations are conducting most—if not all—of their businesses online.

For example, TLG Research Inc. was founded as a virtual organization focused on marketing research for automotive, aviation, marine, and industrial markets for original equipment and replacement parts. Currently, the company consists of an in-house project management staff of 16 people and a virtual network of industry professionals. It also has a global business and research sources in Europe, Latin America, and Asia–Pacific to refer to for consulting and research services as needed.

6-5c The Learning Organization

Another recent approach to organization design is the so-called learning organization. Organizations that adopt this approach work to integrate continuous improvement with continuous employee learning and development. Specifically, a learning organization is one that works to facilitate the lifelong learning and personal development of all its employees while continually transforming itself to respond to changing demands and needs.[45]

Although managers might approach the concept of a learning organization from a variety of perspectives, improved quality, continuous improvement, and performance measurement are frequent goals. The idea is that the most consistent and logical strategy for achieving continuous improvement is by constantly upgrading employee talent, skill, and knowledge. For example, if each employee in an organization learns one new thing each day and can translate that knowledge into work-related practice, continuous improvement will logically follow. Indeed, organizations that wholeheartedly embrace this approach believe that only through constant learning by employees can continuous improvement really occur.[46]

In recent years, many different organizations have implemented this approach. For example, Royal Dutch Shell owns and operates a conference center in Rijswijk, Norway, which it calls the Learning Centre for Technical Courses. The center boasts state-of-the-art classrooms with instructional technology and drilling simulators, lodging facilities, a restaurant and a sandwich shop, a prayer room, and quiet spaces where people can go to reflect and meditate. The Learning Centre can accommodate 270 students per day and more than 5,000 per year. Line managers at the firm rotate through the Shell Learning Centre and serve as teaching faculty. Such teaching assignments last anywhere from a few days to several months. At the same time, all Shell employees routinely attend training programs, seminars, and related activities, all the while learning the latest information that they need to contribute more effectively to the firm. Recent seminar topics have ranged from time management, to the latest oil drilling techniques, to balancing work and family demands, to international trade theory. The idea is that by continuously immersing people in shared learning experiences the firm will promote an organic design populated by people with common knowledge, goals, and expectations.

---

virtual organization
One that has little or no formal structure

learning organization
One that works to facilitate the lifelong learning and personal development of all its employees while continually transforming itself to respond to changing demands and needs

SUMMARY OF LEARNING OUTCOMES AND KEY POINTS

6-1. Identify the basic elements of organizations.

- Organizations are made up of a series of elements:
  - Designing jobs
  - Grouping jobs
  - Establishing reporting relationships
  - Distributing authority
  - Coordinating activities

6-2. Describe the bureaucratic perspective on organization design.

- The bureaucratic model attempted to prescribe how all organizations should be designed.
- It is based on the presumed need for legitimate, logical, and formal rules, regulations, and procedures.

6-3. Explain key situational influences on organization design.

- The situational view of organization design is based on the assumption that the optimal organization design is a function of situational factors.

- Four important situational factors are:
  - Technology
  - Environment
  - Size
  - Organizational life cycle

6-4. Describe the basic forms of organization design that characterize many organizations.

- Many organizations today adopt one of four basic organization designs:
  - Functional (U form)
  - Conglomerate (H form)
  - Divisional (M form)
  - Matrix
- Other organizations use a hybrid design derived from two or more of these basic designs.

6-5. Identify emerging issues in organization design.

- Three emerging issues in organization design are:
  - Team organization
  - Virtual organization
  - Learning organization

DISCUSSION QUESTIONS

Questions for Review

1. What is job specialization? What are its advantages and disadvantages?
2. Distinguish between centralization and decentralization, and comment on their relative advantages and disadvantages.
3. Describe the basic forms of organization design. What are the advantages and disadvantages of each?
4. Compare and contrast the matrix organization and the team organization, citing their similarities and differences.

Questions for Analysis

1. How is specialization applied in settings such as a hospital, restaurant, and church?
2. Identify five ways in which digital coordination affects your daily life.
3. What are the benefits of using the learning organization approach to design? Now consider that, to learn, organizations must be willing to tolerate many mistakes because it is only through the effort of understanding mistakes that learning can occur. With this statement in mind, what are some of the potential problems with the use of the learning organization approach?

Questions for Application

1. Learn how your school or business is organized. Analyze the advantages and disadvantages of this form of departmentalization, and then comment on how well or how poorly other forms of organization might work.
2. Each of the organization designs is appropriate for some firms but not for others. Describe the characteristics that a firm using the U form should have. Then do the same for the H form, the M form, and the matrix design. For each item, explain the relationship between that set of characteristics and the choice of organization design.
3. During the 2020 COVID-19 pandemic many organizations required their employees to work remotely and maintained little or no staff at their headquarters. Is this the same as a virtual organization? Why or why not?

BUILDING EFFECTIVE CONCEPTUAL SKILLS

Exercise Overview

Conceptual skills require you to think in the abstract. In this exercise, you'll use your conceptual skills in analyzing organizational structure.

Exercise Background

Looking at its organization chart allows you to understand a company's structure, including its distribution of authority, its divisional breakdown, its levels of hierarchy, and its reporting relationships. The reverse is also true: When you understand the elements of a company's structure, you can draw up an organization chart to reflect it. In this exercise, that's just what you'll do: You'll use online resources to research a firm's structure and then draw an appropriate organization chart.

Exercise Task

1. Alone or with a partner, go online to research a publicly traded U.S. firm in which you're interested.

Focus on information that will help you understand the company's structure. If you research Ford Motor Company, for example, you should look for information about different types of vehicles, different regions in which Ford products are sold, and different functions that the company performs. (*Hint*: The firm's annual report is usually available online and typically contains a great deal of helpful information. In particular, take a look at the section containing an editorial message from the chairman or CEO and the section summarizing financial information. In many cases, "segment" data reveal a lot about divisional structure.)

2. Draw an organization chart based on your research.
3. Share your results with another group or with the class as a whole. Be prepared to explain and justify the decisions that you made in determining the firm's structure.

BUILDING EFFECTIVE DIAGNOSTIC SKILLS

Exercise Overview

Diagnostic skills enable a manager to visualize the most appropriate response to a situation. In this exercise, you're asked to apply your diagnostic skills to the question of centralization versus decentralization in an organization.

Exercise Background

Managers often find it necessary to change an organization's degree of centralization or decentralization. Begin this exercise by reflecting on two very different scenarios in which this issue has arisen:

Scenario A. You're the top manager in a large organization with a long and successful history of centralized operations. For valid reasons beyond the scope of this exercise, however, you've decided to make the firm much more decentralized.

Scenario B. Assume the exact opposite of the situation in Scenario A. You still occupy the top spot in your firm, but this time you're going to centralize operations in an organization that's always been decentralized.

Exercise Task

Now do the following:

1. For Scenario A, list the major barriers to decentralization that you foresee.
2. For Scenario B, list the major barriers to centralization that you foresee.
3. In your opinion, which scenario would be easier to implement in reality? In other words, is it probably easier to move from centralization to decentralization or vice versa? Whatever your opinion in the matter, be ready to explain it.

Given a choice of starting your career in a firm that's either highly centralized or highly decentralized, which would you prefer? Why?

SKILL-BUILDING PERSONAL ASSESSMENT

Delegation Aptitude Survey

Purpose: To help students gain insight into the process of and the attitudes important to delegation.

Introduction: Delegation has a number of advantages for managers, workers, and organizations, but it also presents challenges. Managers who understand the benefits of delegation, who trust their subordinates, and who have the emotional maturity to allow others to succeed are more likely to be effective delegators.

Instructions:

1. Complete the following Delegation Aptitude Survey. You should think of work-related or group situations in which you have had the opportunity to delegate responsibility to others. If you have not had such experiences, try to imagine how you would respond in such a situation. Circle the response that best typifies your attitude or behavior.
2. Score the survey according to the directions that follow. Calculate your overall score.

3. Working with a small group, compare individual scores and prepare group responses to the discussion questions.

4. Calculate a class-average score. Have one member of the group present the group's responses to the discussion questions.

Delegation Aptitude Survey

Statement	Strongly Agree	Slightly Agree	Not Sure	Slightly Disagree	Strongly Disagree
1. I don't think others can do the work as well as I can.	1	2	3	4	5
2. I often take work home with me.	1	2	3	4	5
3. Employees who can make their own decisions tend to be more efficient.	5	4	3	2	1
4. I often have to rush to meet deadlines.	1	2	3	4	5
5. Employees with more responsibility tend to have more commitment to group goals.	5	4	3	2	1
6. When I delegate, I always explain precisely how the task is to be done.	1	2	3	4	5
7. I always seem to have too much to do and too little time to do it in.	1	2	3	4	5
8. When employees have the responsibility to do a job, they usually do it well.	5	4	3	2	1
9. When I delegate, I make clear the end results I expect.	5	4	3	2	1
10. I usually only delegate simple, routine tasks.	1	2	3	4	5
11. When I delegate, I always make sure everyone concerned is so informed.	5	4	3	2	1
12. If I delegate, I usually wind up doing the job over again to get it right.	1	2	3	4	5
13. I become irritated watching others doing a job I can do better.	1	2	3	4	5
14. When I delegate, I feel I am losing the control I need.	1	2	3	4	5
15. When I delegate, I always set specific dates for progress reports.	5	4	3	2	1
16. When I do a job, I do it to perfection.	1	2	3	4	5

(Continued)

Statement	Strongly Agree	Slightly Agree	Not Sure	Slightly Disagree	Strongly Disagree
17. I honestly feel that I can do most jobs better than my subordinates can.	1	2	3	4	5
18. When employees make their own decisions, it tends to cause confusion.	1	2	3	4	5
19. It's difficult for subordinates to make decisions because they don't know the organization's goals.	1	2	3	4	5
20. When employees are given responsibility, they usually do what is asked of them.	5	4	3	2	1

Discussion Questions

1. In what respects do the survey responses agree or disagree?
2. What might account for some of the differences in individual scores?
3. How can you make constructive use of the survey results?

Bureaucratic System 1	20–29
	30–39
Mixed Systems 2 and 3	40–49
	50–59
	60–69
	70–79
Organic System 4	80–89
	90–100

Scoring: The higher the score, the more organic and participative the organization. The lower the score, the more mechanistic and bureaucratically managed the organization.

Scores in the 20–39 range suggest that the organization is relatively bureaucratic and mechanistic. Scores above 80 suggest that the organization is relatively organic and participative. Scores in the 40–79 range suggest a mixed design. Students should compare the type of organization identified with the type of environment in which it is most likely to be successful as described in the book.

Source: Linda Morable, *Exercises in Management*, 8th ed., pp. 82–84. 2005.

MANAGEMENT AT WORK

Alshaya's Matrix Design

"Because of the breadth of our brands portfolio, it is relatively easy for us to redeploy staff and resources to support our strongest brands. . . ."

—Mohammed Alshaya, Chairman
of M. H. Alshaya

Most likely you have never heard of a business called Alshaya; the Kuwait-based business M. H. Alshaya Company does not have great name recognition. But that's exactly how the privately held company owned by the Alshaya family wants to keep it. To gain insight into the far-reaching nature of the Alshaya empire, however, assume for a moment that you are visiting Bahrain, Dubai, or Kuwait City on business but have a little free time. As it turns out you also need to do a little shopping so you decide to take in one of the huge megamalls that have sprung up in those places in recent years. During your outing you would see and might decide to eat and shop in stores such as The Cheesecake Factory, Pinkberry, IHOP, American Eagle Outfitters, Victoria's Secret, Pottery Barn, Williams-Sonoma, and Starbucks. Perhaps surprisingly, as it turns out, each of those stores and restaurants throughout the entire region are owned and managed by none other than M. H. Alshaya Company.

The Alshaya enterprise dates back to 1890. For much of its history the firm concentrated in the real estate and construction industries. In 1983, though, Alshaya acquired the Kuwait franchise for U.K. retailer Mothercare. The firm's managers immediately began to recognize that the profitability of its new business exceeded their projections and, with approval from the franchisor, started expanding Mothercare into other countries, including Turkey and Russia. As revenues and profits from Mothercare continued to grow, Alshaya began to prospect for other brands to add to its portfolio. In 2006 it acquired the Middle Eastern franchising rights for international clothing retailer H&M, followed quickly by regional franchising rights to Dean and Deluca (in 2008) and P.F. Chang's, Pinkberry, and Payless Shoesource (all in 2009).

Alshaya has continued to grow rapidly as a franchisee for dozens of retailer and restaurant chains, concentrating in the Middle East but recently branching out into Europe and Asia as well. Alshaya offers strong regional expertise—scouting locations, negotiating leases, hiring and training employees, and helping modify foods and other products to meet local religious amd cultural requirements. For example, foods with alcohol-based content must have their ingredients modified, but Alshaya tries to find alternative ingredients that produce the same appearance and taste. Although Alshaya modifies its stores to meet local customs,

it also strives to maintain the character and experience that customers enjoy regardless of their locations. So, a Starbucks latte made in Dubai tastes just like a Starbucks latte made in Seattle and IHOP pancakes in Dubai look and taste the same as IHOP pancakes in Atlanta. And the store and customer "buying experiences" are also the same.

The firm currently operates more than 4,500 stores comprising more than 90 brands in 19 countries, and its stores occupy over 14 million square feet of retail space. Although much of its operations are based in the Middle East, Alshaya also has stores in Poland, Russia, the Czech Republic, the United Kingdom, and Morocco. The firm also employs approximately 60,000 people of 120 different nationalities.

To help staff its stores, Alshaya has also taken the unusual approach of opening its own training academies. Its first was the Alshaya Retail Academy in Riyadh, Saudi Arabia and its mission was to provide retail training and employment on graduation for young Saudi women. The firm has since opened two more academies in Jeddah and Dammam.

The firm is now looking to integrate some of its original real estate and construction businesses with its more recent retailing successes. For example, Alshaya is developing and constructing a major mixed-use development called Burj Alshaya in Kuwait. Several of Alshaya's more up-scale brands will be represented in the retailing sections of the development, but there will also be many other non-Alshaya products represented as well. As just one example, one major tenant will be a new Four Seasons hotel, that company's first hotel in Kuwait.

Alshaya uses a matrix design to manage its diverse and far-flung retail operations. The basic structure is centered on seven business units: fashion and footwear, food, health and beauty, pharmacy, optics, home furnishings, and office supplies. Each of these business units has its own president who reports directly to the CEO. So, for example, the food business unit president oversees Alshaya's Starbucks, Cheesecake Factory, IHOP, Texas Roadhouse, P. F Chang's, and other food businesses across all of their markets (23 food brands in all).

The matrix "overlay" consists of what Alshaya calls cross-border functional teams and includes human resources, finance, legal, property, supply chain, audit, IT, and customer care specialists. The firm's logic for this arrangement is that it enables Alshaya to rely on common metrics, policies, and reporting systems in a consistent manner. For instance, a common metric to measure retail sales is revenue per square foot of floor space and sales at the same location compared from one time period to the same time period a year later. By using common metrics such as these, Alshaya can then judge the performance of an IHOP restaurant in

Kuwait City and compare it to the performance of IHOPs in Warsaw, Dubai, and Doha. All in all, then, Alshaya seems to be performing well, and its matrix design seems well suited for such a complex organization.[47]

Case Questions

1. What situational elements most directly impact Alshaya's organization design?

2. How have both corporate- and business-level strategies influenced Alshaya's organization design?

3. What specific advantages and disadvantages does the matrix structure pose for Alshaya? Do the advantages more than offset the disadvantages? In what ways?

4. As Alshaya continues to grow, how might its organization design need to be changed? Will the matrix design continue to be appropriate or will it need to be changed to something else altogether?

You Make the Call

The Stress of Screening

1. Using the job characteristics theory as a framework, propose changes to the job of Transportation Security Officer to make it more engaging and motivating.

2. The opening case lists the five major units within the Transportation Security Administration (TSA). Review that list of these units from the case and describe the basis of departmentalization apparently being used by the TSA (you may need to consult online resources to completely answer this question).

3. Analyze and describe the levels of hierarchy that exist within TSA. Why do you think the organization has these levels? In your judgment, is the organization too tall, too flat, or does it have the optimum number of levels?

4. Within the passenger screening function at an airport, what kind of interdependence seems to exist among TSAs? What coordination requirements are necessary? How is coordination achieved?

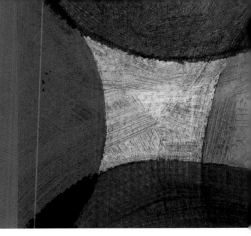

CHAPTER 7

Organization Change and Innovation

Learning Outcomes

After studying this chapter, you should be able to:

7-1   Describe the nature of organization change, including forces for change and planned versus reactive change.

7-2   Discuss the steps in organization change and how to manage resistance to change.

7-3   Describe the major areas of organization change and the assumptions, techniques, and effectiveness of organization development.

7-4   Discuss the innovation process, forms of innovation, failure to innovate, and how organizations can promote innovation.

This chapter describes how organizations manage change. We first examine the nature of organization change and identify the basic issues of managing change. We then identify and describe major areas of change, including business process change, a major type of change undertaken by many firms. We then examine organization development and conclude by discussing organizational innovation as a vital form of change. First, though, let's examine some of the potential effects of ineffective change management.

Management in Action

A Picture Says it All

"[Kodak] . . . overflowed with complacency."

—John Kotter, Organization Change Expert

Imagine that you are a manager at a business that is ranked among the top 20 companies in the *Fortune 500*. Your company, over a hundred years old, employs 145,000 workers and enjoys annual revenues of more than $13 billion. The name of your firm is synonymous with technology and market domination and is as widely known and recognized as such brand names as Coca-Cola, McDonald's, and Levi's. Your company has a 90 percent market share and controls hundreds of lucrative patents. And one of your scientists has just invented a new technology that will revolutionize the market. What could go wrong? Well, fast-forward to the present. Only 30 years later the same company has only around 5,000 employees and is worth less than $150 million. Your company is Kodak and its story represents an extended pattern of either resisting change or implementing change ineffectively.

Former Kodak executive Larry Matteson says that the company was hit by a perfect storm: "I can't think of another major company in the U.S. that has undergone as tough a transformation as Kodak. When IBM changed," explains Matteson, "its core capabilities remained essentially the same; at Kodak, everything changed, right through research, to marketing, to sales."

So—more to the point—what changed everything and reduced a blue-chip corporation to a shadow of itself in just three decades? Most analysts approach this question by citing the advent of *digital technology*—the capacity to store and process data as computerized bits and bytes rather than as streams of electronic signals loaded onto such physical materials as magnetic tape or silver halide film (known as *analog technology*). The so-called *Digital Revolution*—the widespread transition from analog to digital—took off in the 1980s and 1990s, as cellphones became ubiquitous and the Internet became a fixture in business operations. Amazingly, though, it was Kodak scientists who actually created the first digital camera!

According to Harvard's John Kotter, a widely acknowledged authority on organizational change, "Kodak's problem . . . is that it did not move into the digital world well enough and fast enough." It's pretty much a consensus opinion, but Kotter is careful to add the qualifier "on the surface." Below the surface, suggests Kotter, where Kodak made the business decisions that led to its decline, it's an opinion that needs further investigation. Kodak, for example, pioneered digital technologies throughout the 1970s and 1980s, including innovations in color digital cameras, digital print kiosks, and digital image compression. Kodak, says Bill Fischer, CEO of the private equity firm Manzanita Capital, "played along the entire 'imaging' value chain and was certainly in an excellent position to be intimately familiar with whatever was going on within and around the imaging business."

Unfortunately, says Fischer, top Kodak managers "failed to take advantage of their unique perspective." Fischer concludes that Kodak ultimately succumbed to "creeping disruption by digital imaging." As for Kotter, he argues that Kodak was facing a "technological discontinuities challenge," which occurs when a new technology features "low margins and cannibalizes your high-margin core business." In Kotter's estimation, "Kodak did not take decisive action to combat the inevitable challenges" posed by such technologies.

The challenge can be particularly difficult when the discontinuity comes from an unexpected source. The first "smartphone" was rolled out in 1994 and the first camera-equipped smartphone in 2000. By 2010, smartphone manufacturers were shipping more units (100.9 million) than PC makers (92.1 million). A year later, the iPad 2 hit the market. Says Bill Fischer: "We can suspect that Kodak, while recognizing the impending threat of a digital 'something,' probably did not immediately imagine that it would be a 'telephone' that would ultimately be the most damaging agent of disruption" to its core film- and camera-making businesses.

Some of the company's critics charge that, even on the brink of its 2012 bankruptcy, Kodak managers failed—or refused—to acknowledge that many of the company's products had been marginalized by digital substitutions. According to George T. Conboy, chairman of Brighton Securities, Kodak "made a big mistake of riding the cash cow—film—to the point that there was simply no more milk coming from it." During the bankruptcy process, for example, Kodak management hoped to sell one of the firm's prized assets—a package of 1,100 digital-imaging patents— for as much as $2.6 billion. Ultimately, the portfolio brought in only $527 million. Says Jay T. Westbrook, a bankruptcy specialist at the University of Texas School of Law: "What that situation signified—which was part of the problem with the whole business model—is that they thought their technology and their patents were more valuable than they really were. They clung to that belief right until the end."

Kotter agrees with the consensus opinion that Kodak's demise was a result of "strategic decisions either avoided or made poorly." He reminds us, however, that there's still an underlying question to be answered: *"Why* did Kodak managers make the poor strategic decisions they made?" His own answer is fairly simple—on the surface: "The organization," he charges, "overflowed with complacency." In particular, says Kotter, Kodak failed to recognize that digital was a "huge opportunity" only if the company acted with equally "huge urgency." As a matter of fact, Kodak had developed the first digital photographic camera in 1975, and as of 2005, it was the number-one seller of digital cameras in the United States. Within two years, however, it had slipped to fourth, and by 2010 it had plummeted to number seven.

Kodak, it seems, was too slow in realizing that in order to make the transition to digital, it would have to give up the comfort of dominance in an analog technology, which was facing a rapidly diminishing market. In 1976, for instance, Kodak commanded 90 percent of film sales and 85 percent of camera sales in the United States. As of 1996, it controlled over two-thirds of global market share in both categories. According to Andrew Salzman, former Kodak VP for worldwide marketing, top managers at the company were well aware that its markets were "being reinvented" but failed to recognize the need to change. And so, today, Kodak has been reduced to a shell of its former self, a small company that makes specialized products for the film and professional photography markets, as well as home photo printers and image-processing software. Its future, though, still remains blurry.[1]

7-1 THE NATURE OF ORGANIZATION CHANGE

organization change
Any substantive modification to some part of the organization

Organization change is any substantive modification to some part of the organization.[2] Thus, change can involve virtually any dimension or element of an organization: work schedules, bases for departmentalization, span of management, technology, machinery and equipment, organization design, people themselves, and so on. It is also important to keep in mind that any change in an organization may have effects extending beyond the actual area where the change is implemented. For example, when Airbus recently installed a new automated production system at one of its plants, employees needed to be trained to operate new equipment, the compensation system was adjusted to reflect new skill levels, the span of management for supervisors was altered, and several related jobs were redesigned. Selection criteria for new employees were also changed and a new quality-control system was installed. In addition, it is quite common for multiple organization change activities to be going on simultaneously.[3]

7-1a Forces for Change

Why do organizations find change necessary? The basic reason is that something relevant to the organization either has changed or is likely to change in the foreseeable future. The organization therefore may have little choice but to change as well. Indeed, a primary reason for the problems that organizations often face is failure to anticipate or respond properly to changing circumstances. Kodak, for example, failed to recognize the impact that the advent of digital photography and smartphones would have on its products. The forces that compel change may be external or internal to the organization.[4]

External Forces   External forces for change derive from the organization's general and task environments. For example, U.S. automobile companies like General Motors, Ford, Chrysler, and American Motors once dominated the global automobile market and operated as if in a vacuum. However, multiple energy crises, an aggressive Japanese automobile industry led by Toyota, Nissan, and Honda, and floating currency exchange rates and international interest rates—all manifestations of the international dimension of the general environment—profoundly changed U.S. automobile companies. New rules of production and competition forced them to dramatically alter the way they do business. In the political arena, new laws, court decisions, and regulations also affect organizations. The technological dimension may yield new production techniques that the organization needs to explore. The economic

Boeing simultaneously underwent many organization change activities when it installed a new automated production system at one of its plants.

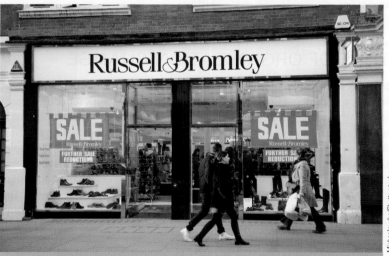

The task environment is a force for change along this busy shopping street. Often when one apparel store advertises a sale, other nearby stores must follow suit. Similarly, if a new restaurant opens, more customers may visit the area and benefit all retail outlets.

dimension is affected by inflation, the cost of living, and money supplies. The sociocultural dimension, reflecting societal values, determines what kinds of products or services will be accepted in the market. Most recently, the COVID-19 pandemic in 2020 forced virtually every organization to change how it conducts business from myriad perspectives.

Because of its proximity to the organization, the task environment is an even more powerful force for change. Competitors influence an organization through their price structures and product lines. When HP lowers notebook prices, Dell may have little choice but to follow suit. Because customers determine what products can be sold at what prices, organizations must be concerned with consumer tastes and preferences. Suppliers affect organizations by raising or lowering prices or changing product lines. Regulators can have dramatic effects on an organization. For example, if OSHA rules that a particular production process is dangerous to workers, it can force a firm to close a plant that uses that process until it meets stricter safety standards. Unions can force change when they have the clout to negotiate for higher wages or if they go on strike.[5]

Internal Forces   A variety of forces inside the organization may also cause change. If top management revises the organization's strategy, organization change is likely to result. A decision by an electronics company to enter the home security market or a decision to increase a 10-year product sales goal by 3 percent would likely necessitate many organization changes. Other internal forces for change may be reflections of external forces. As sociocultural values shift, for example, workers' attitudes toward their jobs may also shift—and workers may demand a change in working hours or working conditions. During the shelter-in-place mandates in early 2020, many workers who previously were not permitted to work remotely found it necessary to quickly adapt to new ways to get their jobs done. As the economy gradually reopened, some of these same workers resisted the requirement that they return to normal working conditions and pushed to maintain the autonomy to work remotely. In cases like this, even though the force is rooted in the external environment, the organization must respond directly to the internal pressure it generates.[7]

> **"The things that an organization stands for should remain firm and fixed, but how it does things should be adjusted constantly."**
> —Jim Collins, Management Consultant[6]

planned change
Change that is designed and implemented in an orderly and timely fashion in anticipation of future events

reactive change
A piecemeal response to circumstances as they develop

7-1b Planned versus Reactive Change

Some change is planned well in advance; other change comes about as a reaction to unexpected events. **Planned change** is change that is designed and implemented in an orderly and timely fashion in anticipation of future events. **Reactive change** is a piecemeal response to circumstances as they develop. Because reactive change may be hurried, the potential for poorly conceived and executed change is increased. Planned change is almost always preferable to reactive change.[8]

Georgia-Pacific, a large forest products business, is an excellent example of a firm that went through a planned and well-managed change process. When the firm appointed a new CEO, he quickly became alarmed at the firm's high accident rate—nine serious injuries per 100 employees each year, and 26 deaths during the most recent five-year period. Although the forest products business is inherently dangerous, the new CEO believed that the accident rate was far too high and set out on a major change effort to improve things. He and other top managers developed a multistage change program intended to educate workers about safety, improve safety equipment in the plant, and eliminate a long-standing part of the firm's culture that made injuries almost a badge of courage. As a result, Georgia-Pacific soon achieved the best safety record in the industry, with relatively few injuries.[9]

On the other hand, many businesses were caught flat-footed by the 2020 COVID-19 pandemic. Some, like Disney and Viking Cruises, had well-conceived contingency and crisis plans already in place and were able to implement those plans (with some modification, of course). On the other hand, firms like Macy's and Carnival Cruises were not nearly as well prepared and had to scramble to determine what to do. In Macy's case, for example, 130,000 workers were furloughed with little advance notice and no guidance about their future employment prospects. For its part, as reports of COVID-19 infections on-board cruise ships began to escalate, Carnival had no plans in place for how to treat those passengers, where their ships could dock, or how they could safely disembark passengers who tested negative for the virus.

MarinaGrigorivna/Shutterstock.com

Accident rates in sawmills and other forest product businesses are often high. One company, Georgia-Pacific, initiated a multistage change process to educate workers, improve safety equipment, and adjust corporate culture.

The importance of approaching change from a planned perspective is reinforced by the frequency of organization change. Most companies or divisions of large companies implement some form of moderate change at least every year and one or more major changes every four to five years.[10] Managers who sit back and respond only when they have to are likely to spend a lot of time hastily changing and re-changing things. A more effective approach is to anticipate forces urging change and plan ahead to deal with them.[11]

Manager's Checklist

- ☐ Managers should understand the primary forces for change that might affect their organization.

- ☐ You should also remember, though, that no amount of foresight or awareness will totally eliminate the chances that reactive change may be necessary.

7-2 MANAGING CHANGE IN ORGANIZATIONS

Organization change is a complex phenomenon. A manager cannot simply wave a wand and implement a planned change like magic. Instead, any change must be systematic and logical to have a realistic opportunity to succeed.[12] To carry this off, the manager needs to understand the steps of effective change and how to counter employee resistance to change.[13]

7-2a Steps in the Change Process

Researchers have over the years developed a number of models or frameworks outlining steps for change.[14] The Lewin model was one of the first, although a more comprehensive approach is usually more useful in today's complex business environment.

The Lewin Model   Kurt Lewin, a noted organizational theorist, suggested that every change requires three steps.[15] The first step is *unfreezing*—individuals who will be affected by the impending change must be led to recognize why the change is necessary. Next, the *change itself* is implemented. Finally, *refreezing* involves reinforcing and supporting the change so that it becomes a part of the system.[16] For example, during a major downturn in the construction industry, Caterpillar experienced a significant drop in revenue. In response, the firm developed a plan to reduce the size of its workforce. The first step in this change (unfreezing) was convincing the United Auto Workers (UAW) to support the reduction because of its importance to the firm's long-term survival. After this unfreezing was accomplished, 30,000 jobs were eliminated (implementation). Then Caterpillar worked to improve its strained relationship with its workers (refreezing) by agreeing to guaranteed future pay hikes and promising no more cutbacks for the next five years. While Lewin's model is appealing in its simplicity, however, it unfortunately lacks operational specificity. Thus, a more comprehensive perspective is often needed.

A Comprehensive Approach to Change   The comprehensive approach to change takes a systems view and delineates a series of specific steps that often lead to successful change. This expanded model is illustrated in Figure 7.1. The first step is recognizing the need for change. Reactive change might be triggered by employee complaints, declines in productivity

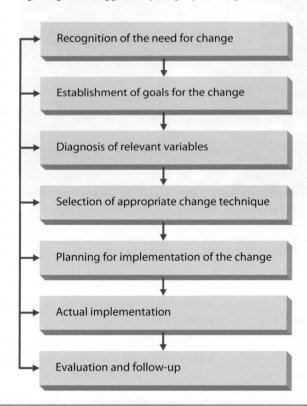

FIGURE 7.1

Steps in the Change Process

Managers must understand how and why to implement change. A manager who, when implementing change, follows a logical and orderly sequence like the one shown here is more likely to succeed than a manager whose change process is haphazard and poorly conceived.

or turnover, court injunctions, sales slumps, or labor strikes. Recognition may simply be managers' awareness that change in a certain area is inevitable. For example, managers may be aware of the general frequency of organizational change undertaken by most organizations and recognize that their organization should probably follow the same pattern. The immediate stimulus might be the result of a forecast indicating new market potential, the accumulation of a cash surplus for possible investment, or an opportunity to achieve and capitalize on a major technological breakthrough. Managers might also initiate change today because indicators suggest that it will be necessary in the near future.[17]

Managers must next set goals for the change. To increase market share, to enter new markets, to restore employee morale, to settle a strike, and to identify investment opportunities all might be goals for change. Third, managers must diagnose what brought on the need for change. Employee turnover, for example, might be caused by below-market pay, substandard working conditions, inadequate supervision, or employee dissatisfaction with benefits. Thus, although turnover may be the immediate stimulus for change, managers must understand its causes in order to make the right changes.

The next step is to select a change technique that will accomplish the intended goals. If turnover is caused by below-market pay, a new reward system may be needed. If the cause is inadequate supervision, interpersonal skills training may be called for. (Various change techniques are summarized later in this chapter.) After the appropriate technique has been chosen, its implementation must be planned. Issues to consider include the costs of the change, its effects on other areas of the organization, and the degree of employee participation appropriate for the situation. If the change is implemented as planned, the results should then be evaluated. If the change was intended to reduce turnover, managers should measure turnover after the change has been in effect for a while. If turnover is still too high, other changes may be necessary.[18] It could be that the wrong change was implemented or that other measures are needed in addition to the initial change, for example.

7-2b Understanding Resistance to Change

Another element in the effective management of change is understanding the resistance that often accompanies change.[19] Managers need to know why people resist change and what can be done about their resistance. Resistance is common for a variety of reasons.[20]

Uncertainty   Perhaps the biggest cause of employee resistance to change is uncertainty. In the face of impending change, employees may become anxious and nervous. They may worry about their ability to meet new job demands, they may think that their job security is threatened, or they may simply dislike ambiguity. Nabisco was once the target of an extended and confusing takeover battle, and during the entire time, employees were nervous about the impending change. The *Wall Street Journal* described them this way: "Many are angry at their leaders and fearful for their jobs. They are swapping rumors and spinning scenarios for the ultimate outcome of the battle for the tobacco and food giant. Headquarters staffers in Atlanta know so little about what's happening in New York that some call their office 'the mushroom complex,' where they are kept in the dark."[21] In another example, 12,500 British Airways cabin crew members voted to participate in a strike over a heavily traveled holiday season. The action against the airline was spurred by high levels of uncertainty as British Airways planned to merge with Iberia Airlines and proposed cutting 1,700 jobs and freezing employee wages in the process.[22]

Threatened Self-Interests   Many impending changes potentially threaten the self-interests of some managers within the organization. A change might diminish their power or influence within the company, so they fight it. Managers at Kodak resisted numerous changes that might have allowed the firm to maintain its market dominance due to threatened self-interests. For instance, until the advent of digital photography, people took rolls of film to a processing center to be "developed" and their photos were then printed on paper. Kodak made the film people bought for their cameras, the chemicals used to develop pictures, and the paper on which the pictures were printed. Managers in the paper division, however, resisted the move to digital because they felt it would render their division much less important to the firm.

Olga Besnard/Shutterstock.com

When companies such as Iberia Airlines and British Airways plan to merge, it can leave existing employees of both firms uncertain and resistant to change. Threats of layoffs and frozen wages often circulate among workers.

Different Perceptions   A third reason that people resist change is due to different perceptions. A manager may make a decision and recommend a plan for change on the basis of her own assessment of a situation. Others in the organization may resist the change because they do not agree with the manager's assessment or they perceive the situation differently.[23] Executives at 7-Eleven once battled this problem as they tried to enact a major organizational change. The corporation wanted to take its convenience stores a bit "upscale" and begin selling fancy fresh foods to go, the newest hardcover novels, some gourmet products, and higher-quality coffee. But many franchisees balked because they saw this move as taking the firm away from its core blue-collar customers.

Feelings of Loss   Many changes involve altering work arrangements in ways that disrupt existing social networks. Because social relationships are important, most people resist any change that might adversely affect those relationships. Other intangibles threatened by change include power, status, security, familiarity with existing procedures, and self-confidence. Many people who had to quickly move to remote work and alternative work locations during the COVID-19 pandemic experienced a feeling of loss due to their inability to meet and interact with their coworkers.

7-2c Overcoming Resistance to Change

Of course, a manager should not give up in the face of resistance to change. Although there are no sure-fire cures, there are several techniques that at least have the potential to overcome resistance.[24]

Participation   Participation is often the most effective technique for overcoming resistance to change. Employees who participate in planning and implementing a change are better able to understand the reasons for the change. Uncertainty is reduced, and self-interests and social relationships are less threatened. Having had an opportunity to express their ideas and assume the perspectives of others, employees are more likely to accept the change gracefully. A classic study of participation monitored the introduction of a change in production methods among four groups in a Virginia pajama factory.[25] The two groups that were allowed to fully participate in planning and implementing the change improved significantly in their productivity and satisfaction relative to the two groups that did not participate. Allstate Technology created the Allstate Change Agent Network to involve employees in change by fostering their understanding and input. Those involved spend about four hours per month for one year taking part in task forces to develop ideas for change, which go directly to leadership.

> **"People often resent change when they have no involvement in how it should be implemented. So, contrary to popular belief, people do not resist change, they resist being controlled."**
> —Ken Blanchard, Management Consultant and Leadership Expert[26]

Education and Communication   Educating employees about the need for and the expected results of an impending change should reduce their resistance. If open communication is established and maintained during the change process, uncertainty can be minimized. Caterpillar used these methods to reduce resistance during many of its cutbacks. First, it informed and educated UAW representatives about the need for and potential value of the planned changes. Then management told all employees what was happening, when it would happen, and how it would affect them individually.

Facilitation   Several facilitation procedures are also advisable. For instance, making only necessary changes, announcing those changes well in advance, and allowing time for people to adjust to new ways of doing things can help reduce resistance to change.[27] One manager at a Prudential Insurance regional office spent several months systematically planning a change in work procedures and job design. As implementation approached, he got excited and too impatient, coming in over the weekend with a work crew and rearranging the office layout. When employees walked in on Monday morning and saw what he had done, they were hostile, anxious, and resentful. What was a promising change became a disaster, and the manager had to scrap the entire plan.

Force-Field Analysis   Although force-field analysis may sound like something out of a *Star Trek* movie, it can help overcome resistance to change. In almost any change situation, forces are acting for and against the change. To facilitate the change, managers start by listing each set of forces and then trying to tip the balance so that the forces facilitating the change outweigh those hindering it. It is especially important to try to remove or at least minimize some of the forces acting against the change. Suppose, for example, that General Motors is considering a plant closing as part of a change. As shown in Figure 7.2, three factors are reinforcing the change: GM needs to cut costs, it has excess capacity, and the plant has outmoded production facilities. At the same time, there is resistance from the UAW, concern for workers being put out of their jobs, and a feeling that the plant might be needed again in the future. GM might start by convincing the UAW that the closing is necessary by presenting profit-and-loss figures. It could then offer relocation and retraining to displaced workers. And it might shut down the plant and put it in "mothballs" so that it can be renovated later. The three major factors hindering the change are thus eliminated or reduced in importance.[28]

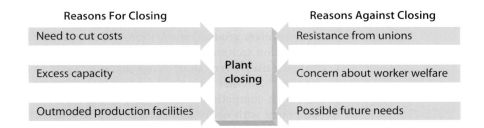

FIGURE 7.2

Force-Field Analysis for Plant Closing at General Motors

A force-field analysis can help a manager facilitate change. A manager able to identify forces acting both for and against a change can see where to focus efforts to remove barriers to change (such as offering training and relocation to displaced workers). Removing the forces against the change can at least partially overcome resistance.

Manager's Checklist

☐ Managers need to understand the importance of implementing change as systematically and logically as possible.

☐ Managers must be aware that people resist change and why this resistance is likely to occur.

☐ They should also know the most effective ways to address resistance to change.

☐ You should have an appreciation of your own tolerance for change.

7-3 AREAS OF ORGANIZATION CHANGE

We noted earlier that change can involve virtually any part of an organization. In general, however, most change interventions involve organization structure and design, technology and operations, or people. The most common areas of change within each of these broad categories are listed in Table 7.1. In addition, many organizations have gone through massive and comprehensive business process change programs.

7-3a Changing Organization Structure and Design

Organization change might be focused on any of the basic components of organization structure or on the organization's overall design. Thus, the organization might change the way it designs its jobs or its bases of departmentalization. Likewise, it might change reporting relationships or the distribution of authority. For example, we noted in Chapter 11 the trend toward flatter organizations. Coordination mechanisms and line-and-staff configurations are also subject to change. On a larger scale, the organization might change its overall design. For example, a growing business could decide to drop its functional design and adopt a divisional design. Or it might transform itself into a matrix. Changes in culture usually involve the structure and design of the organization as well (recall that we discussed changing culture back in Chapter 3). Finally, the organization might change any part of its human resource management system, such as its selection criteria for new employees, its performance appraisal methods, or its compensation package.[29]

7-3b Changing Technology and Operations

Technology is the conversion process used by an organization to transform inputs into outputs. Because of the rapid rate of all technological innovation, technological changes are becoming increasingly important to many organizations. Table 7.1 lists several areas where technological change is likely to be experienced. One important area of change today revolves around information technology. The adoption and institutionalization of information technology innovations is almost constant in most firms today. Oracle, for example, uses a very short-range planning cycle to be best prepared for environmental changes.[30] Another important form of technological change involves equipment. To keep pace with competitors, firms periodically find that replacing existing machinery and equipment with newer models is necessary. Our *Doing Business on Planet Earth* feature discusses how some businesses are focusing new technologies and changes in operations to reduce their waste by-products.

Table 7.1	Areas of Organization Change	
Organization Structure and Design	**Technology and Operations**	**People**
Job design	Information technology	Abilities and skills
Departmentalization	Equipment	Performance
Reporting relationships	Work processes	Perceptions
Authority distribution	Work sequences	Expectations
Coordination mechanisms	Control systems	Attitudes
Line-staff structure	Enterprise resource planning (ERP)	Values
Overall design		
Culture		
Human resource management		

Organization change can affect any part, area, or component of an organization. Most change, however, fits into one of three general areas: organization structure and design, technology and operations, and people.

A change in work processes or work activities may be necessary if new equipment is introduced or new products are manufactured. In manufacturing industries, the major reason for changing a work process is to accommodate a change in the materials used to produce a finished product. Consider a firm that manufactures battery-operated flashlights. For many years, flashlights were made of metal, but now many are made of plastic. A firm might decide to move from metal to plastic flashlights because of consumer preferences, raw materials costs, or other reasons. Whatever the reason, the technology necessary to make flashlights from plastic differs from that used to make flashlights from metal in several different ways. Work process changes may occur in service organizations as well as in manufacturing firms. As traditional barbershops and beauty parlors are replaced by hair salons catering to both sexes, for example, the hybrid organizations have to develop new methods for handling appointments and setting prices.

A change in work sequence may or may not accompany a change in equipment or a change in work processes. Making a change in work sequence means altering the order or sequence of the workstations involved in a particular manufacturing process. For example, a manufacturer might have two parallel assembly lines producing two similar sets of machine parts. The lines might converge at one central quality-control unit, where inspectors verify tolerances. The manager, however, might decide to change to periodic rather than final inspection. Under this arrangement, one or more inspections are established farther up the line. Work sequence changes can also be made in service organizations. The processing of insurance claims, for example, could be changed. The sequence of logging and verifying claims, requesting

DOING BUSINESS ON PLANET EARTH

Toward Zero Waste?

DuPont was once a major generator of trash, routinely dumping thousands of tons of waste materials in landfills each year. But a few years ago, the firm announced its intentions to dramatically reduce the waste it was sending to landfills, with a goal of achieving total recycling wherever possible. To accomplish this goal, the firm used a classic change model. First, it set a standard for each of its business units and facilities. Next, it developed procedures for monitoring progress toward those standards. And finally, it outlined how it would address deviations.

Take DuPont's Building Innovations unit, for example. This business makes such products as kitchen countertops and Tyvek building wrap. In 2008 the business was sending 81 million pounds of waste to landfills each year. But by January 2018 it was not sending anything to landfills! Among the new practices leading to this milestone are:

- Composting cafeteria waste and using it in landscaping
- Repairing shipping pallets to extend their use life and shredding those not repairable for use as animal bedding
- Recycling countertop waste into landscape stone.

There is even a new term that has been coined to reflect this accomplishment: *zero-landfill status*. DuPont is not alone, of course. General Motors recently reported

that 152 of its North American manufacturing plants have achieved zero-landfill status. Moreover, GM also says that it recycles 92 percent of all waste generated by its facilities worldwide. Honda reports that 10 of its 14 North American factories have achieved zero-landfill status. And Toyota claims that its North American operations are at "near-zero"-landfill status.

Outside of the auto industry, Boeing says that a renovated Chinook helicopter plant is at zero-landfill status. And PepsiCo's Frito-Lay facilities are, in the words of the company, approaching zero-landfill status at some of its facilities. For now, though, there are still a few roadblocks and challenges faced by businesses trying to improve their environmental footprint through control procedures. For one thing, some waste products are simply difficult to recycle. DuPont, for example, noted that reducing waste by 80 percent was surprisingly easy, but the last 20 percent posed real challenges. For another, there is no independent resource for verifying zero-landfill status. Regardless, though, critics agree that even if a firm takes small liberties in reporting waste reductions, progress is nevertheless being made.

References: "Companies Aim for Zero Success in Waste Recycling," *USA Today*, www.usatoday.com on April 25, 2020; "Ford to Accelerate Waste Reduction Effort," March 4, 2013, www.greenbiz.com/news on April 25, 2020; "Waste Reduction," March 5, 2020, www.gm.com/vision/waste_reduction on April 25, 2020.

checks, getting countersignatures, and mailing checks could be altered in several ways, such as combining the first two steps or routing the claims through one person while another handles checks. Organizational control systems may also be targets of change.[31] For example, a firm trying to improve the quality of its products might develop and implement a set of more rigorous and comprehensive quality-control procedures.

Finally, many businesses have been working to implement technological and operations change by installing and using complex and integrated software systems. Such systems—called *enterprise resource planning*—link virtually all facets of the business, making it easier for managers to keep abreast of related developments. Enterprise resource planning, or ERP, is a large-scale information system for integrating and synchronizing the many activities in the extended enterprise. In most cases these systems are purchased from external vendors who then tailor their products to the client's unique needs and requirements. Companywide processes—such as materials management, production planning, order management, and financial reporting—can all be managed via ERP. In effect, these are the processes that cut across product lines, departments, and geographic locations.

Developing the ERP system starts by identifying the key processes that need critical attention, such as supplier relationships, materials flows, or customer order fulfillment. The system could result, for instance, in sales processes being integrated with production planning and then integrating both of these into the firm's financial accounting system. For example, a customer in Rome can place an order that is to be produced in Ireland, schedule it to be shipped via air cargo to Rome, and then have it picked up by a truck at the airport and delivered to the customer's warehouse by a specified date. All of these activities are synchronized by activities linkages in one massive database.

The ERP integrates all activities and information flows that relate to the firm's critical processes. It also keeps updated real-time information on their current status, reports recent past transactions and upcoming planned transactions, and provides electronic notices that action is required on some items if planned schedules are to be met. It coordinates internal operations with activities by outside suppliers and notifies business partners and customers of current status and upcoming deliveries and billings. It can integrate financial flows among the firm, its suppliers, its customers, and commercial bank deposits for up-to-the-minute status reports that can be used to create real-time financial reports at a moment's notice, rather than in the traditional one-month (or longer) time span for producing a financial statement. ERP's multilanguage capabilities also allow real-time communication in different languages to facilitate international transactions.

7-3c Changing People, Attitudes, and Behaviors

A third area of organization change has to do with people. For example, an organization might decide to change the skill level of its workforce. This change might be prompted by changes in technology or by a general desire to upgrade the quality of the workforce. Thus, training programs and different selection criteria for new employees might be needed. The organization might also decide to increase its workers' performance level. In this case, a new incentive system or performance-based training might be in order. Due to intense competition for talent from competitors, Microsoft has increased its employees' compensation by shifting a portion of their stock awards to their base salaries, as well as boosting funding for bonuses and stock awards to reward its top performers. Volvo Construction Equipment laid off roughly 25 percent of its workforce globally (the lowest performers), leaving the company with employees who are focused and understand the urgency necessary to facilitate change.

Perceptions and expectations are also a common focus of organization change. Workers in an organization might believe that their wages and benefits are not as high as they should be. Management, however, might have evidence that shows the firm is paying a competitive wage and providing a superior benefit package. The change, then, would be centered on informing and educating the workforce about the comparative value of its compensation package. A common way to do this is to publish a statement that places an actual dollar value on each benefit provided and compares that amount to what other local organizations are providing their workers. Change might also be directed at employee attitudes and values. Many managers,

---

enterprise resource planning (ERP)
A large-scale information system for integrating and synchronizing the many activities in the extended enterprise

for example, are more attuned to the benefits of eliminating adversarial relationships with workers and adopting a more collaborative relationship. In many ways, changing attitudes and values is perhaps the hardest thing to do.[32]

7-3d Changing Business Processes

business process change (reengineering)
The radical redesign of all aspects of a business to achieve major gains in cost, service, or time

Many organizations today also find it useful to periodically go through large-scale comprehensive change programs involving all aspects of organization design, technology, and people. Although various descriptions are used, the most common general terms for these changes are *business process change* or *reengineering*. Specifically, business process change, or reengineering, is the radical redesign of all aspects of a business to achieve major gains in cost, service, or time.[33] ERP, as described previously, is a common platform for changing business processes. However, business process change is a more comprehensive set of changes that goes beyond software and information systems.

Corning, for example, has undergone major reengineering over the last several years. Whereas the 160-year-old business once manufactured cookware and other durable consumer goods, it has transformed itself into a high-tech powerhouse, making such products as the ultra-thin screens used in products like smartphones and laptop computers. Similarly, the dramatic overhauls of Apple to shift away from personal computers to other digital devices, of Yellow Roadway Corporation into a sophisticated freight delivery firm, and of UPS into a major international delivery giant all required business process changes throughout these organizations.

Yellow Roadway Corporation has used business process change and cutting-edge technology to transform itself from an old-line trucking company into a modern and competitive freight delivery firm. This Yellow Roadway truck is awaiting a customs inspection as it crosses the border into Finland.

Taina Sohlman/Shutterstock.com

The Need for Business Process Change Why do so many organizations find it necessary to undergo business process change? We note in Chapter 2 that all systems, including organizations, are subject to entropy—a normal process leading to system decline. An organization is behaving most typically when it maintains the status quo, does not change in sync with its environment, and starts consuming its own resources to survive. In a sense, that is what happened to Kodak. During the early days of digital photography, the firm believed that its brand name would somehow carry it forward and, as a result, displayed no urgency to adapt to the changing environment. The key for a business in this situation, however, is to recognize the beginning of a major shift in the environment and immediately move toward changing relevant business processes. For instance, Netflix required business process changes throughout the organization as it began to create its own content and as it shifted its focus to delivering movies and TV programs through its streaming service rather than through the mail. But these changes were all approached in a planned and strategic fashion.[34] Major problems occur when managers either do not recognize the onset of environmental shifts or entropy until it is well advanced or are complacent about taking steps to correct it.[35]

Approaches to Business Process Change Figure 7.3 shows general steps in changing business processes, or reengineering. The first step is setting goals and developing a strategy for the changes. The organization must know in advance what new business processes are supposed to accomplish and how those accomplishments will be achieved. Next, top managers must begin and direct the reengineering effort. If a CEO simply announces that business process change is to occur but does nothing else, the program is unlikely to be successful. But if the CEO is constantly and visibly involved in the process, underscoring its importance and taking the lead, business process change stands a much better chance of success.

The Reengineering Process

Reengineering is a major redesign of all areas of an organization. To be successful, reengineering requires a systematic and comprehensive assessment of the entire organization. Goals, top management support, and a sense of urgency help the organization re-create itself and blend both top-level and bottom-up perspectives.

Most experts also agree that successful business process change is usually accompanied by a sense of urgency. People in the organization must be persuaded to see the clear and present need for the changes being implemented and appreciate their importance. In addition, most successful reengineering efforts start with a new, clean slate. In other words, rather than assuming that the existing organization is a starting point and then trying to modify it, business process change usually starts by asking questions such as how customers are best served and competitors best neutralized. New approaches and systems are then created and imposed in place of existing ones.

Finally, business process change requires a careful blend of top-down and bottom-up involvement. On the one hand, strong leadership is necessary, but too much involvement by top management can make the changes seem autocratic. Similarly, employee participation is also important, but too little involvement by leaders can undermine the program's importance and create a sense that top managers do not care. Thus, care must be taken to carefully balance these two countervailing forces. Our next section explores more fully one related but distinct approach to change called *organization development*.

7-3e **Organization Development**

We have noted in several places the importance of people and change. Beyond those change interests discussed previously, a special area of interest that focuses almost exclusively on people is organization development.

OD Assumptions   Organization development is concerned with changing attitudes, perceptions, behaviors, and expectations of people in an organization. More precisely, **organization development (OD)** is a planned effort that is organization-wide and managed from the top, intended to increase organizational effectiveness and health through planned interventions in the organization's process, using behavioral science knowledge.[36] The theory and practice of OD are based on several very important assumptions. The first is that

organization development (OD)
An effort that is planned, organization-wide, and managed from the top, intended to increase organizational effectiveness and health through planned interventions in the organization's process, using behavioral science knowledge

employees have a desire to grow and develop. Another is that employees have a strong need to be accepted by others within the organization. Still another critical assumption of OD is that the total organization and the way it is designed will influence the way individuals and groups within the organization behave. Thus, some form of collaboration between managers and their employees is necessary to (1) take advantage of the skills and abilities of the employees and (2) eliminate aspects of the organization that retard employee growth, development, and group acceptance. Because of the intensely personal nature of many OD activities, many large organizations rely on one or more OD consultants (either full-time employees assigned to this function or outside experts hired specifically for OD purposes) to implement and manage their OD programs.[37]

OD Techniques   Several kinds of interventions or activities are generally considered part of organization development.[38] Some OD programs may use only one or a few of these; other programs use several of them at once.

- *Diagnostic activities.* Just as a physician examines patients to diagnose their current condition, an OD diagnosis analyzes the current condition of an organization. To carry out this diagnosis, managers use questionnaires, opinion or attitude surveys, interviews, archival data, and meetings to assess various characteristics of the organization. The results of this diagnosis may generate profiles of the organization's activities, which can then be used to identify problem areas in need of correction.
- *Team building.* Team-building activities are intended to enhance the effectiveness and satisfaction of individuals who work in groups or teams and to promote overall group effectiveness. Given the growing use of teams today, these activities have taken on increased importance. An OD consultant might interview team members to determine how they feel about the group; then an off-site meeting could be held to discuss the issues that surfaced and iron out any problem areas or member concerns. Caterpillar used team building as one method for changing the working relationships between workers and supervisors from confrontational to cooperative. There are also a number of unusual approaches to team building that presumably help managers learn the importance of interdependence and coordination. Examples include outdoor "adventure" activities such as rafting and group cooking classes.[39]
- *Survey feedback.* In survey feedback, each employee responds to a questionnaire intended to measure perceptions and attitudes (e.g., satisfaction and supervisory style). Everyone involved, including the supervisor, receives the results of the survey. The aim of this approach is usually to change the behavior of supervisors by showing them how their subordinates view them. After the feedback has been provided, meetings and workshops may be conducted to evaluate results and suggest constructive changes.
- *Education.* Educational activities focus on classroom training. Although such activities can be used for technical or skill-related purposes, an OD educational activity typically focuses on "sensitivity skills"—that is, it teaches people to be more considerate and understanding of the people they work with. Participants often go through a series of experiential or role-playing exercises to learn better how others in the organization feel.[40]
- *Intergroup activities.* The focus of intergroup activities is on improving the relationships between two or more groups. We noted in Chapter 11 that, as group interdependence increases, so do coordination difficulties. Intergroup OD activities are designed to promote cooperation or resolve conflicts that arose as a result of interdependence. Experiential or role-playing activities are often used to bring this about.
- *Third-party peacemaking.* Another approach to OD is through third-party peacemaking, which is most often used when substantial conflict exists within the organization. Third-party peacemaking can be appropriate on the individual, group, or organizational level. The third party, usually an OD consultant, uses a variety of mediation or negotiation techniques to resolve any problems or conflicts among individuals or groups.

- *Technostructural activities.* Technostructural activities are concerned with the design of the organization, the technology of the organization, and the interrelationship of design and technology with people on the job. A structural change such as an increase in decentralization, a job design change such as an increase in the use of automation, and a technological change involving a modification in work flow all qualify as technostructural OD activities if their objective is to improve group and interpersonal relationships within the organization.

- *Process consultation.* In process consultation, an OD consultant observes groups in the organization to develop an understanding of their communication patterns, decision-making and leadership processes, and methods of cooperation and conflict resolution. The consultant then provides feedback to the involved parties about the processes he or she has observed. The goal of this form of intervention is to improve the observed processes. A leader who is presented with feedback outlining deficiencies in his or her leadership style, for example, might be expected to change to overcome them but also need some coaching and guidance to do so.

- *Life and career planning.* Life and career planning helps employees formulate their personal goals and evaluate strategies for integrating their goals with the goals of the organization. Such activities might include specification of training needs and plotting a career map. General Electric has a reputation for doing an outstanding job in this area.

- *Coaching and counseling.* Coaching and counseling provide nonevaluative feedback to individuals. The purpose is to help people develop a better sense of how others see them and learn behaviors that will assist others in achieving their work-related goals. The focus is not on how the person is performing today; instead, it is on how the person can perform better in the future.

- *Planning and goal setting.* More pragmatic than many other interventions are activities designed to help managers improve their planning and goal setting. Emphasis still falls on the individual, however, because the intent is to help individuals and groups integrate themselves into the overall planning process. The OD consultant might use the same approach as in process consultation, but the focus is more technically oriented on the mechanics of planning and goal setting.

The Effectiveness of OD   Given the diversity of activities encompassed by OD, it is not surprising that managers report mixed results from various OD interventions. Organizations that actively practice some form of OD include American Airlines, Texas Instruments, Procter & Gamble, and BF Goodrich. Goodrich, for example, has trained 60 people in OD processes and techniques. These trained experts have subsequently become internal OD consultants to assist other managers in applying the techniques. Many other managers, in contrast, report that they have tried OD but discarded it.

OD will probably remain an important part of management theory and practice. Of course, there are no sure things when dealing with social systems such as organizations, and the effectiveness of many OD techniques is difficult to evaluate. Because all organizations are open systems interacting with their environments, an improvement in an organization after an OD

These two functional groups are involved in an intergroup activity. As part of a companywide initiative to improve dialogue between all facets of the company, retreats such as this one filled with team-building exercises are occurring on a quarterly basis.

ESB Professional/Shutterstock

intervention may be attributable to the intervention, but it may also be attributable to changes in economic conditions, luck, or other factors.[41]

 **Manager's Checklist**

☐ All managers need to be aware of the different areas of change that may be necessary in their organizations.

☐ When planning and implementing change in one area you should be aware that changes may then be necessary in other areas as well.

7-4 ORGANIZATIONAL INNOVATION

innovation
The managed effort of an organization to develop new products or services or new uses for existing products or services

Another critical form of organization change is innovation. Innovation is the managed effort of an organization to develop new products or services or new uses for existing products or services. Innovation is clearly important because, without new products or services, any organization will fall behind its competition.[42]

7-4a The Innovation Process

The organizational innovation process consists of developing, applying, launching, growing, and managing the maturity and decline of creative ideas.[43] This process is depicted in Figure 7.4.

Innovation Development Innovation development involves the evaluation, modification, and improvement of creative ideas. Innovation development can transform a product or service with only modest potential into a product or service with significant potential. Parker Brothers, for example, decided during innovation development not to market an indoor volleyball game but instead to sell separately the appealing little foam ball designed for the game. The firm will never know how well the volleyball game would have sold, but the Nerf ball and numerous related products generated millions of dollars in revenues for Parker Brothers.

Innovation Application Innovation application is the stage in which an organization takes a developed idea and uses it in the design, manufacturing, or delivery of new products, services, or processes. At this point the innovation emerges from the laboratory and is transformed into tangible goods or services. One example of innovation application is the use of radar-based focusing systems in instant cameras made by a firm called Polaroid. The idea of using radio waves to discover the location, speed, and direction of moving objects was first applied extensively by Allied forces during World War II. As radar technology developed

FIGURE 7.4

The Innovation Process

Organizations actively seek to manage the innovation process. These steps illustrate the general life cycle that characterizes most innovations. Of course, as with creativity, the innovation process will suffer if it is approached too mechanically and rigidly.

Application launch is a critical element in the success or failure of a new product. Google spent over $10 million developing Google Glass but the initial launch of the product was a failure and it was quickly pulled from the market.

Peppinuzzo/Shutterstock.com

during the following years, the electrical components needed became smaller and more streamlined. Researchers at Polaroid applied this well-developed technology in a new way.[44] Kodak, meanwhile, developed digital camera technology but failed to capitalize on it.

Application Launch   Application launch is the stage at which an organization introduces new products or services to the marketplace. The important question is usually not "Does the innovation work?" but "Will customers want to buy the innovative product or service?" History is full of creative ideas that did not generate enough interest among customers to be successful. Some notable innovation failures include a portable seat warmer from Sony, "New" Coke, Amazon's Fire Phone, Cheeto-flavored lip balm, and Google Glass. Thus, despite development and application, new products and services can still fail at the launch phase.

Application Growth   Once an innovation has been successfully launched, it then enters the stage of application growth. This is a period of high economic performance for an organization because demand for the product or service is often greater than supply. Organizations that fail to anticipate this stage may unintentionally limit their growth. At the same time, overestimating demand for a new product can be just as detrimental to performance. Unsold products can sit in warehouses for years.

Innovation Maturity   After a period of growing demand, an innovative product or service often enters a period of maturity. Innovation maturity is the stage at which most organizations in an industry have access to an innovation and are applying it in approximately the same way. The technological application of an innovation during this stage of the innovation process can be very sophisticated. Because most firms have access to the innovation, however, either as a result of their developing the innovation on their own or copying the innovation of others, it does not provide competitive advantage to any one of them. The time that elapses between innovation development and innovation maturity varies notably depending on the particular product or service. Whenever an innovation involves the use of complex skills (such as a complicated manufacturing process or highly sophisticated teamwork), moving from the growth phase to the maturity phase will take longer. In addition, if the skills needed to implement these innovations are rare and difficult to imitate, then strategic imitation may be delayed, and the organization may enjoy a period of sustained competitive advantage.

Innovation Decline   Every successful innovation bears the seeds of its own decline. Because an organization does not maintain a competitive advantage from an innovation at maturity, it must encourage its creative scientists, engineers, and managers to begin looking for new innovations. This continued search for competitive advantage usually leads new products and services to move from the creative process through innovation maturity, and finally to innovation decline. Innovation decline is the stage during which demand for an innovation decreases and substitute innovations are developed and applied. It was at the innovation decline stage that Kodak failed most dramatically.

7-4b Forms of Innovation

Each creative idea that an organization develops poses a different challenge for the innovation process. Innovations can be radical or incremental, technical or managerial, and product or process.

radical innovation
A new product, service, or technology that completely replaces an existing one

incremental innovation
A new product, service, or technology that modifies an existing one

technical innovation
A change in the appearance or performance of products or services or of the physical processes through which a product or service passes

Radical versus Incremental Innovations   Radical innovations are new products, services, or technologies developed by an organization that completely replace the existing products, services, or technologies in an industry.[45] Incremental innovations are new products or processes that modify existing ones. Firms that implement radical innovations fundamentally shift the nature of competition and the interaction of firms within their environments. Firms that implement incremental innovations alter, but do not fundamentally change, competitive interaction in an industry.

Over the last several years, organizations have introduced many radical innovations. For example, compact disc technology replaced long-playing vinyl records in the recording industry, digital downloading supplanted CDs, and digital downloading is already being replaced by Spotify and SoundCloud; DVDs have replaced videocassettes but are now being supplanted by Blu-rays and streaming video; and high-definition television has replaced analog television technology. Whereas radical innovations like these tend to be very visible and public, incremental innovations are actually more numerous. For instance, each new generation of the iPhone and the iPad represent relatively minor changes over previous versions.

Technical versus Managerial Innovations
Technical innovations are changes in the physical appearance or performance of a product or service, or of the physical processes through which a product or service is manufactured. Many of the most important innovations over the last 75 years have been technical. For example, the serial replacement of the vacuum tube with the transistor, the transistor with the integrated circuit, and the integrated circuit with the microchip has greatly enhanced the power, ease of use, and speed of operation of a wide variety of electronic products. Not all innovations developed by organizations are technical, however. Managerial innovations are changes in the management process by which products and services are conceived, built, and delivered to customers.[46] Managerial innovations do not necessarily affect the physical appearance or performance of products or services directly. In effect, business process change or reengineering, as we discuss earlier, represent a managerial innovation.

Amazon has pioneered several new processes for selling and distributing products. One of its most recent experiments involves the potential use of drones such as this one to deliver products to customers the same day as their order.

managerial innovation
A change in the management process in an organization

product innovation
A change in the physical characteristics or performance of an existing product or service or the creation of a new product or service

process innovation
A change in the way a product or service is manufactured, created, or distributed

Product versus Process Innovations   Perhaps the two most important types of technical innovations are product innovations and process innovations. Product innovations are changes in the physical characteristics or performance of existing products or services or the creation of brand-new products or services. Process innovations are changes in the way products or services are manufactured, created, or distributed. Whereas managerial innovations generally affect the broader context of development, process innovations directly affect manufacturing.

The implementation of robotics, as we discussed earlier, is a process innovation. As Figure 7.5 shows, the effect of product and process innovations on economic return depends on the stage of the innovation process that a new product or service occupies. At first, during development, application, and launch, the physical attributes and capabilities of an innovation most affect organizational performance. Thus, product innovations are particularly important during these beginning phases. Later, as an innovation enters the phases of growth, maturity, and decline, an organization's ability to develop process innovations, such as fine-tuning manufacturing, increasing product quality, and improving product distribution, becomes important to maintaining economic return.

Japanese organizations have often excelled at process innovation. The market for 35-mm cameras was once dominated by German and other European manufacturers. However, Japanese camera companies such as Canon and Nikon began an aggressive push to increase

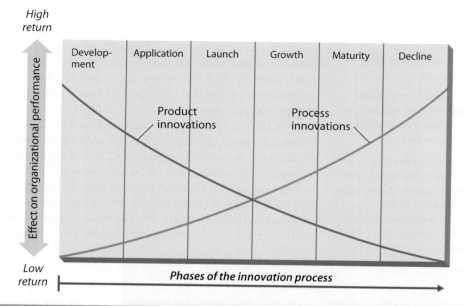

FIGURE 7.5

Effects of Product and Process Innovation on Economic Return

As the innovation process moves from development to decline, the economic return from product innovations gradually declines. In contrast, the economic return from process innovations increases during this same process.

their global market shares. Some of the early Japanese products were not very successful, but these companies continued to invest in their process technology and eventually were able to increase quality and decrease manufacturing costs. The Japanese organizations eventually came to dominate the worldwide market for 35 mm cameras, and the German companies, because they were not able to maintain the same pace of process innovation, struggled to maintain market share and profitability. And as film technology gave way to digital photography, the same Japanese firms have effectively transitioned to leadership in this market as well. Indeed, unlike Kodak, one of its earlier rivals, Fujifilm, has successfully diversified into pharmaceuticals and chemicals while still maintaining a presence in the photography market.

This Nikon camera is an example of Japan's ability to innovate in a speedy manner. Other camera manufacturers were not able to keep up with customers' changing desires and technological advances.

7-4c The Failure to Innovate

To remain competitive in today's economy, organizations must be innovative. And yet many organizations that should be innovative are not successful at bringing out new products or services or do so only after innovations created by others are very mature. Organizations may fail to innovate for at least three reasons.

Lack of Resources Innovation is expensive in terms of dollars, time, and energy. If a firm does not have enough money to fund a program of innovation or does not currently employ the kinds of employees it needs in order to be innovative, it may lag behind in innovation. Even highly innovative organizations cannot become involved in every new product or service its employees think up. For example, numerous other commitments in the electronic instruments and computer industry forestalled HP from investing in Steve Jobs and Steve Wozniak's original idea for a personal computer. With infinite resources of money, time, and technical and managerial expertise, HP might have entered this market early. Because the firm did not have this flexibility, however, it had to make some difficult choices about which innovations to invest in.[47]

Failure to Recognize Opportunities   Because firms cannot pursue all innovations, they need to develop the ability to carefully evaluate innovations and to select the ones that hold the greatest potential. To obtain a competitive advantage, an organization usually must make investment decisions before the innovation process reaches the mature stage. The earlier the investment, however, the greater the risk. If organizations are not skilled at recognizing and evaluating opportunities, they may be overly cautious and fail to invest in innovations that later turn out to be successful for other firms.

"Dynamic corporations of the future should simultaneously be trying alternative ways of doing things in competition within themselves."

—Norman Macrae, Economist[48]

Resistance to Change   As we discuss earlier, many organizations tend to resist change. Innovation means giving up old products and old ways of doing things in favor of new products and new ways of doing things. These kinds of changes can be personally difficult for managers and other members of an organization. Thus, resistance to change can slow the innovation process.

TECH WATCH

Breaking the Mold

Jeff Applegate, CEO of Texas Injection Molding (TIM), appreciates flexibility: "The thing I love about this business," he says, "is the fact that everyday I'm working with a different industry, a different company, a different entrepreneur."

Applegate purchased TIM, a Houston company that manufactures products and parts by injecting thermoplastic and thermosetting polymers into specially designed molds, but he's no novice in the industry: For 10 years, he'd been president of Blackwell Plastics, a leader in Houston's thriving plastics-injection industry. Applegate had just left Blackwell to run his own company when Manufacturing.Net named Blackwell one of its "Most Innovative Industrial Companies." What Manufacturing. Net liked about Blackwell was its flexibility—its ability to make plastics products with applications ranging from the kitchen to aerospace.

Companies like Blackwell and TIM, explains Applegate, "own no tools; we make no products. We're contract manufacturers for other people who bring their ideas to us." Obviously, it helps to be responsive to innovative product designs and to have an open mind about untried manufacturing techniques. Back in 1971, for instance, an inventor named George Ballas brought founder L. D. Blackwell the crude prototype of a product for use around residential lawns—a set of handlebars and a small motor fixed to one

end of a wooden pole and a string-laced tin can attached to the other. Blackwell bought a stake in Ballas's invention and figured out how to turn his demonstration model into a commercial appliance featuring molded plastic components. Within five years, sales had topped $40 million, and the next year Ballas sold the Weed Eater to Emerson Electric for an undisclosed sum (widely understood to be a fortune).

Blackwell has since transformed product designs into product realities for such clients as renowned cardiac surgeon Michael DeBakey (the first disposable tools for open-heart surgery) and NASA (parts for sensors worn by astronauts on America's first manned spaceflights). Along the way, it's also produced such smaller-margin products as the screw-pull wine opener, nylon slides for venetian blinds, liners for water coolers, and holders for iPads. Today, Blackwell's top 10 customers are in 10 different industries, and no single client accounts for more than 10 percent of the firm's revenues.

"We don't target" industries or markets, says Applegate. The injection molder's turn to innovate comes when the company buys into the vision of an entrepreneur and takes on the task of turning a concept into a molded-plastic reality. Thus, its customer diversity is reflected in the flexibility of its manufacturing machines, which range in size from 20 to 550 tons and have over the years been modified to turn out everything from automotive parts to toothbrushes.

(Continued)

TECH WATCH (CONTINUED)

According to Applegate, managerial flexibility is also a good thing to cultivate. "We're a pretty small company," he explains, "and I don't have teams of people to go out and solve problems. So my solution is finding ways to cross disciplines and cross industries to solve problems." A few years ago, for example, when "we were at the end of our rope" in seeking the right material for a faceplate on a frozen drink dispenser, Applegate turned to Eastman Chemical, whose new copolymer was being used to produce pitchers that kept drinks chilled without ice and coffee makers that could go in the dishwasher. With a little modification on Blackwell's part,

the same resin produced a faceplate that performed at the required heat ranges while resisting chemical and impact damage and magnifying visuals displayed by the dispenser.

References: "Most Innovative Industrial Companies" Manu-facturing.Net, www.manufacturing.net on April 25, 2020; Frank Esposito, "Texas Injection Molding Sees Rapid Growth after Recent Sale, *Plastics News*, August 4, 2014, www.plasticsnews.com on April 25, 2020; Rachel Leisemann Immel, "Dream, Build, Create," *IMPO*, August 12, 2013, www.impomag.com on April 25, 2020; Rhoda Miel, "Eastman's Tritan Shines at Housewares Show," www.eastman.com on April 25, 2020.

7-4d Promoting Innovation in Organizations

A wide variety of ideas for promoting innovation in organizations have been developed over the years. Three specific ways for promoting innovation are through the reward system, through the organizational culture, and through a process called intrapreneurship.[49]

The Reward System   A firm's reward system is the means by which it encourages and discourages certain behaviors by employees. Major components of the reward system include salaries, bonuses, and perquisites. Using the reward system to promote innovation is a fairly mechanical but nevertheless effective management technique. The idea is to provide financial and nonfinancial rewards to people and groups who develop innovative ideas. Once the members of an organization understand that they will be rewarded for such activities, they are more likely to work creatively. With this end in mind, Bayer gives a $50,000 award each year to the scientist or group of scientists who develop the biggest commercial breakthrough. 3M's Genesis Grant offers awards between $35,000 and $75,000 to innovators whose projects may have trouble attaining financial backing through normal means and provides a total of $750,000 each year.

It is important for organizations to reward creative behavior, but it is vital to avoid punishing creativity when it does not result in highly successful innovations. It is the nature of the creative and innovative processes that many new product ideas will simply not work out in the marketplace. Each process is fraught with too many uncertainties to generate positive results every time. A person may have prepared him- or herself to be creative, but an insight may not be forthcoming. Or managers may try to apply a developed innovation, only to recognize that it does not work. Indeed, some organizations operate according to the assumption that, if all their innovative efforts succeed, then they are probably not taking enough risks in research and development. At 3M, nearly 60 percent of the creative ideas suggested each year do not succeed in the marketplace.

Managers need to be very careful in responding to innovative failure. If innovative failure is due to incompetence, systematic errors, or managerial sloppiness, then a firm should respond appropriately, for example, by withholding raises or reducing promotion opportunities. People who act in good faith to develop an innovation that simply does not work out, however, should not be punished for failure. If they are, they will probably not be creative in the future. A punitive reward system will discourage people from taking risks and therefore reduce the organization's ability to obtain competitive advantages.

Organization Culture   As we discussed in Chapter 3, an organization's culture is the set of values, beliefs, and symbols that help guide behavior. A strong, appropriately focused organizational culture can be used to support innovative activity. A well-managed culture can communicate a sense that innovation is valued and will be rewarded and that occasional failure in the pursuit of new ideas is not only acceptable but even expected. In addition to reward systems and intrapreneurial activities, firms such as Apple, Google, Nintendo, Sony, Walt Disney, Vodafone, and HP are all known to have strong, innovation-oriented cultures that value individual creativity, risk taking, and inventiveness.[50] Google, for instance, allows employees to use 20 percent of their time (one day per week) to work on their own side projects in order to foster innovation. Our *Tech Watch* feature illustrates the importance of organization culture in innovation.

intrapreneurs
Similar to entrepreneurs except that they develop new businesses in the context of a large organization

Intrapreneurship in Larger Organizations   In recent years, many large businesses have realized that the entrepreneurial spirit that propelled their growth becomes stagnant after they transform themselves from a small but growing concern into a larger one.[51] To help revitalize this spirit, some firms today encourage what they call "intrapreneurship." Intrapreneurs are similar to entrepreneurs except that they develop a new business in the context of a large organization. There are three intrapreneurial roles in large organizations.[52] To successfully use intrapreneurship to encourage creativity and innovation, the organization must find one or more individuals to perform these roles.

The *inventor* is the person who actually conceives of and develops the new idea, product, or service by means of the creative process. Because the inventor may lack the expertise or motivation to oversee the transformation of the product or service from an idea into a marketable entity, however, a second role comes into play. A *product champion* is usually a middle manager who learns about the project and becomes committed to it. He or she helps overcome organizational resistance and convinces others to take the innovation seriously. The product champion may have only limited understanding of the technological aspects of the innovation. Nevertheless, product champions are skilled at knowing how the organization works, whose support is needed to push the project forward, and where to go to secure the resources necessary for successful development. A *sponsor* is a top-level manager who approves of and supports a project. This person may fight for the budget needed to develop an idea, overcome arguments against a project, and use organizational politics to ensure the project's survival. With a sponsor in place, the inventor's idea has a much better chance of being successfully developed.

Several firms have embraced intrapreneurship as a way to encourage creativity and innovation. Colgate-Palmolive has a separate unit, Colgate Venture Company, staffed with intrapreneurs who develop new products. SC Johnson & Son established a $250,000 fund to support new product ideas. Texas Instruments refuses to approve a new innovative project unless it has an acknowledged inventor, champion, and sponsor. Lockheed Martin's Advanced Development Programs, also known as Skunk Works, focuses on innovative aerospace technologies and aircraft.[53]

Manager's Checklist

☐ Managers should be knowledgeable about the basic forms of innovation.

☐ Managers should also have a clear understanding of their organization's approach to innovation.

SUMMARY OF LEARNING OUTCOMES AND KEY POINTS

7-1. Describe the nature of organization change, including forces for change and planned versus reactive change.

- Organization change is any substantive modification to some part of the organization.

- Change may be prompted by forces internal or external to the organization.

- In general, planned change is preferable to reactive change.

7-2. Discuss the steps in organization change and how to manage resistance to change.

- The Lewin model provides a general perspective on the steps involved in change.

- A comprehensive model is usually more effective.

- People tend to resist change because of uncertainty, threatened self-interests, different perceptions, and feelings of loss.

- Participation, education and communication, facilitation, and force-field analysis are methods for overcoming this resistance.

7-3. Describe the major areas of organization change and the assumptions, techniques, and effectiveness of organization development.

- The most common areas of change involve changing organizational structure and design, technology, and people.

- Business process change is a more massive and comprehensive change.

- Organization development is concerned with changing attitudes, perceptions, behaviors, and expectations. Its effective use relies on an important set of assumptions.

- There are conflicting opinions about the effectiveness of several OD techniques.

7-4. Discuss the innovation process, forms of innovation, failure to innovate, and how organizations can promote innovation.

- The innovation process has six steps: development, application, launch, growth, maturity, and decline.

- Basic categories of innovation include radical, incremental, technical, managerial, product, and process innovations.

- Despite the importance of innovation, many organizations fail to innovate because they lack the required creative individuals or are committed to too many other creative activities, fail to recognize opportunities, or resist the change that innovation requires.

- Organizations can use a variety of tools to overcome these problems, including the reward system, organizational culture, and intrapreneurship.

DISCUSSION QUESTIONS

Questions for Review

1. What forces or kinds of events lead to organization change? Identify each force or event as a planned or a reactive change.

2. Compare planned and reactive change. What are the advantages of planned change, as compared to reactive change?

3. In a brief sentence or just a phrase, describe each of the organizational development (OD) techniques.

4. Consider the following list of products. Categorize each along all three dimensions of innovation, if possible (radical versus incremental, technical versus managerial, and product versus process). Explain your answers.

- Moving traditional college classes to an online platform and teaching them in a virtual format
- The rise in popularity of virtual organizations (discussed in Chapter 11)
- Checking the security of packages on airlines with the type of MRI scanning devices that are common in health care
- A device combining features of a cellphone and a handheld computer with Internet capability
- Robotic arms that can perform surgery that is too precise for a human surgeon's hands

- Hybrid automobiles, which run on both batteries and gasoline
- Using video games to teach soldiers how to plan and execute battles

Questions for Analysis

1. What are the symptoms that a manager should look for in determining whether an organization needs to change? What are the symptoms that indicate that an organization has been through too much change?

2. Assume that you are the manager of an organization that has a routine way of performing a task and now faces a major change in how it performs that task. Using Lewin's model, tell what steps you would take to implement the change. Using the comprehensive approach, tell what steps you would take. For each step, give specific examples of actions you would take at that step.

3. Think back to a time when a professor announced a change that you, the student, did not want to adopt. What were the reasons for your resistance to the change? Was the professor able to overcome your resistance? If so, tell what he or she did. If not, tell what he or she could have done that might have been successful.

Questions for Application

1. Some people resist change, whereas others welcome it enthusiastically. To deal with the first group, one needs to overcome resistance to change; to deal with the second, one needs to overcome resistance to stability. What advice can you give a manager facing the latter situation?

2. Can a change made in one area of an organization—in technology, for instance—not lead to change in other areas? If you think that change in one area must lead to change in other areas, describe an example of an organization change to illustrate your point. If you think that change can occur in just one area without causing change in other areas, describe an example of an organization change that illustrates your point.

3. Using online resources, identify a significant innovation that came about as a result of the 2020 COVID-19 pandemic. Describe the process by which the innovation was developed. Did the actual process follow the ideal process described in the chapter? Why or why not?

BUILDING EFFECTIVE DECISION-MAKING SKILLS

Exercise Overview

Decision-making skills include the ability to recognize and define problems or opportunities and then select the proper course of action. This exercise provides a format for analyzing the phases in a decision-making process. As you'll see, the condition prompting the decision can be characterized as either a problem or an opportunity.

Exercise Task

At the risk of oversimplifying, let's begin by supplementing our discussion of "Force-Field Analysis" on page 333 by dividing the process of change making—both personal and organizational—into three broad phases:

1. *Unfreezing*: Recognizing the need for change—identifying the problem(s) that make change necessary
2. *Changing*: Making the change—designing and implementing a plan for a new way of doing things
3. *Refreezing*: Locking in the change—replacing old attitudes and behaviors with new ones that become just as habitual

Step 1: Individual Preparation
This step should be done in writing. Think of a change at work or in your personal life that you would like to make. Now develop a plan for making it, using the three phases of the change process:

1. *Unfreezing*: Briefly describe the change and explain why you think it's needed.

2. *Changing*: Decide upon a date on which you intend to initiate the change and a date by which you want to feel that you've accomplished your goal. Describe your plan for making the change.
3. *Refreezing*: Describe your plans for *maintaining* the change.

Step 2: In-Class Exercise (10–30 minutes)
Your instructor will choose an in-class procedure from among these two options:

- *Option A:* Break the class into three to six groups in which members share their plans and offer suggestions for improvement.
- *Option B:* Break the class into three to six groups in which members share their plans. The group selects and shares its best plan with the class.

Your instructor may offer some concluding remarks.

Step 3: Application (2–4 minutes)
This step should be done in writing. Respond to the following questions:

- What did I learn from this experience?
- How will I use the knowledge that I gained in the future?

You may also want to restate the dates in your original plan.

Adapted from Robert N. Lussier and Christopher F. Achua, *Leadership: Theory, Application, and Skill Development*, 4th ed. (Mason, OH: South-Western Cengage Learning, 2010), pp. 435–438, 448.

BUILDING EFFECTIVE DIAGNOSTIC SKILLS

Exercise Overview

Diagnostic skills, which enable a manager to visualize the most appropriate response to a situation, are especially important during periods of organizational change.

Exercise Background

You're the general manager of a hotel situated along a beautiful stretch of beach on a tropical island. One of the oldest of six large resorts in the immediate area, your hotel is owned by a group of foreign investors. For several years, it's been operated as a franchise unit of a large international hotel chain, as have all the other hotels on the island (such as Hilton, Hyatt, Marriott, and Sheraton).

For the past few years, the hotel's franchisee-owners have been taking most of the profits for themselves and putting relatively little back into the hotel. They've also let you know that their business is not in good financial health and that the revenue from the hotel is being used to offset losses incurred elsewhere. In contrast, most of the other hotels on the island have recently been refurbished and plans for two brand-new hotels have been announced for the near future.

A team of executives from franchise headquarters has just visited your hotel. They're quite disappointed in the property, particularly because it's failed to keep pace with other resorts on the island. They've informed you that if the property isn't brought up to standards, the franchise agreement, which is up for review in a year, will be revoked. You realize that this move would be a potential disaster because you can ill afford to lose the franchisor's brand name, access to its reservation system, or any other benefits of the franchise arrangement.

Sitting alone in your office, you've identified several seemingly viable courses of action:

1. Convince the franchisee-owners to remodel the hotel. You estimate that it will take $8 million to meet the franchisor's minimum standards and another $10 million to bring the hotel up to the standards of the island's top resort.
2. Convince the franchisor to give you more time and more options for upgrading the facility.
3. Allow the franchise agreement to terminate and try to succeed as an independent hotel.
4. Assume that the hotel will fail and start looking for another job. You have a pretty good reputation, but you're not terribly happy about the possibility of having to accept a lower-level position (say, as an assistant manager) with another firm.

Exercise Task

Having mulled over your options, do the following:

1. Rank-order your four alternatives in terms of probable success. Make any necessary assumptions.
2. Identify alternatives other than the four that you identified above.
3. Can more than one alternative be pursued simultaneously? Which ones?
4. Develop an overall strategy for trying to save the hotel while protecting your own interests.

SKILL-BUILDING PERSONAL ASSESSMENT

Innovation and Learning Styles

Introduction: David Kolb, a professor at Case Western University, has described a learning model that tells about different learning styles. While individuals move through all four activities, most express a preference for either hands-on learning or learning by indirect observation, and most express a preference for either learning about abstract concepts or learning about concrete experience. When these two dimensions are combined, the following learning styles are created.

	Active Experimentation	Reflective Observation
Concrete Experience	Accommodator	Diverger
Abstract Conceptualization	Converger	Assimilator

Individuals with any of these styles can be creative and their learning innovative, although the way they will approach creativity and the contribution they can make to the innovation process differ. If you understand style, you'll be better equipped to participate in innovation.

Rank from 1 to 4 (1 = least like you, 4 = most like you)

1. **(a)** I want to try something out first.
   (b) I need to feel personally involved with things.
   (c) I focus on useful practical applications.
   (d) I look for differences and distinctions.

(Continued)

	Active Experimentation	Reflective Observation
		Rank from 1 to 4 (1 = least like you, 4 = most like you)
2. (a) I work mainly by intuition. **(b)** I tend to ask myself questions. **(c)** I always try to think logically. **(d)** I am very result oriented.		
		Rank from 1 to 4 (1 = least like you, 4 = most like you)
3. (a) I let everything filter through my head and think about it. **(b)** I am interested in the here and now. **(c)** I mainly have a practical nature. **(d)** I am mostly interested in the future.		
		Rank from 1 to 4 (1 = least like you, 4 = most like you)
4. (a) I consider the facts, and then I act. **(b)** I act. **(c)** I ponder until I have evaluated every option, and then I act. **(d)** I would rather dream or imagine than think about the facts.		

Scoring: According to Kolb, Accommodators learn and work by doing, Divergers learn and work through imagination, Convergers learn and work by problem solving, and Assimilators learn and work using inductive reasoning. Each of these types, then, has a specific role to play in innovation.

Accommodators would be best at innovation tasks such as designing and building prototypes or testing product features and functions. They would excel as product champions because they are energetic and enthusiastic.

Divergers would be best at brainstorming and generating new products. They would excel as inventors, whether of an entirely new product or of an improvement to an existing product.

Convergers would be best at testing products through experimentation or at developing additional features or enhancements to existing products. They would excel as technical advisors to the innovation process.

Assimilators would be best at thought experiments. They would excel at observing users and then generalizing from the specific observations to more general principles or ideas. They would excel as champions because they enjoy organizing people and information toward a practical outcome.

For more information about Kolb's styles and their implications for learning and work, look online. One interesting site is www.businessballs.com/self-awareness/kolbs-learning-styles/.

MANAGEMENT AT WORK

Mining a New Organization Design

Although some observers might assume that Anglo American PLC is a U.S. company, in reality the company has never been American. Instead, Anglo American is based in the United Kingdom but has substantial operations in other parts of the world, most notably Africa, South America, and Australia. The firm is the world's fourth-largest diversified mining company and the largest producer of platinum. It has annual revenues of more than $20 billion, earned $4 billion in profit in 2019, and has around 90,000 employees.

The last several years have been a period of change for Anglo American. The major upheavals started when Cynthia Carroll was appointed as CEO. The *Times* of London expressed shock at the appointment, referring to mining as "an irredeemably macho industry." Not only was she not a man, Carroll was neither a mining industry veteran nor British (she's an American). When her appointment was announced, Anglo's stock immediately dropped $0.80 per share. The dice, observed the *Times*, were "probably loaded against her from the start," and to make her job even more difficult, she was soon forced to embark on a $2-billion efficiency program involving a number of changes guaranteed to rile the old guard of the century-old company. Her whirlwind campaign to cut costs by $450 million in a 6-month period earned her the nickname "Cyclone Cynthia," but many analysts and investors were unimpressed by the savings: Because the entire industry was struggling with high costs during the recession, Carroll's cost-cutting was seen as little more than the logical and obvious strategy to pursue.

Then, the Swiss–British mining company Xstrata proposed a merger with Anglo—a move that would create a $68 billion firm to compete with industry giants like BHP Billiton, Vale, and Rio Tinto. Xstrata said in a statement that it was seeking "a merger of equals that would realize significant value for both companies' shareholders" and cited "substantial operational synergies" that could amount to savings of $1 billion a year in combined costs. From Anglo's perspective, there were drawbacks to the deal—its portfolio was worth more than Xstrata's and would be diluted by a merger of the two—but the appeal to Anglo shareholders was clear: Depending on how the new company distributed the cost savings among its investors, Anglo shareholders stood to realize an increase in the market value of their holdings of 26–37 percent.

Carroll and the Anglo board quickly rejected Xstrata's offer as "totally unacceptable," and in August, Carroll presented both Anglo's mid-year financial results and its argument for remaining independent. Once again, however, the numbers were underwhelming: Because of the global economy, profits were off 69 percent and revenues 38 percent. Anglo investors wanted to know what management was doing to deliver the kind of returns promised by the Xstrata merger, and an analyst at Barclays Capital, Britain's biggest investment bank, announced that "in our view, Anglo American has not yet presented a strong argument as to why a merger with Xstrata is not strategically sensible and value-creating for its shareholders." "Frankly," replied Carroll,

I know what it is that we need to do. . . . We have a strategy, we have clear goals, we have tremendous assets . . . in the most attractive commodities in the world. The opportunities are massive. . . . We're well aware of what Xstrata does, but I'm very confident of what we can do in the future.

Soon thereafter Xstrata withdrew its offer in the face of resistance from the Anglo board. Anglo, said a company spokesman, "can now move forward and run our business without further distraction." One analyst predicted that Anglo "will likely show a renewed sense of urgency . . . and pull out all the stops to win shareholders over." A few days later Carroll did indeed announce a major overhaul of Anglo's organization design intended to improve efficiency and make the firm more profitable. In making the announcement, she asked shareholders for more time to develop the firm's assets and prove its value as an independent company. "The portfolio changes we have announced," she argued, ". . . will position Anglo American well for sustained, profitable growth in the commodities we have identified as being the most attractive." She also projected that it would take three years to complete the reorganization.

The central element in the new organization design was referred to as *delayering*—eliminating a layer of its structure and reorganizing operations into resource-based units. At the time of the announcement the company was organized into two global product divisions—Coal and Ferrous Metals, each with its own CEO, both of whom reported directly to the CEO of Anglo American. Below the divisional level were Anglo's various global business operations, each dealing with a different commodity (e.g., coal, platinum, iron ore) and each headed by its own CEO and functional support staff. The CEOs of these units reported directly to the CEO of his or her respective division. As a result of what Carroll called "simplification and delayering," these businesses were reorganized into seven "commodity business units" (BUs), each of which is now "profit accountable"—that is, responsible for its own performance. The major criteria for this reorganization were geography and asset status. The platinum unit, for example, is headquartered in South Africa, the copper unit in Chile, and the metallurgical-coal unit in Australia.

In addition, Anglo focused BUs only on its *core assets*—operations that are essential to producing revenue, cash flow, or profit. Going hand in hand with the company's delayering strategy is thus a strategy to divest its noncore assets: Having already shed its interests in gold and aluminum, Anglo also sold its holdings in such commodities as phosphates and zinc as well as a company that manufactures steel products for the construction industry. The decision to delayer and divest, said Anglo chairman Sir John Parker, "represents an important step in creating a more streamlined business, with enhanced focus on operational effectiveness. . . . We have a truly world-class portfolio of assets, and these initiatives further improve our ability to deliver its full potential."

As projected, Anglo American's overhaul was completed in the three-year window. During the years spent changing the firm's organization design, Carroll oversaw a number of new efficiency measures and a reduction in the number of employees from more than 162,000 to around 100,000. Carroll left Anglo American after she finished implementing these massive changes. However, the firm continues to alter its design. Two years later, for example, top managers announced a new overhaul that would result in three large business units, one each for platinum, diamonds, and all other minerals. No timetable was announced for implementation of this next round of changes, however.[54]

Case Questions

1. Identify the basic organization change issues at Anglo American.
2. What basic elements of organization design were changed? What elements were probably not changed?
3. What other aspects of organization change can be identified in this case?
4. What issues related to resistance to change did Anglo American most likely encounter?
5. What role does innovation play in a company like Anglo American?

A Picture Says It All

1. Explain how—theoretically, anyway—making "change innovations" in each of the following *Areas of Organizational Change* might have helped Kodak ease the severity of both the conditions that led it to bankruptcy and the challenges facing it now that it's emerged from bankruptcy: *changing organization structure and design, changing people and attitudes,* and *changing processes.*

2. Judging from the case, explain how, at one point or another, each of the following reasons for *Failure to Innovate* played a role in the process that brought Kodak to bankruptcy: *lack of resources, failure to recognize opportunities, resistance to change.*

3. You can still buy a digital camera with the Kodak name on it, and you can still print pictures at digital kiosks in your local drugstore. These businesses, however, are no longer owned by Kodak. In addition, Kodak no longer publishes photos online or makes pocket video cameras, camera film, or photographic paper. Having emerged from bankruptcy, Kodak intends to focus on the commercial side of the imaging business, such as packaging labels and graphics and printing solutions to client businesses. It also plans to make components and products that other companies can sell under their own brands.

   In what ways does each of the following *Forms of Innovation* figure to play a role in Kodak's efforts to rebuild itself after bankruptcy: *radical innovations, incremental innovations, technical innovations, product innovations,* and *process innovations*?

4. How about you? How surprised are you to learn how fast a blue-chip corporation with a line of household-name products can collapse? Do you think that we live in times that make such stories as Kodak's more or less likely? In your opinion, what's the most important downside of the demise of a company such as Kodak? What's the most important upside?

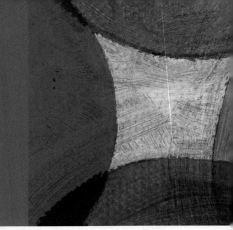

CHAPTER 8

Managing Human Resources in Organizations

Learning Outcomes

After studying this chapter, you should be able to:

8-1 Describe the environmental context of human resource management, including its strategic importance and its relationship with legal and social factors.

8-2 Discuss how organizations attract human resources, including human resource planning, recruiting, and selection.

8-3 Describe how organizations develop human resources, including training and development, performance appraisal, and performance feedback.

8-4 Discuss how organizations maintain human resources, including the determination of compensation and benefits and career planning.

8-5 Discuss labor relations, including how employees form unions and the mechanics of collective bargaining.

8-6 Describe the key issues associated with managing knowledge and contingent and temporary workers.

This chapter is about how organizations manage the people who comprise them. As we will see, the kinds of jobs people have and how they perform those jobs continues to change rapidly. It is critical, therefore, that managers understand the jobs in their organizations, who is available to perform those jobs, and how both jobs and workers will change in the future. The set of processes by which companies manage their employees is called "human resource management," or HRM. We start by describing the environmental context of HRM. We then discuss how organizations attract human resources. Next, we describe how organizations seek to further develop the capacities of their human resources. We also examine how the most valuable human resources are developed and rewarded by organizations. We conclude by discussing labor relations. To start, let's learn about a company that does an exemplary job of managing its human resources.

Management in Action

No Company for Old-Fashioned Management

"Anything that requires knowledge and service gives us a reason to be."

—Danny Wegman, Founder of Wegmans Food Markets

If you're looking for the best Parmesan cheese for your chicken parmigiana recipe, you might try Wegmans, especially if you happen to live in the vicinity of Pittsford, New York. Cheese department manager Carol Kent will be happy to recommend the best brand because her job calls for knowing cheese as well as managing some 20 subordinates. Kent is a knowledgeable employee, and knowledgeable employees, says Wegmans founder Danny Wegman, are "something our competitors don't have and our customers couldn't get anywhere else."

Wegmans Food Markets, a family-owned East Coast chain with more than 100 stores in six states, prides itself on its commitment to customers, and it shows: It ranks at the top of the latest *Consumer Reports* survey of the best national and regional grocery stores. But commitment to customers is only half of Wegmans' overall strategy, which calls for reaching its customers through its employees. "How do we differentiate ourselves?" asks Danny Wegman, who then proceeds to answer his own question: "If we can sell products that require knowledge in terms of how you use them, that's our strategy. Anything that requires knowledge and service gives us a reason to be." That's the logic behind one of Carol Kent's recent assignments—one that she understandably regards as a perk: Wegmans sent her to Italy to conduct a personal study of Italian cheese. "We sat with the families" that make the cheeses, she recalls, and "broke bread with them. It helped me understand that we're not just selling a piece of cheese. We're selling a tradition, a quality."

Kent and the employees in her department also enjoy the best benefits package in the industry, including fully paid health insurance. And that includes part-timers, who make up about two-thirds of the company's workforce of more than 58,000. In part, the strategy of extending benefits to this large segment of the labor force is intended to make sure that stores have enough good workers for crucial peak periods, but there's no denying that the costs of employee-friendly policies can mount up. At 15–17 percent of sales, for example, Wegmans' labor costs are well above the 12 percent figure for most supermarkets. But according to one company HR executive, holding down labor costs isn't necessarily a strategic priority: "We would have stopped offering free health insurance [to part-timers] a long time ago," she admits, "if we tried to justify the costs."

Besides, employee turnover at Wegmans is about 6 percent—a mere fraction of an industry average that hovers around 19 percent (and can approach 100 percent for part-timers). And this is an industry in which total turnover costs have been known to outstrip total annual profits by 40 percent. Wegmans employees tend to be knowledgeable because about 20 percent of them have been with the company for at least ten years, and many have logged at least a quarter century. Says one 19-year-old college student who works at an upstate New York Wegmans while pursuing a career as a high school history teacher, "I love this place. If teaching doesn't work out, I would so totally work at Wegmans." Edward McLaughlin, who directs the Food Industry Management Program at Cornell University, understands this sort of attitude: "When you're a 16-year-old kid, the last thing you want to do is wear a geeky shirt and work for a supermarket," but at Wegmans, he explains, "it's a badge of honor. You're not a geeky cashier. You're part of the social fabric."

Wegmans has been on *Fortune* magazine's annual list of "100 Best Companies to Work For" every year since the list started in 1998 and was number three on the 2020 list. "It says that we're doing something right," says a company spokesperson, "and that there's no better way to take care of our customers than to be a great place for our employees to work." In addition to its health care package, Wegmans has been cited for such perks as fitness center discounts, compressed workweeks, telecommuting, and domestic-partner benefits (including same-sex partners).

Finally, under the company's Employee Scholarship Program, full-time workers can receive up to $2,200 a year for four years and part-timers up to $1,500. Since its inception in 1984, the program has handed out over $86 million in scholarships to more than 25,000 employees. Like most Wegman policies, this one combines employee outreach with long-term corporate strategy: "This program has made a real difference in the lives of many young people," says CEO Colleen Wegman, who adds that it's also "one of the reasons we've been able to attract the best and the brightest to work at Wegmans."

Granted, Wegmans, which has remained in family hands since its founding in 1915, has an advantage in being as generous with its resources as its family of top executives wants to be: It doesn't have to do everything with quarterly profits in mind, and the firm likes to point out that taking care of its employees is a long-standing priority. Profit sharing and fully funded medical coverage were introduced in 1950 by Robert Wegman, son and nephew of brothers Walter and John, who opened the firm's original flagship store in Rochester, New York, in 1930. Why did Robert Wegman make such generous gestures to his employees way back then? "Because," he says simply, "I was no different from them."[1]

8-1 THE ENVIRONMENTAL CONTEXT OF HUMAN RESOURCE MANAGEMENT

human resource management (HRM)
The set of organizational activities directed at attracting, developing, and maintaining an effective workforce

Human resource management (HRM) is the set of organizational activities directed at attracting, developing, and maintaining an effective workforce.[2] Human resource management takes place within a complex and ever-changing environmental context. Three particularly vital components of this context are HRM's strategic importance and the legal and social environments of HRM.

8-1a The Strategic Importance of HRM

Human resources—the people who comprise an organization—are critical for both effectiveness and competitiveness. HRM (or "personnel," as it is sometimes called) was once relegated to second-class status in many organizations, but its importance has grown dramatically in most modern organizations. (At some firms, of course, like Wegmans, employees have always been a top priority.) Its growing importance stems from increased legal complexities, the recognition that human resources are a valuable means for improving productivity, and the increased awareness of the costs associated with poor human resource management.[3] For example, during the last several years, Microsoft has announced several different layoffs (including one numbering 5,000 employees and another 14,000), mostly individuals working in software development. At the same time, though, the firm has continued to expand and hire thousands of other highly talented people for jobs related to online search and network integration, important growth areas for the company. This careful and systematic approach to talent management, reducing employees in areas where they are no longer needed and adding new talent to key growth areas, reflects a strategic approach to HRM.

Indeed, most managers realize that the effectiveness of their HR function has a substantial impact on the bottom-line performance of their organization. Poor human resource planning can result in spurts of hiring followed by layoffs—costly in terms of unemployment compensation payments, training expenses, and morale. Haphazard compensation systems do not attract, keep, and motivate good employees, and outmoded recruitment practices can expose the firm to expensive and embarrassing discrimination lawsuits. Consequently, the chief human resource executive of most large businesses is a vice president directly accountable to the CEO, and many firms develop strategic HR plans and integrate those plans with other strategic planning activities.[4]

Human resource functions have an enormous impact on most aspects of an organization. Ineffective human resource management can lead to high rates of employee turnover, layoffs, and reduced revenue and profits.

Rawpixel.com/Shutterstock.com

Even organizations with as few as 200 employees usually have a human resource manager and a human resource department charged with overseeing these activities. Responsibility for HR activities, however, is usually shared between the HR department and line managers. The HR department may recruit and initially screen candidates, but the final hiring decision is usually made by managers in the department where the new employee will work. Similarly, although HR specialists may create performance appraisal and procedures and systems, the actual evaluation and coaching of employees is done by their immediate superiors.

human capital
Reflects the organization's investment in attracting, retaining, and motivating an effective workforce

The growing awareness of the strategic significance of human resource management has even led to new terminology to reflect a firm's commitment to people. Human capital reflects the organization's investment in attracting, retaining, and motivating an effective workforce. Hence, just as the phrase *financial capital* is an indicator of a firm's financial resources and reserves, so, too, does *human capital* serve as a tangible indicator of the value of the people who comprise an organization.[5] *Talent management* is also a term that is growing in popularity.

> "Most HR people derive their influence through knowledge of rules and regulations. Our power comes from influence, from the roles we play in helping the business succeed."
>
> —Jessica Neal, VP of Human Resources at Netflix[6]

8-1b The Legal Environment of HRM

Title VII of the Civil Rights Act of 1964
Forbids discrimination on the basis of sex, race, color, religion, or national origin in all areas of the employment relationship

A number of laws regulate various aspects of employee–employer relations, especially in the areas of equal employment opportunity, compensation and benefits, labor relations, and occupational safety and health. Several major ones are summarized in Table 8.1.

Equal Employment Opportunity Title VII of the Civil Rights Act of 1964 forbids discrimination in all areas of the employment relationship. The intent of Title VII is to ensure that employment decisions are made on the basis of a person's qualifications rather than on the basis of personal biases. The law has reduced direct forms of discrimination (refusing to promote African Americans into management, failing to hire men as flight attendants, refusing to hire women as construction workers, for instance) as well as indirect forms of discrimination (using employment tests that whites pass at a higher rate than African Americans).

adverse impact
When minority group members pass a selection standard at a rate less than 80 percent of the pass rate of majority group members

Employment requirements such as test scores and other qualifications are legally defined as having an adverse impact on minorities and women when such individuals meet or pass the requirement at a rate less than 80 percent of the rate of majority group members. Criteria that have an adverse impact on protected groups can be used only when there is solid evidence that they effectively identify those who are better able than others to do the job. The Equal Employment Opportunity Commission is charged with enforcing Title VII as well as several other employment-related laws.

Equal Employment Opportunity Commission
Federal agency charged with enforcing Title VII of the Civil Rights Act of 1964

The Age Discrimination in Employment Act—passed in 1967, amended in 1978, and amended again in 1986—is an attempt to prevent organizations from discriminating against older workers. In its current form, it outlaws discrimination against people older than 40 years on the basis of their age. Both the Age Discrimination in Employment Act and Title VII only require passive nondiscrimination, or equal employment opportunity. Employers are not required to seek out and hire minorities, but they must treat all who apply fairly.

Age Discrimination In Employment Act
Outlaws discrimination against people older than age 40; passed in 1967, amended in 1978 and 1986

affirmative action
Intentionally seeking and hiring qualified or qualifiable employees from racial, sexual, and ethnic groups that are underrepresented in the organization

Several executive orders (orders issued by the president of the United States), however, require that employers holding government contracts engage in affirmative action—intentionally and proactively seeking and hiring employees from groups that are underrepresented in the organization. These organizations must have a written affirmative action plan that spells out employment goals for underutilized groups and how those goals will be met. These employers are also required to act affirmatively in hiring Vietnam-era veterans (as a result of the Vietnam Era Veterans Readjustment Assistance Act) and qualified individuals with a disability. Finally, the Pregnancy Discrimination Act forbids discrimination against women who are pregnant.

Americans with Disabilities Act
Prohibits discrimination against people with disabilities

In 1990 Congress passed the Americans with Disabilities Act, which forbids discrimination on the basis of disabilities and requires employers to provide reasonable accommodations for

Table 8.1	The Legal Environment of Human Resource Management

Equal Employment Opportunity

Title VII of the Civil Rights Act of 1964 (as amended by the Equal Employment Opportunity Act of 1972). Forbids discrimination in all areas of the employment relationship.

Age Discrimination in Employment Act. Outlaws discrimination against people older than age 40.

Various executive orders, especially Executive Order 11246 in 1965. Requires employers with government contracts to engage in affirmative action.

Pregnancy Discrimination Act. Specifically outlaws discrimination on the basis of pregnancy.

Vietnam Era Veterans Readjustment Assistance Act. Extends affirmative action mandate to military veterans who served during the Vietnam War.

Americans with Disabilities Act. Specifically outlaws discrimination against persons with a disability.

Civil Rights Act of 1991. Makes it easier for employees to sue an organization for discrimination but limits punitive damage awards if they win.

Compensation and Benefits

Fair Labor Standards Act. Establishes minimum wage and mandated overtime pay for work in excess of 40 hours per week.

Equal Pay Act of 1963. Requires that men and women be paid the same amount for doing the same job.

Employee Retirement Income Security Act of 1974 (ERISA). Regulates how organizations manage their pension funds.

Family and Medical Leave Act of 1993 (FMLA). Requires employers to provide up to 12 weeks of unpaid leave for family and medical emergencies.

Labor Relations

National Labor Relations Act. Spells out procedures by which employees can establish labor unions and requires organizations to bargain collectively with legally formed unions; also known as the Wagner Act.

Labor-Management Relations Act. Limits union power and specifies management rights during a union-organizing campaign; also known as the Taft-Hartley Act.

Health and Safety

Occupational Safety and Health Act of 1970. Mandates the provision of safe working conditions.

As much as any area of management, HRM is subject to wide-ranging laws and court decisions. These laws and decisions affect the human resource function in many areas. For example, AT&T was once fined several million dollars for violating Title VII of the Civil Rights Act of 1964.

Contrary to popular belief, discrimination *per se* is not illegal. Businesses routinely—and legally—discriminate on the basis of performance, experience, education, seniority, and other job-related criteria. That is, it is legal to hire a person with more experience rather than someone with less experience or give a salary increase to high performers but not low performers. However, several laws and executive orders make it illegal to discriminate on the basis of non-job-related criteria such as sex, race, color, religion, or national origin.

chris2766/Shutterstock.com

disabled employees. More recently, the Civil Rights Act of 1991 amended the original Civil Rights Act as well as other related laws by both making it easier to bring discrimination lawsuits and simultaneously limiting the amount of punitive damages that can be awarded in those lawsuits.

Compensation and Benefits Laws also regulate compensation and benefits. The Fair Labor Standards Act, passed in 1938 and amended frequently since then, sets a minimum wage and requires the payment of overtime rates for work in excess of 40 hours per week. The current federal minimum wage is $7.25 an hour. Salaried professional, executive, and administrative employees are exempt from the minimum hourly wage and overtime provisions. The Equal Pay Act of 1963 requires that men and women be paid the same amount for doing the same job. Attempts to circumvent the law by having different job titles and pay rates for men and women who perform the same work are

This employee heads her company's labor union. This firm provides security services for a major city's railway system. As such, it falls under the National Emergency Strike provision, as part of the Tart-Hartley Act.

Civil Rights Act of 1991
Amends the original Civil Rights Act, making it easier to bring discrimination lawsuits while also limiting punitive damages

Fair Labor Standards Act
Sets a minimum wage and requires overtime pay for work in excess of 40 hours per week; passed in 1938 and amended frequently since then

Equal Pay Act of 1963
Requires that men and women be paid the same amount for doing the same job

Employee Retirement Income Security Act of 1974 (ERISA)
Regulates how organizations manage their pension funds

Family and Medical Leave Act of 1993 (FMLA)
Requires employers to provide up to 12 weeks of unpaid leave for family and medical emergencies

National Labor Relations Act
Passed in 1935 to set up procedures for employees to vote on whether to have a union; also known as the *Wagner Act*

also illegal. Basing an employee's pay on seniority or performance is legal, however, even if it means that a man and woman are paid different amounts for doing the same job.

The provision of benefits is also regulated in some ways by state and federal laws. Certain benefits are mandatory—for example, workers' compensation insurance for employees who are injured on the job. Employers who provide a pension plan for their employees are regulated by the Employee Retirement Income Security Act of 1974 (ERISA). The purpose of this act is to help ensure the financial security of pension funds by regulating how they can be invested. The Family and Medical Leave Act of 1993 (FMLA) requires employers to provide up to 12 weeks of unpaid leave for family and medical emergencies.

Labor Relations   Union activities and management's behavior toward unions constitute another heavily regulated area. The National Labor Relations Act (also known as the *Wagner Act*), passed in 1935, set up a procedure for employees to vote on whether to have a union. If they vote for a union, management is required to bargain collectively with the union. The National Labor Relations Board (NLRB) was established by the Wagner Act to enforce its provisions. Following a series of severe strikes in 1946, the Labor-Management Relations Act (also known as the *Taft-Hartley Act*) was passed in 1947 to limit union power. The law increases management's rights during an organizing campaign. The Taft-Hartley Act also contains the National Emergency Strike provision, which allows the president of the United States to prevent or end a strike that endangers national security. Taken together, these laws balance union and management power. Employees can be represented by a legally created and managed union, but the business can make nonemployee-related business decisions without interference.

Health and Safety   The Occupational Safety and Health Act of 1970 directly mandates the provision of safe working conditions. It requires that employers (1) provide a place of employment that is free from hazards that may cause death or serious physical harm and (2) obey the safety and health standards established by the Department of Labor. Safety standards are intended to prevent accidents, whereas occupational health standards are concerned with preventing occupational disease. For example, standards limit the concentration of cotton dust in the air because this contaminant has been associated with lung disease in textile workers. The standards set by provisions of the Occupational Safety and Health Act (OSHA) are enforced by inspectors from the Department of Labor and are initiated when an employee files a complaint of unsafe conditions or when a serious accident occurs.

Spot inspections of plants in especially hazardous industries such as mining and chemicals are also made. Employers who fail to meet OSHA standards may be fined. For instance, in December 2018 a construction worker in New York died after a roof collapsed where he was installing solar panels. An OSHA investigation concluded that the worker's employer, Northridge Construction, failed to provide fall protection devices and protective helmets, did not assess the structural integrity of the roof, and misused a ladder. The firm was fined $224,620. Similarly, Donghee Alabama LLC, an automobile parts manufacturer, was charged with numerous violations leading to the death of one of its employees. This firm was fined $145,438.[7] There were also many complaints about unsafe working conditions filed during the 2020 COVID-19 pandemic.

Emerging Legal Issues   Several other areas of legal interest and concern have emerged during the past few years. One is sexual harassment. Although sexual harassment is forbidden under Title VII, it has received additional attention in the courts and the media recently, as more and more victims have decided to publicly confront the problem as part of the "Me Too" movement. Another emerging human resource management issue is alcohol and drug abuse. Both alcoholism and drug dependence are major problems today. Recent court rulings have tended to define those with an alcohol or drug addiction as disabled, protecting them under the same laws that protect other people with a disability. AIDS is an important legal issue as

National Labor Relations Board (NLRB)
Established by the Wagner Act to enforce its provisions

Labor-Management Relations Act
Passed in 1947 to limit union power; also known as the *Taft-Hartley Act*

Occupational Safety and Health Act of 1970
Directly mandates the provision of safe working conditions

employment-at-will
A traditional view of the workplace that says organizations can fire their employees for whatever reason they want; recent court judgments are limiting employment-at-will

well. AIDS victims, too, are most often protected under various laws protecting the disabled. Employee privacy is also becoming a controversial issue in the HR arena. For instance, can employers refuse to hire an otherwise qualified applicant because of information that person posts on social networking sites?

In the last few years some large employers, most notably Walmart, have come under fire because they do not provide health care for all of their employees. In response to this, the state of Maryland passed a law, informally called the "Walmart bill," that required employers with more than 10,000 workers to spend at least 8 percent of their payrolls on health care or else pay a comparable amount into a general fund for uninsured workers. This law was subsequently found to be illegal by a U.S. District Court, but the issue of benefits for part-time workers will almost certainly continue to be discussed.

Another emerging legal issue involves how organizations deal with LGBTQ employees. Some businesses have implicitly extended equal opportunity to these employees while other businesses have routinely discriminated against them. In June 2020, however, the U.S. Supreme Court ruled that Title VII protections provided by the Civil Rights Act of 1964 extend to LGBTQ employees, therefore making discriminatory actions against them illegal.

8-1c Social Change and HRM

Beyond the objective legal context of HRM, various social changes are also affecting how organizations interact with their employees. First, many organizations are using more and more temporary workers today. This trend, discussed more fully later, allows them to add workers as necessary without the risk that they may have to eliminate their jobs in the future. Second, dual-career families are much more common today than just a few years ago. Organizations are finding that they must make accommodations for employees who are dual-career partners. These accommodations may include delaying transfers, offering employment to the spouses of current employees to retain them, and providing more flexible work schedules and benefits packages.

Employment-at-will is also becoming an important issue. Although employment-at-will has legal implications, its emergence as an issue is socially driven. Employment-at-will is a traditional view of the workplace that says organizations can fire an employee for any reason. Increasingly, however, people are arguing that organizations should be able to fire only people who are poor performers or who violate rules and, conversely, should not be able to fire people who report safety violations to OSHA or refuse to perform unethical activities. Several court cases in recent years have upheld this view and have limited many organizations' ability to terminate employees to those cases where there is clear and just cause or there is an organizationwide cutback. Furthermore, in the wake of massive layoffs during the COVID-19 pandemic in 2020, several ex-workers sued their former employers, citing alleged violations of various severance laws.[8]

Finally, discussions continue to take place regarding the minimum wage. While there is a federal minimum wage, as noted earlier, some states have established higher minimum wages. For example, in California the minimum wage is $12 an hour, in Florida it's $8.46, and in Nebraska it's $9. In Oregon some cities have minimum wages that are higher than the state's minimum of $12 an hour. In Portland, for instance, the minimum is $13.25. The rationale for all of these variations is partially based on the fact that the cost of living is higher in some places than in others and partially because the federal minimum of $7.25 an hour is felt to simply be too low.

The Occupational Safety and Health Act, passed in 1970, mandates that organizations provide their employees with a workplace that is free from hazards, provide necessary safety equipment, and follow guidelines to minimize potential occupational diseases. This worker, for instance, is using several forms of safety equipment while performing a potentially hazardous job. All of this equipment meets Occupational Safety and Health Act requirements.

Hywit Dimyadi/Shutterstock.com

Manager's Checklist

☐ Managers need a clear understanding of the strategic role human resource management plays in their organization.

☐ All managers should be able to identify and briefly summarize the key laws that affect human resource management.

☐ To the extent that you are involved in human resource management activities, such as interviewing potential new employees, you should be very familiar with laws and regulations that affect those activities.

8-2 ATTRACTING HUMAN RESOURCES

With an understanding of the environmental context of human resource management as a foundation, we are now ready to address its first substantive concern—attracting qualified people who are interested in working for the organization.

> **"We are in the midst of a major structural shift in manufacturing.... The number of good-paying, middle-class jobs that have been the bulk of manufacturing is likely going to be less in the future."**
> —Harley Shaiken, Professor of Labor Relations at The University of California, Berkeley[9]

job analysis
A systematized procedure for collecting and recording information about jobs within an organization

8-2a Human Resource Planning

The starting point in attracting qualified human resources is planning. HR planning, in turn, involves job analysis and forecasting the demand and supply of labor.

Job Analysis   Job analysis is a systematic analysis of jobs within an organization. A job analysis is made up of two parts. The job description lists the duties of a job, the job's working conditions, and the tools, materials, information, and equipment used to perform it. The job specification lists the skills, abilities, and other credentials needed to do the job. Job analysis information is used in many human resource activities. For instance, knowing about job content and job requirements is necessary to develop appropriate selection methods and job-relevant performance appraisal systems and to set equitable compensation rates.

Forecasting Human Resource Demand and Supply   When managers fully understand the work and jobs to be performed within the organization, they can more effectively plan for the organization's future human resource needs. Figure 8.1 summarizes the general steps most often followed. The manager starts by assessing trends in past human resources needs, future organizational plans, and general economic trends. A good sales forecast is often the foundation, especially for smaller organizations. Historical ratios can then be used to predict demand for such employees as operating employees, sales representatives, and customer support professionals. For instance, a regional restaurant chain may know that it needs a general manager, four assistant managers, 15 full-time employees, and 20 part-time employees to staff each of its restaurants. If the company plans to add ten new restaurants in the next three years it knows it will need ten new general managers, 40 new assistant managers, and so forth. By factoring in its experiences related to time-to-hire, training requirements, and so forth it will then have a good framework from which to start planning to hire and develop new employees.

Of course, large organizations use much more complicated models to predict their future human resource needs. A major corporation has tens of thousands of employees across hundreds of different jobs and spread across many different countries. A few years ago, Walmart went through an exhaustive planning process that projected that the firm would need to hire 1 million people over the next decade. Of this projected total, 800,000 would be new positions created as the firm grows, and the other 200,000 would replace current workers who are expected to leave for various reasons.[10] As time passes and conditions change, of course, Walmart adjusts these figures both up and down.

Forecasting the supply of labor is really two tasks: forecasting the internal supply (the number and types of employees who will be in the firm at some future date) and forecasting the external

replacement chart
Lists each important managerial position in the organization, who occupies it, how long he or she will probably remain in the position, and who is or will be a qualified replacement

employee information system (skills inventory)
Contains information on each employee's education, skills, experience, and career aspirations; usually computerized

supply (the number and types of people who will be available for hiring in the labor market at large).[11] The simplest approach merely adjusts present staffing levels for anticipated turnover and promotions. Again, though, large organizations use extremely sophisticated models to make these forecasts. Chevron, for example, has a complex forecasting system for keeping track of the present and future distributions of professionals and managers. The Chevron system can spot areas where there will eventually be too many qualified professionals competing for too few promotions or, conversely, too few good people available to fill important positions.[12]

At higher levels of the organization, managers plan for specific people and positions. The technique most commonly used is the **replacement chart**, which lists each important managerial position, who occupies it, how long he or she will probably stay in it before moving on, and who (by name) is now qualified or soon will be qualified to move into the position. This technique allows ample time to plan developmental experiences for persons identified as potential successors to critical managerial jobs.[13] Halliburton, for instance, has a detailed replacement system that the firm calls its Executive Succession System (ESS). When a manager has his or her performance reviewed each year, notations are placed in the system about the person's readiness for promotion, potential positions for promotion, and what development activities are needed to prepare the individual for promotion. Other managers throughout the firm can access the system whenever they have positions available.

To facilitate both planning and identifying persons for current transfer or promotion, some organizations also have an **employee information system**, or **skills inventory**. Such systems are usually computerized and contain information on each employee's education, skills, work experience, and career aspirations. Such a system can quickly locate all the employees in the

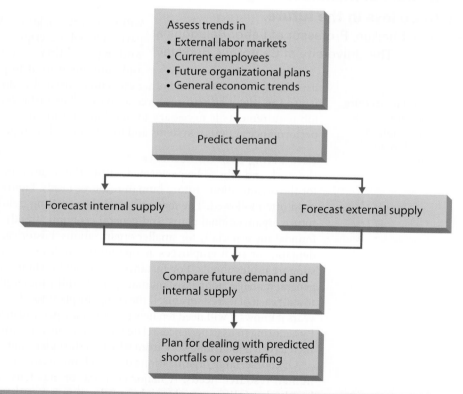

Human Resource Planning

Attracting human resources cannot be left to chance if an organization expects to function at peak efficiency. Human resource planning involves assessing trends, forecasting demand and supply of labor, and then developing appropriate strategies for addressing any differences.

organization who are qualified to fill a position requiring, for instance, a degree in chemical engineering, three years of experience in an oil refinery, and fluency in Spanish. Enterprise resource planning (ERP) systems, as described in Chapter 12, generally include capabilities for measuring and managing the internal supply of labor in ways that best fit the needs of the organization.

Forecasting the external supply of labor is a different problem altogether. How does a manager, for example, predict how many electrical engineers will be seeking work in Georgia three years from now? To get an idea of the future availability of labor, planners must rely on information from such outside sources as state employment commissions, government reports, and figures supplied by colleges on the number of students in major fields.

"We overlooked our own people. It was easier to go to the outside. [But insiders] know our firm and in some cases they already know the client."

—Lucy Sorrentini, Principal in People Services at Booz Allen Hamilton, On Switching Hiring Practices

Matching Human Resource Demand and Supply   After comparing future demand and internal supply, managers can make plans to manage predicted shortfalls or overstaffing. If a shortfall is predicted, new employees can be hired, present employees can be retrained and transferred into the understaffed area, individuals approaching retirement can be convinced to stay on, or labor-saving or productivity-enhancing systems can be installed. For the regional restaurant chain mentioned earlier, for example, the new general managers might come from the ranks of current assistant managers who are interested in advancement.

If the organization needs to hire, the external labor supply forecast helps managers plan how to recruit, based on whether the type of person needed is readily available or scarce in the labor market. As we noted earlier, the trend in temporary workers also helps managers in staffing by affording them extra flexibility. If overstaffing is expected to be a problem, the main options are transferring the extra employees, choosing not to replace individuals who quit, encouraging early retirement, and laying people off.

There are many methods for recruiting employees. At one time, the "Help Wanted" section in daily newspapers was the only way, but today recruiters have many different methods available for attracting job applicants.

Many different issues regarding the supply and demand of labor arose during the COVID-19 pandemic in 2020, but in both directions. Many firms such as traditional retailers and restaurants like Macy's and Olive Garden were hurt by various "shelter-in-place" requirements and laid off thousands of people. Similarly, as global travel plunged, so too did the demand for oil and gas, causing energy-related firms like Chevron and BP to also reduce their workforces. On the other hand, as demand for such products as toilet tissue and cleaning supplies surged, companies like Procter & Gamble and Clorox hired new employees to help meet this demand and, as fewer people ventured out to shop, online retailing skyrocketed and companies like Amazon went into an aggressive hiring mode.

8-2b Recruiting Employees

recruiting
The process of attracting individuals to apply for jobs that are open

Once an organization has an idea of its future human resource needs, the next phase is usually recruiting new employees.[14] **Recruiting** is the process of attracting qualified persons to apply for jobs that are open. Where do recruits come from? Some recruits are found internally; others come from outside the organization.

TECH WATCH

Using Tech to Find Talent

In 2010, Ian Siegel was working as an executive in the latest of a string of start-ups, including Ticketmaster, Stamps.com, and Rent.com. He was frustrated with the slow work of hiring, going through the traditional process of sorting through applications and resumés. He knew there must be a better way and remembers thinking to himself, "This is exactly what the web is designed to make easy." And so, with the help of three other co-founders, Siegel set about to build ZipRecruiter, which has become the nation's fastest-growing online job marketplace.

Siegel took his experience as a market disruptor and applied it to the business of recruiting and job searching. He says, "There is no employer in the country right now who looks forward to hiring or understands how to run the process efficiently, If you surveyed job-seekers, you would find that they, also, do not enjoy their experience. Today, with so much technology, this process should be easier." Determined to maintain autonomy and build their business from the ground up, Siegel and his co-founders fended off multiple purchase and takeover offers to "bootstrap" their business, focusing on small- and medium-sized businesses and internal growth.

When the ZipRecruiter team was satisfied that they had established a strong culture and business model, they sought outside funding, starting with $63 million in venture capital funding in 2014. As of October 2018, ZipRecruiter had raised $219 million in total, making its value $1.9 billion and connecting over 430 million job-seekers with 1.5 million employers. In 2020, ZipRecruiter was the top-rated Android job-search app.

Ironically, in an enterprise that relies on making good matches between people, ZipRecruiter relies on artificial intelligence to make an astonishing number of lightning-quick matches between job-seekers and employers. "The rise of AI has transformed how employers source talent and job-seekers find work," says Siegel. The latest round of funding acquisition will be focused on improving and expanding the company's AI capabilities.

Reference: Joel Cheesman, "ZipRecruiter Raised 156 Million, Now Valued at $1.5 Billion," ERE, October 5, 2018, www.ere .net on April 19, 2020;

---

internal recruiting
Considering current employees as applicants for higher-level jobs in the organization

Internal recruiting means considering present employees as candidates for openings. Promotion from within can help build morale and keep high-quality employees from leaving the firm. In unionized firms, the procedures for notifying employees of internal job change opportunities are usually spelled out in the union contract. For higher-level positions, a skills inventory system may be used to identify internal candidates, or managers may be asked to recommend people who should be considered. Most businesses today routinely post job openings on their internal communication network, or intranet. One disadvantage of internal recruiting is its ripple effect. When an employee moves to a different job, someone else must be found to take his or her old job. For the regional restaurant chain, each of the assistant managers promoted to manager will need to be replaced. They might come from the ranks of current employees, who also must then be replaced. In one organization, 454 job movements were necessary as a result of filling 195 initial openings!

external recruiting
Getting people from outside the organization to apply for jobs

External recruiting involves attracting persons outside the organization to apply for jobs. External recruiting methods include online resources like LinkedIn, traditional advertising, campus interviews, employment agencies or executive search firms, union hiring halls, referrals by present employees, and hiring "walk-ins" or "gate-hires" (people who show up without being solicited). Increasingly, firms are using the internet to post job openings and to solicit applicants. Of course, a manager must select the most appropriate methods—using the state employment service to find maintenance workers but not a nuclear physicist, for example. Private employment agencies can be a good source of clerical and technical employees, and executive search firms specialize in locating top-management talent. Newspaper ads are often used because they reach a wide audience and thus allow minorities equal opportunity to find out about and apply for job openings.

The organization must also keep in mind that recruiting decisions often go both ways—the organization is recruiting an employee, but the prospective employee is also selecting a job.[15] For instance, when unemployment is low (meaning there are fewer people seeking work), businesses may have to work harder to attract new employees. During 2019, when unemployment dropped to a 25-year low, some recruiters at firms such as Sprint, Workday, and Cognex stressed how much "fun" it was to work for them, reinforcing this message with ice cream socials, karaoke contests, softball leagues, and free movie nights.[16] But when unemployment is higher (meaning there are more people looking for work), organizations may find it easier to recruit prospective employees without having to resort to expensive hiring incentives. For example, during the 2020 COVID-19 pandemic, as noted earlier, many firms reduced jobs and/or cut back on labor hours. As a result, in the aftermath of the pandemic, firms that needed to hire new workers found it much easier to do so because there were many qualified people looking for work.

Nevertheless, even if a firm can take its pick of the best potential employees, it still should put its best foot forward, treat all applicants with dignity, and strive for a good person–job fit. Hiring the wrong employee can cost the company about half of a low-skilled worker's annual wages or three to five times upper-level employees' annual wages. Therefore, hiring the "wrong" employee for $50,000 per year could cost the company at least $25,000. These costs stem from training, counseling, low productivity, termination, and recruiting and hiring a replacement.

One generally successful method for facilitating a good person–job fit is what is known as the realistic job preview (RJP). As the term suggests, the RJP involves providing the applicant with a real picture of what performing the job that the organization is trying to fill would be like.[17] For example, it would not make sense for a firm to tell an applicant that the job is exciting and challenging when in fact it is routine and straightforward, yet some managers do just this in order to hire the best people. The likely outcome, though, will be a dissatisfied employee who will quickly be looking for a better job. If the company is more realistic about a job, though, the person hired will be more likely to remain in the job for a longer period of time. Since it might be awkward to tell someone that a job is routine, most RJPs are accomplished by letting an applicant perform a sample of the work or watch others doing the job and then draw their own conclusions about their interest.

realistic job preview (RJP)
Provides the applicant with a real picture of what performing the job that the organization is trying to fill would be like

8-2c Selecting Employees

Once the recruiting process has attracted a pool of applicants, the next step is to select whom to hire. The intent of the selection process is to gather from applicants information that will predict their job success and then to hire the candidates likely to be most successful.[18] Of course, the organization can only gather information about factors that are predictive of future performance. The process of determining the predictive value of information is called validation.

Two basic approaches to validation are predictive validation and content validation. *Predictive validation* involves collecting the scores of employees or applicants on the selection method to be validated and correlating their scores with actual job performance. A significant correlation means that the selection device is a valid predictor of job performance. While not an employment test, SAT or ACT scores are often used in making college admissions decisions because these tests have been shown to be good predictors of academic success. That is, test scores usually correlate positively with grades. *Content validation* uses logic and job analysis data to establish that the selection device measures the exact skills needed for successful job performance. The most critical part of content validation is a careful job analysis showing exactly what duties are to be performed. The test is then developed to measure the applicant's ability to perform those duties.

validation
Determining the extent to which a selection device is really predictive of future job performance

Application Forms and Resumes   The first step in selection for most jobs is asking the candidate to fill out an application form. For higher-level and professional positions, a resumé is usually substituted for the traditional application form. Application forms and resumés are an efficient method of gathering information about the applicant's previous work history, educational background, and other job-related demographic data. They should not contain questions about areas not related to the job, such as gender, religion, or national origin. Application form data and resumés are generally used informally to decide whether a candidate merits further evaluation, and interviewers use application forms and resumés to familiarize themselves with candidates before interviewing them. Unfortunately,

In this interview, the HR representative is explaining to the candidate how to perform a test. All candidates have been asked to perform the same test. The test requires them to analyze sales data and research to propose a marketing plan for a new product. Their performance on this test will be used as one measure to determine the best candidate for the job.

in recent years there has been a trend toward job applicants either falsifying or inflating their credentials to stand a better chance of getting a job. Indeed, one survey of 2.6 million job applications found that an astounding 44 percent of them contained some false information.[19] Another survey conducted by Accu-Screen found that 53 percent of resumés and job applications have false information and 78 percent have misleading information.[20]

Tests   Tests of ability, skill, aptitude, or knowledge that are relevant to the particular job are usually the best predictors of job success, although tests of general intelligence or personality are occasionally useful as well. In addition to being validated, tests should be administered and scored consistently. All candidates should be given the same directions, should be allowed the same amount of time, and should experience the same testing environment (temperature, lighting, distractions).[21]

Interviews   Although a popular selection device, interviews are sometimes poor predictors of job success. For example, biases inherent in the way people perceive and judge others at a first meeting affect subsequent evaluations by the interviewer. Interview validity can be improved by training interviewers to be aware of potential biases and by increasing the structure of the interview. In a structured interview, questions are written in advance, and all interviewers follow the same question list with each candidate they interview. This procedure introduces consistency into the interview procedure and allows the organization to validate the content of the questions to be asked.[22]

For interviewing managerial or professional candidates, a somewhat less structured approach is usually used. Question areas and information-gathering objectives are still planned in advance, but the specific questions vary with the candidates' backgrounds. Trammell Crow Real Estate Investors uses a novel approach in hiring managers. Each applicant is interviewed not only by two or three other managers but also by an administrative assistant or young leasing agent. This provides information about how the prospective manager relates to nonmanagers.

Assessment Centers   Assessment centers are a popular method used to select managers and are particularly good for selecting current employees for promotion.[23] The assessment center is a content-valid simulation of major parts of the managerial job. A typical center lasts one or two days, with groups of 6–12 persons participating in a variety of managerial exercises. Centers may also include interviews, public speaking, and standardized ability tests. Candidates are assessed by several trained observers, usually managers several levels above the job for which the candidates are being considered. Assessment centers can be valid predictors of future managerial performance if they are properly designed and fair to members of minority groups and women.[24] For some firms, the assessment center is a permanent facility created for these activities. For other firms, the assessment activities are performed in a multipurpose location such as a conference room. AT&T pioneered the assessment center concept. For years the firm has used assessment centers to make virtually all of its selection decisions for management positions.

Other Techniques   Organizations also use other selection techniques depending on the circumstances. Polygraph tests, once popular, are declining in popularity. On the other hand, more and more organizations are requiring that applicants in whom they are interested take physical exams. Organizations are also increasingly using drug tests, especially in situations in which drug-related performance problems could create serious safety hazards. For example, applicants for jobs in a nuclear power plant or with access to expensive jewelry would likely be tested for drug use. And some organizations today even run credit checks on prospective employees. Overall, many of these tests now are subsumed under a general background check.

 **Manager's Checklist**

- ☐ Managers should be familiar with the processes of human resource planning, recruiting, and selection.

- ☐ Managers should also understand that selection techniques provide useful information but none is perfect.

- ☐ You should also remember that recruiting and selection are two-way streets: Just as you are trying to find the best employee, prospective employees are also looking for the best jobs.

8-3 DEVELOPING HUMAN RESOURCES

Regardless of how effective a selection system is, however, most employees need additional training if they are to grow and develop in their jobs. Evaluating their performance and providing feedback are also necessary.

8-3a Training and Development

training
Teaching operational or technical employees how to do the job for which they were hired

development
Teaching managers and professionals the skills needed for both present and future jobs

In HRM, training usually refers to teaching operational or technical employees how to do the job for which they were hired. Development refers to teaching managers and professionals the skills needed for both present and future jobs.[25] Most organizations provide regular training and development programs for managers and employees. For example, IBM spends more than $574 million annually on programs and has a vice president in charge of employee education. The FBI recently conducted a large-scale training program to help 30,000 agents better prepare themselves for confronting active shooters in schools, businesses, and public places.[26] U.S. businesses spend more than $85 billion annually on training and development programs away from the workplace. And this figure does not include wages and benefits paid to employees while they are participating in such programs. As various shelter-in-place and closure mandates were eased and then lifted in the wake of the 2020 COVID-19 pandemic, many organizations advertised that their employees and cleaning crews had all been trained in how to enforce social distancing and provide enhanced cleaning and hygiene practices.

"Whether you have 30 employees or 300, creating a culture of opportunity at your business will make a huge difference for your staff. Learning won't be restricted to set training periods, but will happen in all areas of your business, all day long."
—Richard Branson, Founder of Virgin Group[27]

Assessing Training Needs The first step in developing a training plan is to determine what needs exist. For example, if employees do not know how to operate the equipment necessary to do their jobs, a training program on how to operate that equipment is clearly needed. On the other hand, when a group of office workers is performing poorly, training may not be the answer. The problem could be motivation, aging equipment, inadequate access to information, weak supervision, inefficient work design, or a deficiency of skills and knowledge. Only the last could be remedied by training. As training programs are being developed, the manager should set specific and measurable goals specifying what participants are to learn. Managers should also plan to evaluate the training program after employees complete it. The training process from start to finish is diagrammed in Figure 8.2.

Common Training Methods Many different training and development methods are available. Selection of methods depends on many considerations, but perhaps the most

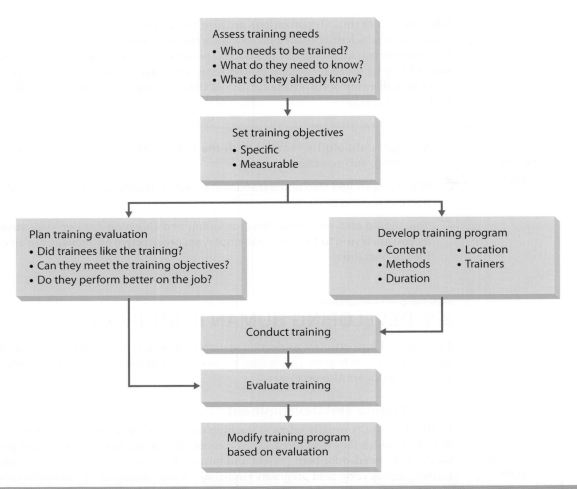

The Training Process

Managing the training process can go a long way toward enhancing its effectiveness. If training programs are well conceived and well executed, both the organization and its employees benefit. Following a comprehensive process helps managers meet the objectives of the training program.

important is training content. When the training content is factual material (such as company rules or explanations of how to fill out forms), assigned reading or presentations work well. When the content is interpersonal relations or group decision making, however, firms must use a method that allows interpersonal contact, such as role-playing or case discussion groups. When employees must learn a physical skill, methods allowing practice and the actual use of tools and materials are needed, as in on-the-job training or vestibule training. (Vestibule training enables participants to focus on safety, learning, and feedback rather than on productivity.)

Web-based and other forms of digital training have become very popular. Such methods allow a mix of training content, are relatively easy to update and revise, let participants use a variable schedule, and lower travel costs.[28] On the other hand, they are limited in their capacity to simulate real activities and facilitate face-to-face interaction. Xerox, Massachusetts Mutual Life Insurance, and Ford have all reported success with these methods. In addition, most training programs actually rely on a mix of methods. Boeing, for example, sends managers to an intensive two-week training seminar involving tests, simulations, role-playing exercises, and flight-simulation exercises.

Training refers to teaching operational or technical employees how to better perform the jobs for which they were hired. This manager is showing two new employees how to monitor a complex production system and what steps to take in the event of a system malfunction.

Nopphon_1987/Shutterstock.com

Finally, some larger businesses have their own self-contained training facilities, often called *corporate universities.* McDonald's was among the first to start this practice with its so-called Hamburger University in Illinois. All management trainees for the firm attend training programs there to learn exactly how long to grill a burger, how to maintain good customer service, and so on. The cult hamburger chain In-N-Out Burger also has a similar training venue it calls In-N-Out University. Other firms that use this approach include Shell Oil and General Electric.[29]

Evaluation of Training Training and development programs should always be evaluated. Typical evaluation approaches include measuring one or more relevant criteria (such as attitudes or performance) before and after the training and determining whether the criteria changed. Evaluation measures collected at the end of training are easy to get, but actual performance measures collected when the trainee is on the job are more important. Trainees may say that they enjoyed the training and learned a lot, but the true test is whether their job performance improves after their training.

8-3b Performance Appraisal

performance appraisal
A formal assessment of how well an employee is doing his or her job

Once employees are trained and settled into their jobs, one of management's next concerns is performance appraisal.[30] Performance appraisal is a formal assessment of how well employees are doing their jobs. Employees' performance should be evaluated regularly for many reasons. One reason is that performance appraisal may be necessary for validating selection devices or assessing the impact of training programs. A second reason is to serve as a basis for making decisions about pay raises, promotions, and training. Still another reason is to provide feedback to employees to help them improve their current performance and plan their future careers.[31]

"The only thing worse than training your employees and having them leave is not training them and having them stay."
—Henry Ford, Founder of Ford Motor Company[32]

Because performance evaluations often help determine wages and promotions, they must be fair and nondiscriminatory. In the case of appraisals, content validation is used to show that the appraisal system accurately measures performance on important job elements and does not measure traits or behavior that are irrelevant to job performance.

Common Appraisal Methods Two basic categories of appraisal methods commonly used in organizations are objective methods and judgmental methods. Objective measures of performance include actual output (i.e., number of units produced), scrap rate, dollar volume of sales, and number of claims processed. Objective performance measures may be contaminated by "opportunity bias" if some persons have a better chance to perform than others. For example, a sales representative selling snow blowers in Michigan has a greater opportunity to generate revenue than does a colleague selling the same product in Alabama. Fortunately, adjusting raw performance figures for the effect of opportunity bias and thereby arriving at figures that accurately represent each individual's performance is often possible.

Another type of objective measure, the special performance test, is a method by which each employee is assessed under standardized conditions. This kind of appraisal also eliminates opportunity bias. For example, Dell Computer call centers record telephone conversations between technical support employees and customers who call with questions or problems. The technical support employees are periodically graded on speed, accuracy, and courtesy in handling the calls. Performance tests measure ability but do not measure the extent to which one is motivated to use that ability on a daily basis. (A high-ability person may be a lazy performer except when being tested.) Special performance tests must therefore be supplemented by other appraisal methods to provide a complete picture of performance.

Judgmental methods, including ranking and rating techniques, are the most common way to measure performance. Ranking compares employees directly with one another and orders them from best to worst. Ranking has a number of drawbacks. Ranking is difficult for large groups because the individuals in the middle of the distribution may be hard to distinguish from one another accurately. Comparisons of people in different work groups are also difficult. For example, an employee ranked third in a strong group may be more valuable and actually performing at a higher level than an employee ranked first in a weak group. Another criticism of ranking is that the manager must rank people on the basis of overall performance, even though each person likely has both strengths and weaknesses. Furthermore, rankings do not provide useful information for feedback. To be told that one is ranked third is not nearly as helpful as to be told that the quality of one's work is outstanding, its quantity is satisfactory, one's punctuality could use improvement, or one's paperwork is seriously deficient.

Rating differs from ranking in that it compares each employee against a fixed standard rather than with other employees. A rating scale provides the standard. Figure 8.3 gives examples of three graphic rating scales for a bank teller. Each consists of a performance

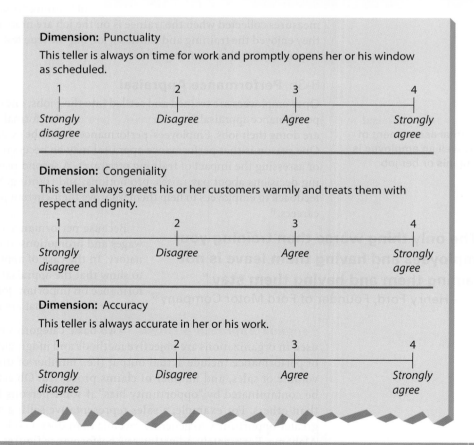

FIGURE 8.3

Graphic Rating Scales for a Bank Teller

Graphic rating scales are very common methods for evaluating employee performance. The manager who is doing the rating circles the point on each scale that best reflects her or his assessment of the employee on that scale. Graphic rating scales are widely used for many different kinds of jobs.

behaviorally anchored rating scale (BARS)
A sophisticated rating method in which supervisors construct a rating scale associated with behavioral anchors

dimension to be rated (punctuality, congeniality, and accuracy) followed by a scale on which to make the rating. In constructing graphic rating scales, performance dimensions that are relevant to job performance must be selected. In particular, they should focus on job behaviors and results rather than on personality traits or attitudes.

The behaviorally anchored rating scale (BARS) is a sophisticated and useful rating method. Supervisors construct rating scales with associated behavioral anchors. They first identify relevant performance dimensions and then generate anchors—specific, observable behaviors typical of each performance level. Figure 8.4 shows an example of a behaviorally anchored rating scale for the dimension "Inventory control."

The other scales in this set, developed for the job of department manager in a chain of specialty stores, include "Handling customer complaints," "Planning special promotions," "Following company procedures," "Supervising sales personnel," and "Diagnosing and solving special problems." The BARS can be effective because it requires that management take proper care in constructing the scales, and it provides useful anchors for supervisors to use in evaluating people. It can also be costly, however, because outside expertise is usually needed and because scales must be developed for each job within the organization.

Errors in Performance Appraisal   Errors or biases can occur in any kind of rating or ranking system.[33] One common problem is *recency error*—the tendency to base judgments on the subordinate's most recent performance because it is most easily recalled. Often a rating or ranking is intended to evaluate performance over an entire time period, such as six months or a year, so the recency error does introduce error into the judgment. Other errors include overuse of one part of the scale—being too lenient, being too severe, or giving everyone a rating of "average."

Halo error is allowing the assessment of an employee on one dimension to "spread" to ratings of that employee on other dimensions. For instance, if an employee is outstanding on quality of output, a rater might tend to give her or him higher marks than deserved on other dimensions. Errors can also occur because of race, sex, or age discrimination, intentionally or unintentionally. For instance, a manager might feel that one of her subordinates is getting too old to perform effectively and should be thinking about retirement. In reality, though,

Job: Specialty store manager
Dimension: Inventory control

7 — Always orders in the right quantities and at the right time

6 — Almost always orders at the right time but occasionally orders too much or too little of a particular item

5 — Usually orders at the right time and almost always in the right quantities

4 — Often orders in the right quantities and at the right time

3 — Occasionally orders at the right time but usually not in the right quantities

2 — Occasionally orders in the right quantities but usually not at the right time

1 — Never orders in the right quantities or at the right time

FIGURE 8.4

Behaviorally Anchored Rating Scale

Behaviorally anchored rating scales help overcome some of the limitations of standard rating scales. Each point on the scale is accompanied by a behavioral anchor—a summary of an employee behavior that fits that spot on the scale.

the employee might still be performing effectively. But because his manager has formed an impression that he is getting too old to work, she unconsciously evaluates him lower than he might deserve. The best way to offset these errors is to ensure that a valid rating system is developed at the outset and then to train managers in how to use it.

One interesting innovation in performance appraisal used in some organizations today is called 360-degree feedback, in which managers are evaluated by everyone around them—their boss, their peers, and their subordinates. Such a complete and thorough approach provides people with a far richer array of information about their performance than does a conventional appraisal given by just the boss. Of course, such a system also takes considerable time and must be handled so as not to breed fear and mistrust in the workplace.[34]

360-degree feedback
Performance appraisal of managers done by their boss, peers, and subordinates

8-3c Performance Feedback

The last step in most performance appraisal systems is giving feedback to subordinates about their performance. This is usually done in a private meeting between the person being evaluated and his or her boss. The discussion should generally be focused on the facts—the assessed level of performance, how and why that assessment was made, and how it can be improved in the future. Feedback interviews are not easy to conduct. Many managers are uncomfortable with this part of the process, though, especially if feedback is negative and subordinates are disappointed by what they hear. Properly training managers, however, can help them conduct more effective feedback interviews.

Because traditional performance appraisal methods and approaches to performance feedback are often criticized and are subject to numerous flaws and shortcomings, managers have started looking for alternative methods for assessing performance. One of the most promising newer methods is what is known as the "check-in" approach. Rather than conducting formal reviews on an annual basis and using a very structured methodology, the traditional method, the check-in method involves managers and their direct reports having regularly scheduled "conversations" where the primary goal is to provide feedback on both how the subordinate is doing and what she or he may need to do to improve. These conversations occur as often as monthly but at least once per quarter. The outcomes are also documented for future reference.

In this meeting, the manager is sharing the 360-degree feedback she has gathered. This feedback is useful to the employee because it relates to all aspects of his day-to-day job. He can use that feedback to improve his performance and more effectively calibrate his goals.

OneStockPhoto/Shutterstock.com

Manager's Checklist

☐ Managers should be familiar with the most common methods for training employees and assessing their performance.

☐ All managers need to understand the advantages and limitations of training and development.

☐ You should understand the strengths and weaknesses of the performance appraisal methods used in your organization

8-4 MAINTAINING HUMAN RESOURCES

After organizations have attracted and developed an effective workforce, they must also make every effort to maintain that workforce. To do so requires effective compensation and benefits as well as career planning.

8-4a Determining Compensation

compensation
The financial remuneration given by the organization to its employees in exchange for their work

Compensation is the financial remuneration given by the organization to its employees in exchange for their work. There are three basic forms of compensation. *Wages* are the hourly compensation paid to operating employees. The minimum hourly wage paid in the United States today is $7.25 (though several states have minimum-wage levels that exceed this federal minimum). *Salary* refers to compensation paid for total contributions, as opposed to pay based on hours worked. For example, managers earn an annual salary, usually paid monthly. They receive the salary regardless of the number of hours they work. Some firms have started paying all their employees a salary instead of hourly wages. For example, all employees at Chaparral Steel earn a salary, starting at $45,000 a year for entry-level operating employees. Finally, *incentives* represent special compensation opportunities that are usually tied to performance. Sales commissions and bonuses are among the most common incentives.

Compensation is an important and complex part of the organization–employee relationship.[35] Basic compensation is necessary to provide employees with the means to maintain a reasonable standard of living. Beyond this, however, compensation also provides a tangible measure of the value of the individual to the organization. If employees do not earn enough to meet their basic economic goals, they will seek employment elsewhere. Likewise, if they believe that their contributions are undervalued by the organization, they may leave or exhibit poor work habits, low morale, and little commitment to and engagement with the organization. Thus, designing an effective compensation system is clearly in the organization's best interests.[36]

A good compensation system can help attract qualified applicants, retain present employees, and stimulate high performance at a reasonable cost relative to an organization's industry and geographic area. To set up a successful system, management must make decisions about wage levels, the wage structure, and the individual wage determination system. Some firms used the 2020 COVID-19 pandemic as an opportunity to refine their compensation systems. While many firms reduced their workforces through layoffs, others used targeted salary cuts to avoid layoffs. For instance, Disney cut the pay of its senior executives by 20–30 percent. Other firms adopted a practice called *furloughing*. Workers in this situation had their hours and pay reduced but retained their full benefits. At Halliburton's headquarters in Houston, for example, about 3,500 employees were told that they would work one week on and one week off for half pay but retain full benefits for a period of two months.

Wage-Level Decision   The wage-level decision is a management policy decision about whether the firm wants to pay above, at, or below the going rate for labor in the industry or the geographic area. Most firms choose to pay near the average, although those that cannot afford more pay below average. Large, successful firms may like to cultivate the image of being "wage leaders" by intentionally paying more than average and thus (presumably) attracting and keeping high-talent employees. Google, IBM, and Microsoft, for example, pay above market rates to get the new employees they want. McDonald's, on the other hand, often pays close to minimum wage. The level of unemployment in the labor force also affects wage levels. Pay declines when labor is plentiful and increases when labor is scarce.

Once managers make the wage-level decision, they need information to help set actual wage rates. Managers need to know what the maximum, minimum, and average wages are for particular jobs in the appropriate labor market. This information is usually collected by means of a wage survey. Area wage surveys can be conducted by individual firms or by local HR or business associations. Professional and industry associations often conduct surveys and make the results available to employers.

job evaluation
An attempt to assess the worth of each job relative to other jobs

Wage-Structure Decision   Wage structures are usually set up through a procedure called job evaluation—an attempt to assess the worth of each job relative to other jobs. At Ben & Jerry's Homemade, company policy once dictated that the highest-paid employee in the firm could not make more than seven times what the lowest-paid employee earned. But this policy had to be modified when the company found that it was simply unable to hire a new CEO without paying more than this amount. Nucor Steel pays close attention to the wage differentials paid across different levels of the organization to make sure they are fair. More details about Nucor's approach to compensation is found in our *Leading the Way* feature. The simplest method for creating a wage structure is to rank jobs from those that should be paid the most (e.g., the president) to those that should be paid the least (e.g., a mail clerk or a custodian).

In a firm with relatively few jobs (like Netflix, for example), this method is quick and practical, but larger firms with thousands of job titles require more sophisticated methods. The next step is setting actual wage rates on the basis of a combination of survey data and the wage structure that results from job evaluation. Jobs of equal value are often grouped into wage grades for ease of administration.

Individual Wage Decisions   After wage-level and wage-structure decisions are made, the individual wage decision must be addressed. This decision concerns how much to pay each employee in a particular job. Although the easiest decision is to pay a single rate for each job, more typically a range of pay rates is associated with each job. For example, the hourly pay range for an individual job might be $10.00 to $15.40 per hour, with different employees earning different rates within the range.

A system is then needed for setting individual rates. This may be done on the basis of seniority (enter the job at $10.00, for example, and increase 50 cents per hour every six months on the job), initial qualifications (inexperienced people start at $10.00; more experienced people start at a higher rate), or merit (raises above the entering rate are given for good performance). Combinations of these bases may also be used.

Online resources also play a key role in compensation patterns today because both job-seekers and current employees can more easily get a sense of what their true market value is. If they can document the claim that their value is higher than what their current employer now pays or is offering, they are in a position to request a higher salary. Consider the case of one compensation executive who met with a subordinate to discuss her raise. He was surprised when she produced data from five different websites backing up her claim for a bigger raise than he had intended to offer.

8-4b **Determining Benefits**

benefits
Things of value other than compensation that an organization provides to its workers

Benefits are things of value other than compensation that the organization provides to its workers. (Benefits are sometimes called *indirect compensation*.) The average company spends an amount equal to more than one-third of its cash payroll on employee benefits. Thus, a typical employee who is paid, say, $60,000 per year also averages a bit over $20,000 more per year in benefits.

Benefits come in several forms. Pay for time not worked includes sick leave, vacation, holidays, and unemployment compensation. Insurance benefits often include life and health insurance for employees and their dependents. Workers' compensation is a legally required insurance benefit that provides medical care and disability income for employees injured on the job. Social Security is a government pension plan to which both employers and employees contribute. Many employers also provide a retirement plan, most commonly a 401(k), to which they and their employees contribute. Employee service benefits include such extras as tuition reimbursement and recreational opportunities.

Some organizations provide what are called "cafeteria benefit plans," whereby basic coverage is provided for all employees but employees are then allowed to choose which additional benefits they want (up to a cost limit based on salary). An employee with five children might choose enhanced medical and dental coverage for dependents, a single employee might prefer more vacation time, and an older employee might elect long-term care benefits. Flexible systems are expected to encourage people to stay in the organization and even help the company attract new employees.[37]

In recent years, companies have also started offering more innovative benefits as a way of accommodating different needs. On-site childcare, mortgage assistance, and paid-leave programs are interesting newer benefits that some firms offer. A good benefits plan may encourage people to join and stay with an organization, but it seldom stimulates high performance, because benefits are tied more to membership in the organization than to performance. To manage their benefits programs effectively, companies should shop carefully, avoid redundant coverage, and provide only those benefits that employees want. Benefits programs should also be explained to employees in clear and straightforward language so that they can use the benefits appropriately and appreciate what the company is providing.

Finally, as a result of economic pressures and escalating costs, some firms have started to reduce employee benefits in the last few years. In 2002, for example, 17 percent of employees in the United States with employer health care coverage saw their benefits cut. The 2008–2009 recession led to further reductions; it is also very likely that more firms will reduce their benefits in the wake of the 2020 COVID-19 pandemic. A Prudential survey found that 60 percent of firms surveyed said their companies had eliminated defined benefits plans or closed their defined benefits plan to new employees.[38]

LEADING THE WAY

Holding True at Nucor Steel

Nucor, the country's largest steelmaker, has never laid employees off or eliminated jobs for economic reasons. During the last recession the U.S. steel industry laid off some 10,000 workers in January 2009 alone. And thousands more were laid off during the 2020 COVID-19 pandemic. But while Nucor employees had few steel orders to fill, they were still working—busy rewriting safety manuals, getting a head start on maintenance jobs, mowing the lawns, and cleaning the bathrooms—and still drawing paychecks. How has Nucor been able to pull this off? Experts point to two things: the firm's employees and its culture. The firm's culture originated in the 1960s as the result of policies established by Ken Iverson, who brought a radical perspective on how to manage a company's human resources to the job of CEO. Iverson figured that workers would be much more productive if an employer went out of its way to share authority with them, respect what they accomplished, and compensate them as handsomely as possible. Today, the basics of the company's HR model are summed up in its "Employee Relations Principles":

- Management is obligated to manage Nucor in such a way that employees will have the opportunity to earn according to their productivity.
- Employees should feel confident that if they do their jobs properly, they will have a job tomorrow.
- Employees have the right to be treated fairly and must believe that they will be.
- Employees must have an avenue of appeal when they believe they are being treated unfairly.

The Iverson approach is based on a highly original pay system. Base pay is actually below the industry average, but the Nucor compensation plan is designed to pay more if employees perform better. For example, if a shift can turn out a defect-free batch of steel, every worker is entitled to a bonus that's paid weekly and that can potentially triple his or her take-home pay. In addition, there are one-time annual bonuses and profit-sharing payouts. In a good year, for example, the average steelworker can take home $85,000 in base pay and weekly bonuses, plus a $2,000 year-end bonus and as much as $19,000 more in profit-sharing money. The system, however, cuts both ways. Take that defect-free batch of steel, for example. If there's a problem with a batch, workers on the shift obviously don't get any weekly bonus. And that's if they catch the problem before the batch leaves the plant. If it reaches the customer, they may *lose* up to three times what they would have received as a bonus.

Everybody in the company, from janitors to the CEO, is covered by some form of incentive plan tied to various goals and targets. Bonuses for department managers are based on a return-on-assets formula tied to divisional performance, as are bonuses under the non-production and non-department–manager plan, which covers everyone, except senior officers, not included in either of the first two plans; bonuses under both manager plans may increase base pay by 75–90 percent. Senior officers don't work under contracts or get pension or retirement plans, and their base salaries are below industry average. In a world in which the typical CEO makes more than 400 times what a factory worker makes, Nucor's CEO makes considerably less. In 2019, for example, his combined salary and bonus (about $2.4 million) came to 23 times the total taken home by the average Nucor factory worker. His bonus and those of other top managers are based on a ratio of net income to stockholder's equity.

References: "Employee Relations Principles," www.nucor.com on April 25, 2020; Nanette Byrnes, "Pain, but No Layoffs at Nucor," *Bloomberg Businessweek*, March 26, 2009, www.bloomberg.com on April 25, 2020; "The Art of Motivation," *Bloomberg Businessweek*, May 1, 2006, www.bloomberg.com on April 25, 2020; "About Us," www.nucor.com on April 25, 2020.

8-4c Career Planning

A final aspect of maintaining human resources is career planning. Few people work in the same jobs their entire careers. Some people change jobs within one organization, others change organizations, and many do both. When these movements are haphazard and poorly conceived, both the individual and the organization suffer. Thus, planning career progressions in advance is in everyone's best interests. Of course, planning a 30-year career for a newcomer just joining the organization is difficult. But planning can help map out what areas one is most interested in and help that person see what opportunities are available within the organization.[39]

Manager's Checklist

☐ Managers need to know the fundamental components and issues involved in determining compensation in organizations.

☐ You should have a clear understanding of your organization's approach to compensation (including benefits).

8-5 MANAGING LABOR RELATIONS

labor relations
The process of dealing with employees who are represented by a union

Labor relations is the process of dealing with employees who are represented by a union.[40] At one time, almost a third of the entire U.S. labor force belonged to a labor union. Unions enjoyed their largest membership between 1940 and 1955. Membership began to decline steadily in the mid-1950s, however, for several reasons: (1) increased standards of living made union membership seem less important; (2) traditionally unionized industries in the manufacturing sector began to decline; and (3) the globalization of business operations caused many unionized jobs to be lost to foreign workers. This downward trend continued until 2008, when union membership rose by the largest amount in over a quarter century, a gain of 428,000 members (12.4 percent of all U.S. workers).

However, union membership again declined in the following few years, dropping to 10.31 percent in 2019. Much of this fluctuation was attributable to fears of job insecurity due to the recession that hit in 2008, but as the economy bottomed out and started to rebound, membership again declined. (While it is too soon to know, it is possible that the dramatic surge in unemployment in 2020 may also stimulate renewed interest in union membership.) Interestingly, while most people associate unions with the manufacturing sector, they are beginning to show up in newer industries as well. For example, workers at Gawker Media, an online publisher of news and blog sites, recently voted to unionize.[41] Managing labor relations is an important part of HRM. However, most large firms have separate labor relations specialists to handle these activities apart from other human resource functions.

Labor relations is the process of dealing with employees who are represented by a union. In recent years, though, labor relations experts have had to address issues that go beyond traditional labor unions. Some of these issues relate to highly mobile knowledge workers. Other issues involve immigrant workers who may not always receive the same employment protections as other workers.

Ken Wolter/Shutterstock.com

8-5a How Employees Form Unions

For employees to form a new local union, several things must occur. First, employees must have an interest in having a union. Nonemployees who are professional organizers employed by a national union (such as the Teamsters or United Auto Workers) may generate interest by making speeches, distributing literature outside the workplace, and/or contacting people via email and/or social media platforms. Inside, employees who want a union try to convince other workers of the benefits of a union.

The second step is to collect employees' signatures on authorization cards. These cards state that the signer wishes to vote to determine whether the union will represent him or her. To show the National Labor Relations Board (NLRB) that interest is sufficient to justify holding an election, 30 percent of the employees in the potential bargaining unit must sign these cards. (Sign-ups are increasingly being done online, of course, although traditional "paper" cards are also still in use in some settings.) Before an election can be held, however, the bargaining unit must be defined. The bargaining unit consists of all employees who will be eligible to vote in the election and to join and be represented by the union if one is formed.

The election is supervised by an NLRB representative (or, if both parties agree, the American Arbitration Association—a professional association of arbitrators) and is conducted by secret ballot. If a simple majority of those voting (not of all those eligible to vote) votes for the union, then the union becomes certified as the official representative of the bargaining unit.[42] The new union then organizes itself by officially signing up members and electing officers; it will soon be ready to negotiate the first contract. The union-organizing process is diagrammed in Figure 8.5. If workers become disgruntled with their union or if management presents strong evidence that the union is not representing workers appropriately, the NLRB can arrange a decertification election. The results of such an election determine whether the union remains certified.

Organizations usually prefer that employees not be unionized because unions limit management's freedom in many areas. Management may thus wage its own campaign to convince employees to vote against the union. "Unfair labor practices" are often committed at this point. For instance, it is an unfair labor practice for management to promise to give employees a raise (or any other benefit) if the union is defeated. Experts agree that the best way to avoid unionization is to simply practice good employee relations all the time—not just when threatened by a union election. Providing absolutely fair treatment with clear standards in the areas of pay, promotion, layoffs, and discipline; having a complaint or appeal system for persons who feel unfairly treated; and avoiding any kind of favoritism will help make employees feel that a union is unnecessary. Walmart strives to avoid unionization through these practices.

8-5b Collective Bargaining

collective bargaining
The process of agreeing on a satisfactory labor contract between management and a union

The intent of collective bargaining is to agree on a labor contract between management and the union that is satisfactory to both parties. The contract contains agreements about such issues as wages, work hours, job security, promotion, layoffs, discipline, benefits, methods of allocating overtime, vacations, rest periods, and the grievance procedure. The process of bargaining may go on for several weeks, several months, or longer, with representatives of management and the union meeting to make proposals and counterproposals. The resulting agreement must be ratified by the union membership. If it is not approved, the union may strike to put pressure on management, or it may choose not to strike and simply continue negotiating until a more acceptable agreement is reached.

Between 2010 and 2019 there was a total of 154 major work stoppages, an average of 15 per year. In 2019 the United Auto Workers (UAW) went on strike against General Motors for several weeks. The UAW's goals for the strike included increased job security and a clearer path for temporary workers to transition to permanent status. Occasionally circumstances arise that cause management and labor to bargain over changes in existing contracts even before a new contract is needed. This is most likely to happen when unforeseen problems jeopardize the future of the business, and hence the jobs of union members. For example, during the 2020 COVID-19 pandemic Disney negotiated terms with its unions that allowed the firm to furlough thousands of workers when its theme parks closed. As one part of the negotiation Disney agreed to continue to provide those employees with their benefits until the parks reopened and people could return to work.

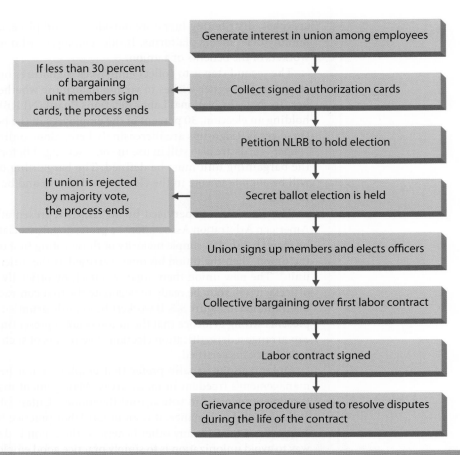

The Union-Organizing Process

If employees of an organization want to form a union, the law prescribes a specific set of procedures that both employees and the organization must follow. Assuming that these procedures are followed and the union is approved, the organization must engage in collective bargaining with the new union.

grievance procedure
The means by which a labor contract is enforced

The grievance procedure is the means by which the contract is enforced. Most of what is in a contract concerns how management will treat employees. When employees feel that they have not been treated fairly under the contract, they file a grievance to correct the problem. The first step in a grievance procedure is for the aggrieved employee to discuss the alleged contract violation with her immediate superior. Often the grievance is resolved at this stage. If the employee still believes that she is being mistreated, however, the grievance can be appealed to the next level. A union official can help an aggrieved employee present her case. If the manager's decision is also unsatisfactory to the employee, additional appeals to successively higher levels are made until, finally, all in-company steps are exhausted. The final step is to submit the grievance to binding arbitration. An arbitrator is a labor law expert who is paid jointly by the union and management. The arbitrator studies the contract, hears both sides of the case, and renders a decision that both parties must obey. The grievance system for resolving disputes about contract enforcement prevents any need to strike during the term of the contract.

Manager's Checklist

☐ Managers need to know the basic steps employees follow to form a union.

☐ If you work in an organization where unions have a presence, you need a clear understanding of how union contracts affect what you can and cannot do.

8-6 NEW CHALLENGES IN THE CHANGING WORKPLACE

As we have seen throughout this chapter, human resource managers face several ongoing challenges in their efforts to keep their organizations staffed with effective workforces. To complicate matters, new challenges arise as the economic and social environments of business change. We conclude this chapter with a look at two of the most important human resource management issues facing business today.

8-6a Managing Knowledge Workers

Employees traditionally added value to organizations because of what they did or because of their experience. Today, however, many employees add value because of what they know.[43]

knowledge workers
Workers whose contributions to an organization are based on what they know

The Nature of Knowledge Work   These employees are usually called knowledge workers, and the skill with which they are managed is a major factor in determining which firms will be successful in the future. Knowledge workers, including computer scientists, engineers, and physical scientists, provide special challenges for the HR manager. These professionals typically require extensive and highly specialized training. Once they are on the job, retraining and training updates are critical to prevent their skills from becoming obsolete. It has been suggested, for example, that currency of a technical education in engineering is about three years.

Knowledge Worker Management and Labor Markets   The demand for knowledge workers continues to grow. As a result, organizations that need these workers must introduce regular market adjustments (upward) in order to pay them enough to motivate them to stay. This is especially critical in areas in which demand is growing, as even entry-level salaries for these employees are high. Once an employee accepts a job with a firm, the employer faces yet another dilemma. Once hired, workers are more subject to the company's internal labor market, which is not likely to be growing as quickly as the external market for knowledge workers as a whole. Consequently, the longer an employee remains with a firm, the further behind the market his or her pay falls—unless, of course, it is regularly adjusted (upward).

"The world is not the same as it used to be. Companies pay for skills in an era where brains are more important than brawn, and the forces of automation, globalization, deregulation, and competition have changed what this kind of work is worth in the world."
—John Challenger, Founder of Outplacement Firm Challenger, Gray, & Christmas[44]

Not surprisingly, strong demand for these workers has inspired some fairly extreme measures for attracting them in the first place.[45] High starting salaries and sign-on bonuses are common. BP Exploration pays petroleum engineers with undersea platform-drilling knowledge—not experience, just knowledge—salaries in the six figures, plus sign-on bonuses of over $50,000 and immediate profit sharing. Even with these incentives, HR managers complained that, in the Gulf Coast region, they cannot retain specialists because young engineers soon leave to accept sign-on bonuses with competitors.

8-6b Contingent and Temporary Workers

A final contemporary HR issue of note involves the use of contingent or temporary workers.[46] Indeed, recent years have seen an explosion in the use of such workers by organizations. The FBI, for example, routinely employs a cadre of retired agents in various temporary jobs.[47]

Trends in Contingent and Temporary Employment   In recent years, the number of contingent workers in the workforce has increased dramatically. A contingent worker is a person who works for an organization on something other than a permanent or full-time basis. Categories of contingent workers include independent contractors, on-call workers, temporary employees (usually hired through outside agencies), and contract and leased employees. Another category is part-time workers. The financial services giant Citigroup, for example, makes extensive use of part-time sales agents to pursue new clients. In 2019, around 40 percent of employed U.S. workers fell into one of these categories, up from 20 percent in 2017.[48]

Managing Contingent and Temporary Workers   Given the widespread use of contingent and temporary workers, HR managers must understand how to use such employees most effectively. In other words, they need to understand how to manage contingent and temporary workers.

One key is careful planning. Even though one of the presumed benefits of using contingent workers is flexibility, it is still important to integrate such workers in a coordinated fashion. Rather than having to call in workers sporadically and with no prior notice, organizations try to bring in specified numbers of workers for well-defined periods of time. The ability to do so comes from careful planning. A second key is understanding contingent workers and acknowledging both their advantages and their disadvantages. In other words, the organization must recognize what it can and cannot achieve from the use of contingent and temporary workers. Expecting too much from such workers, for example, is a mistake that managers should avoid.

Third, managers must carefully assess the real cost of using contingent workers. We noted previously, for example, that many firms adopt this course of action to save labor costs. To justify this perspective, though, the organization should be able to document precisely its labor-cost savings. How much would it be paying people in wages and benefits if they were permanent employees? How does this cost compare with the amount spent on contingent workers? This difference, however, could be misleading. We also noted, for instance, that contingent workers might be less effective performers than permanent and full-time employees. Comparing employee for employee on a direct-cost basis, therefore, is not necessarily valid. Organizations must learn to adjust the direct differences in labor costs to account for differences in productivity and performance.

Finally, managers must fully understand their own strategies and decide in advance how they intend to manage temporary workers, specifically focusing on how to integrate them into the organization. On a very simplistic level, for example, an organization with a large contingent workforce must make some decisions about the treatment of contingent workers relative to the treatment of permanent, full-time workers. Should contingent workers be invited to the company events like parties and other celebrations? Should they have the same access to such employee benefits as counseling services and childcare? There are no right or wrong answers to such questions. Managers must understand that they need to develop a strategy for integrating contingent workers according to some sound logic and then follow that strategy consistently over time.[49]

Indeed, this last point has become part of a legal battleground in recent years as some workers hired under the rubric of contingent workers have subsequently argued that this has been a title in name only and that their employers use this title to discriminate against them in various ways. For instance, FedEx relies on over 13,000 "contract" drivers. These individuals wear FedEx uniforms, drive FedEx trucks, and must follow FedEx rules and procedures. However, because the firm has hired them under a different employment agreement than its "regular" employees, it does not provide them with benefits. Groups of these individuals across the country sued FedEx on the grounds that, for all practical purposes, they are employees and should enjoy the same benefits as other drivers. A U.S. district judge in Indiana ruled in favor of FedEx, upholding the drivers' status as independent contractors in 20 of 28 class-action cases. However, the court has ruled against FedEx on at least one claim and others are still pending.[50]

Manager's Checklist

☐   Managers need to be aware of the fundamental issues and considerations regarding the use of contingent and temporary employees.

☐   You should be aware of trends and challenges in employment for knowledge workers.

SUMMARY OF LEARNING OUTCOMES AND KEY POINTS

8-1. Describe the environmental context of human resource management, including its strategic importance and its relationship with legal and social factors.

- Human resource management is concerned with attracting, developing, and maintaining the human resources an organization needs.

- Its environmental context consists of its strategic importance and the legal and social environments that affect human resource management.

8-2. Discuss how organizations attract human resources, including human resource planning, recruiting, and selection.

- Attracting human resources is an important part of the HRM function.

- Human resource planning starts with job analysis and then focuses on forecasting the organization's future need for employees, forecasting the availability of employees both within and outside the organization, and planning programs to ensure that the proper number and type of employees will be available when needed.

- Recruitment and selection are the processes by which job applicants are attracted, assessed, and hired.

- Methods for selecting applicants include application blanks, tests, interviews, and assessment centers.

- Any method used for selection should be properly validated.

8-3. Describe how organizations develop human resources, including training and development, performance appraisal, and performance feedback.

- Organizations must also work to develop their human resources.

- Training and development enable employees to perform their present jobs effectively and to prepare for future jobs.

- Performance appraisals are important for validating selection devices, assessing the impact

of training programs, deciding pay raises and promotions, and determining training needs.

- Both objective and judgmental methods of appraisal can be applied, and a good system usually includes several methods.

- The validity of appraisal information is always a concern because it is difficult to accurately evaluate the many aspects of a person's job performance.

8-4. Discuss how organizations maintain human resources, including the determination of compensation and benefits and career planning.

- Maintaining human resources is also important.

- Compensation rates must be fair compared with rates for other jobs within the organization and with rates for the same or similar jobs in other organizations in the labor market.

- Properly designed incentive or merit pay systems can encourage high performance, and a good benefits program can help attract and retain employees.

- Career planning is also a major aspect of human resource management.

8-5. Discuss labor relations, including how employees form unions and the mechanics of collective bargaining.

- If a majority of a company's nonmanagement employees so desire, they have the right to be represented by a union.

- Management must engage in collective bargaining with the union in an effort to agree on a contract.

- While a union contract is in effect, the grievance system is used to settle disputes with management.

8-6. Describe the key issues associated with managing knowledge and contingent and temporary workers.

- Two important new challenges in the workplace include the management of knowledge workers and issues associated with the use of contingent and temporary workers.

DISCUSSION QUESTIONS

Questions for Review

1. Describe the steps in the process of human resource planning. Explain the relationships between the steps.
2. Describe the common selection methods. Which method or methods are the best predictors of future job performance? Which are the worst? Why?
3. Compare training and development, noting any similarities and differences. What are some commonly used training methods?
4. Define wages and benefits. List different benefits that organizations can offer. What are the three decisions that managers must make to determine compensation and benefits? Explain each decision.

Questions for Analysis

1. The Family and Medical Leave Act of 1993 is seen as providing much-needed flexibility and security for families and workers. Others think that it places an unnecessary burden on business. Yet another opinion is that the act hurts women, who are more likely to ask for leave, and shuffles them off to a low-paid "mommy track" career path. In your opinion, what are the likely consequences of the act? You can adopt one of the viewpoints expressed above or develop another. Explain your answer.
2. How do you know a selection device is valid? What are the possible consequences of using invalid selection methods? How can an organization ensure that its selection methods are valid?
3. In a right-to-work state, workers are permitted to decide for themselves whether to join a union. In other states, workers may be required to join a union to obtain certain types of employment. If you live in a right-to-work state, do you agree that the choice to join a union should be made by each worker? If you do not live in a right-to-work state, do you agree that workers should be required to join a union? Finally, if the choice were yours to make, would you join a union? Explain your answers. (*Hint*: Right-to-work states are generally in the South, Midwest, and parts of the West. If you do not know whether you live in a right-to-work state, visit the National Right to Work Legal Defense Foundation website at *www.nrtw.org/rtws.htm*.)

Questions for Application

1. Choose three occupations that interest you. (The Labor Department's website has a full list, if you need help choosing.) Then access the Department of Labor, Bureau of Labor Statistics, online *Occupational Outlook Handbook* at *www.bls.gov/oco*. What are the job prospects like in each of these fields? Based on what you read on the website, do you think you would enjoy any of these occupations? Why or why not?
2. Consider a job that you have held or with which you are familiar. Describe how you think an organization could best provide a realistic job preview for that position. What types of information and experiences should be conveyed to applicants? What techniques should be used to convey the information and experiences?
3. Interview an HR manager and ask (1) what role did HR play in managing employees during the 2020 COVID-19 pandemic and (2) what permanent changes, if any, did the firm make in HR practices and procedures in the aftermath of the pandemic?

BUILDING EFFECTIVE DECISION-MAKING SKILLS

Exercise Overview

Decision-making skills refer to the ability to recognize and define problems and opportunities correctly and then to select an appropriate course of action for solving problems or capitalizing on opportunities. For obvious reasons, these skills should be important to you in making career choices.

Exercise Background

If you're in the process of making a career choice, you need to have a firm grip on your own abilities, preferences, and limitations. This is particularly true for recent college graduates, who are often preparing to enter career fields that are largely unknown to them. Fortunately, there are many sources of helpful information out there. The Bureau of Labor Statistics, for example, maintains data about occupations, employment prospects, compensation, working conditions, and many other issues of interest to job-seekers. Information is available by industry, occupation, employer type, and region.

Exercise Task

1. Access a summary of the Department of Labor's *National Compensation Survey* at *https://www.bls.gov/ncs/*. (If the page has moved, search by the survey title.) Find detailed data related to the occupation that you regard as your most likely career choice when you graduate. Then locate detailed data about two other occupations that you might consider—one with a salary that's higher than that of your number-one career choice and one with a salary that's lower.

2. Next, record the hourly salary data for each of your three choices, and then use the hourly salary to project an expected annual income. (*Hint:* Full-time jobs require about 2,000 hours annually.)
3. Based *purely on salary information*, which occupation would be "best" for you?
4. Now go to *www.bls.gov/oco* and access job descriptions for various occupations. Review the description for each of the three career choices that you've already investigated.

5. Based *purely on job characteristics*, which occupation would be "best" for you?
6. Is there any conflict between your answers to questions 3 and 5? If so, how do you plan to resolve it?
7. Are there any job characteristics that you desire strongly enough to sacrifice compensation in order to get them? What are they? What are the limits, if any, on your willingness to sacrifice pay for these job characteristics?

BUILDING EFFECTIVE TECHNICAL SKILLS

Exercise Overview

Technical skills are necessary to understand or perform the specific kind of work that an organization does. In many organizations, this work includes hiring appropriate people to fill positions. This exercise will help you apply certain technical skills to the process of employee selection.

Exercise Background

You may choose either of the following exercise variations. We tend to favor Variation 1 because the exercise is usually more useful if you can relate to real job requirements on a personal level.

Variation 1. If you currently work or have worked in the past, select two jobs with which you have some familiarity. Try to select one job that entails relatively low levels of skill, responsibility, education, and pay and one job that entails relatively high levels in the same categories.

Variation 2. If you've never worked or you're not personally familiar with an array of jobs, assume that you're a manager of a small manufacturing plant. You need to hire

people to fill two jobs. One job is for a plant custodian to sweep floors, clean bathrooms, empty trash cans, and so forth. The other job is for an office manager who will supervise a staff of three clerks and secretaries, administer the plant payroll, and coordinate the administrative operations of the plant.

Exercise Task

Keeping in mind what you've done so far, do the following:

1. Identify the most basic skills needed to perform each of the two jobs effectively.
2. Identify the general indicators or predictors of whether a given person can perform each job.
3. Develop a brief set of interview questions that you might use to determine whether an applicant has the qualifications for each job.
4. How important is it for you, as a manager hiring an employee to perform a job, to possess the technical skills needed to perform the job that you're trying to fill?

SKILL-BUILDING PERSONAL ASSESSMENT

What Do Students Want from Their Jobs?

Purpose: This exercise investigates the job values held by college students at your institution. Then it asks the students to speculate about employers' perceptions of college students' job values. This will help you understand how college students can be recruited effectively. It also gives you insight into the difficulties of managing and motivating people with different values and perceptions.

Introduction: Employees choose careers that match their job values. Employers try to understand employee values to better recruit, manage, and motivate them. Job values are important therefore, in every HR process, from job advertisements and interviews, to performance appraisals, to compensation planning.

Instructions:

1. Complete the following Job Values Survey. Consider what you want from your future career. Using Column 1, rank the 14 job values from 1 to 14, with 1 being the most important to you and 14 being the least important.
2. In your opinion, when potential employers try to attract students, how much importance do they think students give to each of the values? For Column 2, respond with a 1 (plus) if you think employers would rank it higher than students or with a 2 (minus) if you think employers would rate it lower. This is the employers' perception of students' values, not of their own values.

3. In small groups or a class, compute an average ranking for each value. Then discuss the results.

Discussion Questions

1. How much variation do you see in the job value rankings in Column 1? That is, are students' values quite different, moderately different, or very similar overall?

2. If there are significant differences between individuals, what impact might these differences have on the recruiting process? On the training process? On the performance evaluation and compensation process?

3. How much variation do you see in the responses for Column 2? That is, does your group or class agree on how employers perceive college students?

4. Is there a large difference between how you think employers perceive college students and your group's or class's reported job values? If there is a large difference, what difficulties might this create for job-seekers and potential employers? How might these difficulties be reduced or eliminated?

Job Values Survey

	Column 1 Your Ranking	Column 2 Employer Ranking
Working conditions		
Working with people		
Employee benefits		
Challenge		
Location of job		
Self-development		
Type of work		
Job title		
Training program		
Advancement		
Salary		
Company reputation		
Job security		
Autonomy on the job		

Scoring: This survey was administered to a large group, and the average results follow. Responses to this survey vary quite a bit.

If your individual scores fit the pattern of a typical student, then you will likely have an easy time explaining your job values to potential employers.

If your individual scores vary in one or more significant ways, this is not a cause for concern. Many employers seek students with job values that match those of their organizations, which can vary considerably. However, you should plan ahead about ways to effectively communicate with potential employers. Without your self-knowledge and ability to communicate your unique job values, employers would likely assume that you are typical, resulting in a poor understanding of your needs and possibly a poor person–job fit. On the other hand, good self-knowledge and communication skills can result in a superior person–job fit.

The second column of the table demonstrates that recruiters are not able to perfectly predict the relative importance of various job values to potential recruits. Again, self-knowledge and communication are the keys to finding a good person–job fit.

Job Values Survey

Job Value	Student Average	Employer Perceptions
Working conditions	12	–
Work with people	7	–
Employee benefits	11	–
Challenge	2	–
Location of job	13	–
Self-development	3	–

(Continued)

Job Value	Student Average	Employer Perceptions
Type of work	4	–
Job title	14	–
Training program	9	+
Advancement	1	+
Salary	6	–
Company reputation	10	+
Job security	8	–
Autonomy on the job	5	–

MANAGEMENT AT WORK

Elementary, Watson

About a decade ago Geoff Colvin, a long-time editor at *Fortune* magazine and a respected commentator on economics and information technology, agreed to play a special game of *Jeopardy*. The occasion was the annual convention of the National Retail Federation in New York, and Colvin's opponents were a woman named Vicki and an empty podium with the name tag "Watson." Watson's sponsors at IBM wanted to show retailers how smart Watson is. "I wasn't expecting this to go well," recalls Colvin, who knew that Watson had already defeated *Jeopardy*'s two greatest champions. As it turned out, it was even worse than he had expected. "I don't remember the score," says Colvin, "but at the end of our one round I had been shellacked."

Obviously, Watson isn't your average *Jeopardy* savant. It's a *cognitive computing system* that can handle complex problems in which there is ambiguity and uncertainty and draw inferences from data in a way that mimics the human brain. In short, it can deal with the kinds of problems faced by real people. Watson, explains Colvin, "is not connected to the Internet. It's a freestanding machine just like me, relying only on what it knows. . . . So let's confront reality: Watson is smarter than I am."

Watson is also smarter than anyone who's ever been on *Jeopardy*, but it's not going to replace human game-show contestants any time soon. Watson, however, has quite an impressive skill set beyond its game-playing prowess. For example, it has a lot to offer to medical science. At the University of Texas, Watson is employed by the MD Anderson Cancer Center's "Moon Shots" program, whose stated goal is the elimination of cancer. This version of Watson, says IBM's John Kelly, is already "dramatically faster" than the one that was introduced on *Jeopardy*—about three times as fast.

Already, reports Kelly, "Watson has ingested a large portion of the world's medical information" and it's currently "in the final stages of learning the details of cancer." Then what? "Then Watson has to be trained," explains Kelly. Here's how it works: Watson is presented with complex health care problems where the treatment and outcome are known. So you literally have Watson try to determine the best diagnosis or therapy. And then you look to see whether that was the proper outcome. You do this several times, and

the learning engines in Watson begin to make connections between pieces of information. The system learns patterns, it learns outcomes, it learns what sources to trust.

Working with Watson, doctors at Anderson, who are especially interested in leukemia, have made significant headway in their efforts to understand and treat the disease. Watson's role in this process has been twofold:

1. *Expanding capacity*: It helps to make sense out of so-called *big data*—the mountain of text, images, and statistics that, according to Kelly, "is so large that traditional databases and query systems can't deal with it." Moreover, says Kelly, big data is "unstructured" and flows "at incredible speeds. . . . With big data, we're not always looking for precise answers; we're looking for information that will help us make decisions."

2. *Increasing speed*: Kelly also points out that "Watson can do in seconds what would take people years." The system can, for example, process 2000 GB of information—the equivalent of four million books—per second. When it comes to making sense out of the enormous amount of data concerning the genetic factors in cancer, says Kelly, "Watson is like big data on steroids."

Clearly, however, Watson is not *replacing* "knowledge workers" (doctors) at the Anderson Center. Rather, it's being used to support their knowledge work. In this respect, argues Thomas H. Davenport, a widely recognized specialist in knowledge management, Watson is confirming "one of the great clichés of cognitive business technology—that it should be used not to replace knowledge workers, but rather to augment them." On the one hand, even Davenport admits that some jobs have been lost to cognitive technology. In the field of financial services, for instance, many "lower-level" decision makers—loan and insurance-policy originators, credit-fraud detectors—have been replaced by automated systems. At the same time, however, Davenport observes that "experts" typically retain the jobs that call for "reviewing and refining the rules and algorithms [generated by] automated decision systems."

Likewise, human data analysts can create only a few statistical models per week, while machines can churn out a couple of thousand. Even so, observes Davenport, "there are still hundreds of thousands of jobs open for quantitative analysts and big data specialists." Why? "Even though machine learning systems can do a lot of the grunt work," suggests Davenport, "data modeling is complex enough that humans still have to train the systems in the first place and check on them occasionally to see if they're making sense."

Colvin, however, isn't sure that these trends will hold true for much longer. Two years after he competed against Watson, Colvin reported that "Watson is [now] 240 percent faster. I am not." He adds that by 2034—when Watson will probably be an antiquated curiosity—its successors will be another 32 times more powerful. "For over two centuries," admits Colvin, "practically every advance in technology has sparked worries that it would destroy jobs, and it did. . . . But it also created even more new jobs, and the improved technology made those jobs more productive and higher paying. . . . Technology has lifted living standards spectacularly."

Today, however, Colvin is among many experts who question the assumption that the newest generations of technologies will conform to the same pattern. "Until a few years ago," acknowledges former Treasury Secretary Larry Summers, "I didn't think [technological job loss] was a very complicated subject. I'm not so completely certain now." Microsoft founder Bill Gates, on the other hand, is not quite so ambivalent: "Twenty years from now," predicts Gates, "labor demand for lots of skill sets will be substantially lower. I don't think people have that in their mental model."

According to Colvin, today's technology already reflects a different pattern in job displacement: Its "advancing steadily into both ends of the spectrum" occupied by knowledge workers, replacing both low- and high-level positions and "threatening workers who thought they didn't have to worry." Take lawyers, for instance. In the legal-discovery process of gathering information for a trial, computers are already performing the document-sorting process that can otherwise require small armies of attorneys. They can scan legal literature for precedents much more thoroughly and will soon be able to identify relevant matters of law without human help. Before long, says Colvin, they "will move nearer to the heart of what lawyers do" by offering better advice on such critical decisions as whether to sue or settle or go to trial.

So what appears to be the long-term fate of high-end knowledge workers? Davenport thinks that the picture is "still unclear," but he suggests that, in order to be on the safe side, would-be knowledge workers should consider reversing the cliché about technology as a means of augmenting human activity: "If there is any overall lesson" to be learned from current trends, "it is to make sure you are capable of augmenting an automated system. If the decisions and actions that you make at work are remarkably similar to those made by a computer, that computer will probably be taking your paycheck before long."[51]

Case Questions

1. Consider the definition of *knowledge workers* in the text: "workers whose contributions to an organization are based on what they know." In what sense might just about any employee qualify as a "knowledge worker"? For example, what qualifies as "knowledge" in an organization's operational activities (i.e., in the work of creating its products and services)? What's the advantage to an organization of regarding all employees as knowledge workers?

2. Review the sections in Chapter 4 titled "Decision-Making Defined" and "Decision-Making Conditions." Why are computers, especially cognitive computing systems, so effective in assisting the decision-making process? In particular, how can they increase the likelihood of good decisions under conditions of *risk* and *uncertainty*?

3. Think of a few jobs in which the application of "human-relationship skills" is important—even absolutely necessary. Explain why these jobs require more than just decision-making skills. How about you? Does the job that you want require good human-relationship skills? Do your human-relationship skills need some improvement? What sorts of things can you do to improve them?

No Company for Old-Fashioned Management

1. If you were an HR executive at Wegmans, would you focus more on *internal recruiting* or on *external recruiting*? Would your strategy for higher-level positions differ from your strategy for lower-level positions? How would current economic conditions influence your strategy?

2. As an HR executive at Wegmans, you need to hire a group of new employees as part of your management-trainee program—people who will be put on a track leading, ultimately, to positions as store managers. Briefly outline your program for developing these employees.

3. If you were an employee at Wegmans, how would you expect your annual performance appraisal to be conducted? Given the company's customer-relations strategy, which appraisal methods do you think would be most appropriate?

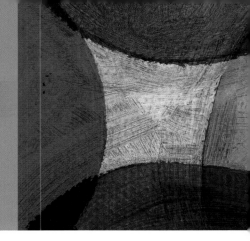

CHAPTER 9

Basic Elements of Individual Behavior in Organizations

Learning Outcomes

After studying this chapter, you should be able to:

9-1 Explain the nature of the individual–organization relationship.

9-2 Describe how personality and personality attributes affect behavior in organizations.

9-3 Discuss individual attitudes in organizations and how they affect behavior.

9-4 Describe basic perceptual processes and the role of attributions in organizations.

9-5 Discuss the causes and consequences of stress and how it can be managed.

9-6 Describe creativity and its role in organizations.

9-7 Explain how workplace behaviors can directly or indirectly influence organizational effectiveness.

The people who populate today's business world are characterized by a wide variety of personalities, behaviors, and attitudes. While most people in business have relatively healthy and constructive personalities and behave in ethical and productive ways, there are some who reflect different profiles. Indeed, myriad different and unique characteristics reside in each and every employee and manager. These affect how they feel about the organization, how they will alter their future attitudes about the firm, and how they perform their jobs. These characteristics reflect the basic elements of individual behavior in organizations. This chapter describes several of these basic elements and is the first of five chapters designed to develop a more complete perspective on the leading function of management. In the first section we investigate the basic relationships that exist between individuals and organizations. The following section introduces the concept of personality and discusses several important personality attributes that can influence behavior in organizations. We then examine individual attitudes and their role in organizations. The role of stress in the workplace is then discussed, followed by a discussion of individual creativity. Finally, we describe a number of basic forms of individual behaviors that are important to organizations. Let's begin by taking a look at one aspect of employee behavior at Burt's Bees.

Management in Action

Engaging with the Company Garbage

"Once you've seen your garbage up close, it's hard to ignore it."

—Shira E. Norman, Sustainability Consultant

A few years ago, Burt's Bees, a maker of natural personal-care products, found to its dismay that it was generating 40 tons of waste every month. Two years later, the company had reduced that amount to 10 tons through a rigorous program of recycling and compositing. It was a start, but at that point, reported John Replogle (CEO at the time), "we were stuck and needed to reinvigorate the effort again." The company's *green team*—a group of volunteer employees who oversee efforts to improve the workplace environment—came up with an employee-oriented trash-appreciation exercise. They stockpiled two weeks' worth of company garbage and dumped it in the parking lot. More than 300 employees then donned hazmat suits and waded through the refuse heap to find everything that should have been recycled and everything that could be recycled if there were someplace to send it.

As a result, Burt's was able to cut waste in half and save $25,000 a year in hauling expenses. "We found money in the dumpster," said Replogle. "We've turned our waste stream from a cost center into a profit center." More importantly, added Replogle, "seeing all that trash in the parking lot translated into a collective 'aha moment,' and we all realized we could do a better job at recycling." In the wake of the dumpster-diving exercise, employee-recycling compliance jumped from 80 percent to 98 percent. "Now," reported Replogle, "we have a shared ethos of taking responsibility."

Burt's isn't the only company that's turned dumpster diving into business as usual. Bentley Prince Street, a commercial carpet maker, has been plumbing its garbage on a monthly basis for more than 15 years. Department-based teams of 20 employees sift through the trash for about 15 minutes looking for recyclable or reusable items. So far, the company has not only saved $50,000 a year in waste hauling but also earns about $150,000 annually from the sales of recyclables to companies that have commercial uses for them.

"The monetary savings," said sustainability director Judy Pike, "are an important aspect of our program, but equally important is . . . educating our employees about recycling and sustainability." Bentley Prince Street coordinates its employee sustainability efforts through its QUEST initiative (for Quality Utilizing Employee Suggestions and Teamwork), a program through which employee teams determine ways of eliminating waste. QUEST has reduced the firm's water intake by 52 percent, its energy use by 40 percent, its greenhouse emissions by 48 percent, and its waste sent to landfill by 97 percent.

The sustainability success of companies like Burt's Bees and Bentley Prince Street isn't entirely surprising to L. Hunter Lovins, president of Natural Capital Solutions, a nonprofit specializing in innovations in environmental practices and economic sustainability. "Let's track the logic," she suggests: "Taking care of your workforce, particularly by engaging them in implementing a corporate commitment to sustainability, will drive greater productivity and thus greater profitability."

Lovins's logic tracks as follows. She starts from the premise that satisfied employees are more productive employees, citing studies reporting that unsatisfied workers currently cost the U.S. economy $300 billion per year. Lovins then proceeds to argue that the most satisfied employees are those who are given the opportunity to "make progress in meaningful work." What constitutes "meaningful work"? For that matter, what constitutes "progress"? Lovins suggests that a good measure of both is the extent to which employees put forth *discretionary effort*— the level *above minimum requirements* that people could put forth if they wanted to. "People who believe their jobs are meaningful," says Lovins, "channel their discretionary effort into their work," such as volunteering to dive into dumpsters or serve on waste-elimination teams.

Lovins also believes that work that involves employees in companywide sustainability efforts is "meaningful" to a lot of Americans. "The American workforce," she contends, no longer views work solely as a means to a paycheck.

To many people, especially the younger generation, their job is an integral part of their lifestyle. . . . Ninety-two percent of Millennials say that they want to work for a socially responsible company. . . . [One] study . . . found that 96 percent of Generation Y respondents are highly concerned about the environment and expect that employers will take steps towards becoming more sustainable."

A recent Gallup survey reported that highly "engaged organizations" returned 3.9 times the earnings-per-share growth rate of companies that rated low on engagement. A similar survey by Hewitt and Associates, a global human resources consulting firm, found that companies with high levels of employee engagement boasted shareholder return 19 percent above average, while those with lower levels were 44 percent below average. The same study identified social and environmental responsibility as a key factor in driving employee engagement.

How do companies foster employee engagement, particularly when it comes to sustainability programs? First, it helps to be genuinely committed to sustainability. A study of employees in the food-processing industry found that "employees' level of organizational commitment is influenced by their perception of their firm's environmental sustainability." More specifically, says Suzanne Tilleman of the University of Montana, engagement is higher when a company turns out a high percentage of organic products and exhibits a *collectivistic identity orientation*— that is, emphasizes companywide contributions to a greater good.

Second, organizational commitment is greater when a company fosters a combination of *top-down leadership* and *bottom-up empowerment* in its sustainability practices. At Burt's Bees, for example, if a department fails to pass certain tests for proper recycling, chronic abusers must go through remedial training. At the same time, the company depends on frontline employees for such ideas as cleaning industrial containers with steam rather than water—an insight that cut water usage for the task by 90 percent. In return, in addition to bonuses tied to companywide sustainability performance, employees receive such "Eco-benefits" as cash compensation for biking or carpooling to work and buying high-efficiency or hybrid vehicles. Then, of course, there are those paid days for volunteering for activities like dumpster diving. Such activities, says Harvard's Bobbi Thomason, "are smart initiatives for showing your people that sustainability is truly important to the organization's central mission." Besides, adds sustainability consultant Shira E. Norman, "once you've seen your garbage up close, it's hard to ignore it."[1]

9-1 UNDERSTANDING INDIVIDUALS IN ORGANIZATIONS

As a starting point in understanding human behavior in the workplace, it is helpful to first consider the basic nature of the relationship between individuals and organizations. An appreciation of the nature of individual differences is also important.

9-1a The Psychological Contract

psychological contract
The overall set of expectations held by an individual with respect to what he or she will contribute to the organization and what the organization will provide in return

Most people have a basic understanding of a contract. Whenever we buy a car or sell a house, for example, both buyer and seller sign a contract that specifies the terms of the agreement. A psychological contract is similar in some ways to a standard legal contract but is less formal and well defined. In particular, a psychological contract is the overall set of expectations held by an individual with respect to what he or she will contribute to the organization and what the organization will provide in return.[2] Thus, a psychological contract does not exist in written form nor are all of its terms explicitly negotiated and specified.

A psychological contract refers to the expectations held by an individual regarding what she or he will contribute to the organization and what the organization will provide in return. This manager and subordinate are reviewing the subordinate's goals for the upcoming year and what rewards are most likely to be provided if those goals are met. These agreements are a part of the psychological contract.

The essential nature of a psychological contract is illustrated in Figure 9.1. The individual employee or manager makes a variety of **contributions** to the organization—effort, skills, ability, time, loyalty, and so forth. These contributions presumably satisfy various needs, expectations, and requirements of the organization. In other words, because the organization may have hired the person because of her skills, it is reasonable for the organization to expect that she will subsequently utilize those skills in the performance of her job.

In return for these contributions, the organization provides **inducements** to the individual employee or manager. Some inducements, like pay and career opportunities, are tangible rewards. Others, like job security and status, are more intangible. Just as the contributions available from the individual must satisfy the needs of the organization, the inducements offered by the organization must serve the needs of the individual. Thus, if a person accepts employment with an organization because he thinks he will earn an attractive salary and have an opportunity to advance, he will expect that those inducements will, in fact, be provided.

contributions
What the individual provides to the organization

inducements
What the organization provides to the individual

If both the individual and the organization perceive that the psychological contract is fair and equitable, they will be satisfied with the relationship and will likely continue it as long as they see it as beneficial to their interests. On the other hand, if either party begins to experience an imbalance or inequity in the contract, they may initiate a change. For example, the worker initially happy with her pay but who hasn't received a pay raise in a long time may decide to request a pay raise or promotion, decrease her contributed effort, or look for a better job elsewhere. The organization can also initiate change by requesting that a worker improve his skills through training, transfer him to another job, or terminate his employment altogether.[3]

A basic challenge faced by the organization, then, is to manage psychological contracts. The organization must ensure that it is getting value from its employees. At the same time, it must be sure that it is providing employees with appropriate inducements. If the organization

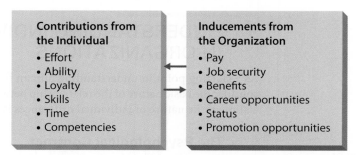

Contributions from the Individual	Inducements from the Organization
• Effort	• Pay
• Ability	• Job security
• Loyalty	• Benefits
• Skills	• Career opportunities
• Time	• Status
• Competencies	• Promotion opportunities

FIGURE 9.1

The Psychological Contract

Psychological contracts are the basic assumptions that individuals have about their relationships with their organization. Such contracts are defined in terms of contributions by the person relative to inducements from the organization.

is underpaying its employees for their contributions, for example, they may perform poorly or leave for better jobs elsewhere. On the other hand, if they are being overpaid relative to their contributions, the organization is incurring unnecessary costs.[4]

9-1b The Person–Job Fit

person–job fit
The extent to which the contributions made by the individual match the inducements offered by the organization

One specific aspect of managing psychological contracts is understanding the person–job fit. **Person–job fit** is the extent to which the contributions made by the individual match the inducements offered by the organization. In theory, each employee has a specific set of needs that he wants fulfilled and a set of job-related behaviors and abilities to contribute. Thus, if the organization can take perfect advantage of those behaviors and abilities and exactly fulfill his needs, it will have achieved a perfect person–job fit.

"Whether someone rock climbs, plays the cello, or enjoys film noir may seem trivial but these leisure pursuits are crucial for assessing someone as a cultural fit."

—Lauren Rivera, Professor at Northwestern University

Of course, such a precise level of person-job fit is seldom achieved. There are several reasons for this. For one thing, organizational selection procedures are imperfect. Organizations can make approximations of employee skill levels, motivation, and potential when making hiring decisions and can improve them through training. But even simple performance dimensions are often hard to measure in objective and valid ways.

Another reason for imprecise person–job fits is that both people and organizations change. A person who finds a new job stimulating and exciting may find the same job boring and monotonous once it has been mastered. And when the organization adopts new technology, it changes the skills it needs from its employees. Still another reason for imprecision in the person–job fit is that each individual is unique. Measuring skills and performance is difficult enough. Assessing needs, attitudes, and personality is far more complex. Each of these individual differences serves to make matching individuals with jobs a challenging and complex process.[5]

individual differences
Personal attributes that vary from one person to another

naito29/Shutterstock.com

Person–job fit is the extent to which the contributions made by an individual match the inducements offered by the organization. These workers, for instance, are cleaning and repairing the windows on the upper floors of an office tower. Some people would find a job such as this exciting, interesting and rewarding, whereas others would be nervous or scared to work under these conditions. These feelings contribute to person–job fit.

9-1c The Nature of Individual Differences

Individual differences are personal attributes that vary from one person to another. Individual differences may be physical, psychological, or emotional. Taken together, all of the individual differences that characterize any specific person serve to make that person unique from everyone else. Much of the remainder of this chapter is devoted to individual differences. Before proceeding, however, we must also note the importance of the situation in assessing the behavior of individuals.

Are specific differences that characterize a given person good or bad? Do they contribute to or detract from performance? The answer, of course, is that it depends on the circumstances. One person may be very dissatisfied, unengaged, withdrawn, and negative in one job setting, but very satisfied, engaged, outgoing, and positive in another. Working conditions, coworkers, and leadership are all important ingredients.

Thus, whenever an organization tries to assess or account for individual differences among its employees, it must also be sure to consider the situation in which behavior occurs. Individuals who are satisfied or productive workers in one context may prove to be dissatisfied or unproductive workers in another context. Attempting to consider both individual differences and contributions in relation to inducements and contexts, then, is a major challenge for organizations as they try to establish effective psychological contracts with their employees and achieve optimal fits between people and jobs.[6] Many people and their employers found it necessary to adjust their psychological contacts during the 2020 COVID-19 pandemic because of changes in work places, work schedules, and work expectations.

Manager's Checklist

☐ Managers need to understand the concepts and importance of a psychological contract.

☐ You should also appreciate the importance of person-job fit.

☐ Managers must also remember that no two people are the same.

personality
The relatively permanent set of psychological and behavioral attributes that distinguish one person from another

"Big Five" personality traits
A popular personality framework based on five key traits

agreeableness
A person's ability to get along with others

conscientiousness
The number of things a person can effectively work on at one time

9-2 PERSONALITY AND INDIVIDUAL BEHAVIOR

Personality traits represent some of the most fundamental sets of individual differences in organizations. Personality is the relatively stable set of psychological attributes that distinguish one person from another.[7] Managers should strive to understand basic personality attributes and the ways they can affect people's behavior in organizational situations, not to mention their perceptions of and attitudes toward the organization.

9-2a The "Big Five" Personality Traits

Psychologists have identified literally thousands of personality traits and dimensions that differentiate one person from another. But researchers have now identified five fundamental personality traits that are especially relevant to organizations. Because these five traits are so important and because they have been the subject of so much attention, they are commonly referred to as the "Big Five" personality traits.[8] Figure 9.2 illustrates the Big Five traits.

Agreeableness refers to a person's ability to get along with others. Agreeableness causes some people to be gentle, cooperative, forgiving, understanding, and good-natured in their dealings with others. But it results in others' being irritable, short-tempered, uncooperative, and generally antagonistic toward other people. Note that being agreeable does not mean that an individual automatically "agrees" with everything. It does mean, though, that an agreeable individual is cordial and more pleasant than someone who is less agreeable. Research suggests that highly agreeable people will be better able to develop good working relationships with coworkers, subordinates, and higher-level managers, whereas less agreeable people will not have particularly good working relationships. This same pattern might also extend to relationships with customers, suppliers, and other key organizational constituents.

Conscientiousness refers to the number of things a person can effectively work on at one time. In one sense, then, conscientiousness can be taken as a surrogate for the ability to effectively multitask. People who focus on relatively fewer tasks and projects are likely to be organized, systematic, careful, thorough, responsible, and self-disciplined as they work to complete those tasks and projects.

Agreeableness—a person's ability to get along with others—is one of the "Big Five" personality traits. This man would appear to be very agreeable, given his happy and positive display of emotions.

Pressmaster/Shutterstock.com

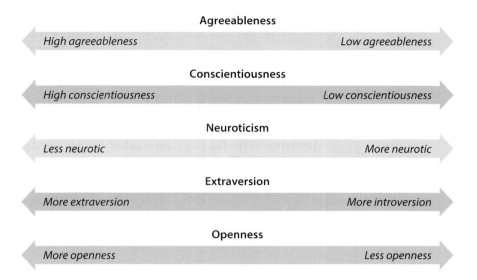

FIGURE 9.2

The "Big Five" Model Of Personality

The "Big Five" personality model represents an accepted framework for understanding personality traits in organizational settings. In general, experts tend to agree that personality traits toward the left end of each dimension, as illustrated in this figure, are more positive in organizational settings, whereas traits closer to the right are less positive.

Others, however, tend to take on too many tasks and projects and/or to procrastinate and, as a result, are more disorganized, careless, and irresponsible, as well as less thorough and self-disciplined. Research has found that more conscientious people tend to be higher performers than less conscientious people across a variety of different jobs. This pattern seems logical, of course, because more conscientious people will take their jobs seriously and will approach the performance of their jobs in highly responsible fashions.

The third of the Big Five personality dimensions is Neuroticism. People who are less neurotic will be relatively poised, calm, resilient, and secure. But people who are more neurotic will be more excitable, insecure, reactive, and subject to extreme mood swings. People with less neuroticism might be expected to better handle job stress, pressure, and tension. Their stability might also lead them to be seen as more reliable than their less-stable counterparts.

Extraversion refers to a person's comfort level with relationships. People who are called "extraverts" are sociable, talkative, assertive, and open to establishing new relationships. Introverts are much less sociable, talkative, assertive, and less open to establishing new relationships. Research suggests that extraverts generally tend to be higher overall job performers than introverts and that they are also more likely to be attracted to jobs based on personal relationships, such as sales and marketing positions.

Finally, Openness refers to a person's rigidity of beliefs and range of interests. People with high levels of openness are willing to listen to new ideas and to change their own ideas, beliefs, and attitudes as a result of new information. They also tend to have broad interests and to be curious, imaginative, and creative. On the other hand, people with low levels of openness tend to be less receptive to new ideas and less willing to change their minds. Furthermore, they tend to have fewer and narrower interests and to be less curious and creative. People with more openness might be expected to be better performers, owing to their flexibility and the likelihood that they will be better accepted by others in the organization. Openness may also encompass an individual's willingness to accept change. For example, people with high levels of openness may be more receptive to change, whereas people with low levels of openness may be more likely to resist change.

neuroticism
Extent to which a person is poised, calm, resilient, and secure

extraversion
A person's comfort level with relationships

openness
A person's rigidity of beliefs and range of interests

The Big Five framework continues to attract the attention of both researchers and managers. The potential value of this framework is that it encompasses an integrated set of traits that appear to be valid predictors of work-related behaviors in a variety of situations. Thus, managers who can develop both an understanding of the framework and the ability to assess these traits in their employees will be in a good position to understand how and why employees behave as they do.[9] On the other hand, managers must also be careful not to overestimate their ability to assess the Big Five traits in others. Even assessment using the most rigorous and valid measures, for instance, is still likely to be somewhat imprecise. Another limitation of the Big Five framework is that it is based primarily on research conducted in the United States. Thus, there are unanswered questions as to how accurately it applies to workers in other cultures. And even within the United States, a variety of other factors and traits are also likely to affect behavior in organizations.[10]

9-2b The Myers-Briggs Framework

Another interesting approach to understanding personalities in organizations is the Myers-Briggs framework. This framework, based on the classic work of Carl Jung, differentiates people in terms of four general dimensions. These are defined as follows:

- *Extraversion (E) versus Introversion (I).* Extraverts get their energy from being around other people, whereas introverts are worn out by others and need solitude to recharge their energy.
- *Sensing (S) versus Intuition (N).* The sensing type prefers concrete things, whereas intuitives prefer abstract concepts.
- *Thinking (T) versus Feeling (F).* Thinking individuals base their decisions more on logic and reason, whereas feeling individuals base their decisions more on feelings and emotions.
- *Judging (J) versus Perceiving (P).* People who are the judging type enjoy completion or being finished, whereas perceiving types enjoy the process and open-ended situations.

To use this framework, people complete a questionnaire designed to measure their personality on each dimension. Higher or lower scores in each of the dimensions are used to classify people into one of 16 different personality categories.

The Myers-Briggs Type Indicator (MBTI) is one popular questionnaire that some organizations use to assess personality types. Indeed, it is among the most popular selection instruments used today, with as many as 2 million people taking it each year. Research suggests that the MBTI is a useful method for determining communication styles and interaction preferences. In terms of stable personality attributes, however, questions exist about both the validity and the reliability of the MBTI.

9-2c Other Personality Traits at Work

Besides the Big Five and the Myers-Briggs framework, there are several other personality traits that influence behavior in organizations. Among the most important are locus of control, self-efficacy, authoritarianism, Machiavellianism, self-esteem, and risk propensity.

Locus of control is the extent to which people believe that their behavior has a real effect on what happens to them.[11] Some people, for example, believe that if they work hard, they will succeed. They also may believe that people fail do so because they lack ability or motivation. People who believe that individuals are in control of their lives are said to have an *internal locus of control*. Other people think that fate, chance, luck, or other people's behavior determines what happens to them. For example, an employee who fails to get a promotion may attribute that failure to a politically motivated boss or just bad luck, rather than to her or his own lack of skills or poor performance record. People who think that forces beyond their control dictate what happens to them are said to have an *external locus of control*. During the COVID-19 pandemic in 2020 individuals with an internal locus of control were more likely to take seriously "shelter-in-place" advisories and to exercise caution in their social interactions. This was due to their beliefs that such behaviors on their part would improve their chances

locus of control
The degree to which a person believes that his or her behavior has a direct impact on the consequences of that behavior

of avoiding the virus. On the other hand, those who were less cautious attributed their own behavior to a variety of factors, but some expressed the opinion that fate or other factors beyond their control would determine whether or not they became infected. These individuals were also among those less likely to wear face masks.

self-efficacy
An individual's beliefs about her or his capabilities to perform a task

Self-efficacy is a related but subtly different personality characteristic. Self-efficacy is a person's beliefs about his or her capabilities to perform a task.[12] People with high self-efficacy believe that they can perform well on a specific task, whereas people with low self-efficacy tend to doubt their ability to perform a specific task. Although self-assessments of ability contribute to self-efficacy, so, too, does the individual's personality. Some people simply have more self-confidence than do others. This belief in their ability to perform a task effectively results in their being more self-assured and more able to focus their attention on performance.

authoritarianism
The extent to which a person believes that power and status differences are appropriate within hierarchical social systems like organizations

Another important personality characteristic is authoritarianism, the extent to which one believes that power and status differences are appropriate within hierarchical social systems like organizations.[13] For example, a person who is highly authoritarian may accept directives or orders from someone with more authority purely because the other person is "the boss." On the other hand, although a person who is not highly authoritarian may still carry out appropriate and reasonable directives from the boss, he or she is also more likely to question things, express disagreement with the boss, and even refuse to carry out orders if they are for some reason objectionable. A highly authoritarian manager may be autocratic and demanding, and highly authoritarian subordinates will be more likely to accept this behavior from their leader. On the other hand, a less authoritarian manager may allow subordinates a bigger role in making decisions, and less authoritarian subordinates will respond positively to this behavior.

Machiavellianism
Behavior directed at gaining power and controlling the behavior of others

Machiavellianism is another important personality trait. This concept is named after Niccolò Machiavelli, a sixteenth-century Italian political philosopher. In his book *The Prince*, Machiavelli explained how the nobility could more easily gain and use power. *Machiavellianism* is now used to describe behavior directed at gaining power and controlling the behavior of others. Research suggests that Machiavellianism is a personality trait that varies from person to person. More Machiavellian individuals tend to be rational and nonemotional, may be willing to lie to attain their personal goals, may put little weight on loyalty and friendship, and may enjoy manipulating others' behavior. Less Machiavellian individuals are more emotional, less willing to lie to succeed, value loyalty and friendship highly, and get little personal pleasure from manipulating others. By all indicators, Dov Charney, founder and former CEO of American Apparel, has a high degree of Machiavellianism. He apparently came to believe that his position of power in the company gave him the right to do just about anything he wanted with company resources and employees.[14] He was eventually fired but retained as a consultant.

fizkes/Shutterstock.com

This employee is explaining to his boss why he deserves a promotion. His high level of self-efficacy is serving him well in this conversation because he is able to highlight his strengths and point to his positive contributions to the latest project.

self-esteem
The extent to which a person believes that he or she is a worthwhile and deserving individual

Self-esteem is the extent to which a person believes that she is a worthwhile and deserving individual.[15] A person with high self-esteem is more likely to seek high-status jobs, be more confident in her ability to achieve higher levels of performance, and derive greater intrinsic satisfaction from her accomplishments. In contrast, a person with less self-esteem may be more content to remain in a lower-level job, be less confident of his ability, and focus more on extrinsic rewards. Among the major personality dimensions, self-esteem is the one that has been most widely studied in other countries. Although more research is clearly needed, the published evidence does suggest that self-esteem as a personality trait does indeed exist in a variety of countries and that its role in organizations is reasonably important across different cultures.[16]

risk propensity
The degree to which an individual is willing to take chances and make risky decisions

Risk propensity is the degree to which one is willing to take chances and make risky decisions. A manager with a high risk propensity, for example, might be expected to experiment with new ideas and gamble on new products. She might also lead the organization in new and different directions. This manager might also be a catalyst for innovation. On the other hand, the same person might also jeopardize the continued well-being of the organization if the risky decisions prove to be bad ones. A manager with low risk propensity might lead to a stagnant and overly conservative organization or help the organization successfully weather turbulent and unpredictable times by maintaining stability and calm. Thus, the potential consequences of risk propensity to an organization are heavily dependent on that organization's environment. During the 2020 COVID-19 pandemic, individuals with a high risk propensity were more likely to engage in social interactions and venture to places where there might be a higher risk of exposure to the virus whereas those with a lower risk propensity were more likely to rigidly maintain social-distancing guidelines and avoid areas where virus exposure was more likely.

9-2d Emotional Intelligence

emotional intelligence (EQ)
The extent to which people are self-aware, manage their emotions, motivate themselves, express empathy for others, and possess social skills

The concept of emotional intelligence also provides some interesting insights into personality. Emotional intelligence, or EQ, refers to the extent to which people are self-aware, manage their emotions, motivate themselves, express empathy for others, and possess social skills.[17] These various dimensions can be described as follows:

- *Self-Awareness.* This is the basis for the other components. It refers to a person's capacity for being aware of how they are feeling. In general, more self-awareness allows people to more effectively guide their own lives and behaviors.
- *Managing Emotions.* This refers to a person's capacities to balance anxiety, fear, and anger so that they do not overly interfere with getting things accomplished.
- *Motivating Oneself.* This dimension refers to a person's ability to remain optimistic and to continue striving in the face of setbacks, barriers, and failure.
- *Empathy.* Empathy refers to a person's ability to understand how others are feeling, even without being explicitly told.
- *Social Skill.* This refers to a person's ability to get along with others and to establish positive relationships.

Preliminary research suggests that people with high EQ may perform better than others, especially in jobs that require a high degree of interpersonal interaction and that involve influencing or directing the work of others. Moreover, EQ appears to be something that is not biologically based but can be developed.[18]

Manager's Checklist

☐ Managers need to understand personality and the basic personality dimensions most relevant to organizations.

☐ You should also be sufficiently self-aware to understand both your own personality and how your personality affects you at work.

9-3 ATTITUDES AND INDIVIDUAL BEHAVIOR

attitudes
Complexes of beliefs and feelings that people have about specific ideas, situations, or other people

Another important element of individual behavior in organizations is attitudes. Attitudes are complexes of beliefs and feelings that people have about specific ideas, situations, or other people.[19] Attitudes are important because they are the mechanism through which most people express their feelings. An employee's complaint that he feels underpaid by his organization reflects his attitude about his pay. Similarly, when a manager comments that she likes the new advertising campaign, she is expressing her attitude about the company's marketing efforts.

Attitudes have three components. The *affective component* of an attitude reflects feelings and emotions a person has toward a situation. The *cognitive component* of an attitude is derived from knowledge one has about a situation. It is important to note that cognition is subject to individual perceptions (something we discuss more fully later). Thus, one person might "know" that a certain political candidate is better than another, whereas someone else might "know" just the opposite. Finally, the *intentional component* of an attitude reflects how one expects to behave toward or in the situation.

To illustrate these three components, consider the case of a manager who places an order for some supplies for his organization from a new office supply firm. Suppose many of the items he orders are out of stock, others are overpriced, and still others arrive damaged. When he calls someone at the supply firm for assistance, he is treated rudely and gets disconnected before his claim is resolved. When asked how he feels about the new office supply firm, he might respond, "I don't like that company [*affective component*]. They are the worst office supply firm I've ever dealt with [*cognitive component*]. I'll never do business with them again [*intentional component*]."

cognitive dissonance
Caused when an individual has conflicting attitudes

Attitudes are complexes of beliefs and feelings that people have about specific ideas, situations, or people. This woman has just had a damaged package delivered to her door. She is unhappy with the delivery company for damaging the package and is expressing her feelings to the delivery company representative. She most likely now has a negative attitude toward this delivery company.

Andrey_Popov/Shutterstock.com

People generally feel a need to maintain consistency among the three components of their attitudes. However, circumstances sometimes arise that lead to conflicts. The conflict individuals may experience among their own attitudes is called cognitive dissonance.[20] Say, for example, that a person who has vowed never to work for a big, impersonal corporation intends instead to open her own business and be her own boss. Unfortunately, a series of financial setbacks leads her to have no choice but to take a job with a large company and work for someone else. Thus, cognitive dissonance occurs: The affective and cognitive components of the person's attitude conflict with intended behavior. To reduce cognitive dissonance, which is usually an uncomfortable experience for most people, she might tell herself that the situation is only temporary and that she can go back out on her own in the near future. Or she might revise her cognitions and decide that working for a large company is more pleasant than she had expected.

9-3a Work-Related Attitudes

People in organizations form attitudes about many different things. For example, employees are likely to have attitudes about their salaries, promotion possibilities, their bosses, employee benefits, the food in the company cafeteria, the firm's technology, and the color of the company softball team uniforms. Of course, some of these attitudes are more important than others. Especially important attitudes are job satisfaction or dissatisfaction and organizational commitment.[21]

job satisfaction or dissatisfaction
An attitude that reflects the extent to which an individual is gratified by or fulfilled in his or her work

Job Satisfaction or Dissatisfaction   Job satisfaction or dissatisfaction is an attitude that reflects the extent to which an individual is gratified by or fulfilled in his or her work. Extensive research conducted on job satisfaction has indicated that personal factors, such as an individual's needs and aspirations, determine this attitude, along with group and organizational factors, such as relationships with coworkers and supervisors, as well as working conditions, work-related policies, and compensation.[22]

A satisfied employee also tends to be absent less often, to make positive contributions, and to be inclined to stay with the organization.[23] In contrast, a dissatisfied employee may be absent more often, may experience stress that disrupts coworkers, and may be continually looking for another job. Contrary to what many managers believe, however, high levels of job satisfaction do not necessarily lead to higher levels of performance. Our *Leading the Way* feature highlights the importance that one firm, Hilton Hotels, places on employee satisfaction, as well as employee commitment and engagement.

"How can someone say they're successful if they're not happy doing their work? To me, that's not success."
— Nicholas Lore, Founder of the Rockport Institute, A Career Coaching Firm

9-3b Organizational Commitment and Engagement

organizational commitment
An attitude that reflects a person's identification with and attachment to the organization itself

organizational engagement
The extent to which an employee sees him- or herself as part of the organization, actively looks for ways to contribute to the organization, and is involved with the organization in multiple ways

Organizational commitment is an attitude that reflects a person's identification with and attachment to the organization itself. Organizational engagement, similarly, refers to the extent to which an employee sees him- or herself as part of the organization, actively looks for ways to contribute to the organization, and is involved with the organization in multiple ways. A person with high levels of commitment and engagement is likely to see herself as a true member of the organization (e.g., referring to the organization in personal terms like "We make high-quality products"), to overlook minor sources of dissatisfaction with the organization, and to see herself remaining a member of the organization. In contrast, a person with less organizational commitment and engagement is more likely to see himself as an outsider (e.g., referring to the organization in less personal terms like "They don't pay their employees very well"), to express more dissatisfaction about things, and to not see himself as a long-term member of the organization.

Research also suggests that commitment and engagement tend to strengthen with a person's age, years with the organization, sense of job security, and participation in decision making.[24] Employees who feel committed to and engaged with an organization have highly reliable habits, plan a long tenure with the organization, and muster more effort in performance. Although there are few definitive things that organizations can do to create or promote commitment and engagement, there are a few specific guidelines available.[25] For one thing, if the organization treats its employees fairly and provides reasonable rewards and job security, those employees will more likely be satisfied, committed, and engaged. Allowing employees to have a say in how things are done can also promote all three attitudes.[26]

LEADING THE WAY

Happy Hotel Workers at Hilton

At the end of World War I, a young man named Conrad Hilton came home to Cisco, Texas, with money he'd saved up while serving in the U.S. Army Quartermaster Corps. Even though it was a meager $5,000 (roughly equivalent to $70,000 in 2020), he was impatient to invest it rather than spend it, so when he saw the old Mobley Hotel for sale, he bought it. In 1925, Conrad Hilton opened the first Hilton Hotel in Dallas, and in 1927 in Waco, Texas, he opened the first hotel with air conditioning. In 1947 he opened the first hotel with a television in every room.

The corporate mission for Hilton Hotels still reflects the founder's original vision: "Our mission is to be the most hospitable company in the world, and you can't do that without great people, and you can't get great people without being a great workplace," says Matt Schuyler, Hilton's chief human resources officer.

While many companies lovingly attend to the working conditions of white-collar employees—with treadmill desks, soothing quiet rooms, and whimsical common areas—the needs of service workers are all but ignored. Hilton Hotels is attempting to rectify this imbalance with an ambitious program to spruce up employee workspaces in hopes that will improve their experience and, in turn, reduce turnover, improve customer service, and drive profitability.

The initiatives began after Hilton's initial public offering in 2013 (Hilton was owned by private equity firm Blackstone

(Continued)

 **LEADING THE WAY (CONTINUED)**

from 2007 to 2013), under the guidance of CEO Christopher Nassetta. "I put on a housekeeper's jacket and I'm like, 'Wow, this is heavy'," the Hilton CEO told *Fortune* recently. "It didn't feel very comfortable or flexible, and I'm thinking, we got this wrong—we're not giving them the right clothing to wear." Nassetta and his team decided that changes were in order, so in early 2018, the company launched a partnership with Under Armour to have the sports apparel giant redesign lighter, more comfortable workwear.

That's just one of several employee-focused changes that have crowned the 100-year-old Hilton as the *Best Company to Work For in America* for both 2019 and 2020. It's sweet validation for Nassetta, who upon taking the reins at Hilton in 2007 found an organization that "had lost our way a bit," he said. "We forgot that we are a business of people serving people, and the corporate environment got very disconnected from the front line."

Hilton's commitment to making sure the front-line workers reflect the mission of the company harkens back to corporate ideals that developed in the late 1920s, when Western Electric, in Hawthorne, Illinois, hired Elton Mayo, a sociologist, to conduct experiments on worker productivity. Mayo increased the lighting and saw worker output improve. But when he lowered the lighting, the productivity continued to increase. Ultimately, Mayo concluded that it wasn't the actual changes that made a difference, but that workers were responding to the attention they were being shown from management.

Although hotels and resorts across the globe were forced to suspend services due to the COVID-19 pandemic, with approximately 60,000 direct employees in its corporate offices and hotels in the United States and 200,000 more through franchise hotels, the company made the decision to furlough workers, as opposed to laying them off. Furloughed Hilton employees in the United States were given direct access to an online resource center and expedited hiring processes at leading companies including Amazon, CVS, Lidl, Albertsons, Plastics Industry Association, and Sunrise Senior Living.

"The recognized quality of our team members, including their hospitality and service culture training, make them ideal candidates to quickly step in and assist organizations in these temporary assignments," said Nigel Glennie, vice president of corporate communication at Hilton, in an interview with *USA Today.* "We hope to expand the program globally, adding more companies, and we plan to welcome these team members back when travel resumes."

References: Oliver Staley, "Hilton Hotels' Newest Upgrades Are Strictly for Staff," Quartz at Work, April 2, 2018, https://qz.com on April 4, 2020; "100 Best Companies to Work For 2019," *Fortune*, https://fortune.com on April 4, 2019; Josh Rivera, "Furloughed Hilton Workers Offered Access to Other Jobs During Coronavirus Pandemic," *USA Today*, March 23, 2020, www.usatoday.com on April 4, 2020.

9-3c **Affect and Mood in Organizations**

Researchers have recently started to focus renewed interest on the affective component of attitudes. Recall from our preceding discussion that the affective component of an attitude reflects our feelings and emotions. Although managers once believed that emotion and feelings varied among people from day to day, research now suggests that, although some short-term fluctuation does indeed occur, there are also underlying stable predispositions toward fairly constant and predictable moods and emotional states.[27]

positive affectivity
A tendency to be relatively upbeat and optimistic, have an overall sense of well-being, see things in a positive light, and seem to be in a good mood

negative affectivity
A tendency to be generally downbeat and pessimistic, see things in a negative way, and seem to be in a bad mood

Some people, for example, tend to have a higher degree of positive affectivity. This means that they are relatively upbeat and optimistic, have an overall sense of well-being, and usually see things in a positive light. Thus, they always seem to be in a good mood. It's also been proposed that positive affectivity may play a role in entrepreneurial success.[28] Other people, those with more negative affectivity, are just the opposite. They are generally downbeat and pessimistic, and they usually see things in a negative way. They seem to be in a bad mood most of the time.

Of course, as noted above, there can be short-term variations among even the most extreme types. People with a lot of positive affectivity, for example, may still be in a bad mood if they have just received some bad news—being passed over for a promotion, getting extremely negative performance feedback, or being laid off or fired, for instance. Similarly, those with negative affectivity may still be in a good mood—at least for a short time—if they have just been promoted, received very positive performance feedback, or had other positive events occur. After the initial impact of these events wears off, however, those with positive affectivity will generally return to their normal positive mood, whereas those with negative affectivity will gravitate back to their normal bad mood.

Manager's Checklist

☐ Managers should know the three components of an attitude.

☐ Managers should also understand the determinants and consequences of job satisfaction or dissatisfaction, organizational commitment, and organizational engagement.

☐ You should be sufficiently self-aware that you know your own levels of job satisfaction or dissatisfaction, organizational commitment, and organizational engagement and how they affect your behavior.

perception
The set of processes by which an individual becomes aware of and interprets information about the environment

9-4 PERCEPTION AND INDIVIDUAL BEHAVIOR

As noted earlier, an important element of an attitude is the person's perception of the object about which the attitude is formed. Because perception plays a role in a variety of other workplace behaviors, managers need to have a general understanding of basic perceptual processes.[29] The role of attributions is also important.

9-4a Basic Perceptual Processes

Perception is the set of processes through which an individual becomes aware of and interprets information about the environment. As shown in Figure 9.3, basic perceptual processes that are particularly relevant to organizations are selective perception and stereotyping.

Selective Perception Selective perception is the process of screening out information that we are uncomfortable with or that contradicts our beliefs. For example, suppose a manager is exceptionally fond of a particular worker. The manager has a very positive attitude about the worker and thinks he is a top performer. One day the manager notices that the worker seems to be goofing off. Selective perception may cause the manager to quickly forget what he observed. Similarly, suppose a manager has formed a very negative image of a particular worker. She thinks this worker is a poor performer and never does a good job. When she happens to observe an example of high performance from

Selective perception is the process of screening out information that we are uncomfortable with or that contradicts our beliefs. This manager just caught one of her employees napping on the job when he needs to be working on a big project. If she already has a negative opinion of this worker, her opinion will now become even more negative. But if she has always viewed him positively, she may overlook this current incident as an anomaly.

YAKOBCHUK VIACHESLAV/Shutterstock.com

selective perception
The process of screening out information that we are uncomfortable with or that contradicts our beliefs

the worker, she, too, may not remember it for very long. In one sense, selective perception is beneficial because it allows us to disregard minor bits of information. Of course, this is helpful only if our basic perception is accurate. If selective perception causes us to ignore important information, however, it can become quite detrimental.

stereotyping
The process of categorizing or labeling people on the basis of a single attribute

Stereotyping Stereotyping is the process of categorizing or labeling people on the basis of a single attribute. Common attributes on which people often stereotype are race, gender, and age.[30] Of course, stereotypes along these lines are inaccurate and can often be harmful. For example, suppose a manager forms the stereotype that women can perform only certain tasks and that men are best suited for other tasks. To the extent that this affects the manager's hiring practices, the manager is (1) costing the organization valuable talent for both sets of jobs, (2) violating federal law, and (3) behaving unethically. On the other hand, certain forms of stereotyping can be useful and efficient. Suppose, for example, that a manager believes that communication skills are important for a particular job and that speech communication majors tend to have exceptionally good communication skills. As a result, whenever he interviews

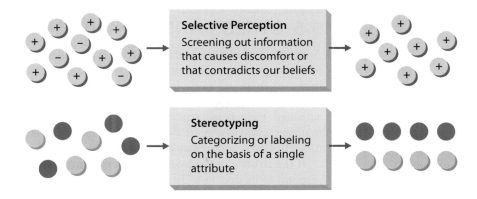

FIGURE 9.3

Perceptual Processes

Two of the most basic perceptual processes are selective perception and stereotyping. As shown here, selective perception occurs when we screen out information (represented by the – symbols) that causes us discomfort or that contradicts our beliefs. Stereotyping occurs when we categorize or label people on the basis of a single attribute, illustrated here by color.

candidates for jobs, he pays especially close attention to speech communication majors. To the extent that communication skills truly predict job performance and that majoring in speech communication does indeed provide those skills, this form of stereotyping can be beneficial.

9-4b Perception and Attribution

attribution

The process of observing behavior and attributing causes to it

Perception is also closely linked with another process called *attribution*. Attribution is a mechanism through which we observe behavior and then attribute causes to it.[31] The behavior that is observed may be our own or that of others. For example, suppose someone realizes one day that she is working fewer hours than before, that she talks less about her work, and that she calls in sick more often. She might conclude from this that she must have become disenchanted with her job and subsequently decide to quit. Thus, she observed her own behavior, attributed a cause to it, and developed what she thought was a consistent response.

More common is attributing cause to the behavior of others. For example, if the manager of the person just described has seen the same behavior, he might form exactly the same attribution. On the other hand, he might instead decide that she has a serious illness, that he is driving her too hard, that she is experiencing too much stress, that she has a drug problem, or that she is having family problems.

The basic framework around which we form attributions is *consensus* (the extent to which other people in the same situation behave the same way), *consistency* (the extent to which the same person behaves in the same way at different times), and *distinctiveness* (the extent to which the same person behaves in the same way in other situations). For example, suppose a manager observes that an employee is late for a meeting. The manager might further realize that he is the only one who is late (low consensus), recall that he is often late for other meetings (high consistency), and subsequently realize that the same employee is sometimes late arriving for work and returning from lunch (low distinctiveness). This pattern of attributions might cause the manager to decide that the person's behavior is something that should be changed. As a result, the manager might meet with the subordinate and establish some punitive consequences for future tardiness.

Manager's Checklist

☐ Managers should understand perception in general, as well as selective perception and stereotyping in particular.

☐ You need to also appreciate the role of attributions in organizations.

9-5 STRESS AND INDIVIDUAL BEHAVIOR

stress
A person's response to a strong stimulus, which is called a *stressor*

general adaptation syndrome (GAS)
General cycle of the stress process

Another important element of behavior in organizations is stress. Stress is a person's response to a strong stimulus.[32] This stimulus is called a *stressor*. Stress generally follows a cycle referred to as the general adaptation syndrome, or GAS,[33] shown in Figure 9.4. According to this view, when a person first encounters a stressor, the GAS is initiated, and the first stage, alarm, is activated. He may feel panic, wonder how to cope, and feel helpless. For example, suppose a manager is told to prepare a detailed evaluation of a plan by his firm to buy one of its competitors. His first reaction may be, "How will I ever get this done by tomorrow?"

If the stressor is too intense, the person may feel unable to cope and never really try to respond to its demands. In most cases, however, after a short period of alarm, the person gathers some strength and starts to resist the negative effects of the stressor. For example, the manager with the evaluation to write may calm down, call home to say he is working late, roll up his sleeves, order out for coffee, and get to work. Thus, at stage 2 of the GAS, the person is resisting the effects of the stressor.

In many cases, the resistance phase may end the GAS. If the manager can complete the evaluation earlier than expected, he may drop it in his briefcase or backpack, smile to himself, and head home tired but satisfied. On the other hand, prolonged exposure to a stressor without resolution may bring on stage 3 of the GAS—exhaustion. At this stage, the person literally gives up and can no longer resist the stressor. The manager, for example, might fall asleep at his desk at 3:00 A.M. and never finish the evaluation.

We should note that stress is not all bad. In the absence of stress, we may experience lethargy and stagnation. An optimal level of stress, on the other hand, can result in motivation and excitement. Too much stress, however, can have negative consequences. It is also important to understand that stress can be caused by "good" as well as "bad" things. Excessive pressure, unreasonable demands on our time, and bad news can all cause stress. But even receiving a bonus and then having to decide what to do with the money can be stressful. So, too, can receiving a promotion, gaining recognition, and similar good things.

Type A
Individuals who are extremely competitive, very devoted to work, and have a strong sense of time urgency

Type B
Individuals who are less competitive, less devoted to work, and have a weaker sense of time urgency

One important line of thinking about stress focuses on Type A and Type B personalities.[34] Type A individuals are extremely competitive, very devoted to work, and have a strong sense of time urgency. They are likely to be aggressive, impatient, and very work oriented. They have a lot of drive and want to accomplish as much as possible as quickly as possible. Type B individuals are less competitive, less devoted to work, and have a weaker sense of time urgency. Such people are less likely to experience conflict with others and more likely to have a

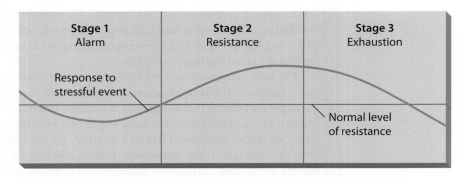

FIGURE 9.4

The General Adaptation Syndrome

The general adaptation syndrome represents the normal process by which we react to stressful events. At stage 1—alarm—we feel panic and alarm, and our level of resistance to stress drops. Stage 2—resistance—represents our efforts to confront and control the stressful circumstance. If we fail, we may eventually reach stage 3—exhaustion—and just give up or quit.

Stress is a person's response to a strong stimulus. This woman is behind on a major project (a strong stimulus). Her response (stress) is anxiety and worry over her ability to get the project completed.

balanced, relaxed approach to life. They can work at a constant pace without time urgency. Type B people are not necessarily more or less successful than are Type A people, but they are less likely to experience stress.

9-5a Causes and Consequences of Stress

Stress is obviously not a simple phenomenon. *A World of Difference* clearly illustrates its complexity. Several different things can cause stress, as listed in Figure 9.5. Note that this list includes only work-related conditions. We should keep in mind that stress can also be the result of personal circumstances.[35]

Causes of Stress   Work-related stressors fall into one of four categories—task, physical, role, and interpersonal demands. *Task demands* are associated with the task itself. Some occupations are inherently more stressful than others. Having to make fast decisions, decisions with less than complete information, or decisions that have relatively serious consequences are some of the things that can make some jobs stressful. The jobs of surgeon, airline pilot, and stockbroker are relatively more stressful than the jobs of general practitioner, baggage handler, and office receptionist. Although a general practitioner makes important decisions, he is also likely to have time to make a considered diagnosis and fully explore a number of different treatments. But during surgery, the surgeon must make decisions quickly while realizing that the wrong one may endanger her patient's life. Many health care professionals and first responders experienced a surge in task demand–related stress during the 2020 COVID-19 pandemic.

> **"Increasing store hours increases the hours that the bad guys can rob you. Darkness to dawn is the highest time of exposure to armed robberies."**
> —Bill Wise, Former Manager of Safety and Security for Wendy's

Physical demands are stressors associated with the job setting. Working outdoors in extremely hot or cold temperatures, or even in an improperly heated or cooled office, can lead to stress. Likewise, jobs that have rotating work shifts make it difficult for people to have stable sleep patterns. A poorly designed office—one that, for example, makes it difficult for people to have privacy or promotes too little social interaction—can result in stress, as can poor lighting and inadequate work surfaces. Even more severe are actual threats to health. Examples include jobs like coal mining, poultry processing, and toxic waste handling. Similarly, some jobs carry risks associated with higher incident rates of violence, such as armed robberies. Examples include law enforcement officers, taxi drivers, and convenience store clerks. Again, during the 2020 pandemic, many health care workers and first responders experienced an increase in physical demands as they had to work longer hours and, in many cases, in compromised work locations.

Role demands can also cause stress. (Roles are discussed more fully in Chapter 18.) A role is a set of expected behaviors associated with a position in a group or organization. Stress can result from either role conflict or role ambiguity that people can experience in groups. For example, an employee who is feeling pressure from her boss to work longer hours or to travel more, while also being asked by her family for more time at home, will almost certainly experience stress as a result of role conflict.[36] Similarly, a new employee experiencing role ambiguity because of poor orientation and training practices by the organization will also suffer from stress. Excessive meetings are also a potential source of stress.[37] While job cuts and layoffs during the 2020 pandemic focused attention on the stress experienced by those losing their jobs (and appropriately so), it's also the case that many of the managers imposing the layoffs experienced stress as well.[38]

FS Stock/Shutterstock.com

FIGURE 9.5

Causes of Work Stress

There are several causes of work stress in organizations. Four general sets of organizational stressors are task demands, physical demands, role demands, and interpersonal demands.

Interpersonal demands are stressors associated with relationships that confront people in organizations. For example, group pressures regarding restriction of output and norm conformity can lead to stress. Leadership styles may also cause stress. An employee who feels a strong need to participate in decision making may feel stress if his boss refuses to allow such participation. And individuals with conflicting personalities may experience stress if required to work too closely together. For example, a person with an internal locus of control might be frustrated when working with someone who prefers to wait and just let things happen.[39]

> **"Some of [the people I laid off] I'd worked with for a very long time. I saw such pain in their faces, but felt I couldn't show my emotions to them.... As soon as I could, I'd close the door, draw the blinds, and have a good sob."**
>
> —Alicia Sanera, HR Executive

A WORLD OF DIFFERENCE

Differences Can Lead to Stress

Aimee Stephens agonized for months over how to inform her employer, RG & GR Harris Funeral Homes, in Garden City, Michigan, that she was transgender and would begin dressing as a woman at work. She had worked as an exemplary employee for them for nearly six years. Stephens was fired two weeks after her disclosure. Stephens's case is before the Supreme Court after being upheld by a court of appeals in March 2018.

Scott Phillips Gartner worked in the Norfolk, Virginia, fire department for nearly 30 years. After marrying in 2014 and adding his husband's name to his personnel records, the way he was treated within the department changed radically. Gartner sued the fire department for gender discrimination, hostile work environment, and retaliation.

Don Zarda was participating in a team skydive, where an instructor is strapped to a team member. As he was securing his connection to a female client, he attempted to reassure her by telling her "Don't worry; I'm gay." Immediately after the dive, Zarda was fired. He sued Altitude, Inc. for wrongful termination.

These three cases, all under review by the Supreme Court, illustrate both the changing nature of rights in the workplace and the need for companies to have clear and fair workplace policies to protect their employees. Furthermore, if employees don't feel that their basic rights are protected, it's impossible to create a workplace culture that fosters good morale and bolsters productivity.

(Continued)

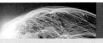

A WORLD OF DIFFERENCE (CONTINUED)

As of 2020, 23 states and the District of Columbia had LGBTQ-specific nondiscrimination laws on the books. In spite of this growing legal protection, a 2018 Harris poll showed that over 50 percent of LGBTQ employees surveyed had experienced harassment or discrimination in the workplace. The same research showed that 25 percent of LGBTQ employees had left a company that they felt did not support their rights and inclusion.

From celebrating Pride Month to donating to The Trevor Project, companies are looking for ways to support LGBTQ employees and customers. The Human Rights Campaign has a Trans Toolkit for employers, providing guidance on how to support an employee undergoing transition. Glassdoor, one of the world's largest job recruiting websites, offers information about an employer's level of support for LGBTQ equality.

Increasingly, companies are responding to the needs not only of their LGBTQ customers but also their employees. No matter the outcome of the three cases before the Supreme Court, it is undeniable that the landscape of employee rights is changing, and companies must pay attention.

References: "R.G. & G.R. Harris Funeral Homes v. EEOC and Aimee Stephens," ACLU, September 10, 2019, www.aclu.org on May 1, 2020; Kathryn Vasel, "Fired for Being Transgender: The Fight for LGBTQ Workers' Rights," Action News Now, June 15, 2019, www.actionnewsnow.com on May 1, 2020; "Altitude Express, Inc. v. Zarda," Freedom for All Americans, August 28, 2019, www.freedomforallamericans.org on May 1, 2020; Susan Miller, "'Shocking Numbers': Half of LGBTQ Adults Live in States Where No Laws Ban Job Discrimination," *USA Today*, October 8, 2019, www.usatoday.com on May 1, 2020.

Consequences of Stress   As noted earlier, the results of stress may be positive or negative. The negative consequences may be behavioral, psychological, or medical. Behaviorally, for example, stress may lead to detrimental or harmful actions, such as smoking, alcohol or drug abuse, and overeating. Other stress-induced behaviors are accident proneness, violence toward self or others, and eating disorders. Substance abuse is also a potential consequence.[40] Many people reported that during the shelter-in-place phase of the 2020 pandemic they exercised less and ate more, in part because it helped them cope with stress.

Stress can also result in psychological consequences. These can interfere with a person's mental health and well-being. Problems include sleep disturbances, depression, family problems, and sexual dysfunction. Managers are especially prone to sleep disturbances when they experience stress at work.[41] Medical consequences of stress affect an individual's physiological well-being. Heart disease and stroke have been linked to stress, as have headaches, backaches, ulcers and related disorders, and skin conditions such as acne and hives.

Individual stress also has direct consequences for businesses. For an operating employee, stress may translate into poor-quality work and lower productivity. For a manager, it may mean faulty decision making and disruptions in working relationships.[42] Withdrawal behaviors can also result from stress. People who are having difficulties with stress in their jobs are more likely to call in sick or to leave the organization. More subtle forms of withdrawal may also occur. A manager may start missing deadlines, for example, or taking longer lunch breaks. Employees may also withdraw by developing feelings of indifference. The irritation displayed by people under great stress can make them difficult to get along with. Job satisfaction, morale, and commitment can all suffer as a result of excessive levels of stress. So, too, can motivation to perform.

burnout
A feeling of exhaustion that may develop when someone experiences too much stress for an extended period of time

Another consequence of stress is burnout—a feeling of exhaustion that may develop when someone experiences too much stress for an extended period of time. Burnout results in constant fatigue, frustration, and helplessness. Increased rigidity follows, as do a loss of self-confidence and psychological withdrawal. The individual dreads going to work, often puts in longer hours but gets less accomplished than before and exhibits mental and physical exhaustion. Because of the damaging effects of burnout, some firms are taking steps to help avoid it. For example, British Airways provides all of its employees with training designed to help them recognize the symptoms of burnout and develop strategies for avoiding it.

9-5b **Managing Stress**

Given the potential consequences of stress, it follows that both people and organizations should be concerned about how to limit its more damaging effects. Numerous ideas and approaches have been developed to help manage stress. Some are strategies for individuals; others are strategies for organizations.[43]

One way people manage stress is through exercise. People who exercise regularly feel less tension and stress, are more self-confident, and feel more optimistic. Their better physical condition also makes them less susceptible to many common illnesses. People who do not exercise regularly, on the other hand, tend to feel more stress and are more likely to be depressed. They are also more likely to have heart attacks. And, because of their physical condition, they are more likely to contract other illnesses as well.

Another method people use to manage stress is relaxation. Relaxation allows individuals to adapt to, and therefore better deal with, their stress. Relaxation comes in many forms, such as taking regular vacations and engaging in nonwork activities on the weekends. One study found that people's attitudes toward a variety of workplace characteristics improved significantly following a weekend when they were able to fully disengage from their work.[44] People can also learn to relax while on the job. For example, some experts recommend that people take regular rest breaks during their normal workday. Google has gone so far as to offer "nap pods" at work where employees can take brief naps during the workday.

People can also use time management to control stress. The idea behind time management is that many daily pressures can be reduced or eliminated if people do a better job of managing time. One approach to time management is to make a list every morning of the things to be done that day. The items on the list are then grouped into three categories: critical activities that must be performed, important activities that should be performed, and optional or trivial things that can be delegated or postponed. The individual performs the items on the list in their order of importance.

Finally, people can manage stress through support groups. A support group can be as simple as a group of family members or friends to enjoy leisure time with. Going out after work with a couple of coworkers to a basketball game or a movie, for example, can help relieve stress built up during the day. Family and friends can help people cope with stress on an ongoing basis and during times of crisis. For example, an employee who has just learned that she did not get the promotion she has been working toward for months may find it helpful to have a good friend to lean on, talk to, or yell at. People also may make use of more elaborate and formal support groups. Community centers or churches, for example, may sponsor support groups for people who have recently gone through a divorce, the death of a loved one, or some other tragedy. During the 2020 COVID-19 pandemic many people formed online groups with friends, coworkers, and/or family members and then used platforms like Zoom or Facebook to "meet" for social interaction.

Organizations are also beginning to realize that they should be involved in helping employees cope with stress. One argument for this is that because the business is at least partially responsible for stress, it should also help relieve it. Another is that stress-related insurance claims by employees can cost the organization considerable sums of money. Still another is that workers experiencing lower levels of detrimental stress will be able to function more effectively. AT&T uses a variety of seminars and workshops to help its employees cope with the stress they face in their jobs. The firm was prompted to develop these seminars for all three of the reasons noted here.

A wellness stress program is a special part of the organization specifically created to help deal with stress. Organizations have adopted stress-management programs, health promotion programs, and other kinds of programs for this purpose. The AT&T seminar program noted earlier is similar to this idea, but true wellness programs are ongoing activities that have a number of different components. They commonly include exercise-related activities as well as classroom instruction programs dealing with smoking cessation, weight reduction, and general stress management. Corning has adopted a stress management program providing workers with resources to help them understand stress and its health effects, as well as how to adopt skills for coping with stress. As part of the program, the company offers various classes in tai chi, biofeedback, meditation, yoga, muscle relaxation, guided imagery, and cognitive restructuring.

Some companies have developed their own programs or use existing programs of this type. Concho Resources, for example, has a gym at its corporate headquarters. Other firms negotiate discounted health club membership rates with local establishments. For the instructional part of the program, the organization can again either sponsor its own training or perhaps jointly sponsor seminars with a local YMCA, civic organization, or church. Organization-based fitness programs facilitate employee exercise, a very positive consideration, but such programs are also quite costly. Still, more and more companies are developing fitness programs for employees. Similarly, some companies are offering their employees periodic sabbaticals—extended breaks from work that presumably allow people to get revitalized and reenergized. Intel and McDonald's are among the firms offering this benefit.[45]

 **Manager's Checklist**

☐ Managers need to understand the nature of stress, especially its primary causes and consequences.

☐ You should know if you are more of a Type A or a Type B person.

9-6 CREATIVITY IN ORGANIZATIONS

creativity
The ability of an individual to generate new ideas or to conceive of new perspectives on existing ideas

Creativity is yet another important component of individual behavior in organizations. Creativity is the ability of a person to generate new ideas or to conceive of new perspectives on existing ideas. What makes a person creative? How do people become creative? How does the creative process work? Although psychologists have not yet discovered complete answers to these questions, examining a few general patterns can help us understand the sources of individual creativity within organizations.[46]

9-6a The Creative Individual

Numerous researchers have focused their efforts on trying to describe the common attributes of creative people. These attributes generally fall into three categories: background experiences, personal traits, and cognitive abilities.

Background Experiences and Creativity Researchers have observed that many creative people were raised in environments in which creativity was nurtured. Mozart was raised in a family of musicians and began composing and performing music at age six. Pierre and Marie Curie, great scientists in their own right, also raised a daughter, Irene, who won the Nobel Prize in chemistry. Thomas Edison's creativity was nurtured by his mother. Elon Musk was encouraged by his mother to develop competencies in programming; he sold the rights to a video game he created when he was 12 years old. However, people with background experiences very different from theirs have also been creative. Frederick Douglass was born into slavery in Tuckahoe, Maryland, and had very limited opportunities for education. Nonetheless, his powerful oratory and creative thinking helped lead to the Thirteenth Amendment to the U.S. Constitution, which outlawed slavery in the United States.

Personal Traits and Creativity Certain personal traits have also been linked to creativity in individuals. The traits shared by most creative people are openness, an attraction to complexity, high levels of energy, independence and autonomy, strong self-confidence, and a strong belief that one is, in fact, creative. People who possess these traits are more likely to be creative than are those who do not have them. Elon Musk has high self-efficacy and self-esteem; these traits no doubt influenced his creative pursuits.

Cognitive Abilities and Creativity Cognitive abilities are an individual's power to think intelligently and to analyze situations and data effectively. Intelligence may be a precondition for individual creativity—although most creative people are highly intelligent, not all intelligent people are necessarily creative. Creativity is also linked with the ability to think divergently and convergently. *Divergent thinking* is a skill that allows people to see differences among situations, phenomena, or events. *Convergent thinking* is a skill that allows people to see similarities among situations, phenomena, or events. Creative people are generally very skilled at both divergent and convergent thinking. Elon Musk has done extremely well in such diverse fields as software development, financial management applications, space exploration, mining, and automobile production.

9-6b The Creative Process

Although creative people often report that ideas seem to come to them "in a flash," individual creative activity actually tends to progress through a series of stages. Not all creative activity has to follow these four stages, but much of it does.

Wolfgang Amadeus Mozart is acknowledged as one of the most creative musical composers of all time. He began composing at the age of five and could play both violin and keyboard. Both of his parents were musicians, and they both motivated him to work in the music field and provided a nurturing environment to support his passion.

Preparation   The creative process normally begins with a period of *preparation*. To make a creative contribution to business management or business services, a person must usually receive formal training and education in business. Formal education and training are usually the most efficient ways of becoming familiar with this vast amount of research and knowledge. This is one reason for the strong demand for undergraduate- and master's-level business education. Formal business education can be an effective way for a person to get "up to speed" and begin making creative contributions quickly. Experiences that managers have on the job after their formal training has ended can also contribute to the creative process. In an important sense, the education and training of creative people never really ends. It continues as long as they remain interested in the world and curious about the way things work. Bruce Roth earned a PhD in chemistry and then spent years working in the pharmaceutical industry learning more and more about chemical compounds and how they work in human beings.

Incubation   The second phase of the creative process is *incubation*—a period of less intense conscious concentration during which the knowledge and ideas acquired during preparation mature and develop. A curious aspect of incubation is that it is often helped along by pauses in concentrated rational thought. Some creative people rely on physical activity such as jogging or swimming to provide a break from thinking. Others may read or listen to music. Sometimes sleep may even supply the needed pause. Bruce Roth eventually joined Warner-Lambert, an up-and-coming drug company, to help develop medication to lower cholesterol. In his spare time, Roth read mystery novels and hiked in the mountains. He later acknowledged that this was when he did his best thinking. Similarly, when he was running Microsoft, Bill Gates retreated to a secluded wooded cabin twice a year to reflect on trends in technology; it is during these weeks, he says, that he developed his best insights into where Microsoft should be heading.[47]

Insight   Usually occurring after preparation and incubation, *insight* is a spontaneous breakthrough in which the creative person achieves a new understanding of some problem or situation. Insight represents a coming together of all the scattered thoughts and ideas that were maturing during incubation. It may occur suddenly or develop slowly over time. Insight can be triggered by some external event, such as a new experience or an encounter with new data, which forces the person to think about old issues and problems in new ways, or it can be a completely internal event in which patterns of thought finally coalesce in ways that generate new understanding. One day Bruce Roth was reviewing data from some earlier studies that had found the new drug under development to be no more effective than other drugs already available. But this time he saw some statistical relationships that had not been identified previously. He knew then that he had a major breakthrough on his hands.

Verification   Once an insight has occurred, *verification* determines the validity or truthfulness of the insight. For many creative ideas, verification includes scientific experiments to determine whether the insight actually leads to the results expected. Verification may also include the development of a product or service prototype. A prototype is one product, or a very small number of products, built just to see if the ideas behind this new product actually work. Product prototypes are rarely sold to the public but are very valuable in verifying the insights developed in the creative process. Once the new product or service is developed, verification in the marketplace is the ultimate test of the creative idea behind it. Bruce Roth and his colleagues set to work testing the new drug compound and eventually won FDA approval. The drug, named Lipitor, is already the largest-selling pharmaceutical in history. And Pfizer, the firm that bought Warner-Lambert in a hostile takeover, earns more than $10 billion a year on the drug.

9-6c Enhancing Creativity in Organizations

Managers who wish to enhance and promote creativity in their organizations can do so in a variety of ways.[48] One important method for enhancing creativity is to make it a part of the organization's culture, often through explicit goals. Firms that truly want to stress creativity—Google, 3M, and Rubbermaid, for example—state goals that some percentage of future revenues is to be gained from new products. This clearly communicates that creativity and innovation are valued. Best Buy once picked four groups of salespeople in their 20s and early 30s and asked them to spend 10 weeks living together in a Los Angeles apartment complex (with expenses paid by the company and still earning their normal pay). Their job? Sit around and brainstorm new business ideas that could be rolled out quickly and cheaply.[49]

Another important part of enhancing creativity is to reward creative successes, while being careful not to punish creative failures. Many ideas that seem worthwhile on paper fail to pan out in reality. If the first person to come up with an idea that fails is fired or otherwise punished, others in the organization will become more cautious in their own work. And, as a result, fewer creative ideas will emerge. Steve Jobs encouraged creativity throughout Apple's culture by reinforcing debate when discussing new ideas and removing passive-aggressive behaviors. Dealing with conflict head-on and embracing the tension spurs new ideas and different angles and reduces risks.[50]

Manager's Checklist

☐   Managers need to know the basic elements of creativity and its likely causes.

☐   You should also have a clear understanding of how creativity is valued and fostered in your organization.

9-7 TYPES OF WORKPLACE BEHAVIOR

Now that we have looked closely at how individual differences can influence behavior in organizations, let's turn our attention to what we actually mean by workplace behavior. Workplace behavior is a pattern of action by the members of an organization that directly or indirectly influences organizational effectiveness. Important workplace behaviors include performance and productivity, absenteeism and turnover, and organizational citizenship. Unfortunately, a variety of dysfunctional behaviors can also occur in organizations.

9-7a Performance Behaviors

Performance behaviors are the total set of work-related behaviors that the organization expects the person to display. Therefore, they are essentially derived from the psychological contract. For some jobs, performance behaviors can be narrowly defined and easily measured.

workplace behavior
A pattern of action by the members of an organization that directly or indirectly influences organizational effectiveness

performance behaviors
The total set of work-related behaviors that the organization expects the person to display

For example, an assembly-line worker who sits by a moving conveyor and attaches parts to a product as it passes by has relatively few performance behaviors. He or she is expected to remain at the workstation and correctly attach the parts. Performance can often be assessed quantitatively by counting the percentage of parts correctly attached.

For many other jobs, however, performance behaviors are more diverse and much more difficult to assess. For example, consider the case of a research and development scientist at Merck. The scientist works in a lab trying to find new scientific breakthroughs that have commercial potential. The scientist must apply knowledge learned in graduate school with experience gained from previous research. Intuition and creativity are also important elements. And the desired breakthrough may take months or even years to accomplish. As we discussed in Chapter 13, organizations rely on a number of different methods for evaluating performance. The key, of course, is to match the evaluation mechanism with the job being performed.

9-7b Withdrawal Behaviors

Another important type of work-related behavior is that which results in withdrawal-absenteeism and turnover. Absenteeism occurs when a person does not show up for work. The cause may be legitimate (illness, jury duty, death in the family, and so forth) or feigned (reported as legitimate but actually just an excuse to stay home). When an employee is absent, her or his work does not get done at all, or a substitute must be hired to do it. In either case, the quantity or quality of actual output is likely to suffer. Obviously, some absenteeism is expected. The key goal of organizations is to minimize feigned absenteeism and to reduce legitimate absences as much as possible. High absenteeism may be a symptom of other problems as well, such as job dissatisfaction and low morale.

Turnover occurs when people quit their jobs. An organization usually incurs costs in replacing individuals who have quit, but if turnover involves especially productive people, it is even more costly. Turnover seems to result from a number of factors, including aspects of the job, the organization, the individual, the labor market, and family influences. In general, a poor person–job fit is also a likely cause of turnover.[51] When unemployment is high, this tends to reduce employee-driven turnover, given that fewer jobs are available. But when unemployment is low (and there are many open jobs), turnover may naturally increase as people seek better opportunities, higher pay, and so forth.

Efforts to directly manage turnover are often fraught with difficulty, even in organizations that concentrate on rewarding good performers. Of course, some turnover is inevitable, and in some cases it may even be desirable. For example, if the organization is trying to cut costs by reducing its staff, having people voluntarily choose to leave is preferable to having to terminate their jobs. And if the people who choose to leave are low performers or express high levels of job dissatisfaction, the organization may also benefit from turnover.

9-7c Organizational Citizenship

Organizational citizenship is the behavior of individuals that makes a positive overall contribution to the organization.[52] Consider, for example, an employee who does work that is acceptable in terms of both quantity and quality. However, she refuses to work beyond precise hours, will not help newcomers learn the ropes and is generally unwilling to make any contribution to the organization beyond the strict performance of her job. Although this person may be seen as a good performer, she is not likely to be seen as a good organizational citizen.

Another employee may exhibit a comparable level of performance. In addition, however, he will always work late or come in early when he needs to, will take time to help newcomers learn their way around, and is perceived as being helpful and committed to the organization's success. Although his level of performance may be seen as equal to that of the first worker, he is also likely to be seen as a better organizational citizen.

The determinant of organizational citizenship behaviors is likely to be a complex mosaic of individual, social, and organizational variables. For example, the personality, attitudes, and needs of the individual will have to be consistent with citizenship behaviors. Similarly, the social context in which the person works, or the work group, will need to facilitate and

absenteeism
When a person does not show up for work

turnover
When people quit their jobs

organizational citizenship
The behavior of individuals that makes a positive overall contribution to the organization

promote such behaviors (we discuss group dynamics in Chapter 18). And the organization itself, especially its culture, must be capable of promoting, recognizing, and rewarding these types of behaviors if they are to be maintained. Research suggests that organizational citizenship may play an important role in organizational effectiveness.[53]

9-7d Dysfunctional Behaviors

dysfunctional behaviors
Those that detract from, rather than contribute to, organizational performance

Some work-related behaviors, however, are dysfunctional in nature. Dysfunctional behaviors are those that detract from, rather than contribute to, organizational performance.[54] Two of the more common ones, absenteeism and turnover, have already been discussed. But other forms of dysfunctional behavior may be even more costly for an organization. Theft and sabotage, for example, result in direct financial costs for an organization. Sexual and racial harassment also cost an organization, both indirectly (by lowering morale, producing fear, and driving off valuable employees) and directly (through financial liability if the organization responds inappropriately). So, too, can politicized behavior, intentionally misleading others in the organization, spreading malicious rumors, and similar activities. Incivility and rudeness can result in conflict and damage to morale and the organization's culture.[55]

Workplace violence is also a growing concern. Violence by disgruntled workers or former workers results in dozens of deaths and hundreds of injuries each year.[56] The factors that contribute to workplace violence—not to mention the factors involved in increases and decreases—are difficult to pin down. However, many factors appear to contribute to potential violent behavior, including psychological disorders, a feeling of being disrespected by the organization, and a sense of hopelessness.

 **Manager's Checklist**

☐ Managers need to be able to distinguish between performance behaviors, withdrawal behaviors, organizational citizenship, and dysfunctional behaviors.

☐ You should be able to candidly assess your own performance behaviors, withdrawal behaviors, organizational citizenship, and dysfunctional behaviors.

SUMMARY OF LEARNING OUTCOMES AND KEY POINTS

9-1. Explain the nature of the individual–organization relationship.

- A basic framework that can be used to facilitate this understanding is the psychological contract—the set of expectations held by people with respect to what they will contribute to the organization and what they expect to get in return.

- Organizations strive to achieve an optimal person–job fit, but this process is complicated by the existence of individual differences.

9-2. Describe how personality and personality attributes affect behavior in organizations.

- Personality is the relatively stable set of psychological and behavioral attributes that distinguish one person from another.

- The "Big Five" personality traits are:
  - Agreeableness
  - Conscientiousness

  - Neuroticism
  - Extraversion
  - Openness

- The Myers-Briggs framework can also be a useful mechanism for understanding personality.

- Other important traits are:
  - Locus of control
  - Self-efficacy
  - Authoritarianism
  - Machiavellianism
  - Self-esteem
  - Risk propensity

- Emotional intelligence, a fairly new concept, may provide additional insights into personality.

9-3. Discuss individual attitudes in organizations and how they affect behavior.

- Attitudes are based on emotion, knowledge, and intended behavior.

- Whereas personality is relatively stable, some attitudes can be formed and changed easily. Others are more constant.
- Job satisfaction or dissatisfaction, organizational commitment, and organizational engagement are important work-related attitudes.

9-4. Describe basic perceptual processes and the role of attributions in organizations.

- Perception is the set of processes by which a person becomes aware of and interprets information about the environment.
- Basic perceptual processes include selective perception and stereotyping.
- Perception and attribution are also closely related.

9-5. Discuss the causes and consequences of stress and how it can be managed.

- Stress is a person's response to a strong stimulus.
- The general adaptation syndrome outlines the basic stress process.
- Stress can be caused by task, physical, role, and interpersonal demands.
- Consequences of stress include organizational and individual outcomes as well as burnout.
- Several things can be done to manage stress.

9-6. Describe creativity and its role in organizations.

- Creativity is the capacity to generate new ideas.
- Creative people tend to have certain profiles of background experiences, personal traits, and cognitive abilities.
- The creative process itself includes preparation, incubation, insight, and verification.

9-7. Explain how workplace behaviors can directly or indirectly influence organizational effectiveness.

- Workplace behavior is a pattern of action by the members of an organization that directly or indirectly influences organizational effectiveness.
- Performance behaviors are the set of work-related behaviors that the organization expects the person to display to fulfill the psychological contract.
- Basic withdrawal behaviors are absenteeism and turnover.
- Organizational citizenship refers to behavior that makes a positive overall contribution to the organization.
- Dysfunctional behaviors can be very harmful to an organization.

DISCUSSION QUESTIONS

Questions for Review

1. What is a psychological contract? List the things that might be included in individual contributions. List the things that might be included in organizational inducements.
2. Describe the three components of attitudes and tell how the components are related. What is cognitive dissonance? How do individuals resolve cognitive dissonance?
3. Identify and discuss the steps in the creative process. What can an organization do to increase employees' creativity?
4. Identify and describe several important workplace behaviors.

Questions for Analysis

1. Organizations often use personality tests to screen job applicants. What are the advantages and disadvantages of this approach? What can managers do to avoid some of the potential pitfalls?

2. As a manager, how can you tell that an employee is experiencing job satisfaction? How can you tell that employees are highly committed to the organization? If a worker is not satisfied, what can a manager do to improve satisfaction? What can a manager do to improve organizational commitment and engagement?
3. Managers cannot pay equal attention to every piece of information, so selective perception is a fact of life. How does selective perception help managers? How does it create difficulties for them? How can managers increase their "good" selective perception and decrease the "bad"?

Questions for Application

1. Write the psychological contract you have in this class. In other words, what do you contribute, and what inducements are available? Ask your professor to tell the class about the psychological contract that he or she intended to establish with the students in your class. How does the professor's intended contract compare with the one you wrote? If there are differences, why

do you think the differences exist? Share your ideas with the class.

2. Assume that you are going to hire three new employees for the department store you manage. One will sell shoes, one will manage the toy department, and one will work in the stockroom. Identify the basic characteristics you want in each of the people to achieve a good person–job fit.

3. Did you feel increased stress during the 2020 COVID-19 pandemic? Why? How did you cope with it? Are you still using any of those stress management methods today?

BUILDING EFFECTIVE INTERPERSONAL SKILLS

Exercise Overview

Interpersonal skills refer to the ability to communicate with, understand, and motivate individuals and groups. This exercise introduces you to a widely used tool for personality assessment and shows how an understanding of personality can be of use in developing effective interpersonal relationships within organizations.

Exercise Background

Of the many different ways of interpreting personality, the widely used Myers-Briggs Type Indicator categorizes individual personality types along four dimensions:

1. *Extraversion (E) versus Introversion (I).* Extraverts get their energy from being around other people, whereas introverts are worn out by others and need solitude to recharge their energy.
2. *Sensing (S) versus Intuition (N).* The sensing type prefers concrete things, whereas the intuitivist prefers abstract concepts.
3. *Thinking (T) versus Feeling (F).* Thinking individuals base their decisions more on logic and reason, whereas feeling individuals base their decisions more on feelings and emotions.
4. *Judging (J) versus Perceiving (P).* Judging types enjoy completion or being finished, whereas perceiving types enjoy process and open-ended situations.

Using the Myers-Briggs Type Indicator, researchers use survey answers to classify individuals into 16 personality types—all the possible combinations of the four Myers-Briggs dimensions. The resulting personality type is then expressed as a four-character code, such as *ESTP* for *Extravert-Sensing-Thinking-Perceiving.* These four-character codes are then used to describe an individual's preferred way of interacting with others.

Exercise Task

1. Use a Myers-Briggs assessment form to gain insights into your own personality type. You can find a form at *https://keirsey.com/temperament-overview/*, a website that also contains additional information about personality type. This assessment is not a direct measure of Myers-Briggs personality types but does offer measures on similar categories. (*Note:* There are no fees for taking the Temperament Sorter, nor must you agree to receive email.)

2. When you've determined the four-letter code for your personality type, visit the website of the Myers Briggs Foundation at *https://www.myersbriggs.org/my-mbti-personality-type/mbti-basics/the-16-mbti-types.htm?bhcp=1*. This will help explain how your personality type affects not only your preferred style of working but your leadership style as well.

3. Conclude by responding to the following questions:

   - How easy is it to measure personality?
   - Do you feel that the online test accurately assessed your personality?
   - Why or why not? Share your assessment results and your responses with the class.

BUILDING EFFECTIVE TIME-MANAGEMENT SKILLS

Exercise Overview

Time-management skills refer to the ability to prioritize tasks, to work efficiently, and to delegate appropriately. Among other reasons, they're important because poor time-management skills may result in stress. This exercise shows you how effective time-management skills can help reduce stress.

Exercise Background

List several of the major events or expectations that tend to be stressful for you. Common stressors include school (classes, exams), work (finances, schedules), and personal circumstances (friends, romance, family). Try to be as specific as possible and try to identify at least 10 different stressors.

Exercise Task

Using your list, do each of the following:

1. Evaluate the extent to which poor time-management skills on your part play a role in the way each stressor affects you. Do exams cause stress, for example, because you tend to put off studying?

2. For each stressor that's affected by your time-management habits, develop a strategy for using your time more efficiently.

3. Note the interrelationships among different kinds of stressors to see if they revolve around time-related problems. For example, financial pressures may cause you to work, and work may interfere with school. Can you manage any of these interrelationships more effectively by managing your time more effectively?

4. How do you typically manage the stress in your life? Can you manage stress in a more time-effective manner?

SKILL-BUILDING PERSONAL ASSESSMENT

Understanding Your Personality

This self-assessment helps you develop a better understanding of your own personality. It will also give you an appreciation of the complexities involved in trying to measure personality traits.

Introduction: Personality traits represent some of the most fundamental individual differences in organizations. Research has identified literally thousands of personality traits and dimensions that differentiate one person from another. But, in recent years, researchers have identified five fundamental personality traits that are especially relevant to organizations. Because these five traits are so important and because they are currently the subject of so much attention, they are now commonly referred to as the "Big Five" personality traits.

Instructions: The following survey consists of 15 statements. Answer each statement as candidly as possible by circling the best response. After completing the survey, score your responses.

Big Five Personality Assessment

1. How likely are you to make sure other people are happy and comfortable?

Very Likely	Moderately Likely	Neither Likely Nor Unlikely	Moderately Unlikely	Very Unlikely
5	4	3	2	1

2. How likely are you to prepare for things in advance?

Very Likely	Moderately Likely	Neither Likely Nor Unlikely	Moderately Unlikely	Very Unlikely
5	4	3	2	1

3. How likely are you to feel blue or depressed for no real reason?

Very Likely	Moderately Likely	Neither Likely Nor Unlikely	Moderately Unlikely	Very Unlikely
5	4	3	2	1

4. How likely are you to start a conversation with a stranger?

Very Likely	Moderately Likely	Neither Likely Nor Unlikely	Moderately Unlikely	Very Unlikely
5	4	3	2	1

5. How likely are you to use difficult or unusual words?

Very Likely	Moderately Likely	Neither Likely Nor Unlikely	Moderately Unlikely	Very Unlikely
5	4	3	2	1

6. How likely are you to forgive someone for a mistake they have made?

Very Likely	Moderately Likely	Neither Likely Nor Unlikely	Moderately Unlikely	Very Unlikely
5	4	3	2	1

7 How likely are you to set a schedule and then keep to that schedule?

Very Likely	Moderately Likely	Neither Likely Nor Unlikely	Moderately Unlikely	Very Unlikely
5	4	3	2	1

(Continued)

8. How likely are you to feel insecure about something?

Very Likely	Moderately Likely	Neither Likely Nor Unlikely	Moderately Unlikely	Very Unlikely
5	4	3	2	1

9. How likely are you to have many different friends at the same time?

Very Likely	Moderately Likely	Neither Likely Nor Unlikely	Moderately Unlikely	Very Unlikely
5	4	3	2	1

10. How likely are you to change your mind about something when you learn more about it?

Very Likely	Moderately Likely	Neither Likely Nor Unlikely	Moderately Unlikely	Very Unlikely
5	4	3	2	1

11. How likely are you to go along with what other people want to do?

Very Likely	Moderately Likely	Neither Likely Nor Unlikely	Moderately Unlikely	Very Unlikely
5	4	3	2	1

12. How likely are you to make a "to-do" list and then mark everything off as you get things done?

Very Likely	Moderately Likely	Neither Likely Nor Unlikely	Moderately Unlikely	Very Unlikely
5	4	3	2	1

13. How likely are you to feel stressed or worried?

Very Likely	Moderately Likely	Neither Likely Nor Unlikely	Moderately Unlikely	Very Unlikely
5	4	3	2	1

14. How likely are you to plan parties or other social events?

Very Likely	Moderately Likely	Neither Likely Nor Unlikely	Moderately	Very Unlikely
5	4	3	2	1

15. How likely are you to listen carefully when other people express their opinions?

Very Likely	Moderately Likely	Neither Likely Nor Unlikely	Moderately Unlikely	Very Unlikely
5	4	3	2	1

Scoring: To score your self-assessment add up the three numbers you circled for the following questions.

Q 1, 6, 11 = Your level of Agreeableness

Q 2, 7, 12 = Your level of Conscientiousness

Q 3, 8, 13 = Your level of Neuroticism

Q 4, 9, 14 = Your level of Extraversion

Q 5, 10, 15 = Your level of Openness

Interpretation: For each of the five traits, a score of 3, 4, 5, or 6 should be considered low, a score of 7, 8, 9, 10, or 11 is moderate, and a score of 12, 13, 14, 05 15 is high. Using your scores, now address the discussion questions that follow. (Note: This instrument is a brief variation of several other much longer ones. Your scores actually only reflect general tendencies. If you want a more valid and precise assessment, there are several online instruments that are available at no charge. You can locate these by searching for "big five measures" or similar phrases.)

Discussion Questions

1. How accurately or inaccurately do you think this assessment is describing your personality as you believe it to be?

2. Based on the results of this assessment, what kind of job(s) might you want to seek when you graduate?

3. Do you think it's possible to change one or more of your traits? If so, how might you try to do so?

MANAGEMENT AT WORK

Can't Get No Job Satisfaction?

"For the most part, the employer contract is dead."

—Rebecca Ray, Executive VP of Knowledge Organization, The Conference Board

News flash: American workers aren't happy with rec-room ping-pong tables and free massages. Or, to be a little more precise: Such perks aren't enough to make them satisfied with their jobs. According to Gallup's most recent State of the American Workplace Report, a mere 34 percent of U.S. workers are "engaged" in their work. That's up from 30 percent from 2018, but it doesn't amount to much, especially when you consider that more than half of all workers (52 percent) show up every morning but have very little interest in what they do all day. What's worse, the 13 percent that's left are *actively disengaged*—which means, says Gallup CEO Jim Clifton, that "they roam the halls spreading discontent." According to the report, those actively disengaged employees cost the U.S. economy $550 billion a year in lost productivity.

Admittedly, younger workers tend to find workplace perks, such as Google's nap pods and onsite roller-hockey rink, more attractive than their older counterparts. "They're often looking for things they can brag about to their peers," explains Bob Nelson, author of *1,501 Ways to Reward Employees*. But if the boss is a jerk or tasks aren't stimulating, cautions Nelson, "perks aren't going to fix it. You may keep [younger workers] for a while, but at some point, they're going to leave."

Nelson's opinion would seem to be confirmed by another major survey. According to The Conference Board's most recent report on job satisfaction, while satisfaction among workers age 25–34 came in at 50.5 percent, only 37.8 percent of workers under age 25 were satisfied with their jobs—down from 46 percent in 2012 and about 60 percent 20 years earlier. Baby Boomers, observes The Conference Board's Linda Barrington, "will compose a quarter of the U.S. workforce [by 2024], and since 1987 we've watched them increasingly losing faith in the workplace." Nelson reports that younger workers tend to leave jobs after about a year, compared to 4.4 years for older employees, and John Gibbons, another Conference Board researcher, notes that 22 percent of all respondents to the survey don't expect to be in their current jobs for more than a year. "These data," he concludes, "throw up a red flag because widespread job dissatisfaction" and the resulting turnover "can impact enterprise-level success." Recent studies indicate, for example, that it can cost an employer from 16 percent to 213 percent of average annual salary to replace every employee who leaves a company.

How do workers become dissatisfied, and what happens when they do? Danielle Lee Novack of Penn State University has created an instructive scenario that we've simplified to fit the needs of our case:

> *A woman named Megan has coordinated the onstage portions of dance competitions for three years. From January through June, Megan has to travel to different competition venues, including three weekends per month. This demanding half year is offset by the other six-month period, when her schedule is much more relaxed. Because she likes what she does, she's willing to deal with the unusual schedule, especially as her manager has assured her that, should something important come up on a weekend, she'll try to accommodate Megan. Her manager has recognized her excellent work in each of her three years, and Megan is satisfied with her job responsibilities, coworkers, and salary.*
>
> *Megan learns in December that her best friend is getting married in June and asks her boss for the wedding weekend off. Despite her promises, her manager refuses to accommodate Megan. Needless to say, Megan is frustrated. As it happens, she's also bothered by her manager's tendency to micromanage subordinates and feels that she has no freedom to make any key decisions on her own. Besides, everything has to be approved before Megan can act on any of her own initiatives—a situation that's already cost her two promotional partnerships that she'd worked personally to develop. Not only did she receive no recognition for her efforts, but she missed out on two bonuses. Finally, because the company is small and Megan already works directly under a high-ranking manager, she feels that there's no chance for her to advance or take on new responsibilities in the future.*
>
> *Before long, Megan is resentful about giving up weekends, about her manager's habit of controlling every aspect of every project, and about the feeling that there's little point in trying to excel if she's merely going to be doing the same thing over and over again. In short, Megan is dissatisfied with her job, and she's thinking about finding another one.*

A review of both surveys shows that the sources of Megan's dissatisfaction are pretty much the same as those cited by most dissatisfied American workers. At first glance, for example, some people may find it surprising that her pay doesn't figure into Megan's current discontent, but The Conference Board survey found that employees are slightly happier with pay scales than they have been in the past.

Not everybody, however, is equally "satisfied" with his or her income. Not surprisingly, The Conference Board says that 64 percent of people earning more than $125,000 are satisfied with their jobs, as are 57.6 percent of those with incomes between $75,000 and $100,000. However, only 24.4 percent of those earning under $15,000 could say the same thing. In the shrinking middle—where Megan no doubt falls—only 32 percent of those making $15,000–35,000 and 45 percent of those making $35,000–75,000 are satisfied.

Danielle Kurtzleben, however, a former business and economics reporter for *U.S. News and World Report*, observes a contradiction between two survey findings: (1) that "growth in employee compensation has fallen off sharply since the 1980s and 1990s"; and (2) that workers are "not much less satisfied today with their wages than they were 25 years ago." Workers, she cautions, may be more satisfied with *wages* than with total *compensation*, noting that the deepest levels of dissatisfaction between 1987 and 2013 is in such compensation-related areas as health coverage and sick-leave policies.

In fact, worker satisfaction with compensation plans are at a ten-year low—primarily because such compensation benefits as pension, 401(k), and health plans are fast disappearing. "For the most part," says The Conference Board's Rebecca Ray, "the employer contract is dead." It's a serious matter, she adds, because such benefits have long served to cement long-term employer–employee relationships.

So, according to the Gallup and Conference Board reports, what aspects of their jobs are most workers most dissatisfied with? As it happens, the two areas that received the lowest scores are consistent, whether directly or indirectly, with the sources of Megan's dissatisfaction: According to The Conference Board, only 23.8 percent of workers are satisfied with their employers' promotion policies and only 24.2 percent with their bonus plans. Conversely, the most important drivers of satisfaction include growth potential, recognition, and satisfaction with one's supervisor. It may also be interesting to note that although such areas as promotion policies and bonus plans are typically more important to men, women are significantly less satisfied than men on both counts.

At bottom, the results of both surveys are somewhat paradoxical—and perhaps even misleading. The apparent good news is that, at 47.7 percent, overall job satisfaction in 2013 was up from 47.3 percent in 2012. Obviously that's very little, and the bad news is that both figures are meaningful only in the context of a 42.6 percent level in 2010—the lowest level ever. The worse news is that recent levels of job satisfaction represent a significant drop from 61.1 percent in 1987, the first year in which The Conference Board began tracking the phenomenon.[57]

Case Questions

1. What about you? If you're employed, are you (relatively) satisfied or dissatisfied with your job? If you're not working (or haven't yet held down a job), focus on the areas in which you're satisfied or dissatisfied with what you *are* doing (e.g., going to school).

2. Next is a table listing 22 factors in job satisfaction *in order of importance* to the U.S. workers surveyed by The Conference Board. Create your own list of factors *in order of their importance to you at this stage of your life*. Be prepared to discuss the differences between your list and (1) the list below and (2) the lists drawn up by various classmates.

1. Growth potential	11. Quality of equipment
2. Communication channels	12. Wages
3. Recognition	13. Training
4. Performance reviews	14. People at work
5. Interest in work	15. Family leave
6. Workload	16. Flextime
7. Work/life balance	17. Bonus
8. Supervisor	18. Sick days
9. Physical environment	19. Vacation
10. Promotion policy	20. Pension
	21. Health coverage
	22. Commute

3. What about Megan? First, draw up a list of job-dissatisfaction factors for Megan. Second, regard the following as applicable to Megan's situation:

- She likes the type of work she does and has good relationships with coworkers.
- More than a few of her coworkers are also frustrated by the company's tight supervision and demanding work schedule.
- She is a cheerful and positive person.
- She performs well and gets positive feedback because she looks for solutions to problems rather than dwelling on the negative aspects of things.

What do you think Megan should do? If you think that she should find another job, be prepared to explain why you think it's the best move. If you think that she should try to resolve her frustrations before looking for another job, explain the points that she should try to get across in conversations with her boss.

Gad Levanon, an economist who coauthored The Conference Board report, makes this observation: "Based on macro trends worker satisfaction should be on the rise. But job dissatisfaction may remain entrenched until we see improvements in worker compensation, which has grown abysmally in recent years despite historically high corporate profits." Levanon is expressing an opinion and making a related prediction. Explain his opinion and his prediction in your own words. Do you agree or disagree with this opinion and prediction? In particular, do you expect things to get better economically? Whether you answer yes or no, how do you see your prospects for getting a job that you're satisfied with?

Engaging with the Company Garbage

1. What about you? *Millennials* and *Generation Y* refer to the same thing—generally speaking, people born between the early 1980s and early 2000s. Does this range of birth years include you? Whether it does or doesn't, how would you characterize your personal attitude toward *sustainability*, especially in the workplace? How does your attitude toward sustainability reflect your attitudes toward such matters as the country's economic future and your own?

2. Hunter Lovins defines *employee engagement* as "the goal of creating supportive, collaborative, and rewarding work environments." Compare her understanding of employee engagement with the principle of *organizational commitment* as it's characterized in the text. In what sense is developing employee engagement intended to go a step beyond fostering organizational commitment in workplace attitudes?

   Lovins also talks about *employee integration*, by which she means a company's goal of "integrating its sustainability strategies into employee job descriptions and employees' everyday jobs." In your opinion, what sort of policies and practices would be important in achieving employee integration over and above employee engagement?

3. "Again, what about you? Consider the definition of *employee engagement* in Question 2. Do you think that you'd be responsive to an employer's efforts to engage you in your job? What kind of values—in terms of both company objectives and employee rewards—would be most likely to engage you? Where would *sustainability* rank among those values? Or do you think that other factors would probably weigh more heavily in your attitude toward your job? What might they be?

4. Some experts report that *employee engagement* "has become the new Holy Grail for many organizations" or that it "has long been the Holy Grail for creating thriving and successful organizations." Robert A. Cooke, however, believes that achieving and optimizing employee engagement is more complicated than it may seem. Cooke, who's CEO of Human Synergistics International, a consultancy specializing in organizational culture and leadership and group and individual behavior, charges that the human capital consulting industry continues to sell the idea that a few sips from the Holy Grail of employee engagement will magically transform organizations and heal whatever ails them. While this is a good start, companies should go beyond this and get to the root of their organizational ills by using a true organizational culture survey to define, activate, and reinforce the behaviors that drive the right kind of engagement and optimize organizational performance. Review our discussion of *organization culture* in Chapter 2. Discuss the pros and cons of Cooke's statement that "truly understanding how to optimize performance in your organization requires understanding your culture."

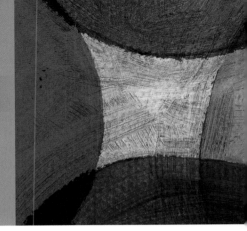

CHAPTER 10

Managing Employee Motivation and Performance

Learning Outcomes

After studying this chapter, you should be able to:

10-1 Discuss the nature of motivation, including its importance and historical perspectives.

10-2 Describe the major *content* perspectives on motivation.

10-3 Describe the major *process* perspectives on motivation.

10-4 Describe *reinforcement* perspectives on motivation.

10-5 Discuss popular motivational strategies.

10-6 Describe the role of organizational reward systems in motivation.

As the business world gets increasingly complex, so too are the challenges in motivating people to perform in various ways. For example, just a few years ago no one would have predicted the complications of retaining talented employees when business was booming and unemployment was extremely low, which was the case in 2019, followed by the challenges of motivating people during a global pandemic and resulting economic collapse as managers had to do in 2020. Regardless of the context, though, much of what managers today deal with is motivating, engaging, and retaining their most valued employees, the subject of this chapter. We first examine the nature of employee motivation and then explore major perspectives on motivation. Newly emerging approaches to motivating employees are then discussed. We conclude with a description of rewards and their role in motivation. Let's start with a discussion of a firm that does a great job keeping its employees motivated and engaged.

Management in Action

What Makes SAS a Great Place to Work?

"95 percent of our assets drive out of the gate every evening"

—James Goodnight, CEO of SAS

SAS is a fixture among *Fortune*'s annual list of the "100 Best Places to Work in America." It's also among the largest privately held software development companies in the world. And it's no surprise that the firm is in both groups. SAS and its senior leadership team consistently go to unusual lengths to make sure they attract a great workforce and then motivate those employees to work hard and in the best interests of the company while also maintaining a good work–life balance.

SAS (originally called Statistical Analysis System) was formed in 1966 as a consortium of eight universities. Its purpose was to develop and market software that researchers could use to analyze data in an efficient, reliable, and accessible manner. At the time, North Carolina State University (NCSU) had the most powerful mainframe computer among the partners and was designated as the consortium host; NCSU professors Jim Goodnight and Jim Barr were appointed as project leads. The firm's products quickly started to generate revenue and its employees saw significant business opportunities. Within just a few years, operations outgrew the offices at NCSU so the core team moved operations across the street to form SAS Institute, Inc. and became an independent privately owned business. Goodnight assumed the role of CEO while Barr focused on new product development.

By 1978, SAS had 21 employees and a growing customer base. From the very beginning the founders recognized the importance of employee recognition. For example, when the firm hit its first 100 customers Jim Goodnight bought pizza for all of the firm's employees and organized a Friday afternoon celebration. Everyone was so appreciative that he continued that practice for every 100 new customers. During this early stage of growth Goodnight also began placing bowls of M&Ms around the office in case anyone wanted a quick treat.

In 1980, the headquarters moved from Raleigh to Cary, North Carolina, with bowls of free M&M's and breakfast goodies to welcome employees to the new location. In keeping with their growing employee-centric practices, SAS opened a corporate-sponsored daycare at the new headquarters office in 1981. Corporate daycare was practically unheard of at the time, but SAS did not stop there. They would later add a recreation and fitness center, health care center, and an on-site gourmet café. Beyond these tangible benefits, though, SAS also developed a reputation for treating its employees fairly. Collectively, all of these things resulted in the firm winning its first "Best Places to Work" award.

With innovative products and a loyal and motivated workforce, SAS continued to grow and prosper. The new headquarters in Cary expanded from one building with offices for 50 employees to 18 buildings, and by the end of 1989, the company had nearly 1,500 employees worldwide. By the end of the 1990s, the workforce for SAS grew to over 7,000 employees worldwide supporting 3 million users in 120 countries. The firm had also established offices on every continent, in every major United States city, and most international business centers.

The SAS operation in Australia was the first company unit outside of the United States recognized as a "Best Place to Work" in 1999, clearly suggesting that SAS's culture was capable of making cross-country moves. The "Best Place to Work" honors continued to roll in from places such as the United Kingdom, Mexico, Portugal, Finland, China, the Netherlands, Belgium, Norway, and Sweden. Aside from keeping employee satisfaction and engagement at the forefront, the company also prioritized business expansion and celebrated 17 years of double-digit growth in revenue from 1976 until 1999. From that time on, growth continued, albeit at a slower pace. By the early 2000s, SAS was well established as a "Best Place to Work" regardless of location. Indeed, its consistent recognition earned the company a place as one of the inaugural 22 members of the "Best Places to Work Hall of Fame" introduced by *Fortune* in 2005.

During the onset of the 2008–2009 recession, employees at SAS were understandably nervous about potential layoffs and reductions in the workforce. The firm's competitors were already announcing massive layoffs, but CEO Jim Goodnight held a global webcast to announce that none of SAS's 13,000 employees would lose their jobs. Goodnight was effectively putting the firm's track record of annual profit increases on the line. But by keeping an eye on other areas for cost reductions, the risk paid off and the company still had a year of growth in 2009.

Because they are paid an equitable salary, have great benefits, and are respected and valued by SAS, the firm's employees are incredibly loyal to the company and highly motivated to continue to contribute. Beyond the recognition and continual growth, for example, SAS has annual turnover that is a fraction of the turnover experienced by other software development companies—SAS's average turnover is 2–3 percent while the industry average is 22 percent (and most of the turnover at SAS is attributable to retirements rather than people leaving for other jobs).

SAS does not pay high salaries, with compensation only slightly above average. However, it does offer a generous profit-sharing program. To help minimize the stress and pressures coming from life outside work, the company also focuses on employee health and well-being and providing resources for employees to thrive. They emphasize employees having a work–life balance because they believe this will "further encourage employee creativity." Employees and their families have free access to amenities such as work–life offices where eight social workers can assist with drawing up wills, arranging elder care, providing counseling on work–life balance, and so forth; an on-site health clinic staffed by 57 doctors, nurses, physical therapists, nutritionists, and psychotherapists; and an on-site pharmacy. SAS also offers the services of a company concierge to help employees plan special family events.

There is a state-of-the-art gymnasium on the SAS campus featuring a weight room, cardiovascular equipment, soccer and softball fields, tennis courts, tracks, an aquatic center with a 75-foot pool, an aerobics studio, indoor basketball and racquetball, and pool tables. They also have a hair salon, modern collaborative workspaces, subsidized cafeterias, and art and sculptures decorating the building. The facilities also have common work areas and breakrooms on every floor, routinely filled with snacks, treats, M&Ms, and built-in soda fountains. Finally, SAS also provides generous time off and flexibility options because the company trusts employees to set their own hours as needed to get their work done. Perhaps not surprisingly, then, employees at SAS are uniformly motivated and engaged to do their best every day.[1]

10-1 THE NATURE OF MOTIVATION

motivation
The set of forces that cause people to behave in certain ways

Motivation is the set of forces that cause people to behave in certain ways.[2] On any given day, for instance, an employee may choose to work as hard as possible at a job, work at a moderate pace to meet performance expectations, do just enough to avoid a reprimand, or do as little as possible. The goal for the manager is to maximize the likelihood of the first behavior and minimize the likelihood of the last. This goal becomes all the more important when we understand how important motivation is in the workplace.

10-1a The Importance of Employee Motivation in the Workplace

Individual performance is generally determined by three things: motivation (the desire to do the job), ability (the capability to do the job), and work environment (the resources needed to do the job). If an employee lacks ability, the manager can provide training or replace the worker. If there is a resource problem, the manager can correct it. But if motivation is the problem, the task for the manager is more challenging.[3] Individual behavior is a complex phenomenon (as we saw in our last chapter), and the manager may be hard pressed to figure out the precise nature of the problem and how to solve it. Thus, motivation is important because of its significance as a determinant of performance and because of its intangible nature.[4]

The motivation framework in Figure 10.1 is a good starting point for understanding how motivated behavior occurs. The motivation process begins with a need deficiency. For example, when a worker feels that she is underpaid, she experiences a need for more income. In response, the worker searches for ways to satisfy the need, such as working harder to try

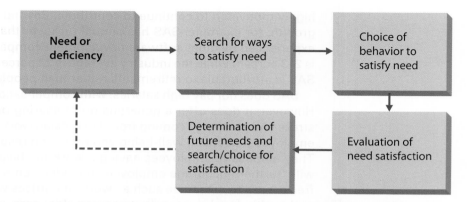

The Motivation Framework

The motivation process progresses through a series of discrete steps. Content, process, and reinforcement perspectives on motivation address different parts of this process.

Frederick Taylor, an early management pioneer, advocated an incentive pay system that would pay workers a set amount of money for each unit of output they produced. One of his earliest projects was studying the craft of brick laying, developing the most efficient steps to perform this job, teaching workers his method, and then paying them based on the number of bricks they laid each hour.

to earn a raise or seeking a new job. Next, she chooses an option to pursue. After carrying out the chosen option—working harder and putting in more hours for a reasonable period of time, for example—she then evaluates her success. If her hard work results in a pay raise, she probably feels good about things and will continue to work hard. But if her increased performance is not recognized and no raise is provided, she is likely to try another option.

10-1b Historical Perspectives on Motivation

To appreciate what we know about employee motivation, it is helpful to first review earlier approaches. The traditional, human relations, and human resource approaches have each shed partial (but incomplete) light on motivation.[5]

The Traditional Approach The traditional approach is best represented by the work of Frederick W. Taylor.[6] As noted in Chapter 2, Taylor advocated an incentive pay system. He believed that managers knew more about the jobs being performed than did workers, and he assumed that economic gain was the primary thing that motivated everyone. Other assumptions of the traditional approach were that work is inherently unpleasant for most people and that the money they earn is more important to employees than the nature of the job they are performing. Hence, people could be expected to perform any kind of job if they were paid enough. Although the role of money as a motivating factor cannot be dismissed, proponents of the traditional approach took too narrow a view of the role of monetary compensation and failed to consider other motivational factors.

The Human Relations Approach The human relations approach was also summarized in Chapter 2.[7] Human relations advocates emphasized the role of social processes in the workplace.

In contrast to the traditional approach, the human relations approach suggests that social processes are of paramount importance in employee motivation. Hence, these employees, who appear to like each other and enjoy working together, should presumably be motivated to perform at a high level.

Their basic assumptions were that employees want to feel useful and important, that employees have strong social needs, and that these needs are more important than money in motivating them. Advocates of the human relations approach advised managers to make workers feel important and allow them a minor degree of self-direction and self-control in carrying out routine activities. The illusion of involvement and importance was expected to satisfy workers' basic social needs and result in higher motivation to perform. For example, a manager might allow a work group to participate in making a decision even though he or she had already determined what the decision would be. The symbolic gesture of seeming to allow participation was expected to enhance motivation, even though no real participation took place.

The Human Resource Approach The human resource approach to motivation carries the concepts of needs and motivation one step further. Whereas human relations advocates believed that the illusion of contribution and participation would enhance motivation, the human resource view assumes that the contributions themselves are valuable to both individuals and organizations. It assumes that people want to contribute and are able to make genuine contributions. Management's task, then, is to encourage participation and to create a work environment that makes full use of the human resources available. This philosophy guides most contemporary thinking about employee motivation. At Ford, Apple, Texas Instruments, and HP, for example, work teams are used to solve a variety of problems and to make substantive contributions to the organization.

Manager's Checklist

☐ Managers need to appreciate the historical perspectives on employee motivation.

☐ You should also be familiar with the various parts of the motivational cycle.

10-2 CONTENT PERSPECTIVES ON MOTIVATION

content perspectives
Approach to motivation that tries to answer the question, What factor or factors motivate people?

Content perspectives on motivation deal with the first part of the motivation process—needs and need deficiencies. More specifically, content perspectives address this question: What factor or factors in the workplace motivate people? Labor leaders often argue that workers can be motivated by more pay, shorter working hours, and improved working conditions. Meanwhile, some experts suggest that motivation can be more effectively enhanced by providing employees with more autonomy and greater responsibility.[8] Both of these views represent content views of motivation. The former asserts that motivation is a function of pay, working hours, and working conditions; the latter suggests that autonomy and responsibility are the causes of motivation. Two widely known content perspectives on motivation are the needs hierarchy and the two-factor theory.

10-2a The Needs Hierarchy Approach

The needs hierarchy approach has been advanced by many theorists. Needs hierarchies assume that people have different needs that can be arranged in a hierarchy of importance. The two best known are Maslow's hierarchy of needs and the ERG theory.

"Happiness lies not in the mere possession of money; it lies in the joy of achievement, in the thrill of creative effort."

—Franklin D. Roosevelt, Former U.S. President[9]

Maslow's hierarchy of needs
Suggests that people must satisfy five groups of needs in order—physiological, security, belongingness, self-esteem, and self-actualization

Maslow's Hierarchy of Needs Abraham Maslow, a human relationist, argued that people are motivated to satisfy five need levels.[10] **Maslow's hierarchy of needs** is shown in Figure 10.2. At the bottom of the hierarchy are the *physiological needs*—things like food, sex, and air, which represent basic issues of survival and biological function. In organizations, these needs are generally satisfied by adequate wages and the work environment itself, which provides restrooms, adequate lighting, comfortable temperatures, and ventilation. Next are the *security needs* for a secure physical and emotional environment. Examples include the desire for housing and clothing and the need to be free from worry about money and job security. These needs can be satisfied in the workplace by job continuity (no layoffs), a grievance system (to protect against arbitrary supervisory actions), and an adequate insurance and retirement benefit package (for security against illness and provision of income in later life).

Belongingness needs relate to social processes. They include the need for love and affection and the need to be accepted by one's peers. These needs are satisfied for most people by family and community relationships outside of work and by friendships on the job. A manager can help satisfy these needs by allowing social interaction and by making employees feel like part of a team or work group.

Esteem needs actually comprise two different sets of needs: the need for a positive self-image and self-respect and the need for recognition and respect from others. A manager can help address these needs by providing a variety of extrinsic symbols of accomplishment, such as job titles, nice offices, and similar rewards, as appropriate. At a more intrinsic level, the manager can provide challenging job assignments and opportunities for the employee to feel a sense of accomplishment.

At the top of the hierarchy are the *self-actualization needs*. These involve realizing one's potential for continued growth and individual development. The self-actualization needs

FIGURE 10.2

Maslow's Hierarchy of Needs

Maslow's hierarchy suggests that human needs can be classified into five categories and that these categories can be arranged in a hierarchy of importance. A manager should understand that an employee may not be satisfied with only a salary and benefits; he or she may also need challenging job opportunities to experience self-growth and satisfaction.

Source: Adapted from Abraham H. Maslow, "A Theory of Human Motivation," *Psychology Review*, 1943, Vol. 50, pp. 370–396.

Jelena Zelen/Shutterstock.com

Abraham Maslow suggests that esteem needs play an important role in employee motivation. Esteem needs include the desire to be recognized and respected by others. One avenue for satisfying esteem needs for some individuals is a large and impressive office such as this one.

"I wanted to do something with my life where I felt I was contributing. Somehow, selling more tacos and margaritas than the week before wasn't."

—Cathey Gardner, Former Restaurant Manager, On her Decision to Become a Nurse[11]

ERG theory of motivation
Suggests that people's needs are grouped into three possibly overlapping categories— existence, relatedness, and growth

are perhaps the most difficult for a manager to address. In fact, it can be argued that these needs must be met entirely from within the individual. But a manager can help by promoting a culture wherein self-actualization is possible. For instance, a manager could give employees a chance to participate in making decisions about their work and the opportunity to learn new things.

Maslow suggests that the five need categories constitute a hierarchy. A person is motivated first and foremost to satisfy physiological needs. As long as these remain unsatisfied, the person is motivated to fulfill only them. When satisfaction of physiological needs is achieved, they cease to act as primary motivational factors, and the person moves "up" the hierarchy and becomes concerned with security needs. This process continues until the person reaches the self-actualization level. Maslow's concept of the needs hierarchy has a certain intuitive logic and has been accepted by many managers. But research has revealed certain shortcomings and defects in the theory. Some research has found that five levels of need are not always present and that the order of the levels is not always the same as postulated by Maslow.[12] In addition, people from different cultures are likely to have different need categories and hierarchies.

The ERG Theory In response to these and similar criticisms, an alternative hierarchy of needs, called the **ERG theory of motivation**, was developed.[13] This theory collapses the needs hierarchy developed by Maslow into three levels. *Existence needs* correspond to the physiological and security needs. *Relatedness needs* focus on how people relate to their social environment. In Maslow's hierarchy, these would encompass both the need to belong and the need to earn the esteem of others. *Growth needs*, the highest level in this schema, include the needs for self-esteem and self-actualization.

Although the ERG theory assumes that motivated behavior follows a hierarchy in somewhat the same fashion as suggested by Maslow, there are two important differences. First, the ERG theory suggests that more than one level of need can cause motivation at the same time. For example, it suggests that people can be motivated by a desire for money (existence), friendship (relatedness), and the opportunity to learn new skills (growth) all at once. Second, the ERG theory has what has been called a *frustration-regression* element. Thus, if needs remain unsatisfied, the person will become frustrated, regress to a lower level, and begin to pursue those things again. For example, a worker previously motivated by money (existence needs) may have just been awarded a pay raise sufficient to satisfy those needs. Suppose that he then tries to establish more friendships to satisfy relatedness needs. If for some reason he finds that it is impossible to become better friends with others in the workplace, he eventually gets frustrated and regresses to being motivated to earn even more money.

The basic premises of both Maslow's hierarchy of needs and the ERG theory were clearly illustrated by the events of 2019 and 2020. In 2019, the job market was robust, and many workers had relatively secure jobs with reasonable wages, benefits, job security, and viable professional networks. As a result, most were probably focused largely on trying to satisfy esteem and growth needs. However, as the impact of COVID-19 spread and the economy collapsed in 2020, many of these same workers feared losing their jobs, grew concerned about their health, and worried about their financial future. They also experienced a loss of social interaction due to various shelter-in-place and social-distancing requirements. As a result, esteem and growth probably became less important while physiological, security, and relatedness needs again became prominent.

10-2b The Two-Factor Theory

two-factor theory of motivation
Suggests that people's satisfaction and dissatisfaction are influenced by two independent sets of factors—motivation factors and hygiene factors

Another popular content perspective is the two-factor theory of motivation.[14] Frederick Herzberg developed his theory after interviewing 200 accountants and engineers. He asked them to recall occasions when they had been satisfied and motivated and occasions when they had been dissatisfied and unmotivated. Surprisingly, he found that different sets of factors were associated with satisfaction and with dissatisfaction—that is, a person might identify "low pay" as causing dissatisfaction but would not necessarily mention "high pay" as a cause of satisfaction. Instead, different kinds of factors—such as recognition or accomplishment—were cited as causing satisfaction and motivation.

This finding led Herzberg to conclude that the traditional view of job satisfaction was incomplete. That view implicitly assumed that satisfaction and dissatisfaction are at opposite ends of a single continuum. People might be satisfied, dissatisfied, or somewhere in between. But Herzberg's interviews had identified two different dimensions altogether: one ranging from satisfaction to no satisfaction and the other ranging from dissatisfaction to no dissatisfaction. This perspective, along with several examples of factors that affect each continuum, is shown in Figure 10.3. Note that the factors influencing the satisfaction continuum—called *motivation factors*—are related specifically to the work content. The factors presumed to cause dissatisfaction—called *hygiene factors*—are related to the work environment.

Based on these findings, Herzberg argued that there are two stages in the process of motivating employees. First, managers must ensure that the hygiene factors are not deficient. Pay and security must be appropriate, working conditions must be safe, technical supervision must be acceptable, and so on. By providing hygiene factors at an appropriate level, managers do not necessarily stimulate motivation but merely ensure that employees are "not dissatisfied." Employees whom managers try to "satisfy" through hygiene factors alone will usually do just enough to get by. Thus, managers should proceed to stage two—giving employees the opportunity to experience motivation factors such as achievement and recognition. The result is predicted to be higher levels of satisfaction and motivation. Herzberg also went a step further than most other theorists and described exactly how to use the two-factor theory in the workplace. Specifically, he recommended job enrichment, as discussed in Chapter 10. He argued that jobs should be redesigned to provide higher levels of the motivation factors.

Motivation Factors
- Achievement
- Recognition
- The work itself
- Responsibility
- Advancement and growth

Hygiene Factors
- Supervisors
- Working conditions
- Interpersonal relations
- Pay and security
- Company policies and administration

Satisfaction ← → No satisfaction   Dissatisfaction ← → No dissatisfaction

FIGURE 10.3

The Two-Factor Theory of Motivation

The two-factor theory suggests that job satisfaction has two dimensions. A manager who tries to motivate an employee using only hygiene factors, such as pay and good working conditions, will likely not succeed. To motivate employees and produce a high level of satisfaction, managers must also offer factors such as responsibility and the opportunity for advancement (motivation factors).

Although widely known among many managers, Herzberg's two-factor theory is not without its critics. One criticism is that the findings in Herzberg's initial interviews are subject to different explanations. Another charge is that his sample was not representative of the general population and that subsequent research has often failed to uphold the theory.[15] Herzberg's theory is not held in high esteem by researchers in the field today but it has had a major impact on managers and has played a key role in increasing their awareness of motivation and its importance in the workplace.

10-2c Individual Human Needs

In addition to these theories, research has focused on specific individual human needs that are important in organizations. The three most important individual needs are achievement, affiliation, and power.[16]

need for achievement
The desire to accomplish a goal or task more effectively than in the past

The need for achievement, the best known of the three, is the desire to accomplish a goal or task more effectively than in the past. People with a high need for achievement have a desire to assume personal responsibility, a tendency to set moderately difficult goals, a desire for specific and immediate feedback, and a preoccupation with their task. David C. McClelland, the psychologist who first identified this need, has argued that only about 10 percent of the U.S. population truly have a high need for achievement while almost one-quarter of the workers in Japan have a high need for achievement.

fizkes/Shutterstock.com

The need for achievement is the desire to accomplish a goal or task more effectively than in the past. This man's need for achievement has motivated him to perform at the highest level possible, and his efforts are being recognized by his boss and acknowledged by his colleagues.

The need for affiliation is less well understood. Like Maslow's belongingness need, the need for affiliation is a desire for human companionship and acceptance. People with a strong need for affiliation are likely to prefer (and perform better in) a job that entails a lot of social interaction and offers opportunities to make friends. One recent survey found that workers with one or more good friends at work are much more likely to be committed to their work. United Airlines, for instance, allows flight attendants to form their own teams; those who participate tend to form teams with their friends.[17] Individuals with a strong need for affiliation may have been more prone to anxiety and feelings of sadness and loss during the social-distancing measures taken during the COVID-19 pandemic in 2020. On the other hand, people with a lower need for affiliation may have adapted more easily.

The need for power has also received considerable attention as an important ingredient in managerial success. The need for power is the desire to be influential in a group and to control one's environment.

need for affiliation
The desire for human companionship and acceptance

need for power
The desire to be influential in a group and to control one's environment

Research has shown that people with a strong need for power are likely to be superior performers, have good attendance records, and occupy supervisory positions. One study found that managers as a group tend to have a stronger power motive than the general population and that successful managers tend to have stronger power motives than less successful managers.[18] The need for power might explain why Mark Hurd, a former CEO of HP, took advantage of his power and role as head of the company several years ago. Hurd was forced to resign after a sexual harassment claim by a female contractor alleging that Hurd had used corporate funds for personal gains in attempts to woo her. The former CEO had submitted personal receipts ranging from $1,000 to $20,000 over a two-year period.[19]

10-2d Implications of the Content Perspectives

Managers should remember that Maslow's needs hierarchy, the ERG theory, the two-factor theory, and the needs for achievement, affiliation, and power all provide useful insights into factors that cause motivation. What they do not do is shed much light on the process of motivation. They do not explain why people might be motivated by one factor rather than by another at a given level or how people might go about trying to satisfy their different needs. These questions involve behaviors or actions, goals, and feelings of satisfaction—concepts that are more effectively addressed by various process perspectives on motivation.

Manager's Checklist

☐ Managers need to remember that needs and need deficiencies are the catalyst in stimulating motivated behavior.

☐ Managers should recognize, however, that different people have different needs.

☐ Finally, you should also remember that any given person's needs change over time.

10-3 PROCESS PERSPECTIVES ON MOTIVATION

process perspectives
Approaches to motivation that focus on why people choose certain behavioral options to fulfill their needs and how they evaluate their satisfaction after they have attained these goals

Process perspectives are concerned with how motivation occurs. Rather than attempting to identify motivational stimuli, process perspectives focus on why people choose certain behavioral options to satisfy their needs and how they evaluate their satisfaction after they have attained these goals. Three useful process perspectives on motivation are the expectancy, equity, and goal-setting theories.

10-3a Expectancy Theory

expectancy theory
Suggests that motivation depends on two things—how much we want something and how likely we think we are to get it

Expectancy theory suggests that motivation depends on two things—how much we want something and how likely we think we are to get it.[20] Assume that you are approaching graduation and looking for a job as a management trainee. You see in the want ads that General Motors is seeking a new vice president with a starting salary of $950,000 per year. Even though you might aspire to have this type of job one day, you will not waste your time applying now because you realize that you have no real chance of getting it. The next ad you see is for someone to scrape bubble gum from underneath theater seats for a starting wage of $8 an hour. Even though you could probably get this job, you do not apply because you do not want it. Then you see an ad for a management trainee at a big company, with a starting salary of $65,000. You may apply for this job because you want it and because you think you have a reasonable chance of getting it.

Expectancy theory rests on four basic assumptions. First, it assumes that behavior is determined by a combination of forces in the individual and in the environment. Second, it assumes that people make decisions about their own behavior in organizations. Third, it assumes that different people have different types of needs, desires, and goals. Fourth, it assumes that people make choices from among alternative plans of behavior, based on their perceptions of the extent to which a given behavior will lead to desired outcomes.

Figure 10.4 summarizes the basic expectancy model. The model suggests that motivation leads to effort and that effort, combined with employee ability and environmental factors, results in performance. Performance, in turn, leads to various outcomes, each of which has an associated value, called its *valence*. The most important parts of the expectancy model cannot be shown in the figure, however. These are the individual's expectation that effort will lead to high performance, that performance will lead to outcomes, and that each outcome will have some kind of value.

effort-to-performance expectancy
The individual's perception of the probability that effort will lead to high performance

Effort-to-Performance Expectancy   The effort-to-performance expectancy is the individual's perception of the probability that effort will lead to high performance. When the person believes that effort will lead directly to high performance, this expectancy will be quite strong (close to 1.00). When the person believes that effort and performance are unrelated, the effort-to-performance expectancy is very weak (close to 0). The belief that effort is somewhat but not strongly related to performance carries with it a moderate expectancy (somewhere between 0 and 1.00).

performance-to-outcome expectancy
The individual's perception that performance will lead to a specific outcome

Performance-to-Outcome Expectancy   The performance-to-outcome expectancy is the individual's perception that performance will lead to a specific outcome. For example, if the person believes that high performance *will* result in a pay raise, the performance-to-outcome

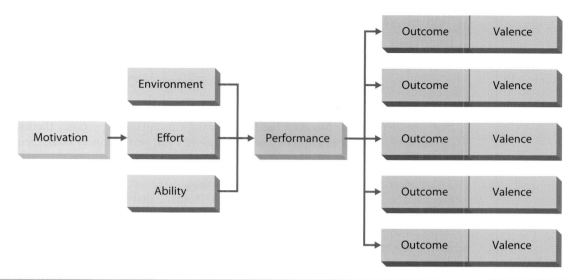

The Expectancy Model of Motivation

The expectancy model of motivation is a complex but relatively accurate portrayal of how motivation occurs. According to this model, a manager must understand what employees want (such as pay, promotions, or status) to begin to motivate them.

outcomes
Consequences of behaviors in an organizational setting, usually rewards

valence
An index of how much a person wants a particular outcome; the attractiveness of the outcome to the individual

expectancy is high (approaching 1.00). The person who believes that high performance *may* lead to a pay raise has a moderate expectancy (between 1.00 and 0). The person who believes that performance has no relationship to rewards has a low performance-to-outcome expectancy (close to 0).

Outcomes and Valences   Expectancy theory recognizes that a person's behavior results in a variety of outcomes, or consequences, in an organizational setting. A high performer, for example, may get bigger pay raises, faster promotions, and more praise from the boss. On the other hand, she may also be subject to more stress and incur resentment from coworkers. Each of these five outcomes also has an associated value, or valence—an index of how much a person values a particular outcome. If the individual wants the outcome, its valence is positive; if the individual does not want the outcome, its valence is negative; and if the individual is indifferent to the outcome, its valence is zero.

It is this part of expectancy theory that goes beyond the content perspectives on motivation. Different people have different needs, and they will try to satisfy these needs in different ways. For an employee who has a high need for achievement and a low need for affiliation, the pay raise and promotions that are outcomes of high performance might have positive valences, the praise and resentment zero valences, and the stress a negative valence. For a different employee, with a low need for achievement and a high need for affiliation, the pay raise, promotions, and praise might all have positive valences, whereas both resentment and stress could have negative valences.

For motivated behavior to occur, three conditions must be met. First, the effort-to-performance expectancy must be greater than 0 (the person must believe that if effort is expended, high performance will result). The performance-to-outcome expectancy must also be greater than 0 (the person must believe that if high performance is achieved, certain outcomes will follow). And the sum of the valences for the outcomes must be greater than 0. (One or more outcomes may have negative valences if they are more than offset by the positive valences of other outcomes. For example, the attractiveness of a pay raise, a promotion, and praise from the boss may outweigh the unattractiveness of more stress and resentment from coworkers.) Expectancy theory suggests that when these conditions are met, the person is motivated to expend effort.

"When we're productive and we've done something good together (and we are recognized for it), we feel satisfied, not the other way around."

—J. Richard Hackman, Pioneer in Organizational Psychology[21]

Starbucks credits its unique stock ownership program with maintaining a dedicated and motivated workforce. Based on the fundamental concepts of expectancy theory, Starbucks employees earn stock as a function of their seniority and performance. Thus, their hard work helps them earn shares of ownership in the company.[22]

The Porter-Lawler Extension   An interesting extension of expectancy theory has been proposed by Porter and Lawler.[23] Recall from Chapter 2 that the human relationists assumed that employee satisfaction causes good performance. We also noted that research has not consistently supported such a relationship. Porter and Lawler suggested that there may indeed be a relationship between satisfaction and performance but that it goes in the opposite direction—that is, high performance may lead to high satisfaction. Figure 10.5 summarizes Porter and Lawler's logic. Performance results in rewards for an individual. Some of these are extrinsic (such as pay and promotions); others are intrinsic (such as self-esteem and accomplishment). The person evaluates the equity, or fairness, of the rewards relative to the effort expended and the level of performance attained. If the rewards are perceived to be equitable, the person is satisfied.

10-3b Equity Theory

After needs have stimulated the motivation process and the person has chosen an action that is expected to satisfy those needs, he or she assesses the fairness, or equity, of the resultant outcome. Equity theory contends that people are motivated to seek social equity in the rewards they receive for performance.[24] Equity is an individual's belief that the treatment he or she is receiving is fair relative to the treatment received by others. According to equity theory, outcomes from a job include pay, recognition, promotions, social relationships, and intrinsic rewards. To get these rewards, the individual makes inputs to the job, such as time, experience, effort, education, and loyalty. The theory suggests that people view their outcomes and inputs as a ratio and then compare it to someone else's ratio. This other "person" may be someone in the work group or some sort of group average or composite. The process of comparison looks like this:

> **equity theory**
> Suggests that people are motivated to seek social equity in the rewards they receive for performance

$$\frac{\text{Individual Inputs}}{\text{Individual Outcomes}} = \frac{\text{Other's Inputs}}{\text{Other's Outcomes}}$$

Both the formulation of the ratios and comparisons between them are very subjective and based on individual perceptions. Even so, however, as a result of comparisons three conditions may result: The person may feel equitably rewarded, underrewarded, or overrewarded. A feeling of equity will result when the two ratios are equal. This may occur even though the other person's outcomes are greater than the individual's own outcomes—provided that the other's inputs are also proportionately greater. Suppose that Mark has a high school education and earns $40,000. He may still feel equitably treated relative to Susan, who earns $60,000 because she has a college degree and more experience.

People who feel underrewarded try to reduce the inequity. Such a person might decrease her inputs by exerting less effort, increase her outcomes by asking for a raise, distort the original ratios by rationalizing, try to get the other person to change her or his outcomes or inputs, leave the situation, or change the object of comparison. An individual may also feel overrewarded relative to another person. This is not likely to be terribly disturbing to most people, but research suggests that some people who experience inequity under these conditions are somewhat motivated to reduce it. Under such a circumstance, the person might increase his inputs by exerting more effort, reduce his outcomes by producing fewer units (if paid on a per-unit basis), distort the original ratios by rationalizing, or try to reduce the inputs or increase the outcomes of the other person.

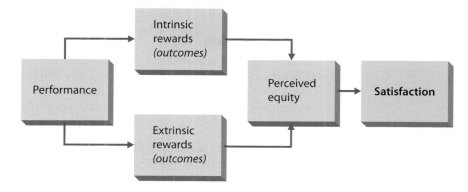

FIGURE 10.5

The Porter-Lawler Extension of Expectancy Theory

The Porter-Lawler extension of expectancy theory suggests that if performance results in equitable rewards, people will be more satisfied. Thus, performance can lead to satisfaction. Managers must therefore be sure that any system of motivation includes rewards that are fair, or equitable, for all.

Source: Edward E. Lawler III and Lyman W. Porter, "The Effect of Performance on Job Satisfaction," *Industrial Relations*, October 1967, Vol. 7, p. 23.

Equity is the extent to which an individual feels fairly treated relative to others. Take these two women, for example. The woman at the second desk has just received news that she is being promoted and is excited, engaged, and highly motivated because she believes she deserves the promotion. The woman at the first desk, though, now feels unhappy because she thought she would be getting the promotion.

"People have long memories. They'll remember whether they think they were dealt with equitably."

—William Conaty, Former Director of HR at General Electric[28]

Managers today may need to pay even greater attention to equity theory and its implications. Many firms, for example, have moved toward performance-based reward systems (discussed later in this chapter) as opposed to standard or across-the-board salary increases. Hence, they must ensure that the bases for rewarding some people more than others are clear and objective. Beyond legal issues such as discrimination, managers need to be sure that they are providing fair rewards and incentives to those who do the best work.[25] Moreover, they must be sensitive to cultural differences that affect how people may perceive and react to equity and inequity.[26]

10-3c Goal-Setting Theory

The goal-setting theory of motivation assumes that behavior is a result of conscious goals and intentions.[27] Therefore, by setting goals for people in the organization, a manager should be able to influence their behavior. Given this premise, the challenge is to develop a thorough understanding of the processes by which people set goals and then work to reach them. In the original version of goal-setting theory, two specific goal characteristics—goal difficulty and goal specificity—were expected to shape performance.

Goal Difficulty   *Goal difficulty* is the extent to which a goal is challenging and requires effort. If people work to achieve goals, it is reasonable to assume that they will work harder to achieve more difficult goals. But a goal must not be so difficult that it is unattainable. If a new manager asks her sales force to increase sales by 300 percent, the group may become disillusioned because they see no change of achieving such a huge increase. A more realistic but still difficult goal—perhaps a 30 percent increase—would be a better incentive. A substantial body of research supports the importance of goal difficulty. In one study, for example, managers at Weyerhaeuser set difficult goals for truck drivers hauling loads of timber from cutting sites to wood yards. Over a nine-month period, the drivers increased the quantity of wood they delivered by an amount that would have required $250,000 worth of new trucks at the previous per-truck average load.[29]

Goal Specificity   *Goal specificity* is the clarity and precision of the goal. A goal of "increasing productivity" is not very specific; a goal of "increasing productivity by 3 percent in the next six months" is quite specific. Some goals, such as those involving costs, output, profitability, and growth, are readily amenable to specificity. Other goals, however, such as improving employee job satisfaction, morale, company image and reputation, ethics, and socially responsible behavior, may be much harder to state in specific terms. Like difficulty, specificity has been shown to be consistently related to performance. The study of timber truck drivers just mentioned, for example, also examined goal specificity. The initial loads the truck drivers were carrying were found to be 60 percent of the maximum weight each truck could haul. The managers set a new goal for drivers of 94 percent, which the drivers were soon able to reach. Thus, the goal was both specific and difficult.

> **"Your vision is your destination, and small, manageable goals are the motor that will get you there. Without the vision you're on a road to nowhere. Without the goals, you have a destination but no motor. They work in tandem, and you need both."**
> —Dr. Frank Murtha, Counseling Psychologist[30]

Because the theory attracted so much widespread interest and research support from researchers and managers alike, an expanded model of the goal-setting process was eventually proposed. The expanded model, shown in Figure 10.6, attempts to capture more fully the complexities of goal setting in organizations.

The expanded theory argues that goal-directed effort is a function of four goal attributes: difficulty and specificity, as already discussed, and acceptance and commitment. *Goal acceptance* is the extent to which a person accepts a goal as his or her own. *Goal commitment* is the extent to which she or he is personally interested in reaching the goal. The

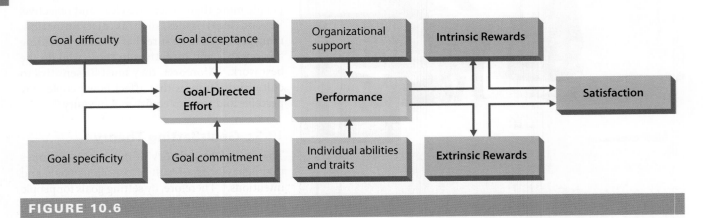

FIGURE 10.6

The Expanded Goal-Setting Theory of Motivation

One of the most important emerging theories of motivation is goal-setting theory. This theory suggests that goal difficulty, specificity, acceptance, and commitment combine to determine an individual's goal-directed effort. This effort, when complemented by appropriate organizational support and individual abilities and traits, results in performance. Finally, performance is seen as leading to intrinsic and extrinsic rewards that, in turn, result in employee satisfaction.

Source: Gary P. Latham and Edwin A. Locke, "A Motivational Technique That Works," *Organizational Dynamics*, Autumn 1979, Vol. 8, Issue 2, p. 79.

manager who vows to take whatever steps are necessary to cut costs by 10 percent has made a commitment to achieve the goal. Factors that can foster goal acceptance and commitment include participating in the goal-setting process, making goals challenging but realistic, and believing that goal achievement will lead to valued rewards.

The interaction of goal-directed effort, organizational support, and individual abilities and traits determines actual performance. Organizational support is whatever the organization does to help or hinder performance. Positive support might mean making available adequate talent, access to information and technology, and a sufficient supply of raw materials; negative support might mean failing to fix damaged equipment, relying only on outdated technology, and denying access to critical information. Individual abilities and traits are the skills and other personal characteristics necessary for doing a job. As a result of performance, a person receives various intrinsic and extrinsic rewards, which in turn influence satisfaction. Note that the latter stages of this model are quite similar to the Porter and Lawler expectancy model discussed earlier.[31]

10-3d Implications of the Process Perspectives

Expectancy theory can be useful for managers who are trying to improve the motivation of their subordinates. A series of steps can be followed to implement the basic ideas of the theory. First, figure out the outcomes each employee is likely to want. Second, decide what kinds and levels of performance are needed to meet organizational goals. Then make sure that the desired levels of performance are attainable. Also, make sure that desired outcomes and desired performance are linked. Next, analyze the complete situation for conflicting expectancies and ensure that the rewards are large enough. Finally, make sure the total system is equitable (that is, fair to everyone). The single most important idea for managers to remember from equity theory is that if rewards are to motivate employees, they must be perceived as being equitable and fair. A second implication is that managers need to consider the nature of the "other" to whom the employee is comparing her- or himself. Goal-setting theory can be used to implement both expectancy and equity theory concepts.

Manager's Checklist

☐ Managers need to remember that people are motivated both by how much they want a particular outcome and by how likely they think it is that their performance will lead to that outcome.

☐ Managers should also recognize the importance of equity—employees' feeling that they are being treated and rewarded equitably.

☐ You should also understand that goal difficulty and goal specificity can play a major role in motivating employees.

10-4 REINFORCEMENT PERSPECTIVES ON MOTIVATION

reinforcement theory
Approach to motivation that argues that behavior that results in rewarding consequences is likely to be repeated, whereas behavior that results in punishing consequences is less likely to be repeated

A third element of the motivational process addresses why some behaviors are maintained over time and why other behaviors change. As we have seen, content perspectives deal with needs, whereas process perspectives explain why people choose various behaviors to satisfy needs and how they evaluate the equity of the rewards they get for those behaviors. Reinforcement perspectives explain the role of those rewards as they cause behavior to change or remain the same over time. Specifically, reinforcement theory argues that behavior that results in rewarding consequences is likely to be repeated, whereas behavior that results in punishing consequences is less likely to be repeated.[32] The *Leading the Way* feature provides some interesting insights into reinforcement theory.

LEADING THE WAY

To Reward, or to Punish?. . . That Is the Question

Suppose you are the general manager of a supermarket and you've just finished a department-by-department year-end review of your managers' performance. Every department—meats, dairy, seafood, deli, bakery, and so forth—has performed up to or beyond expectations. All except one: Produce fell 12 percent short of your forecast. You decide to reward all your managers with healthy bonuses except for your produce manager. In other words, you plan to use *punishment* in order to motivate your produce manager and *positive reinforcement* to motivate all of your other managers. You congratulate yourself for having reached a fair and logical decision.

According to Daniel Kahneman, a psychologist who won the Nobel Prize in economics for his work on behavioral and decision-making models, your decision is probably not fair (at least not altogether), and it's certainly not logical—at least not when the reality of the situation is taken into consideration. Here's how Kahneman sees your two-pronged decision-making model:

- *Manager's department performs well → You reward manager → Department continues to perform well*
- *Manager's department performs poorly → You punish manager → Department performs better*

The key to Kahneman's perspective is called *regression to the mean*—the principle that, from one performance measurement to the next, the change in performance will be toward the overall average level of performance. Say, for example, that you're an average golfer and that par for your course is 72. If you shoot 68 in one round, your next round will probably be *in the direction* of 72—not necessarily 72 exactly, which is your average, or 76, which would bring you exactly back to a two-round average of 72. Technically, regression to the mean is a *law* and not a *rule*: You could shoot a second round of 70 or even 67, but *most of the time*, your second-round score won't be as good as your first-round score.

Why does regression to the mean occur? Because a complex combination of factors usually determines any outcome. And because this combination is complex, it's not likely that the same combination will repeat itself the next time you measure the outcome. Which brings us back to your produce manager: *It's not likely that his managerial performance was the sole (or even necessarily the primary) factor in his department's poor performance.* Other factors might include variations in competition, economic and market conditions, and decisions made by managers above him—all of which are largely random and which will undoubtedly be different from one performance measurement to the next.

Now that you understand a little about the reality of regression to the mean, compare your decision-making model to a model that reflects reality:

- *Manager's department performs well → Department probably does not perform as well*
- *Manager's department performs poorly → Department probably performs better*

Your reinforcement decision will *probably* have little or nothing to do with next year's outcome in any of your store's departments. And you've *probably* been unfair to your produce manager. Kahneman isn't inclined to be overly critical of your mistaken belief that you've made a logical, fair, and effective decision: "It's very difficult for people to detect their own errors," he admits. "You're too busy making a mistake to detect it at the same time." He does, however, reserve the right to be pessimistic: "The failure to recognize the import of regression," he warns,

can have pernicious consequences. . . . We normally reinforce others when their behavior is good and punish them when their behavior is bad. By regression alone [however], they are most likely to improve after being punished and most likely to deteriorate after being rewarded. Consequently, we are exposed to a lifetime schedule in which we are most often rewarded for punishing others and punished for rewarding [them].

References: Bryan Burke, "Fighter Pilots and Firing Coaches," *Advanced NFL Stats*, February 19, 2009, www.advancednflstats.com on May 8, 2020; David Hall, "Daniel Kahneman Interview," *New Zealand Listener*, January 20, 2012, www.listener.co.nz on May 8, 2020; Steve Miller, "We're Not Very Good Statisticians," *Information Management*, March 26, 2012, www.information-management.com on May 8, 2020; Galen Strawson, "*Thinking, Fast and Slow* by Daniel Kahneman—Review," *The Guardian*, December 13, 2011, www.guardian.co.uk on May 8, 2020; and *Judgment under Uncertainty: Heuristics and Biases*, eds. Daniel Kahneman, Paul Slovic, and Amos Tversky (Cambridge, UK: Cambridge University Press, 1982).

10-4a Kinds of Reinforcement in Organizations

positive reinforcement
A method of strengthening behavior with rewards or positive outcomes after a desired behavior is performed

There are four basic kinds of reinforcement that can result from behavior—positive reinforcement, avoidance, punishment, and extinction.[33] These are summarized in Table 10.1. Two kinds of reinforcement strengthen or maintain behavior, whereas the other two weaken or decrease behavior.

Positive reinforcement, a method of strengthening behavior, is a reward or a positive outcome that an individual experiences after a desired behavior is performed. When a

avoidance
Used to strengthen behavior by avoiding unpleasant consequences that would result if the behavior were not performed

punishment
Used to weaken undesired behaviors by using negative outcomes or unpleasant consequences when the behavior is performed

extinction
Used to weaken undesired behaviors by simply ignoring or not reinforcing them

manager observes an employee doing an especially good job and offers praise, the praise serves to positively reinforce the behavior of good work. Other positive reinforcers in organizations include pay raises, promotions, and awards tied to desired behaviors. Employees who work at General Electric's customer service center receive clothing, sporting goods, and even trips to Disney World as rewards for outstanding performance. The other method of strengthening desired behavior is through avoidance. An employee may come to work on time to avoid a reprimand. In this instance, the employee is motivated to perform the behavior of punctuality to avoid an unpleasant consequence that is likely to follow tardiness.

Punishment is used by some managers to weaken the incidence of undesired behaviors. When an employee is loafing, coming to work late, doing poor work, or interfering with the work of others, the manager might resort to reprimands, discipline, or fines. The logic is that the unpleasant consequence will reduce the likelihood that the employee will choose that particular behavior again. Given the counterproductive side effects of punishment (such as resentment and hostility), though, it is often advisable to use the other kinds of reinforcement if at all possible. Extinction can also be used to weaken behavior, especially behavior that has previously been rewarded. When an employee tells an inappropriate joke and the boss laughs, the laughter reinforces the behavior and the employee may continue to tell inappropriate jokes. By simply ignoring this behavior and not reinforcing it, however, the boss may cause the behavior to subside and eventually become "extinct."

10-4b Providing Reinforcement in Organizations

Not only is the kind of reinforcement important, but so is when or how often it occurs. Various strategies are possible for providing reinforcement. These are also listed in Table 10.1. The fixed-interval schedule provides reinforcement at fixed intervals of time, regardless of behavior. A good example of this schedule is the weekly or monthly paycheck. This method provides the least incentive for good work because employees know they will be paid regularly regardless of their

Positive reinforcement is a reward or other desired outcome. This employee has just gotten assigned to a prestigious new project and is getting a pay raise. Both serve as positive reinforcement (assuming, of course, that prestige and pay are both valuable to her).

fizkes/Shutterstock.com

Table 10.1	Elements of Reinforcement Theory

Arrangement of the Reinforcement Contingencies

1. *Positive Reinforcement.* Strengthens behavior by providing a desirable consequence.	3. *Punishment.* Weakens behavior by providing an undesirable consequence.
2. *Avoidance.* Strengthens behavior by allowing escape from an undesirable consequence.	4. *Extinction.* Weakens behavior by ignoring it.

Schedules for Applying Reinforcement

1. *Fixed-Interval.* Reinforcement is applied at fixed time intervals, regardless of behavior.	1. *Fixed-Ratio.* Reinforcement is applied after a fixed number of behaviors, regardless of time.
2. *Variable-Interval.* Reinforcement is applied at variable time intervals.	2. *Variable-Ratio.* Reinforcement is applied after a variable number of behaviors.

A manager who wants the best chance of reinforcing a behavior would likely offer the employee a positive reinforcement after a variable number of behaviors (variable-ratio reinforcement). For example, the manager could praise the employee after the third credit card application was received. Additional praise might be offered after the next five applications, then again after the next three, the next seven, the next four, and so on.

fixed-interval schedule
Provides reinforcement at fixed intervals of time, such as regular weekly paychecks

variable-interval schedule
Provides reinforcement at varying intervals of time, such as occasional visits by the supervisor

fixed-ratio schedule
Provides reinforcement after a fixed number of behaviors regardless of the time interval involved, such as a bonus for every fifth sale

variable-ratio schedule
Provides reinforcement after varying numbers of behaviors are performed, such as the use of compliments by a supervisor on an irregular basis

behavior modification (OB Mod)
Method for applying the basic elements of reinforcement theory in an organizational setting

efforts. A variable-interval schedule also uses time as the basis for reinforcement, but the time interval varies from one reinforcement to the next. This schedule is appropriate for praise or other rewards based on visits or inspections. When employees do not know when their boss is going to drop by, they tend to maintain a reasonably high level of effort all the time.

A fixed-ratio schedule gives reinforcement after a fixed number of behaviors, regardless of the time that elapses between behaviors. This results in an even higher level of effort. For example, when Macy's is recruiting new credit card customers, salespersons get a small bonus for every fifth application returned from their department. Under this arrangement, motivation will be high because each application gets the person closer to the next bonus. The variable-ratio schedule, the most powerful schedule in terms of maintaining desired behaviors, varies the number of behaviors needed for each reinforcement. A supervisor who praises an employee for her second order, the seventh order after that, the ninth after that, then the fifth, and then the third is using a variable-ratio schedule. The employee is motivated to increase the frequency of the desired behavior because each performance increases the probability of receiving a reward. Of course, a variable-ratio schedule is difficult (if not impossible) to use for formal rewards such as pay because it would be too complicated to keep track of who was rewarded when.

Managers wanting to explicitly use reinforcement theory to motivate their employees generally do so with a technique called behavior modification, or OB Mod.[34] An OB Mod program starts by specifying behaviors that are to be increased (such as producing more units) or decreased (such as coming to work late). These target behaviors are then tied to specific forms or kinds of reinforcement. Although many organizations (such as Procter & Gamble and Ford) have used OB Mod, the best-known application was at Emery Air Freight (now a part of Consolidated Freightways). Management felt that the containers used to consolidate small shipments into fewer, larger shipments were not being packed efficiently. Through a system of self-monitored feedback and rewards, Emery increased container usage from 45 to 95 percent and saved over $3 million during the first three years of the program.[35]

10-4c Implications of the Reinforcement Perspectives

Reinforcement in organizations can be a powerful force for maintaining employee motivation. Of course, for reinforcement to be truly effective, managers need to use it in a manner consistent with the various types and schedules of reinforcement discussed above. In addition, managers must understand that they may be inadvertently motivating undesired or dysfunctional behaviors. For instance, if an employee routinely comes to work late but experiences no consequences, both that worker and others will see that it is all right to be late for work.

 **Manager's Checklist**

☐ Managers should be familiar with the basic kinds and schedules of reinforcement that are available to them.

☐ Managers should also know the kinds of effects that are most likely to follow from any given form of reinforcement.

10-5 POPULAR MOTIVATIONAL STRATEGIES

Although the various theories discussed thus far provide a solid explanation for motivation, managers must use various techniques and strategies to actually apply them. Among the most popular motivational strategies today are empowerment and participation and alternative forms of work arrangements. Various forms of performance-based reward systems, discussed in the next section, also reflect efforts to boost motivation and performance.

empowerment
The process of enabling workers to set their own work goals, make decisions, and solve problems within their sphere of responsibility and authority

10-5a Empowerment and Participation

Empowerment and participation represent important methods that managers can use to enhance employee motivation. Empowerment is the process of enabling workers to set their own work goals, make decisions, and solve problems within their sphere of responsibility and

participation
The process of giving employees a voice in making decisions about their own work

authority. Participation is the process of giving employees a voice in making decisions about their own work. Thus, empowerment is a somewhat broader concept that promotes participation in a wide variety of areas, including but not limited to work itself, work context, and work environment.[36]

The role of participation and empowerment in motivation can be expressed in terms of both content perspectives and expectancy theory. Employees who participate in decision making may be more committed to executing decisions properly. Furthermore, the successful process of making a decision, executing it, and then seeing the positive consequences can help satisfy one's need for achievement, provide recognition and responsibility, and enhance self-esteem. Simply being asked to participate in organizational decision making also may enhance an employee's self-esteem. In addition, participation should help clarify expectancies; that is, by participating in decision making, employees may better understand the linkage between their performance and the rewards they want most.

Participation and empowerment are popular strategies for improving employee motivation. This manager is giving his team autonomy to make an important decision—that is, he is empowering them.

Monkey Business Images/Shutterstock.com

Areas of Participation   At one level, employees can participate in addressing questions and making decisions about their own jobs. Instead of just telling them how to do their jobs, for example, managers can ask employees to make their own decisions about how to do them. Based on their own expertise and experience with their tasks, workers might be able to improve their own productivity. In many situations, they might also be well qualified to make decisions about what materials to use, what tools are needed, and so forth.

It might also be motivational to let workers make decisions about administrative matters, such as work schedules. If jobs are relatively independent of one another, employees might decide when to change shifts, take breaks, go to lunch, and so forth. A work group or team might also be able to schedule vacations and days off for all of its members. Furthermore, employees are getting increasing opportunities to participate in broader issues of product quality. Such participation has become a hallmark of successful Japanese and other international firms, and many U.S. companies have followed suit.

Techniques and Issues in Empowerment   In recent years, many organizations have actively sought ways to extend participation beyond the traditional areas. Simple techniques, such as suggestion boxes and question-and-answer meetings, allow a certain degree of participation, for example. The basic motive has been to better capitalize on the assets and capabilities inherent in all employees. Thus, many managers today prefer the term *empowerment* to *participation* because of its more comprehensive character.

One method used to empower workers is the use of work teams. Such teams are collections of employees empowered to plan, organize, direct, and control their own work. Their supervisor, rather than being a traditional "boss," plays more the role of a coach. The other method for empowerment is to change the team's overall method of organizing. The basic pattern is for an organization to eliminate layers from its hierarchy, thereby becoming much more decentralized. Power, responsibility, and authority are subsequently delegated as far down the organization as possible, placing control over work squarely in the hands of those who actually do it.[37]

Regardless of the specific technique or method used, however, empowerment will enhance organizational effectiveness only if certain conditions exist. First of all, the organization must be sincere in its efforts to spread power and autonomy to lower levels of the organization. Token efforts to promote participation in only a few areas are not likely to succeed. Second, the organization must be committed to maintaining participation and empowerment. Workers will be resentful if they are given more control, only to later have it reduced or taken away altogether. Third, workers must truly believe that they and their managers are working together in their joint best interests. In some factory settings, for instance, high-performing workers have been found to routinely conceal the secrets of their high output. They fear that if management learns those secrets, it will use them to ratchet up performance expectations.[38]

In addition, the organization must be systematic and patient in its efforts to empower workers. Turning over too much control too quickly can spell disaster. And finally, the organization must be prepared to increase its commitment to training and development. Employees given more freedom in how they work will quite likely need additional training to help them exercise that freedom most effectively.[39]

10-5b Alternative Forms of Work Arrangements

Many organizations today have also been experimenting with a variety of alternative work arrangements. These alternative arrangements are generally intended to enhance employee motivation and performance by providing employees with greater flexibility in how and when they work. Among the more popular alternative work arrangements are variable work schedules, flexible work schedules, job sharing, and telecommuting.[40]

Variable Work Schedules   Although there are many exceptions, of course, the traditional work schedule starts at 8:00 or 9:00 in the morning and ends at 5:00 or so in the evening, five days a week (and, of course, many managers work additional hours outside of these times). Unfortunately, this schedule makes it difficult to attend to routine personal business—going to the bank, seeing a doctor or dentist for a routine checkup, having a parent–teacher conference, getting an automobile serviced, and so forth. At a surface level, then, employees locked into this sort of arrangement may find it necessary to take a sick day or a vacation day to handle these activities. At a more unconscious level, some people may also feel so powerless and constrained by their job schedule as to feel increased resentment and frustration.

> **"These guidelines . . . effectively mean that as long as they do their work, our employees can work whenever they want, from wherever they want."**
> —Richard Branson, Founder of Virgin Group[41]

compressed work schedule
Working a full 40-hour week in fewer than the traditional five days

To help counter these problems, some businesses have adopted a **compressed work schedule**, working a full 40-hour week in fewer than the traditional five days.[42] One approach involves working 10 hours a day for four days, leaving an extra day off. Another alternative is for employees to work slightly less than 10 hours a day, but to complete the 40 hours by lunch time on Friday (many medical practices use this schedule). And a few firms have tried having employees work 12 hours a day for three days, followed by four days off. Organizations that have used these forms of compressed workweeks include John Hancock, BP Amoco, and Philip Morris. One problem with this schedule is that when employees put in too much time in a single day, they tend to get tired and perform at a lower level later in the day.

A schedule that some organizations have adopted is what they call a "nine-eighty" schedule. Under this arrangement, employees work a traditional schedule one week and a compressed schedule the next, getting every other Friday off. In other words, they work 80 hours (the equivalent of two weeks of full-time work) in nine days. By alternating the regular and compressed schedules across half of its workforce, the organization can be fully staffed at all times, while still giving employees two full weekdays off each month. Shell Oil and BP Amoco Chemicals are two of the firms that currently use this schedule.

flexible work schedule
Work schedule in which employees have some control over the hours they choose to work; also called *flextime*

Flexible Work Schedules   Another popular alternative work arrangement is **flexible work schedule**, sometimes called *flextime*. Flextime gives employees more personal control over the times they work. The workday is typically broken down into two categories: flexible time and core time. All employees must be at their workstations during core time, but they can choose their own schedules during flexible time. Thus, one employee may choose to start work early in the morning and leave in midafternoon, another to start in the late morning and work until late afternoon, and still another to start early in the morning, take a long lunch break, and work until late afternoon. Organizations that have used the flexible work schedule method for arranging work include HP, Microsoft, and Texas Instruments.

"I get to sit here and look out my window while I talk to customers [by telecommuting]—and watch the leaves changing, squirrels running around, and kids going off to school."
—Walt Swanson, Customer Service Representative at Agilent Technologies

job sharing
When two part-time employees share one full-time job

Job Sharing   Yet another potentially useful alternative work arrangement in some settings is job sharing. In job sharing, two part-time employees share one full-time job. One person may perform the job from 8:00 A.M. to noon and the other from 1:00 P.M. to 5:00 P.M. Job sharing may be desirable for people who want to work only part time or when job markets are tight. For its part, the organization can accommodate the preferences of a broader range of employees and may benefit from the talents of more people.

telecommuting
Allowing employees to spend part of their time working offsite, usually at home

Telecommuting   An increasingly popular approach to alternative work arrangements is telecommuting—allowing employees to spend part of their time working offsite, usually at home. Another term for this approach is "alternative work locations." By using digital technology for remote connectivity, such as Zoom, Microsoft Meeting, and other remote conferencing platforms, many employees can maintain close contact with their organization and still get just as much (or even more) work done at home as they would if they were in the office. The increased power and sophistication of modern communication technology are making telecommuting easier and easier. One recent study found that nearly half of the U.S. workforce (64 million workers) are in jobs that allow for at least partial telecommuting.[43] Nearly half of AT&T's employees have received mobile and remote access technologies that provide them with the flexibility to work from various locations. And 40 percent of IBM's employees currently telecommute. (In the case of IBM, not only are employees more satisfied with the arrangement but the firm has saved close to $2.9 billion in office space needs.[44]) There was a surge in telecommuting during the 2020 COVID-19 pandemic as many workplaces shut down or restricted access and people were encouraged or even required to work remotely. For example, like their counterparts at many firms, employees at Twitter were allowed to work remotely during the pandemic. Even as businesses were reopening, though, Twitter's CEO, Jack Dorsey, saw the benefits of working remotely and so announced that everyone at the company could continue to work from home indefinitely.[45]

imtmphoto/Shutterstock.com

Telecommuting is a motivational technique that allows employees to spend part of their time working from home or some other alternative workplace. This man is working from his home office.

 **Manager's Checklist**

☐ Managers need to know the role that employee empowerment and participation play in employee motivation.

☐ You should also know the various work schedules used by organizations and how those schedules can affect motivation.

10-6 USING REWARD SYSTEMS TO MOTIVATE PERFORMANCE

reward system
The formal and informal mechanisms by which employee performance is defined, evaluated, and rewarded

Aside from these types of motivational strategies, an organization's reward system is its most basic tool for managing employee motivation. An organizational reward system is the formal and informal mechanisms by which employee performance is defined, evaluated, and rewarded. Rewards that are tied specifically to performance, of course, have the greatest impact on enhancing both motivation and actual performance.

Performance-based rewards play a number of roles and address a variety of purposes in organizations. The major purposes involve the relationship of rewards to motivation and to performance. Specifically, organizations want employees to perform at relatively high levels and need to make it worth their effort to do so. When rewards are associated with higher levels of performance, employees will presumably be motivated to work harder to achieve those awards. At that point, their own self-interests coincide with the organization's interests. Performance-based rewards are also relevant regarding other employee behaviors, such as engagement, retention, and citizenship.

10-6a Merit Reward Systems

Merit reward systems are among the most fundamental forms of performance-based rewards.[46] Merit pay generally refers to pay awarded to employees on the basis of the relative value of their contributions to the organization. Employees who make greater contributions are given higher pay than those who make lesser contributions. Merit pay plan, then, are compensation plans that formally base at least some meaningful portion of compensation on merit.

The most general form of merit pay plan is to provide annual salary increases to employees based on their relative merit. Merit, in turn, is usually determined or defined based on the person's performance and overall contributions to the organization. For example, an organization using such a traditional merit pay plan might instruct its supervisors to give all their employees an average pay raise of, say, 4 percent. But the individual supervisor is further instructed to differentiate among high, average, and low performers. Under a simple system, for example, a manager might give the top 25 percent of her employees a 6 percent pay raise, the middle 50 percent a 4 percent or average pay raise, and the bottom 25 percent a 2 percent pay raise.

10-6b Incentive Reward Systems

Incentive reward systems are among the oldest forms of performance-based rewards. For example, some companies were using individual piece-rate incentive plans over 100 years ago.[47] Under a piece-rate incentive plan, the organization pays an employee a certain amount of money for every unit she or he produces. For example, an employee might be paid $1 for every dozen units of product that are successfully completed. But such simplistic systems fail to account for such facts as minimum-wage levels and rely very heavily on the assumptions that performance is totally under a worker's control and that the employee does a single task continuously throughout his or her work time. Thus, most organizations today that try to use incentive compensation systems use more sophisticated methodologies.

Some variations on a piece-rate system are, however, still fairly popular. Although many of these still resemble the early plans in most ways, a well-known piece-rate system at Lincoln Electric illustrates how an organization can adapt the traditional model to achieve better results. For years, Lincoln's employees were paid individual incentive payments based on their performance. However, the amount of money shared (the incentive pool) was based on the company's profitability. There was also a well-organized system whereby employees could make suggestions for increasing productivity. There was motivation to do this because the employees received one-third of the profits (another third went to the stockholders, and the last share was retained for improvements and seed money). Thus, the pool for incentive payments was determined by profitability, and an employee's share of this pool was a function of his or her base pay and rated performance based on the piece-rate system. Lincoln Electric was most famous, however, because of the stories (which were apparently typical) of production workers receiving a year-end bonus payment that equaled their yearly base pay.[48] In recent years, Lincoln has partially abandoned its famous system for business reasons, but it still serves as a benchmark for other companies seeking innovative piece-rate pay systems.

Incentive Pay Plans   Generally speaking, *individual incentive plans* reward individual performance on a real-time basis. In other words, rather than increasing a person's base salary at the end of the year, the worker instead receives some level of salary increase or financial

---

merit pay
Pay awarded to employees on the basis of the relative value of their contributions to the organization

merit pay plan
Compensation plan that formally bases at least some meaningful portion of compensation on merit

piece-rate incentive plan
Reward system wherein the organization pays an employee a certain amount of money for every unit she or he produces

reward in conjunction with demonstrated outstanding performance in close proximity to when that performance occurred. Individual incentive systems are most likely to be used in cases in which performance can be objectively assessed in terms of number of units of output or similar measures, rather than on a subjective assessment of performance by a superior. WD-40 Company uses an individual incentive plan that covers almost its entire workforce. The firm's managers credit the incentive plan with motivating and engaging its employees to perform at high levels during both good and bad times. For instance, even during the 2008–2009 recession, the firm achieved record profits.[49]

Perhaps the most common forms of individual incentives today are *sales commissions* that are paid to people engaged in sales work. For example, sales representatives for consumer products firms and retail sales agents may be compensated under this type of commission system. In general, the person might receive a percentage of the total volume of attained sales as her or his commission for a period of time. Some sales jobs are based entirely on commission, whereas others use a combination of base minimum salary with additional commission as an incentive. Notice that these plans put a considerable amount of the salespersons' earnings "at risk." In other words, although organizations often have drawing accounts to allow the salesperson to live during lean periods (the person then "owes" this money back to the organization), if he or she does not perform well, he or she will not be paid much. The portion of salary based on commission is simply not guaranteed and is paid only if sales reach some target level.

Adam Gregor/Shutterstock.com

Sales commissions are among the most common forms of incentive pay plans. This smartphone sales professional, for example, earns a base salary. However, she also earns additional income based on the total volume of sales she generates each week. So, she is incentivized to sell as many smartphones and related products and services as possible because doing so increases her own pay.

Other Forms of Incentive   Occasionally organizations may also use other forms of incentives to motivate people. For example, a nonmonetary incentive, such as additional time off or a special perk, might be a useful incentive. For example, a company might establish a sales contest in which the sales group that attains the highest level of sales increase over a specified period of time will receive an extra week of paid vacation, perhaps even at an prearranged place, such as a tropical resort or a ski lodge, or on a cruise.[50]

A major advantage of incentives relative to merit systems is that incentives are typically a one-time reward and do not accumulate by becoming part of the individual's base salary. Stated differently, a person whose outstanding performance entitles him or her to a financial incentive gets the incentive only one time, based on that level of performance. If the person's performance begins to erode in the future, then she or he may receive a lesser incentive or perhaps no incentive in the future. As a consequence, his or her base salary remains the same or is perhaps increased at a relatively moderate pace; he or she receives one-time incentive rewards as recognition for exemplary performance. Furthermore, because these plans, by their very nature, focus on one-time events, it is much easier for the organization to change the focus of the incentive plan. At a simple level, for example, an organization can set up an incentive plan for selling one product during one quarter, but then shift the incentive to a different product the next quarter, as the situation requires. Automobile companies like Ford and GM routinely do this by reducing sales incentives for models that are selling very well and increasing sales incentives for models that are selling below expectations or are about to be discontinued.

DOING BUSINESS ON PLANET EARTH

M(otivation) p(er) G(allon)

Drivers for private truck fleets log about 20,000 miles a year. They drive 82 percent of all medium- and heavy-duty vehicles in the United States and account for 52 percent of the total miles traveled by commercial motor vehicles (CMVs). "The way these employees drive," says veteran industry journalist Mike Antich, "can either increase or decrease fuel economy and greenhouse gas emissions." "If you change driving behavior," Antich argues, "you have a direct impact on the amount of fuel consumed and the amount of emissions produced. Even small increases in mpg [miles per gallon]" can make a big difference, and Antich points out that fuel-conscious fleet managers have reported up to 30 percent reductions in fuel consumption by changing driver behavior.

How? By motivating drivers to comply with company sustainability policies. Unfortunately, of course, it's not that simple. Most drivers, according to Antich, "want to do the right thing but don't see sustainability as part of their job responsibilities. In fact, the No. 1 reason corporate sustainability programs are not 'sustainable' is driver noncompliance. A successful sustainability initiative," says Antich, "requires developing programs that motivate employees to comply." He goes on to argue that effective motivational programs often involve *gainsharing*— programs designed to share company cost savings with employees.

Again, however, implementing the solution isn't quite as easy as identifying it. Traditionally, observes Antich, gainsharing involves *financial incentives*, but he admits that "in today's cost-constrained business environment, offering financial incentives [may not be] a realistic option." Consequently, many firms have found that *individual recognition* can be an effective alternative to financial incentives: "Repeatedly," says Antich, "respondents to employee surveys rate 'individual recognition' as a key factor that motivates them to want to excel or achieve corporate objectives."

Both scientific studies and the experiences of various companies show that the importance of employee recognition—including financial rewards—should not be underestimated in sustainability efforts, primarily because the importance of *individual behavior* should not

be underestimated. According to a report by Jones Lang LaSalle (JLL), a professional-services and investment-management company, many companies with active efficiency programs are finding that further improvements in sustainability can be achieved only by turning to the people who are responsible for implementing those programs. "The low-hanging fruit has been plucked," JLL's Michael Jordan advises clients. "You now need the participation of humans."

Nussbaum Transportation, for example, has developed a software program called Driver Excelerator, which collects and analyzes fuel-related data from various sources, including electronic control devices for capturing mpg numbers. Using the resulting data, managers award points to drivers of the 230-truck fleet for beating the company's mpg goal. If, for instance, a driver achieves an average quarterly mpg of 8.5 against a goal of 6.5, he or she receives 200 points, which are allotted according to a three-tier system: Bronze pays $0.50 per point, Silver $5.00 per point, and Gold $8.00 per point. Some drivers in the Gold tier earn an extra $1,600 every three months.

Illinois-based Nussbaum was careful to reject an "all-or-nothing" system in which drivers received a bonus for meeting a target and nothing for falling short. "Our experience," says HR Director Jeremy Stickling, "shows that that's a big de-motivator" because drivers who miss out tend to blame external circumstances such as weather or load weights. In fact, Nussbaum plans to make mileage-based performance rewards a bigger portion of drivers' base-pay rate. The idea is for drivers to get higher monthly checks instead of big quarterly bonus checks. "Guys want their money now," notes Stickling.

References: Mike Antich, "Using 'Gainsharing' to Achieve Sustainability Goals," Automotive Fleet, April 2, 2014, www.automotive-fleet.com on May 8, 2020; Jones Lang LaSalle, "Employee Sustainability Engagement," www.joneslanglasalle.com on May 8, 2020; American Transportation Research Institute, "The Role of Truck Drivers in Sustainability," http://atri-online.org on May 8, 2020; and Aaron Huff, "Performance-Based Pay, Part 1: The Science of Scoring Drivers," *Commercial Carrier Journal*, December 18, 2013, www.ccjdigital.com on May 8, 2020.

10-6c Team and Group Incentive Reward Systems

The merit compensation and incentive compensation systems described in the preceding sections deal primarily with performance-based reward arrangements for individuals. There also exists a different set of performance-based reward programs that are targeted for teams and groups. These programs are particularly important for managers to understand today, given the widespread trends toward team- and group-based methods of work and organization.[51]

Common Team and Group Reward Systems   There are two commonly used types of team and group reward systems. One type used in many organizations is an approach called *gainsharing*. Gainsharing programs are designed to share the cost savings from productivity improvements with employees. The underlying assumption of gainsharing is that employees and the employer have the same goals and thus should appropriately share in incremental economic gains.[52] The *Doing Business on Planet Earth* feature provides an interesting example of an innovative gainsharing program.

gainsharing programs Designed to share the cost savings from productivity improvements with employees

In general, organizations that use gainsharing start by measuring team- or group-level productivity. It is important that this measure be valid and reliable and that it truly reflect current levels of performance by the team or group. The team or work group itself is then given the task of trying to lower costs and otherwise improve productivity through any measures that its members develop and its manager approves. Resulting cost savings or productivity gains that the team or group is able to achieve are then quantified and translated into dollar values. A predetermined formula is then used to allocate these dollar savings between the employer and the employees themselves. A typical formula for distributing gainsharing savings is to provide 25 percent to the employees and 75 percent to the company.

One specific type of gainsharing plan is an approach called the Scanlon plan. This approach was developed by Joseph Scanlon in 1927. The Scanlon plan has the same basic strategy as gainsharing plans, in that teams or groups of employees are encouraged to suggest strategies for reducing costs. However, the distribution of these gains is usually tilted much more heavily toward employees, with employees usually receiving between two-thirds and three-fourths of the total cost savings that the plan achieves. Furthermore, the distribution of cost savings resulting from the plan is given not just to the team or group that suggested and developed the ideas but across the entire organization.

Scanlon plan Similar to gainsharing, but the distribution of gains is tilted much more heavily toward employees

Other Types of Team and Group Rewards   Although gainsharing and Scanlon-type plans are among the most popular group incentive reward systems, there are other systems that are also used by some organizations. Some companies, for example, have begun to use true incentives at the team or group level. Just as with individual incentives, team or group incentives tie rewards directly to performance increases. And, like individual incentives, team or group incentives are paid as they are earned rather than being added to employees' base salaries. The incentives are distributed at the team or group level, however, rather than at the individual level. In some cases, the distribution may be based on the existing salary of each employee, with incentive bonuses being given on a proportionate basis. In other settings, each member of the team or group receives the same incentive pay.

Some companies also use nonmonetary rewards at the team or group level—most commonly in the form of prizes and awards. For example, a company might visibly recognize and celebrate the particular team in a plant or subunit of the company that achieves the highest level of productivity increase, the highest level of reported customer satisfaction, or a similar index of performance. The reward itself might take the form of additional time off, as described earlier in this chapter, or a tangible award, such as a trophy or plaque. In any event, the idea is that the reward is at the team level and serves as recognition of exemplary performance by the entire team.

There are also other kinds of team- or group-level incentives that go beyond the contributions of a specific work group. These are generally organizationwide kinds of incentives. One longstanding method for this approach is *profit sharing*. In a profit-sharing approach, at the end of the year some portion of the company's profits is paid into a profit-sharing pool that is then distributed to all employees. Either this amount is distributed at that time or it is put into an escrow account and payment is deferred until the employee retires.

The basic rationale behind profit-sharing systems is that everyone in the organization can expect to benefit when the company does well. But, on the other side of the coin, during bad economic times, when the company is earning little or no profit, then there is little or no contribution to the profit-sharing fund. This sometimes results in negative reactions from employees, who have perhaps come to feel that profit sharing is really a part of their annual compensation.

Employee stock ownership plans (ESOPs) also represent a group-level reward system that some companies use. Under the employee stock ownership plan, employees are gradually given a meaningful stake in ownership of a corporation. The typical form of this plan involves the company taking out a loan, which is then used to buy a portion of its own stock in the open market. Over time, company profits are then used to pay off this loan. Employees, in turn, receive a claim on ownership of some portion of the stock held by the company, usually based on their seniority and sometimes on their performance. Eventually, each individual becomes an owner of the company. One study found that 20 percent of employees in the private sector (25 million Americans) reported owning stock in their companies, with 10 percent holding stock options.[53]

Employee stock ownership plans are a group-level reward plan that some companies use. Publix is a Florida-based regional grocery chain with around 193,000 employees and 1,239 locations across the Southeast. Publix is jointly owned by the family of its founder (George Jenkins) and current and former employees and is the largest employee-owned company in the United States. In 2019 the firm was also number 39 on *Fortune*'s list of the "100 Best Places to Work."

John Mantell/Shutterstock.com

10-6d Executive Compensation

The top-level executives of most companies have separate compensation programs and plans. These are intended to reward these executives for their performance and for the performance of the organization.

Standard Forms of Executive Compensation   Most senior executives receive their compensation in two forms. One form is a *base salary*. As with the base salary of any staff member or professional member of an organization, the base salary of an executive is a guaranteed amount of money that the person will be paid. For example, in 2019 General Motors paid its CEO, Mary Barra, $2.1 million in base salary.[54]

Above and beyond this base salary, however, most executives also receive one or more forms of incentive pay. The traditional method of incentive pay for executives is in the form of bonuses. Bonuses, in turn, are usually determined by the performance of the organization. Thus, at the end of the year, some portion of a corporation's profits may be diverted into a bonus pool. Senior executives then receive a bonus expressed as a percentage of this bonus pool. The chief executive officer and president are obviously likely to get a larger percentage bonus than a vice president. The exact distribution of the bonus pool is usually specified ahead of time in the individual's employment contract. Some organizations intentionally leave the distribution unspecified, so that the board of directors has the flexibility to give larger rewards to those deemed to be most deserving. GM's Mary Barra received a cash bonus of $2.73 million in 2019.[55]

Special Forms of Executive Compensation   Beyond base salary and bonuses, many executives receive other kinds of compensation as well. A form of executive compensation that has received a lot of attention in recent years has been various kinds of stock and stock options. A **stock option plan** is established to give senior managers the option to buy company stock in the future at a predetermined fixed price. The basic idea underlying stock option plans is that if the executives contribute to higher levels of organizational performance, then the company stock should increase in value. Then the executive will be able to purchase the stock at the predetermined price, which theoretically should be lower than its future market price. The difference then becomes profit for the individual. GM awarded Mary Barra $12.14 million in direct stock payments and additional stock options with a potential value of $3.5 million.[56]

Stock and stock options continue to grow in popularity as a means of compensating top managers. Options, especially, are seen as a means of aligning the interests of the manager with those of the stockholders and, given that they do not cost the organization much (other than some possible dilution of stock values), they will probably be even more popular in the future.

stock option plan
Established to give senior managers the option to buy company stock in the future at a predetermined fixed price

Top executives often get perquisites, or "perks," in addition to their salary, bonuses, and stock options. Access to corporate planes is a common perk in some companies.

Tom Kuest - Fotograf/Shutterstock.com

In fact, a recent study by KPMG Peat Marwick indicates that for senior management whose salary exceeds $250,000, stock options represent the largest share of the salary mix (relative to salary and other incentives). Furthermore, when we consider all of top management (annual salary over $750,000), stock options comprise a full 60 percent of their total compensation. And the Peat Marwick report indicates that even among exempt employees at the $50,000-a-year level, stock options represent 13 percent of total compensation.

But events in recent years have raised serious questions about the use of stock options as incentives for executives. For example, several executives at Enron allegedly withheld critical financial information from the markets, cashed in their stock options (while Enron stock was trading at $80 a share), and then watched as the financial information was made public and the stock fell to less than $1 a share. Of course, actions such as these (if proven) are illegal, but they still raise questions in the public's mind about the role of stock options and about the way organizations treat stock options from an accounting perspective. Most organizations have *not* treated stock options as liabilities, even though, when exercised, they are exactly that. There is concern that by not carrying stock options as liabilities, the managers are overstating the value of the company, which, of course, can help raise the stock price. Finally, when stock prices fall below the option price, they become essentially worthless.

Aside from stock option plans, other kinds of executive compensation are also used by some companies. Among the more popular are such perquisites as memberships in private clubs, access to company recreational facilities, and similar considerations. Some organizations also make available to senior executives low- or no-interest loans. These are often given to new executives whom the company is hiring from other companies and serve as an incentive for the person to leave his or her current job to join a new organization. GM's Mary Barra received $1.5 million in other compensation during 2019 for things such as perks, tax reimbursement, and payments for life insurance.[57]

Criticisms of Executive Compensation   In recent years, executive compensation has come under fire for a variety of reasons. One major reason is that the levels of executive compensation attained by some managers seem simply too large for the average shareholder to understand. It is not uncommon, for instance, for a senior executive of a major corporation to earn total income from his or her job in a given year of well in excess of $1 million and sometimes the income of chief executive officers can be substantially more than this. Mary Barra's total compensation from GM in 2019 was 203 times the compensation for the median GM employee that year. Thus, just as the typical person may have difficulty comprehending the income of some movie stars and sports stars, so, too, would the average person be surprised at the astronomical salaries paid to some senior executives.

Compounding the problem created by perceptions of executive compensation is the fact that there often seems to be little or no relationship between the performance of the organization and the compensation paid to its senior executives.[58] Certainly, if an organization is performing at an especially high level and its stock price is increasing consistently, then most observers would agree that the senior executives responsible for this growth should be entitled to attractive rewards.[59] However, it is more difficult to understand a case in which executives are paid large salaries and other forms of rewards when their company is performing at only a marginal level, yet this is fairly common today. For example, two years before his departure, former General Electric CEO Jeffrey Immelt received stock options that increased his total compensation to $28.5 million from a base salary of $9.8 million, an increase of 188 percent. However, during that same year shareholder returns fell behind those of similar companies (24.33 percent compared to 32.21 percent).[60]

10-6e New Approaches to Performance-Based Rewards

Some organizations have started to recognize that they can leverage the value of the incentives they offer to their employees and to groups in their organization by allowing those individuals and groups to have a say in how rewards are distributed. For example, at the extreme, a company could go so far as to grant salary increase budgets to work groups and then allow the members of those groups themselves to determine how the rewards are going to be allocated among the various members of the group. This strategy would appear to hold considerable promise if everyone understands the performance arrangements that exist in the work group and everyone is committed to being fair and equitable. Unfortunately, it can also create problems if people in a group feel that rewards are not being distributed fairly.[61]

Organizations are also getting increasingly innovative in their incentive programs. For example, some now offer stock options to all their employees, rather than just to top executives. In addition, some firms are looking into ways to purely individualize reward systems. For instance, a firm might offer one employee a paid three-month sabbatical every two years in exchange for a 20 percent reduction in salary. Another employee in the same firm might be offered a 10 percent salary increase in exchange for a 5 percent reduction in company contributions to the person's retirement account. Corning, General Electric, and Microsoft are among the firms that have indicated potential interest in these kinds of options.[62]

Regardless of the method used, however, it is also important that managers in an organization effectively communicate what rewards are being distributed and the basis for that distribution. In other words, if incentives are being distributed on the basis of perceived individual contributions to the organization, then members of the organization should be informed of that fact. This will presumably better enable them to understand the basis on which pay increases and other incentives and performance-based rewards have been distributed.

Manager's Checklist

☐ Managers need to know the essential elements of merit and incentive reward systems.

☐ You should also be aware of the various issues associated with executive compensation.

SUMMARY OF LEARNING OUTCOMES AND KEY POINTS

10-1. Discuss the nature of motivation, including its importance and historical perspectives.

- Motivation is the set of forces that cause people to behave in certain ways.

- Motivation is an important consideration for managers because, along with ability and environmental factors, it determines individual performance.

- Thinking about motivation has evolved from the traditional view through the human relations approach to the human resource view.

10-2. Describe the major *content* perspectives on motivation.

- Content perspectives on motivation are concerned with what factor or factors cause motivation.

- Popular content theories include Maslow's needs hierarchy, the ERG theory, and Herzberg's two-factor theory.
- Other important needs are the needs for achievement, affiliation, and power.

10-3. Describe the major *process* perspectives on motivation.

- Process perspectives on motivation deal with how motivation occurs.
- Expectancy theory suggests that people are motivated to perform if they believe that their effort will result in high performance, that this performance will lead to rewards, and that the positive aspects of the outcomes outweigh the negative aspects.
- Equity theory is based on the premise that people are motivated to achieve and maintain social equity.
- Attribution theory is a new process theory.

10-4. Describe *reinforcement* perspectives on motivation.

- The reinforcement perspective focuses on how motivation is maintained.
- Its basic assumption is that behavior that results in rewarding consequences is likely to be

repeated, whereas behavior resulting in negative consequences is less likely to be repeated.

- Reinforcement contingencies can be arranged in the form of positive reinforcement, avoidance, punishment, and extinction, and they can be provided on fixed-interval, variable-interval, fixed-ratio, or variable-ratio schedules.

10-5. Discuss popular motivational strategies.

- Managers use a variety of motivational strategies derived from the various theories of motivation.
- Common strategies include empowerment and participation and alternative forms of work arrangements, such as variable work schedules, flexible work schedules, and telecommuting.

10-6. Describe the role of organizational reward systems in motivation.

- Reward systems also play a key role in motivating employee performance.
- Popular methods include merit reward systems, incentive reward systems, and team and group incentive reward systems.
- Executive compensation is also intended to serve as motivation for senior managers but has currently come under close scrutiny and criticism.

DISCUSSION QUESTIONS

Questions for Review

1. Each historical perspective on motivation built on the earlier perspectives and differed from them in some ways. Describe the similarities and differences between the traditional approach and the human relations approach. Then describe the similarities and differences between the human relations approach and the human resource approach.
2. Compare and contrast content, process, and reinforcement perspectives on motivation.
3. Explain how goal-setting theory works. How is goal setting different from merely asking a worker to "do your best"?
4. Describe some new forms of working arrangements. How do these alternative arrangements increase motivation?

Questions for Analysis

1. Choose one theory from the content perspectives and one from the process perspectives. Describe actions that a manager might take to increase worker motivation

under each of the theories. What differences do you see between the theories in terms of their implications for managers?
2. Can factors from both the content and the process perspectives be acting on a worker at the same time? Explain why or why not. Whether you answered yes or no to the previous question, explain the implications for managers.
3. How do rewards increase motivation? What would happen if an organization gave too few rewards? What would happen if it gave too many?

Questions for Application

1. Think about the worst job you have held. What approach to motivation was used in that organization? Now think about the best job you have held. What approach to motivation was used there? Can you base any conclusions on this limited information? If so, what are they?
2. Interview both a manager and a worker (or administrator and faculty member) from a local organization. What

views of or approaches to motivation seem to be in use in that organization? Do the manager's views differ from the worker's? If so, how do you explain the differing perceptions?

3. Consider a class you have taken. Using just that one class, offer examples of times when the professor used positive reinforcement, avoidance, punishment, and extinction to manage students' behavior.

BUILDING EFFECTIVE INTERPERSONAL SKILLS

Exercise Overview

Interpersonal skills refer to your ability to communicate with, understand, and motivate both individuals and groups. This exercise gives you a chance to see whether the factors that motivate you come primarily from you and your work itself or from factors that are external to you and the nature of your work.

Exercise Task

Following is a list of 12 factors that contribute to job satisfaction and motivation. To find out how important each factor is to you, select a number from 1 to 5 according to the following scale:

1. _____ An interesting job that I enjoy doing
2. _____ A boss who treats everyone the same regardless of the circumstances
3. _____ Getting praise and other recognition and appreciation for my work

4. _____ A job that's routine without much change from day to day
5. _____ Opportunity for advancement
6. _____ A nice title regardless of pay
7. _____ Job responsibility that gives me the freedom to do things my way
8. _____ Good working conditions (e.g., safe environment, convenient cafeteria, etc.)
9. _____ Opportunity to learn new things
10. _____ Emphasis on following rules, regulations, procedures, and policies
11. _____ A job that I can do well and succeed at
12. _____ Job security; a job with one company

5	4	3	2	1
Very Important		**Somewhat Important**		**Not Important**

Scoring: Next, the 12 factors are divided into two lists. For each factor, record the number (from 1 to 5) that you put in the blank before it. Then add up each column (each column score should be from 6 to 30 points):

Motivating factor	Maintenance factor
1. _____	2. _____
3. _____	4. _____
5. _____	6. _____
7. _____	8. _____
9. _____	10. _____
11. _____	12. _____
Totals _____	_____

Which factors tend to be more important to you—internal (motivating) or external (maintenance)? *The closer your column score to a total of 30, the more important that factor is to you.*

Adapted from Robert N. Lussier and Christopher F. Achua, *Leadership: Theory, Application, and Skill Development*, 4th ed. (Mason, OH: South-Western Cengage Learning, 2010), pp. 82–84.

BUILDING EFFECTIVE DECISION-MAKING SKILLS

Exercise Overview

Decision-making skills refer to the ability to recognize and define problems and opportunities correctly and then to select an appropriate course of action for solving problems or capitalizing on opportunities. This exercise allows you to build your decision-making skills while applying goal-setting theory to the task of planning your career.

Exercise Background

Lee Iacocca started his career at Ford in 1946 in an entry-level engineering job. By 1960 he was a vice president and in charge of the group that designed the Mustang, and 10 years later he was a president of the firm. After being fired from Ford in 1978, he became president at Chrysler and eventually rose to the CEO spot, a job he held until he retired in 1992.

What's really remarkable about Iacocca's career arc—at least the upward trajectory—is the fact that he apparently had it all planned out, even before he finished college.

The story goes that, while he was still an undergraduate, Iacocca wrote out a list of all the positions that he'd like to hold during his career. Number one was "engineer at an auto maker," followed by all the career steps that he planned to take until he was a CEO. He also included a timetable for his climb up the corporate ladder. Then he put his list on a three-by-five-inch card that he folded and stowed in his wallet, and we're told that every time he took out that card and looked at it, he gained fresh confidence and drive. He apparently reached the top several years ahead of schedule, but otherwise he followed his career path and timetable faithfully. As you can see, Iacocca used goal-setting theory to motivate himself, and there's no reason why you can't do the same.

Exercise Task

1. Consider the position that you'd like to hold at the peak of your career. It may be CEO, owner of a chain of clothing stores, partner in a law or accounting firm, or president of a university. Then again, it may be something less lofty. Whatever it is, write it down.

2. Now describe a career path that will lead you toward that goal. It may help to work "back"—that is, starting with your final position and working backward in time to some entry-level job. If you aren't sure about the career path that will lead to your ultimate goal, do some research. Talk to someone in your selected career field, ask an instructor who teaches in it, or go online. The website of the American Institute of Certified Public Accountants, for example, has a section titled "Career Resources," which includes information about career paths and position descriptions for accounting.

3. Write down each step in your path on a card or a sheet of paper.

4. If, like Lee Iacocca, you were to carry this piece of paper with you and refer to it often as you pursued your career goals, do you think it would help you achieve them? Why or why not?

SKILL-BUILDING PERSONAL ASSESSMENT

Assessing Your Needs

Introduction: Needs are one factor that influences motivation. The following assessment surveys your judgments about some of your personal needs that might be partially shaping your motivation.

Instructions: Judge how descriptively accurate each of the following statements is about you. You may find making a decision difficult in some cases, but you should force yourself to make a choice. Record your answers next to each statement according to the following scale:

Rating Scale

5 Very descriptive of me

4 Fairly descriptive of me

3 Somewhat descriptive of me

2 Not very descriptive of me

1 Not descriptive of me at all

1. _____ I aspire to accomplish difficult tasks and maintain high standards and am willing to work toward distant goals.

2. _____ I enjoy being with friends and people in general and accept people readily.

3. _____ I am easily annoyed and am sometimes willing to hurt people to get my way.

4. _____ I try to break away from restraints or restrictions of any kind.

5. _____ I want to be the center of attention and enjoy having an audience.

6. _____ I speak freely and tend to act on the spur of the moment.

7. _____ I assist others whenever possible, giving sympathy and comfort to those in need.

8. _____ I believe in the saying that "there is a place for everything and everything should be in its place." I dislike clutter.

9. _____ I express my opinions forcefully, enjoy the role of leader, and try to control my environment as much as I can.

10. _____ I want to understand many areas of knowledge and value synthesizing ideas and generalization.

After responding to the questions, reflect on the kinds of jobs and careers most and least likely to help you fulfill these needs.

Scoring: This set of needs was developed in 1938 by H. A. Murray, a psychologist, and operationalized by another psychologist, I. W. Atkinson. Known as Murray's Manifest Needs because they are visible through behavior, they are the following:

1. Achievement
2. Affiliation
3. Aggression
4. Autonomy
5. Exhibition

6. Impulsivity
7. Nurturance
8. Order
9. Power
10. Understanding

To score your results, look at each question individually—the needs correspond one-to-one to the items on the assessment questionnaire.

Although little research has evaluated Murray's theory, the different needs have been investigated. People seem to have a different profile of needs underlying their motivations at different ages. The more any one or more of these needs are descriptive of you, the more you see that particular need as being active in your motivational makeup.

For more information, see H. A. Murray, *Explorations in Personality* (New York: Oxford University Press, 1938); and J. W. Atkinson, *An Introduction to Motivation* (Princeton, NJ: Van Nostrand, 1964).

MANAGEMENT AT WORK

Engaged to Be Motivated

"I don't mind people throwing darts at higher ed, but it doesn't have to take the blame for everything."

—Philip D. Gardner, Director of Michigan State University's Collegiate Employment Research Institute

Fact 1: If you graduate from college, you're more likely to get a full-time job than if you hadn't. *Fact 2*: If you graduate from college, you'll probably enjoy higher lifetime earnings than if you hadn't. *Fact 3*: If you graduate from college, you're *less* likely to be engaged in your work than if you hadn't.

That's right—*less* likely. To be fair, Fact 3 doesn't reflect much of a difference: According to a Gallup survey released in 2018, only 28.3 percent of graduates are "involved in and enthusiastic about" their work, compared to 32.7 percent of people who didn't go beyond high school. Even so, Brandon Busteed of Gallup Education finds the survey results "really stunning. Given that what we all expect out of college is something better," he explains, "you'd think that college graduates are way more engaged in careers than everybody else."

Does the apparent problem lie with colleges or with workplaces? Not surprisingly, the answer is both. Let's start with colleges. First of all, it doesn't appear to make any difference what kind of college a person went to—large or small, public or private, prestigious or mid-tier public: The percentages not only of those engaged at work but of those "thriving" in all areas of personal "well-being" are roughly the same (with graduates of for-profit schools faring not quite as well).

It would appear, then, that colleges of all types are failing to provide the kinds of experiences that result in high levels of workplace engagement. Have you, for example, encountered a professor who cared about you personally, got you excited about learning, or encouraged you to pursue your dreams? If so, you have been "emotionally supported," and your odds of being engaged at work (and of thriving in your well-being) have probably doubled. Have you had a job or internship that let you apply what you've been learning in college, worked on any projects that took a semester or more to complete, or been involved in extracurricular activities? If you've had the advantage of these forms of "experiential and deep learning," you're also twice as likely to be engaged and thriving. Unfortunately, only 14 percent of graduates could answer yes to the first set of criteria and only 6 percent to the second set. As for all six experiences, a mere 3 percent said yes. On individual measures, although 63 percent said that a teacher had fired them up about a subject, only 32 percent had ever worked on a long-term project, and only 22 percent had found mentors who encouraged them.

"It's literally about higher education in general," suggests Busteed. "There's something about the process and the experience that's preventing graduates from getting to a place where they're doing what they're best at." Busteed suspects that, without strong mentorship, college students fail to set clear career paths and, as a result, too many of them fall into one of two traps: (1) getting stuck in jobs for which they're overqualified or (2) resorting to such "fall-back" career paths as law school and investment banking. "I think we're kind of caught up in preconceived notions of what success should look like," says Busteed, "and it's landing a lot of college graduates in the wrong place." Some educators agree. "The particular value of [the Gallup] survey," says Harold V. Hartley III, senior VP of the Counsel of Independent Colleges, "is that it looks at outcomes that are different from the outcomes that we typically look at—like did you get a job, what's your salary, and those kinds of things."

Not surprisingly, however, many educators are unconvinced that colleges should bear the brunt of the survey's findings. "There's kind of a half-empty, half-full story here," says Alexander McCormick, director of the National Survey of Student Engagement. He points out, for instance, that the survey classifies 55 percent of the respondents as "not engaged" and argues that although these people are not emotionally connected to their workplaces, neither are they dissatisfied with them. Philip D. Gardner, director of Michigan State University's Collegiate Employment Research Institute, adds that the Gallup survey fails to account for differences in individual goals and goal-oriented behavior. Highly educated people, he observes, don't settle into jobs as quickly as most people, and younger workers are less likely to consider work critical to their identities or well-being.

Mark Schneider, VP of the American Institutes for Research, a nonprofit organization that conducts social-science and behavioral research, contends that the Gallup survey reveals interesting *correlations* (between, for example, college and workplace experiences) but falls short in providing any *causative* explanations. Take, for example, a graduate who reports the following correlation: She had an internship at college and is engaged in her work. What if this graduate was personally motivated to find the internship and is engaged in her work because she brings the same level of personal motivation to her job? The Gallup survey suggests that there is a cause-and-effect relationship between the college experience (the internship) and the workplace experience (engagement). The conclusion, however, does not necessarily follow because personal motivation may be the most significant factor in both experiences.

A critical question, it would seem, remains unaddressed: Which motivational behavior came first—acting on *personal motivation* (such as seeking the experience of the internship) or acting on *learned motivation* (such as applying the lessons learned through the internship to the postgraduation workplace)? Even Busteed admits that the survey's results may suffer from a "chicken-and-egg problem."

Which brings us to the implications of the survey results for business. As we've already seen, the survey is ultimately as much concerned with productivity and motivation in the workplace as with workplace preparation in college. According to Busteed, the survey's findings provide "a formula for something that alters life and career trajectory. … It's all actionable, by way of who we hire and how we incentivize and reward." The report thus suggests that colleges should do a better job of preparing students to get jobs in workplaces in which they'll be *engaged*—that is, in which they'll be working at something that they're good at and like for organizations that care about their work.

Philip Gardner, for one, thinks that the problem reflects workplace experiences as much as higher-education experiences. "I don't mind people throwing darts at higher ed, but it doesn't have to take the blame for everything," he says, and many researchers and consultants feel that employers should focus more clearly on the *personal motivation* that each individual brings to the workplace. According to The Fortune Group, for instance, which provides personal-development training for businesses, "motivation is internal and personal. Within each person, there has to be that drive or will to succeed, and if it's not there, *no one* can synthetically put it there."

If a company wants to increase "motivation and engagement in the workplace," says the consultancy, it must "create a climate or an environment in which people's natural abilities and internal motivations are allowed to come to the fore." In fact, The Fortune Group operates on the assumption that "employees don't perform because someone or something interferes with their desire or ability to perform." *Task interference*, for example, "could be something the employee *doesn't* have, such as proper resources, tools, or training." Another form of interference, *consequence imbalance*, occurs when employees are "doing the right things but aren't getting recognition for it." Like task interference, it should be classified as "mismanagement" because it "creates an imbalance that interferes with people's desire and/or ability to perform."[63]

Case Questions

1. Consider each of the following *perspectives on motivation*: *needs hierarchy, two-factor theory, expectancy theory, equity theory,* and *goal-setting theory*. How does each of these perspectives depend on *learned motivation*? On *personal motivation*?

2. What about you? Which form of motivation—*learned motivation* or *personal motivation*—has played a greater role in your pursuit of your goals, whether in school, at work, or in both areas? Given this assessment of your own experience with motivation, which of the motivational perspectives listed in Question 1 is most likely to help you in your work life? Whatever your answers to these questions, be sure to give examples from your own experience.

3. The theory that too few students get the help they need in setting clear career paths suggests that colleges should provide more career counseling. However, according to the National Survey of Student Engagement, only 43 percent of college seniors talked *very often* or *often* about career plans with a faculty member or adviser; 39 percent did *sometimes*, and 17 percent *never* did. How about you? Have you sought career advice or counseling from resources available at your school? Do you plan to? Have you sought advice elsewhere? If so, where elsewhere and why elsewhere?

4. The Gallup survey measured levels of engagement by asking respondents whether they *agreed* or *disagreed* with several statements about postgraduation work experiences. Here are six of those statements:

   • I have opportunities to learn and grow.
   • My opinions seem to count.
   • I have the opportunity to do what I do best every day.
   • I have the tools and resources I need to do my job.

- My supervisor encourages my development.
- I know what is expected of me.

List these six statements *in their order of importance to you as probable factors in your satisfaction with a job*. Be prepared to discuss your priorities.

[*Note*: One of these statements proved to be the strongest predictor of workplace engagement among all of the statements in the survey. Your instructor can tell you which one it is after you've drawn up and discussed your list.]

You Make the Call

What Makes SAS a Great Place to Work?

1. Consider each of the following *perspectives on motivation*: *needs hierarchy*, *two-factor theory*, and *reinforcement theory*. How would each of these perspectives contribute to an understanding of why employees at SAS are motivated and engaged?

2. Note that all but one of the perspectives in Question 1 fall into the *content* category. What about *process perspectives—expectancy theory*, *equity theory*, and *goal-setting theory*? Answering the same question with regard to process perspectives would probably prove a little more difficult. Why? In other words, explain what this exercise might tell us about some basic differences between content and process perspectives.

3. Consider the benefits that help make SAS a great place to work in terms of *incentive reward systems*. In what sense, for instance, can benefits be regarded as an incentive reward system, whether as an *incentive pay plan* or as some other form of incentive? What, if any, advantages does it have over the various types of incentive reward systems mentioned in the text? What disadvantages does it share?

4. In both this chapter and previous chapters we have examined firms that consistently make various lists of "best place to work." What strategic advantages do these firms enjoy? Why don't more firms pursue this kind of recognition?

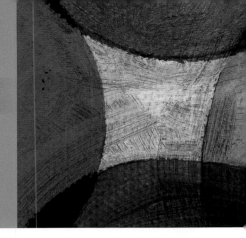

CHAPTER 11

Leadership and Influence Processes

Learning Outcomes

After studying this chapter, you should be able to:

11-1 Describe the nature of leadership and how it relates to management.

11-2 Discuss the two generic approaches to leadership.

11-3 Describe the major situational approaches to leadership.

11-4 Describe three related approaches to leadership.

11-5 Discuss three emerging approaches to leadership.

11-6 Discuss political behavior in organizations and how it can be managed.

This chapter examines leadership in organizations and looks at both effective leaders and less effective ones. We start by characterizing the nature of leadership and discuss the three major approaches to studying leadership: traits, behaviors, and situations. After examining other perspectives on leadership, we conclude by describing another approach to influencing others: political behavior in organizations. We begin with a discussion of Steve Jobs and Tim Cook, who have both led Apple but in somewhat different ways.

Management in Action

Two Bites from the Same Apple

"Innovation distinguishes between a leader and a follower."

—**Steve Jobs, Co-Founder and Former CEO of Apple**

Steve Jobs is considered to have been one of the greatest innovators and managers in the history of American business. Was he also a great leader? Many people would agree that he was, although there would also be dissent. Really, it all depends on how you define leadership and what you consider to determine leadership greatness. In 2011 Jobs turned over the reins at Apple to his hand-picked successor, Tim Cook. Is Cook a great innovator? Manager? Leader? Once again, it depends on definitions and perspectives.

Jobs was born in 1955. During his childhood he was fascinated by his father's interest in mechanics and electrical devices. He was not, however, a model student. He was advanced for his age, and most likely bored in a traditional classroom. Jobs resisted authority, often misbehaved, and was suspended more than once. In high school he was subjected to bullying, because he was so smart, and described himself as being socially awkward.

Different leadership styles are illustrated by Tim Cook (left) and Steve Jobs. However, each is considered to have been extremely effective in helping build Apple into one of the world's greatest companies.

When Jobs was age 13, he had an internship at Hewlett-Packard (now HP), further reinforcing his interest in electronics. He met Steve Wozniak in high school and the two became friends. After college Jobs took a job at Atari and began developing video games. He also continued to work with Wozniak on a variety of electronics projects. The two finished developing their prototype for what would become the Apple I personal computer in 1976 and then formed their company to begin selling them. The Apple II, however, was the product that really put Apple on the map. Unfortunately, Wozniak suffered serious injuries in an airplane accident and resigned from Apple in 1985.

Jobs continued to expand the company and soon led it to become a major player in the home computer market. He continued to push new product introductions as opposed to actually managing the firm to the point that he and other members of the board of directors decided the firm needed a more experienced manager to serve as CEO. After a long search Apple hired John Sculley, a highly respected CEO at PepsiCo, to run the company. Unfortunately, Jobs and Sculley began clashing almost immediately. Jobs wanted to continue to focus on innovation and future product development while Sculley wanted to concentrate more on current products, profitability, and market share. Things finally came to a climax when Sculley convinced the board of directors to fire Jobs.

Not to be deterred, Jobs soon started another computer firm called NeXT. NeXT, in turn, would eventually transform itself into Pixar and ultimately be acquired by Disney. Meanwhile, back at Apple, Scully did indeed help grow the company, going from $800 million to $8 billion in revenue. However, following a power struggle with board members over strategic issues and as growth slowed, Sculley was forced out of Apple in 1993. In 1997 Apple bought NeXT and Jobs rejoined the firm he had helped create. He was subsequently named CEO once again later that year.

During his second stint at Apple Jobs led the way in pushing for such developments as the MacBook, iPod, iPhone, iPad, and iTunes. And along the way Apple became a dominant force in the digital products market and Jobs himself became a legend. There was considerable debate, though, about his leadership style. Most observers agree that he was passionate but abrasive and aloof. Jobs also insisted on both excellence and perfection from everyone at Apple. He was also reportedly secretive and did little to promote teamwork.

As one observer put it, Jobs "violated every rule of management. He was not a consensus builder but a dictator who listened mainly to his own intuition. He was a maniacal micromanager. He had an astonishing aesthetic sense, which businesspeople almost always lack. . .. He never mellowed, never let up on Apple employees, never stopped relying on his singular instincts in making decisions about how Apple products should look and how they should work." And either because of or despite these behaviors, Apple continued to grow at a rapid pace. Unfortunately, however, Jobs developed serious health problems and was diagnosed with pancreatic cancer in 2003.

When his health first began to decline, Jobs had promoted Tim Cook to the position of COO and made it clear that he was to be the next leader to run Apple. Early in his career Cook spent 12 years working for IBM and then accepted a senior position at Compaq. In 1997 he was personally recruited by Jobs to join Apple and moved through a succession of senior positions as Jobs recognized that he might be his heir apparent. When Cook did take over as CEO, he quickly made several changes to the senior leadership team, in part to cut down on what he saw as political behavior. He also worked to develop a calmer, more benign culture and emphasized the needs for greater transparency and improved teamwork. Cook is reportedly also less prone to berating people, although his standards are just as high as the expectations always voiced by Jobs.

In 2014 Cook came out as gay in a Bloomberg Business editorial, noting that "I'm proud to be gay, and I consider being gay among the greatest gifts God has given me." With this announcement he became the first (and still only) openly gay leader of a *Fortune* 500 company. He has since been held up as a role model for diversity and inclusion in business and serves as an advocate for LGBTQ rights. Meanwhile, Apple continues to hum along and shows no signs of slowing down. And just as Steve Jobs developed a carefully crafted plan to identify who would eventually replace him, Cook has also commented that he probably already knows who will someday replace *him*.[1]

11-1 THE NATURE OF LEADERSHIP

In Chapter 15, we described various models and perspectives on employee motivation. From the manager's standpoint, trying to motivate people is an attempt to influence their behavior. In many ways, leadership, too, is an attempt to influence the behavior of others. Consequently, motivation and leadership are complementary activities in organizations. In this section, we first define leadership, then differentiate it from management, and conclude by relating it to power.

11-1a The Meaning of Leadership

leadership
As a process, the use of noncoercive influence to shape the group's or organization's goals, motivate behavior toward the achievement of those goals, and help define group or organizational culture; as a property, the set of characteristics attributed to individuals who are perceived to be leaders

leaders
People who can influence the behaviors of others without having to rely on force; those accepted by others as leaders

Leadership is both a process and a property.[2] As a process—focusing on what leaders actually do—leadership is the use of noncoercive influence to shape the group or organization's goals, motivate behavior toward the achievement of those goals, and help define group or organizational culture.[3] As a property, leadership is the set of characteristics attributed to individuals who are perceived to be leaders. Thus, leaders are (1) people who can influence the behaviors of others without having to rely on coercion or (2) people whom others accept as leaders. Both Steve Jobs and Tim Cook are acknowledged as leaders by most people even though their styles are different.

11-1b Leadership and Management

From these definitions, it should be clear that leadership and management are related, but they are also not the same. A person can be a manager, a leader, both, or neither.[4] Some of the basic distinctions between the two are summarized in Table 11.1. At the left side of the table are four activities that differentiate leadership from management. The other two columns show how each element differs when considered from a management and from a leadership point of view. For example, when executing plans, managers focus on monitoring results, comparing them with goals, and correcting deviations. In contrast, leaders focus on energizing people to overcome bureaucratic hurdles to reach goals.

Management and leadership are not necessarily the same thing. The manager on the left is reviewing financial documents in order to make a decision. These activities are a part of management, but not leadership. However, the manager on the right is engaging in leadership as she is working to motivate her team to meet their new performance expectations.

Organizations need both management and leadership if they are to be effective. Leadership is necessary to create change, and management is necessary to achieve orderly results. Management in conjunction with leadership can produce orderly change, and leadership in conjunction with management can keep the organization properly aligned with its environment. Indeed, perhaps part of the reason why executive compensation has soared in recent years is the belief that management and leadership skills reflect a critical but rare combination that can lead to organizational success.

Table 11.1	Distinctions Between Management and Leadership	
Activity	**Management**	**Leadership**
Creating an agenda	*Planning and Budgeting* Establishing detailed steps and timetables for achieving needed results; allocating the resources necessary to make those needed results happen	*Establishing Direction* Developing a vision of the future, often the distant future, and strategies for producing the changes needed to achieve that vision
Developing a human network for achieving the agenda	*Organizing and Staffing* Establishing some structure for accomplishing plan requirements, staffing that structure with individuals, delegating responsibility and authority for carrying out the plan, providing policies and procedures to help guide people, and creating methods or systems to monitor implementation	*Aligning People* Communicating the direction by words and deeds to everyone whose cooperation may be needed to influence the creation of teams and coalitions that understand the visions and strategies and accept their validity
Executing plans	*Controlling and Problem Solving* Monitoring results versus planning in some detail, identifying deviations, and then planning and organizing to solve these problems	*Motivating and Inspiring* Energizing people to overcome major political, bureaucratic, and resource barriers by satisfying very basic, but often unfulfilled, human needs
Outcomes	Producing a degree of predictability and order and having the potential to produce consistently major results expected by various stakeholders (e.g., for customers, always being on time; for stockholders, being on budget)	Producing change, often to a dramatic degree, and having the potential to produce extremely useful change (e.g., new products that customers want, new approaches to labor relations that help make a firm more competitive)

Management and leadership are related, but independent, constructs. Managers and leaders differ in how they create an agenda, develop a rationale for achieving the agenda, and execute plans, and they differ in the types of outcomes they achieve.

Source: The Free Press, a division of Simon & Schuster Adult Publishing Group, from *A Force for Change: How Leadership Differs from Management* by John P. Kotter. 1990.

11-1c Leadership and Power

power
The ability to affect the behavior of others

To fully understand leadership, it is also necessary to understand power. Power is the ability to affect the behavior of others. It is also important to note that one can have power without actually using it. For example, a basketball coach has the power to bench a player who is not performing up to par. The coach seldom has to use this power, though, because players recognize that the power exists and work hard to keep their starting positions. In organizational settings, there are usually five kinds of power: legitimate, reward, coercive, referent, and expert power.[5]

legitimate power
Power granted through the organizational hierarchy; the power defined by the organization to be accorded to people occupying particular positions

Legitimate Power   Legitimate power is power granted through the organizational hierarchy; it is the power defined by the organization to be accorded to people occupying a particular position. A manager can assign job-relevant tasks to a subordinate, and a subordinate who refuses to do them or does them poorly can be reprimanded or even fired. Such outcomes stem from the manager's legitimate power as defined and vested in her or him by the organization. Legitimate power, then, is essentially the same as authority. All managers have legitimate power over their subordinates. The mere possession of legitimate power, however, does not by itself make someone a leader. Some subordinates follow only orders that are strictly within the letter of organizational rules and policies. If asked to do something not in their job descriptions, they may refuse or do a poor job. In this situation the manager is exercising authority but not leadership. There were questions during the 2020 COVID-19 pandemic about the extent to which government leaders had the legitimate power to order people to shelter in place, wear masks, exercise social distancing, and so forth. Some people, for instance, agreed with these kinds of mandates whereas others rebelled against them.

"I want the government to go away. They are taking away our future."
—Unidentified German Protester during 2020 COVID-19 Lockdown[6]

reward power
The power to give or withhold rewards, such as salary increases, bonuses, promotions, praise, recognition, and interesting job assignments

Reward Power   Reward power is the power to give or withhold rewards. Rewards that a manager may control include salary increases, bonuses, promotion recommendations, praise, recognition, and interesting job assignments. In general, the greater the number of rewards a manager controls and the more important the rewards are to subordinates, the greater is the manager's reward power. If the subordinate sees as valuable only the formal organizational rewards controlled by the manager, then he or she is not a leader. If the subordinate also wants and appreciates the manager's informal rewards, such as praise, gratitude, and recognition, however, then the manager is also exercising leadership.

coercive power
The power to force compliance by means of psychological, emotional, or physical threat

Coercive Power   Coercive power is the power to force compliance by means of psychological, emotional, or physical threat. In the past, physical coercion in organizations was relatively common. In most organizations today, however, coercion is limited to verbal reprimands, written reprimands, disciplinary layoffs, fines, demotion, and termination. Some managers occasionally go so far as to use verbal abuse, humiliation, and psychological coercion in an attempt to manipulate subordinates. (Of course, most people would agree that these are not appropriate leadership behaviors.) James Dutt, a legendary former CEO of Beatrice Company, once told a subordinate that if his wife and family got in the way of his working a 24-hour day seven days a week, he should get rid of them.[7] Charlie Ergen, founder and chairman of Dish Network, is also known to be an abrasive and hard-nosed leader. Dish is often cited as one of the worst places to work in America.[8] While not going to these extremes, there have been reports that Steve Jobs occasionally used coercion to get things done. The more punitive the elements under a manager's control and the more important they are to subordinates, the more coercive power the manager possesses. On the other hand, the more managers use coercive power, the more likely they are to provoke resentment and hostility and the less likely they are to be seen as leaders.[9]

referent power
The personal power that accrues to someone based on identification, imitation, loyalty, or charisma

"[Dish Network's Charlie Ergen's leadership style is] . . . pounding people into submission."
—Former Dish Executive[10]

Referent Power   Compared with legitimate, reward, and coercive power, which are relatively concrete and grounded in objective facets of organizational life, referent power is abstract. It is based on identification, imitation, loyalty, or charisma. Followers may react favorably because they

Coercive power is the power to force compliance by means of psychological, emotional, or physical threat. This manager is using coercive power by yelling at his assistant. While this may produce immediate results, in the long run it will breed resentment and lead to low morale and turnover.

NDAB Creativity/Shutterstock.com

identify in some way with a leader, who may be like them in personality, background, or attitudes. In other situations, followers might choose to imitate a leader with referent power by wearing the same kind of clothing, working the same hours, or espousing the same management philosophy. Steve Jobs usually wore jeans and black turtlenecks in public appearances, and some Apple employees adopted the same style because they admired him so much. Referent power may also take the form of charisma, an intangible attribute of the leader that inspires loyalty and enthusiasm. Thus, a manager might have referent power, but it is more likely to be associated with leadership.

Expert Power **Expert power** is derived from information or expertise. A manager who knows how to interact with an eccentric but important customer, a scientist who is capable of achieving an important technical break-through that no other company has dreamed

expert power
The personal power that accrues to someone based on the information or expertise they possess

of, and an administrative assistant who knows how to unravel bureaucratic red tape all have expert power over anyone who needs that information. During the 2020 COVID-19 pandemic, people who already knew how to use online communication platforms like Microsoft Teams and Zoom held expert power as they helped others learn those same skills. The more important the information and the fewer the people who have access to it, the greater is the degree of expert power possessed by any one person. In the case of the COVID-19 situation the expert power mentioned previously was short-lived as most people found it relatively easy to learn the new skills needed for virtual meetings. In general, people who are both leaders and managers tend to have a lot of expert power.

Expert power is derived from information or expertise. This manager is showing his colleagues how to interpret some complex statistical analyses. At this point, at least, he has expert power.

Goodluz/Shutterstock.com

Using Power How does a manager or leader use power? Several methods have been identified. One method is the *legitimate request*, which is based on legitimate power. The manager requests that the subordinate comply because the subordinate recognizes that the organization has given the manager the right to make the request. Most day-to-day interactions between manager and subordinate are of this type. Another use of power is *instrumental compliance*, which is based on the reinforcement theory of motivation. In this form of exchange, a subordinate complies to get a reward the manager controls. Suppose that a manager asks a subordinate to do something outside the range of the subordinate's normal duties, such as working extra hours on the weekend, terminating a relationship with a longstanding buyer, or delivering bad news. The subordinate complies and, as a direct result, reaps praise and a bonus from the manager. The next time the subordinate is asked to perform a similar activity, that subordinate will recognize that compliance will be instrumental in her getting more rewards. Hence, the basis of instrumental compliance is clarifying important performance–reward contingencies.

A manager is using *coercion* when she suggests or implies that the subordinate will be punished, fired, or reprimanded if he does not do something. *Rational persuasion* occurs when the manager can convince the subordinate that compliance is in the subordinate's best interests. For example, a manager might argue that the subordinate should accept a transfer because it would be good for the subordinate's career. In some ways, rational persuasion is like reward power, except that the manager does not directly control the reward.

Still another way a manager can use power is through *personal identification*. A manager who recognizes that she has referent power over a subordinate can shape the behavior of that subordinate by engaging in desired behaviors: The manager consciously becomes a model for the subordinate and exploits personal identification. Sometimes a manager can induce a subordinate to do something consistent with a set of higher ideals or values through *inspirational appeal*. For example, pleas for loyalty and teamwork (such as "we really need to support our company on this" or "we all need to pull together as a team to get this done") represent inspirational appeals. Referent power plays a role in determining the extent to which an inspirational appeal is successful because its effectiveness depends at least in part on the persuasive abilities of the leader.

An ill-advised method of using power is through *information distortion*. In this case a manager may withhold or distort information to influence subordinates' behavior. For example, if a manager has agreed to allow everyone to participate in choosing a new group member but subsequently finds one person whom she really prefers, she might withhold some of the credentials of other qualified applicants so that the desired member is selected. This use of power is very risky and in many cases unethical. For example, if subordinates find out that the manager has deliberately misled them or withheld information, they will lose their confidence and trust in that manager's leadership.[11]

Manager's Checklist

☐ All managers should understand the distinctions between leadership and management.

☐ Managers should also be familiar with the five bases of power.

11-2 GENERIC APPROACHES TO LEADERSHIP

Early approaches to the study of leadership adopted what might be called a "universal" or "generic" perspective. Specifically, they assumed that there was one set of answers to the leadership puzzle. One generic approach focused on leadership traits, and the other looked at leadership behavior.

11-2a Leadership Traits

The first organized approach to studying leadership analyzed the personal, psychological, and physical traits of strong leaders. The trait approach assumed that some basic trait or set of traits existed that differentiated leaders from nonleaders. If those traits could be defined, they reasoned, potential leaders could be identified based on those traits. Researchers thought that leadership traits might include intelligence, assertiveness, above-average height, good vocabulary, attractiveness, self-confidence, and similar attributes.[12]

During the first half of the twentieth century, hundreds of studies were conducted in an attempt to identify important leadership traits. For the most part, the results of the studies were disappointing. For every set of leaders who possessed a common trait, a long list of exceptions was also found, and the list of suggested traits soon grew so long that it had little practical value. Alternative explanations usually existed even for relationships between traits and leadership that initially appeared valid. For example, it was observed that many leaders have good communication skills and are assertive. Rather than those traits being the cause of leadership, however, successful leaders may begin to display those traits after they have achieved a leadership position.

job-centered leader behavior
The behavior of leaders who pay close attention to the job and work procedures involved with that job

employee-centered leader behavior
The behavior of leaders who develop cohesive work groups and ensure employee satisfaction

Although most researchers gave up trying to identify traits as predictors of leadership ability, many people still explicitly or implicitly adopt a trait orientation.[13] For example, politicians are all too often elected on the basis of personal appearance, public speaking abilities, or an aura of self-confidence. In addition, though, traits like honesty and integrity may very well be fundamental leadership traits that serve an important purpose and should obviously be considered. Intelligence also seems to play a meaningful role in leadership.[14]

11-2b Leadership Behaviors

Spurred on by their lack of success in identifying useful leadership traits, researchers soon began to investigate other variables, especially the actual behaviors or actions of leaders. The new assumption was that effective leaders somehow behaved differently than less effective leaders. Thus, the goal was to develop a fuller understanding of leadership behaviors.

> "It is wise to persuade people to do things and make them think it was their own idea."
> —Nelson Mandela, Former President of South Africa

initiating-structure behavior
The behavior of leaders who define the leader–subordinate role so that everyone knows what is expected, establish formal lines of communication, and determine how tasks will be performed

Michigan Studies Researchers at the University of Michigan, led by Rensis Likert, began studying leadership several decades ago.[15] Based on extensive interviews with both leaders (managers) and followers (subordinates), this research identified two basic forms of leader behavior: job centered and employee centered. Managers using job-centered leader behavior pay close attention to subordinates' work, explain work procedures, and are keenly interested in performance. Managers using employee-centered leader behavior are interested in developing a cohesive work group and ensuring that employees are satisfied with their jobs. Their primary concern is the welfare of subordinates.

The two styles of leader behavior were presumed to be at the ends of a single continuum. Although this suggests that leaders may be extremely job centered, extremely employee centered, or somewhere in between, Likert studied only the two end styles for contrast. He argued that employee-centered leader behavior generally tends to be more effective. We should also note the similarities between Likert's leadership research and his Systems 1 through 4 organization designs (discussed in Chapter 11). Job-centered leader behavior is consistent with the System 1 design (rigid and bureaucratic), whereas employee-centered leader behavior is consistent with the System 4 design (organic and flexible). When Likert advocated moving organizations from System 1 to System 4, he was also advocating a transition from job-centered to employee-centered leader behavior throughout the organization.

Ohio State Studies At about the same time that Likert was beginning his leadership studies at the University of Michigan, a group of researchers at Ohio State University also began studying leadership.[16] The extensive questionnaire surveys conducted during the Ohio State studies also suggested that there are two basic leader behaviors or styles: initiating-structure behavior and consideration behavior. When using initiating-structure behavior, the leader clearly defines the leader–subordinate role so that everyone knows what is expected, establishes formal lines of communication, and determines how tasks will be performed. Leaders using consideration behavior show concern for subordinates and try to establish a warm, friendly, and supportive climate. The behaviors identified at Ohio State are similar to those described at Michigan, but there are important differences. One major difference is that the Ohio State researchers did not interpret leader behavior as being one-dimensional; each behavior was assumed to be independent of the other. Presumably, then, a leader could exhibit varying levels of initiating structure and at the same time varying levels of consideration.

At first, the Ohio State researchers thought that leaders who exhibit high levels of both behaviors would tend to be more effective than

Abraham Lincoln is considered to have been a great leader. Part of this image came from how effectively he made decisions and led the United States during the Civil War. But some people also (erroneously) attributed his leadership to the fact that he was very tall—a physical trait.

Everett Historical/Shutterstock.com

consideration behavior
The behavior of leaders who show concern for subordinates and attempt to establish a warm, friendly, and supportive climate

other leaders. A study at International Harvester (now Navistar International), however, suggested a more complicated pattern.[17] The researchers found that employees of supervisors who ranked high on initiating structure were high performers but expressed low levels of satisfaction and had a higher absence rate. Conversely, employees of supervisors who ranked high on consideration had low performance ratings but high levels of satisfaction and few absences from work. Later research isolated other variables that made consistent prediction difficult and determined that situational influences also occurred. (This body of research is discussed in the section on situational approaches to leadership.[18])

Job-centered leader behavior focuses on jobs and work procedures. This manager is exhibiting job-centered behavior as he demonstrates how to perform a task to two of his workers.

concern for production
The part of the Leadership Grid that deals with the job and task aspects of leader behavior

concern for people
The part of the Leadership Grid that deals with the human aspects of leader behavior

Leadership Grid Yet another behavioral approach to leadership is the *Leadership Grid* (formerly called the *Managerial Grid*).[19] The Leadership Grid provides a means for evaluating leadership styles and then training managers to move toward an ideal style of behavior. The Leadership Grid is shown in Figure 11.1. The horizontal axis represents concern for production (similar to job-centered and initiating-structure behaviors), and the vertical axis represents concern for people (similar to employee-centered and consideration behaviors). Note the five extremes of managerial behavior: the 1,1 manager (impoverished management), who exhibits minimal concern for both production and people; the 9,1 manager (authority–compliance), who is highly concerned about production but exhibits little concern for people; the 1,9 manager (country club management), who has exactly opposite concerns from the 9,1 manager; the 5,5 manager (middle-of-the-road management), who maintains adequate concern for both people and production; and the 9,9 manager (team management), who exhibits maximum concern for both people and production.

According to this approach, the ideal style of leadership behavior is 9,9. There is a six-phase program to assist managers in achieving this style of behavior. A.G. Edwards, Westinghouse, the FAA, Equicor, and other companies have used the Leadership Grid and reported that it was reasonably successful. However, there is little published independent scientific evidence regarding its true effectiveness and most leadership scholars see it as being useful for descriptive purposes but not of true substantive value.

These leader-behavior theories have played an important role in the development of contemporary thinking about leadership. In particular, they suggest the need to focus on

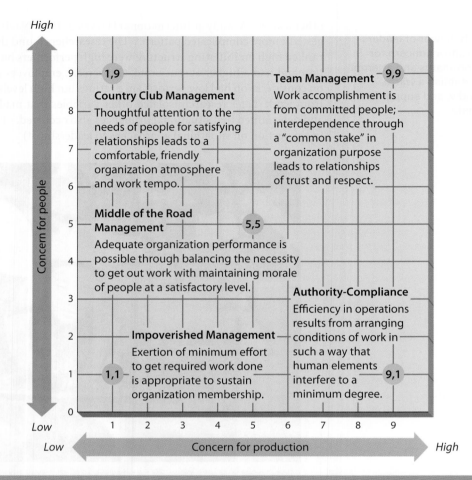

FIGURE 11.1

The Leadership Grid

The Leadership Grid® is a method of evaluating leadership styles. The overall objective of an organization using the Grid is to train its managers using organization development techniques so that they are simultaneously more concerned for both people and production (9,9 style on the Grid).

Source: The Leadership Grid figure from *Leadership Dilemmas—Grid Solutions* by Robert R. Blake and Anne Adams McCanse.

what leaders do (their behaviors) as opposed to with what leaders are (the trait approach). Unfortunately, these theories also make universal generic prescriptions about what constitutes effective leadership. When we are dealing with complex social systems composed of complex individuals, however, few, if any, relationships are consistently predictable, and certainly no formulas for success are infallible. Yet the behavior theorists tried to identify consistent relationships between leader behaviors and employee responses in the hope of finding a dependable prescription for effective leadership. As we might expect, they often failed. Other approaches to understanding leadership were therefore needed. The catalyst for these new approaches was the realization that although interpersonal and task-oriented dimensions might be useful for describing the behavior of leaders, they were not useful for predicting or prescribing it. The next step in the evolution of leadership theory was the creation of situational models.

leadership. Locus of control is a personality trait (as discussed in Chapter 14). People who have an internal locus of control believe that what happens to them is a function of their own efforts and behavior. Those who have an external locus of control assume that fate, luck, or "the system" determines what happens to them. A person with an internal locus of control may prefer participative leadership, whereas a person with an external locus of control may prefer directive leadership. Managers can do little or nothing to influence the personal characteristics of subordinates, but they can shape the environment to take advantage of these personal characteristics by, for example, providing rewards and structuring tasks.

Environmental characteristics include factors outside the subordinates' control. Task structure is one such factor. When structure is high, directive leadership is less effective than when structure is low. Employees do not usually need their leader to continually tell them how to do an extremely routine job. The formal authority system is another important environmental characteristic. Again, the higher the degree of formality, the less directive is the leader behavior that will be accepted by subordinates. The nature of the work group also affects appropriate leader behavior. When the work group provides the employee with social support and satisfaction, supportive leader behavior is less critical. When social support and satisfaction cannot be derived from the group, the worker may look to the leader for this support. Greater leadership support may also be an important factor in times of change or under unusually stressful conditions. For instance, many workers needed extra support from their leaders during the COVID-19 pandemic in 2020.

The basic path–goal framework as illustrated in Figure 11.4 shows that different leader behaviors affect subordinates' motivation to perform. Personal and environmental characteristics are seen as defining which behaviors lead to which outcomes. The path–goal theory of leadership is a dynamic and incomplete model. The original intent was to state the theory in general terms so that future research could explore a variety of interrelationships and modify the theory. Research that has been done suggests that the path–goal theory is a reasonably good description of the leadership process and that future investigations along these lines should enable us to discover more about the link between leadership and motivation.

11-3c **Vroom's Decision Tree Approach**

Vroom's decision tree approach
Predicts what kinds of situations call for different degrees of group participation

The third major contemporary approach to leadership is Vroom's decision tree approach. The earliest version of this model was proposed by Victor Vroom and Philip Yetton and later revised and expanded by Vroom and Arthur Jago.[26] Vroom subsequently developed yet

FIGURE 11.4

The Path–Goal Framework

The path–goal theory of leadership suggests that managers can use four types of leader behavior to clarify subordinates' paths to goal attainment. Personal characteristics of the subordinate and environmental characteristics within the organization both must be taken into account when determining which style of leadership will work best for a particular situation.

another refinement of the original model.[27] Like the path–goal theory, this approach attempts to prescribe a leadership style appropriate to a given situation. It also assumes that the same leader may display different leadership styles. But Vroom's approach concerns itself with only a single aspect of leader behavior: subordinate participation in decision making.

Basic Premises   Vroom's decision tree approach assumes that the degree to which subordinates should be encouraged to participate in decision making depends on the characteristics of the situation. In other words, no one decision-making process is best for all situations. After evaluating a variety of problem attributes (characteristics of the problem or decision), the leader determines an appropriate decision style that specifies the amount of subordinate participation.

Vroom suggests that managers use one of two different decision trees.[28] To do so, the manager first assesses the situation in terms of several factors. This assessment involves determining whether the given factor is high or low for the decision that is to be made. For instance, the first factor is decision significance. If the decision is extremely important and may have a major impact on the organization (such as choosing a location for a new distribution center), its significance is high. But if the decision is routine and its consequences are not terribly important (selecting a name for the firm's fantasy football league), its significance is low. This assessment guides the manager through the paths of the decision tree to a recommended course of action. One decision tree is to be used when the manager is interested primarily in making the decision as quickly as possible; the other is to be used when time is less critical and the manager is interested in helping subordinates to improve and develop their own decision-making skills.

The two decision trees are shown in Figures 11.5 and 11.6. The problem attributes (situational factors) are arranged along the top of the decision tree. To use the model, the decision maker starts at the left side of the diagram and assesses the first problem attribute (decision significance). The answer determines the path to the second node on the decision tree, where the next attribute (importance of commitment) is assessed. This process continues until a terminal node is reached. In this way, the manager identifies an effective decision-making style for the situation.

Vroom's decision tree approach focuses on helping leaders decide how much participation to encourage among subordinates when a decision is being made. This leader is actively seeking input from his team in making a decision.

Mego studio/Shutterstock.com

Decision-Making Styles   The various decision styles reflected at the ends of the tree branches represent different levels of subordinate participation that the manager should try to adopt in a given situation. The five styles are defined as follows:

- *Decide.* The manager makes the decision alone and then announces or "sells" it to the group.
- *Consult (individually).* The manager presents the situation to group members individually, obtains their suggestions, and then makes the decision.
- *Consult (group).* The manager presents the situation to group members at a meeting, gets their suggestions, and then makes the decision.
- *Facilitate.* The manager presents the situation to the group at a meeting, defines the problem and its boundaries, and then facilitates group member discussion as they make the decision.
- *Delegate.* The manager allows the group to define for itself the exact nature and parameters of the situation and then to develop a solution.

Decision Significance	Importance of Commitment	Leader Expertise	Likelihood of Commitment	Group Support	Group Expertise	Team Competence	
H	H	H	H	—	—	—	Decide
H	H	H	L	H	H	H	Delegate
H	H	H	L	H	H	L	Consult (group)
H	H	H	L	H	L	—	Consult (group)
H	H	H	L	L	—	—	Consult (group)
H	H	L	H	H	H	H	Facilitate
H	H	L	H	H	H	L	Consult (individually)
H	H	L	H	H	L	—	Consult (individually)
H	H	L	H	L	—	—	Consult (individually)
H	H	L	L	H	H	H	Facilitate
H	H	L	L	H	H	L	Consult (group)
H	H	L	L	H	L	—	Consult (group)
H	H	L	L	L	—	—	Consult (group)
H	L	H	—	—	—	—	Decide
H	L	L	—	H	H	H	Facilitate
H	L	L	—	H	H	L	Consult (individually)
H	L	L	—	H	L	—	Consult (individually)
H	L	L	—	L	—	—	Consult (individually)
L	H	—	H	—	—	—	Decide
L	H	—	L	—	—	H	Delegate
L	H	—	L	—	—	L	Facilitate
L	L	—	—	—	—	—	Decide

FIGURE 11.5

Vroom's Time-Driven Decision Tree

This matrix is recommended for situations when time is of the highest importance in making a decision. The matrix operates like a funnel. You start at the left with a specific decision problem in mind. The column headings denote situational factors that may or may not be present in that problem. You progress by selecting high or low (H or L) for each relevant situational factor. Proceed along the funnel, judging only those situational factors for which a judgment is needed, until you reach the recommended process.

Source: Adapted from *Leadership and Decision-Making*, by Victor H. Vroom and Philip W. Yetton.

Vroom's decision tree approach represents a very focused but quite complex perspective on leadership. To compensate for this difficulty, Vroom has developed elaborate expert system software to help managers assess a situation accurately and quickly and then to make an appropriate decision regarding employee participation.[29] Many firms, including Halliburton, Raytheon, Lennox, and Avis, have provided their managers with training in how to use the various versions of this model.

Evaluation and Implications Vroom's original model and its subsequent refinement attracted a great deal of attention and generally have been supported by research.[30] For example, there is support for the idea that individuals who make decisions consistent with the

Decision Significance	Importance of Commitment	Leader Expertise	Likelihood of Commitment	Group Support	Group Expertise	Team Competence	
H	H	—	H	H	H	H	Decide
						L	Facilitate
					L	—	Consult (group)
				L	—	—	Consult (group)
			L	H	H	H	Delegate
						L	Facilitate
					L	—	Facilitate
				L	—	—	Consult (group)
	L	—	—	H	H	H	Delegate
						L	Facilitate
					L	—	Consult (group)
				L	—	—	Consult (group)
L	H	—	H	—	—	—	Decide
			L	—	—	—	Delegate
	L	—	—	—	—	—	Decide

(Left margin label spanning the table: PROBLEM STATEMENT)

FIGURE 11.6

Vroom's Development-Driven Decision Tree

This matrix is to be used when the leader is more interested in developing employees than in making the decision as quickly as possible. Just as with the time-driven tree shown in Figure 11.5, the leader assesses up to seven situational factors. These factors, in turn, funnel the leader to a recommended process for making the decision.

Source: Adapted *Leadership and Decision-Making*, by Victor H. Vroom and Philip W. Yetton.

predictions of the model are more effective than those who make decisions inconsistent with it. The model therefore appears to be a tool that managers can apply with some confidence in deciding how much subordinates should participate in the decision-making process.

11-3d The Leader–Member Exchange Approach

Because leadership is such an important area, managers and researchers continue to study it. As a result, new ideas, theories, and perspectives are continuously being developed. The **leader–member exchange (LMX) model** of leadership, conceived by George Graen and Fred Dansereau, stresses the importance of variable relationships between leaders and each of their subordinates.[31] Each superior–subordinate pair is referred to as a "vertical dyad." The model differs from earlier approaches in that it focuses on the differential relationship leaders often establish with different subordinates. Figure 11.7 shows the basic concepts of the leader–member exchange theory.

The model further suggests that supervisors establish a special relationship with a small number of trusted subordinates, referred to as the "in-group." The in-group usually receives special duties requiring responsibility and autonomy; they may also receive special privileges. Subordinates who are not a part of this group are called the "out-group," and they receive less of the supervisor's time and attention. Note in the figure that the leader has a dyadic, or one-to-one, relationship with each of the five subordinates.

leader–member exchange (LMX) model
Stresses that leaders have different kinds of relationships with different subordinates

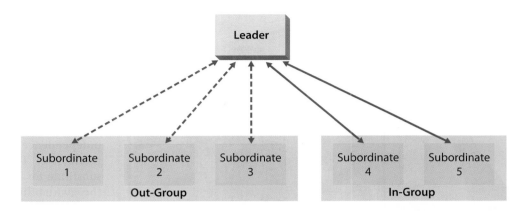

FIGURE 11.7

The Leader–Member Exchange (LMX) Model

The LMX model suggests that leaders form unique independent relationships with each of their subordinates. As illustrated here, a key factor in the nature of this relationship is whether the individual subordinate is in the leader's out-group or in-group.

Early in his or her interaction with a given subordinate, the supervisor initiates either an in-group or an out-group relationship. It is not clear how a leader selects members of the in-group, but the decision may be based on personal compatibility and subordinates' competence. Research has confirmed the existence of in-groups and out-groups. In addition, studies generally have found that in-group members have a higher level of performance and satisfaction than do out-group members.[32]

Manager's Checklist

☐ Managers should be familiar with the essential elements of each of the situational approaches to leadership.

☐ You should also have a sense of which situational approach is most useful and least useful for you personally.

☐ Essentially, all managers should know that there is no one set of leadership behaviors that will be universally effective.

11-4 RELATED APPROACHES TO LEADERSHIP

Because of its importance to organizational effectiveness, leadership continues to be the focus of a great deal of research and theory building. Other approaches that have attracted attention are the concepts of substitutes for leadership and transformational leadership.[33]

11-4a Substitutes for Leadership

substitutes for leadership
A concept that identifies situations in which leader behaviors are neutralized or replaced by characteristics of subordinates, the task, and the organization

The concept of substitutes for leadership was developed because existing leadership models and theories do not account for situations in which leadership is not needed.[34] They simply try to specify what kind of leader behavior is appropriate. The substitutes concept, however, identifies situations in which leader behaviors are neutralized or replaced by characteristics of the subordinate, the task, and the organization. For example, when a patient is delivered to a hospital emergency room, the professionals on duty do not wait to be told what to do by a leader. Nurses, doctors, and attendants all go into action without waiting for directive or supportive leader behavior from the emergency room supervisor.

Substitutes for leadership are things that neutralize or replace the need for formal leadership. The professionalism and training of these emergency medical technicians, for example, allows them to respond and carry out their responsibilities without waiting for someone to tell them what to do.

Characteristics of the subordinate that may serve to neutralize leader behavior include ability, experience, need for independence, professional orientation, and indifference toward organizational rewards. For example, employees with a high level of ability and experience may not need to be told what to do. Similarly, a subordinate's strong need for independence may render leader behavior ineffective. Task characteristics that may substitute for leadership include routineness, the availability of feedback, and intrinsic satisfaction. When the job is routine and simple, the subordinate may not need direction. When the task is challenging and intrinsically satisfying, the subordinate may not need or want social support from a leader.

Organizational characteristics that may substitute for leadership include formalization, group cohesion, inflexibility, and a rigid reward structure. Leadership may not be necessary when policies and practices are formal and inflexible, for example. Similarly, a rigid reward system may rob the leader of reward power and thereby decrease the importance of the role. Research has provided support for the concept of substitutes for leadership.[35]

11-4b Charismatic Leadership

charismatic leadership
Assumes that charisma is an individual characteristic of the leader

charisma
A form of interpersonal attraction that inspires support and acceptance

The concept of charismatic leadership, like trait theories, assumes that charisma is an individual characteristic of the leader. Charisma is a form of interpersonal attraction that inspires support and acceptance. All else being equal, someone with charisma is more likely to be able to influence others than is someone without charisma. For example, a highly charismatic manager will be more successful in influencing subordinate behavior than a manager who lacks charisma. Thus, influence is again a fundamental element of this perspective.

Robert House first proposed a theory of charismatic leadership, based on research findings from a variety of social science disciplines.[36] His theory suggests that charismatic leaders are likely to have a lot of self-confidence, a firm conviction in their beliefs and ideals, and a strong need to influence people. They also tend to communicate high expectations about follower performance and express confidence in followers. Steve Jobs clearly had charisma, whereas Tim Cook is somewhat less charismatic (but still very effective).

There are three elements of charismatic leadership in organizations that most experts acknowledge.[37] First, the leader needs to be able to envision the future, set high expectations, and model behaviors consistent with meeting those expectations. Next, the charismatic leader must be able to energize others through a demonstration of personal excitement, personal confidence, and patterns of success. And, finally, the charismatic leader enables others by supporting them, empathizing with them, and expressing confidence in them.[38]

Charismatic leadership ideas are quite popular among managers today and are the subject of numerous books and articles. Unfortunately, few studies have tried to specifically test the meaning and impact of charismatic leadership. There are also lingering ethical issues about charismatic leadership, however, that trouble some people. For instance, President Bill Clinton was a charismatic leader. But some of his critics argued that this very charisma caused his supporters to overlook his flaws and to minimize some of his indiscretions. In contrast, President George W. Bush was not particularly charismatic, and this may have enabled his critics to magnify his shortcomings.

A WORLD OF DIFFERENCE

Following Her Own Path

In the small Pakistani community where Ruzwana Bashir was born and raised, women were expected to aspire to marriage and children, not college and entrepreneurship. Bashir, however, was encouraged by teachers who urged her to pursue higher education. She broke through those gender and culture barriers and continues to work against them as the founder and CEO of the travel site Peek.

As she began her career in the financial services industry, Bashir felt pressure to act like her male counterparts. At a recent conference she explained, "In that environment as a woman, you can feel crowd-forced to conform." While earning her MBA at Harvard's Business School as a Fulbright Scholar, she realized that traditionally feminine attributes can be an advantage. "Those 'female' traits of empathy and compassion—of being collaborative—are true business strengths."

At Oxford, she became president of the Oxford Union, a debating society famed for hosting speakers such as Senator John McCain and fashion designer Tom Ford. She was only the second female Asian president of that prestigious society, following in the footsteps of former Pakistani President Benazir Bhutto, who became the union's leader in 1977. It was at Oxford that Bashir first wore Western clothing, but although she excelled in school, she always felt different in race, gender, and class. It was in 2012, after spending over 20 frustrating hours trying to arrange a getaway with friends to Turkey, she and cofounder Oskar Bruening launched Peek.com, adding yet another benchmark to her already impressive social resumé—that of a woman-founded tech company. Although there are already several travel websites, Peek occupies a unique space in the market. Peek helps travelers to plan the perfect trip, including itineraries for a "Perfect Day" in your destination.

At Peek.com, the company has maintained a staffing mix of 50 percent men and 50 percent women, with considerable ethnic diversity. Bashir encourages female employees and introduces them to mentors. She also practices what she preaches—allowing herself to show vulnerability rather than presenting the traditionally male decisive and authoritative style. In addition, she is an outspoken advocate for women's rights worldwide. For instance, she recently published a groundbreaking essay that drew attention to the abuse of women in the United Kingdom's Asian communities. "Growing up the way I did gave me empathy and understanding for different walks of life," Bashir says. "It inspired me to choose the kind of company I wanted to build."

References: Leena Rao, "How Ruzwana Bashir Became Silicon Valley's Favorite British Import," *Fortune*, November 11, 2016, www.fortune.com on May 16, 2020; https://www.peek.com on May 16, 2020; "Ruzwana Bashir," *Wikipedia*, https://en.wikipedia.org on May 16, 2020.

11-4c Transformational Leadership

transformational leadership
Leadership that goes beyond ordinary expectations by transmitting a sense of mission, stimulating learning experiences, and inspiring new ways of thinking

Another newer perspective on leadership has been called by a number of labels: charismatic leadership, inspirational leadership, symbolic leadership, and transformational leadership. We use the term transformational leadership and define it as leadership that goes beyond ordinary expectations by transmitting a sense of mission, stimulating learning experiences, and inspiring new ways of thinking.[39] Because of rapid change and turbulent environments, transformational leaders are increasingly being seen as vital to the success of business.[40]

A widely circulated popular press article once identified seven keys to successful leadership: trusting one's subordinates, developing a vision, keeping cool, encouraging risk, being an expert, inviting dissent, and simplifying things.[41] Although this list was the result of a simplistic survey of the leadership literature, it is nevertheless consistent with the premises underlying transformational leadership. So, too, are recent examples cited as effective leadership. Take the case of 3M. The firm's current CEO is working to make the firm more efficient and profitable while simultaneously keeping its leadership role in new product innovation. He has also changed the reward system, overhauled procedures, and restructured the entire firm. And so far, at least, analysts have applauded these changes.

"Turnaround or growth, it's getting your people focused on the goal that is still the job of leadership."

—Anne Mulcahy, Former CEO of Xerox

Manager's Checklist

☐ Managers should be aware that leadership substitutes and neutralizers may affect their ability to lead.

☐ You should also be familiar with the importance of charisma and the nature of transformational leadership.

11-5 EMERGING APPROACHES TO LEADERSHIP

Recently, three potentially very important new approaches to leadership have emerged. One is called "strategic leadership;" the others are cross-cultural leadership and ethical leadership.

11-5a Strategic Leadership

strategic leadership
The ability to understand the complexities of both the organization and its environment and to lead change in the organization in order to achieve and maintain a superior alignment between the organization and its environment

Strategic leadership is a new concept that explicitly relates leadership to the role of top management. We define strategic leadership as the ability to understand the complexities of both the organization and its environment and to lead change in the organization in order to achieve and maintain a superior alignment between the organization and its environment. This definition reflects an integration of the leadership concepts covered in this chapter with our discussion of strategic management in Chapter 7.

To be effective as a strategic leader, a manager needs to have a thorough and complete understanding of the organization—its history, its culture, its strengths, and its weaknesses. In addition, the leader needs a firm grasp of the organization's environment. This understanding must encompass current conditions and circumstances as well as significant trends and issues on the horizon. The strategic leader also needs to recognize how the firm is currently aligned with its environment—where it relates effectively and where it relates less effectively with that environment. Finally, looking at environmental trends and issues, the strategic leader works to improve both the current alignment and the future alignment.[42]

Reed Hastings (founder and CEO of Netflix), Jeff Bezos (CEO of Amazon), W. Craig Jelinek (CEO of Costco), Michael Dell (founder and CEO of Dell Computer), and Mary Barra (CEO of General Motors) are generally seen today as strong strategic leaders.[43] On the other hand, Ken Lewis (former CEO of Bank of America) and Fran Horowitz (CEO of Abercrombie & Fitch) have recently been cited as less effective strategic leaders.[44]

DOING BUSINESS ON PLANET EARTH

Leading Sustainably

In 1980, John DeJoria was homeless, living in an old Rolls-Royce in L.A. He had just invested all of his savings—amounting to just $700—in a little venture with his Scottish-American hairstylist, Paul. With a bare-bones budget, they sold their self-branded hair care products to salons by going door-to-door. While the first two years were difficult, they had almost $1 million in annual sales in their third year of operation. Today, Paul Mitchell's products are sold in more than 150,000 beauty salons in 87 countries and annual sales exceed $1 billion.

DeJoria is a serial entrepreneur, having started more than a dozen businesses, including House of Blues, DeJoria Diamonds, and Patrón Spirits. In each of his

businesses, DeJoria makes high quality and sustainability a priority. In an interview with *Fortune* magazine, he explains, "A lot of people make things to sell. But when the product is old, the consumer tosses it out and buys something else. If you make things with the highest quality, you'll be in the reorder business, which keeps the sales growing." Sustainability is particularly important in the Paul Mitchell product line. Paul Mitchell was the first beauty products company to reject animal testing and labels itself "Cruelty-Free since 1980."

While much of DeJoria's success can be attributed to hard work, his charisma and message inspire others. One of his mottos is "Success unshared is failure." He is committed

(Continued)

DOING BUSINESS ON PLANET EARTH (CONTINUED)

to giving back through organizations such as Habitat for Humanity and Food4Africa and Paul Mitchell Schools raised over $20 million for charity in 15 years. He is also the founder of Grow Appalachia, an organization that helps those in rural areas to overcome food insecurity by growing their own food. Not surprisingly, DeJoria signed Warren Buffett and Bill Gates's Giving Pledge, through which the world's wealthiest citizens commit to giving most of their wealth to philanthropy.

References: Emily Canal, "FORBES 400: Meet the American Billionaires Attending the Forbes Under 30 Summit," *Forbes*, September 29, 2014, www.forbes.com on May 16, 2020; Dinah Eng, "Adventures of a Serial Entrepreneur," *Fortune*, April 24, 2012, www.fortune.com on May 16, 2020; Chase Peterson-Withorn, "After Building Two Billion-Dollar Brands, John Paul DeJoria Shares His Success," *Forbes*, September 11, 2014, www.forbes.com on May 16, 2020.

11-5b Cross-Cultural Leadership

Another new perspective on leadership is based on cross-cultural issues. In this context, culture is used as a broad concept to encompass both international differences and diversity-based differences within one culture. For instance, when a Japanese firm sends an executive to head the firm's operations in the United States, that person will need to become acclimated to the cultural differences that exist between the two countries and to change his or her leadership style accordingly. Japan is generally characterized by collectivism, whereas the United States is based more on individualism. The Japanese executive, then, will find it necessary to recognize the importance of individual contributions and rewards, as well as the differences in individual and group roles, that exist in Japanese and U.S. businesses.

> **"Challenges are global. . . . They require people from every country, every background, every area of expertise, pulling together."**
> —Indra Krishnamurthy Nooyi, Former CEO of Pepsico

Similarly, cross-cultural factors play a growing role in organizations as their workforces become more and more diverse. Most leadership research, for instance, has been conducted on samples or case studies involving white male leaders (until several years ago, most business leaders were white males). But as more females, African Americans, and Latinos achieve leadership positions, it may be necessary to reassess how applicable current theories and models of leadership are when applied to an increasingly diverse pool of leaders.

11-5c Ethical Leadership

Most people have long assumed that top managers are ethical people. But in the wake of recent corporate scandals, faith in top managers has been shaken. Perhaps now more than ever, high standards of ethical conduct are being held up as a prerequisite for effective leadership. More specifically, top managers are being called on to maintain high ethical standards for their own conduct, to exhibit ethical behavior unfailingly, and to hold others in their organizations to the same standards.

> **"Reputation is everything."**
> —Ken Chenault, Former CEO of American Express[45]

The behaviors of top leaders are being scrutinized more than ever, and those responsible for hiring new leaders for a business are looking more and more closely at the background of those being considered. And the emerging pressures for stronger corporate governance models are likely to further increase commitment to selecting only those individuals with high ethical standards and to hold them more accountable than in the past for both their actions and the consequences of those actions.[46]

Manager's Checklist

☐ Managers should recognize the growing importance of strategic leadership.

☐ Managers should also know that cross-cultural differences can affect leadership.

☐ You should understand the importance of ethics in leadership.

11-6 POLITICAL BEHAVIOR IN ORGANIZATIONS

political behavior
Activities carried out for the specific purpose of acquiring, developing, and using power and other resources to obtain one's preferred outcomes

Another common influence on behavior is politics and political behavior. **Political behavior** describes activities carried out for the specific purpose of acquiring, developing, and using power and other resources to obtain one's preferred outcomes.[47] Political behavior may be undertaken by managers dealing with their subordinates, subordinates dealing with their managers, and managers and subordinates dealing with others at the same level. In other words, it may be directed upward, downward, or laterally. Decisions ranging from where to locate a manufacturing plant to where to put the company coffee maker are subject to political action. In any situation, individuals may engage in political behavior to further their own ends, to protect themselves from others, to further goals they sincerely believe to be in the organization's best interests, or simply to acquire and exercise power. And power may be sought by individuals, by groups of individuals, or by groups of groups.[48]

"In our company, we don't want any politics. If you see or smell anything like politics, kill it."
—Dinesh C. Paliwal, Former CEO of Harman International Industries

Although political behavior is difficult to study because of its sensitive nature, one important survey found that many managers believed that politics influenced salary and hiring decisions in their firm. Many also believed that the incidence of political behavior was greater at the upper levels of their organization and lesser at the lower levels. More than half of the respondents felt that organizational politics was bad, unfair, unhealthy, and irrational, but most suggested that successful executives have to be good politicians and be political to get ahead.[49]

11-6a Common Political Behaviors

Research has identified four basic forms of political behavior widely practiced in organizations.[50] One form is *inducement*, which occurs when a manager offers to give something to someone else in return for that person's support. For example, a product manager might suggest to another product manager that she will put in a good word with his boss if he supports a new marketing plan that she has developed. By most accounts, former WorldCom CEO Bernard Ebbers made frequent use of this tactic to retain his leadership position in the company. For example, he allowed board members to use the corporate jet whenever they wanted and invested heavily in their pet projects.

A second tactic is *persuasion*, which relies on both emotion and logic. An operations manager wanting to construct a new plant on a certain site might persuade others to support his goal on grounds that are objective and logical (it's less expensive; taxes are lower) as well as subjective and personal. Ebbers also used this approach. For instance, when one board member tried to remove him from his position, he worked behind the scenes to persuade the majority of board members to allow him to stay on.

A third political behavior involves the *creation of an obligation*. For example, one manager might support a recommendation made by another manager for a new advertising campaign. Although he might really have no opinion on the new campaign, he might think that by going along, he is incurring a debt from the other manager and will be able to "call in" that debt when he wants to get something done and needs additional support. Ebbers loaned WorldCom board members money, for example, but then forgave the loans in exchange for their continued support.

Coercion is the use of force to get one's way. For example, a manager may threaten to withhold support, rewards, or other resources as a way to influence someone else. This, too, was a common tactic used by Ebbers. He reportedly belittled any board member who dared question him, for example. In the words of one former director, "Ebbers treated you like a prince—as long as you never forgot who was king."[51]

impression management
A direct and intentional effort by someone to enhance his or her image in the eyes of others

11-6b Impression Management

Impression management is a subtle form of political behavior that deserves special mention. **Impression management** is a direct and intentional effort by someone to enhance his or her image in the eyes of others. People engage in impression management for a variety of reasons.

"You never get a second chance to make a first impression."
—Will Rogers, American Humorist and Philospher

Impression management is a direct and intentional effort to enhance how others see us. While there is nothing wrong with wanting to look good and present ourselves in a positive manner like this manager, of course, some people take impression management too far and create unrealistic or false impressions.

For one thing, they may do so to further their own careers. By making themselves look good, they think they are more likely to receive rewards, to be given attractive job assignments, and to receive promotions. They may also engage in impression management to boost their self-esteem. When people have a solid image in an organization, others make them aware of it through compliments, respect, and so forth. Still another reason people use impression management is in an effort to acquire more power and hence more control.

People try to manage how others perceive them through a variety of mechanisms. Appearance is one of the first things people think of. Hence, a person motivated by impression management will pay close attention to the choice of attire, selection of language, and use of manners and body posture. People interested in impression management are also likely to try to associate themselves only with successful projects. By being assigned to high-profile projects led by highly successful managers, a person can begin to link his or her own name with such projects in the minds of others.

Impression management, of course, is common and not inherently inappropriate. To the contrary, most career advisors stress the importance of making good impressions. Sometimes, however, people too strongly motivated by impression management become obsessed with it and may resort to dishonest or unethical means. For example, some people have been known to take credit for others' work in an effort to make themselves look better. People have also been known to exaggerate or even falsify their personal accomplishments in an effort to build an enhanced image.[52]

11-6c Managing Political Behavior

By its very nature, political behavior is tricky to approach in a rational and systematic way. But managers can handle political behavior so that it does not do excessive damage.[53] First, managers should be aware that, even if their actions are not politically motivated, others may assume that they are. Second, by providing subordinates with autonomy, responsibility, challenge, and feedback, managers reduce the likelihood of political behavior by subordinates. Third, managers should avoid using power if they want to avoid charges of political motivation. Fourth, managers should get disagreements out in the open so that subordinates will have less opportunity for political behavior by using conflict for their own purposes. Finally, managers should avoid covert activities. Behind-the-scenes activities give the impression of political intent, even if none really exists.[54] Other guidelines include clearly communicating the bases and processes for performance evaluation, tying rewards directly to performance, and minimizing competition among managers for resources.[55]

Of course, these guidelines are much easier to list than they are to implement. The well-informed manager should not assume that political behavior does not exist or, worse yet, attempt to eliminate it by issuing orders or commands. Instead, the manager must recognize that political behavior exists in virtually all organizations and that it cannot be ignored or stamped out. It can, however, be managed in such a way that it will seldom inflict serious damage on the organization. It may even play a useful role in some situations.[56] For example, a manager may be able to use his or her political influence to stimulate a greater sense of social responsibility or to heighten awareness of the ethical implications of a decision.

"Every time I turn around, there is someone sticking their head in my office reminding me what they are doing for me."
—Trevor Traina, Silicon Valley Entrepreneur[57]

Manager's Checklist

☐ All managers need to be familiar with the various forms of political behavior in organizations.

☐ You should also recognize impression management and know when it is acceptable behavior and when it is unacceptable behavior.

SUMMARY OF LEARNING OUTCOMES AND KEY POINTS

11-1. Describe the nature of leadership and how it relates to management.

- As a process, leadership is the use of noncoercive influence to shape the group's or organization's goals, motivate behavior toward the achievement of those goals, and help define group or organization culture.
- As a property, leadership is the set of characteristics attributed to those who are perceived to be leaders.
- Leadership and management are often related but are also different.
- Managers and leaders use legitimate, reward, coercive, referent, and expert power.

11-2. Discuss the two generic approaches to leadership.

- The trait approach to leadership assumed that some basic trait or set of traits differentiated leaders from nonleaders.
- The leadership behavior approach to leadership assumed that the behavior of effective leaders was somehow different from the behavior of nonleaders.
- Research at the University of Michigan and Ohio State University identified two basic forms of leadership behavior—one concentrating on work and performance and the other concentrating on employee welfare and support.
- The Leadership Grid attempts to train managers to exhibit high levels of both forms of behavior.

11-3. Describe the major situational approaches to leadership.

- Situational approaches to leadership recognize that appropriate forms of leadership behavior are not universally applicable and attempt to specify situations in which various behaviors are appropriate.

- The LPC theory suggests that a leader's behaviors should be either task oriented or relationship oriented, depending on the favorableness of the situation.
- The path–goal theory suggests that directive, supportive, participative, or achievement-oriented leader behaviors may be appropriate, depending on the personal characteristics of subordinates and the environment.
- Vroom's decision tree approach maintains that leaders should vary the extent to which they allow subordinates to participate in making decisions as a function of problem attributes.
- The leader–member exchange model focuses on individual relationships between leaders and followers and on in-group versus out-group considerations.

11-4. Describe three related approaches to leadership.

- Related leadership perspectives are the concept of substitutes for leadership, charismatic leadership, and the role of transformational leadership in organizations.

11-5. Discuss three emerging approaches to leadership.

- Emerging approaches include strategic leadership, cross-cultural leadership, and ethical leadership.

11-6. Discuss political behavior in organizations and how it can be managed.

- Political behavior is another influence process frequently used in organizations.
- Impression management, one especially important form of political behavior, is a direct and intentional effort by someone to enhance his or her image in the eyes of others.
- Managers can take steps to limit the effects of political behavior.

DISCUSSION QUESTIONS

Questions for Review

1. What activities do managers perform? What activities do leaders perform? Do organizations need both managers and leaders? Why or why not?
2. What are the situational approaches to leadership? Briefly describe each and compare and contrast their findings.
3. Describe the subordinate's characteristics, leader behaviors, and environmental characteristics used in path–goal theory. How do these factors combine to influence motivation?
4. In your own words, define political behavior. Describe four political tactics and give an example of each.

Questions for Analysis

1. Even though the trait approach to leadership has no empirical support, it is still widely used. In your opinion, why is this so? In what ways is the use of the trait approach helpful to those who use it? In what ways is it harmful to those who use it?
2. The behavioral theories of leadership claim that an individual's leadership style is fixed. Do you agree or disagree? Give examples to support your position. The behavioral theories also claim that the ideal style is the same in every situation. Do you agree or disagree? Again, give examples.
3. A few universities are experimenting with alternative approaches, such as allowing students to design their own majors, develop a curriculum for that major, choose professors and design courses, or self-direct and self-evaluate their studies. These are examples of substitutes for leadership. Do you think this will lead to better outcomes for students than a traditional approach? Would you personally like to have that type of alternative approach at your school? Explain your answers.

Questions for Application

1. Consider the following list of leadership situations. For each situation, describe in detail the kinds of power the leader has. If the leader were the same but the situation changed—for example, if you thought of the president as the head of his family rather than of the military—would your answers change? Why?

   - The president of the United States is commander-in-chief of the U.S. military
   - An airline pilot is in charge of a particular flight
   - Fans look up to a movie star
   - Your teacher is the head of your class

2. Reflect on the 2020 COVID-19 pandemic. Recall two or three leaders you thought were very effective and one or two others you thought were less effective. Why did you see each in this light? What are the implications of your thoughts for leadership?
3. Describe a time when you or someone you know was part of an in-group or an out-group. What was the relationship between each of the groups and the leader? What was the relationship between the members of the two different groups? What was the outcome of the situation for the leader? For the members of the two groups? For the organization?

BUILDING EFFECTIVE INTERPERSONAL SKILLS

Exercise Overview

Interpersonal skills refer to your ability to communicate with, understand, and motivate both individuals and groups. This exercise asks you to examine the ways in which your attitudes toward work relationships reflect your political behavior in the workplace.

Exercise Task

Following is a series of 20 statements. To what extent does each statement describe your use—actual or planned—of the described behavior when you're on the job? To address this question, rate your response to each statement according to the following scale:

1	2	3	4	5
Rarely		Occasionally		Usually

1. _____ I use personal contacts to get jobs and promotions.
2. _____ I try to find out what's going on in every organizational department.
3. _____ I dress the same way as the people in power and develop the same interests (e.g., watch or play sports, join the same clubs, etc.).
4. _____ I purposely seek contacts and network with higher-level managers.
5. _____ If upper management offered me a raise and promotion requiring me to move to a new location, I'd say yes even if I didn't want to move.
6. _____ I get along with everyone, even people regarded as difficult to get along with.
7. _____ I try to make people feel important by complimenting them.

8. _____ I do favors for other people and ask favors in return, and I thank people, often sending thank-you notes.

9. _____ I work at developing a good working relationship with my supervisor.

10. _____ I ask my supervisor and other people for advice.

11. _____ When someone opposes me, I still work to maintain a positive working relationship with that person.

12. _____ I'm courteous, positive, and pleasant in my relationships with other people.

13. _____ When my supervisor makes a mistake, I never point it out publicly.

14. _____ I'm more cooperative (I compromise) than competitive (I try to get my own way).

15. _____ I tell the truth.

16. _____ I avoid saying negative things about my supervisor or other people behind their backs.

17. _____ I work at getting people to know me by name and face by continually introducing myself.

18. _____ I ask satisfied customers and other people familiar with my work to let my supervisor know how good a job I'm doing.

19. _____ I try to win contests and get prizes, pins, and other awards.

20. _____ I send notices of my accomplishments to higher-level managers and such outlets as company newsletters.

Scoring

1. Add up the 20 numbers in the blanks before all the questions. Your total will range between 20 and 100. This number reflects your overall political behavior: *The higher your score, the greater your political behavior.*

2. Record your score here _____ and on the scale that follows:

   20__30__40__50__60__ 70__80__90__100
   Nonpolitical   *Political*

3. Now you want to determine your use of political power in *four different areas* (e.g., learning organizational culture, being a team player, etc.). To do this, add up your numbers for each of the following sets *of questions* and then divide by 5. You will then have your average score for each area:

   A. *Learning the organizational culture and getting to know the power players:*

      Questions 1–5 total ____ divided by 5 = ____

   B. *Developing good working relationships, especially with your boss:*

      Questions 6–12 total ____ divided by 5 = ____

   C. *Being a loyal, honest team player:*

      Questions 13–16 total ____ divided by 5 = ____

   D. *Gaining recognition:*

      Questions 16–20 total ____ divided by 5 = ____

The higher your average score for each set of questions, the greater your use of political power in that area. Do you rate about the same in each area, or do you rate more highly in some areas more than others?

Adapted from Robert N. Lussier and Christopher F. Achua, *Leadership: Theory, Application, and Skill Development*, 4th ed. (Mason, OH: SouthWestern Cengage Learning, 2010), pp. 120–121.

BUILDING EFFECTIVE CONCEPTUAL SKILLS

Exercise Overview

Conceptual skills require you to think in the abstract. This exercise introduces you to one approach to assessing leadership skills and relating leadership theory to practice.

Exercise Background

At any given time, there's no shortage of publications offering practical advice on management and leadership. Recent business bestsellers included such titles as *Good to Great,* by Jim Collins; *First, Break All the Rules,* by Marcus Buckingham; and *The 21 Irrefutable Laws of Leadership,* by John C. Maxwell. Some of these books, such as *Winning,* by former General Electric CEO Jack Welch, are written by managers with years of experience. Others are written by consultants, professors, or business reporters.

Granted, a lot of these books—okay, most of them—don't have much theoretical foundation, and many are basically compendiums of opinions and suggestions unsupported by scientific evidence. Even so, many touch upon ideas that may well be worth the time it takes a busy manager to read them.

Thus, a real issue for contemporary managers is knowing how to analyze what they read in the popular press and how to separate the practical wheat from the pop-culture chaff. This exercise gives you a little practice in doing just that.

Exercise Task

1. Visit *https://www.mindtools.com/pages/article/leadership-style-quiz.htm* and take the leadership style assessment there (if this URL is no longer working, use an

online search engine to find another leadership assessment you can take for free).

2. Review carefully each question and each suggested answer. Do you see any correlation between the questions and the theoretical models of leadership discussed in this chapter? Which model or models do you think was used to construct this assessment? What details in the questions, answers, or both led you to that conclusion?

3. Think of a book you have read about leadership. How valid or invalid do you think its views on leadership were? Do you see any connection between the book and the items on the quiz you completed earlier? Explain.

4. Based on what you've learned from this exercise, how confident are you that an assessment or questionnaire is an accurate measure of leadership ability? Explain.

SKILL-BUILDING PERSONAL ASSESSMENT

Managerial Leader Behavior Questionnaire

Introduction: Leadership is often seen as consisting of a set of characteristics that is important for managers in an organization to develop. The following assessment surveys the practices or beliefs that you would apply in a management role—that is, your managerial leadership.

Instructions: The following statements refer to different ways in which you might behave in a managerial leadership role. For each statement, indicate how you do behave or how you think you would behave. Describing yourself may be difficult in some cases, but you should force yourself to make a selection. Record your answers next to each statement according to the following scale:

Rating Scale

5 Very descriptive of me

4 Fairly descriptive of me

3 Somewhat descriptive of me

2 Not very descriptive of me

1 Not descriptive of me at all

1. _____ I emphasize the importance of performance and encourage everyone to make a maximum effort.

2. _____ I am friendly, supportive, and considerate toward others.

3. _____ I offer helpful advice to others on how to advance their careers and encourage them to develop their skills.

4. _____ I stimulate enthusiasm for the work of the group and say things to build the group's confidence.

5. _____ I provide appropriate praise and recognition for effective performance and show appreciation for special efforts and contributions.

6. _____ I reward effective performance with tangible benefits.

7. _____ I inform people about their duties and responsibilities, clarify rules and policies, and let people know what is expected of them.

8. _____ Either alone or jointly with others, I set specific and challenging but realistic performance goals.

9. _____ I provide any necessary training and coaching or arrange for others to do it.

10. _____ I keep everyone informed about decisions, events, and developments that affect their work.

11. _____ I consult with others before making work-related decisions.

12. _____ I delegate responsibility and authority to others and allow them discretion in determining how to do their work.

13. _____ I plan in advance how to efficiently organize and schedule the work.

14. _____ I look for new opportunities for the group to exploit, propose new undertakings, and offer innovative ideas.

15. _____ I take prompt and decisive action to deal with serious work-related problems and disturbances.

16. _____ I provide subordinates with the supplies, equipment, support services, and other resources necessary to work effectively.

17. _____ I keep informed about the activities of the group and check on its performance.

18. _____ I keep informed about outside events that have important implications for the group.

19. _____ I promote and defend the interests of the group and take appropriate action to obtain necessary resources for the group.

20. _____ I emphasize teamwork and try to promote cooperation, cohesiveness, and identification with the group.

21. _____ I discourage unnecessary fighting and bickering within the group and help settle conflicts and disagreements in a constructive manner.

22. _____ I criticize specific acts that are unacceptable, find positive things to say, and provide an opportunity for people to offer explanations.

23. _____ I take appropriate disciplinary action to deal with anyone who violates a rule, disobeys an order, or has consistently poor performance.

Scoring: These statements represent 23 behavior categories that research has identified as descriptive of managerial leadership. Not all 23 are important in any given situation. Typically, fewer than half of these behaviors are associated with effective performance in particular situations; thus, there is no "right" or "wrong" set of responses on this questionnaire. The behavior categories are as follows:

1. Emphasizing performance
2. Showing consideration
3. Providing career counseling
4. Inspiring subordinates
5. Providing praise and recognition
6. Structuring reward contingencies
7. Clarifying work roles
8. Setting goals
9. Training or coaching
10. Disseminating information
11. Encouraging participation in decisions
12. Delegating
13. Planning
14. Innovating
15. Problem solving
16. Facilitating the work
17. Monitoring operations
18. Monitoring the environment
19. Representing the unit
20. Facilitating cooperation and teamwork
21. Managing conflict
22. Providing criticism
23. Administering discipline

In military organizations at war, inspiring subordinates, emphasizing performance, clarifying work roles, problem solving, and planning seem most important. In military organizations during peacetime, inspiring subordinates, emphasizing performance, clarifying work roles, showing consideration, providing criticism, and administering discipline seem most important. In business organizations, emphasizing performance, monitoring the environment, clarifying work roles, setting goals, and sometimes innovating seem to be most important. In each of these instances, however, the level of organization, type of technology, environmental conditions, and objectives sought help determine the exact mix of behaviors that will lead to effectiveness. You should analyze your particular situation to determine which subset of these behavior categories is most likely to be important and then strive to develop that subset.

Source: David D. Van Fleet and Gary A. Yukl, *Military Leadership: An Organizational Behavior Perspective*, pp. 38–39.

MANAGEMENT AT WORK
The Road to Leadership

"Your title makes you a manager, people decide if you're a leader."
—Bill Campbell, Leadership Coach

On November 14, 1970, a plane crash took the lives of 37 Marshall University football players, their coach, and 27 other staff and community members who were returning from a game in North Carolina. Brad Smith stood on a small hill near his hometown of Kenova, West Virginia, watching his cousins and other community members fighting to contain the fiery aftermath. That event, of course, left an indelible impression on him, while also showing him the value of teamwork, community, and resilience.

Smith graduated from Marshall in 1986, and later added a master's degree in management from Aquinas College in Michigan while working a full-time day job for Pepsi. After a few career changes, he landed at Intuit in 2003. Smith started out working in Plano, Texas, running the accountant relations portion of the professional tax business. Thanks to his success there, Intuit asked him to move to San Diego to run TurboTax, the company's flagship consumer tax business. In 2005, Smith moved to Silicon Valley to help lead a team that would fend off an attempt by Microsoft to steal market share from QuickBooks. Having proven that he was more than just a manager, the board of directors named him CEO in 2008, succeeding Intuit founder Scott Cook.

As a leader, Smith melds innovation with profit-motive. For instance, based on Google's innovative model, he implemented unstructured time where employees can use 10 percent of their time to work on any project they choose. His theory is sound. Smith says, ". . . people who focus on things they love will work harder and get more done. We're looking for great ideas that will improve our workers' skills and efficiency. We're also hoping to foster innovation—if someone has an idea for a new product that our customers would love, then we encourage them to go for it." Since introducing unstructured time, Intuit has seen more than 200 initiatives go to market, resulting in $100 million in new revenue.

Another one of Smith's strategies was to focus on design in order to overcome the perception that financial software is boring and dull. He even reconfigured the layout of the physical space within the organization, making fewer cubicles and more open spaces, encouraging collaboration. In 2015, his vision was to make Intuit one of the most design-driven companies in the world by 2020, and although there may be no objective measure of success for such a goal, Intuit's constant innovation and design strategies have paid off. When he took the helm of Intuit at the age of 43, the company had 8,000 employees and annual revenues of $2.6 billion. By early 2020, as well as being a long-term member of *Fortune* magazine's "100 Best Places to Work," the company's revenues had tripled, and the stock price had risen from under $25 to over $260 per share (NASDAQ: INTU).

Smith attributes his success as a leader to lessons he gathered along the way: from his parents, who instilled a sense of community, family, and leadership; to his academic career; and to his extracurricular experiences, such as teaching martial arts. In high school, he'd played football until his sophomore year when he decided to dedicate his time to studying martial arts. By the time Smith was a senior he had earned his black belt, and soon after, he notes, "I was teaching an entire school, with about 150 students. You get measured on the progress of the students you're teaching. It's no longer about your own abilities; it's about building the capability in others. I fall back on that to this day."

College was formative as well. Of his alma mater, Smith says, "Marshall has a sense of purpose and values that I love. Look at what it has accomplished since the plane crash. Champions aren't defined by whether they hit the canvas, but by how quickly they get back up. Marshall University just perseveres. It's a university that has been hit with tragedy and fought its way through, and it just keeps coming back. And I think that is the secret to life."

In late 2018, at the relatively young age of 54 and after 11 years at the helm of Intuit, Smith announced that he was turning over the top spot to Executive Vice President Sasan Goodarzi on January 1, 2019, so he could focus on his duties as a board member of Intuit as well as Nordstrom and Survey Monkey, and pursue a passion for improving public education, especially in often "overlooked" zip codes, like his hometown in West Virginia. Even though his leadership certainly played a key role in the company's success so far, Smith would be the first to tell you that he didn't do it all on his own. One of his favorite quotes comes from Bill Campbell, a well-known business coach and one of Smith's early mentors, who said, "Your title makes you a manager, people decide if you're a leader."[58]

Case Questions

1. What personal traits does Brad Smith possess that aid him as a leader? Are these traits consistent with the early trait perspectives on leadership?
2. How would you describe Brad Smith's leadership style? Which leadership concepts, models, or theories best reflect how he leads?
3. Do you believe that Smith's gender played a part in his success? Why or why not?
4. What are three important leadership lessons that you can learn from Smith's career path?

You Make the Call

Two Bites from the Same Apple

1. Was Steve Jobs a better leader or a better manager? Why? Is Tim Cook a better leader or a better manager? Why?
2. Compare and contrast the leadership styles exhibited by Steve Jobs and Tim Cook.
3. Which leadership concepts and models are most illustrative of how Steve Jobs led? Which leadership concepts and models are most illustrative of how Tim Cook leads now?
4. In your opinion, if you had to choose either Steve Jobs or Tim Cook to lead your company, who would you choose? Why?

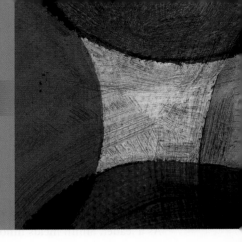

CHAPTER **12**

Communication in Organizations

Learning Outcomes

After studying this chapter, you should be able to:

12-1 Describe the interpersonal nature of organizations.

12-2 Describe the role and importance of communication in the manager's job.

12-3 Identify the basic forms of communication in organizations.

12-4 Discuss informal communication, including its various forms and types.

12-5 Describe how the communication process can be managed to recognize and overcome barriers.

This chapter is the first of two that focuses on interpersonal processes in organizations. We first establish the interpersonal nature of organizations and then discuss communication, one of the most basic forms of interaction among people. We begin by examining communication in the context of the manager's job. We then identify and discuss forms of interpersonal, group, and organizational communication. After discussing informal means of communication, we describe how organizational communication can be effectively managed. In our next chapter, we discuss other important elements of interpersonal relations: group and team processes and conflict. We begin with a description of how easily communication and its messages can be misunderstood and how one organization has dealt with this.

Management in Action

A Big Desk May Say it All

"It's a strange phenomenon. People have literally been doing it all their lives, but when it comes to communicating with staff we are falling short."

—**Miguel Angel Garcia, Senior Vice President at Univision**

In 2012 managers at Univision Communications determined that they had a problem. For many years, the company had promoted people the way that most companies tend to do. Miguel Angel Garcia, Senior Vice President for Live Events, noted, "You take the best technical person at a given position, and it stands to reason that that same person can take the reins and manage all of the people that do that same technical job." However, after years of promoting people in this same way problems began to arise across various departments. The problem: The people being promoted to management roles had little idea how to manage and their greatest deficit by far was their inability to effectively communicate with those they managed.

"In the beginning we did not know what was happening. It seemed like morale and overall employee satisfaction just dropped through the floor," added Garcia. In the end the company, desperate to solve the problem and restore morale, hired a consulting firm to attempt to diagnose the problem and come up with a way to fix it. "We just could not figure it out. We were way too close to it, and we needed a fresh set of eyes to look at it," Garcia noted. The consulting firm began interviewing employees and a consensus among responses pointed to one clear answer: The new managers were not communicating effectively with their staff. To correct the problem, a new training program for managers was devised and implemented.

The problem at Univision is not unique to their organization. Communication is one of the skills that is most often taken for granted in the business world. And, if we think about it a little, we can certainly understand why. We have, as human beings, been communicating all of our lives, so it stands to reason that if we do something every day of our lives that by the time we enter the workplace we should all be experts at it. The problem is that we rarely give much thought to *how* we communicate with others . . . we just do it and hope that it works. Thus, the challenge is to begin thinking differently about the communication process and approach it thoughtfully, tactically, and with our end goals in mind. As we will see, this is a process of getting managers to construct their messages based on the needs of the audience that they will address.

Garcia notes, "At the beginning of our new training program our consulting team had a serious challenge to face. The first thing that they had to convince people of was that they were not nearly as gifted at communication as they thought that they were." Again, this is a common element of management-level communication training. As we saw above, people generally take the idea of communication for granted, thus the first element of any good training program is to convince the audience that they will benefit from beginning to think about communication efforts in a different, more strategic way.

"The key to effective communication at the management level is to begin to think, not just of what you want to say, but how your audience is going to receive the information that you are about to share. Every employee that one faces is different in some way from all others. Thus, our first fundamental error is thinking that what works for us will work for everyone else that we run into," Dr. Brad Wesner, one of the consultants, notes. "And this was our experience working with Univision. We do this by pitching management scenarios to the staff and asking them what we would do. Then, after hearing their directives, we react in ways that they do not expect. This freaks them out a lot, and it forces them to rethink their directives and present them in another way. In the end, they keep doing it over and over until the message they construct is finally received and understood."

Univision, a major media company, uses consultants to assist with communication training for new managers.

Ken Wolter/Shutterstock.com

This type of role play is essential to training new managers how to tactically create their message and verify that their message was received as intended. The process involves some trial and error early on, but over time the managers learn that certain people (their audience) receive messages differently than others. Furthermore, by adapting their communication practices based on their audience, the managers get the response from their audience that they want.

The process at Univision also began to add some nonverbal elements that the new managers had never considered. Garcia notes, "I remember on the second day of training I was sitting in the back just watching the consultants work when we took a short break. During the break one of the managers approached Dr. Wesner and asked about a particular employee he was having difficulty reaching. Wesner listened intently to the conversation and then, out of the blue, asked the manager to take him to his office. I thought this was about the strangest request ever, but I decided to follow along to see where it went. Dr. Wesner walked into the office and started laughing. He walked back into the hall, shook the hand of the new manager, and said, "We need to get you a smaller desk."

"The desk was this massive old oak desk. I was intimidated just looking at it. It looked like something out of the Oval Office. Imagine that you are an employee who gets summoned to your boss's office. You have a seat in front of this massive desk that clearly says, "Hey, I am the boss and you are not." The poor employees had no chance to have an open dialogue with that thing in the room. It simply was not designed with open lines of communication in mind. Rather, it was designed so that the guy behind it could convey authority. It had to go. In the end, the guy really liked the desk and wanted to keep it so we compromised. I told him that when he had an employee come into the office to step from behind the desk and sit directly across from the employee. The guy started doing it, and all of a sudden communication just opened up. Problem solved."

Normally when individuals consider communication they tend to think of the message that they are sending with words. However, an incredible amount of information is sent and received based on things like the setting in which the communication takes place, the tone of voice we use when communicating, how fast we talk, and even how much eye contact that the receiver gets from the sender. These nonverbal cues have an incredible amount of meaning, and we must consider how to use them tactically.

Dr. Wesner recalls, "I remember the very first time that I saw this [the use of tactical nonverbal communication] in action. One of the first jobs that I ever had out of college was working with this lady who we will call Dianne. Dianne was short, maybe 5 feet tall, and she knew it. She also knew that everyone that she managed was taller than she was. Dianne made the decision that she had to do something to make sure that her authority was conveyed. So, every time she had you into her office, the very first thing she would do is ask you to sit down. The next thing she would do is stand up so that she would be taller than you were. Dianne did this every time without fail. It was a while before I recognized what she was doing. In the end, she was simply using body position to convey her authority."

Six months after Univision started training managers on tactical communication practices, follow-up interviews with employees and surveys of the newly trained managers showed a dramatic change in organizational performance. Managers reported that turnover had reduced dramatically and that error rates within their span of control had dramatically reduced. Even more impressive, employees who were interviewed said that they felt as if their managers had become much more relationship oriented and that they had started to really understand the needs of employees. In short, tactical communication proved vital in turning management practices around and producing better results.[1]

Organizations today are continually looking for ways to improve communication among their employees, customers, and other stakeholders. Some, like Univision, are looking to communication consultants to take the next step in the evolution of communication. But communication has always been a vital part of managerial work. Indeed, managers around the world agree that communication is one of their most important tasks. It is important for them to communicate with others in order to convey their vision and goals for the organization and to clearly direct those that report to them on the day-to-day challenges that they face. Additionally, it's important for others to communicate with them so that they will better understand what is going on in their environment and how they and their organization can become more effective.

12-1 THE INTERPERSONAL NATURE OF ORGANIZATIONS

In Chapter 1, we noted how much of a manager's job involves scheduled and unscheduled meetings, telephone calls, email, and related activities. Indeed, a great deal of what all managers do involves interacting with other people, both directly and indirectly and both inside and outside of the organization. The schedule that follows is a typical day for the president of a Houston-based company. He kept a log of his activities for several different days so that you could better appreciate the nature of managerial work.

6:00–6:30 A.M.	Read and respond to email from home; scan major news stories online.
7:45–8:15 A.M.	Arrive at work; review hardcopy mail sorted by assistant.
8:15–8:30 A.M.	Scan digital version of the *Wall Street Journal*; read and respond to email; scan online sources for business news and updates.
8:30–9:00 A.M.	Meet with labor officials and plant manager to resolve minor labor disputes.
9:00–9:30 A.M.	Review internal report; read and respond to new email; read and respond to new text messages.
9:30–10:00 A.M.	Meet with two marketing executives to review advertising campaign; instruct them to send approvals to advertising agency.
10:00–11:30 A.M.	Meet with company executive committee to discuss strategy, budgetary issues, and competition (this committee meets weekly).
11:30–12:00 noon.	Send several emails; read and respond to new email and texts.
12:00–1:15 P.M.	Lunch with the financial vice president and two executives from another subsidiary of the parent corporation; primary topic of discussion is the Houston Rockets basketball team; place three hands-free phone calls en route to lunch and receive one call en route back to office.
1:15–1:45 P.M.	Meet with human resource director and assistant about a recent OSHA inspection; establish a task force to investigate the problems identified and to suggest solutions.
1:45–2:00 P.M.	Read and respond to new email and texts.
2:00–2:30 P.M.	Video conference (Zoom) with four other company presidents.
2:30–3:00 P.M.	Meet with financial vice president about a confidential issue that came up at lunch (unscheduled).
3:00–3:30 P.M.	Work alone in office; read and respond to new email and texts; send several emails and texts.
3:30–4:15 P.M.	Meet with a group of sales representatives and the company purchasing agent.

4:15–5:30 P.M.	Work alone in office.
5:30–7:00 P.M.	Play racquetball at nearby athletic club with marketing vice president.
9:00–9:30 P.M.	Read and respond to email and texts from home; send text to assistant about an emergency meeting to be scheduled for the next day.

How did this manager spend his time? He spent most of it working, communicating, and interacting with other people. And this compressed daily schedule does not include several other brief telephone calls, brief conversations with his assistant, and brief conversations with other managers. Clearly, interpersonal relations, communication, and group processes are a pervasive part of all organizations and a vital part of all managerial activities.[2]

12-1a Interpersonal Dynamics

The nature of interpersonal relations in an organization is as varied as the individual members themselves.[3] At one extreme, interpersonal relations can be personal and positive. This occurs when the parties know each other, have mutual respect and affection, and enjoy interacting. Let's look at two examples. First, two managers who have known each other for years, socialize together on weekends, and are close personal friends will likely interact at work in a positive fashion. At the other extreme, interpersonal dynamics can be personal but negative. This most likely occurs when the parties dislike each other, do not have mutual respect, and do not enjoy interacting. In this second example, consider the case of a manager who fought openly to block the promotion of another manager within the organization. Over the objections of the first manager, however, the other manager still gets promoted to the same rank. When the two of them must interact, it will most likely be in a negative manner. And, as we will see, in order for the two to interact productively, that negative interpersonal perception must be overcome.

Most interactions fall between these extremes, as members of the organization interact in a professional way focused primarily on goal accomplishment. The interaction deals with the job at hand, is relatively formal and structured, and is task directed. Consider this third example. Two managers may respect each other's work and recognize the professional competence that each brings to the job. However, they may also have few common interests and little to talk about besides the job they are doing. These different types of interactions may occur between individuals, between groups, or between individuals and groups, and they can change over time. The two managers in the second scenario in the previous paragraph, for example, might decide to bury the hatchet and adopt a professional but detached manner. The two managers in the third example could find more common ground than they anticipated and evolve to a personal and positive interaction.

Interpersonal dynamics pervade virtually every facet of organizations. People talk, exchange facial expressions, message, text, or email throughout their work days. In general, interpersonal relations can range from personal and positive to personal and negative or anywhere in between.

Monkey Business Images/Shutterstock.com

"You Have to Read People Quickly to Fit into the Social Network."
—Stephen Miles, Executive Coach

12-1b Outcomes of Interpersonal Behaviors

A variety of things can happen as a result of interpersonal behaviors.[4] Recall from Chapter 15, for example, that many perspectives on motivation suggest that people have social needs. Interpersonal relations in organizations can be a primary source of need satisfaction for many people. For a person with a strong need for affiliation, high-quality interpersonal relations can be an important positive element in the workplace. However, when this same person is confronted with poor-quality working relationships, the effect can be just as strong but in the other direction.

Interpersonal relations also serve as a solid basis for social support. Suppose that an employee receives a poor performance evaluation or is denied a promotion. Others in the organization can lend support because they share a common frame of reference—an understanding of the causes and consequences of what happened. Good interpersonal relations throughout an organization can also be a source of synergy. People who support one another and who work well together can accomplish much more than people who do not support one another and who do not work well together. Another outcome, implied earlier, is conflict—people may leave an interpersonal exchange feeling angry or hostile. Finally, from a managerial perspective, strong interpersonal relationships with employees allow managers to know how employees will react to specific challenges, where their strengths lie, and what strategies for motivation of employees will be successful. But a common thread is woven through all of these outcomes: communication between people in the organization.[5]

Manager's Checklist

☐ Managers should be aware of the various kinds of interpersonal interactions that can be identified in organizational settings.

☐ You should have an appreciation of how much of your daily life involves interacting with other people.

☐ Managers should use an individualized approach for interaction with others in the organization based on knowledge gained from repeated interactions.

12-2 COMMUNICATION AND THE MANAGER'S JOB

As evidenced by the daily log presented earlier, a typical day for a manager includes doing desk work, attending scheduled meetings, placing and receiving telephone calls, reading and answering correspondence, attending unscheduled meetings, and making tours. Most of these activities involve communication. In fact, managers usually spend over half their time on some form of communication. Communication always involves two or more people, so other behavioral processes—such as motivation, leadership, and group and team interactions—all come into play. Top executives must handle communication effectively if they are to be true leaders.[6] Indeed, communication took on even great importance during the COVID-19 pandemic in 2020 as managers had to quickly adapt to new forms of communication, adjust to employees working remotely, and respond to new expectations about both managerial and organizational messaging and communication.

12-2a The Problems with Communication

Communication happens almost from the moment we are born. We emerge into the world cold, hungry, and in need of comfort, so what is the very first thing that we do? We cry. And in response to our crying we are immediately warmed, fed, and comforted by our parents. We quickly learn that when something is wrong, crying will get us the attention that we need to correct the problem. This is what Pavlov might have referred to as our first ever conditioned response to stimuli, as when we quickly equate crying as a method to achieve satisfaction of our desires.[7] However, in this very basic interaction there is a problem that can haunt our communication efforts for years: even at birth the problem we are experiencing is obvious to us, but may not always be obvious to those around us. Consider the same baby for a moment, but this time a few months older. The baby is still unable to speak and begins to get sick. The baby knows that it does not feel well, so it starts to cry. After all, crying has always brought relief in the past. However, this time the parents try all of the normal tricks to comfort the child with no success. In this case, the baby knows what is wrong but efforts to communicate in an effort to fix the problem fall flat. Simply put, to us, our communication is perfect, because to us it makes perfect sense, yet the challenge in communication is to make what makes sense to us also make sense to others. As we will see, that takes more effort than we may initially imagine.

The second, and equally troubling, problem with communication is that we have been doing it all our lives. As the old saying goes, "Practice makes perfect," and if that statement was true then we all should be experts after years of practicing communication every day. The problem is that we are not. Communication takes a significant amount of thought, planning, and work. Furthermore, the work never really ends. The reason for this is that every situation we face, and every communication partner that we interact with, is different. So, what worked for us in the past is not a guarantee of what will work in the present. To be successful, we must endeavor to gain an ever greater understanding of what makes communication successful and work diligently each day to improve.

12-2b A Definition of Communication

Imagine three managers working in an office building. The first manager is all alone but is nevertheless yelling for a subordinate to come help. No one appears, but he continues to yell. The second manager is talking to a subordinate on a smartphone, but a poor signal causes the subordinate to misunderstand some important numbers being provided by the manager. As a result, the subordinate sends 1,500 crates of eggs to 150 Fifth Street, when he should have sent 150 crates of eggs to 1500 Fifteenth Street. The third manager is talking in her office with a subordinate who clearly hears and understands what is being said. Each of these managers is attempting to communicate, but with different results.

Communication is the process of transmitting information from one person to another. Did any of our three managers communicate? The last did, and the first did not. How about the second? In fact, she did communicate. She transmitted information, and information was received. The problem was that the message transmitted and the message received were not the same. The words spoken by the manager were distorted by a poor phone connection. Effective communication, then, is the process of sending a message in such a way that the message received is as close in meaning as possible to the message intended. Although the second manager engaged in communication, it was not effective.

Our definition of effective communication is based on the ideas of meaning and consistency of meaning. Meaning is the idea that the individual who initiates the communication exchange wishes to convey. In effective communication, the meaning is transmitted in such a way that the receiving person understands it. As noted earlier, it is important to realize that communication is never perfect in that none of us has the capacity to read another person's mind; thus, we can never see or experience things in the exact same way as someone else. However, by working to create common methods to facilitate understanding, we can facilitate enough meaning exchange to make understanding possible. One of the main ways that we do this is through the use of common language. For example, consider these messages:

1. The high today will be only 40 degrees.
2. It will be cold today.
3. *Ceteris paribus.*
4. Xn1gpbo5cz4ikab19.

You probably understand the meaning of the first statement. The second statement may seem clear at first, but it is somewhat less clear than the first statement because cold is a relative condition and the word can mean different things to different people. Fewer still understand the third statement because it is written in Latin. None of you understands the last statement because it is written in a secret code that the author developed as a child.

12-2c The Role of Communication in Management

We noted earlier the variety of activities that fill a manager's day. Meetings, telephone calls, emails, texts, and various other kinds of correspondence are all a necessary part of every manager's job—and all clearly involve communication. To better understand the linkages

communication
The process of transmitting information from one person to another

effective communication
The process of sending a message in such a way that the message received is as close in meaning as possible to the message intended

CHAPTER 12 | COMMUNICATION IN ORGANIZATIONS

fizkes/Shutterstock.com

Communication and effective communication are not necessarily the same thing. This woman is reading a document, so communication is taking place. At the same time, though, her expression suggests that the communication may not be effective. She may not understand the message, for instance, or she may be angered or confused by it.

between communication and management, recall the variety of roles that managers must fill. Each of the 10 basic managerial roles discussed in Chapter 1 would be impossible to accomplish without communication. Interpersonal roles involve interacting with supervisors, subordinates, peers, and others outside the organization. Decisional roles require managers to seek out information to use in making decisions and then communicate those decisions to others. Informational roles focus specifically on acquiring and disseminating information.

Communication also relates directly to the basic management functions of planning, organizing, leading, and controlling. Environmental scanning, integrating planning-time horizons, and decision making, for example, all necessitate communication. Delegation, coordination, and organization change and development also entail communication. Developing reward systems and interacting with subordinates as a part of the leading function would be impossible without some form of communication.

And communication is essential to establishing standards, monitoring performance, and taking corrective actions as a part of control. Clearly, then, communication is a pervasive part of virtually all managerial activities.[8]

12-2d The Communication Process

Figure 12.1 illustrates how communication generally takes place between people. The process of communication begins when one person (the sender) wants to transmit a fact, idea, opinion, or other information to someone else (the receiver). This fact, idea, or opinion has meaning to the sender, whether it be simple and concrete or complex and abstract. For example, Linda Porter, a marketing representative at Canon, recently landed a new account and wanted to tell her boss about it. This fact and her motivation to tell her boss represented meaning.

The next step is to encode the meaning into a form appropriate to the situation. The encoding might take the form of words, facial expressions, gestures, or even artistic expressions and physical actions. The choice of how to encode the message is a very conscious decision based on the sender's knowledge of the situation and the receiver. The sender must also make sure that the message has enough information that it will not be misinterpreted by the receiver. For example, Linda might choose to say, "I just landed the Acme account," "We just got some good news from Acme," "I just spoiled Xerox's day," "Acme just made the right decision," or any number of other things. She actually chose the second message. Clearly, the encoding process is influenced by the content of the message, the familiarity of sender and receiver, and other situational factors.

After the message has been encoded, it is transmitted through the appropriate channel or medium. The channel is most simply defined as the method for transmission that we choose to use when communicating. For example, the channel by which this encoded message is being transmitted to you is the printed page in the context of a physical textbook or a digital image if you are using an e-book. This channel makes the most sense as the author is not present with you at the moment, and this message is only one in the larger context of the entire management text that you are reading. Common channels in organizations include meetings, email or text messages, memos, letters, reports, telephone calls, and face-to-face interactions. Linda Porter might have written her boss a note, sent him an email or text, called him on the telephone, or dropped by his office to convey the news. Because both she and her boss were out of the office when she got the news, she sent him a text.

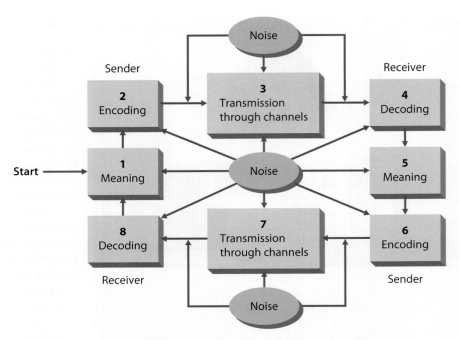

The numbers indicate the sequence in which steps take place.

FIGURE 12.1

The Communication Process

This figure diagrams the communication process. Notice that the process is cyclical, with a message being conceived, transmitted, decoded, and feedback returning to the sender. The process continues until the message is received and understood as intended. Notice also that noise can impact the message at any point; thus, the manager must understand that the conversation in the next office, the printer that is out of paper, and the receiver's worries may all negatively impact the manager's best efforts to communicate.

After the message is received, it is decoded by the receiver, who then interprets the meaning to the best of his or her ability. As noted earlier, the consistency of meaning transmission can vary dramatically. Upon hearing about the Acme deal, the sales manager at Canon might have thought, "This'll mean a big promotion for both of us," "This is great news for the company," "This is going to mean a lot of extra hours and will ruin my vacation plans," or "She's blowing her own horn too much again." His actual feelings were closest to the second statement. In many cases, the meaning prompts a response, and the cycle is continued when a new message is sent by the same steps back to the original sender. The manager might have called the sales representative to offer congratulations, written her a personal note of praise, offered praise in an email or text, or sent a formal letter of acknowledgment. Linda's boss sent her a text and then wrote her a personal note as a follow-up.

As noted earlier, communication is never perfect and often requires several attempts to get it right. Consider the previous example, but this time let's assume that the manager gets Linda's message and his reaction is that the extra work is likely to jeopardize his vacation plans. As we might assume, his response to Linda may be very different here. In this scenario it may take several attempts by Linda to really convey the message she intended. Thus, consider the interaction below:

Linda: We just got some good news from Acme.

Boss: Oh man, when are we going to need to start working on that.

Linda: Acme would like us to be up and running in two weeks.

Boss: Ouch, that is going to really mess me up. I was planning on leaving next week for vacation with my family. My kids are going to be bummed to miss out on Disney.

![image of a man in a suit looking at a smartphone while sitting at a desk with a laptop]

Noise can take many forms—people talking in the background, construction taking place outside an office, and so on. But noise comes in other forms. This manager was just talking with his manager about an important project and his call was dropped.

fizkes/Shutterstock.com

![image of two women working together at a laptop]

Communication is often a cyclical process involving information passing back and forth between participants until understanding of the message is achieved. These colleagues are discussing information as they work to solve a problem. They both appear to be actively engaged in the process.

Monkey Business Images/Shutterstock.com

Linda: No problem. I knew you had plans. I am already coordinating with the team here so that we can handle everything in your absence. All that I need from you is a final approval of the total work plan, and I can have that in your email inbox by 3:00 today. So, you can say hello to Mickey for me!

Boss: Outstanding! Way to go on nailing this new account, and I appreciate that you took my personal needs into consideration in your planning!

In this scenario, Linda's first message did not get the reaction from her boss that she expected. She was expecting him to be ecstatic, but he responded in a way that indicated he was clearly concerned about something. It takes a few exchanges before all of the information is fleshed out and Linda's message is fully understood.

It is also vital that we understand the concept of "noise." *Noise* is any phenomenon that may disrupt communication anywhere along the way. Noise comes in two varieties: internal and external. External noise is noise that is outside of the individuals involved in the communication interaction: the sound of someone coughing, a truck driving by, or two people talking close at hand. It can also include disruptions such as a letter lost in the mail, an interrupted cellphone call, an email misrouted or infected with a virus, or a text not being received because of poor service. Internal noise is noise that is "inside" of one of the individuals in the interaction that causes them to be distracted and makes sending and decoding messages difficult. For example, if you have ever had a headache or been sick at work, the discomfort that you were experiencing makes it difficult to focus, making concentration on communication difficult.

Upon getting Linda's text, her boss immediately began experiencing internal noise as he considered how the additional workload would impact his vacation plans. This noise distracted him from the original intent of Linda's message and, as we noted above, it took repeated communication interactions to break through the noise and complete an accurate transmission.

Manager's Checklist

☐ Managers should recognize the difference between communication and effective communication.

☐ You should also understand the basic elements of the communication process, especially the role of noise.

☐ Recognize that communication is never perfect, so we must continuously verify that messages are received as intended.

12-3 FORMS OF COMMUNICATION IN ORGANIZATIONS

Managers need to understand several kinds of communication that are common in organizations today.[9] These include interpersonal communication, communication in networks and teams, organizational communication, and virtual communication.

12-3a Interpersonal Communication

Interpersonal communication generally takes one of three typologies: oral, nonverbal, and written.

oral communication
Face-to-face conversation, group discussions, telephone calls, and other circumstances in which the spoken word is used to transmit meaning

Oral Communication Oral communication takes place in conversations, group discussions, telephone calls, Skype, Zoom, FaceTime, or other situations in which the spoken word is used to express meaning. Oral communication is so prevalent for several reasons. The primary advantage of oral communication is that it promotes prompt feedback and interchange in the form of verbal questions or agreement, facial expressions, and gestures. Due to the numerous kinds of immediate feedback, oral communication is often referred to as being "rich" in that there are numerous communication channels occurring simultaneously. This richness allows participants to immediately determine if their message has been received and interpreted correctly or if further clarification is necessary. Oral communication is also easy (all the sender needs to do is talk), and it can be done with little preparation (though careful preparation is advisable in certain situations). The sender does not need pencil and paper, a printer, or other equipment. In one survey, 55 percent of the executives sampled felt that their own written communication skills were fair or poor, so they chose oral communication to avoid embarrassment![10]

However, oral communication also has drawbacks. It may suffer from problems of inaccuracy if the speaker chooses the wrong words to convey meaning or leaves out pertinent details, if noise disrupts the process, or if the receiver forgets part of the message.[11] In a two-way discussion, there is seldom time for a thoughtful, considered response or for introducing many new facts and, unless there is some form of recording being used, there is no permanent record of what has been said. In addition, although most managers are comfortable talking to people individually or in small groups, fewer enjoy speaking to larger audiences.[12]

nonverbal communication
Any communication exchange that does not use words or uses words to carry more meaning than the strict definition of the words themselves

Nonverbal Communication Nonverbal communication is a communication exchange that does not use words or uses words to carry more meaning than the strict definition of the words themselves. Nonverbal communication is a powerful but little-understood form of communication in organizations. It often relies on facial expressions, body movements, physical contact, proximity between communicators, and gestures. One study found that as much as 55 percent of the content of a message is transmitted by facial expressions and body posture and that another 38 percent derives from inflection and tone. Words themselves may account for only 7 percent of the content of the message.[13]

Research has identified three kinds of nonverbal communication practiced by managers: images, settings, and body language.[14] In this context, images are the kinds of words or phrases people elect to use. "Damn the torpedoes, full speed ahead" and "Even though there are some potential hazards, we should proceed with this course of action" may convey the same

Nonverbal communication often relies on body language—facial expressions, posture, gestures, and so forth. This man, for example, is conveying through his crossed arms and demeanor that he is unhappy or impatient.

InesBazdar/Shutterstock.com

meaning, but how they are interpreted in a particular context can be radically different. The person who uses the first expression may be perceived as a maverick, a courageous hero, an individualist, or a reckless and foolhardy adventurer. The person who uses the second might be described as aggressive, forceful, diligent, or narrow minded and resistant to change. At a meeting of Walmart executives, former CEO Lee Scott once announced that "I can tell everyone what color underwear they're wearing." His meaning? There was an issue dividing the group, and Scott wanted those in attendance to know that he was aware of which executives were on each side of the issue.[15] In short, our choice of words conveys much more than just the strict meaning of the words themselves.

> **"Make no mistake. I can tell everyone what color underwear they're wearing."**
> —Former Walmart CEO Lee Scott, Meaning That He Knew Who in a Group of Executives Was On His Side

Extending the image concept a bit further, not only are the words we choose important in determining how meaning will be interpreted, but other aspects play into our choices as well. For example our tone and volume convey vastly different meanings depending on how we use them. Imagine a manager walking into the office of a subordinate and calmly announcing, "We need to call the client." This conveys that there is an issue that needs attention and that contacting the client should resolve the issue. Now imagine the same manager walking into the same office but this time exclaiming at high volume, "We need to call the client!" In this case the volume and tone change and so does the meaning. Now there is the impression of some immediate pending emergency that has to be resolved to avoid disastrous consequences.

The setting for communication also plays a major role in nonverbal communication. Boundaries, familiarity, the home turf, and other elements of the setting are all important. Much has been written about the symbols of power in organizations. The size and location of an office, the kinds of furniture in the office, and the accessibility of the person in the office all communicate useful information. For example, Mary Barra, CEO of GM, positions her desk so that it is always between her and a visitor. This keeps her in charge. When she wants a less formal dialogue, she moves around to the front of the desk and sits beside her visitor. Michael Dell of Dell Computer, in contrast, has his desk facing a side window so that, when he turns around to greet a visitor, there is never anything between them.

A third form of nonverbal communication is body language.[16] For example, the distance we stand from someone as we speak, known as *proxemics*, has meaning. In the United States, standing very close to someone you are talking to generally signals either familiarity or aggression. The English and Germans stand farther apart than Americans when talking, whereas the Arabs, Japanese, and Mexicans stand closer together.[17] Eye contact is another effective means of nonverbal communication. For example, prolonged eye contact might suggest either hostility or romantic interest, whereas a lack of eye contact can be associated with dishonesty or disinterest. Other kinds of body language include body and hand movement, pauses in speech, and mode of dress.

The manager should be aware of the importance of nonverbal communication and recognize its potential impact. Giving an employee good news about a reward with the wrong nonverbal cues can destroy the reinforcement value of the reward. Likewise, reprimanding an employee but providing inconsistent nonverbal cues can limit the effectiveness of the sanctions. The tone of the message, where and how the message is delivered, facial expressions, and gestures can all amplify or weaken the message or change the message altogether. During the COVID-19 pandemic people occasionally noted when leaders would be encouraging people to socially distance, wear face coverings, and so forth while they (the leaders) were not themselves doing those same things.

Emoticons also play a growing role in nonverbal communication. For instance, in a face-to-face conversation we can use a facial expression to indicate that we are kidding or being sarcastic with our words. In an email or text, though, the context clues provided by facial expressions are lost. But now people can attach emoticons—smiling faces, frowning faces, winks, and so forth—to emails, texts, or other digital messages to convey additional information.

written communication
Memos, letters, reports, notes, and other circumstances in which the written word is used to transmit meaning

Written Communication   "Putting it in writing" in a letter, report, memorandum, handwritten note, or email or text message can solve many of the problems inherent in oral communication. Nevertheless, and perhaps surprisingly, written communication is not as common as one might imagine, nor is it a mode of communication much respected by managers. Over 80 percent of the managers who responded to one survey indicated that the written communication they received was of fair or poor quality. In a different study, 65 percent of the executives surveyed indicated they preferred to interact with customers, business partners, and vendors with email or text messaging rather than by phone.[18]

The biggest single drawback of traditional forms of written communication is that they inhibit feedback and interchange. This lack of immediate feedback to the message is often referred to as message "leanness." For example, when one manager sends another manager a letter, it must be written or dictated, printed, mailed, received, routed, opened, and read. If there is a misunderstanding, it may take several days for it to be recognized, let alone rectified. Although the use of email or texts is, of course, much faster, both sender and receiver must still have access to a computer or other device, and the receiver must open and read the message for it to actually be received. The lag time between the sending of a message and receiving feedback from it can, and in many cases does, result in inaccurate interpretation of the original sender's meaning. Thus, written communication often inhibits feedback and interchange and is usually more difficult and time-consuming than oral communication.

Of course, written communication offers some advantages. It is often very accurate and provides a permanent record of the exchange. The sender can take the time to collect and assimilate the information and can draft and revise it before it is transmitted. This process allows the sender to carefully consider both the content of the message and how the receiver is likely to interpret the message as written. When done skillfully, the ability to strategically construct a message can be a powerful way of making sure a message is received as intended. The receiver can take the time to read it carefully and can refer to it repeatedly, as needed. For these reasons, written communication is generally preferable when important details are involved or in situations in which the receiver will likely need to reference the details of the message repeatedly. At times it is important to one or both parties to have a written record available as evidence of exactly what took place. This is why, for instance, most legal contracts are in written form. In the event either party questions responsibilities, the contract can be used to clearly determine the answers. Susan Li lives in the United States but owns two factories in China that manufacture uniforms and protective clothing for health care workers. While she uses email for casual communication, she also relies heavily on formal business letters in communicating with the managers of her factories and with her major customers. Li believes that such letters give her an opportunity to carefully think through what she wants to say, tailor her message to each person, and avoid subsequent misunderstandings.

Choosing the Right Form   Which form of interpersonal communication should the manager use? The best medium will be determined by the situation. Oral communication is most effective when the richness of the message is of the greatest importance and immediate feedback is needed in order to make sure that the sender's message has been interpreted correctly. Less formal written communication such as email or text messaging is often preferred when the message is personal, nonroutine, and brief. However, email has played a prominent role in several recent court cases, so managers should always use discretion when sending messages electronically.[19] For example, private emails made public during legal proceedings have played major roles in litigation involving Enron, Tyco, WorldCom, and Morgan Stanley.[20] More formal written communication is usually best when the message is more impersonal, routine, and longer.

The manager can also combine media to capitalize on the advantages of each. For example, a quick phone call or text to set up a meeting is easy and gets an immediate response. Following up the call or text with a reminder email, digital meeting invitation, or handwritten note helps ensure that the recipient will remember the meeting, and it provides a record that the meeting was, in fact, scheduled. Digital communication, discussed more fully later, blurs the differences between oral and written communication and can help each be more effective. In some instances, digital communication itself is also the most appropriate way to send a message.

"I'm not a big emailer. I prefer face-to-face whenever possible."

—A. G. Lafley, Former Chairman at Procter & Gamble

12-3b **Communication in Networks and Work Teams**

Although communication among team members in an organization is clearly interpersonal in nature, substantial research also focuses specifically on how people in networks and work teams communicate with one another. A communication network is the pattern through which the members of a group or team communicate. Researchers studying group dynamics have identified several typical networks in groups and teams consisting of three, four, and five members. Representative networks among five-member teams are shown in Figure 12.2.[21]

In the wheel pattern, all communication flows through one central person, who is probably the group's leader. In a sense, the wheel is the most centralized network because one person receives and disseminates all information. The Y pattern is slightly less centralized—two people are close to the center. The chain offers a more even flow of information among members, although two people (the ones at each end) interact with only one other person. This path is closed in the circle pattern. Finally, the all-channel network, the most decentralized, allows a free flow of information among all group members. Everyone participates equally, and the group's leader, if there is one, is not likely to have excessive power. Most social media platforms such as Facebook and LinkedIn allow individual users to form groups; these groups, in turn, then communicate like an all-channel network.

Research conducted on networks suggests some interesting connections between the type of network and group performance. For example, when the group's task is relatively simple and routine, centralized networks tend to perform with greatest efficiency and accuracy. The dominant leader facilitates performance by coordinating the flow of information. When a group of accounting clerks is logging incoming invoices and distributing them for payment, for example, one centralized leader can coordinate things efficiently. When the task is complex and nonroutine, such as making a major decision about organizational strategy, decentralized networks tend to be most effective because open channels of communication permit more interaction and a more efficient sharing of relevant information. Managers should recognize the effects of communication networks on group and organizational performance and should try to structure networks appropriately.

12-3c **Organizational Communication**

Still other forms of communication in organizations are those that flow among and between organizational units or groups. Each of these involves oral or written communication, but each also extends to broad patterns of communication across the organization.[22] As shown in Figure 12.3, two of these forms of communication follow vertical and horizontal linkages in the organization.

communication network The pattern through which the members of a group communicate

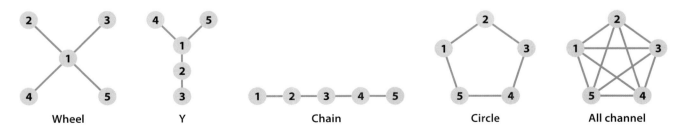

Wheel Y Chain Circle All channel

FIGURE 12.2

Types of Communication Networks

Research on communication networks has identified five basic networks for five-person groups. These networks vary in terms of information flow, position of the leader, and effectiveness for different types of tasks. Managers might strive to create centralized networks when group tasks are simple and routine. Alternatively, managers can foster decentralized groups when group tasks are complex and nonroutine.

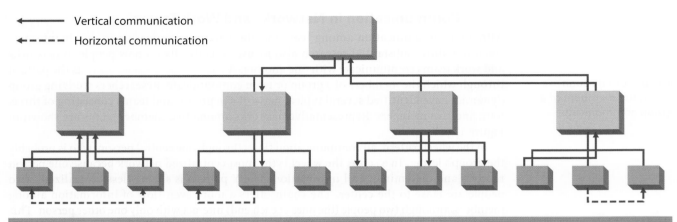

← Vertical communication

←---- Horizontal communication

FIGURE 12.3

Formal Communication in Organizations

Formal communication in organizations follows official reporting relationships or prescribed channels. For example, vertical communication, shown here with the solid lines, flows between levels in the organization and involves subordinates and their managers. Horizontal communication, shown with dashed lines, flows between people at the same level and is usually used to facilitate coordination.

vertical communication
Communication that flows up and down the organization, usually along formal reporting lines; takes place between managers and their superiors and subordinates and may involve several different levels of the organization

Vertical Communication Vertical communication is communication that flows up and down the organization, usually along formal reporting lines—that is, it is the communication that takes place between managers and their superiors and subordinates. Vertical communication may involve only two people, or it may flow through several different organizational levels. *Upward communication* consists of messages from subordinates to superiors. This flow is usually from subordinates to their direct superior, then to that person's direct superior, and so on up the hierarchy. Occasionally, a message might bypass a particular superior. The typical content of upward communication is requests, information that the lower-level manager thinks is of importance to the higher-level manager, responses to requests from the higher-level manager, suggestions, complaints, and financial information. Research has shown that upward communication is more subject to distortion than is downward communication. For example, subordinates may tend to withhold or distort information that makes them look bad. The greater the degree of difference in status between superior and subordinate and the greater the degree of distrust, the more likely the subordinate is to suppress or distort information. For instance, subordinates might choose to withhold information about problems from their boss if they think the news will make him angry and if they think they can solve the problem themselves without his ever knowing about it. Finally, it should also be noted that with regard to oral retelling of a message, the more individuals that the message passes through, the more the message is prone to distortion from one telling to the next.[23] Thus, as a message moves from one level of the organization to the another, the original sender's meaning is ever more prone to distortion.

A lot of communication in organizations is vertical—passing up and down the hierarchy between people at different levels. This manager is explaining a new project to her team. As she discusses what the team will be doing and answers questions from her team members, vertical communication is taking place. As the team engages with each other, the communication is horizontal, since the team members are all at the same level of the hierarchy.

Monkey Business Images/Shutterstock.com

Downward communication occurs when information flows down the hierarchy from superiors to subordinates. The typical content of these messages is directives on how something is to be done, the assignment of new responsibilities, performance feedback, and general information that the higher-level manager thinks will be of value to the lower-level manager. Vertical communication can and usually should be two-way in nature. In other words, give-and-take communication with active feedback is generally likely to be more effective than one-way communication.[24]

Horizontal Communication   Whereas vertical communication involves a superior and a subordinate, horizontal communication involves colleagues and peers at the same level of the organization. For example, an operations manager might communicate to a marketing manager that inventory levels are running low and that projected delivery dates should be extended by two weeks. This type of communication serves a number of purposes. It facilitates coordination among interdependent units. For example, a manager at Motorola was once researching the strategies of Japanese semiconductor firms in Europe. He found a great deal of information that was relevant to his assignment. He also uncovered some additional information that was potentially important to another department, so he passed it along to a colleague in that department, who used it to improve his own operations. Horizontal communication can also be used for joint problem solving, as when two plant managers at Northrop Grumman got together to work out a new method to improve productivity. Finally, horizontal communication plays a major role in work teams with members drawn from several departments.

horizontal communication
Communication that flows laterally within the organization; involves colleagues and peers at the same level of the organization and may involve individuals from several different organizational units

12-3d **Digital Communication**

Finally, as already noted, digital communication has become the norm in organizations today. Both formal information systems and personal information technology have reshaped how managers communicate with one another. Some of the perils of pervasive digital communication are explored in our *Tech Watch* box.

Formal Information Systems   Most larger businesses manage at least a portion of their organizational communication through information systems. Some firms go so far as to create a position for a chief information officer, or CIO. General Mills, Disney, Walmart, Xerox, and Burlington Industries all have such a position. The CIO is responsible for determining the information-processing needs and requirements of the organization and then putting in place systems that facilitate smooth and efficient organizational communication.

TECH WATCH

Thinking (and Talking) on Your Feet

A few years ago, MIT psychologist Sherry Turkle contributed an opinion piece to the *New York Times*. In her opinion, "we live in a technological universe in which . . . we have sacrificed conversation for mere connection," and it's a habit fraught with psychological and philosophical pitfalls. "We are tempted to think," Turkle argues, "that our little sips of online connection add up to a big gulp of real conversation. But they don't." Why? Because "human relationships are rich; they're messy and demanding. We have learned the habit of cleaning them up with technology. And the move from conversation to connection is part of this [habit]."

Unfortunately, Turkle contends, it's a habit by which "we shortchange ourselves." For one thing, we tend to forget the fact that relationships with other people are inherently complicated matters. "Face-to-face conversation," explains Turkle,

unfolds slowly. It teaches patience. When we communicate on our digital devices, we learn different habits. As we ramp up the volume and velocity of online connections, we start to expect faster answers. To get these, we ask one another simpler questions; we dumb down our communications, even on the most important matters.

(Continued)

TECH WATCH (CONTINUED)

In a practical sense, these habits fail to engage one of the most significant factors in effective interpersonal communication: the willingness to *listen*. By its very nature, for example, conversation demands responsiveness to the messages—verbal and nonverbal—being sent by another person. We must constantly adjust to the fluidity—the "messiness"—of conversational give-and-take, and Turkle observes that because conversation requires us to respond to "tone and nuance," we must also "see things from another's point of view." As conversations "tend to play out in person," adds journalist Megan Garber, "they are messy—full of pauses and interruptions and topic changes and assorted awkwardness. But the messiness is what allows for true exchange. It gives participants the time—and, just as important, the permission—to think and react and glean insights."

According to Paul Barnwell, responding to nuance and tone is a habit—and a skill—that we can ill afford to lose. Barnwell, who teaches Digital Media at a high school specializing in communications and media, wonders if "there is any 21st-century skill more important than being able to sustain a confident, coherent conversation." Unfortunately, he notes,

kids spend hours each day engaging with ideas and one another through screens, but rarely do they have an opportunity to truly hone their interpersonal communication skills. . . . Students' reliance on screens for communication is detracting—and distracting—from their engagement in real-time talk.

For example, says Barnwell,

when it's time to negotiate pay raises and discuss projects with employers, students will have to exude a thoughtful presence and demonstrate the ability to think on their feet. But if the majority of their conversations are based on fragments pinballed back and forth through a screen, how will they develop the ability to truly communicate in person?

Donna Lubrano, of the Newbury College School of Business Management, agrees. More and more businesses, she says, are becoming frustrated by entry-level employees who "lack the ability to speak to customers and present ideas, as well as the communication skills to work in the team environment. . . In terms of verbal communication," she adds, "too many students cannot think on their feet."

References: Sherry Turkle, "The Flight from Conversation," *New York Times*, April 21, 2012, www.nytimes.com on May 16, 2020; Megan Garber, "Saving the Lost Art of Conversation," *The Atlantic*, January/February 2014, www.theatlantic.com on May 16, 2020; Paul Barnwell, "My Students Don't Know How to Have a Conversation," *The Atlantic*, April 22, 2014, www.theatlantic.com on May 16, 2020; Jamar Ramos, "Communication Breakdown: Interpersonal Skills in the Digital Age," *WorldWideLearn*, www.worldwidelearn.com on May 14, 2020.

Part of the CIO's efforts also involves the creation of one or more formal information systems linking all relevant managers, departments, and facilities in the organization. Most enterprise resource planning systems play this role very effectively. In the absence of such a system, a marketing manager, for example, may need to call a warehouse manager to find out how much of a particular product is in stock before promising shipping dates to a customer. An effective formal information system allows the marketing manager to get the information more quickly, and probably more accurately, by plugging directly into a computerized information system.

Personal Electronic Technology In the last decade, the nature of organizational communication has changed dramatically, mainly because of breakthroughs in personal electronic communication technology, and the future promises even more change. Electronic typewriters and then photocopying machines were early breakthroughs. The photocopier, for example, made it possible for a manager to have a typed report distributed to large numbers of

Digital communication has fundamentally changed how people communicate. Members of this team, for example, are literally scattered around the world but are able to carry on a conversation almost as easily as if they were in the same room.

Travelerpix/Shutterstock.com

other people in an extremely short time. Personal computers accelerated the process even more. Email networks, the internet, corporate intranets, social networking sites, wireless communication systems, social media platforms, and other breakthroughs are carrying communication technology even further.

It is also becoming common to have teleconferences in which managers stay at their own locations (such as home offices or offices in different cities) but meet via Skype, Microsoft Team, Zoom, and similar methods. The COVID-19 pandemic in 2020 saw these methods become even more popular. Managers can also record messages and deliver them to thousands of colleagues around the world in seconds. Highly detailed information can be retrieved with ease from large electronic databanks. These new technologies are behind the rise of a new version of an old work arrangement—the cottage industry. In a cottage industry, people work at home (in their "cottage") and periodically bring the products of their labors in to the company. *Telecommuting* is the label given to a new electronic cottage industry. In telecommuting, people work at home on their computers or other devices and transmit their work to their companies digitally.

Mobile phones have also made it even easier for managers to communicate with one another. Most now use cellphones to make calls while commuting to and from work and carry them in their pockets, bags, and briefcases so that they can receive calls regardless of where they are. Indeed, many people today don't even have landline phones any longer, relying instead on their mobile phones. Indeed, smartphones such as Apple iPhones and Samsung Android devices, as well as iPads and Microsoft Surface tablets, have truly revolutionized how people communicate with one another. Smartwatches and virtual keyboards are also beginning to take things to yet the next level.

Psychologists, however, are beginning to associate some problems with these communication advances. For one thing, managers who are seldom in their "real" offices are likely to fall behind in the inner workings of the organization and may even be victimized by organizational politics because they are not present to keep in touch with what is going on. They drop out of the organizational grapevine and miss out on much of the informal communication that takes place. Moreover, the use of digital communication at the expense of face-to-face meetings and conversations makes it hard to build a strong culture, develop solid working relationships, and create a mutually supportive atmosphere of trust and cooperativeness.[25] Finally, digital communication has also opened up new avenues for dysfunctional employee behavior, such as the passing of threatening, lewd, or offensive materials to others. For example, the *New York Times* once fired almost 10 percent of its workers at one of its branch offices for sending inappropriate emails at work.[26]

 **Manager's Checklist**

☐ Managers must make strategic choices about what form of communication is appropriate while remaining attentive to message feedback.

☐ Managers should be aware of the primary forms of communication that are used by their colleagues.

☐ You should also keep abreast of breakthroughs and new forms of digital communication technologies, as well as being cognizant of the pros and cons of digital communication.

12-4 INFORMAL COMMUNICATION IN ORGANIZATIONS

The forms of organizational communication discussed in the previous section all represent planned and relatively formal communication mechanisms. However, in many cases some of the communication that takes place in an organization transcends these formal channels and instead follows any of several informal methods. Figure 12.4 illustrates many examples of informal communication. Common forms of informal communication in organizations include the grapevine and management by wandering around.

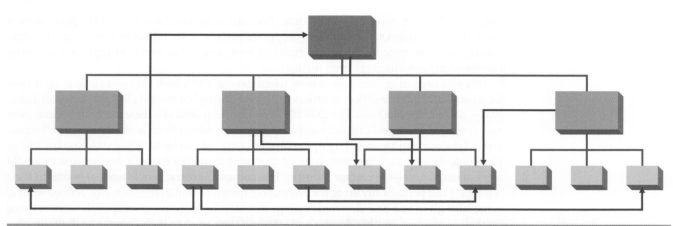

FIGURE 12.4

Informal Communication in Organizations

Informal communication in organizations may or may not follow official reporting relationships or prescribed channels. It may cross different levels and different departments or work units, and may or may not have anything to do with official organizational business.

12-4a The Grapevine

grapevine

An informal communication network among people in an organization

The **grapevine** is an informal communication network that can permeate an entire organization. Grapevines are found in all organizations except the very smallest, but they do not always follow the same patterns as, nor do they necessarily coincide with, formal channels of authority and communication. Research has identified several kinds of grapevines.[27] The two most common are illustrated in Figure 12.5. The gossip chain occurs when one person spreads the message to many other people. Each one, in turn, may either keep the information confidential or pass it on to others. The *gossip chain* is likely to carry personal information. The other common grapevine is the *cluster chain*, in which one person passes the information to a selected few individuals. Some of the receivers pass the information to a few other individuals; the rest keep it to themselves.

"The only way to address uncertainty is to communicate and communicate. And when you think you've just about got to everybody, then communicate some more."

—Terry Lundgren, Chairman and Former CEO of Macy's

There is some disagreement about how accurate the information carried by the grapevine is, but research is increasingly finding it to be fairly accurate, especially when the information is based on fact rather than speculation. One study found that the grapevine may be between 75 and 95 percent accurate.[28] That same study also found that informal communication is increasing in many organizations for several basic reasons. One contributing factor is the recent increase in merger, acquisition, and takeover activity. Because such activity can greatly affect the people within an organization, it follows that they may spend more time talking about it.[29] The second contributing factor is that as more and more corporations move facilities from inner cities to suburbs, employees tend to talk less and less to others outside the organization and more and more to one another. Yet another contributing factor is simply the widespread availability of information technology that makes it easier than ever before for people to communicate quickly and easily.

More recently, another study looked at the effects of the recent recession and large-scale job losses on informal communication. Over half of the survey participants reported a sharp increase in gossip and rumors in their organizations. The same survey also reported an increase in the amount of eavesdropping in most businesses.[30] Furthermore, in another

Gossip Chain
One person tells many

Cluster Chain
Many people tell a few

FIGURE 12.5

Common Grapevine Chains Found in Organizations

The two most common grapevine chains in organizations are the gossip chain (in which one person communicates messages to many others) and the cluster chain (in which many people pass messages to a few others).

Source: From Keith Davis and John W. Newstrom, *Human Behavior at Work: Organizational Behavior*, 8th ed., 1989.

management by wandering around
An approach to communication that involves the manager's literally wandering around and having spontaneous conversations with others

Gossip and the grapevine are a natural part of organizational life. These two people are exchanging secrets. Their conversation may be personal or work related. It might also be positive and constructive or negative and destructive. Managers need to know that they cannot eliminate gossip but can minimize its dysfunctional consequences by maintaining open and effective formal communication channels.

survey, 32 percent of people claimed to use their work email inappropriately and 48 percent admitted gossiping with other employees through their email.[31] Finally, in another survey conducted, over half of the participants reported that they had overheard confidential conversations at work.[32]

Attempts to eliminate the grapevine are not likely to succeed, but fortunately the manager does have some control over it. By maintaining open channels of communication and responding vigorously to inaccurate information, the manager can minimize the damage the grapevine can do. And if used carefully, in some situations the grapevine can actually be an asset. By learning who the key people in the grapevine are, for example, the manager can use it to sound out employee reactions to new ideas, such as a change in human resource policies or benefit packages. The manager can also get valuable information from the grapevine and use it to improve decision making.[33]

> "Especially in this climate with job security, any time there's budget talk my ears perk up."
>
> —Anonymous Employee Working in a Cubicle Environment

12-4b Management by Wandering Around

Another popular form of informal communication is called, interestingly enough, management by wandering around.[34] The basic idea is that some managers keep in touch with what is going on by wandering around and talking with people—immediate subordinates, subordinates far down the organizational hierarchy, delivery people, customers, or anyone else who is involved with the company in some way. Bill Marriott, for example, frequently visited the kitchens, loading

docks, and custodial work areas whenever he toured a Marriott hotel. He claimed that, by talking with employees throughout the hotel, he got new ideas and had a better feel for the entire company. And when United Airlines CEO Scott Kirby travels, he makes a point of talking to flight attendants and other passengers to gain continuous insights into how the business can be run more effectively.

A related form of organizational communication that really has no specific term is simply the informal interchange that takes place outside the normal work setting. Employees attending a company picnic, playing on the company softball team or in a fantasy football league, or just hanging out together on the weekend will almost always spend part of their time talking about work. For example, Texas Instruments engineers at the Lewisville, Texas, facility often frequent a local bar in town after work. On any given evening, they talk about the Dallas Cowboys, the newest government contract received by the company, the weather, their boss, the company's stock price, local politics, and problems at work. There is no set agenda, and the key topics of discussion vary from group to group and from day to day. Still, the social gatherings serve an important role. They promote a strong culture and enhance understanding of how the organization works.

Management by wandering around can be an effective method for managers to communicate with customers and others in the organization. This hotel manager, for instance, is having an impromptu conversation with the hotel restaurant chef. There is a good chance that they will both learn things from their conversation.

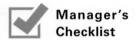 **Manager's Checklist**

- ☐ All managers need to understand the three fundamental kinds of informal communication that occur in an organization.
- ☐ Managers should also remember that they cannot eliminate informal communication.

12-5 MANAGING ORGANIZATIONAL COMMUNICATION

In view of the importance and pervasiveness of communication in organizations, it is vital for managers to understand how to manage the communication process.[35] Managers should understand how to maximize the potential benefits of communication and minimize the potential problems. We begin our discussion of communication management by considering the factors that might disrupt effective communication and how to deal with them.

12-5a Barriers to Communication

Several factors may disrupt the communication process or serve as barriers to effective communication.[36] As shown in Table 12.1, these may be divided into two classes: individual barriers and organizational barriers.

"It has taken a lot of work, including cross-cultural understanding and awareness, to help us be productive. The work has paid off. We learned communication was the key. Through communication we discovered our commonalities."
—Debra Nelson, Executive at Mercedes-Benz, United States

Table 12.1	Barriers to Effective Communication	
Individual Barriers		**Organizational Barriers**
Conflicting or inconsistent signals		Semantics
Credibility about the subject		Status or power differences
Reluctance to communicate		Different perceptions
Poor listening skills		Noise
Predispositions about the subject		Overload
		Language differences

Many barriers can disrupt effective communication. Some of these barriers involve individual characteristics and processes. Others are functions of the organizational context in which communication is taking place.

Individual Barriers　　Several individual barriers may disrupt effective communication. One common problem is conflicting or inconsistent signals. A manager is sending conflicting signals when she says on Monday that things should be done one way, but then prescribes an entirely different procedure on Wednesday. Inconsistent signals are being sent by a manager who says that he has an "open door" policy and wants his subordinates to drop by, but keeps his door closed and becomes irritated whenever someone stops in. In many cases, this kind of inconsistency in message results in employees who are reluctant to communicate at all, bringing about a lack of vertical communication that eventually results in information not being available to the people that need it most.

Another barrier is lack of credibility. Credibility problems arise when the sender is not considered a reliable source of information. He may not be trusted or may not be perceived as knowledgeable about the subject at hand. When a politician is caught withholding information or when a manager makes a series of bad decisions, the extent to which he or she will be listened to and believed thereafter diminishes. In extreme cases, people may talk about something they obviously know little or nothing about.

Some people are simply reluctant to initiate a communication exchange. This reluctance may occur for a variety of reasons. A manager may be reluctant to tell subordinates about an impending budget cut because he knows they will be unhappy about it. Likewise, a subordinate may be reluctant to transmit information upward for fear of reprisal or because it is felt that such an effort would be futile. For managers to maintain open lines of communication, these areas of reluctance must be overcome. While bad news is always unpleasant, it is still essential to get the news in the hands of the people who can come together as a team and work to make the necessary corrections. The key to overcoming reluctance is to create a culture in which bad news is viewed as a challenge that the team must work together in order to overcome rather than simply an end point after which someone has to be disciplined. Establishing this kind of cultural perspective rests in the hands of managers and how they communicate about how bad news will be handled by the organization as well as their ability to consistently follow through on that plan. Telling the team one day that "we will overcome challenges by working together" and then firing the first person who brings you bad news sends an inconsistent message that destroys the kind of open communication culture you are trying to create.

Poor listening habits can be a major barrier to effective communication. Some people are simply poor listeners. When someone is talking to them, they may be daydreaming, looking around, reading, or listening to another conversation. Because they are not concentrating on what is being said, they may not comprehend part or all of the message. They may even think that they really are paying attention, only to realize later that they cannot remember parts of the conversation.

Receivers may also bring certain predispositions to the communication process. They may already have their minds made up, firmly set in a certain way. For example, a manager may have heard that his new boss is unpleasant and hard to work with. When she calls him in for an introductory meeting, he may go into that meeting predisposed to dislike her and discount what she has to say.

". . . a synergy-related headcount adjustment goal."
—Jargon-Ladden Wording used in a Nokia Press Release to Announce the
Reduction of 9,000 Jobs[37]

Organizational Barriers   Other barriers to effective communication involve the organizational context in which the communication occurs. Semantics problems arise when words have different meanings for different people. Words and phrases such as *profit*, *increased output*, and *return on investment* may have positive meanings for managers but less positive meanings for labor.

Communication problems may also arise when people of different power or status try to communicate with each other. The company president may discount a suggestion from an operating employee, thinking, "How can someone at that level help me run my business?" Or, when the president goes out to inspect a new plant, workers may be reluctant to offer suggestions because of their lower status. The marketing vice president may have more power than the human resource vice president and consequently may not pay much attention to a staffing report submitted by the human resource department.

If people perceive a situation differently, they may have difficulty communicating with one another. When two managers observe that a third manager has not spent much time in her office lately, one may believe that she has been to several important meetings, and the other may think she is "hiding out." If they need to talk about her in some official capacity, problems may arise because one has a positive impression and the other a negative impression.

Environmental factors may also disrupt effective communication. As mentioned earlier, noise may affect communication in many ways. If a manager's phone loses power or connectivity, communication may be disrupted. Similarly, overload may be a problem when the receiver is being sent more information than he or she can effectively handle. Many managers report getting so many email and text messages each day that they sometimes feel overwhelmed.[38] And when the manager gives a subordinate many jobs on which to work and at the same time the subordinate is being told by family and friends to do other things, overload may result and communication effectiveness diminishes.

Finally, as businesses become more and more global, different languages can create problems. To counter this problem, some firms are adopting an "official language." For example, when the German chemical firm Hoechst merged with the French firm Rhone-Poulenc, the new company adopted English as its official language. Indeed, English is increasingly becoming the standard business language around the world.[39]

12-5b Improving Communication Effectiveness

Considering how many factors can disrupt communication, it is fortunate that managers can resort to several techniques for improving communication effectiveness.[40] As shown in Table 12.2, these techniques include both individual and organizational skills.

Individual Skills   The single most important individual skill for improving communication effectiveness is being a good listener.[41] Being a good listener requires that the person be prepared to listen, not interrupt the speaker, concentrate on both the words and the meaning being conveyed, be patient, and ask questions

There are many ways that communication effectiveness can be improved. One of the most powerful ways to be a better communicator is by being a good listener. The man on the left is paying close attention and carefully listening to his colleague on the right. As a result, their conversation will likely end with productive results.

Pressmaster/Shutterstock.com

Table 12.2	Overcoming Barriers to Communication
Individual Skills	**Organizational Skills**
Develop good listening skills	Follow up
Encourage two-way communication	Regulate information flows
Be aware of language and meaning	Understand the richness of media
Maintain credibility	
Be sensitive to receiver's perspective	
Be sensitive to sender's perspective	

Because communication is so important, managers have developed several methods of overcoming barriers to effective communication. Some of these methods involve individual skills, whereas others are based on organizational skills.

as appropriate.[42] This concept is known as "active listening," and as the definition suggests, to be effective the listener must be an active participant in the conversation. The higher the level of the listener's engagement in the conversation, the more likely the listener is to understand, retain, and productively respond to the information received. Active listening requires conscious effort on the part of the listener, and doing it for extended periods is mentally fatiguing. However, the efforts are worth it as it allows the receiver to verify that the message received was the message intended. So important are good listening skills that companies like Delta, IBM, and Boeing conduct programs to train their managers to be better listeners. Figure 12.6 illustrates the characteristics of poor listeners versus good listeners. Our *Leading the Way* feature provides additional insights into the importance of listening.

In addition to being a good listener, several other individual skills can promote effective communication. Feedback, one of the most important, is facilitated by two-way communication. Two-way communication allows the receiver to ask questions, request clarification, summarize their understanding of information that they receive, and express opinions that let the sender know whether he or she has been understood. In general, the more complicated the message, the more useful two-way communication is. In addition, the sender should be aware of the meanings that different receivers might attach to various words. For example, when addressing stockholders, a manager might use the word *profits* often. When addressing labor leaders, however, she may choose to use *profits* less often.

> "... being a good listener for as long as you can stand it is the most important thing [for a new leader] to do."
> —Henry Schacht, Former CEO of Lucent Technologies

Furthermore, the sender should try to maintain credibility. This can be accomplished by not pretending to be an expert when one is not, by "doing one's homework" and checking facts, and by otherwise being as accurate and honest as possible. Additionally, because nobody is correct all the time, when mistakes are made, credibility can be maintained if managers take ownership of their mistakes.[43]

The sender should also try to be sensitive to the receiver's perspective. A manager who must tell a subordinate that she has not been recommended for a promotion should recognize that the subordinate will be frustrated and unhappy. The content of the message and its method of delivery should be chosen accordingly. The manager should be primed to accept a reasonable degree of hostility and bitterness without getting angry in return.[44]

Finally, the receiver should also try to be sensitive to the sender's point of view. Suppose that a manager has just received some bad news—for example, that his position is being eliminated next year. Others should understand that he may be disappointed, angry, or even depressed for a while. Thus they might make a special effort not to take too much offense if he snaps at them, and they might look for signals that he needs someone to talk to.[45]

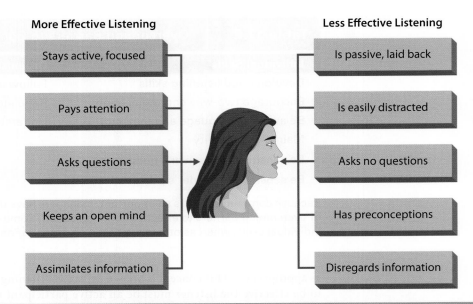

More Effective Listening

- Stays active, focused
- Pays attention
- Asks questions
- Keeps an open mind
- Assimilates information

Less Effective Listening

- Is passive, laid back
- Is easily distracted
- Asks no questions
- Has preconceptions
- Disregards information

FIGURE 12.6

More and Less Effective Listening Skills

Effective listening skills are a vital part of communication in organizations. There are several barriers that can contribute to poor listening skills in organizations. Fortunately, there are also several practices for improving listening skills.

LEADING THE WAY

In Communication We Trust

When James E. Rogers was CEO of the energy company Cinergy, he held regular "listening sessions" in which, among other things, he sought feedback about his own performance, even asking employees at one session to grade him on a scale of A to F. When fewer than half of his employees gave him an A, Rogers started asking open-ended questions about his performance. Ironically, the area in which the most employees suggested improvement was "internal communications."

According to the authors of *Talk, Inc.: How Trusted Leaders Use Conversation to Power Their Organizations*, what Rogers's employees wanted was more "intimacy" in "organizational conversation." Explain Boris Groysberg of Harvard Business School and communications consultant Michael Slind,

Where conversational intimacy prevails, those with decision-making authority seek and earn the trust (and hence the careful attention) of those who work under that authority. They do so by cultivating the art of listening to people at all levels of the organization

and by learning to speak with employees directly and authentically.

The key factor in conversational intimacy, say Groysberg and Slind, is *trust*: "Where there is no trust," they argue, "there can be no intimacy. . . . No one will dive into a heartfelt exchange of views with someone who seems to have a hidden agenda or a hostile manner." Research shows that it's a point well taken: One study found that fewer than half of workers trust senior managers, and only 28 percent consider them a credible source of information.

The need for leaders to cultivate trust, says management expert Peter Drucker, accounts for a notable shift in contemporary leadership practice: Organizations, he explains, "are no longer built on force but on trust." He hastens to add, "Trust does not necessarily mean that people like each other. It means they understand one another." In today's workplace, says Drucker, a leader's effectiveness in meeting organizational goals depends on making optimum use of employees' knowledge about the work that's being done (and about how

(Continued)

LEADING THE WAY (CONTINUED)

to improve it). Thus, "the first secret of effectiveness is to understand the people you work with so that you can make use of their strengths." Communication, therefore, must be a medium of understanding, and it must support the mutual understanding of each party to the conversation.

Groysberg and Slind agree. "The sound of one person talking," they point out, "is obviously not a conversation." Organizational conversation means that "leaders talk *with* employees and not just *to* them." It thus requires *interactivity* as well as intimacy, and employees must have "the institutional support they need to speak up and (where appropriate) talk back."

Not surprisingly, James Rogers is a good case in point. "I think that, as the years have gone on," says Rogers,

I've really honed my ability to listen and understand everybody's story and to help them build a story

around their capabilities—a story that plays to their strengths. . . . At the end of the day, [employees] have to trust . . . that you wouldn't be asking them to do this unless you had confidence in them. They have to trust that you see something in them that they may not see completely in themselves.

References: Boris Groysberg and Michael Slind, "Leadership Is a Conversation," *Harvard Business Review*, June 2012, https://hbr.org on May 16, 2020; Kellie Cummings, "Trust, Communication, and Leadership: The Three Laws of Influence," American Society for Training & Development, April 9, 2013, www.td.org on May 16, 2020; Stephen M. R. Covey, "How the Best Leaders Build Trust," *Leadership Now*, www.leadership.now.com on May 16, 2020; Adam Bryant, "The C.E.O. as General (and Scout)," *New York Times*, October 10, 2009, www.nytimes.com on May 16, 2020.

Organizational Skills   Three useful organizational skills can also enhance communication effectiveness for both the sender and the receiver—following up, regulating information flow, and understanding the richness of different media. Following up simply involves checking at a later time to be sure that a message has been received and understood. After a manager sends a report to a colleague, she might send a follow-up message a few days later to make sure the report was received. If it was, the manager might ask whether the colleague has any questions about it.

Regulating information flow means that the sender or receiver takes steps to ensure that overload does not occur. For the sender, this could mean not passing too much information through the system at one time. For the receiver, it might mean calling attention to the fact that he is being asked to do too many things at once. Many managers limit the influx of information by periodically weeding out the list of journals and routine reports they receive or they train their assistant to screen phone calls and visitors. Indeed, some executives now get so much email that they have it routed to an assistant. That person reviews the email, discards those that are not useful (such as "spam"), responds to those that are routine, and passes on to the executive only those that require her or his personal attention.

Both parties should also understand the richness associated with different media. When a manager is going to lay off a subordinate temporarily, the message should be delivered in person. A face-to-face channel of communication gives the manager an opportunity to explain the situation and answer questions. When the purpose of the message is to grant a pay increase, written communication may be appropriate because it can be more objective and precise. The manager could then follow up the written notice with personal congratulations.

Manager's Checklist

☐ Managers need to be aware of the primary barriers to communication in organizations.

☐ You should also be aware of how to most effectively overcome those barriers.

SUMMARY OF LEARNING OUTCOMES AND KEY POINTS

12-1. Describe the interpersonal nature of organizations.

- Communication is the process of transmitting information from one person to another.
- Effective communication is the process of sending a message in such a way that the message received is as close in meaning as possible to the message intended.

12-2. Describe the role and importance of communication in the manager's job.

- Communication is a pervasive and important part of the manager's world.
- The communication process consists of a sender's encoding meaning and transmitting it to one or more receivers, who receive the message and decode it into meaning.
- In two-way communication, the process continues with the roles reversed.
- Noise can disrupt any part of the overall process.

12-3. Identify the basic forms of communication in organizations.

- Several forms of organizational communication exist. Interpersonal communication focuses on communication among a small number of people.
- Two important forms of interpersonal communication, oral and written, both offer unique advantages and disadvantages.
- The manager should weigh the pros and cons of each when choosing a medium for communication.
- Nonverbal communication includes facial expressions, body movement, physical contact, gestures, and inflection and tone.

- Communication networks are recurring patterns of communication among members of a group or work team.
- Vertical communication between superiors and subordinates may flow upward or downward.
- Horizontal communication involves peers and colleagues at the same level in the organization.
- Organizations also use information systems to manage communication.
- Electronic communication is having a profound effect on managerial and organizational communication.

12-4. Discuss informal communication, including its various forms and types.

- There is also a great deal of informal communication in organizations.
- The grapevine is the informal communication network among people in an organization.
- Management by wandering around is also a popular informal method of communication.

12-5. Describe how the communication process can be managed to recognize and overcome barriers.

- Managing the communication process necessitates recognizing the barriers to effective communication and understanding how to overcome them.
- Barriers can be identified at both the individual and the organizational levels.
- Both individual and organizational skills can be used to overcome these barriers.

DISCUSSION QUESTIONS

Questions for Review

1. Describe the difference between communication and effective communication. How can a sender verify that a communication was effective? How can a receiver verify that a communication was effective?

2. Which form of interpersonal communication is best for long-term retention? Why? Which form is best for getting across subtle nuances of meaning? Why?

3. What are the similarities and differences of oral and written communication? What kinds of situations call for the use of oral methods? What situations call for written communication?

4. Describe the individual and organizational barriers to effective communication. For each barrier, describe one action that a manager could take to reduce the problems caused by that barrier.

Questions for Analysis

1. How did the 2020 COVID-19 pandemic impact how you communicate? What have been the most positive

changes you've made or have observed others making as a result of the pandemic?"

2. At what points in the communication process can problems occur? Give examples of how noise can interfere with the communication process. What can managers do to reduce problems and noise?

3. In what ways does communication differ when it occurs in the digital format? What are the drawbacks of digital communication? What are some of the benefits of digital communication?

Questions for Application

1. What forms of communication have you experienced today? What form of communication is involved in a face-to-face conversation with a friend? A telephone call from a customer? A traffic light or crossing signal? A picture of a cigarette in a circle with a slash across it? An area around machinery defined by a yellow line painted on the floor?

2. Keep track of your own activities over the course of a few hours of leisure time to determine what forms of communication you encounter. Which forms were most common? If you had been tracking your communications while at work, how would the list be different? Explain why the differences occur.

3. For each of the following situations, tell which form of communication you would use. Then ask the same question of someone who has been in the workforce for at least 10 years. For any differences that occur, ask the worker to explain why his or her choice is better than yours. Do you agree with his or her assessment? Why or why not?

- Describing complex changes in how health care benefits are calculated and administered to every employee of a large firm
- Asking your boss a quick question about how she wants something done
- Telling customers that a new two-for-one promotion is available at your store
- Reprimanding an employee for excessive absences on the job
- Reminding workers that no smoking is allowed in your facility

BUILDING EFFECTIVE TECHNICAL SKILLS

Exercise Overview

Technical skills are necessary to understand or perform the specific kind of work that an organization does. This exercise will help you develop and apply technical skills in using the internet to gather information for making important decisions.

Exercise Background

The management of a large retailer wants to leverage the company's enormous purchasing power to buy products in bulk quantities at relatively low prices. The plan calls for individual stores to order specific quantities from a single warehouse and distribution center, and as the company's operations manager, it's your job to identify potential locations for the new facility.

First, you know that you'll need quite a lot of land; the warehouse itself will occupy more than four acres. In addition, because incoming shipments will arrive by both rail and truck, you'll need to be close to railroads and major highways. Land price is important, of course, and the cost of living should be relatively low. Finally, you want relatively mild weather conditions so that shipping disruptions are minimal.

Experience has shown that small to midsize communities work best. Moreover, because the company already maintains warehouses in the West and East, the new one will probably be located in the central or south-central area of the country. Your boss wants you to identify three or four possible sites.

Exercise Task

With all of this information in mind, do the following:

1. Use online resources to identify as many as ten possible locations.

2. Using additional information gathered from online resources, narrow your set of ten locations to three or four.

3. Continuing to use online resources, find out as much as you can about each of the three or four finalists on your list and be ready to discuss the pros and cons of each as they relate to your selection criteria.

BUILDING EFFECTIVE INTERPERSONAL SKILLS

Exercise Overview

Interpersonal skills refer to the ability to communicate with, understand, and motivate individuals and groups. This in-class demonstration gives you some practice in understanding the roles played by verbal and nonverbal elements in the interaction between two people.

Exercise Background

Because more than half the information in any face-to-face exchange is conveyed by nonverbal means, body language is a significant factor in any interpersonal communication. Consider, for example, the impact of a yawn or a frown (never mind a shaken fist). At the same time, however, most people pay relatively little conscious attention to the nonverbal elements of an exchange, especially the more subtle ones. And if you misread the complete set of signals that someone is sending you, you're not likely to receive that person's message in the way that's intended.

In this exercise, you'll examine some interactions between two people from which we've eliminated sound; in other words, you'll have only visual clues to help you decipher the meaning of the messages being sent and received. Then you'll be asked to examine those same interactions with both visual and verbal clues intact.

Exercise Task

1. Observe the silent video segments that your professor shows to the class. For each segment, describe the nature of the relationship and interaction between the two people. What nonverbal clues did you rely on in reaching your conclusions?
2. Next, observe the same video segments with audio included. Describe the interaction again, this time indicating any verbal clues that you relied on.
3. How accurate were your assessments when you had only visual information? Explain why you were or were not accurate in your assessment of the situation.
4. What does this exercise show you about the role of nonverbal factors in interpersonal communication? What advice would you now give managers about the importance of these factors?

SKILL-BUILDING PERSONAL ASSESSMENT

Gender Talk Quiz

Introduction: Research shows that men and women sometimes have trouble communicating effectively with one another at work because they have contrasting values and beliefs about differences between genders. The following assessment surveys your beliefs and values about each gender. (The authors reviewed available scholarly literature on this topic and found no current work that covers the full gender continuum. The existing sources provide insight into binary male and female tendencies in workplace communication. With more research, our understanding of differences in gender identification may help to further inform and evolve workplace communications.)

If you think a statement below is an accurate description of communication patterns, mark it true. If you think it isn't, mark it false.

1. Men talk more than women.
2. Men are more likely to interrupt women than to interrupt other men.
3. During conversations, women spend more time looking at their partner than men do.
4. Nonverbal messages carry more weight than verbal messages.
5. Female managers communicate with more emotional openness and drama than male managers.
6. Men not only control the content of conversations, they also work harder in keeping conversations going.
7. When people hear generic words, such as *mankind* and *he*, they respond inclusively, indicating that the terms apply to both sexes.
8. In classroom communications, male students receive more reprimands and criticism.
9. Women are more likely than men to disclose information about intimate personal concerns.
10. Female speakers are more animated in their style than are males.
11. Women use less personal space than men.
12. When a male speaks, he is listened to more carefully than a female speaker, even when she makes the identical presentation.
13. In general, women speak in a more tentative style than do men.
14. Women are more likely to answer questions that are not addressed to them.
15. There is widespread gender segregation in schools, and it hinders effective classroom communication.
16. Female managers are seen by both male and female subordinates as better communicators than male managers.
17. In classroom communications, teachers are more likely to give verbal praise to female than to male students.
18. In general, men smile more often than women.

Scoring:

1. True. Despite the stereotype, the research is consistent and clear. In classrooms, in offices, in group discussions, and in two-person conversations, men talk more than their fair share of the time. For example, in one experiment, male and female subjects were asked to verbally describe pictures and engravings. The women's average description was approximately three minutes. For a man, the average time was 13 minutes.

2. True. When women talk with other women, interruptions are evenly distributed.

   When men talk with other men, interruptions are evenly distributed. However, when men and women talk with one another, almost all interruptions are by male speakers.

   Sociologists Candace West and Donald Zimmerman analyzed conversations in university settings, both on and off campus. They found that males interrupt females much more often than they interrupt other males and more often than females interrupt either males or females. These sociologists think that interrupting is a way of exercising power. They say, "Here we are dealing with a class of speakers, females, whose right to speak appears to be casually infringed upon by males."

3. True. Many studies—with subjects ranging from infants to older adults—have shown that women are more likely than men to look at their partner. One reason may be that men talk more and women listen more. Research shows that a listener of either sex looks more at a speaker than the speaker looks at the listener. Another possible reason women look more frequently at a partner may be their need for and expertise in decoding nonverbal cues. In a direct staring confrontation, however, women will be more likely to avert their eyes, especially when stared at by men. Frequently, a woman will tilt her head back rather than look directly at a man. Researchers call this a presenting gesture that reflects friendliness and submission.

4. True. Nonverbal messages carry over four times the weight of verbal messages. Other research shows that in most two-person conversations, nonverbal messages convey more than 65 percent of the meaning. Women seem to communicate more effectively on this nonverbal channel. They are better than men at decoding nonverbal cues. They are also more likely to reflect their feelings through facial expressions.

5. False. Research conducted at a Midwest hospital and in the clerical departments and production lines of manufacturing firms show that both female and male managers score higher than the general population in communicating friendliness and approval to subordinates. Furthermore, women managers are no more emotionally open or dramatic than their male counterparts. Both sexes appear to feel that managers should not demonstrate these characteristics. However,

there were some communication differences. Male managers were more dominant in style and more likely to direct the content and flow of the conversation.

6. False. While men do exert power and authority in controlling the course of conversations, women exert more effort in maintaining communication. Sociologist Pamela Fishman placed tape recorders in homes of couples who described themselves as free of traditional sex role stereotypes. Fishman recorded over 50 hours of conversations that occurred naturally. Over 96 percent of the topics men introduced were developed into conversations. Only 36 percent of the topics women introduced were similarly developed. Women asked more questions and were more willing to develop a topic introduced by men. In contrast, men "killed" conversational topics that women introduced by giving a minimal response, such as "um," and failing to ask questions or make more extended comments about the topic. In studies of mock jury deliberations, it has been found that women are more likely to make understanding and supportive comments.

7. False. Words such as *mankind*, *man*, and *he* are supposed to be generic and are presumed to include both men and women. Research shows that this isn't really the case. People are more literal in their thinking. Studies with elementary, secondary, and college students show that when the supposed generic word *man* is used, people envision males, even when the content implies both men and women. In another study, students illustrated supposedly generic references (e.g., urban man) with males' pictures more than they did when references were neutral (e.g., urban life). Other researchers found that when male generic nouns and pronouns were used to describe the job of psychologists, female students described the job as less attractive to them than when sex-neutral terms were used. Women who were exposed to the feminine generic ("she" to include everybody) reported feelings of pride, importance, and power. Yet another researcher reports that when an applicant for an executive position was described as a "girl," subjects rated her as less "tough," "mature," "brilliant," and "dignified," and they gave her approximately 6 percent less in salary than when the word *woman* was used.

8. True. The research is very consistent on this issue. From preschool through high school, male students are more likely than female students to be reprimanded for misbehavior. Some studies say they are eight to ten times as likely to be scolded. Sometimes they get reprimanded more because they are misbehaving more. But other studies show that when females and males are misbehaving equally, the males are still more likely to get scolded and receive harsher penalties.

9. True. There is some inconsistency in the research here, but most studies show that women are more likely to reveal personal information about themselves. This

pattern may reflect differences in power or status between males and females. For example, in work situations, subordinates tend to reveal more personal information about themselves than their superiors reveal to them.

The more power a person has, the more personal information he or she is likely to receive.

10. True. Female speakers display more animated behavior, including amount and intensity of eye contact, gestures, facial expressions, and body movement. Furthermore, they are more likely to use a wider range of pitch and more variable intonations than male speakers. However, men appear to be more dramatic in their verbal behavior. They are more likely to tell anecdotes and jokes.

11. True. Women's space is far more likely to be intruded on by others. Women are approached more closely than men by both women and men. When women and men approach each other on the street, women are more likely to walk around men or move out of their way. In homes, men are more likely to have a room, study, or den—an inviolate area where nothing is to be touched. Women also use space in a more confining way. While men are more likely to sit with arms and legs apart, women cross legs at ankles and sit with hands in their laps, taking up far less space. This reduced control of space or territory is characteristic of those with less power and status.

12. True. Both female and male members of audiences pay more attention to male speakers than female speakers. Audience members recall more information from presentations given by males. This appears to occur whether the information is stereotyped as appropriate for males or stereotyped as associated with females. And it occurs even when male and female speakers make an identical presentation.

13. True. According to linguist Robin Lakoff, "women's language" is characterized by certain patterns:

- Making statements that end in a questioning intonation or putting tag questions at the end of declarative sentences ("This is a good movie, isn't it?").
- Using qualifiers such as "kind of" or "I guess."
- Use of "empty adjectives" (*divine* or *lovely*) and use of *so* with adjectives (*so thoughtful*).

While not all studies support Lakoff's notion of women's speech, several show that women do express themselves with more diffidence and less assertion than men. Many researchers claim that tentative speech patterns do not characterize the speech of women so much as they characterize the speech of those who lack power. For example, one group of researchers analyzed communication in a police station. They found that both male and female clients who came to the station were more likely to use "women's language" than were either male or female police personnel. There are consequences to using "women's language." Both men and women who speak in a tentative, nonassertive style are less likely to be believed by a jury. In fact, only recently has the British Broadcasting Corporation (BBC) allowed women to read the news over the air because they were perceived to lack credibility or authority.

14. False. Men manage to capture more than their fair share of talk time. Sometimes women actually help men gain this advantage because they are more likely to ask questions, whereas men are more likely to give answers. However, men often take this advantage for themselves by interrupting women and by answering questions that are not addressed to them.

15. True. When people hear the word *segregation*, they usually think about racial discrimination. Gender segregation may occur in more subtle ways, but it is widespread. Teachers, or students themselves, frequently form separate boy and girl lines, seating arrangements, work groups, play areas, and even science lab work teams. Even college classrooms display gender segregation in student seating arrangements. Children cross racial lines more often than gender lines in classroom communication. Some researchers have found that students are often unwilling to work together on science projects. However, teachers can encourage boys and girls to play and work together simply by praising children engaged in cross-gender interaction. An important implication of the research is that when girls and boys work and play together, they are less likely to hold stereotyped attitudes.

16. True. Despite the stereotypes, when employees work for a female supervisor, they vote their approval. Female managers are seen as giving more attention to subordinates, as more open to new ideas, and as more supportive of worker effort than male managers. Both female and male subordinates report that morale and job satisfaction are higher when supervised by women. Others report that women are more dependable, show greater concern, and pay better attention to detail. Research on female managers in the business world is related to research in elementary schools. Studies on elementary schools with female principals show that these schools are warmer, more democratic, and are characterized by higher student achievement and higher pupil and parental satisfaction.

17. False. Although girls get better grades than boys, they receive less verbal praise from teachers. When girls do get praise from teachers, it is likely to be for neatness and appearance ("That's an attractive paper," "You have very neat handwriting"). In contrast, when boys get praise, it is more likely to be for the intellectual quality of their ideas. Not only do teachers praise boys more, but they also criticize them more, ask them more questions, and give them more attention in general.

18. False. Women are far more likely to smile than men. They do this in many different social situations, even though they are not necessarily happy or amused. In one field study, researchers smiled at approximately 150 males and 150 females in public. In general, women returned the smiles more often than men. Women returned the smiles to men 93 percent of the time and to other women 86 percent of the time. Males smiled back at women 67 percent of the time, and they returned smiles to men 58 percent of the time.

Source: From Myra Sadker and Joyce Kaser, *The Communications Gender Gap.* Mid-Atlantic Center for Sex Equity.

MANAGEMENT AT WORK
Standing Up for Warmth

"Let your body tell you that you're powerful and deserving, and you become more present, enthusiastic, and authentically yourself."
—Social Psychologist Amy Cuddy

In 2012, Amy Cuddy, a social psychologist who teaches at Harvard Business School, delivered a presentation at the prestigious TEDGlobal Conference in Edinburgh, Scotland. Her subject was body language and its effect on "the way your life unfolds." TED presentations are offered for free online viewing, and since 2006, they've been watched more than a billion times worldwide. Cuddy's talk has the distinction of being the second-most-watched TED presentation of all time, with nearly 26 million views and counting. *Time* magazine immediately put Cuddy on its list of "Game Changers," and *Business Insider* ranked her 37th among "50 Women Who Are Changing the World."

What did Cuddy have to say that was so important? Basically, "Smile and sit up straight." The advice, of course, is pretty simple, but the reason why it's good advice is not. Cuddy had research to back her up, and that research had led her to a series of significant insights into the significance of body language. What inspired Cuddy's research? "I noticed in class," she recalls,

> that women tended to make themselves small, holding their wrists, wrapping their arms around themselves. Guys tended to make themselves bigger. They're leaning back, stretching out, draping their arms around chairs. We know from studies of facial feedback that if you smile, you fake yourself into feeling happier. We wondered whether just asking people to spread out would help them feel more powerful.

So Cuddy and her colleagues invited students into the social-psych laboratory for a few experimental exercises. Participants were asked to spend two minutes alone in a room striking what Cuddy calls "power poses," either "high power" or "low power." For *high-power poses*, think superhero posture—chest lifted, head held high, arms either raised or propped on the hips. (Cuddy prefers "the Wonder Woman"—hands on hips, legs wide.) *Low-power poses* include putting your hands on your neck and crossing your limbs. In general, says Cuddy, "expansive, open postures reflect high power, whereas contractive, closed postures reflect low power."

Before and after the posing exercises, Cuddy's team recorded participants' levels of two hormones: testosterone, which is known to increase feelings of power and confidence, and cortisol, which is associated with feelings of anxiety and stress. After just two minutes of posing, high-power posers experienced a 20 percent increase in testosterone and a 25 percent drop in cortisol. "Not only do these postures reflect power," explains Cuddy, "they also *produce* it." In addition, high-power posers displayed behavior associated with the exercise of power in the real world—a fact that didn't surprise Cuddy: "Effective leaders," she points out, "have a classic hormone profile: high levels of testosterone, low levels of cortisol.... When people take over the alpha role, their testosterone rises and their cortisol drops."

The study's findings show not only that our hormonal levels can change, but that we can take the initiative in changing them. The process engages a series of feedback loops. As we've seen, for example, the principle is evident in the effect of a smile: "Feeling happy makes us smile, and smiling makes us happy," observes Cuddy. But what if you don't feel like smiling? "Fake it till you become it," she advises: *Faking* happiness, it seems, has pretty much the same effect as *being* happy. The key is the smile: Using the muscles of your face to communicate nonverbally sends a message to your brain, and as with smiling, so with standing up straight. Thus the purpose of power posing, explains Cuddy, "is to optimize your brain"—to balance your hormones in the way that you want them balanced. "Let your body tell you that you're powerful and deserving," she says, and when you pass that message along to your brain, "you become more present, enthusiastic, and authentically yourself."

Perhaps even more importantly, adds Cuddy, the feedback that you get from such nonverbal behavior as smiling "is also contagious. We tend to mirror one another's nonverbal expressions and emotions, so when we see someone beaming and emanating genuine warmth, we can't resist smiling ourselves." In addition, such responses typically reflect first impressions and often contribute to snap judgments about people—what Cuddy calls "spontaneous trait inferences." Her research has thus extended to the effect of body language on first impressions, and she's found that there are two critical variables: *warmth* and *competence*. These two factors, she says, account for 90 percent of our evaluations of other people and, more importantly, shape the way we feel about and act toward them.

Unfortunately, projections of both warmth and competence can produce seemingly contradictory behavior in other people. According to Cuddy,

> people judged to be competent but lacking in warmth often elicit envy in others, an emotion involving both respect and resentment that cuts both ways. When we respect someone, we want to cooperate or affiliate ourselves with him or her, but resentment can make that person vulnerable to harsh reprisal. . . . On the other hand, people judged as warm but incompetent tend to elicit pity, which also involves a mix of emotions: Compassion moves us to help those we pity, but our lack of respect leads us ultimately to neglect them.

The first type that Cuddy describes here falls into the category *cold/competent* and the second into the category *warm/incompetent*—two of four categories into which people may fit in Cuddy's warmth/competence matrix. At the extremes are *warm/competent*, which elicits admiration, helping, and cooperation, and *cold/incompetent*, which elicits contempt, neglect, and harassment (and even violence).

As revealing as it is, this matrix raises further questions: Is there any difference between, say, *warm/competent* and *competent/warm* and, if so, which is optimum, particularly if one's job involves leading other people? According to Cuddy, "putting competence first undermines leadership" because doing so fails to prioritize the most important factor in any relationship—*trust*. "Prioritizing warmth," she says

> helps you connect immediately with those around you, demonstrating that you hear them, understand them, and can be trusted by them . . . . In management settings, trust increases information sharing, openness, and cooperation . . . . Most important, it provides the opportunity to change people's attitudes and beliefs, not just their outward behavior. That's the sweet spot when it comes to the ability to get people to fully accept your message.

So, how can you project warmth? First, says Cuddy, "Find the right level . . . . Aim for a tone that suggests that you're leveling with people—that you're sharing the straight scoop, with no pretense or emotional adornment." Second, "validate feelings": Begin by agreeing with people, letting them know

right off that "you hold roughly the same worldview that they do." Last but not least, "Smile—and mean it."

Cuddy hastens to add that coming across effectively is a matter of prioritizing, not of minimizing one trait in favor of the other. The best way to lead, she concludes, "is to combine warmth and strength. . . . The traits can actually be mutually reinforcing: Feeling a sense of personal strength helps us to be more open, less threatened, and less threatening in stressful situations. When we feel confident and calm, we project authenticity and warmth."[46]

Case Questions

1. What about you? How do you sit in class? Does Cuddy's description of students' classroom body language seem to apply to you? Specifically, what might you do to improve your classroom body language? How about your body language in other situations?

2. Review the section in the text on "Individual Barriers" to communication. How might Cuddy's analysis of the impressions that we make on people help in understanding these barriers? More specifically, how might that analysis be used in helping to overcome them? Now ask yourself which of these barriers seem to affect your own communication habits. How might Cuddy's analysis help you to understand and deal with the barriers to your own communication habits?

3. Here's a list of Cuddy's four ideal types in the warmth/competence matrix, along with examples of people who, according to her research, tend to fall into each category:

   - Warm/competent—fathers
   - Warm/incompetent—working mothers
   - Cold/competent—Asian students
   - Cold/incompetent—economically disadvantaged people

   Bearing in mind that these examples reflect generalized *perceptions* of people, explain why each group falls into its respective category. Add another group to each category. Explain the role played by *stereotyping* in assigning people to each category. Finally, to what extent do you yourself tend to succumb to these generalizations?

4. As we've seen, Cuddy has observed "a gender grade gap" in her MBA classes at Harvard, in which classroom participation accounts for a significant portion of students' grades. "It's competitive—you really have to get in there," she says, and women aren't quite as successful at contributing to discussions as men. Men, she reports, volunteer to answer questions by shooting their arms in the air while women tend toward a polite bent-elbow wave. Women often touch their faces and necks while talking and tend to sit with

tightly crossed ankles. "These postures," says Cuddy, "are associated with powerlessness and intimidation and keep people from expressing who they really are." Cuddy's research also reveals that nonwhite males are often subject to the same disadvantages and exhibit similar behaviors when participating in classroom discussion.

Why does this "gender gap" exist in the classroom?

You Make the Call

A Big Desk May Say it All

1. At Univision, a manager was having trouble communicating because of always sitting behind a large desk. Recall and discuss an office or home you may have been in recently that communicated specific things about the person occupying the home or office.
2. For a firm like Univision, identify the most common forms of *vertical communication* and *horizontal communication* flow.
3. Dr. Brad Wesner, cited as a consultant for Univision, said "Everybody thinks that communication is just something you do. Our challenge is getting them to believe that it is something you really need to think about tactically." What do you think this means? Do you communicate tactically?
4. One recent survey found that employees wanted to engage with senior managers through internal social media: 42 percent, for example, would be willing to talk with line managers or team leaders over Facebook, and 20 percent would be happy to tweet a department head or even the CEO. Twenty percent of managers said that they'd be happy to reciprocate. At the same time, the survey revealed that two-thirds of employees had no involvement in their companies' social media activities, and more than a quarter were not permitted access to their employers' internal communications networks. Why do you think there's such a disparity between employee attitudes and organizational practice?

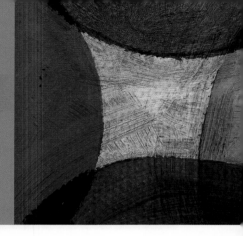

CHAPTER 13

Managing Work Groups and Teams

Learning Outcomes

After studying this chapter, you should be able to:

13-1 Describe types of groups and teams in organizations, why people join groups and teams, and the stages of group and team development.

13-2 Discuss four essential characteristics of groups and teams.

13-3 Describe interpersonal and intergroup conflict in organizations.

13-4 Discuss how organizations manage conflict.

As we noted in Chapter 17, groups and teams are found throughout most organizations. It stands to reason, then, that managers should be interested in making sure those groups and teams are as productive as possible. This chapter is about all of the processes that affect group and team performance. We first introduce basic concepts of group and team dynamics. Subsequent sections explain the characteristics of groups and teams in organizations. We then describe interpersonal and intergroup conflict. Finally, we conclude with a discussion of how conflict can be managed. First, however, let's explore how diversity within groups and teams may be one factor that boosts group and team performance

Management in Action

An Open Invitation to Innovation

"Any five-year-old has no trouble turning an old blanket and a couple of chairs into an impenetrable fort."

—Andy Zynga, CEO of NineSigma

A few years ago, a well-known multinational company hired an innovation consulting firm called NineSigma to draw up a *request for proposal (RFP)* titled "Nanoparticle Halide Salt: Formulation and Delivery." According to NineSigma CEO Andy Zynga, providing an RFP means "crafting a very precise written needs statement for vetted solution providers who have known expertise in specific areas." In this case, the client was in the market for a chemically designed salt with specific properties—a compound for which its own R&D department didn't have the necessary expertise. So NineSigma, reports Zynga, "marketed" its RFP "to a broad audience of technical experts. Proposals came in from a variety of industries and organization types, including energy and fuels, pharma, and engineering services." The winning proposal was submitted by a team of orthopedics researchers who had created nanoparticles of salt for studies of osteoporosis.

And that's how PepsiCo developed a way to reduce the sodium content of Lay's Classic potato chips without sacrificing the flavor that consumers were used to. This approach to an expanded search for solutions is sometimes called *open innovation*, which Zynga defines as "the process of reaching beyond your team, company, or industry for technologies, solutions, ideas, and knowledge available through global solution-provider networks. . . . The rationale," he explains, "is that partnering with outside innovators may lead to something even better and will undoubtedly accelerate the process if a more advanced solution exists elsewhere."

In a very real sense, although it's a "process of reaching beyond your team," open innovation is also an extension of the principle of building teams with a greater diversity of input. David Feitler, senior program manager at NineSigma, points to a parallel between team building as a means of breaking down *internal* barriers to problem solving and open innovation as a means of breaking down *external* barriers. Feitler explains that another NineSigma client, Dutch-based multinational paint manufacturer AzkoNobel, was already practicing open innovation as a means of breaching external barriers when it approached NineSigma about improving internal collaboration. The company was divided into 11 autonomous divisions, and it had grown mainly by means of acquisition. As a result, says Feitler, it "had the typical silos, with organizational and geographical boundaries inhibiting the diffusion of knowledge.

"The solution," he reports,

> was to implement the request for proposal process inside the organization, broadly training large numbers of technical staff in the process and more intensively training a core group of "Internal Program Managers" to provide the coaching and guidance required for a well-specified search [for collaborative ideas].

Two years later, adds Feitler, AzkoNobel had developed a process of assembling "ad hoc SWAT teams," which allows "individuals with challenging problems ... to tap into a system that gives them rapid access to colleagues in other divisions and countries."

The idea of "ad hoc SWAT teams," argues Feitler, is consistent with the findings of studies on the role of so-called *cross-pollination*—the recombination of previously unrelated ideas—in the diffusion of innovation. In particular, Feitler cites research led by Harvard University's Lee Fleming, who culled data from every U.S. patent granted since 1975. What did Fleming and his team want to find out from all of this data? First, they wanted to know what kind of networks among inventors and researchers had been developed to foster significant cross-pollination. Second, they were interested in how different networks contribute to "creativity," which is commonly defined as the combining of familiar ideas in unexpected ways.

Fleming's team identified two different network models that tend to result in "novel combinations": (1) the *broker*, which revolves around an influential person who's connected to many other people who don't know each other, and (2) the *connector*, which revolves around an influential person who often introduces his collaborators to each other. The researchers found that organizations functioning as brokers were more likely to generate new ideas because they occupied a central position through which information and ideas travel. By the same token, brokers typically found it harder than connectors to get their ideas publicized.

Some related research goes into more practical detail. Gratton and Erickson, for instance, found that cross-pollination "almost always requires the input and expertise of people with disparate views and backgrounds." In other words, *diversity* of expertise and experience is critical, but Gratton and Erickson also concluded that it can "inhibit collaboration": "Diversity," they observe, *often means that team members are working with people that they know only superficially or have never met before—colleagues drawn from other divisions of the company, perhaps, or even from outside it. We have found that the higher the proportion of strangers on the team and the greater the diversity of background and experience, the less likely the team members are to share knowledge or exhibit other collaborative behaviors.*

In turn, these findings are consistent with Fleming's conclusion that "the evidence linking breakthroughs with multidisciplinary collaborations remains mixed. On average," advises Fleming, "it's more productive to search within established disciplines. Or, when trying to cross-pollinate between fields, the more appropriate approach is to combine areas that have some common ground." Fleming limits the term "breakthrough" to those "very, very few" inventions or innovations that ultimately produce the highest level of value. Thus, when it comes to diversity or "multidisciplinary collaboration," the issue is whether "the divergence between collaborators' fields of expertise" is more or less likely to yield a breakthrough. In this respect, the results were in fact mixed. Fleming found, for example, that the greater this divergence, "the lower the *overall* quality" of a team's output. At the same time, however, outputs will vary more widely from useless to extremely valuable, thus making breakthroughs more likely.

Finally, let's go back to NineSigma's Andy Zynga, who attributes the impasse faced by PepsiCo's internal problem solvers to a "cognitive bias" that psychologists call *functional fixedness*. "Any five-year-old," observes Zynga, "has no trouble turning an old blanket and a couple of chairs into an impenetrable fort. But as we get older, knowledge and experience increasingly displace imagination and our ability to see an object for anything other than its original purpose."

Adult-run organizations, Zynga argues, encounter functional fixedness on a much more complex level: "Technologists, engineers, and designers," he says, "not only have their own expertise, they have their own way of applying their expertise. Ironically, the more success they've had with their approach to a solution, the harder it is to imagine a different one." As Zynga sees it, open innovation "replicates the process that a five-year-old goes through to see the potential of a fort in a couple of chairs and a blanket." It's all a matter of making connections between what you want to create and objects—or ideas—that apparently have unrelated applications. "Open innovation practitioners," explains Zynga, "source solutions to specific problems in [an analogous] way—by enabling a connection between a need and potential solutions that reside in unrelated industries."[1]

13-1 GROUPS AND TEAMS IN ORGANIZATIONS

Groups are a ubiquitous part of organizational life. They are the basis for much of the work that gets done, and they evolve both inside and outside the normal structural boundaries of the organization. We define a group as two or more people who interact regularly to accomplish a common purpose or goal.[2] The purpose of a group or team may range from preparing a new marketing plan, to informally sharing information, to making important decisions, to fulfilling social needs.

13-1a **Types of Groups and Teams**

In general, three basic kinds of groups are found in organizations—functional groups, informal or interest groups, and task groups and teams.[3] These are illustrated in Figure 13.1.

Functional Groups   A functional group is a permanent group created by the organization to accomplish a number of organizational purposes with an unspecified time horizon. The

group
Consists of two or more people who interact regularly to accomplish a common purpose or goal

functional group
A permanent group created by the organization to accomplish a number of organizational purposes with an unspecified time horizon

A functional group is a permanent group created by the organization. The staff of this hospital emergency room would be considered a functional group comprised of doctors, nurses, and technicians.

advertising department at Target, the management department at Florida Atlantic University, and the nursing staff at the Mayo Clinic are functional groups. The advertising department at Target, for example, seeks to plan effective advertising campaigns, increase sales, run in-store promotions, and develop a unique identity for the company. It is assumed that the functional group will remain in existence after it attains its current objectives; those objectives will then be replaced by new ones.

Informal or Interest Groups　　An **informal or interest group** is created by its own members for purposes that may or may not be relevant to organizational goals. It also has an unspecified time horizon. A group of employees who lunch together every day may be discussing productivity, money embezzling, or local politics and sports.[4] As long as the group members enjoy eating together, they will probably continue to do so. When lunches cease to be pleasant, they will seek other company or a different activity.

informal or interest group
Created by its members for purposes that may or may not be relevant to those of the organization

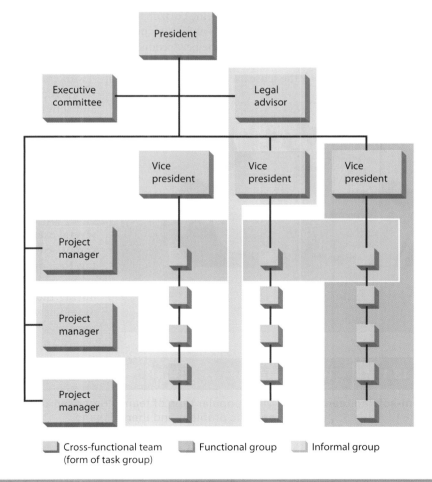

President

Executive committee

Legal advisor

Vice president

Vice president

Vice president

Project manager

Project manager

Project manager

▮ Cross-functional team　　▮ Functional group　　▮ Informal group
(form of task group)

FIGURE 13.1

Types of Groups in Organizations

Every organization has many different types of groups. In this hypothetical organization, a functional group is shown within the purple area, a cross-functional team within the yellow area, and an informal group within the green area.

task group
A group created by the organization to accomplish a relatively narrow range of purposes within a stated or implied time horizon

team
A group of workers that functions as a unit, often with little or no supervision, to carry out work-related tasks, functions, and activities

virtual team
Team comprised of people from remote worksites who work together online

Informal groups can be a powerful force that managers cannot ignore.[5] One writer described how a group of employees at a furniture factory subverted their boss's efforts to increase production. They tacitly agreed to produce a reasonable amount of work but not to work too hard. One man kept a stockpile of completed work hidden as a backup in case he got too far behind. In another example, unhappy auto workers described how they left out gaskets and seals and put soft-drink bottles inside doors to cause customer complaints.[6] Of course, informal groups can also be a positive force, as when people work together to help out a colleague who has suffered a personal tragedy. For example, many examples of this form of behavior were reported in the wake of the COVID-19 pandemic in 2020.

In recent years, online platforms and social media have served as vehicles for the emergence of more and different kinds of informal or interest groups. As one example, Facebook includes a wide array of interest groups that bring together people with common interests. And increasingly, workers who lose their jobs as a result of layoffs are banding together digitally to offer moral support to one another and to facilitate networking as they all look for new jobs.[7]

Task Groups   A **task group** is a group created by the organization to accomplish a relatively narrow range of purposes within a stated or implied time horizon. Most committees and task forces are task groups. The organization specifies group membership and assigns a relatively narrow set of goals, such as developing a new product or evaluating a proposed grievance procedure. The time horizon for accomplishing these purposes is either specified (a committee may be asked to make a recommendation within 60 days) or implied (the project team will disband when the new product is developed).

Teams are a special form of task group that are widespread in most organizations today.[8] In the sense used here, a **team** is a group of workers that functions as a unit, often with little or no supervision, to carry out work-related tasks, functions, and activities. Table 13.1 lists and defines some of the various types of teams that are being used today. Earlier forms of teams included autonomous work groups and quality circles. Today, teams are also sometimes called "self-managed teams," "cross-functional teams," or "high-performance teams." Many firms today are routinely using teams to carry out most of their daily operations.[9] *Doing Business on Planet Earth* provides several examples. Furthermore, **virtual teams**—teams comprised of people from remote worksites who work together online—are also becoming more and more common.[10] Virtual teams became increasingly popular during the 2020 COVID-19 pandemic as people had to find new ways to interact on projects while working remotely,

There are many different kinds of groups in organizations today. This virtual group includes members from three different locations. They are interacting together—some in person and some using virtual technology—to review and discuss their unit's performance.

Andrey_Popov/Shutterstock.com

Table 13.1	Types of Teams
Problem-solving team	Most popular type of team; comprises knowledge workers who gather to solve a specific problem and then disband
Management team	Consists mainly of managers from various functions like sales and production; coordinates work among other teams
Work team	An increasingly popular type of team; work teams are responsible for the daily work of the organization; when empowered, they are self-managed teams
Virtual team	A newer type of work team whose members interact in a virtual arena; members enter and leave the network as needed and may take turns serving as leader
Quality circle	Declining in popularity, quality circles, comprising workers and supervisors, meet intermittently to discuss workplace problems

Source: From *Fortune*, September 5, 2004. Time Inc.

DOING BUSINESS ON PLANET EARTH

Cooking Up Sustainability

How much does it cost to cook pasta? It depends on how you do it—and, of course, on how much pasta you want to cook. Olive Garden, for example, cooks a lot of pasta: The Italian-food chain has almost 900 locations worldwide and offers an annual "Never Ending Pasta Bowl" deal in which customers can pack all the pasta they want into their own customized creations. On the other hand, the pasta-cooking process is basically the same one that you use in your own kitchen: bring cold water to a boil, put in the hard pasta, and bring the water to a second boil. Back in 2015, however, Olive Garden tweaked the process by modifying the cold- and hot-water inlet valves on its pasta cookers so that the process uses hot water only. Since then, the chain has saved $2.9 million in energy costs, mostly in the cost of heating and reheating water.

How does a company come up with such sustainable ideas? At Darden Restaurants, Olive Garden's parent corporation, many such ideas originate with in-house Sustainability Teams, which Darden describes as "groups of employees in each restaurant who implement programs to reduce waste and energy and water usage." The company hastens to point out that "they are also responsible for many of the ideas we have used to improve sustainability at our restaurants" and, in the spring of 2018, Darden took a step further in seeking out grassroots input by surveying 12,000 employees to gather both feedback on current sustainability efforts and ideas for improvement.

By and large, however, the job of implementing these efforts falls to each restaurant's Sustainability Team, which typically includes three to five members. Individual efforts are important to Darden's overall sustainability strategy because the company has discovered that the regular performance of some basic tasks can make a big difference. Michele Smith, for example, is in charge of thermostats at an Olive Garden restaurant. "When I come to work in the morning," she says, "I make sure all the thermostats are set where they're supposed to be. . . . It gives me a chance," she adds, "to feel like I'm helping out and doing something good." Generally speaking,

Smith's attitude toward workplace sustainability reflects that of her generation: So-called *Millennials*—the roughly one-fourth of Americans born between 1980 and the mid-2000s—are the most sustainability-conscious segment of the population and, according to one recent survey, 80 percent of them want to work for sustainability-conscious companies.

Take Pam Martin, for instance, who is a Sustainability Team member at a Bahama Breeze restaurant. "When I heard about the team," she recalls, "I felt like it was almost a personal obligation ... to make sure ... our environment is protected and maintained instead of creating a larger carbon footprint. I want to make sure we're doing the most that we can to make sure our impact on the environment is minimal." According to Brandon Tidwell, Manager of Sustainability at Darden, the initiatives that the company launched in 2017 were in part a response to the interest of young employees in stepping up sustainability practices. "The idea of doing more," says Tidwell,

> came out of our millennial workforce. Seventy percent of our employees are 30 and under, and they are very interested in this issue. This millennial generation grew up with environmental education in school, and they want to make a difference in their careers and be actively engaged. They grew up recycling at home and separating their trash, so when they can't do the same thing in the restaurant, it's frustrating for them. They want their workplace to share their same values.

References: Mike Hower, "Here's What's On Olive Garden's Sustainability Menu," *GreenBiz,* www.greenbiz.com on May 22, 2020; Darden Restaurants Inc., "Planet," *Darden Sustainability,* 2020, www.darden.com on May 22, 2020; Sherleen Mahoney, "Leading an Industry while Making a Difference," RFMA *Facilitator,* February–March, 2013, http://c.ymcdn.com on May 22, 2020; Darden Restaurants Inc., "Reporting Library" (videos), *Darden Sustainability,* 2020, www.darden.com on May 24, 2020; Aarthi Rayapura, "Millennials Most Sustainability-Conscious Generation Yet, But Don't Call Them 'Environmentalists,'" *Sustainable Brands,* March 11, 2014, www.sustainablebrands. com on May 28, 2020.

Organizations create teams for a variety of reasons. For one thing, they give more responsibility for task performance to the workers who are actually performing the tasks. They also empower workers by giving them greater authority and decision-making freedom. In addition, they allow the organization to capitalize on the knowledge and motivation of their workers. Finally, they enable the organization to shed its bureaucracy and to promote flexibility and responsiveness. Ford used teams to design its newest version of the Mustang. Similarly, General Motors used a team to develop its Chevrolet Volt. And both Universal Studios and Disney used teams to develop plans for reopening theme parks in the wake of the COVID-19 pandemic in 2020.

When an organization decides to use teams, it is essentially implementing a major form of organization change, as discussed in Chapter 12. Thus, it is important to follow a logical and systematic approach to planning and implementing teams in an existing organization design. It is also important to recognize that resistance may be encountered. This resistance is often from first-line managers who will be giving up some of their authority to the team. Many organizations find that they must change the whole management philosophy of such managers away from being supervisors to being coaches or facilitators.[11]

After teams are in place, managers should then continue to monitor their contributions and how effectively they are functioning. In the best circumstances, teams will become very cohesive groups with high performance norms. To achieve this state, the manager can use any or all of the techniques described later in this chapter for enhancing cohesiveness. If implemented properly, and with the support of the workers themselves, performance norms will likely be relatively high. In other words, if the change is properly implemented, the team participants will understand the value and potential of teams and the rewards they may expect to get as a result of their contributions. On the other hand, poorly designed and implemented teams will do a less effective job and may even detract from organizational effectiveness.[12]

> **"If a team can't be fed by two pizzas, it's too large."**
>
> —Jeff Bezos, Founder and CEO of Amazon.com

People join groups and teams for many different reasons. For instance, people might join a group in order to participate in social activities such as playing pool, throwing darts, bowling, softball, bridge, and so forth.

13-1b Why People Join Groups and Teams

People join groups and teams for a variety of reasons. They join functional groups simply by virtue of joining organizations. People accept employment to earn money or to practice their chosen professions. Once inside the organization, they are assigned to jobs and roles and thus become members of functional groups. People in existing functional groups are told, are asked, or volunteer to serve on committees, task forces, and teams. People join informal or interest groups for a variety of reasons, most of them quite complex.[13] Indeed, the need to be a team player has grown so strong today that many organizations will actively resist hiring someone who does not want to work with others.[14]

Interpersonal Attraction One reason why people choose to form informal or interest groups is that they are attracted to one another. Many different factors contribute to interpersonal attraction. When people see a lot of each other, pure proximity increases the likelihood that interpersonal attraction will develop. Attraction is increased when people have similar attitudes, personalities, or shared life experiences.

Group Activities Individuals may also be motivated to join a group because the activities of the group appeal to them. Jogging, playing video games, bowling, discussing poetry or books, playing fantasy football, and flying model airplanes are all activities that some people enjoy. Many of them are more enjoyable to participate in as a member of a group, and most require more than one person. Many large firms like Shell Oil and Apple Computer have a flag football, softball, or bowling league. A person may join a bowling team not because of any particular attraction to other group members, but simply because being a member of the group allows that person to participate in a pleasant activity. Of course, if the group's level of interpersonal attraction is very low, a person may choose to forgo the activity rather than join the group.

> **"Give us people who are dedicated to making the team work, as opposed to a bunch of talented people with big egos, and we'll win every time."**
>
> —John McConnell, CEO of Worthington Industries

AS photo studio/Shutterstock.com

Group Goals   The goals of a group may also motivate people to join. The Sierra Club, which is dedicated to environmental conservation, is a good example of this kind of interest group. Various fundraising groups are another illustration. Members may or may not be personally attracted to the other fundraisers, and they probably do not enjoy the activity of knocking on doors or calling people to ask for money, but they join the group because they subscribe to its goal. Workers join unions like the United Auto Workers because they support its goals.

Need Satisfaction   Still another reason for joining a group is to satisfy the need for affiliation. New residents in a community may join the "Newcomers Club" (or a similar organization targeted at new residents) partially as a way to meet new people and partially just to be around other people. Likewise, newly single people may join support groups as a way to have companionship.

Instrumental Benefits   A final reason why people join groups is that membership is sometimes seen as instrumental in providing other benefits to the individual. For example, it is fairly common for college students entering their senior year to join several professional clubs or associations because they believe that listing such memberships on a resumé is a good way to enhance their chances of getting a job. Similarly, a manager might join a certain racquet club not because she is attracted to its members (although she might be) and not because of the opportunity to play tennis (although she may enjoy it). The club's goals are not relevant, and her affiliation needs may be satisfied in other ways. However, she may feel that being a member of this club will lead to important and useful business contacts. The racquet club membership is instrumental in establishing those contacts. Membership in civic groups such as the Junior League and Rotary may be solicited for similar reasons.

13-1c Stages of Group and Team Development

Imagine the differences between a collection of five people who have just been brought together and told by their boss that they will form a group or team and a group or team that has functioned like a well-oiled machine for years. Members of a new group or team are unfamiliar with how they will function together and are tentative in their interactions. In a group or team with considerably more experience, members are familiar with one another's strengths and weaknesses and are more secure in their roles in the group. The former group or team is generally considered to be immature; the latter, mature. To progress from the immature phase to the mature phase, a group or team must go through certain stages of development, as shown in Figure 13.2.[15]

The first stage of development is called *forming*. The members of the group or team get acquainted and begin to test which interpersonal behaviors are acceptable and which are unacceptable to the other members. The members are very dependent on others at this point to provide cues about what is acceptable. The basic ground rules for the group or team are established, and a tentative group structure may emerge.[16] At Adidas, for example, a merchandising team was created to handle a new line of sportswear. The team leader and his members were barely acquainted and had to spend some time getting to know one another.

The second stage of development, often slow to emerge, is *storming*. During this stage, there may be a general lack of unity and uneven interaction patterns. At the same time, some members of the group or team may begin to exert themselves to become recognized as the group leader or at least to play a major role in shaping the group's agenda. In Adidas's team, some members advocated a rapid rollout of the new sportswear line; others argued for a slower rollout. The first faction won, with disastrous results. Because of the rush, product quality was poor and deliveries were late. As a result, the team leader was fired and a new manager placed in charge.

The third stage of development, called *norming*, usually begins with a burst of activity. During this stage, each person begins to recognize and accept her or his role and to understand the roles of others. Members also begin to accept one another and to develop a sense of unity. There may also be temporary regressions to the previous stage. For example, the group or team might begin to accept one particular member as the leader. If this person later violates important

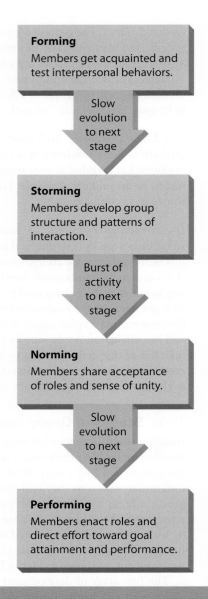

Stages of Group Development

As groups mature, they tend to evolve through four distinct stages of development. Managers must understand that group members need time to become acquainted, accept one another, develop a group structure, and become comfortable with their roles in the group before they can begin to work directly to accomplish goals.

norms or otherwise jeopardizes his or her claim to leadership, conflict might reemerge as the group rejects this leader and searches for another. Adidas's new team leader transferred several people away from the team and set up a new system and structure for managing things. The remaining employees accepted his new approach and settled into doing their jobs.

Performing, the final stage of group or team development, is also slow to develop. The team really begins to focus on the problem at hand. The members enact the roles they have accepted, interaction occurs, and the efforts of the group are directed toward goal attainment. The basic structure of the group or team is no longer an issue but has become a mechanism for accomplishing the purpose of the group. Adidas's new product line is now growing consistently and has successfully avoided the problems that plagued it at first.

competition reduces cohesiveness. When members are competing among themselves, they focus more on their own actions and behaviors than on those of the group.

Fourth, domination by one or more persons in the group or team may cause overall cohesiveness to decline. Other members may feel that they are not being given an opportunity to interact and contribute, and they may become less attracted to the group as a consequence. The *Leading the Way* feature provides more insights into this aspect of group dynamics. Finally, unpleasant experiences that result from group membership may reduce cohesiveness. A marketing group that comes in last in a sales contest, an athletic team that sustains a long losing streak, and a work group reprimanded for poor-quality work may all become less cohesive as a result of their unpleasant experiences.

LEADING THE WAY

Primed for Power

For a long time, observes industrial/organizational psychologist Liane Davey, we were brought up on the idea that "power is useful in driving performance. You defer to your boss because that's how the hierarchy works. It creates clarity and alignment and keeps things moving." Not surprisingly, then, when bosses function as leaders in group decision-making situations, power encourages them to assume dominant roles. Davey points out, however, that the criteria for successful group performance are no longer what they used to be: "In our innovation economy," she says, "where tasks require creative problem solving, information sharing, and collaboration, we need to get the value of all the members of a team—not just the limited perspective of the boss.

"The research," Davey adds, "bears this out." The research she has in mind was conducted by a team of business professors. In various experiments, Tost, Gino, and Larrick tested the effect of two variables on team performance: (1) In some cases, they appointed a formal leader, and in others, they did not; (2) in some cases, leaders were "primed" by being asked to recall past exercises of power, and in others, leaders were not primed. In one experiment, teams were asked to solve a murder mystery. The two groups *without formal leaders* were successful 60 percent of the time; the group *with a formal leader primed to feel powerful* had the worst success rate—about 25 percent.

"The problem," says Rick Larrick of Duke University, "is that people who are in a power mindset don't stop to ask what others know and think. And this [habit] is facilitated by formal roles and titles, because it means that those in a less powerful position tend to defer to the person with the higher position." This doesn't mean, however, that leaderless teams are the best way to go. The key factor in team success—or the lack of it—appears to be the way leaders *perceive* their power. "The best teams," Larrick points out, "had leaders who were not reminded of power. This makes sense in that leaders do play an essential role by providing structure

to teams. But the structure has to ensure participation. A facilitative leader is one way to create this desirable structure."

As Larrick reminds us, the best success rate in solving the murder mystery—80 percent—was posted by the group *with a formal leader who was not primed to feel powerful ahead of time*. With this team, notes co-researcher Francesca Gino of Harvard University, "the leader is sort of stepping back. It's more of what you like to see, where the leader is orchestrating the conversation, but everyone is talking."

In other words, differences in team leadership, response, and performance seem to depend in large part on *perceptions* on the part of both leaders and team members. Leaders, for example, were "primed" to heighten their perception of themselves as powerful: "With the rush that comes with having control," explains Gino, "it's easy for a manager to hog the floor—even feel obligated to play this role." In turn, reports Larrick, when leaders acted on the basis of self-perceived empowerment, team members, who perceived themselves to be "in less powerful positions, tended to defer to the person with the higher position."

"Oftentimes," concludes Gino, "we behave the way we do because we're not aware of the effects of our actions. Bringing this type of awareness to leaders in group decision-making situations could set up a different process whereby they benefit from what others have to offer."

References: Liane Davey, "Don't Let Your Voice Be Silenced by Your Boss," *Psychology Today*, February 18, 2014, www.psychologytoday.com on May 20, 2020; Leigh Plunkett Tost, Francesca Gino, and Richard P. Larrick, "When Power Makes Others Speechless: The Negative Impact of Leader Power on Team Performance" (abstract), *Academy of Management Journal*, 2012, Vol. 56, No. 5, https://journals.aom.org on May 20, 2020; Michael Blanding, "Pulpit Bullies: Why Dominating Leaders Kill Teams," *Harvard Business School Working Knowledge*, November 18, 2013, http://hbswk.hbs.edu on May 18, 2020; Erin Medlyn, "New Research Finds Overbearing Leaders Can Hurt Their Team's Performance," Duke University Fuqua School of Business, May 18, 2020.

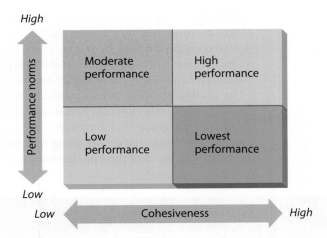

FIGURE 13.4

The Interaction Between Cohesiveness and Performance Norms

Group cohesiveness and performance norms interact to determine group performance. From the manager's perspective, high cohesiveness combined with high performance norms is the best situation, and high cohesiveness with low performance norms is the worst situation. Managers who can influence the level of cohesiveness and performance norms can greatly improve the effectiveness of a work group.

Consequences of Cohesiveness   In general, as teams become more cohesive, their members tend to interact more often, conform more to norms, and become more satisfied with the team. Cohesiveness may also influence team performance. However, performance is also influenced by the team's performance norms. Figure 13.4 shows how cohesiveness and performance norms interact to help shape team performance.

When both cohesiveness and performance norms are high, high performance should result because the team wants to perform at a high level (norms) and its members are engaged and working together toward that end (cohesiveness). When norms are high and cohesiveness is low, performance will be moderate. Although the team wants to perform at a high level, its members are not necessarily working well together. When norms are low, performance will be low, regardless of whether group cohesiveness is high or low. The least desirable situation occurs when low performance norms are combined with high cohesiveness. In this case, all team members embrace the standard of restricting performance (owing to the low performance norm), and the group is united in its efforts to maintain that standard (owing to the high cohesiveness). If cohesiveness were low, the manager might be able to raise performance norms by collaboratively establishing higher goals and then rewarding goal attainment or by bringing in new group members who are high performers. But a highly cohesive group is likely to resist these interventions.[25]

13-2d Formal and Informal Leadership

Most functional groups and teams have a formal leader—that is, one appointed by the organization or chosen or elected by the members of the group. Because friendship and interest groups are formed by the members themselves, however, any formal leader must be elected or designated by the members. Although some groups do designate such a leader (a softball team may elect a captain, for example), many do not. Moreover, even when a formal leader is designated, the group or team may also look to others for leadership. An informal leader is a person who engages in leadership activities but whose right to do so has not been formally recognized. The formal and the informal leader in any group or team may be the same person, or they may be different people. We noted earlier the distinction between the task

informal leader
A person who engages in leadership activities but whose right to do so has not been formally recognized by the organization or group

This group has just learned that it has exceeded its performance goals for the quarter. As a result, the group will likely become more cohesive and feel a greater commitment to high performance norms in the future.

specialist and socioemotional roles within groups. An informal leader is likely to be a person capable of carrying out both roles effectively. If the formal leader can fulfill one role but not the other, an informal leader often emerges to supplement the formal leader's functions. If the formal leader can fill neither role, one or more informal leaders may emerge to carry out both sets of functions.

Is informal leadership desirable? In many cases informal leaders are quite powerful because they draw from referent or expert power. When they are working in the best interests of the organization, they can be a tremendous asset. Notable athletes like LeBron James and Megan Rapinoe are examples of informal leaders. However, when informal leaders work counter to the goals of the organization, they can cause significant difficulties. Such leaders may lower performance norms, instigate walkouts or wildcat strikes, or otherwise disrupt the organization.

Manager's Checklist

☐ Identify and describe the fundamental characteristics of groups and teams.

☐ Assume you were assigned to manage a highly cohesive group with low performance norms. What would you do to try to change things?

13-3 INTERPERSONAL AND INTERGROUP CONFLICT

Of course, when people work together in an organization, things do not always go smoothly. Indeed, conflict is an inevitable element of interpersonal relationships in organizations. In this section, we look at how conflict affects overall performance. We also explore the causes of conflict between individuals, between groups, and between an organization and its environment.

13-3a The Nature of Conflict

conflict
A disagreement among two or more individuals or groups

Conflict is a disagreement among two or more individuals, groups, or organizations. This disagreement may be relatively superficial or very strong. It may be short-lived or exist for months or even years, and it may be work related or personal. Conflict may manifest itself in a variety of ways. People may compete with one another, glare at one another, shout, or withdraw. Groups may band together to protect popular members or oust unpopular members. Organizations may seek legal remedies.

Most people assume that conflict is something to be avoided because it connotes antagonism, hostility, unpleasantness, and dissension. Indeed, managers and management theorists have traditionally viewed conflict as a problem to be avoided.[26] Now, however, experts have come to recognize that, although conflict can be a major problem, certain kinds of conflict may also be beneficial.[27] For example, when two members of a site selection committee disagree over the best location for a new plant, each may be forced to more thoroughly study and defend his or her preferred alternative. As a result of more systematic analysis and discussion, the committee may make a better decision and be better prepared to justify it to others than if everyone had agreed from the outset and accepted an alternative that was perhaps less well analyzed.

As long as conflict is being handled in a cordial and constructive manner, it is probably serving a useful purpose in the organization. On the other hand, when working relationships are being disrupted and the conflict has reached destructive levels, it has likely become

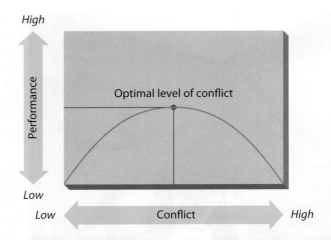

FIGURE 13.5

The Nature of Organizational Conflict

Either too much or too little conflict can be dysfunctional for an organization. In either case, performance may be low. However, an optimal level of conflict that sparks motivation, creativity, innovation, and initiative can result in higher levels of performance.

dysfunctional and needs to be addressed.[28] We discuss ways of dealing with such conflict later in this chapter.

Figure 13.5 depicts the general relationship between conflict and performance for a group or organization. If there is absolutely no conflict in the group or organization, its members may become complacent and apathetic. As a result, group or organizational performance and innovation may begin to suffer. A moderate level of conflict among group or organizational members, on the other hand, can spark motivation, creativity, innovation, and initiative and raise performance. Too much conflict, though, can produce such undesirable results as hostility and lack of cooperation, which lower performance. The key for managers is to find and maintain the optimal amount of conflict that fosters performance. Of course, what constitutes optimal conflict varies with both the situation and the people involved.[29]

13-3b Causes of Conflict

Conflict may arise in both interpersonal and intergroup relationships. Occasionally, conflict between individuals and groups may be caused by particular organizational strategies and practices. A third arena for conflict is between an organization and its environment.

Interpersonal Conflict   Conflict between two or more people is almost certain to occur in any organization, given the great variety in perceptions, goals, attitudes, and so forth among its members. Bill Gates, founder and former CEO of Microsoft, and Kazuhiko Nishi, a former business associate from Japan, once ended a lucrative long-term business relationship because of interpersonal conflict. Nishi accused Gates of becoming too political, while Gates charged that Nishi became too unpredictable and erratic in his behavior.[30] During the COVID-19 pandemic in 2020, Amazon vice president Tim Bray resigned, accusing the company of firing warehouse employees who complained about health and safety procedures at their worksites. Another Amazon vice president, Brad Porter, then accused Bray of sensationalism and indicated that the accusations were false. Many of these charges and countercharges were posted online, suggesting high levels of interpersonal conflict.[31]

A frequent source of interpersonal conflict in organizations is what many people call a "personality clash"—when two people distrust each other's motives, dislike each other, or for some other reason simply cannot get along.[32] Conflict may also arise between people who have different beliefs or perceptions about some aspect of their work or their organization. For example, one manager might want the organization to require that all employees use Microsoft Office software, to promote standardization. Another manager might believe that a variety of software packages should be allowed, in order to recognize individuality. Similarly, one manager may disagree with a colleague over whether the organization is guilty of discriminating against women in promotion decisions. Conflict can also result from excess competitiveness among individuals. Two people vying for the same job, for example, may resort to political behavior in an effort to gain an advantage. If either competitor sees the other's behavior as inappropriate, accusations are likely to result. Even after the "winner" of the job is determined, such conflict may continue to undermine interpersonal relationships, especially if the reasons given for selecting one candidate are ambiguous or open to alternative explanations.

Sometimes, of course, conflicts can't be resolved from within the organization, and when parties—both individuals and companies—are forced to seek resolution outside corporate headquarters, they usually find themselves in a courtroom or the offices of a governmental agency. Once in a great while, conflicts escalate to the point at which they end up in the halls of Congress.

Intergroup Conflict   Conflict between two or more organizational groups is also quite common. For example, the members of a firm's marketing group may disagree with the production group over product quality and delivery schedules. Two sales groups may disagree over how to meet sales goals, and two groups of managers may have different ideas about how best to allocate organizational resources.

Many intergroup conflicts arise more from organizational causes than from interpersonal causes. In Chapter 11, we described three forms of group interdependence—pooled, sequential, and reciprocal. Just as increased interdependence makes coordination more difficult, it also increases the potential for conflict. For example, recall that in sequential interdependence, work is passed from one unit to another. Intergroup conflict may arise if the first group turns out too much work (the second group will fall behind), too little work (the second group will not meet its own goals), or poor-quality work.

At one Macy's department store, conflict arose between stockroom employees and sales associates. The sales associates claimed that the stockroom employees were slow in delivering merchandise to the sales floor so that it could be priced and shelved. The stockroom employees, in turn, claimed that the sales associates were not giving them enough lead time to get the merchandise delivered and failed to understand that they had additional duties besides carrying merchandise to the sales floor.

Just like people, different departments often have different goals. Furthermore, these goals may often be incompatible. A marketing goal of maximizing sales, achieved partially by offering many products in a wide variety of sizes, shapes, colors, and models, probably conflicts with a production goal of minimizing costs, achieved partially by long production runs of a few items. These kinds of conflict played a role in the demise of Eastman Kodak. The divisions responsible for film and for photo paper resisted the shift to digital photography even though the technology division was pushing to make an aggressive shift to digital. The film and paper divisions had more power, though, slowing the move to digital but eventually pushing Kodak into bankruptcy.

Competition for scarce resources can also lead to intergroup conflict. Most organizations—especially universities, hospitals, government agencies, and businesses in depressed industries—have limited resources. In one New England town, for example, the public works department and the library battled over funds from a federal construction grant. The Buick, Pontiac, and Chevrolet divisions of General Motors frequently fought over the right to manufacture various new products developed by the company. This in-fighting was identified as one of many factors that led to GM's problems during the Great Recession of 2007–2009. As part of the solution, the Pontiac brand was eventually discontinued.

Conflict Between Organization and Environment   Conflict that arises between one organization and another is called *interorganizational conflict*. A moderate amount of interorganizational conflict resulting from business competition is expected, of course, but sometimes conflict becomes more extreme. For example, on multiple occasions Apple and Samsung have each accused the other of copying proprietary technology as they compete to gain competitive advantage and grow market share for their iPhone and Galaxy smartphones.

Conflict can also arise between an organization and other elements of its environment. An organization may conflict with a consumer group over claims it makes about its products. McDonald's faced this problem a few years ago when it published nutritional information about its products that omitted details about fat content. A manufacturer might conflict with a governmental agency such as the federal Occupational Safety and Health Administration (OSHA). For example, the firm's management may believe it is in compliance with OSHA regulations, whereas officials from the agency itself believe that the firm is not in compliance. Or a firm might conflict with a supplier over the quality of raw materials. The firm may think the supplier is providing inferior materials, while the supplier thinks the materials are adequate. Finally, individual managers obviously may have disagreements with groups of workers. A manager may think her workers are doing poor-quality work and that they are unmotivated. The workers, on the other hand, may believe they are doing good jobs and that the manager is doing a poor job of leading them.

 **Manager's Checklist**

☐ Define conflict and identify its primary causes.

☐ Try to think of a time when you were involved in conflict that had a positive outcome.

13-4 MANAGING CONFLICT IN ORGANIZATIONS

How do managers cope with all this potential conflict? Fortunately, as Table 13.3 shows, there are ways to stimulate conflict for constructive ends, to control conflict before it gets out of hand, and to resolve it if it does. Below we look at ways of managing conflict.[33]

13-4a Stimulating Conflict

In some situations, an organization may stimulate conflict by placing individual employees or groups in competitive situations. Managers can establish sales contests, incentive plans, bonuses, or other competitive stimuli to spark competition. As long as the ground rules are

Table 13.3	Methods for Managing Conflict
Stimulating Conflict	
Increase competition among individuals and teams.	
Hire outsiders to shake things up.	
Change established procedures.	
Controlling Conflict	
Expand resource base.	
Enhance coordination of interdependence.	
Set superordinate goals.	
Match personalities and work habits of employees.	
Resolving and Eliminating Conflict	
Avoid conflict.	
Convince conflicting parties to compromise.	
Bring conflicting parties together to confront and negotiate conflict.	

Conflict is a powerful force in organizations and has both negative and positive consequences. Thus, managers can draw on several different techniques to stimulate, control, or resolve and eliminate conflict, depending on their unique circumstances.

equitable and all participants perceive the contest as fair, the conflict created by the competition is likely to be constructive because each participant will work hard to win (thereby enhancing some aspect of organizational performance).

Another useful method for stimulating conflict is to bring in one or more outsiders who will shake things up and present a new perspective on organizational practices. Outsiders may be new employees, current employees assigned to an existing work group, or consultants or advisors hired on a temporary basis. Of course, this action can also provoke resentment from insiders who feel they were qualified for the position. The Anglo American Mining Company, based in South Africa and England, once hired an executive from the United States for its CEO position, expressly to change how the company did business. Her arrival brought with it new ways of doing things and a new enthusiasm for competitiveness. Unfortunately, some valued employees also chose to leave Anglo American because they resented some of the changes that were made. Changing established procedures, especially procedures that have outlived their usefulness, can also stimulate conflict. Such actions cause people to reassess how they perform their jobs and whether they perform them correctly. For example, one university president announced that all vacant staff positions could be filled only after written justification had received his approval. Conflict arose between the president and the department heads, who felt they were having to do more paperwork than was necessary. Most requests were approved, but because department heads now had to think through their staffing needs, a few unnecessary positions were appropriately eliminated.

13-4b Controlling Conflict

One method of controlling conflict is to expand the resource base. Suppose a top manager receives two budget requests for $100,000 each. If she has only $180,000 to distribute, the stage is set for conflict because each group will believe its proposal is worth funding and will be unhappy if it is not fully funded. If both proposals are indeed worthwhile, it may be possible for the manager to come up with the extra $20,000 from some other source and thereby avoid difficulty.

Leaders can use a variety of methods to manage conflict. Some methods focus on stimulating conflict whereas other techniques help control or resolve conflict. These two managers have been in conflict over a pending decision. However, they have just negotiated an understanding that makes both of them happy and are "sealing the deal" with a handshake.

ESB Professional/Shutterstock.com

As noted earlier, pooled, sequential, and reciprocal interdependence can all result in conflict. If managers use an appropriate technique for enhancing coordination, they can reduce the probability that conflict will arise. Techniques for coordination (described in Chapter 11) include making use of the managerial hierarchy, relying on rules and procedures, enlisting liaison people, forming task forces, and integrating departments. At the Macy's store mentioned earlier, the conflict was addressed by providing salespeople with clearer forms on which to specify the merchandise they needed and in what sequence. If one coordination technique does not have the desired effect, a manager might shift to another one.[34]

Competing goals can also be a source of conflict among individuals and groups. Managers can sometimes focus employee attention on higher-level, or superordinate, goals as a way of eliminating lower-level conflict. When labor unions like the United Auto Workers make wage concessions to ensure the survival of the automobile industry, they are responding to a superordinate goal. Their immediate goal may be higher wages for members, but they realize that, without the automobile industry, their members would not even have jobs.

Finally, managers should try to match the personalities and work habits of employees so as to avoid conflict between individuals. For instance, two valuable subordinates, one who loves to talk while working and the other a much quieter person easily distracted by conversation, probably should not be required to work together in an enclosed space. If conflict does arise between incompatible people, a manager might seek an equitable transfer for one or both of them to other units.

13-4c Resolving and Eliminating Conflict

Despite everyone's best intentions, conflict sometimes flares up. If it is disrupting the workplace, creating too much hostility and tension, or otherwise harming the organization, attempts must be made to resolve it.[35] Some managers who are uncomfortable dealing with conflict choose to avoid it and hope it will go away. Avoidance may sometimes be effective in the short run for some kinds of interpersonal disagreements, but it does little to resolve long-run or chronic conflicts. Even more unadvisable, though, is "smoothing"—minimizing the conflict and telling everyone that things will "get better." Often the conflict only worsens as people continue to brood over it.

Compromise is striking a middle-range position between two extremes. This approach can work if it is used with care, but in most compromise situations, someone wins and someone loses. Budget problems are one of the few areas amenable to compromise because of their objective nature. Assume, for example, that additional resources are not available to the manager mentioned earlier. She has $180,000 to divide, and each of two groups claims to need $100,000. If the manager believes that both projects warrant funding, she can allocate $90,000 to each. The fact that the two groups have at least been treated equally may minimize the potential conflict.

The confrontational approach to conflict resolution—also called *interpersonal problem solving*—consists of bringing the parties together to confront the conflict. The parties discuss the nature of their conflict and try to reach an agreement or a solution. Confrontation requires a reasonable degree of maturity on the part of the participants, and the manager must structure the situation carefully. If handled well, this approach can be an effective means of resolving conflict. In recent years, many organizations have experimented with a technique called *alternative dispute resolution*, using a team of employees to arbitrate conflict in this way.[36] Negotiation, a closely related method, is discussed in our final section.

Regardless of the approach, organizations and their managers should realize that conflict must be addressed if it is to serve constructive purposes and be prevented from bringing about destructive consequences. Conflict is inevitable in organizations, but its effects can be constrained with proper attention. For example, Dow Chemical Company sent 200 of its managers to a three-day workshop on conflict management. The managers engaged in a variety of exercises and discussions to learn with whom they were most likely to come in conflict and how they should try to resolve it. As a result, managers at the firm later reported that hostility and resentment in the organization had been greatly diminished and that people in the firm reported more pleasant working relationships.[37]

13-4d Negotiation

negotiation
The process in which two or more parties (people or groups) reach agreement on an issue even though they have different preferences regarding that issue

Negotiation is the process in which two or more parties (people or groups) reach agreement on an issue even though they have different preferences regarding that issue. In its simplest form the parties involved may be two individuals who are trying to decide who will pay for lunch. A little more complexity is involved when two people, such as an employee and a manager, sit down to decide on personal performance goals for the next year against which the employee's performance will be measured. Even more complex are the negotiations that take place between labor unions and the management of a company or between two companies as they negotiate the terms of a joint venture. The key issues in such negotiations are that at least two parties are involved, their preferences are different, and they need to reach agreement. Interest in negotiation has grown steadily in recent years.[38] Four primary approaches to negotiation have dominated this study: individual differences, situational characteristics, game theory, and cognitive approaches.

Early psychological approaches concentrated on the personality traits of the negotiators.[39] Traits investigated have included demographic characteristics and personality variables. Demographic characteristics have included age, gender, and race, among others. Personality variables have included risk taking, locus of control, tolerance for ambiguity, self-esteem, authoritarianism, and Machiavellianism. The assumption of this type of research was that the key to successful negotiation was selecting the right person to do the negotiating, one who had the appropriate demographic characteristics or personality. This assumption seemed to make sense because negotiation is such a personal and interactive process. However, the research rarely showed the positive results expected because situational variables negated the effects of the individual differences.[40]

Situational characteristics are the context within which negotiation takes place. They include such things as the types of communication between negotiators, the potential outcomes of the negotiation, the relative power of the parties (both positional and personal), the time frame available for negotiation, the number of people representing each side, and the presence of other parties. Some of this research has contributed to our understanding of the negotiation process. However, the shortcomings of the situational approach are similar to those of the individual characteristics approach. Many situational characteristics are external to the negotiators and beyond their control. Often the negotiators cannot change their relative power positions or the setting within which the negotiation occurs. So, although we have learned a lot from research on the situational issues, we still need to learn much more about the process.

Game theory was developed by behavioral economists using mathematical models to predict the outcome of negotiation situations (as illustrated in the Academy Award–winning movie A *Beautiful Mind*). It requires that every alternative and outcome be analyzed with probabilities and numerical outcomes reflecting the preferences for each outcome. In addition, the order in which different parties can make choices and every possible move are predicted, along with associated preferences for outcomes. The outcomes of this approach are exactly what negotiators want: a predictive model of how negotiation should be conducted. One major drawback is that it requires the ability to describe all possible options and outcomes for every possible move in every situation before the negotiation starts. This is often very tedious, if possible at all. Another problem is that this theory assumes that negotiators are rational at all times. Other research in negotiation has shown that negotiators often do not act rationally. Therefore, this approach, although elegant in its prescriptions, is usually unworkable in a real negotiation situation.

The fourth approach is the cognitive approach, which recognizes that negotiators often depart from perfect rationality during negotiation; it tries to predict how and when negotiators will make these departures. Howard Raiffa's decision analytic approach focuses on providing advice to negotiators actively involved in negotiation.[41] Bazerman and Neale have added to Raiffa's work by specifying eight ways in which negotiators systematically deviate from rationality.[42] The types of deviations they describe include escalation of commitment to a previously selected course of action, overreliance on readily available information, assuming that the negotiations can produce fixed-sum outcomes, and anchoring negotiation in irrelevant information. These cognitive approaches have advanced the study of negotiation a long way beyond the early individual and situational approaches. Negotiators can use them to attempt to predict in advance how the negotiation might take place.

Manager's Checklist

☐ What techniques are available to managers to stimulate, control, and resolve conflict?

☐ What are the primary risks involved if a manager decides to stimulate conflict?

SUMMARY OF LEARNING OUTCOMES AND KEY POINTS

13-1. Describe types of groups and teams in organizations, why people join groups and teams, and the stages of group and team development.

- A group is two or more people who interact regularly to accomplish a common purpose or goal.

- General kinds of groups in organizations are
  - functional groups,
  - task groups and teams, and
  - informal or interest groups.

- A team is a group of workers that functions as a unit, often with little or no supervision, to carry out organizational functions.

13-2. Discuss four essential characteristics of groups and teams.

- People join functional groups and teams to pursue a career.

- Their reasons for joining informal or interest groups include interpersonal attraction, group activities, group goals, need satisfaction, and potential instrumental benefits.

- The stages of team development include testing and dependence, intragroup conflict and hostility, development of group cohesion, and focusing on the problem at hand.

- Four important characteristics of teams are role structures, behavioral norms, cohesiveness, and informal leadership.

  - Role structures define task and socioemotional specialists and may be disrupted by role ambiguity, role conflict, or role overload.

- Norms are standards of behavior for group members.

- Cohesiveness is the extent to which members are loyal and committed to the team and to one another.

- Informal leaders are those leaders whom the group members themselves choose to follow.

13-3. Describe interpersonal and intergroup conflict in organizations.

- Conflict is a disagreement between two or more people, groups, or organizations.

- Too little or too much conflict may hurt performance, but an optimal level of conflict may improve performance.

- Interpersonal and intergroup conflict in organizations may be caused by personality differences or by particular organizational strategies and practices.

13-4. Discuss how organizations manage conflict.

- Organizations may encounter conflict with one another and with various elements of the environment.

- Three methods of managing conflict are
  - to stimulate it,
  - to control it, and
  - to resolve and eliminate it.

DISCUSSION QUESTIONS

Questions for Review

1. What is a group? Describe the several different types of groups and indicate the similarities and differences among them. What is the difference between a group and a team?

2. What are the stages of group development? Do all teams develop through all the stages discussed in this chapter? Why or why not? How might the management of a mature team differ from the management of teams that are not yet mature?

3. Describe the development of a role within a group. Tell how each role leads to the next.

4. Describe the causes of conflict in organizations. What can a manager do to control conflict? To resolve and eliminate conflict?

Questions for Analysis

1. Individuals join groups for a variety of reasons. Most groups contain members who joined for different reasons. What is likely to be the result when members join a group for different reasons? What can a group leader do to reduce the negative impact of a conflict in reasons for joining the group?

2. Consider the case of a developed group, where all members have been socialized. What are the benefits to the individuals of norm conformity? What are the benefits of not conforming to the group's norms? What are the benefits to an organization of conformity? What are the benefits to an organization of nonconformity?

3. During the 2020 COVID-19 pandemic there was disagreement about the need for face coverings. Some people thought face masks should be required for everyone all the time, others thought face masks should be entirely optional, and others had opinions somewhere in between. What were the sources of this conflict? What options were used to address it?

Questions for Application

1. Think of several groups of which you have been a member. Why did you join each? Did each group progress through the stages of development discussed in this chapter? If not, why do you think it did not?

2. Describe the behavioral norms that are in effect in your management class. To what extent are the norms generalized; in other words, how severely are students "punished" for not observing norms? To what extent is there norm variation; that is, are some students able to "get away" with violating norms to which others must conform?

3. Describe a case of interpersonal conflict that you have observed in an organization. Describe a case of intergroup conflict that you have observed. (If you have not observed any, interview a worker or manager to obtain examples.) In each case, was the conflict beneficial or harmful to the organization, and why?

BUILDING EFFECTIVE CONCEPTUAL SKILLS

Exercise Overview

Conceptual skills require you to think in the abstract. This exercise will allow you to practice your conceptual skills as they apply to the activities of work teams in organizations.

Exercise Background

Business organizations, of course, don't have a monopoly on effective groups. Basketball teams and military squadrons are teams, as is a government policy group such as the president's cabinet, the leadership of a church or civic organization, or even a student committee.

Exercise Task

1. Use online resources to identify an example of a real-life team. Be sure to choose one that meets two criteria:

(a) it's not part of a for-profit business and **(b)** you can argue that it's highly effective.

2. Determine the reasons for the team's effectiveness. (*Hint:* You might look for websites sponsored by the group itself, review online news sources for current articles about it, or enter the group name in a search engine.) Consider team characteristics and activities, such as role structures, norms, cohesiveness, and conflict management.

3. What can a manager learn from the characteristics and activities of this particular team? How might the factors that contribute to this team's success be adopted in a business setting?

BUILDING EFFECTIVE COMMUNICATION SKILLS

Exercise Overview

Communication skills refer not only to the ability to convey information and ideas to others but to handle information and ideas received from them. They're essential to effective teamwork because teams depend on the ability of members to send and receive information that's accurate. This exercise invites you to play a game designed to demonstrate how good communication skills can lead to improved teamwork and team performance.

Exercise Background

You'll play this game in three separate rounds. In round 1, you're on your own. In round 2, you'll work in a small group and share information. You'll also work in a small group in

round 3, but this time, you'll have the additional benefit of some suggestions for improving the group's performance. Typically, students find that performance improves over the course of the three rounds. In particular, they find that creativity is enhanced when information is shared.

Exercise Task

1. Play the "Name Game" that your professor will explain to you. In round 1, work out your answers individually and then report your individual score to the class.

2. For round 2, you'll join a group of three to five students. Work out your answers together and write your group answers on a single sheet of paper. Now allow each group member to look at the answer sheet. If you can do so without being overheard by other groups, have each group member whisper the answers on the sheet to the group. Report your group score to the class.

3. Your professor will then ask the highest-performing individuals and groups to share their methods with the class. At this point, your professor will make some suggestions. Be sure to consider at least two strategies for improving your score.

4. Now play round 3, working together in the same small groups in which you participated in round 2. Report your group scores to the class.

5. Did average group scores improve upon average individual scores? Why or why not?

6. Did average group scores improve after methods for improvement were discussed at the end of round 2? Why or why not?

7. What has this game taught you about teamwork and effectiveness? Share your thoughts with the class.

SKILL-BUILDING PERSONAL ASSESSMENT

Using Teams

Introduction: The use of groups and teams is becoming more common in organizations throughout the world. The following assessment surveys your beliefs about the effective use of teams in work organizations.

Instructions: You will agree with some of the statements and disagree with others. In some cases you may find making a decision difficult, but you should force yourself to make a choice. Record your answers next to each statement according to the following scale:

Rating Scale

4 Strongly agree

3 Somewhat agree

2 Somewhat disagree

1 Strongly disagree

1. _____ Each person in a work team should have a clear assignment so that individual accountability can be maintained.

2. _____ For a team to function effectively, the team must be given complete authority over all aspects of the task.

3. _____ One way to get teams to work is simply to assemble a group of people, tell them in general what needs to be done, and let them work out the details.

4. _____ Once a team gets going, management can turn its attention to other matters.

5. _____ To ensure that a team develops into a cohesive working unit, managers should be especially careful not to intervene in any way during the initial startup period.

6. _____ Training is not critical to a team because the team will develop any needed skills on its own.

7. _____ It's easy to provide teams with the support they need because they are basically self-motivating.

8. _____ Teams need little or no structure to function effectively.

9. _____ Teams should set their own direction, with managers determining the means to the selected end.

10. _____ Teams can be used in any organization.

Scoring: Judging on the basis of research conducted by J. Richard Hackman and others, all the statements are false.

1. An emphasis on individual accountability essentially undermines any effort to develop a team.

2. Complete authority is likely to lead to anarchy. Limits should be set.

3. Teams should be kept small, should have clear boundaries, and should have an enabling structure that ensures member motivation.

4. Teams need coaching, counseling, and support at certain intervals during their functioning.

5. The start-up period is critical, which is why managers must spend time and energy coaching and counseling the team during this period. Once the team gets going, the manager should pull back until the team reaches a natural break or completes a performance cycle.

6. Training is absolutely critical and should be done before the team is assembled or shortly thereafter. If the needed skills and knowledge change, management should be ready to assist in training to help the team learn the new skills and acquire the new knowledge quickly.

7. Providing support for teams is difficult. A reward system must recognize and reinforce team performance, an educational system must provide needed skills and knowledge, an information system must provide necessary information, and physical and fiscal resources must be available as needed.

8. Teams need some structure to work effectively.

9. The opposite is true. Managers should set the direction and establish wide limits on constraints, whereas the means to the end should be determined by the team.

10. Teams cannot effectively be used in organizations that have strong individualistic cultures.

Source: *Test adapted from J. Richard Hackman, ed.,* Groups That Work (and Those That Don't) (*San Francisco: Jossey-Bass, 1990),* pp. 493–504.

MANAGEMENT AT WORK
Promoting the Cause of Diversity

"The findings are clear: for groups that value innovation and new ideas, diversity helps."
—Katherine W. Phillips, Former Professor at Columbia University Business School

In a review of the research on workplace diversity, Beryl Nelson, a former software-engineering manager at Google, referred to several studies showing that teams "whose members are heterogeneous"—diverse—"have a higher potential for innovation than teams whose members are homogeneous." According to Nelson, "diverse teams are more effective" in two key respects: "They produce better financial results and results in innovation." She cites, for example, the financial benefits to companies at which women serve in senior positions: Companies in the top quartile—those ranking better than 75 percent of all companies—enjoyed 41 percent greater return on equity and 56 percent greater earnings before taxes. Among companies with at least three women on their boards of directors, return on equity was 16.7 percent, as opposed to an average of 11.5 percent; return on sales was 16.8 percent, as opposed to an average of 11.5 percent.

Racial diversity also has significant benefits: Studies show that greater racial diversity corresponds to better results in market share, sales revenue, and profits. A study of 366 companies by the consulting firm McKinsey & Co., for example, reveals that for every 10 percent increase in racial diversity among senior executive teams, earnings before taxes increased by 0.8 percent.

Research also indicates that the presence of women contributes to the "collective intelligence and creativity" of teams—and thus to their potential for innovation. One study divided participants into teams of three to five members and assigned each team tasks involving brainstorming, decision making, and problem solving. Individual intelligence tests were given beforehand and used to ensure intellectual equality among teams, which were given collective intelligence scores after they had performed their assigned tasks. There was only one predictor of collective intelligence: the presence of women on a team. All the high-scoring teams

were composed of about 50 percent women, while all groups with less gender mix had lower scores. Why did women make a difference? The researchers concluded that higher-scoring teams did a better job of applying the contributions of all members because they displayed better social skills—skills on which, according to additional research, women tend to score more highly.

Note, however, that this study was based on small groups. When we're talking about organizations, as opposed to teams, we're talking about much larger groups, and this difference has an important implication for the study of workplace diversity. One research team, for instance, looked at the top firms on the Standard & Poor's Composite 1500 list in order to see if there was a relationship between the makeup of their top-management teams and their financial results. The researchers concluded that "female representation in top management leads to an increase of $42 million in firm value." Another team analyzed eight years of employee survey data provided by a company with more than 60 offices worldwide. They found that by shifting from an all-male or all-female staff to a staff split 50–50 by gender, an office could increase revenue by 41 percent.

Obviously, large-scale studies like these also suggest a correspondence between greater diversity and better financial performance. But as Katherine W. Phillips, formerly of the Columbia University Business School, pointed out, large-scale studies "show only that diversity is *correlated* with better performance, not that it *causes* better performance." Two things may *correlate* with one another simply because we find some reason to associate them, but it doesn't mean that one necessarily causes the other. Nelson acknowledged the same drawback in studies of workplace diversity. Many studies, she reminds us, "show a correlation between diverse organizational composition, financial success, and innovation" but demonstrate no "clear causal relationship between diversity and success."

Before going any further, we need to understand what the issue is. The problem has to do with the kinds of conclusions that can be drawn from what Phillips calls "large data-set studies," which involve so many variables that it's difficult to isolate those that indicate cause and effect from those that indicate mere correlation. A firm that enjoys a 41 percent greater return on equity than comparable companies may have given itself a competitive advantage by putting more women in senior positions, but it clearly has additional competitive advantages as well.

Because there are fewer variables involved in smaller-scale studies of teams (as opposed to larger organizations), these studies may reveal a causal relationship that might also be present in larger groups. Phillips thus recommends closer analysis of "diversity in small groups" as a valid means of focusing on possible cause-and-effect relationships between diversity and performance. In fact, she says, "the findings are clear: for groups that value innovation and new ideas, diversity helps."

Phillips cites a study in which she teamed with fellow researchers "to examine the impact of racial diversity on small decision-making groups." The team assembled three-person groups with two different racial compositions—all white and two white members plus one nonwhite member. Each group had to solve a murder mystery. All groups shared certain common information, but individual members were given important clues that only he or she knew. In order to solve the mystery, each group had to share all of its collective information, including the clues known only to one member. "The groups with racial diversity," reports Phillips, "significantly outperformed the groups with no racial diversity." Why? The researchers concluded that members teamed with "similar others" tended to assume that everyone shared the same information and the same perspective. As a result, all-white groups were less diligent in processing all of their available information—a sure hindrance to creativity and innovation.

Phillips also cites a study designed "to examine the influence of racial and opinion composition in small-group discussions." Groups were given 15 minutes to discuss some relevant social issue (e.g., the death penalty). The researchers created a dissenting opinion on each issue and had one group member present it as part of the discussion. Phillips reports that

> *when a black person presented a dissenting perspective to a group of whites, the perspective was perceived as more novel and led to broader thinking and consideration of alternatives than when a white person introduced* that same dissenting perspective. The *lesson: when we hear dissent from someone who is different from us, it provokes more thought than when it comes from someone who looks like us.*

Roy Y. J. Chua, an organizational behavior specialist at Harvard, has studied a specific kind of workplace team—multicultural teams. He has found that, for certain types of tasks, culturally diverse teams exhibit greater creativity, mainly because cultural diversity supplies "unique access to a range of knowledge systems." Chua has also discovered, however, that

"it's inevitable to have conflict when you bring people from different cultural backgrounds together." Neither teams nor organizations are more creative when the organization suffers from what Chua calls "ambient cultural disharmony"—the effect on individuals and groups of cultural conflict in an organizational environment. If people perceive diversity as a source of conflict, says Chua, they tend to "shut down the search for connections involving ideas from different cultures" and thus miss opportunities for creativity and innovation afforded by diversity of ideas and information.[43]

Case Questions

1. According to Katherine W. Phillips,

   Research has shown that social diversity in a group can cause discomfort, rougher interactions, a lack of trust, greater perceived interpersonal conflict, lower communication, less cohesion, more concern about disrespect, and other problems. So what is the upside?

   Provide a cogent answer to Phillips's closing question—that is, one that reflects what you've learned about diversity, group dynamics, workplace teams, and creativity /innovation.

2. Discuss the pros and cons of socially diverse teams in terms of *behavioral norms*. What, for example, is likely to be the extent of *norm variation* in a diverse team? What sorts of variations are likely to affect team performance? How might group leaders deal with such variations? How might they manage variations to the team's benefit? To what extent should group leaders encourage *norm conformity*? What steps can leaders take to encourage conformity?

3. Among "Challenges Faced by Diverse Teams," Beryl Nelson include *unconscious bias* and *stereotype threat*. We define *stereotyping* in Chapter 14 as "the process of categorizing people on the basis of a single attribute." Nelson explains that stereotypes

   are learned through cultural messages and stories, comments from family and friends, portrayals in the media, and so forth. Despite our best intentions, they can bias our impressions of, and affect our actions toward, others in our environment. . . . They shape our expectations of what people should be doing, especially at work. . . . The stereotypes especially relevant in work situations include not only those characteristics that are visible, such as sex, race, weight, and age, but also those not visible but relatively easy to discern, such as educational background and nationality.[†]

   Nelson also points out that "almost everyone has measurable biases." An ongoing test conducted by Harvard's Project Implicit has found, for example, that

70–80 percent of all participants have a bias against women in technology. Findings such as those by Project Implicit indicate the *stereotype threat* to teams composed of diverse members.

First, explain various ways in which *stereotype threat* can keep a diverse team from being as effective as it could be.

Second, suggest a few strategies that group and organizational leaders can take to reduce stereotype threat.

Finally, think about your own biases: What biases do you harbor about women (e.g., they don't have an aptitude for math)? About men (e.g., they aren't altruistic or eager to help others)? What biases do you harbor about Asians, African Americans, Hispanics, and older people? Bear in mind, by the way, that even people who are subject to a given bias can actually share it.[‡]

4. *Beware of lurking variables.* In the following two examples, cause-and-effect conclusions have been drawn from evidence of correlation. In each case, the conclusion is false because there is a so-called "lurking variable"—an unstated third variable that affects *both* causes of the correlation. Identify a *probable*

lurking variable in each example and explain why each conclusion is false.

a. When ice cream sales increase, drowning deaths also increase. Therefore, ice cream consumption causes drowning.

b. A great many people who sleep with their shoes on often wake up with headaches. Therefore, sleeping with one's shoes on causes headaches.

In the next two examples, matters are complicated because the correlation may work both ways. First, provide both *yes* and *no* answers to the question posed by each statement. Next, identify a *probable* lurking variable in each case and explain why both *yes* and *no* answers are *likely* to be false.

c. Surveys show that workers who say that they're happy with their jobs tend to be quite productive. Does being happy cause workers to be more productive?

d. Surveys show that couples who live together before marriage have a higher rate of divorce than couples who don't live together before marriage. Does living together cause divorce?

An Open Invitation to Innovation

1. How good are you at "thinking outside the box"? Are you fixated on functionality? Try solving the following problem before googling the solution.

You have the three items pictured here: a book of matches, a box of thumbtacks, and a candle.

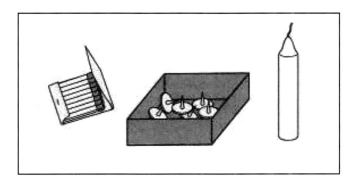

How can you attach the candle to a wall so that, when it's lit, wax doesn't drip on the floor?[†]

2. Explain the advantages and disadvantages of open innovation and multidisciplinary collaboration in

terms of team *cohesion*. What aspects of such teams, for example, may increase cohesiveness? Which aspects may reduce cohesiveness?

3. Consider teams formed for multidisciplinary collaboration or as a result of open innovation in terms of *role structure*. Is role structure, for example, likely to be set or to evolve differently than it usually does in internal functional or task groups? How might the transmission of *sent roles* be more complicated? Is *role ambiguity* likely to be more prevalent? How about *role conflict* (in particular, *intrarole conflict*)?

4. Gratton and Erickson describe two *leadership styles* among leaders of multidisciplinary teams:

- *Relationship-oriented leaders* tend to foster "an environment of trust and goodwill in which people are more likely to share knowledge";
- *Task-oriented leaders* help "to make objectives clear, to create a shared awareness of the dimensions of the task, and to provide monitoring and feedback."

First of all, ask yourself which of these two leadership styles you're more comfortable with. In other words, if you were assigned to lead a team, which leadership style would you probably bring to the task?

Now assume that you have been assigned to lead a team of fellow students in drafting a proposed curriculum of required courses for freshmen and sophomores at your college. Naturally, the team consists of students with a broad range of majors. What will probably be your strengths as leader of your group? What will probably be your weaknesses?

Finally, in trying to determine which style—relationship or task oriented—was most effective in leading collaborative teams, Gratton and Erickson concluded that

an emphasis throughout a project on one style at the expense of the other inevitably hindered the long-term performance of the team. . . . The most productive, innovative teams were typically led by people who were both task and relationship oriented. What's more, these leaders changed their style during the project.

Under what circumstances will you most likely have to change your leadership style in order to keep the group working effectively? Try to be specific in identifying circumstances that might arise over the course of your team project. What do you need to do in order to adjust your style to shifting circumstances?

1. Remove the tacks from the box.
2. Tack the box to the wall.
3. Put the candle in the box.
4. Light the candle.

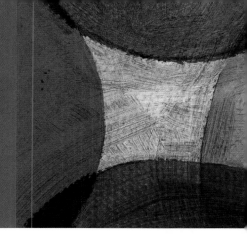

CHAPTER 14

Basic Elements of Control

Learning Outcomes

After studying this chapter, you should be able to:

14-1 Explain the purpose of control, including different types of control and the steps in the control process.

14-2 Identify the three forms of operations control.

14-3 Describe budgets and other tools for financial control.

14-4 Distinguish between two opposing forms of structural control.

14-5 Discuss the relationship between strategy and control, including international strategic control.

14-6 Identify characteristics of effective control including why people resist control and how managers can overcome this resistance.

As we discussed in Chapter 1, control is one of the four basic managerial functions that provide the organizing framework for this book. This is the first of two chapters devoted to this important area. In the first section of the chapter we explain the purpose of control. We then look at types of control and the steps in the control process. The rest of the chapter examines the four levels of control that most organizations must employ to remain effective: operations, financial, structural, and strategic control. We conclude by discussing the characteristics of effective control, noting why some people resist control and describing what organizations can do to overcome this resistance. Let's start by looking at how control is used at one popular restaurant chain.

Management in Action

Controlling the Cheesecakes

"[Cheesecake managers are] scanning the screens for a station stacking up red flags, indicating orders past the target time, and deciding whether to give the cooks at the station a nudge or an extra pair of hands. . . ."

—Atul Gawande, Popular Writer

In 1972, Evelyn and Oscar Overton took the last of their savings and moved from their home in Detroit, Michigan, to Los Angeles, California, to try their hand, one last time, to create a growing entrepreneurial venture. Evelyn had been selling cheesecakes from a small setup in her basement for almost 30 years, but the business never really took off. Still, she dreamed of something bigger. But it was their son David who finally made that dream come true when

Eric Glenn/Shutterstock.com

he opened a little shop in Beverly Hills in 1978 showcasing his mom's products. On opening day, confident that the store would be a huge success, he decided to open after the lunch crowd. A line formed at the door at 2 o'clock and business has grown ever since. By 2019, The Cheesecake Factory had expanded to 360 restaurants throughout the world.

The Cheesecake Factory's current lunch and dinner menus include seafood, pasta, burgers, steaks, and more, designed to appeal to a broad audience, and most of the food is made from scratch. The only thing not made on-demand, ironically, is the cheesecake. The iconic dessert comes from the company's bakery division, which operates two bakery production facilities, one in Calabasas Hills, California, and one in Rocky Mount, North Carolina, that produce quality cheesecakes and other baked products for its restaurants, international licensees, and third-party bakery customers.

One of the strategic goals of The Cheesecake Factory is to provide a product that looks, tastes, and feels homemade, and so, despite the incredible volume of desserts it makes and sells, the company resists going to full automation in its operations. That's not to say that the operations of the bakery for the world-famous restaurant chain are in any way antiquated. Rather, the company has learned to be very selective in where, how, and why it applies new technologies. For instance, production managers use state-of-the-art inventory systems to label and track all items from raw materials to finished products, and the company has automated processes that make sense to automate, like mixing, baking, and freezing. But finishing is still done by hand.

In the restaurants themselves, kitchens are organized as a production line. Orders, accompanied by standardized recipes and images of how the dishes should look, appear on computer monitors above the food prep stations. Along the line the prep cooks chop vegetables, slice meat, and arrange seasonings while a timer counts down. Each order then moves down the line to the cooks. The cooks are responsible for cooking the food and finalizing the orders. Finally, each order is reviewed and quality-checked by a head cook before going out to the customer.

In the background, kitchen managers are also monitoring how efficient orders are being processed. For instance, each new order is supposed to move through the process according to predetermined times. If an order is taking too long to fill, a red flag pops up on a monitor. When they see these flags, managers might encourage the cook to work a bit faster, move some people around the kitchen to different stations, or step in themselves to help with a backlog.

The system is streamlined, efficient, and highly replicable across restaurants. Every Cheesecake Factory follows the same recipes and uses the same system, ensuring both quality of food and quality of service as well as consistent experiences for customers. In addition, the company uses data analytics to forecast not only how many guests to expect on a given night but also what they will likely order. This model allows each restaurant to order the right kinds and the right amount of ingredients and to have just the right number of staff on board.

Atul Gawande, a prominent surgeon and writer, published an article in *The New Yorker* that was a "behind-the-scenes" look at The Cheesecake Factory. The article praised how The Cheesecake Factory had created and maintained highly effective control systems and processes that kept the business on track without being overly bureaucratic or stifling to employees. The article also asked rhetorical questions about why his own industry, health care, couldn't seem to integrate some of the obvious operational efficiencies that the restaurant chain had implemented to combine both profit and service.

In addition to effective quality control, Atul noticed that "the managers monitored the pace, too—scanning the screens for a station stacking up red flags, indicating orders past the target time, and deciding whether to give the cooks at the station a nudge or an extra pair of hands. They watched for waste—wasted food, wasted time, wasted effort. The formula was Business 101: Use the right amount of goods and labor to deliver what customers want and no more. Anything more is waste, and waste is lost profit."

But The Cheesecake Factory isn't just all about efficiency and productivity. Evelyn Overton always claimed that her employees were her greatest asset. David now runs the business as CEO, and he has continued to follow that belief. Cheesecake Factory employees are paid above the industry average and also have benefits that are superior to those of most other restaurant chains. In addition, they can get reimbursed for education expenses and work flexible schedules. And there are clear career paths that can lead to advancement as chefs and as managers. Indeed, in 2020, *Fortune* magazine named The Cheesecake Factory one of the "100 Best Companies to Work For" for the seventh year in a row.[1]

14-1 THE NATURE OF CONTROL

control
The regulation of organizational activities in such a way as to facilitate goal attainment

Control is the regulation of organizational activities so that some targeted element of performance remains within acceptable limits. Without this regulation, organizations have no indication of how well they are performing in relation to their goals. Control, like a ship's rudder, keeps the organization moving in the proper direction. At any point in time, it compares where the organization is in terms of performance (financial, productive, or otherwise) to where it is supposed to be. Like a rudder, control provides an organization with a mechanism for adjusting its course if performance falls outside of acceptable boundaries. For example, FedEx has a performance goal of delivering 98 percent of its packages on time. If on-time deliveries fall below 98 percent, control systems will signal the problem to managers, so that they can make necessary adjustments in operations to regain the target level of performance.[2] An organization without effective control procedures is not likely to reach its goals—or, if it does reach them, to know that it has! Effective control became even more important during and in the aftermath of the 2020 COVID-19 pandemic. Economic pressures pushed many businesses to the brink of closing and only a tighter focus on control allowed some of them to keep their doors open.

14-1a The Purpose of Control

As Figure 14.1 illustrates, control provides an organization with ways to adapt to environmental change, to limit the accumulation of error, to cope with organizational complexity, and to minimize costs. These four functions of control are worth a closer look.

Adapting to Environmental Change In today's complex and turbulent business environment, all organizations must contend with change.[3] If managers could establish goals and achieve them instantaneously, control would not be needed. But between the time a goal is established and the time it is reached, many things can happen in the organization and its environment to disrupt movement toward the goal—or even to change the goal itself. A properly designed control system can help managers anticipate, monitor, and respond to changing circumstances.[4] In contrast, an improperly designed system can result in organizational performance that falls far below acceptable levels.

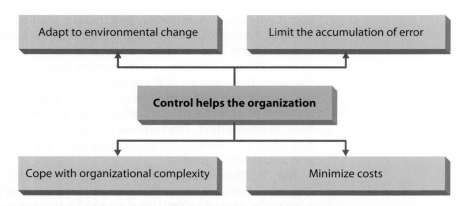

FIGURE 14.1

The Purpose of Control

Control is one of the four basic management functions in organizations. The control function, in turn, has four basic purposes. Properly designed control systems can fulfill each of these purposes.

For example, Michigan-based Metalloy, a 65-year-old, family-run metal-casting company, signed a contract to make engine-seal castings for NOK, a big Japanese auto parts maker. Metalloy was pleased when its first 5,000-unit production run yielded 4,985 acceptable castings and only 15 defective ones. NOK, however, was quite unhappy with this performance and insisted that Metalloy raise its standards. In short, global quality standards in most industries are such that customers demand near-perfection from their suppliers. A properly designed control system can help managers like those at Metalloy stay better attuned to rising standards.

Limiting the Accumulation of Error   Small mistakes and errors do not often seriously damage the financial health of an organization. Over time, however, small errors may accumulate and become very serious. For example, Whistler Corporation, a large radar detector manufacturer, was once faced with such rapidly escalating demand that quality essentially became irrelevant. The defect rate rose from 4 percent to 9 percent to 15 percent and eventually reached 25 percent. One day, a manager realized that 100 of the plant's 250 employees were spending all their time fixing defective units and that $2 million worth of inventory was awaiting repair. Had the company adequately controlled quality as it responded to increased demand, the problem would never have reached such proportions. Similarly, a routine quality control inspection of an early prototype of Boeing's 787 Dreamliner revealed that a fastener had not been installed correctly. Closer scrutiny then revealed that literally thousands of fasteners had been installed wrong in every plane under construction at the time. As a result, the entire project was delayed several months. If the inspection process had been more rigorous to begin with, the error would likely have been found and corrected much earlier, rather than continuing to accumulate and grow into a major problem for Boeing.[5]

Coping with Organizational Complexity   When a firm purchases only one raw material, produces one product, has a simple organization design, and enjoys constant demand for its product, its managers can maintain control with a very basic and simple system. But a business that produces many products from myriad raw materials and has a large market area, a complicated organization design, and many competitors needs a sophisticated system to maintain adequate control. When large firms merge, the short-term results are often disappointing. The typical reason for this is that the new enterprise is so large and complex that the existing control systems are simply inadequate. HP and Compaq Computer faced just this problem when HP acquired Compaq and had to address myriad issues to transform the two firms into one. Similarly, when American Airlines and US Airways merged, the entire process took over two years, in large part because of the complexity of each firm.

Minimizing Costs   When it is practiced effectively, control can also help reduce costs and boost output. For example, Georgia-Pacific Corporation, a large wood-products company, learned of a new technology that could be used to make thinner blades for its saws. The firm's control system was used to calculate the amount of wood that could be saved from each cut made by the thinner blades relative to the costs used to replace the existing blades. The results have been impressive—the wood that is saved annually by the new blades each year fills 800 rail cars. As Georgia-Pacific discovered, effective control systems can eliminate waste, lower labor costs, and improve output per unit of input. Starbucks recently instructed its coffee shops to stop automatically brewing decaffeinated coffee after lunch. Sales of decaf plummet after lunch, and Starbucks realized that baristas were simply pouring most of it down the drain when it became stale. Now, between noon and early evening they brew decaf only by the cup and only when a customer orders it.[6] A Cadbury chewing gum factory located in Taiwan significantly lowered its operating expenses through the simple replacement of its dehumidifier. Moisture and temperature control are critical to the gum manufacturing process, so Cadbury adopted the new dehumidifying system to reduce these costs. With the system, Cadbury reduced its energy usage by 60 percent and its operating expenses by 50 percent.[7] Similarly, many businesses are cutting back on everything from employee health insurance coverage to overnight shipping to business lunches for clients in their quest to lower costs.[8]

14-1b Types of Control

The examples of control given thus far have illustrated the regulation of several organizational activities, from producing quality products to coordinating complex organizations. Organizations practice control in a number of different areas and at different levels, and the responsibility for managing control is widespread.

Areas of Control   Control can focus on any area of an organization. Most organizations approach areas of control in terms of the four basic types of resources they use: physical, human, information, and financial.[9] Control of physical resources includes inventory management (stocking neither too few nor too many units in inventory), quality control (maintaining appropriate levels of output quality), and equipment control (maintaining the necessary facilities and machinery). Control of human resources includes selection and placement, training and development, performance appraisal, and compensation. Relatedly, organizations also try to control the behavior of their employees—directing them toward higher performance, for example, and away from unethical behaviors.[10] Control of information resources includes sales and marketing forecasting, environmental analysis, public relations, production scheduling, and economic forecasting.[11] Financial control involves managing the organization's debt so that it does not become excessive, ensuring that the firm always has enough cash on hand to meet its obligations but does not have excess cash in an idle account, and that receivables are collected and bills are paid on a timely basis.

In many ways, the control of financial resources is the most important area because financial resources are related to the control of all the other resources in an organization. Too much inventory leads to storage costs; poor selection of personnel leads to termination and rehiring expenses; inaccurate sales forecasts lead to disruptions in cash flows and other financial effects. Financial issues tend to pervade most control-related activities.

Levels of Control   Just as control can be broken down by area, Figure 14.2 shows that it can also be broken down by level within the organizational system. Operations control focuses on the processes the organization uses to transform resources into products or services.[12] Quality control is one type of operations control. Financial control is concerned with the organization's financial resources. Monitoring receivables to make sure customers are paying their bills on time is an example of financial control. Structural control is concerned with how the elements of the organization's structure are serving their intended purpose. Monitoring the administrative ratio to make sure staff expenses do not become excessive is an example of structural control. Finally, strategic control focuses on how effectively the organization's

---

operations control
Focuses on the processes the organization uses to transform resources into products or services

financial control
Concerned with the organization's financial resources

structural control
Concerned with how the elements of the organization's structure are serving their intended purpose

strategic control
Focuses on how effectively the organization's strategies are succeeding in helping the organization meet its goals

FIGURE 14.2

Levels of Control

Managers use control at several different levels. The most basic levels of control in organizations are strategic, structural, operations, and financial control. Each level must be managed properly if control is to be most effective.

corporate, business, and functional strategies are succeeding in helping the organization meet its goals. For example, if a corporation has been unsuccessful in implementing its strategy of related diversification, its managers need to identify the reasons and either change the strategy or renew their efforts to implement it. We discuss these four levels of control more fully later in this chapter.

controller
A position in organizations that helps line managers with their control activities

Responsibilities of Control Traditionally, managers have been responsible for overseeing the wide array of control systems and concerns in organizations. They decide which types of control the organization will use, and they implement control systems and take actions based on the information provided by control systems. Thus, ultimate responsibility for control rests with all managers throughout an organization.

Most larger organizations also have one or more specialized managerial positions called *controllers*. A **controller** is responsible for helping line managers with their control activities, for coordinating the organization's overall control system, and for gathering and assimilating relevant information. Many businesses that use an H-form or M-form organization design have several controllers: one for the corporation and one for each division. The job of controller is especially important in organizations where control systems are complex.[13]

In addition, some organizations also use operating employees to help maintain effective control. Indeed, employee participation is often used as a vehicle for allowing operating employees an opportunity to help facilitate organizational effectiveness. For example, Whistler Corporation increased employee participation in an effort to turn its quality problems around. As a starting point, the quality control unit, formerly responsible for checking product quality at the end of the

Often issues can be found in a workplace where employees perceive their manager's control measures to be unreasonable. In this photo an unhappy manager chastises his subordinates over a minor dip in sales. The employees are trying to explain, with not much success, that recent harsh winter conditions negatively affected customers' shopping patterns.

imtmphoto/Shutterstock.com

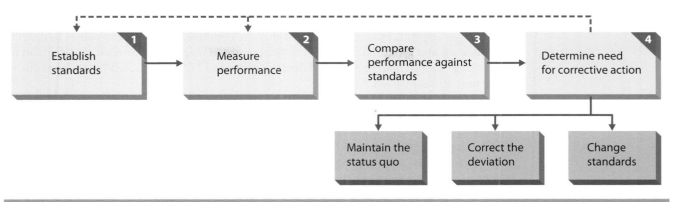

FIGURE 14.3

Steps In The Control Process

Having an effective control system can help ensure that an organization achieves its goals. Implementing a control system, however, is a systematic process that generally proceeds through four interrelated steps.

assembly process, was eliminated. Next, all operating employees were encouraged to check their own work and told that they would be responsible for correcting their own errors. As a result, Whistler eliminated its quality problems and regained profitability.

14-1c Steps in the Control Process

Regardless of the types or levels of control systems an organization needs, there are four fundamental steps in any control process.[14] These are illustrated in Figure 14.3.

Establishing Standards   The first step in the control process is establishing standards. A **control standard** is a target against which subsequent performance will be compared.[15] Employees at a Taco Bell fast-food restaurant, for example, work toward the following service standards:

control standard

A target against which subsequent performance will be compared

1. A minimum of 95 percent of all customers will be greeted within three minutes of their arrival.
2. Preheated tortilla chips will not sit in the warmer more than 30 minutes before they are served to customers or discarded.
3. Empty tables will be cleaned within five minutes after being vacated.

Standards established for control purposes should be expressed in measurable terms. Note that standard 1 above has a time limit of three minutes and an objective target of 95 percent of all customers. In standard 3, the objective target of "all" empty tables is implied.

Control standards should also be consistent with the organization's goals. Taco Bell has organizational goals involving customer service, food quality, and restaurant cleanliness. A control standard for a retailer like Home Depot should be consistent with its goal of increasing its annual sales volume by 25 percent within five years. A hospital trying to shorten the average hospital stay for a patient will have control standards that reflect current averages. A university reaffirming its commitment to academics might adopt a standard of graduating 80 percent of its student athletes within five years of their enrollment. Control standards can be as narrow or as broad as the level of activity to which they apply and must follow logically from

When Boeing and Airbus are assembling airplanes, their managers establish an array of control standards and performance indicators. Maintaining effective control is especially important for massive projects such as these.

Katrina Brown/Shutterstock.com

organizational goals and objectives. When Airbus introduced the A380, the world's largest passenger airplane, managers indicated that the firm needed to ship 270 planes in order to break even and set a goal of delivering 18 per year. Managers also forecast that demand for very large aircraft like the A380 and Boeing's revamped 747 would exceed 1,200 planes during the next 20-year period.[16]

A final aspect of establishing standards is to identify performance indicators. Performance indicators are measures of performance that provide information that is directly relevant to what is being controlled. For example, suppose an organization is following a tight schedule in building a new plant. Relevant performance indicators could be buying a site, selecting a building contractor, and ordering equipment. Monthly sales increases are not, however, directly relevant. On the other hand, if control is being focused on revenue, monthly sales increases are relevant, whereas buying land for a new plant is less relevant.

Measuring Performance   The second step in the control process is measuring performance. Performance measurement is a constant, ongoing activity for most organizations. For control to be effective, performance measures must be valid. Daily, weekly, and monthly sales figures measure sales performance, and production performance may be expressed in terms of unit cost, product quality, or volume produced. Employees' performance is often measured in terms of quality or quantity of output, but for many jobs, measuring performance is not so straightforward.

A research and development scientist at Merck, for example, may spend years working on a single project before achieving a breakthrough. A manager who takes over a business on the brink of failure may need months or even years to turn things around. Valid performance measurement, however difficult to obtain, is nevertheless vital in maintaining effective control, and performance indicators can usually be developed. The scientist's progress, for example, may be partially assessed by peer review, and the manager's success may be evaluated by her ability to convince creditors that she will eventually be able to restore profitability. As Airbus completed the design and manufacture of its A380 jumbo jet, managers recognized that delays and cost overruns had changed its breakeven point. New calculations indicated that the company would need to sell 420 planes before it would become profitable. Its annual sales, of course, remained relatively easy to measure.

Comparing Performance Against Standards   The third step in the control process is comparing measured performance against established standards. Performance may be higher than, lower than, or identical to the standard. In some cases comparison is easy. The goal of each product manager at General Electric is to make the product either number one or number two (on the basis of total sales) in its market. Because this standard is clear and total sales are easy to calculate, it is relatively simple to determine whether this standard has been met. Sometimes, however, comparisons are less clear-cut. If performance is lower than expected, the question is how much deviation from standards to allow before taking remedial action. For example, is increasing sales by 7.9 percent when the standard was 8 percent close enough?

Taking corrective action is a critical part of the control process. For example, as the end of a sales season approaches most retailers start to cut prices in order to clear inventory. Few people will be looking for sweaters in May (because it's getting warmer) or swimsuits in October (because it's getting cooler). But they may buy these items anyway if the prices are reduced. This helps the retailer control inventory costs.

The timetable for comparing performance to standards depends on a variety of factors, including the importance and complexity of what is being controlled. For longer-run and higher-level standards, annual comparisons may be appropriate. In other circumstances, more frequent comparisons are necessary. For example, a business with a severe cash shortage may need to monitor its on-hand cash reserves daily. In its first year of production, Airbus did indeed deliver 18 A380s, just as it had forecast. The *Beyond Traditional Business* feature provides other insights into the control process in the nonprofit sector.

Considering Corrective Action   The final step in the control process is determining the need for corrective action. Decisions regarding corrective action draw heavily on a manager's analytic and diagnostic skills. For example, as health care costs have risen, many firms have sought ways to keep their own expenses in check. Some have reduced benefits; others have opted to pass on higher costs to their employees.[17]

After comparing performance against control standards, one of three actions is appropriate: maintain the status quo (do nothing), correct the deviation, or change the standards. Maintaining the status quo is preferable when performance essentially matches the standards, but it is more likely that some action will be needed to correct a deviation from the standards.

Sometimes, performance that is higher than expected may also cause problems for organizations. For example, when highly anticipated new video games or game systems are first introduced, the demand may be so strong that customers are placed on waiting lists. And even some people who are among the first to purchase such products immediately turn around and list them for sale on eBay for an inflated price. The manufacturer may be unable to increase production in the short term, though, and also knows that demand will eventually drop. At the same time, however, the firm would not want to alienate potential customers. Consequently, it may decide to simply reduce its advertising. This may curtail demand a bit and limit customer frustration.

Changing an established standard is usually necessary if it was set too high or too low at the outset. This is apparent if large numbers of employees routinely beat the standard by a wide margin or if no employees ever meet the standard. Also, standards that seemed perfectly appropriate when they were established may need to be adjusted because circumstances have since changed.

As the 2007–2009 global recession began to take its toll, two major Airbus customers, Qantas and Emirates, indicated that they needed to defer delivery of some previously ordered A380s. As a result, Airbus found it necessary to reduce its production in 2009 from 18 to only 14. In the years that followed, international air travel patterns changed and demand for new, somewhat smaller, and much more fuel-efficient airplanes began to surge. At the same time, demand for the A380 dropped steadily and more and more customers cancelled or delayed orders. Finally, in 2020, Airbus announced that it would cease production of the giant aircraft altogether. The plane had never become profitable.

Carolyn Franks/Shutterstock.com

Retailers often close underperforming stores like this one as part of the control process. This falls under the step of taking corrective action if a particular location is not meeting revenue expectations and the company cannot identify a way to turn things around.

"Closing underperforming stores is a natural part of business of any smart retailer."

—Maria Sceppaguerico, Spokesperson for Ann Taylor

BEYOND TRADITIONAL BUSINESS

The Intelligent Way to Run a Nonprofit

Opportunity International Network (OI) is a nonprofit specializing in *microfinance*—the practice of making small loans (about $200 on average) to help poor clients in developing countries start up small businesses. Back in 2005, OI's focus was on the victims of a tsunami that struck South Asia in December 2004, killing more than a quarter of a million people and devastating local economies. OI planned to add 10,000 clients in Indonesia and 20,000 in India. Meanwhile, the organization was also committed to adding 11,000 clients in AIDS-ravaged Africa. It also intended to increase its client base from 675,000 to 2 million in the next five years.

Needless to say, the addition of so many loans would entail a lot of additional record keeping, and OI's overtaxed IT system was inadequate to the task of managing the extra data. Former CEO Larry Reed admitted that "when you have a loan for $200 that's paid back [a few dollars] weekly, [and it takes] three months before you find out the loan is late, you're behind the curve.... The ability to manage information—especially to track what's happening with clients [in South Asia]—is very important for us to ramp up the program there."

So OI took steps to gain more control over its data-management process as it was planning to grow. Key to the project was the assistance of Hyperion Solutions Corp., a California-based company specializing in software for *business performance management*—technology-supported processes for measuring an organization's performance against its strategic goals. Hyperion donated $250,000 worth of tools and services to enhance OI's ability to consolidate and analyze data from various sources, put the resulting information to work in carrying out strategic initiatives, and then measure the success of those initiatives. OI, for example, was able to develop a program for measuring the impact of its initiatives on the lives of its clients and their children.

OI was perhaps ahead of the curve in adopting programs that now tend to fall under the heading of *business intelligence (BI)*—software programming that helps organizations evaluate their activities by using various specialized tools, including reporting applications. BI can be particularly valuable to nonprofit organizations, which have traditionally focused their reporting efforts on such broad, strictly quantitative data as number of people served and number of dollars raised.

Today, however, nonprofit decision makers need to evaluate a much wider range of information. Let's say, for example, that a nonprofit sponsors an event through social media. The event may attract a lot of participants (easily quantifiable data), but what the organization really needs to know is whether event participation actually translated into successful fund-raising. If so, what social media and which social-media message was most effective? Are there any strategic lessons for the future to be learned from the answers to these questions?

Nurse-Family Partnerships (NFP), for example, is a nonprofit that arranges for registered nurses to make regular home visits to low-income first-time mothers. For the last ten years, NFP has used Efforts to Outcomes (ETO) BI software to monitor and report program performance. The application tracks program outcomes by sorting thousands of data points for the development of each mother and child. It also permits NFP to monitor numbers of in-person visits and nurses' caseloads and compare the data to evidence-based benchmarks. Ultimately, NFP's BI process not only allows it to monitor program outcomes but to report those outcomes more effectively to its stakeholders, thereby enhancing its ability to secure the funding necessary to maintain programs and outcome levels.

References: Heather Havenstein, "BI Tools Help Nonprofit Make Loans to Tsunami Victims," *Computerworld*, March 11, 2005, www.computerworld.com on June 1, 2020; B. J. Cortis, "Business Intelligence Can Drive Nonprofit Sector Decision Making," *Philanthropy Journal*, June 24, 2013, http://philanthropyjournal.blogspot.com on June 1, 2020; Social Solutions Inc., "Customer Case Study: Nurse Family Partnership" (n.d.), www.socialsolutions.com on June 1, 2020; Gil Al louche, "Five Non-profits Using Big Data to Measure and Improve Effectiveness," *BI Insight*, http://businessintelligence.com on June 1, 2020.

Manager's Checklist

☐ All managers should understand the basic purposes of control used in organizations.

☐ Managers need to also be familiar with the various types of control.

☐ You should also know the essential steps in the control process.

---

operations control
Focuses on the processes the organization uses to transform resources into products or services

14-2 OPERATIONS CONTROL

One of the four levels of control practiced by most organizations, **operations control**, is concerned with the processes the organization uses to transform resources into products or services. As Figure 14.4 shows, the three forms of operations control—preliminary, screening,

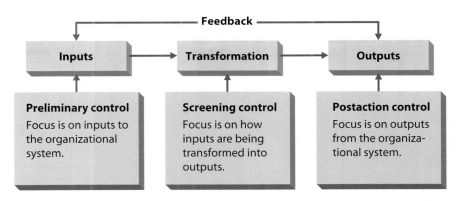

FIGURE 14.4

Forms of Operations Control

Most organizations develop multiple control systems that incorporate all three basic forms of control. For example, the publishing company that produced this book screens inputs by hiring only qualified employees, typesetters, and printers (preliminary control). In addition, quality is checked during the transformation process, such as after the manuscript is typeset (screening control), and the outputs—printed and bound books—are checked before they are shipped from the bindery (postaction control). The same types of control systems are employed in the development of the company's digital products and solutions.

and postaction—occur at different points in relation to the transformation processes used by the organization.

14-2a Preliminary Control

preliminary control
Attempts to monitor the quality or quantity of financial, physical, human, and information resources before they actually become part of the system

Preliminary control concentrates on the resources—financial, material, human, and information—the organization brings in from the environment. Preliminary control attempts to monitor the quality or quantity of these resources before they enter the organization. Firms like PepsiCo and General Mills hire only college graduates for their management training programs, and even then only after applicants satisfy several interviewers and selection criteria. In this way, they control the quality of the human resources entering the organization. When Kroger contracts with other companies to make private-label products to be sold in its stores, it specifies rigid standards of quality, thereby controlling physical inputs. Organizations also control financial and information resources. For example, privately held companies like SAS Institute and Mars limit the extent to which outsiders can buy their stock, and television networks try to verify the accuracy of news stories before they are broadcast.

14-2b Screening Control

screening control
Relies heavily on feedback processes during the transformation process

Screening control focuses on meeting standards for product or service quality or quantity during the actual transformation process itself. Screening control relies heavily on feedback processes. For example, in a Dell Computer assembly factory, computer system components are checked periodically as each unit is being assembled. This is done to ensure that all the components that have been assembled up to that point are working properly. The periodic quality checks provide feedback to workers so that they know what, if any, corrective actions to take. Because they are useful in identifying the causes of problems, screening controls tend to be used more often than other forms of control.

More and more companies are adopting screening controls because they are an effective way to promote employee participation and catch problems early in the overall transformation process. For example, Corning adopted screening controls for use in manufacturing television glass. In the past, finished television screens were inspected only after they were finished.

Screening control focuses on meeting standards for quality or quantity during the production process. This factory makes boots and shoes. At this stage in production the tops and bottoms of the boots have just been attached. This quality-control inspector is making sure that the seals meet the quality standards set by the company before the boots move on to the next stage of production.

Unfortunately, over 4 percent of them were later returned by customers because of defects. Now the glass screens are inspected at each step in the production process, rather than at the end, and the return rate from customers has dropped to .03 percent.

14-2c Postaction Control

Postaction control focuses on the outputs of the organization after the transformation process is complete. Corning's old system was postaction control—final inspection after the product was completed. Although Corning abandoned its postaction control system, this still may be an effective method of control, primarily if a product can be manufactured in only one or two steps or if the service is fairly simple and routine. Although postaction control alone may not be as effective as preliminary or screening control, it can provide management with information for future planning. For example, if a quality check of finished goods indicates an unacceptably high defect rate, the production

postaction control
Monitors the outputs or results of the organization after the transformation process is complete

manager knows that he or she must identify the causes and take steps to eliminate them. Postaction control also provides a basis for rewarding employees. Recognizing that an employee has exceeded personal sales goals by a wide margin, for example, may alert the manager that a bonus or promotion is in order.

Most organizations use more than one form of operations control. For example, Honda's preliminary control includes hiring only qualified employees and specifying strict quality standards when ordering parts from other manufacturers. Honda uses numerous screening controls in checking the quality of components during the assembly of cars. A final inspection and test drive as each car rolls off the assembly line is part of the company's postaction control.[18] Indeed, most successful organizations employ a wide variety of techniques to facilitate operations control.

Manager's Checklist

☐ Managers should be able to distinguish between preliminary, screening, and post-action control.

☐ You should also understand how the various forms of operations control can be used simultaneously.

14-3 FINANCIAL CONTROL

Financial control is the control of financial resources as they flow into the organization (revenues, shareholder investments), are held by the organization (working capital, retained earnings), and flow out of the organization (employee wages and salaries, expenses). Businesses must manage their finances so that revenues are sufficient to cover costs and still return a profit to the firm's owners. Not-for-profit organizations such as universities have the same concerns: Their revenues (from tax dollars or tuition) must cover operating expenses and overhead. U.S. automakers Ford and General Motors have had to face the business reality that they have to reduce the costs of paying employees they do not need but whom they are obligated to keep due to long-standing labor agreements. A few years ago Ford offered to cover the full costs of a college education for employees who met specified criteria if they would resign; GM, for its part, offered lump-sum payments of varying amounts to some of its workers in return for their resignations. A complete discussion of financial management is beyond the scope of this book, but here we examine the control provided by budgets and other financial control tools.

14-3a Budgetary Control

A *budget* is a plan expressed in numerical terms. Organizations establish budgets for work groups, departments, divisions, and the whole organization. The usual time period for a budget is one year, although breakdowns of budgets by the quarter or month are also common. Budgets are generally expressed in financial terms, but they may occasionally be expressed in units of output, time, or other quantifiable factors. When Disney launches the production of a new movie, it creates a budget for how much the movie should cost. Some movies require expensive special effects and high-cost stars, so the budget may well exceed $100 million. Other movies, though, are simpler to make and cast lower-priced actors and thus have a smaller budget. *Avengers: Endgame* had a budget of $365 million, while the live-action remake of *Mulan* had a budget of $90 million. (Of course, Disney's projections were also that each movie would earn revenue above its budget.)

Because of their quantitative nature, budgets provide yardsticks for measuring performance and facilitate comparisons across departments, between levels in the organization, and from one time period to another. Budgets serve four primary purposes. They help managers coordinate resources and projects (because they use a common denominator, usually dollars). They help define the established standards for control. They provide guidelines about the organization's resources and expectations. Finally, budgets enable the organization to evaluate the performance of managers and organizational units.

Types of Budgets   Most organizations develop and make use of three different kinds of budgets: financial, operating, and nonmonetary. Table 14.1 summarizes the characteristics of each of these.

A *financial budget* indicates where the organization expects to get its cash for the coming time period and how it plans to use it. Because financial resources are critically important, the organization needs to know where those resources will be coming from and how they are

Table 14.1	Developing Budgets In Organizations
Types of Budgets	**What Budget Shows**
Financial budget	Sources and uses of cash
Cash flow or cash budget	All sources of cash income and cash expenditures in monthly, weekly, or daily periods
Capital expenditures budget	Costs of major assets such as a new plant, machinery, or land
Balance sheet budget	Forecast of the organization's assets and liabilities in the event all other budgets are met
Operating budget	Planned operations in financial terms
Sales or revenue budget	Income the organization expects to receive from normal operations
Expense budget	Anticipated expenses for the organization during the coming time period
Profit budget	Anticipated differences between sales or revenues and expenses
Nonmonetary budget	Planned operations in nonfinancial terms
Labor budget	Hours of direct labor available for use
Space budget	Square feet or meters of space available for various functions
Production budget	Number of units to be produced during the coming time period

Organizations use various types of budgets to help manage their control functions. The three major categories of budgets are financial, operating, and nonmonetary. There are several different types of budgets in each category. To be most effective, each budget must be carefully matched with the specific function being controlled.

to be used. The financial budget provides answers to both these questions. Usual sources of cash include sales revenue, short- and long-term loans, the sale of assets, and the issuance of new stock.

For years Exxon was very conservative in its capital budgeting. As a result, the firm amassed a huge financial reserve but was overtaken in sales by Royal Dutch/Shell, BP, and other oil producers. Executives at Exxon subsequently made the decision to use their reserves to help finance the firm's acquisition of Mobil, creating ExxonMobil. The firm's newfound size then allowed it to invest more in exploration, building new refineries, and so forth and to regain the number-one sales position. Since that time, the firm has become more aggressive in capital budgeting to stay ahead of its European rivals.

An *operating budget* is concerned with planned operations within the organization. It outlines what quantities of products or services the organization intends to create and what resources will be used to create them. Dell creates an operating budget that specifies how many of each model of its various computers and related products will be produced each period.

A *nonmonetary budget* is simply a budget expressed in nonfinancial terms, such as units of output, hours of direct labor, machine hours, or square-foot allocations. Nonmonetary budgets are most commonly used by managers at the lower levels of an organization. For example, a plant manager can schedule work more effectively knowing that he or she has 8,000 labor hours to allocate in a week, rather than trying to determine how to best spend $86,451 in wages in a week.

Developing Budgets   Traditionally, budgets were developed by top management and the controller and then imposed on lower-level managers. Although some organizations still follow this pattern, most organizations today now allow all managers to participate in the

FIGURE 14.5

Developing Budgets in Organizations

Most organizations use the same basic process to develop budgets. Operating units are requested to submit their budget requests to divisions. These divisions, in turn, compile unit budgets and submit their own budgets to the organization. An organizational budget is then compiled for approval by the budget committee, controller, and CEO.

budget process. As a starting point, top management generally issues a call for budget requests, accompanied by an indication of overall patterns the budgets may take. For example, if sales are expected to drop in the next year, managers may be told up front to prepare for cuts in operating budgets.

As Figure 14.5 shows, the heads of each operating unit typically submit budget requests to the head of their division. An operating unit head might be a department manager in a manufacturing or wholesaling firm or a program director in a social service agency. The division heads might include plant managers, regional sales managers, or college deans. The division head integrates and consolidates the budget requests from operating unit heads into one overall division budget request. Substantial interaction among managers usually takes place at this stage, as the division head coordinates the budgetary needs of the various departments.

Division budget requests are then forwarded to a budget committee. The budget committee is usually composed of top managers. The committee reviews budget requests from several divisions and, once again, duplications and inconsistencies are corrected. Finally, the budget committee, the controller, and the CEO review and agree on the overall budget for the organization, as well as specific budgets for each operating unit. These decisions are then communicated back to each manager.

Strengths and Weaknesses of Budgeting   Budgets offer a number of advantages, but they also have weaknesses. On the plus side, budgets facilitate effective control. Placing dollar values on operations enables managers to monitor operations better and pinpoint problem areas. Budgets also facilitate coordination and communication between departments because they express diverse activities in a common denominator (dollars). Budgets help maintain records of organizational performance and are a logical complement to planning. In other words, as managers develop plans, they should simultaneously consider control measures to accompany them. Organizations can use budgets to link plans and control by first developing budgets as part of the plan and then using those budgets as part of control.

On the other hand, some managers apply budgets too rigidly. Budgets are intended to serve as frameworks, but managers sometimes fail to recognize that changing circumstances may warrant budget adjustments. The process of developing budgets can also be very time-consuming. Finally, budgets may limit innovation and change. When all available funds are allocated to specific operating budgets, it may be impossible to procure additional funds to take advantage of an unexpected opportunity. Indeed, for these very reasons, some organizations are working to scale back their budgeting systems. Although most organizations are likely to continue to use budgets, the goal is to make them less confining and rigid.

14-3b Other Tools for Financial Control

Although budgets are the most common means of financial control, other useful tools are financial statements, ratio analysis, and financial audits.

Financial Statements   A financial statement is a profile of some aspect of an organization's financial circumstances. There are commonly accepted and required ways that financial statements must be prepared and presented. The two most basic financial statements prepared and used by virtually all organizations are a balance sheet and an income statement.

The balance sheet lists the assets and liabilities of the organization at a specific point in time, usually the last day of an organization's fiscal year. For example, the balance sheet may summarize the financial condition of an organization on December 31, 2021. Most balance sheets are divided into current assets (assets that are relatively liquid, or easily convertible into cash), fixed assets (assets that are longer term in nature and less liquid), current liabilities (debts and other obligations that must be paid in the near future), long-term liabilities (payable over an extended period of time), and stockholders' equity (the owners' claim against the assets).

Whereas the balance sheet reflects a snapshot profile of an organization's financial position at a single point in time, the income statement summarizes financial performance over a period of time, usually one year. For example, the income statement might be for the period January 1, 2021, through December 31, 2021. The income statement summarizes the firm's

financial statement
A profile of some aspect of an organization's financial circumstances

balance sheet
List of assets and liabilities of an organization at a specific point in time

income statement
A summary of financial performance over a period of time

revenues less its expenses to report net income (profit or loss) for the period. Information from the balance sheet and income statement is used in computing important financial ratios.

Financial ratios compare different elements of a balance sheet or income statement to one another. Ratio analysis is the calculation of one or more financial ratios to assess some aspect of the financial health of an organization. Organizations use a variety of different financial ratios as part of financial control. For example, *liquidity ratios* indicate how liquid (easily convertible into cash) an organization's assets are. *Debt ratios* reflect ability to meet long-term financial obligations. *Return ratios* show managers and investors how much return the organization is generating relative to its assets. *Coverage ratios* help estimate the organization's ability to cover interest expenses on borrowed capital. *Operating ratios* indicate the effectiveness of specific functional areas rather than of the total organization. Walt Disney and Halliburton each rely heavily on financial ratios to keep their financial operations on track.

Financial Audits   Audits are independent appraisals of an organization's accounting, financial, and operational systems. The two major types of financial audits are the external audit and the internal audit.

External audits are financial appraisals conducted by experts who are not employees of the organization. External audits are typically concerned with determining that the organization's accounting procedures and financial statements are compiled in an objective and verifiable fashion. The organization contracts with a certified public accountant (CPA) for this service. The CPA's main objective is to verify for stockholders, the Internal Revenue Service, and other interested parties that the methods by which the organization's financial managers and accountants prepare documents and reports are legal and proper. External audits are so important that publicly held corporations are required by law to have external audits regularly, as assurance to investors that the financial reports are reliable.

Unfortunately, in a classic example, flaws in the auditing process played a major role in the downfall of Enron (as well as several other major firms) in the early 2000s. The problem can be traced back partially to the auditing groups' problems with conflicts of interest and eventual loss of objectivity. For instance, Enron was such an important client for its auditing firm, Arthur Andersen, that the auditors started letting the firm take liberties with its accounting systems for fear that if they were too strict, Enron might take its business to another auditing firm. In the aftermath of the resulting scandal, Arthur Andersen was forced to close its doors, Enron became a shell of its former self, executives were indicted, and the entire accounting profession was called into question. Unfortunately, some data suggests that even today auditing firms still make errors in their reviews of firm records.[19]

Some organizations also use external auditors to review other aspects of their financial operations. For example, some auditing firms now specialize in checking corporate legal bills. An auditor for the Fireman's Fund Insurance Company uncovered several thousands of dollars in legal fee errors. Other auditors are beginning to specialize in real estate, employee benefits, and pension plan investments.

Whereas external audits are conducted by external accountants, an *internal audit* is handled by employees of the organization. Its objective is the same as that of an external audit: to verify the accuracy of financial and accounting procedures used by the organization. Internal audits also examine the efficiency and appropriateness of financial and accounting procedures. Because the staff members who conduct them are a permanent part of the organization, internal audits tend to be more expensive than external audits. But employees, who are more familiar with the organization's practices, may also point out significant aspects of the accounting system besides its technical correctness. Large organizations like BP and Ford have an internal auditing staff that spends all its time conducting audits of different divisions and functional areas of the organization. Smaller organizations may assign accountants to an internal audit group on a temporary or rotating basis.

Satyam Computer Services in India falsely reported profits of over $1 billion when in reality it had only $66 million. The Indian affiliate of PricewaterhouseCoopers, PW India, was in charge of routinely auditing the firm, but failed to follow basic auditing procedures. Rather than confirming the supposed $1 billion cash balances with the banks, PW India relied solely on the information provided by the firm's management. In some cases, auditors

ratio analysis
The calculation of one or more financial ratios to assess some aspect of the organization's financial health

audit
An independent appraisal of an organization's accounting, financial, and operational systems

failed to follow up on confirmations sent independently by the banks that showed significant differences from the balances reported by management. PW India was eventually fined $7.5 million—the largest penalty ever imposed by India on a foreign accounting firm.[20] Our *Tech Watch* feature presents another perspective on auditing.

Manager's Checklist

☐ Managers should be familiar with the basic kinds of budgets used in their organizations.

☐ You should also understand the budgeting process used in your organization.

☐ All managers should also know how to interpret basic financial statements and understand the meaning of basic financial ratios.

TECH WATCH

Analytics and the Future of Auditing

Following the Stock Market Crash of 1929, the Federal government created the Securities and Exchange Commission (SEC) in order to regulate financial reports from publicly traded companies. Although the SEC has the legal authority to establish Generally Accepted Accounting Principles (GAAP), as financial transactions became more and more complicated, the SEC and the accounting profession partnered to create the Financial Accounting Standards Board (FASB)—the first full-time accounting standards-setting and research board in the world.

In order to enforce the SEC and FASB rules, accounting firms developed audit procedures to apply to company financial statements. As independent auditors, the accounting firms could assure the public that the statements had been prepared in accordance with GAAP. Early audits relied on management assertions and reports, but as they developed and evolved, the auditing procedures began to look at more objective evidence, such as visual inspections of inventory and confirmations of receivables. That was the state of auditing for years. Much of the auditing was done by hand, basic spreadsheets, and some sampling and statistical analysis. But in recent years the audit function has been changing rapidly as audit firms are integrating data analytics, machine learning, and other modern technology in audit work, changing the breadth and depth of audits and clients' expectations.

Just as data analytics and big data help inform what we buy, what news we read, and even whom we date, it is now becoming a big part of audit work. Data analytics enable auditors to examine 100 percent of a client's transactions; track and analyze trends, as well as anomalies and risks, to identify problematic areas or transactions; and benchmark a company's financial information against others based on industry, geography, size, or other factors. The big auditing firms are also integrating artificial intelligence (AI) and natural language processing (NLP) into their systems. Using NLP to extract information and a human-in-the-loop to validate the results, an AI system is three times more consistent and twice as efficient as previous humans-only teams. For instance, a team of a dozen accountants might spend six months combing through hundreds of thousands of legal documents looking for a change of control provisions during a client's sale of a business unit. Now, a team of six to eight members can use an AI system to complete the same task in less than a month.

Just a decade or so ago, many accountants would have scoffed at the idea of using AI to assist in the accounting process and NLP was a research dream. Now, though, smart systems are replacing much of the accounting process, and new cloud technologies and block-chain networking are just the tip of the iceberg of the change that is coming to the industry. Even so, however, experts say that the human element will never be outdated, just used differently. Only time will tell.

References: Raymond Johnson and Laure Wiley, *Auditing: A Practical Approach with Data Analytics* (New York, Wiley, 2019); "How Big Data and Analytics are Transforming the Audit," EY, April 1, 2015, https://www.ey.com on July 6, 2020.

14-4 STRUCTURAL CONTROL

Organizations can create designs for themselves that result in very different approaches to control. Two major forms of structural control, bureaucratic control and decentralized control, represent opposite ends of a continuum, as shown in Figure 14.6.[21] The six dimensions shown in the figure represent perspectives adopted by the two extreme types of structural control.

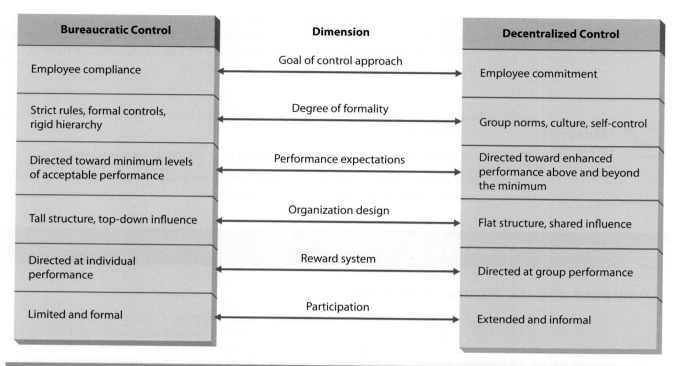

Organizational Control

Organizational control generally falls somewhere between the two extremes of bureaucratic and decentralized control. NBC Television uses bureaucratic control, whereas Levi Strauss uses decentralized control.

In other words, they have different goals, degrees of formality, performance expectations, organization designs, reward systems, and levels of participation. Although a few organizations fall precisely at one extreme or the other, most tend toward one end but may have specific characteristics of either.

14-4a Bureaucratic Control

bureaucratic control
A form of organizational control characterized by formal and mechanistic structural arrangements

Bureaucratic control is an approach to organization design characterized by formal and mechanistic structural arrangements. As the term suggests, it follows the bureaucratic model. The goal of bureaucratic control is employee compliance. Organizations that use it rely on strict rules and a rigid hierarchy, insist that employees meet minimally acceptable levels of performance, and often have a tall structure. They focus their rewards on individual performance and allow only limited and formal employee participation.

NBC Television (owned by NBCUniversal) applies structural controls that reflect many elements of bureaucracy. The organization relies on many rules to regulate employee travel, expense accounts, and other expenses. A new performance appraisal system precisely specifies minimally acceptable levels of performance for everyone. The organization's structure is considerably taller than those of the other major networks, and rewards are based on individual contributions. Perhaps most significantly, many NBC employees have argued that they have too small a voice in how the organization is managed.

In another example, a few years ago a large oil company made the decision to allow employees to wear casual attire to work. But a committee then spent weeks developing a 20-page set of guidelines on what was and was not acceptable. For example, denim jeans are not allowed. Similarly, athletic shoes could be worn as long as they are not white. And all shirts must have a collar. Nordstrom, the department store chain, has also moved toward bureaucratic control of all of its purchasing in an effort to lower costs. Similarly, Home Depot is moving more toward bureaucratic control to cut its costs and to try to blunt the inroads made into its customer base by Amazon.[22]

14-4b Decentralized Control

decentralized control
An approach to organizational control based on informal and organic structural arrangements

Decentralized control, in contrast, is an approach to organizational control characterized by informal and organic structural arrangements. As Figure 14.6 shows, its goal is employee commitment to the organization. Accordingly, it relies heavily on group norms and a strong corporate culture and gives employees the responsibility for controlling themselves. Employees are encouraged to perform beyond minimally acceptable levels. Organizations using this approach are usually relatively flat. They direct rewards at group performance and favor widespread employee participation.

Levi Strauss practices decentralized control. The firm's managers use groups as the basis for work and have created a culture wherein group norms help facilitate high performance. Rewards are subsequently provided to the higher-performing groups and teams. The company's culture also reinforces contributions to the overall team effort, and employees have a strong sense of loyalty to the organization. Levi's has a flat structure, and power is widely shared. Employee participation is encouraged in all areas of operation. Another company that uses this approach is Southwest Airlines. When Southwest made the decision to "go casual," the firm resisted the temptation to develop dress guidelines. Instead, managers decided to allow employees to exercise discretion over their attire and to deal with clearly inappropriate situations on a case-by-case basis. Netflix also uses decentralized control.

 **Manager's Checklist**

☐ Managers need to know the fundamental differences between bureaucratic and decentralized control.

☐ You should also be familiar with the most obvious advantages and disadvantages of bureaucratic versus decentralized control.

14-5 STRATEGIC CONTROL

Given the obvious importance of an organization's strategy, it is also important that the organization assess how effective that strategy is in helping the organization meet its goals.[23] To do this requires that the organization integrate its strategy and control systems. This is especially true for the global organization.

14-5a Integrating Strategy and Control

strategic control
Control aimed at ensuring that the organization is maintaining an effective alignment with its environment and moving toward achieving its strategic goals

Strategic control generally focuses on five aspects of organizations—structure, leadership, technology, human resources, and information and operational control systems. For example, an organization should periodically examine its structure to determine whether it is facilitating the attainment of the strategic goals being sought. Suppose a firm using a functional (U-form) design has an established goal of achieving a 20 percent sales growth rate per year, but performance indicators show that it is currently growing at a rate of only 10 percent per year. Detailed analysis might reveal that the current structure is inhibiting growth in some way (e.g., by slowing decision making and inhibiting innovation) and that a divisional (M-form) design is more likely to bring about the desired growth (by speeding decision making and promoting innovation).

In this way, strategic control focuses on the extent to which implemented strategy achieves the organization's strategic goals. If, as outlined above, one or more avenues of implementation are inhibiting the attainment of goals, that avenue should be changed. Consequently, the firm might find it necessary to alter its structure, replace key leaders, adopt new technology, modify its human resources, or change its information and operational control systems.

For several years, Pfizer, the world's largest pharmaceutical company, invested billions of dollars in research and development. But the firm recently acknowledged that it was not getting an adequate return on its investment and announced that it was laying off 800 senior researchers. Pfizer also signaled a strategic reorientation by suggesting it would look for other drug companies to buy in order to acquire new patents and drug formulas. In contrast, 3M is a company that is known for its innovation and product development, with staples like Scotch tape and Post-it notes. The company recently announced that it would increase its R&D spending to 6 percent of sales, hire 60–80 additional PhD research scientists, and construct a new $150 million R&D lab.

Kohl's department stores essentially redefined how to compete effectively in the mid-tier retailing market and was on a trajectory to leave competitors like JCPenney's and Dillard's in its dust. But then the firm inexplicably stopped doing many of the very things that had led to its success—such as keeping abreast of current styles, maintaining low inventories, and keeping its stores neat and clean—and began to stumble. After recognizing their errors, managers devoted renewed attention to rejuvenating Kohl's strategic focus and get it back on track.[24]

> ## "Some of the work will be to improve the presentation of our national brands because we know that we have slipped with consumers in their perceptions of Kohl's as a place to get great national brands."
>
> —Kevin Mansell, Former CEO PF Kohl's Corporation,
> on "Getting their Mojo Back"

14-5b International Strategic Control

Because they are relatively large firms operating in complex markets, global organizations must take an especially pronounced strategic view of their control systems. One very basic question that has to be addressed is whether to manage control from a centralized or a decentralized perspective.[25] Under a centralized system, each organizational unit around the world is responsible for frequently reporting the results of its performance to headquarters. Managers from the home office often visit foreign branches to observe firsthand how the units are functioning.

BP, Unilever, Procter & Gamble, and Sony all use this approach. They believe centralized control is effective because it allows the home office to stay better informed of the performance of foreign units and to maintain more control over how decisions are made. For example, BP discovered that its Australian subsidiary was not billing its customers for charges as quickly as were its competitors. By shortening the billing cycle, BP now receives customer payments five days faster than before. Managers believe that they discovered this oversight only because of a centralized financial control system.

Organizations that use a decentralized control system require foreign branches to report less often and in less detail. For example, each unit may submit summary performance statements on a quarterly basis and provide full statements only once a year. Similarly, visits from the home office are less frequent and less concerned with monitoring and assessing performance. IBM, Ford, and Shell all use this approach. Because Ford practices decentralized control of its design function, European designers have developed several innovative automobile design features. Managers believe that if they had been more centralized, designers would not have had the freedom to develop their new ideas.

Manager's Checklist

☐ Managers should know how strategy and control are most commonly integrated.

☐ Managers should also know in what ways domestic and international control issues are similar and in what ways they differ.

14-6 MANAGING CONTROL IN ORGANIZATIONS

Effective control, whether at the operations, financial, structural, or strategic level, successfully regulates and monitors organizational activities. To use the control process, managers must recognize the characteristics of effective control and understand how to identify and overcome occasional resistance to control.[26]

14-6a Characteristics of Effective Control

Control systems tend to be most effective when they are integrated with planning and when they are flexible, accurate, timely, and objective.

Integration with Planning   Control should be linked with planning. The more explicit and precise this linkage, the more effective the control system is. The best way to integrate planning and control is to account for control as plans develop. In other words, as goals are set during the planning process, attention should be paid to developing standards that will reflect how well the plan is realized. Managers at Champion Auto Parts Company decided to broaden their product line to include a wider range of automotive accessories—a total of 21 new products. As part of this plan, managers decided in advance what level of sales they wanted to realize from each product for each of the next five years. They established these sales goals as standards against which actual sales would be compared. Thus, by accounting for their control system as they developed their plan, managers at Champion did an excellent job of integrating planning and control.

Flexibility   The control system itself must be flexible enough to accommodate change. Consider, for example, an organization whose diverse product line requires 75 different raw materials. The company's inventory control system must be able to manage and monitor current levels of inventory for all 75 materials. When a change in product line changes the number of raw materials needed, or when the required quantities of the existing materials change, the control system should be flexible enough to handle the revised requirements. The alternative—designing and implementing a new control system—is an avoidable expense. Champion's control system included a mechanism that automatically shipped products to major customers to keep their inventories at predetermined levels. The firm had to adjust this system when one of its biggest customers decided not to stock the full line of Champion products. Because its control system was flexible, though, modifying it for the customer was relatively simple. During the 2020 COVID-19 pandemic, organizations that had flexible control systems were better able to adapt to the rapidly changing environment than were businesses with less flexible control systems.

Accuracy   Managers make a surprisingly large number of decisions based on inaccurate information. Field representatives may hedge their sales estimates to make themselves look better. Production managers may hide costs to meet their targets. Human resource managers may overestimate their minority recruiting prospects to meet affirmative action goals. In each case, the information that other managers receive is inaccurate, and the results of inaccurate information may be quite dramatic. If sales projections are inflated, a manager might cut advertising (thinking it is no longer needed) or increase advertising (to further build momentum). Similarly, a production manager unaware of hidden costs may quote a sales price much lower than desirable. Or a human resources manager may speak out publicly on the effectiveness of the company's minority recruiting, only to find out later that these prospects have been overestimated. In each case, the result of inaccurate information is inappropriate managerial action.

Timeliness   Timeliness does not necessarily mean quickness. Rather, it describes a control system that provides information as often as is necessary. Because Champion has a wealth of historical data on revenue from its original auto product lines, it does not need information on those products as often as it needs sales feedback for its newer products. Retail organizations usually need sales results daily so that they can manage cash flow and adjust advertising and promotion. In contrast, they may need information about physical inventory only quarterly or annually. In general, the more uncertain and unstable the circumstances, the more often measurement is needed.

Objectivity   The control system should provide information that is as objective as possible. To appreciate this, imagine the task of a manager responsible for control of his organization's human resources. He asks two plant managers to submit reports. One manager notes that morale at his plant is "okay," that grievances are "about where they should be," and that turnover is "under control." The other reports that absenteeism at her plant is running at 4 percent, that 16 grievances have been filed this year (compared with 24 last year), and that turnover is 12 percent. The second report will almost always be more useful than the first. Of course, managers also need to look beyond the numbers when assessing performance. For example, a plant manager may be boosting productivity and profit margins by putting too much pressure on workers and using poor-quality materials. As a result, impressive short-run gains may be overshadowed by longer-run increases in employee turnover and customer complaints.

14-6b Resistance to Control

Managers sometimes make the mistake of assuming that the value of an effective control system is self-evident to employees. This is not always so, however. Many employees resist control, especially if they feel overcontrolled, if they think control is inappropriately focused on or that it rewards inefficiency, or if they are uncomfortable with accountability.

Overcontrol   Occasionally, organizations try to control too many things. This becomes especially problematic when the control directly affects employee behavior. An organization that instructs its employees when to come to work, where to park, when to have morning coffee, and when to leave for the day is exerting considerable control over people's daily activities. Yet many organizations try to control not only these but other aspects of work behavior as well. Of particular relevance in recent years is some companies' efforts to control their employees' access to private email and social media during work hours. Some companies have no policies governing these activities, some attempt to limit it, and some attempt to forbid it altogether.[27]

Troubles arise when employees perceive these attempts to limit their behavior as being unreasonable. A company that tells its employees how to dress, how to arrange their desks, and how to wear their hair may be met with more resistance. Employees at Chrysler who drove non-Chrysler vehicles used to complain because they were forced to park in a distant parking lot while those who drove Chrysler products could park closer to their offices. People felt that these efforts to control their personal behavior (what kind of car to drive) were excessive. Managers eventually removed these controls and now allow open parking. Some employees at Abercrombie & Fitch once argued that the firm was guilty of overcontrol because of its strict dress and grooming requirements—for example, no necklaces or facial hair for men and only natural nail polish and earrings no larger than a dime for women. Likewise, Enterprise Rent-A-Car has a set of 30 dress-code rules for women and 26 rules for men. The firm was once sued by one former employee who was fired because of the color of her hair.[28] Disney stipulates that its employees should only wear sunglasses that permit park guests to see their eyes. UBS, a large Swiss bank, had (until recently) a 44-page dress code that prescribed, among other things, that employees should avoid eating garlic and onions (so as to not offend customers), keep their toenails trimmed (so as to not tear their stockings or socks), and wear only skin-colored underwear (so it would not be visible through outer garments). Men were instructed in how to knot a tie, and everyone was encouraged to keep their glasses clean. (When the dress code was made public, UBS indicated that it would be making some revisions!)[29]

"Glasses should always be kept clean. On the one hand this gives you optimal vision, and on the other hand dirty glasses create an appearance of negligence."
—UBS Dress Code

Inappropriate Focus   The control system may be too narrow, or it may focus too much on quantifiable variables and leave no room for analysis or interpretation. A sales standard that encourages high-pressure tactics to maximize short-run sales may do so at the expense of goodwill from long-term customers. Such a standard is too narrow. A university reward system that encourages faculty members to publish large numbers of articles but fails to consider the quality of the work is also inappropriately focused. Employees resist the intent of the control system by focusing their efforts only on the performance indicators being used.

Rewards for Inefficiency Imagine two operating departments that are approaching the end of their fiscal years. Department 1 expects to have $25,000 of its budget left over; department 2 is already $10,000 in the red. As a result, department 1 may have its budget cut for the next year ("They had money left, so they obviously got too much to begin with"), and department 2 may get a budget increase ("They obviously haven't been getting enough money"). Thus, department 1 is punished for being efficient, and department 2 is rewarded for being inefficient. (No wonder departments commonly hasten to deplete their budgets as the end of the year approaches!) As with inappropriate focus, people resist the intent of this control and behave in ways that run counter to the organization's intent.

Too Much Accountability Effective controls allow managers to determine whether employees successfully discharge their responsibilities. If standards are properly set and performance accurately measured, managers know when problems arise and which departments and individuals are responsible. People who do not want to be answerable for their mistakes or who do not want to work as hard as their bosses might therefore resist control. For example, American Express uses a number of techniques to assess the performance of its customer service representatives. One metric in this system is an automated measure of how many calls each of its customer service representatives handles each day. If one representative has typically worked at a slower pace and handled fewer calls than other representatives, that person's deficient performance can now more easily be pinpointed.

14-6c Overcoming Resistance to Control

Perhaps the best way to overcome resistance to control is to create effective control to begin with. If control systems are properly integrated with organizational planning and if the controls are flexible, accurate, timely, and objective, the organization will be less likely to overcontrol, to focus on inappropriate standards, or to reward inefficiency. Two other ways to overcome resistance are encouraging employee participation and developing verification procedures.

Encourage Employee Participation Chapter 12 noted that participation can help overcome resistance to change. By the same token, when employees are involved with planning and implementing the control system, they are less likely to resist it. For instance, employee participation in planning, decision making, and quality control at the Chevrolet Gear and Axle plant in Detroit resulted in increased employee concern for quality and a greater commitment to meeting standards.

Develop Verification Procedures Multiple standards and information systems provide checks and balances in control and allow the organization to verify the accuracy of performance indicators. Suppose a production manager argues that she failed to meet a certain cost standard because of increased prices of raw materials. A properly designed inventory control system will either support or contradict her explanation. Suppose that an employee who was fired for excessive absences argues that he was not absent "for a long time." An effective human resource control system should have records that support the termination. Resistance to control declines because these verification procedures protect both employees and management. If the production manager's claim about the rising cost of raw materials is supported by the inventory control records, she will not be held solely accountable for failing to meet the cost standard, and some action probably will be taken to lower the cost of raw materials.

Manager's Checklist

☐ Managers should know the essential characteristics of effective control.

☐ You should also be familiar with the reasons some people resist control and the best ways to overcome that resistance.

SUMMARY OF LEARNING OUTCOMES AND KEY POINTS

14-1. Explain the purpose of control, including different types of control and the steps in the control process.

- Control is the regulation of organizational activities so that some targeted element of performance remains within acceptable limits.

- Control provides ways to adapt to environmental change, to limit the accumulation of errors, to cope with organizational complexity, and to minimize costs.

- Control can focus on financial, physical, information, and human resources and includes operations, financial, structural, and strategic levels.

- Control is the function of managers, the controller, and, increasingly, of operating employees.

- Steps in the control process are
  - to establish standards of expected performance to measure actual performance,
  - to compare performance to the standards, and
  - to evaluate the comparison and take appropriate action.

14-2. Identify the three forms of operations control.

- Operations control focuses on the processes the organization uses to transform resources into products or services.

- Preliminary control is concerned with the resources that serve as inputs to the system.

- Screening control is concerned with the transformation processes used by the organization.

- Postaction control is concerned with the outputs of the organization.

- Most organizations need multiple control systems because no one system can provide adequate control.

14-3. Describe budgets and other tools for financial control.

- Financial control focuses on controlling the organization's financial resources.

- The foundation of financial control is budgets, which are plans expressed in numerical terms.

- Most organizations rely on financial, operating, and nonmonetary budgets.

- Financial statements, various kinds of ratios, and external and internal audits are also important tools organizations use as part of financial control.

14-4. Distinguish between two opposing forms of structural control.

- Structural control addresses how well an organization's structural elements serve their intended purpose.

- Two basic forms of structural control are bureaucratic and decentralized control.

- Bureaucratic control is relatively formal and mechanistic.

- Decentralized control is informal and organic.

- Most organizations use a form of organizational control somewhere between total bureaucratic and total decentralized control.

14-5. Discuss the relationship between strategy and control, including international strategic control.

- Strategic control focuses on how effectively the organization's strategies are succeeding in helping the organization meet its goals.

- The integration of strategy and control is generally achieved through organization structure, leadership, technology, human resources, and information and operational control systems.

- International strategic control is also important for multinational organizations.

- The foundation of international strategic control is whether to practice centralized or decentralized control.

14-6. Identify characteristics of effective control including why people resist control and how managers can overcome this resistance.

- One way to increase the effectiveness of control is to fully integrate planning and control.

- The control system should also be as flexible, accurate, timely, and objective as possible.

- Employees may resist organizational controls because of overcontrol, inappropriate focus, rewards for inefficiency, and a desire to avoid accountability.

- Managers can overcome this resistance by improving the effectiveness of controls and by allowing employee participation and developing verification procedures.

DISCUSSION QUESTIONS

Questions for Review

1. What is the purpose of organizational control? Why is it important?
2. What are the different levels of control? What are the relationships between the different levels?
3. Describe how a budget is created in most organizations. How does a budget help a manager with financial control?
4. Describe the differences between bureaucratic and decentralized control. What are the advantages and disadvantages of each?

Questions for Analysis

1. How can a manager determine whether his or her firm needs improvement in control? If improvement is needed, how can the manager tell what type of control needs improvement (operations, financial, structural, or strategic)? Describe some steps a manager can take to improve each of these types of control.
2. One company uses strict performance standards. Another has standards that are more flexible. What are the advantages and disadvantages of each system?

3. Are the differences in bureaucratic control and decentralized control related to differences in organization structure? If so, how? If not, why not? (The terms do sound similar to those used to discuss the organizing process.)

Questions for Application

1. Many organizations today are involving lower-level employees in control. Give at least two examples of specific actions that a lower-level worker could take to help his or her organization better adapt to environmental change. Then do the same for limiting the accumulation of error, coping with organizational complexity, and minimizing costs.
2. Select two different kinds of organizations with which you have some familiarity. For each one, identify how its control systems and processes may have changed during the 2020 COVID-19 pandemic.
3. Interview a worker to determine which areas and levels of control exist for him or her on the job. Does the worker resist efforts at control? Why or why not?

BUILDING EFFECTIVE TIME-MANAGEMENT SKILLS

Exercise Overview

Not surprisingly, time-management skills—which refer to the ability to prioritize tasks, to work efficiently, and to delegate appropriately—play a major role in performing the control function: Managers can use time-management skills to control their own work activities more effectively. The purpose of this exercise is to demonstrate the relationship between time-management skills and the process of controlling workplace activities.

Exercise Background

You're a middle manager in a small manufacturing plant. Today is Monday, and you've just returned from a week's vacation. The first thing you discover is that your assistant won't be in today (his aunt died, and he's out of town at the funeral). He did, however, leave you the following note:

Dear Boss:
Sorry about not being here today. I will be back tomorrow. In the meantime, here are some things you need to know:
  Ms. Glinski [your boss] wants to see you today at 4:00.
  The shop steward wants to see you as soon as possible about a labor problem.
  Mr. Bateman [one of your big customers] has a complaint about a recent shipment.

  Ms. Garcia [one of your major suppliers] wants to discuss a change in delivery schedules.
  Mr. Prescott from the Chamber of Commerce wants you to attend a breakfast meeting on Wednesday to discuss our expansion plans.
  The legal office wants to discuss our upcoming OSHA inspection.
  Human resources wants to know when you can interview someone for the new supervisor's position.
  Jack Williams, the machinist you fired last month, has been hanging around the parking lot, and his presence is making some employees uncomfortable.

Exercise Task

Review the preceding information and then do the following:

1. Prioritize the work that needs to be done by sorting the information into three categories: *very timely*, *moderately timely*, and *less timely*. Then address the following questions.
   a. Are *importance* and *timeliness* the same thing?
   b. What additional information do you need before you can begin to prioritize all of these demands on your time?
   c. How would your approach differ if your assistant were in the office?

BUILDING EFFECTIVE TECHNICAL SKILLS

Exercise Overview

Technical skills are necessary to understand or perform the specific kind of work that an organization does. This exercise allows you to develop the technical skills needed to construct and evaluate the effectiveness of a budget.

Exercise Background

Although corporate budgets are obviously much more complicated, the basic processes of creating a corporate budget on the one hand and a personal budget on the other share a few important features. Both, for instance, begin with estimations of inflow and outflow. In addition, both compare actual results with estimated results, and both culminate in plans for corrective action.

Exercise Task

1. Prepare lists of your *estimated* expenditures and income for one month. Remember: You're dealing with budgeted amounts, not the amounts that you actually spend and take in. You're also dealing with figures that represent a typical month or a reasonable minimum. If, for example, you estimate that you spend $300 a month on groceries, you need to ask yourself whether that's a reasonable amount to spend on groceries for a month. If it's not, perhaps a more typical or reasonable figure is, say, $200.

   First, estimate your necessary monthly expenses for tuition, rent, car payments, childcare, food, utilities, and so on. Then estimate your income from all sources, such as wages, allowance, loans, and funds borrowed on credit cards. Calculate both totals.

2. Now write down all of your *actual* expenses and all your *actual* income over the last month. If you don't have exact figures, estimate as closely as you can. Calculate both totals.

3. Compare your *estimates* to your *actual* expenses and actual income. Are there any discrepancies? If so, what caused them?

4. Did you expect to have a surplus or a deficit for the month? Did you actually have a surplus or a deficit? What can you do to make up any deficit or manage any surplus?

5. Do you regularly use a personal budget? If yes, how is it helpful? If no, how might it be helpful?

SKILL-BUILDING PERSONAL ASSESSMENT

Understanding Control

Introduction: Control systems must be carefully constructed for all organizations, regardless of their specific goals. The following assessment surveys your ideas about and approaches to control.

Instructions: You will agree with some of the statements and disagree with others. In some cases, making a decision may be difficult, but you should force yourself to make a choice. Record your answers next to each statement according to the following scale.

Rating Scale

4   Strongly agree

3   Somewhat agree

2   Somewhat disagree

1   Strongly disagree

1. _____ Effective controls must be unbending if they are to be used consistently.

2. _____ The most objective form of control is one that uses measures such as stock prices and rate of return on investment (ROI).

3. _____ Control is restrictive and should be avoided if at all possible.

4. _____ Controlling through rules, procedures, and budgets should not be used unless measurable standards are difficult or expensive to develop.

5. _____ Overreliance on measurable control standards is seldom a problem for business organizations.

6. _____ Organizations should encourage the development of individual self-control.

7. _____ Organizations tend to try to establish behavioral controls as the first type of control to be used.

8. _____ The easiest and least costly form of control is output or quantity control.

9. _____ Short-run efficiency and long-run effectiveness result from the use of similar control standards.

10. _____ Controlling by taking into account ROI and using stock prices in making control decisions are ways of ensuring that a business organization is responding to its external market.

11. _____ Self-control should be relied on to replace other forms of control.

12. _____ Controls such as ROI are more appropriate for corporations and business units than for small groups or individuals.

13. _____ Control is unnecessary in a well-managed organization.

14. _____ The use of output or quantity controls can lead to unintended or unfortunate consequences.

15. _____ Standards of control do not depend on which constituency is being considered.

16. _____ Controlling through the use of rules, procedures, and budgets can lead to rigidity and to a loss of creativity in an organization.

17. _____ Different forms of control cannot be used at the same time. An organization must decide how it is going to control and stick to that method.

18. _____ Setting across-the-board output or quantity targets for divisions within a company can lead to destructive results.

19. _____ Control through rules, procedures, and budgets is generally not very costly.

20. _____ Reliance on individual self-control can lead to problems with integration and communication.

Scoring: The odd-numbered items are all false, and the even-numbered ones are all true. Thus, you should have positive responses for the even-numbered items and negative responses for the odd-numbered items. If you agreed strongly with all of the even-numbered items and disagreed strongly with all of the odd-numbered items, your total score would be zero.

Examine your responses to see which items you responded to incorrectly. Focus on learning why the answers are what they are.

MANAGEMENT AT WORK

The Law of Cheating

"Don't go looking for the perfect performance measure. It doesn't exist."

—Robert D. Behn, Harvard University, Kennedy School of Government

Let's suppose that you're the manager of a factory that manufactures automotive bumpers. When the fourth quarter rolls around, you see that you aren't on track to meet your quota by your year-end deadline. Failure to meet either the quota or the deadline will mean that you won't be getting any bonus or stock options and, in fact, your job might be at risk. So you decide to put off regularly scheduled maintenance and repairs for the quarter and produce bumpers at full capacity—a practice called "storming." You meet your quota and deadline, but catching up with maintenance and repairs during the first quarter of the following year reduces your production capacity for three months. Down the line, of course, you'll be facing yet another quota and another deadline, and in order to recoup the resulting loss in production, you'll have to resort to "storming" once again. Obviously, it won't be long before your operations are completely out of control.

Not fair, you say: Your job is constantly on the line because the quotas and deadlines that you have to meet are too demanding. Unfortunately, as most social scientists could tell you, you are a victim of *Campbell's Law.* Several years ago Donald T. Campbell, a social psychologist specializing in research methodology, came to the following conclusion:

> The more any quantitative social indicator is used for social decision-making, the more subject it will be to corruption pressures and the more apt it will be to distort and corrupt the social processes that it is intended to monitor.

In other words, once a measurement (or *metric*) is specified as a key criterion for the success of a process or project, its ability to measure what it's supposed to will almost inevitably be compromised. Why? If the stakes and the cost of failure are too high, people tend to cheat.

Campbell's Law predicted, for example, what actually happened in Atlanta schools beginning in 2005 and culminating in 2015 when 11 former educators were convicted of racketeering charges stemming from a conspiracy to alter student test scores. The original investigation had extended to nearly 180 principals and teachers at more than 40 schools and had resulted in 35 indictments. The educators, it seems, were motivated and under stress by increasing pressure to meet official performance standards on which bonuses and even employment status depended, and adherents of Campbell's Law argue that the episode reflects the failure of a misguided control process designed to measure student performance too narrowly. According to one report on the Atlanta episode, the dilemma fostered by high-stakes educational standards is an all-too-clear demonstration of Campbell's original formula for control failure:

> School districts are increasingly tying teacher pay to performance, and there's no consensus on the best way to measure student proficiency, so high test scores are starting to look a lot like money. What emerges is bad news: a carrot-and-stick approach to a sector of the workforce that many consider to be underpaid.

We shouldn't be surprised by such responses to impractical performance measures, says Robert D. Behn of Harvard University's Kennedy School of Government: "After all, we have put significant pressure on schools and teachers to improve test scores. . . . When the pressure becomes personal—when a person's job and income are on the line—some people may resort to cheating. Why do you think all of those professional baseball players used steroids?"

Behn distinguishes between "honest cheating" and "dishonest cheating." Like the tactics used by certain educators in Atlanta, "dishonest cheating is illegal, and you can go to jail for it" (most of the convicted principals were served prison sentences of five to 20 years). On the other hand, such practices as "teaching to the test"—focusing one's efforts on standardized testing to the detriment of other educational activities—are merely "honest cheating": "There is nothing illegal about it. No one goes to jail for it. Still, it illustrates how putting pressure on schools, principals, and teachers to improve on very specific performance measures can produce the distortions about which Campbell worried."

According to Behn and other analysts of the impulse to cheat, a common denominator in both types of "honesty" is the imposition of "very specific performance measures." In business, such measures are often called *key performance indicators (KPIs)*—quantifiable metrics that show how well an organization is achieving its goals. KPIs can help an organization focus on its most effective strategies, but if they aren't conceived or executed properly, KPIs can be misleading. Campbell himself offered the example of a city that sets a strategy to reduce crime, designating the crime rate as a KPI. If the crime rate goes down, can city officials be sure that crime has actually been reduced? Not necessarily: What if police, in order to push down the rate, had adopted new criteria for crimes that must be formally reported or systematically downgraded to less serious classifications?

When enforced by such counterstrategic employee behavior, Campbell's Law can sabotage the best-laid plans—as you did when you gamed the process of meeting your quotas and deadlines. You were given a certain amount of discretion in the way you both achieved and reported your results, and you made your decision based on the fact that the stakes and the cost of failure were too high.

Ironically, your employer also gave you incentives to make the decision that you did—literally: In addition to protecting your job, you acted to secure your bonus and stock options. According to EthicalSystems, a nonprofit that compiles research on ethical leadership, conflicts of interest, cheating, and other related issues, extensive research shows that decisions like yours "are frequently distorted by incentives." An example, suggests James Freis Jr., an attorney specializing in financial-industry regulation, "might be a contractor who knows his bonus depends on the fulfillment of certain contracts and so may be tempted to offer a bribe to a foreign official who is responsible for signing off on a license, customs duty, or shipment." Relatedly, some contractors may have a bonus tied to completion dates. As these dates approach and if the project is behind schedule, there may be a tendency to take construction shortcuts.

Freis may well have been thinking about the case of Alcatel-Lucent SA, the world's largest supplier of land-line phone networks. The company agreed to pay $137 million to settle criminal and civil charges stemming from violations of the U.S. Foreign Corrupt Practices Act. According to the Securities and Exchange Commission, "Alcatel and its subsidiaries failed to detect or investigate numerous red flags suggesting that employees were directing sham consultants to provide gifts and payments to foreign government officials to illegally win business." Managers at Alcatel received the bulk of their pay in the form of stock incentives and bonuses tied to short-term profitability.

The problem, suggests Harvard's Behn, is the practice of pegging high-stakes incentives to narrow win-or-lose KPIs. As Campbell's Law shows, cheating—including the violation of an organization's ethics rules—will probably occur under such circumstances. "So get over it," Behn advises organizational strategists. "Don't go looking for the perfect performance measure. It doesn't exist. Don't waste countless meetings debating whose measure is without defects. All measures have them." Instead, he suggests,

> start with a good measure (or two). Not great, not perfect, just good. From the beginning, try to identify its inadequacies. Recognize what problems the measure might create; then, as you implement your performance strategy, be alert for the emergence of flaws and distortions. When suggesting, adopting, or employing a performance measure, all [managers] should be aware of—and beware of—Campbell's Law.

Case Questions

1. **What about you?** Put yourself in the position of the Atlanta educators whose dilemma is described in the case. If there was a real possibility that you'd lose your job because your students performed badly, how would you assess your situation and your options? What if there were a real possibility that you'd lose a pay raise and promotion? How about the possibility that you'd be reassigned to a much less desirable school? Be prepared to argue either side of your case.

2. Think about a class that you're taking now or have taken in the past. What KPI played the most important role in the instructor's evaluation of your performance? What did it tell you about your instructor's strategy for teaching the course? Do you think that it was too narrowly focused or otherwise unreasonable? If so, how do you think your instructor could have improved his performance-evaluation strategy?

3. Again, what about you? After having read this case, have you reconsidered your attitude toward how much control or accountability you'd like to have in a job? If, for example, you're studying to be a teacher, how do you

feel about a career goal such as moving up to principal or even multischool administrator? How does your concept of an ideal work/life relationship affect your thinking on the subject?

4. As we saw in Chapter 13, *incentives* "represent special compensation opportunities that are usually tied to performance"—that is, to a certain form of workplace behavior. They can also be tied to other forms of workplace behavior—such as complying with an employer's policies regarding legal and ethical conduct (its so-called *compliance and ethics, or C&E, program*). Incentives can be either "soft" (consisting of nontangible encouragement or recognition) or "hard" (typically consisting of tangible, often monetary rewards). What "C&E" incentives affect the way you conduct yourself, whether at work or at school? How do they stack up against the incentives to behave in accord with Campbell's Law? Is there any tension between the two sets of incentives? What do you do—or can you do—to resolve any tension as you make decisions affecting your behavior?

You Make the Call

Controlling the Cheesecakes

1. What kinds of control methods and systems does The Cheesecake Factory rely on? Which type of control is most important at the level of an individual restaurant? How about for the company as a whole?

2. Would you categorize The Cheesecake Factory as a service provider or a provider of goods, or both? How would your classification affect your quality-control decisions? How would it affect the way you approach operations?

3. Describe how budgets may be helpful for methods improvement in restaurant operations. What kinds of information would you hope to gain from the budgets?

4. Identify a major U.S. restaurant chain that has recently received *poor quality ratings*. Who are its customers, and what are the basic causes that led to declining quality?

5. U.S. restaurants must comply with local health regulations. The results of periodic inspections have to be posted or published, or both. What actions would you recommend be considered by restaurants to overcome negative perceptions from a less-than satisfactory rating?

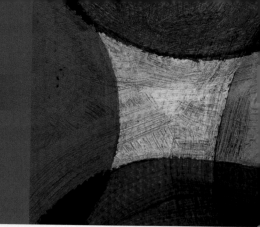

CHAPTER 15

Managing Operations, Quality, and Productivity

Learning Outcomes

After studying this chapter, you should be able to:

15-1   Describe the nature of operations management.

15-2   Discuss the components involved in designing effective operations systems.

15-3   Discuss organizational technologies and their role in operations management.

15-4   Identify the components involved in implementing operations systems through supply chain management.

15-5   Explain the meaning and importance of managing quality and total quality management.

15-6   Explain the meaning and importance of managing productivity, productivity trends, and ways to improve productivity.

In this chapter, we explore operations management, quality, and productivity. We first introduce operations management and discuss its role in general management and organizational strategy. The next three sections discuss the design of operations systems, organizational technologies, and implementing operations systems. We then introduce and discuss various issues in managing for quality and total quality. Finally, we discuss productivity, which is closely related to quality. We begin by analyzing the role of operations management in the retail industry and how Tesco has been using supply chain techniques to boost its global market share.

Management in Action

Out Supply-Chaining the King of Supply Chainers

". . . there isn't a place in the world where Tesco has gone one-on-one with Walmart and Tesco hasn't won."

—Kevin Coupe, Food-Retail Analyst

It's no secret that Walmart is the largest retailer (and indeed, the largest corporation based on revenue) on the planet, with total revenues in 2019 of $524 billion. It's almost five times larger than the number-two retailer in the United States, Home Depot (2019 revenue, $110 billion), and it's bigger than Europe's three largest retailers—France's Carrefour, Britain's Tesco, and Germany's Metro AG—combined. It is, according to the business-information service Hoover's, "an irresistible (or at least unavoidable) retail force that has yet to meet any immovable

Tesco is a master at supply chain management.

objects." One key to Walmart's success has been astute supply chain management. For example, Walmart was among the first to use point-of-sale scanners to track product sales and reorder quickly to meet shifting consumer buying patterns. And Walmart has also been ruthless at forcing its suppliers to continuously lower their own costs.

But some experts have recently noted that Walmart is actually getting beaten at its own game by one of its European rivals, Tesco. Food-retail analyst Kevin Coupe points out that "there isn't a place in the world where Tesco has gone one-on-one with Walmart and Tesco hasn't won." In Britain, for example, U.K.-owned Tesco, one of the world's largest food retailers, commands a 34-percent market share—double that of Walmart-owned Asda.

Tesco's 6,500 stores in 11 countries utilize five basic formats, customized to match the needs of the local market. Its ability to manage stores in multiple formats as well as multiple markets is one of the company's greatest strengths. The key to this core competence is technology—or, more precisely, data management—which is critical in any effort to optimize inventory selection, size, and distribution. Tesco, reports retail-industry analyst Scott Langdoc, "is ruthless in supply-chain management." In the United Kingdom, for instance, a wireless network connecting all Tesco stores facilitates real-time management of distribution and transportation. Workers use handheld PDAs for data entry and reporting, and radio frequency identification (RFID) tags allow them to track crates and pallets carrying anywhere from 3,500 to 60,000 different products going to markets located anywhere from Sussex to Seoul.

Tesco is good not only at applying data management to supply chain management, but it has also developed considerable skill in applying data management to the analysis of consumer preferences in different markets. Tesco relies on a data-mining firm called Dunnhumby (of which it has majority control) to manage everything from targeting sales promotions to designing store formats and, perhaps most importantly, developing private-label products. Along with its ability to manage multiple store formats, many analysts regard Tesco's ability to provide a better and broader range of private brands—products manufactured for retailers who sell them under their own names—as one of the most important factors in the company's marketing success. U.S. retailers, on the other hand, have never been quite able to convince consumers that private-label products are as good as their brand-name counterparts. Walmart, for example, struggles to get 35 percent of its sales from private-label goods. In many countries, however, Tesco gets as much as 60 percent of its revenue from private-label products.

The difference? Tesco, explains New York retail consultant Burt P. Flickinger III, knows which products to develop, how to price them, and how to integrate them into the product lines of its various stores. "[Our] range of high-quality own-label products," says CEO Dave Lewis, ". . . is an integral part of our offer in every market in which we operate." Tesco offers about 12,000 private-label and specialty brands at every price point. Some high-range products, such as Tesco Finest Chocolates, even sell at 50-percent premiums to established brands like Cadbury, and all of them sell at significantly higher margins than national brands.

According to Flickinger, "Tesco is arguably the finest food retailer in the world," and he suggests that, armed with a unique set of competencies, the British grocer may well be "Walmart's worst nightmare." But, like every business, Tesco isn't perfect. In 2007, for instance, it rolled out a new chain of food stores, called Fresh & Easy, in California, Arizona, and Nevada. Unfortunately, its timing and location choice couldn't have been worse. Tesco acquired its properties at the height of the U.S. property boom of the mid-2000s. California, Arizona, and Nevada, however, were among the worst-hit areas when the bubble in the U.S. housing market burst, dooming Fresh & Easy's viability. Tesco has now pulled out of the U.S. market but some experts believe the company will launch a new push in the near future. Indeed, Walmart knows it cannot rest easy, for the U.S. market is too big for a skillful and aggressive rival like Tesco to ignore for long.[1]

15-1 THE NATURE OF OPERATIONS MANAGEMENT

Operations management is at the core of what organizations do as they add value and create products and services. But what exactly are operations? And how are they managed? **Operations management** is the set of managerial activities used by an organization to transform resource inputs into products and services. When Dell Computer buys electronic components, assembles them into PCs, and then ships them to retailers and individual consumers, it is engaging in operations management. When a Pizza Hut employee orders food and paper products and then combines dough, cheese, and tomato paste to create a pizza, he or she is engaging in operations management.

operations management
The total set of managerial activities used by an organization to transform resource inputs into products, services, or both

15-1a The Importance of Operations

Operations is an important functional concern for organizations because efficient and effective management of operations goes a long way toward ensuring competitiveness and overall organizational performance, as well as enhancing quality and productivity. Inefficient or ineffective operations management, on the other hand, will almost inevitably lead to poorer performance and lower levels of both quality and productivity.

In an economic sense, operations management creates value and utility of one type or another, depending on the nature of the firm's products or services. If the product is a physical good, such as a Harley-Davidson motorcycle, operations creates value and provides form utility by combining many dissimilar inputs (sheet metal, rubber, paint, internal combustion engines, and human skills) to make something (a motorcycle) that is more valuable than the actual cost of the inputs used to create it. The inputs are converted from their incoming form into a new physical form. This conversion is typical of manufacturing operations and essentially reflects the organization's technology.

In contrast, the operations activities of Delta Airlines create value and provide time and place utility through its services. The airline transports passengers and freight according to agreed-upon departure and arrival places and times. Other service operations, such as a Coors beer distributorship or a Zara retail store, create value and provide place and possession utility by bringing together the customer and products made by others. Although the organizations in these examples produce different kinds of products or services, their operations processes share many important features.[2]

15-1b Manufacturing and Production Operations

manufacturing
A form of business that combines and transforms resource inputs into tangible outcomes

Because manufacturing once dominated U.S. industry, the entire area of operations management used to be called "production management." **Manufacturing** is a form of business that combines and transforms resources into tangible outcomes that are then sold to others. The Goodyear Tire & Rubber Company is a manufacturer because it combines rubber and chemical compounds and uses blending equipment and molding machines to create tires. Broyhill is a manufacturer because it buys wood and metal components, pads, and fabric and then combines them into furniture.

During the 1970s, manufacturing entered a long period of decline in the United States, primarily because of foreign competition. U.S. firms had grown complacent even as new foreign competitors came onto the scene with better equipment and much higher levels of efficiency. For example, steel companies in the Far East were able to produce high-quality steel for much lower prices than were U.S. companies like Bethlehem Steel and U.S. Steel. At one time these two companies were among the largest steel producers in the world. Bethlehem, though, closed its doors in 2003 while U.S. Steel has undergone several changes and is today a smaller (but much more profitable) company. Indeed, faced with a battle for survival, many companies underwent a long and difficult period of change, eliminating waste and transforming themselves into leaner, more efficient and responsive entities. They reduced their workforces dramatically, closed antiquated or unnecessary plants, and modernized their remaining plants. Since 2000 their efforts have started to pay dividends, as U.S. businesses have regained their competitive positions in many different industries. Although manufacturers from other parts of the world are still formidable competitors, and U.S. firms may never again be competitive in some markets, the overall picture is much better than it was just a few years ago. And prospects continue to look bright.[3]

15-1c Service Operations

service organization
An organization that transforms resources into an intangible output and creates time or place utility for its customers

During the decline of the manufacturing sector, a tremendous growth in the service sector kept the U.S. economy from declining at the same rate. A service organization is one that transforms resources into an intangible output and creates time or place utility for its customers. For example, Merrill Lynch makes stock transactions for its customers, Avis leases cars to its customers, and local hairstylists cut clients' hair. In 1947 the service sector was responsible for less than half of the U.S. gross national product (GNP). By 1975, however, this figure had reached 65 percent. And in 2018 the service sector accounted for nearly 80 percent of the private-sector gross domestic product (GDP) and provided 100 million jobs.[4] Managers in service organizations have come to see that many of the tools, techniques, and methods that are used in a factory are also useful to a service firm. For example, managers of automobile plants and hair salons both have to decide how to design their facilities, identify the best locations for them, determine optimal capacities, make decisions about inventory storage, set procedures for purchasing raw materials, and set standards for productivity and quality.

15-1d The Role of Operations in Organizational Strategy

It should be clear by this point that operations management is very important to organizations. Beyond its direct impact on such factors as competitiveness, quality, and productivity, it also directly influences the organization's overall level of effectiveness. For example, the deceptively simple strategic decision of whether to stress high quality regardless of cost, lowest possible cost regardless of quality, or some combination of the two has many important implications. A highest-possible-quality strategy will dictate state-of-the-art technology and rigorous control of product design and materials specifications. A combination strategy might call for lower-grade technology and less concern about product design and materials specifications. Just as strategy affects operations management, so, too, does operations management affect strategy. Suppose that a firm decides to upgrade the quality of its products or services. The organization's ability to implement the decision is dependent in part on current production capabilities and other resources. If existing technology will not permit higher-quality work, and if the organization lacks the resources to replace its technology, increasing quality to the desired new standards will be difficult. The *A World of Difference* feature illustrates how operations can give a new start-up operation a competitive advantage.

A WORLD OF DIFFERENCE

Dispensing Hope

On the outskirts of Santiago, Chile, food is expensive and options are limited. The lack of population density, coupled with low household incomes, has resulted in very few supermarkets. Most residents shop at small stores with narrow product lines and prices up to 40 percent higher than those found in more populated areas. In the hope of improving the lives of people living in these areas, Algramo, a Santiago-based company, has a unique distribution model. Algramo, whose name means "by the gram," buys products in bulk, keeping its costs low. The company installs high-tech vending machines in local stores and stocks them with beans, lentils, rice, and sugar, as well as other products. Algramo doesn't charge the storeowner for installing the machine and shares the profits from all sales equally with the shopkeeper. In just its first year of operation, Algramo had dispensers in more than 300 locations, serving approximately 36,000 customers.

The company is the brainchild of Chilean student Jose Manuel Moller. He and three friends moved to a small community outside Santiago in hopes of gaining a better understanding of the conditions for residents. While the neighborhood stores are an important meeting place for the community, high prices for food, coupled with low

wages, result in most residents struggling to meet their most basic needs. Moller began to see these high prices as a "poverty tax" imposed on the 70 percent of the Chilean population living outside the major cities, and he was determined to make a difference.

The company estimates that its model has allowed buyers to save up to 40 percent per month on household products, allowing them to use the saved funds to obtain better health care or to provide quality educational opportunities for their children. The benefits of Algramo's business model are not limited to the consumer but also extend to shopkeepers. Algramo's vending machines generate profits for small stores that operate on narrow margins, allowing them to stay in business and improve the owners' quality of life. Benefits of the model even extend to the environment: Algramo dispenses its products in reusable containers, reducing the waste associated with disposable packaging.

Algramo earned a B Company certification in 2014, and in 2015 *Fast Company* selected Algramo as one of the 50 most innovative companies in the world. In 2019, Algramo had a presence in over 1,600 stores, serving 220,000 customers in low-income areas and avoiding an estimated 180,000 kilograms of waste.[5]

Manager's Checklist

☐ Managers should be able to distinguish between manufacturing and production operations and service operations.

☐ You should also have a clear understanding of the operations management strategy or strategies in your organization.

15-2 DESIGNING OPERATIONS SYSTEMS

The problems, challenges, and opportunities faced by operations managers revolve around the acquisition and utilization of resources for conversion. Their goals include both efficiency and effectiveness. A number of issues and decisions must be addressed as operations systems are designed. The most basic ones are product-service mix, capacity, and facilities.

15-2a Determining Product-Service Mix

product–service mix
How many and what kinds of products or services (or both) to offer

A natural starting point in designing operations systems is determining the product–service mix. This decision flows from corporate, business, and marketing strategies. Managers have to make a number of decisions about their products and services, starting with how many and what kinds to offer.[6] Procter & Gamble, for example, makes regular, whitening, tartar-control, and various other formulas of Crest toothpaste; offers each in a variety of flavors; and packages them in several different sizes and kinds of tubes, pumps, and other dispensers. Similarly, workers at Subway sandwich shops (referred to as "Sandwich Artists" by the company) can combine different breads, vegetables, meats, and condiments to create hundreds of different kinds of sandwiches. Decisions also have to be made regarding the level of quality desired, the optimal cost of each product or service, and exactly how each is to be designed. During a review of its manufacturing operations, managers at General Electric figured out how to

A firm's product-service mix is determined in large part by corporate or business strategies. A logical next step is to design operations systems to efficiently produce products to be sold with the desired packaging and sizes. Of course, as shown here, most products are sold in a wide variety of forms and sizes.

reduce the number of parts in its industrial circuit breakers from 28,000 to 1,275. This whole process was achieved by carefully analyzing product design and production methods. Some firms quickly altered their product–service mix during the 2020 COVID-19 pandemic. For example, some restaurants started home-delivery services, some curbside pickup, and some even started selling grocery items like bread and milk. LVMH modified a perfume facility to make hand sanitizer and Ford revamped a plant to make medical ventilators.

capacity
The amount of products, services, or both that can be produced by an organization

15-2b Capacity Decisions

The capacity decision involves choosing the amount of products, services, or both that can be produced by the organization. Determining whether to build a factory capable of making 5,000 or 8,000 units per day is a capacity decision. So, too, is deciding whether to build a restaurant with 100 or 150 seats or a bank with five or 10 teller stations. The capacity decision is truly a high-risk one because of the uncertainties of future product demand and the large monetary stakes involved. An organization that builds capacity exceeding its needs may commit resources (capital investment, space, and so forth) that will never be recovered. Alternatively, an organization can build a facility with a smaller capacity than expected demand. Doing so may result in lost market opportunities, but it may also free capital resources for use elsewhere in the organization.

A major consideration in determining capacity is demand. A company operating with fairly constant monthly demand might build a plant capable of producing an amount each month roughly equivalent to its demand. But if its market is characterized by seasonal fluctuations, building a smaller plant to meet normal demand and then adding extra shifts staffed with temporary workers or paying permanent workers extra to work more hours during peak periods might be the most effective choice. Likewise, a restaurant

Capacity decisions are an important part of operations management. Take this restaurant, for example. Right now, many people are waiting for tables. If the restaurant were larger, more customers could be seated immediately and the restaurant would generate more revenue. However, during other periods when demand might be lower, the restaurant would have unused space and experience higher costs.

In the wake of COVID-19, most entertainment venues like theme parks, movie theaters, and so forth imposed social-distancing measures. Universal Studios, for instance, placed markers on the ground to remind people in ride queues to maintain six feet of space between each party.

iStock.com/anilbolukbas

that needs 150 seats for Saturday night but never needs more than 100 at any other time during the week would probably be foolish to expand to 150 seats. During the rest of the week, it must still pay to light, heat, cool, and clean the excess capacity. Many customer service departments have tried to improve their capacity to deal with customers while also lowering costs by using automated voice prompts to direct callers to the right representative. Many businesses had to adjust their capacities during the 2020 COVID-19 pandemic. For instance, at various times restaurants were restricted to 25 or 50 percent of their normal capacity. Theme parks like Universal Studios and Disney World also limited the number of people who could visit each day. And many factories had to limit the number of employees who could work at the same time.

15-2c Facilities Decisions

Facilities are the physical locations where products or services are created, stored, and distributed. Major decisions pertain to facilities location and facilities layout.

Location   **Location** is the physical positioning or geographic site of facilities and must be determined by the needs and requirements of the organization. A company that relies heavily on railroads for transportation needs to be located close to rail facilities. Nucor Steel, for instance, only locates its mills adjacent to rail lines. General Electric decided that it did not need six plants to make circuit breakers, so it invested heavily in automating one plant and closed the other five. Different organizations in the same industry may have different facilities requirements. Benetton uses only one distribution center for the entire world, whereas Walmart has several distribution centers in the United States alone. A traditional retailer must choose its location very carefully to be convenient for consumers, while an industrial facility can often be located in a less-visible business park or other area where rent is cheaper.

Layout   The choice of physical configuration, or the **layout**, of facilities is closely related to other operations decisions. The three entirely different layout alternatives shown in Figure 15.1 help demonstrate the importance of the layout decision.

A **product layout** is appropriate when large quantities of a single product are needed. It makes sense to custom-design a straight-line flow of work for a product when a specific task is performed at each workstation as each unit flows past. Most assembly lines use this format. For example, Dell's personal computer factories use a product layout.

Process layouts are used in operations settings that create or process a variety of products or activities. Auto repair shops and health care clinics are good examples. Each car and each person is a separate "product." The needs of each incoming job are diagnosed as it enters the operations system, and the job is routed through the unique sequence of workstations needed to create the desired finished product. In a process layout, each type of conversion task is centralized in a single workstation or department. All welding is done in one designated shop location, and any car that requires welding is moved to that area. This setup is in contrast to the product layout, in which several different workstations may perform welding operations if the conversion task sequence so dictates. Similarly, in a hospital, all x-rays are done in one location, all surgeries in another, and all physical therapy in yet another. Patients are moved from location to location to get the services they need.

facilities
The physical locations where products or services are created, stored, and distributed

location
The physical positioning or geographic site of facilities

layout
The physical configuration of facilities, the arrangement of equipment within facilities, or both

product layout
A physical configuration of facilities arranged around the product; used when large quantities of a single product are needed

process layouts
A physical configuration of facilities arranged around the process; used in facilities that create or process a variety of products

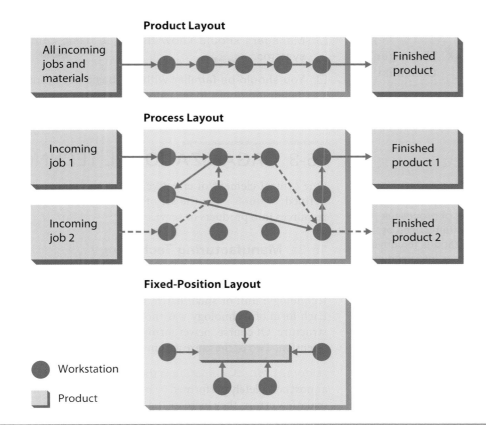

FIGURE 15.1

Approaches to Facilities Layout

When a manufacturer produces large quantities of a product (such as cars or computers), it may arrange its facilities in an assembly line (product layout). In a process layout, the work (such as patients in a hospital or custom pieces of furniture) moves through various workstations. Locomotives and bridges are both manufactured in a fixed-position layout.

fixed-position layout
A physical configuration of facilities arranged around a single work area; used for the manufacture of large and complex products such as airplanes

cellular layouts
A physical configuration of facilities used when families of products can follow similar flow paths

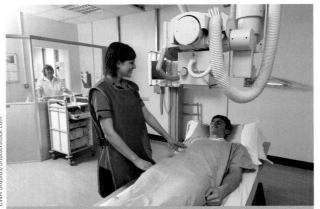

Most hospitals use process layouts to treat patients. This patient, for example, has been brought from his room to the x-ray lab. After imaging is complete, he will return to his room before then moving again to the operating theater to receive the appropriate treatment. Later, he will be taken to the physical therapy center to begin his recovery.

The **fixed-position layout** is used when the organization is creating a few very large and complex products. Aircraft manufacturers like Boeing and shipbuilders like General Dynamics use this method. An assembly line capable of moving one of Boeing's 787 aircraft would require an enormous plant, so instead the airplane itself remains stationary, and people and machines move around it as it is assembled.

The cellular layout is a relatively new approach to facilities design. Cellular layouts are used when families of products can follow similar flow paths. A clothing manufacturer, for example, might create a cell, or designated area, dedicated to making a family of pockets, such as pockets for shirts, coats, blouses, and slacks. Although each kind of pocket is unique, the same basic equipment and methods are used to make all of them. Hence, all pockets might be made in the same area and then delivered directly to different product layout assembly areas where the shirts, coats, blouses, and slacks are actually being assembled.

Manager's Checklist

☐ Managers should know the three basic components in designing operations systems.

☐ You should be familiar with the basic decisions that relate to each component in designing operations systems.

15-3 ORGANIZATIONAL TECHNOLOGIES

technology
The set of processes and systems used by organizations to convert resources into products or services

One central element of effective operations management is technology. In Chapter 3 we defined technology as the set of processes and systems used by organizations to convert resources into products or services.

15-3a Manufacturing Technology

Numerous forms of manufacturing technology are used in organizations. In Chapter 11 we discussed the research of Joan Woodward. Recall that Woodward identified three forms of technology: unit or small batch, large batch or mass production, and continuous process.[7] Each form of technology was thought to be associated with a specific type of organization structure. Of course, newer forms of technology not considered by Woodward also warrant attention. Two of these are automation and computer-assisted manufacturing.

automation
The process of designing work so that it can be completely or almost completely performed by machines

Automation   Automation is the process of designing work so that it can be completely or almost completely performed by machines. Because automated machines operate quickly and make few errors, they increase the amount of work that can be done. Thus, automation helps to improve products and services and fosters innovation. Automation is the most recent step in the development of machines and machine-controlling devices. Machine-controlling devices have been around since the 1700s. James Watt, a Scottish engineer, invented a mechanical speed control to regulate the speed of steam engines in 1787. The Jacquard loom, developed by a French inventor, was controlled by paper cards with holes punched in them. Early accounting and computing equipment were controlled by similar punched cards.

Automation relies on feedback, information, sensors, and a control mechanism. Feedback is the flow of information from the machine back to the sensor. Sensors are the parts of the system that gather information and compare it to preset standards. The control mechanism is the device that sends instructions to the automatic machine. Early automatic machines were primitive, and the use of automation was relatively slow to develop. These elements are illustrated by the example in Figure 15.2. A thermostat has sensors that monitor air temperature and compare it to a preset value. If the air temperature falls below the preset value, the thermostat sends an electrical signal to the furnace, turning it on. The furnace heats the air. When the sensors detect that the air temperature has reached a value higher than the low preset value, the thermostat stops the furnace. The last step (shutting off the furnace) is known as *feedback*, a critical component of any automated operation.

The big move to automate factories began during World War II. The shortage of skilled workers and the development of high-speed computers combined to bring about a tremendous interest in automation. Programmable automation (the use of computers to control machines) was introduced during this era, eventually replacing most conventional automation (the use of mechanical or electromechanical devices to control machines). The automobile industry began to use automatic machines for a variety of jobs. In fact, the term *automation* came into use in the 1950s in the automobile industry. The chemical and oil-refining industries also began to use computers to regulate production. During the 1990s, automation became a major element in the manufacture of computers and computer components, such as electronic chips and circuits. And in the last two decades automation has been extended to clothing manufacturing, package sorting and delivery, and order fulfillment in warehouses. It is this computerized, or programmable, automation that presents the greatest opportunities and challenges for management today.

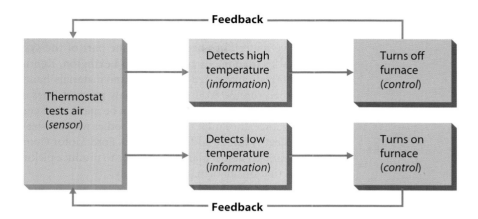

Feedback

FIGURE 15.2

A Simple Automatic Control Mechanism

All automation includes feedback, information, sensors, and a control mechanism. A simple thermostat is an example of automation. Another example is Benetton's distribution center in Italy. Orders are received, items pulled from stock and packaged for shipment, and invoices prepared and transmitted, with no human intervention.

The impact of automation on people in the workplace is complex. In the short term, specific individuals whose jobs are automated may, in fact, end up without a job. In the long term, however, more jobs tend to be added than are lost. This is attributable to the idea that automation improves overall economic growth, spurring business growth and expansion and thus creating more jobs. Nevertheless, not all companies are able to help displaced workers find new jobs, so the human costs are sometimes high, especially in the short run. In the coal industry, for instance, automation has been used primarily in mining. The output per miner has risen dramatically from the 1950s on. The demand for coal, however, has decreased, and productivity gains resulting from automation have lessened the need for miners. Consequently, many workers have lost their jobs, and the industry has not been able to absorb them. In contrast, in the electronics industry, the rising demand for products has led to increasing employment opportunities despite the growing use of automation.[8]

Computer-Assisted Manufacturing   Current extensions of automation generally revolve around computer-assisted manufacturing. Computer-assisted manufacturing is technology that relies on computers to design or manufacture products. One type of computer-assisted manufacturing is *computer-aided design (CAD)*—the use of computers to design parts and complete products and to simulate performance so that prototypes need not be constructed. Boeing uses CAD technology to study hydraulic tubing in its commercial aircraft. Japan's automotive industry uses it to speed up car design. GE used CAD to change the design of circuit breakers, and Benetton uses CAD to design new styles and products. Oneida, the table flatware firm, uses CAD to design new flatware patterns; for example, it can design a new spoon in a single day. CAD is usually combined with *computer-aided manufacturing (CAM)* to ensure that the design moves smoothly to production. The production computer shares the design computer's information and can have machines with the proper settings ready when production is needed. A CAM system is especially useful when reorders come in because the computer can quickly produce the desired product, prepare labels and copies of orders, and send the product out to where it is wanted.

Closely aligned with this approach is *computer-integrated manufacturing (CIM)*. In CIM, CAD and CAM are linked together, and computer networks automatically adjust machine placements and settings to enhance both the complexity and the flexibility of scheduling. In settings that use these technologies, all manufacturing activities are controlled by the computer network. Because the network can access the company's other information systems, CIM is both a powerful and a complex management control tool.

computer-assisted manufacturing
A technology that relies on computers to design or manufacture products

Flexible manufacturing systems (FMS) usually have robotic work units or workstations, assembly lines, and robotic carts or some other form of computer-controlled transport system to move material as needed from one part of the system to another. FMS like the one at Lexmark's manufacturing facility in Lexington, Kentucky, rely on computers to coordinate and integrate automated production and materials-handling facilities. When garment retailers like Abercrombie & Fitch launch new product lines, they often plan several variations of specific products so that changes can be made once consumer demand is better understood. For instance, they might make shirt bodies without sleeves, knowing that long, mid-length, or short sleeves can be added as needed. Ford Motor Company has also been a pioneer in FMS. It can quickly adjust plant capabilities to produce pickups, SUVs, or small hybrids depending on fluctuations in demand and supply.[9]

These systems are not without disadvantages, however. For example, because they represent fundamental change, they also generate resistance. Additionally, because of their tremendous complexity, CAD systems are not always reliable. CIM systems are so expensive that they raise the breakeven point for firms using them. This means that the firm must operate at high levels of production and sales to be able to afford the systems.

"Lean isn't good enough anymore. The new reality requires being both lean and flexible."
—David Cole, Automobile Industry Expert

Robotics   Another trend in manufacturing technology is computerized robotics. A **robot** is any artificial device that can perform functions ordinarily thought to be appropriate for human beings. Robotics refers to the science and technology of the construction, maintenance, and use of robots. The use of industrial robots has steadily increased over the last few decades and is expected to continue to increase slowly as more companies recognize the benefits that accrue to users of industrial robots.

robot
Any artificial device that is able to perform functions ordinarily thought to be appropriate for human beings

Welding was one of the first applications for robots, and it continues to be the area for most applications. A close second is materials handling. Other applications include machine loading and unloading, painting and finishing, assembly, casting, and such machining applications as cutting, grinding, polishing, drilling, sanding, buffing, and deburring. Daimler AG, for instance, replaced about 200 welders with 50 robots on an assembly line and increased productivity about 20 percent. The use of robots in inspection work is increasing. They can check for cracks and holes, and they can be equipped with vision systems to perform visual inspections.

Robots are also beginning to move from the factory floor to other applications. The Dallas police used a robot to apprehend a suspect who had barricaded himself in an apartment building. The robot smashed a window and reached with its mechanical arm into the building. The suspect panicked and ran outside. At the Long Beach Memorial Hospital in California, brain surgeons are assisted by a robot arm that drills into the patient's skull with extreme precision. Some newer applications involve remote work. For example, the use of robot submersibles controlled from the surface can help divers in remote locations. Surveillance robots fitted with microwave sensors can do things that a human guard cannot do, such as "seeing" through nonmetallic walls and in the

Jenson/Shutterstock.com

Many large manufacturers today make use of robots for part of their assembly processes. These robots, for instance, are welding together parts of automobiles moving along an assembly line. The robots can perform these welding tasks faster and more accurately than can human workers. On the other hand, there are many other tasks that humans can perform better than robots.

"Neither workers nor robots can reach their productive potential without interacting more closely."
—Volker Grünenwald, Head of Systems Integration at Pilz, A German Engineering Firm

dark. In other applications, automated farming (called "agrimation") uses robot harvesters to pick fruit from a variety of trees.

Robots are also used by small manufacturers. One robot slices carpeting to fit the inside of custom vans in an upholstery shop. Another stretches balloons flat so that they can be spray-painted with slogans at a novelties company. At a jewelry company, a robot holds class rings while they are engraved by a laser. These robots are lighter, faster, stronger, and more intelligent than those used in heavy manufacturing and are the types that more and more organizations will be using in the future.

15-3b Service Technology

Service technology is also changing rapidly. And it, too, is moving more and more toward automated systems and procedures. In banking, for example, technological breakthroughs led to automated teller machines and made it much easier to move funds between accounts or between different banks. Most people now have their paychecks deposited directly into a checking account from which many of their bills are then automatically paid. Electronic banking—where people can access their accounts, move money between accounts, and pay bills—has become commonplace, and many people deposit checks digitally using imaging from their smartphones.

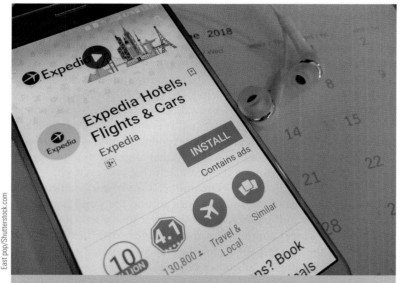

East pop/Shutterstock.com

Hotels use increasingly sophisticated technology to accept and record room reservations. People can now, for instance, check in online and then use their smartphone to enter their room. Universities use digital technologies to electronically store and provide access to books, scientific journals, government reports, and articles. Hospitals and other health care organizations use new forms of service technology to manage patient records, dispatch ambulances and EMTs, and monitor patient vital signs. Restaurants use technology to record and fill customer orders, order food and supplies, and prepare food. If you've ever seen a performance by Cirque du Soleil, you probably have some idea of the role played by technology in its spectacular productions. Given the increased role that service organizations—from restaurants and dry cleaners to hotels and live performances—are playing in today's economy, even more technological innovations are certain to be developed in the years to come.[10]

Hotels are using increasingly sophisticated technology, including apps like Expedia, to enable guests to book reservations and upgrades. These same apps can also be used to book flights, rental cars, and other travel services.

Manager's Checklist

☐ Managers should be familiar with new manufacturing technologies.

☐ Managers also need to be familiar with new service technologies.

☐ You should also understand your organization's approach to manufacturing and/or service technologies.

15-4 IMPLEMENTING OPERATIONS SYSTEMS THROUGH SUPPLY CHAIN MANAGEMENT

After operations systems have been properly designed and technologies developed, they must then be put into use by the organization. Their basic functional purpose is to control transformation processes to ensure that relevant goals are achieved in such areas as quality and costs. Operations management has a number of special purposes within this control framework, including purchasing and inventory management. Indeed, this area of management has become so important in recent years that a new term—*supply chain management*—has been coined. Specifically, supply chain management can be defined as the process of managing operations control, resource acquisition and purchasing, and inventory so as to improve overall efficiency and effectiveness.[11]

15-4a Operations Management as Control

One way of using operations management as control is to coordinate it with other functions. Bayer, for example, established a consumer products division that produces and distributes fertilizers and lawn chemicals. To facilitate control, the operations function was organized as an autonomous profit center. Bayer finds this effective because its manufacturing division is given the authority to determine not only the costs of creating the product but also the product price and the marketing program.

In terms of overall organizational control, a division like the one used by Bayer should be held accountable only for the activities over which it has decision-making authority. It would be inappropriate, of course, to make operations accountable for profitability in an organization that stresses sales and market share over quality and productivity. Misplaced accountability results in ineffective organizational control, to say nothing of hostility and conflict. Depending on the strategic role of operations, then, operations managers are accountable for different kinds of results. For example, in an organization using bureaucratic control, accountability will be spelled out in rules and regulations. In a decentralized system, it is likely to be understood and accepted by everyone.

Within operations, managerial control ensures that resources and activities achieve primary goals such as a high percentage of on-time deliveries, low unit-production cost, or high product reliability. Any control system should focus on the elements that are most crucial to goal attainment. For example, firms in which product quality is a major concern (as it is at Rolex) might adopt a screening control system to monitor the product as it is being created. If quantity is a higher priority (as it is at Timex), a postaction system might be used to identify defects at the end of the system without disrupting the manufacturing process itself.

When Boeing started production of its Boeing 787 Dreamliner, the plane was hailed as the most commercially successful new plane of all time. Airlines around the world preordered over 900 of the planes at a cost of $178 million each before they ever took a test flight, based on its projected fuel efficiency, passenger comfort, low maintenance costs, flexibility, and other major design elements. But the first test flights for the plane were over two years late, largely because of supply chain issues. Boeing subcontracted out the design and assembly of major components of the 787 to firms in Japan, Italy, South Carolina, and Kansas, but did not impose adequate coordination or control standards across these various suppliers. As a result, subassemblies did not fit together properly, there were numerous quality and delivery issues, and myriad other problems. Clearly, then, poor supply chain management can be disastrous, especially for major new products.[12]

Recent events have also underscored the consequences of disruptions to supply chains. In the early days of the 2020 COVID-19 pandemic, for example, many areas experienced shortages of certain products, most notably cleaning products and paper goods. These shortages, though, were not due to the products not being manufactured but instead were caused by breakdowns in one or more elements of their supply chains. Suppose, for example, that a particular company routinely orders and receives various chemicals that are then combined to manufacture hand sanitizer. The finished product is then poured into containers and labels applied to the containers. The bottles are then packed into cardboard boxes. Next, a shipping company picks up boxes of the product from the manufacturer and transports them to a distribution center where they are stored, then picked up again to be delivered to a retailer that has placed an order (and this is actually a very simple supply chain example). Now, further suppose that the company that provides the cardboard boxes was located in an area that was greatly impacted by COVID-19 and closed its doors for several weeks. In reality, there was plenty of hand sanitizer, shipping companies willing to transport it, and retailers wanting to sell it. However, because there were no boxes available near the beginning of the

---

supply chain management
The process of managing operations control, resource acquisition, and inventory so as to improve overall efficiency and effectiveness

The 2020 COVID-19 pandemic resulted in many short-term product shortages. This customer, for example, is facing limited options as she does her shopping. Fortunately, as supply chains recovered, most shortages were eliminated.

purchasing management
Buying materials and resources needed to produce products and services

inventory control
Managing the organization's raw materials, work in process, finished goods, and products in transit

Work-in-process inventories consist of partially completed products that are not yet ready for shipment or sale. This furniture maker, for example, is working on drawers for a new chest. The partially finished chest has value and is considered to be an asset for business purposes but has not yet achieved its final form and full value.

supply chain, customers at the end of the supply chain would not be able to purchase it. Similarly, many companies around the globe use parts and components manufactured in China. China, as you will recall, was the first—and one of the hardest hit—countries by COVID-19. To better control the spread of the virus the Chinese government ordered that most businesses, including factories, shut down for several weeks. This shutdown, in turn, led to shortages of parts that companies in other countries had come to depend on.

15-4b Purchasing Management

Purchasing management, also called *procurement*, is concerned with buying the materials and resources needed to create products and services. In many ways, purchasing is at the very heart of effective supply chain management. The purchasing manager for a retailer like Nordstrom or Target is responsible for buying the merchandise the store will sell. The purchasing manager for a manufacturer buys raw materials, parts, and machines needed by the organization. Large companies like GE, IBM, and Siemens have large purchasing departments.[13] The manager responsible for purchasing must balance a number of constraints. Buying too much ties up capital and increases storage costs. Buying too little might lead to shortages and higher reordering costs. The manager must also make sure that the quality of what is purchased meets the organization's needs, that the supplier is reliable, and that the best financial terms are negotiated.

Many firms have changed their approaches to purchasing over the years as a means of lowering costs and improving quality and productivity. In particular, rather than relying on hundreds or even thousands of suppliers, many companies have reduced their numbers of suppliers and negotiated special production-delivery arrangements.[14] For example, the Honda plant in Marysville, Ohio, found a local business owner looking for a new opportunity. They negotiated an agreement whereby the business owner would start a new company to mount car radio speakers into plastic moldings. He delivers finished goods to the plant three times a day, and Honda buys all he can manufacture. Thus, he has a stable sales base, Honda has a local and reliable supplier, and both companies benefit.

15-4c Inventory Management

Inventory control, also called *materials control*, is essential for effective operations management. The four basic kinds of inventories are *raw materials*, *work-in-process*, *finished-goods*, and *in-transit* inventories. As shown in Table 15.1, the sources of control over these inventories are as different as their purposes. Work-in-process inventories, for example, are made up of partially completed products that need further processing; they are controlled by the shop-floor system. In contrast, the quantities and costs of finished-goods inventories are under the control of the overall production scheduling system, which is determined by high-level planning decisions. In-transit inventories are controlled by the transportation and distribution systems.

Table 15.1	Inventory Types, Purposes, and Sources of Control	
Type	**Purpose**	**Source of Control**
Raw materials	Provide the materials needed to make the product	Purchasing models and systems
Work in process	Enable overall production to be divided into stages of manageable size	Shop-floor control systems
Finished goods	Provide ready supply of products on customer demand and enable long, efficient production runs	High-level production scheduling systems in conjunction with marketing
In transit (pipeline)	Distribute products to customers	Transportation and distribution control systems

just-in-time (JIT) method
An inventory system that has necessary materials arriving as soon as they are needed (just in time) so that the production process is not interrupted

Like most other areas of operations management, inventory management has changed notably over the past few decades. One particularly important breakthrough is the just-in-time (JIT) method. First popularized by the Japanese, the JIT system reduces the organization's investment in storage space for raw materials and in the materials themselves. Historically, manufacturers built large storage areas and filled them with materials, parts, and supplies that would be needed days, weeks, and even months in the future. A manager using the JIT approach orders materials and parts more often and in smaller quantities, thereby reducing investment in both storage space and actual inventory. The ideal arrangement is for materials to arrive just as they are needed—or just in time.[15]

Recall our example about the small firm that assembles radio speakers for Honda and delivers them three times a day, making it unnecessary for Honda to carry large quantities of the speakers in inventory. In an even more significant example, Johnson Controls makes automobile seats for Mercedes and ships them by small truckloads to a Mercedes plant 75 miles away. Each shipment is scheduled to arrive two hours before it is needed. Clearly, the JIT approach requires high levels of coordination and cooperation between the company and its suppliers. If shipments arrive too early, Mercedes has to find a place to store them. If they arrive too late, the entire assembly line may have to be shut down, resulting in enormous expense. When properly designed and used, the JIT method controls inventory very effectively. Our *Tech Watch* feature illustrates how a breakdown in JIT food deliveries resulted in major problems for both KFC and its employees.

TECH WATCH

When the Colonel Ran Out of Chicken

KFC is a division of Yum! Brands, the largest fast-food chain in the world. KFC, founded by Colonel Harland Sanders, originally stood for Kentucky Fried Chicken. Shortly after the chain was acquired by PepsiCo in 1986 its name was shortened to KFC, primarily because of the negative health connotations of the word "fried." In 1997 Pepsi packaged KFC with its other restaurant brands, Taco Bell and Pizza Hut, and spun the business off as Tricon Global Restaurants. Tricon was renamed Yum! Brands in 2002 after it acquired A&W and Long John Silver's.

Today there are more than 17,400 KFC stores in over 100 countries. As you might expect, then, people who walk into any of these 17,400 KFC stores on any given

day expect to be able to buy . . . chicken. But amazingly, one day in early 2018 many KFC stores in the United Kingdom had little or no chicken to sell! What had happened? Had the Colonel overslept? No, not at all. The real problem was a supply chain issue caused by a switch in delivery companies.

KFC's UK operation had for many years relied on a food distribution specialist called Bidvest to deliver chicken products to its 900 UK restaurants. Bidvest has several distribution centers throughout the United Kingdom and a well-oiled distribution network developed over several years of experience. When their delivery contract with KFC came up for renewal, however, they were underbid

(Continued)

TECH WATCH (CONTINUED)

by an international delivery company named DHL. While DHL has years of experience delivering international freight, they were just entering the food delivery business. After DHL won the contract, they, in turn, hired another company called Quick Service Logistics (QSL) to develop software to help them create a network to run their new service.

Unfortunately for both KFC and DHL, there was not enough time to try out the new distribution system and work out all of the bugs. As a result, when the changeover from Bidvest to DHL happened in mid-February 2018 many KFC chicken orders simply went unfulfilled. And when KFC stores began to run out of chicken, they had no choice but to close. At one point almost 600 of the 900 UK KFC stores were closed. Of course, the most "public" issue faced by KFC was that its customers could not buy their chicken. Behind the scenes, though, there was another big problem. What happened to the KFC restaurant employees when they had no jobs to perform?

As it turns out, the answer depended on who they actually worked for. About a third of the KFC restaurants in the United Kingdom are owned by the chain's parent company Yum! Brands. Those employees affected by the chicken shortage were "encouraged" to take holiday, or vacation, but were not forced to do so. Those who chose to not take holiday and who were in salaried positions continued to receive their normal salaries. Hourly workers, meanwhile, received an amount based on the average hours worked per day for the previous 12 weeks.

Other KFC stores, however, are owned and operated by franchisees. KFC's corporate office indicated that "Franchisees will be seeking their own independent advice, but we're encouraging them to adopt this (corporate) policy too." In other words, we hope they will treat their workers in the same way that we are, but they can really do what they want. In the ensuing chaos many KFC workers reported that they were being given zero-hour shifts, essentially meaning that they had jobs but were not working and therefore not getting paid. As one KFC worker told the BBC, "This problem isn't our fault, but we are the ones who can't work. I have bills that come out of my account on Friday and I feel terrible about the whole situation. I am looking for a new job."

In the end, many KFC restaurants were able to open around two weeks after the shortages began, while others remained closed for almost a month. So, how much did this debacle cost KFC? No one can say for sure, of course. There was the actual loss of short-term revenue, which could be estimated. On top of that was the loss of trust in a chicken restaurant that runs out of chicken and the associated public-relations embarrassment. And then, behind the scenes, there were the additional costs associated with reduced employee morale and replacement costs for employees who simply got fed up and found new jobs.

References: "KFC Shortages to Continue All Week," BBC, February 20, 2018, www.bbc.com/news/business.com on June 10, 2020; *Hoovers Handbook of World Business 2020* (Austin, TX: Hoover's Business Press, 2020), pp. 465–467.

Manager's Checklist

☐ Managers should be familiar with supply chain management and its basic components.

☐ You should also be familiar with your organization's approach to supply chain management.

15-5 MANAGING TOTAL QUALITY

Quality and productivity have become major determinants of business success or failure today and are central issues in managing organizations. But, as we will see, achieving higher levels of quality is not an easy accomplishment. Simply ordering that quality be improved is about as effective as waving a magic wand.[16] The catalyst for its emergence as a mainstream management concern was foreign business, especially Japanese. And nowhere was it more visible than in the auto industry. During an early energy crisis back in the 1970s many people bought Toyotas, Hondas, and Nissans because they were more fuel-efficient than U.S. cars. Consumers soon found, however, that not only were the Japanese cars more fuel-efficient, they were also of higher quality than U.S. cars. Parts fit together better, the trim work was neater, and the cars were more reliable. Thus, after the energy crisis subsided, Japanese cars remained formidable competitors because of their reputation for quality.

"You cannot copy high quality, and it takes a long time to get a reputation for quality."
—Millard "Mickey" Drexler, Former CEO of J. Crew

Table 15.2	Eight Dimensions of Quality

1.	*Performance.* A product's primary operating characteristic; examples are automobile acceleration and a television's picture clarity
2.	*Features.* Supplements to a product's basic functioning characteristics, such as power windows on a car
3.	*Reliability. A* probability of not malfunctioning during a specified period
4.	*Conformance.* The degree to which a product's design and operating characteristics meet established standards
5.	*Durability.* A measure of product life
6.	*Serviceability.* The speed and ease of repair
7.	*Aesthetics.* How a product looks, feels, tastes, and smells
8.	*Perceived quality.* As seen by a customer

These eight dimensions generally capture the meaning of quality, which is a critically important contributor to organizational success today. Understanding the basic meaning of quality is a good first step toward managing it more effectively.

Source: Exhibit from "Competing on the Eight Dimensions of Quality," by David A. Garvin, November/December 1987. Harvard Business School Publishing Corporation;

15-5a The Meaning of Quality

quality
The totality of features and characteristics of a product or service that bear on its ability to satisfy stated or implied needs

The American Society for Quality Control defines quality as the totality of features and characteristics of a product or service that bear on its ability to satisfy stated or implied needs.[17] Quality has several different attributes. Table 15.2 lists eight basic dimensions that determine the quality of a particular product or service. For example, a product that has durability and is reliable is of higher quality than a product with less durability and reliability.

Quality is also relative. For example, a Lincoln is a higher-grade car than a Ford Fusion, which, in turn, is a higher-grade car than a Ford Focus. The difference in quality stems from differences in design and other features. The Focus, however, is considered a high-quality car relative to its engineering specifications and price. Likewise, the Fusion and Lincoln may also be high-quality cars, given their standards and prices. Thus, quality is both an absolute and a relative concept. Quality is also relevant for both products and services. Although its importance for products like cars and computers was perhaps recognized first, service firms ranging from airlines to restaurants have also come to see that quality is a vitally important determinant of their success or failure. Service quality, as we discuss later in this chapter, has thus also become a major competitive issue in U.S. industries today.[18]

"[Porsches] . . . cost a lot of money. When you spend that kind of money, you expect things to be right."

—Lynn Kinzig, Porsche Dealer

Malcolm Baldrige Award
Named after a former secretary of commerce, this prestigious award is given to firms that achieve major quality improvements

15-5b The Importance of Quality

To help underscore the importance of quality, the U.S. government created the Malcolm Baldrige Award, named after the former secretary of commerce who championed quality in U.S. industry. The award, administered by an agency of the Commerce Department, is given annually to firms that achieve major improvements in the quality of their products or services. In other words, the award is based on changes in quality, as opposed to absolute quality. In addition, many other quality awards have been created. For example, the Rochester Institute of Technology and *USA Today* award their Quality Cup award not to entire organizations but to individual teams of workers within organizations. Quality is also an important concern for individual managers and organizations for three very specific reasons: competition, productivity, and costs.[19]

Competition   Quality has become one of the most competitive points in business today. Ford, Daimler AG, General Motors, and Toyota, for example, each imply that their cars and trucks are higher in quality than the cars and trucks of the others. And American, Delta, and

United Airlines each claim to provide the best and most reliable service. In the wake of the recent economic recession resulting from the COVID-19 pandemic, many businesses have focused even more attention on service quality as a competitive advantage during lean times. While some firms, for example, cut their staff at customer call centers, others did not. What impact might this have? One study found that cutting four representatives at a call center of three dozen people sent the number of customers put on hold for four minutes from zero to 80. Firms with especially strong reputations for service quality include Amazon, USAA (an insurance firm), Lexus, Ritz-Carlton, Ace Hardware, and Apple.[20]

"During tough times there are plenty of other pressures customers face. We don't want a customer service issue to be what makes them blow a cork."

—John Venhuizen, President and CEO of Ace Hardware

Productivity Managers have also come to recognize that quality and productivity are related. Some managers once thought that they could increase output (productivity) only by decreasing quality. Managers today have learned the hard way that such an assumption is almost always wrong. If a firm installs a meaningful quality enhancement program, three things are likely to result. First, the number of product or service defects is likely to decrease, causing fewer returns and complaints from customers. Second, because the number of defects goes down, resources (materials and people) dedicated to reworking flawed output will be decreased. Third, because making employees responsible for quality reduces the need for quality inspectors, the organization can produce more units with fewer resources.

total quality management (TQM) (quality assurance)
A strategic commitment by top management to change its whole approach to business in order to make quality a guiding factor in everything it does

Costs Improved quality also lowers costs. Poor quality results in higher returns from customers, high warranty costs, and lawsuits from customers injured by faulty products. Future sales are lost because of disgruntled customers. An organization with quality problems often has to increase inspection expenses just to catch defective products. We noted in Chapter 19, for example, how at one point Whistler Corporation was using 40 percent of its workforce just to fix poorly assembled radar detectors made by the other 60 percent.[21]

IGOR_SINUS/Shutterstock.com

Notice the poor quality sewing on this denim jacket.

15-5c Total Quality Management

Once an organization makes a decision to enhance the quality of its products and services, it must then decide how to implement this decision. The most pervasive approach to managing quality has been called total quality management (TQM; sometimes called quality assurance)—a real and meaningful effort by an organization to change its whole approach to business in order to make quality a guiding factor in everything the organization does.[22] Figure 15.3 highlights the major ingredients in TQM.

Strategic Commitment The starting point for TQM is a strategic commitment by top management. Such commitment is important for several reasons. First, the organizational culture must change to recognize that quality is not just an abstract ideal but an objective goal that must be pursued.[23] Second, a decision to pursue the goal of quality carries with it some real costs—for expenditures such as new equipment and facilities. Thus, without a commitment from top management, quality improvement will prove to be just a slogan or gimmick, with little or no real change. Several years ago, Porsche had the lowest reliability of any automobile maker in the world. But a major commitment from top management helped turn the company around. By paying more attention to consumer preferences and using the other methods described below, Porsche shot to the top of global automobile reliability.[24]

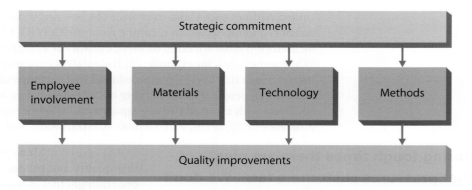

Total Quality Management

Quality is one of the most important issues facing organizations today. Total quality management, or TQM, is a comprehensive effort to enhance an organization's product or service quality. TQM involves the five basic dimensions shown here. Each is important and must be addressed effectively if the organization expects to truly increase quality.

Employee Involvement   Employee involvement is another critical ingredient in TQM. Virtually all successful quality enhancement programs involve making the person doing the job responsible for making sure it is done right.[25] By definition, then, employee involvement is a critical component in improving quality. Work teams, discussed in Chapter 18, are common vehicles for increasing employee involvement.

Technology   New forms of technology are also useful in TQM programs. Automation and robots, for example, can often make products with higher precision and better consistency than can people. Investing in higher-grade machines capable of doing jobs more precisely and reliably often improves quality. For example, Samsung has achieved notable improvements in product quality by replacing many of its machines with new equipment. Similarly, most U.S. manufacturers make regular investments in new technology to help boost quality.

Materials   Another important part of TQM is improving the quality of the materials that organizations use. Suppose that a company that assembles stereos buys chips and circuits from another company. If the chips have a high failure rate, consumers will return defective stereos to the company whose nameplate appears on them, not to the company that made the chips. The stereo firm then loses in two ways: refunds back to customers and a damaged reputation. As a result, many firms have increased the quality requirements they impose on their suppliers as a way of improving the quality of their own products.

Methods   Improved methods can improve product and service quality. Methods are operating systems used by the organization during the actual transformation process. American Express Company, for example, has found ways to cut its approval time for new credit cards from three weeks to only two days. This results in improved service quality.

15-5d TQM Tools and Techniques

Beyond the strategic context of quality, managers can also rely on several specific tools and techniques for improving quality. Among the most popular today are value-added analysis, benchmarking, outsourcing, reducing cycle times, ISO 9000 and ISO 14000, statistical quality control, and Six Sigma.

Value-Added Analysis   Value-added analysis is the comprehensive evaluation of all work activities, materials flows, and paperwork to determine the value that they add for customers. Such an analysis often reveals wasteful or unnecessary activities that can be eliminated

value-added analysis
The comprehensive evaluation of all work activities, materials flows, and paperwork to determine the value that they add for customers

without jeopardizing customer service. For example, during a value-added analysis, HP determined that its contracts were unnecessarily long, confusing, and hard to understand. The firm subsequently cut its standard contract form down from 20 to two pages and experienced an 18 percent increase in its computer sales.

benchmarking
The process of learning how other firms do things in an exceptionally high-quality manner

Benchmarking   Benchmarking is the process of learning how other firms do things in an exceptionally high-quality manner. Some approaches to benchmarking are simple and straightforward. For example, Xerox routinely buys copiers made by other firms and takes them apart to see how they work. This enables the firm to stay abreast of improvements and changes its competitors are making. When Ford was planning the newest version of the Fusion, it identified the 400 features customers considered most important to them. It then found the competing cars that did the best job on each feature. Ford's goal was to equal or surpass each of its competitors on those 400 features. Other benchmarking strategies are more indirect. For example, many firms study how Amazon manages its online business, how Disney recruits and trains employees, and how FedEx tracks packages for applications they can employ in their own businesses.[26]

outsourcing
Subcontracting services and operations to other firms that can perform them more cheaply or better

Outsourcing   Another innovation for improving quality is outsourcing. Outsourcing is the process of subcontracting services and operations to other firms that can perform them more cheaply or better. If a business performs each and every one of its own administrative and business services and operations, it is almost certain to be doing at least some of them in an inefficient or low-quality manner. If those areas can be identified and outsourced, the firm will save money and realize a higher-quality service or operation.[27] For example, until recently Whirlpool handled all of its own computing operations. Now, however, those operations are subcontracted to IBM, which handles all of Whirlpool's computing. The result is higher-quality computing systems and operations at Whirlpool for less money than it was spending before. Firms must be careful in their outsourcing decisions, though, because service or delivery problems can lead to major complications. Boeing's 787 aircraft, for example, ran several months behind schedule because the firms to which Boeing outsourced some of its production ran late.[28]

cycle time
The time needed by the organization to accomplish activities such as developing, making, and distributing products or services

Reducing Cycle Time   Another popular TQM technique is reducing cycle time. Cycle time is the time needed by the organization to develop, make, and distribute products or services.[29] If a business can reduce its cycle time, quality will often improve. A good illustration of the power of cycle-time reduction comes from General Electric. At one point the firm needed six plants and three weeks to produce and deliver custom-made industrial circuit breaker boxes. By analyzing and reducing cycle time, the same product can now be delivered in three days, and only a single plant is involved. Table 15.3 identifies a number of basic suggestions that

Table 15.3	Guidelines for Increasing the Speed of Operations

1. *Start from scratch.* It is usually easier than trying to do what the organization does now faster.

2. *Minimize the number of approvals needed to do something.* The fewer people who have to approve something, the faster approval will get done.

3. *Use work teams as a basis for organization.* Teamwork and cooperation work better than individual effort and conflict.

4. *Develop and adhere to a schedule.* A properly designed schedule can greatly increase speed.

5. *Do not ignore distribution.* Making something faster is only part of the battle.

6. *Integrate speed into the organization's culture.* If everyone understands the importance of speed, things will naturally get done more quickly.

Many organizations today are using speed for competitive advantage. Listed in the table are six common guidelines that organizations follow when they want to shorten the time they need to get things accomplished. Although not every manager can do each of these things, most managers can do at least some of them.

Source: From *Fortune*, February 13, 1989. Time, Inc.

have helped companies reduce the cycle time of their operations. For example, GE found it better to start from scratch with a remodeled plant. GE also wiped out the need for approvals by eliminating most managerial positions and setting up teams as a basis for organizing work. Stressing the importance of the schedule helped Dell build a new plant and start production of a new product in only 18 months. Samsung used to need 12–18 months to design new cellphone models, but can do it now in less than six months.[30] And Ford is aggressively working on techniques that can shorten the development cycle time for new models.[31]

ISO 9000:2000 and ISO 14000 Still another useful technique for improving quality is ISO 9000. ISO 9000:2000 refers to a set of quality standards created by the International Organization for Standardization; the standards were revised and updated in 2000, again in 2015, and yet again in 2019. In addition, several substandards and extensions have also been developed. These include:

- ISO 9001:2008 – sets out the requirements of a quality management system
- ISO 9000:2005 – covers the basic concepts and language
- ISO 9004:2009 – focuses on how to make a quality management system more efficient and effective
- ISO 19011:2011 – sets out guidance on internal and external audits of quality management systems

These standards cover such areas as product testing, employee training, record keeping, supplier relations, and repair policies and procedures. Firms that want to meet these standards apply for certification and are audited by a firm chosen by the organization's domestic affiliate (in the United States, this is the American National Standards Institute). These auditors review every aspect of the firm's business operations in relation to the standards. Many firms report that merely preparing for an ISO 9000 audit has been helpful. Many firms today, including General Electric, DuPont, British Telecom, and Philips Electronics, are urging—or in some cases requiring—that their suppliers achieve ISO 9000 certification. All told, more than 170 countries have adopted ISO 9000 as a national standard, and more than 1 million certificates of compliance have been issued. ISO 14000 is an extension of the same concept to environmental performance. Specifically, ISO 14000 requires that firms document how they are using raw materials more efficiently, managing pollution, and reducing their impact on the environment.

Statistical Quality Control Another quality control technique is statistical quality control (SQC). As the term suggests, SQC is concerned primarily with managing quality.[32] Moreover, it is a set of specific statistical techniques that can be used to monitor quality. *Acceptance sampling* involves sampling finished goods to ensure that quality standards have been met. Acceptance sampling is effective only when the correct percentage of products that should be tested (e.g., 2, 5, or 25 percent) is determined. This decision is especially important when the test renders the product useless. Batteries, wine, and collapsible steering wheels, for example, are consumed or destroyed during testing. Another SQC method is *in-process sampling*. In-process sampling involves evaluating products during production so that needed changes can be made. The painting department of a furniture company might periodically check the tint of the paint it is using. The company can then adjust the color as necessary to conform to customer standards. The advantage of in-process sampling is that it allows problems to be detected before they accumulate.

ISO 9000:2000
A set of quality standards created by the International Organization for Standardization and revised in 2000

ISO 14000
A set of standards for environmental performance

statistical quality control (SQC)
A set of specific statistical techniques that can be used to monitor quality; includes acceptance sampling and in-process sampling

Statistical quality control can play a critical role in improving quality. Acceptance sampling is one useful form of statistical quality control. This inspector has just taken a sample of a new liquid detergent. The sample will be tested for quality and adjustments to the detergent ingredients will be made if needed.

Marcin Balcerzak/Shutterstock.com

Six Sigma   Six Sigma was originally developed by Motorola but has now been refined to the point where it can be used by most manufacturing or service organizations. The Six Sigma method tries to eliminate mistakes. Although firms rarely obtain Six Sigma quality, it does provide a challenging target. *Sigma* refers to a standard deviation, so a Six Sigma defect rate is six standard deviations above the mean rate; 1 sigma quality would produce 690,000 errors per million items. Three sigmas is challenging—66,000 errors per million. Six Sigma is obtained when a firm produces a mere 3.4 mistakes per million. Implementing Six Sigma requires making corrections until errors virtually disappear. At General Electric, the technique saved the firm $8 billion in three years. GE is now teaching its customers, including Walmart and Dell, about the approach.

 **Manager's Checklist**

- [ ] Managers should know the basic components of total quality management.
- [ ] You should also be familiar with the common tools used to manage quality.

15-6 MANAGING PRODUCTIVITY

Although the current focus on quality by U.S. companies is a relatively recent phenomenon, managers have been aware of the importance of productivity for years. The stimulus for this attention was a recognition that the gap between productivity in the United States and that in other industrialized countries was narrowing. This section describes the meaning of productivity and underscores its importance. After summarizing recent productivity trends, we suggest ways that organizations can increase their productivity.

15-6a The Meaning of Productivity

productivity
An economic measure of efficiency that summarizes what is produced relative to resources used to produce it

In a general sense, productivity is an economic measure of efficiency that summarizes the value of outputs relative to the value of the inputs used to create them.[33] Productivity can be and often is assessed at different levels of analysis and in different forms.

Levels of Productivity   By level of productivity we mean the units of analysis used to calculate or define productivity. For example, *aggregate productivity* is the total level of productivity achieved by a country. *Industry productivity* is the total productivity achieved by all the firms in a particular industry. *Company productivity*, just as the term suggests, is the level of productivity achieved by an individual company. *Unit* and *individual productivity* refer to the productivity achieved by a unit or department within an organization and the level of productivity attained by a single person.

Forms of Productivity   There are many different forms of productivity. *Total factor productivity* is defined by the following formula:

$$\text{Productivity} = \frac{\text{Outputs}}{\text{Inputs}}$$

Total factor productivity is an overall indicator of how well an organization uses all of its resources, such as labor, capital, materials, and energy, to create all of its products and services. The biggest problem with total factor productivity is that all the ingredients must be expressed in the same terms—dollars (it is difficult to add hours of labor to number of units of a raw material in a meaningful way). Total factor productivity also gives little insight into how things can be changed to improve productivity. Consequently, most organizations find it more useful to calculate a partial productivity ratio. Such a ratio uses only one category of resource. For example, labor productivity could be calculated by this simple formula:

$$\text{Labor Productivity} = \frac{\text{Outputs}}{\text{Direct Labor}}$$

This method has two advantages. First, it is not necessary to transform the units of input into some other unit. Second, this method provides managers with specific insights into how changing different resource inputs affects productivity. Suppose that a business can manufacture 100 units of a particular product with 20 hours of direct labor. The organization's labor productivity index is 100/20, or 5 (5 units per labor hour). Now suppose that worker efficiency is increased (through one of the ways to be discussed later in this chapter) so that the same 20 hours of labor results in the manufacture of 120 units of the product. The labor productivity index increases to 120/20, or 6 (6 units per labor hour), and the firm's managers can readily see the direct results of a specific managerial action.

15-6b The Importance of Productivity

Managers consider it important that their firm maintain high levels of productivity for a variety of reasons. Firm productivity is a primary determinant of an organization's level of profitability and, ultimately, of its ability to survive. All else equal, if one organization is more productive than another, it will have more products to sell at lower prices and have more profits to reinvest in other areas. Productivity also partially determines people's standard of living within a particular country. At an economic level, businesses consume resources and produce goods and services. The goods and services created within a country can be used by that country's own citizens or exported for sale in other countries. The more goods and services the businesses within a country can produce, the more goods and services the country's citizens will have. Even goods that are exported result in financial resources then flowing back into the home country. Thus, the citizens of a highly productive country are likely to have a notably higher standard of living than are the citizens of a country with low productivity.

15-6c Productivity Trends

The United States has one of the highest levels of productivity in the world. Sparked by gains made in other countries in the 1970s and 1980s, however, U.S. business began to focus more attention on productivity.[34] Indeed, this was a primary factor in the decisions made by U.S. businesses to retrench, retool, and become more competitive in the world marketplace. For example, General Electric's dishwasher plant in Louisville cut its inventory requirements by 50 percent, reduced labor costs from 15 percent to only 10 percent of total manufacturing costs and cut product development time in half. From auto plants to steel companies to washing machine makers, manufacturing productivity is much higher today than was the case 30 years ago. Indeed, as a result of various productivity-related initiatives and programs, productivity trends have now leveled out, and U.S. workers are generally maintaining their lead in most industries.[35]

One important factor that also affects U.S. productivity indices has been the tremendous growth of the service sector in the United States. Although this sector has grown, its productivity growth has been somewhat lower but still consistent. One complication associated with service-sector productivity is measurement. For example, it is fairly simple to calculate the number of tons of steel produced at a steel mill or the number of vehicles made in an automobile plant and divide those totals by the number of labor hours used; it is more difficult to determine the output of an attorney or a certified public accountant. Still, productivity in the service sector has also grown, just at a somewhat slower rate.[36]

Figure 15.4 illustrates manufacturing, service, and total productivity growth from 1987 through 2019 in terms of annual average percentage of increase. Note that productivity percentages are tied to the base year of 2012, a date set by the U.S. Bureau of Labor Statistics. As you can see, manufacturing productivity grew steadily from 1987 through 2012. However, after a small incremental increase in 2013, it has dropped a bit and now remains somewhat steady from year-to-year. On the service side, productivity growth has been more gradual but also continues to increase each year. Overall, then, total productivity growth has continued through 2019.

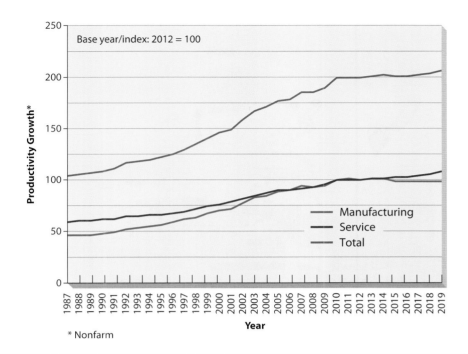

Manufacturing And Service Productivity Growth Trends

Both manufacturing productivity and service productivity in the United States continue to grow, although manufacturing productivity is growing at a faster pace. Total productivity, therefore, also continues to grow.

Source: U.S. Bureau of Labor Statistics

15-6d Improving Productivity

How does a business or industry improve its productivity? Suggestions made by experts generally fall into two broad categories: improving operations and increasing employee involvement.

Improving Operations   One way that firms can improve operations is by spending more on research and development. Research and development (R&D) spending helps identify new products, new uses for existing products, and new methods for making products. Each of these contributes to productivity. For example, Bausch & Lomb almost missed the boat on extended-wear contact lenses because the company had reduced its commitment to R&D. When it became apparent that its major competitors were almost a year ahead of Bausch & Lomb in developing the new lenses, management made R&D a renewed top-priority concern. As a result, the company made several scientific breakthroughs, shortened the time needed to introduce new products, and greatly enhanced both total sales and profits—and all with a smaller workforce than the company used to employ. Even though other countries are greatly increasing their R&D spending, the United States continues to be the world leader in this area.

Another way firms can boost productivity through operations is by reassessing and revamping their transformation facilities. We noted earlier how one of GE's modernized plants does a better job than six antiquated ones. Just building a new factory is no guarantee of success, but Maytag, Ford, Caterpillar, and many other businesses have achieved dramatic productivity gains by revamping their production facilities. Furthermore, facilities refinements are not limited to manufacturers. McDonald's restaurants, for instance, look quite different

Research and development helps identify new products, new uses for existing products, and new methods for making products. Each of these things, in turn, contributes to productivity. The scientists in this R&D lab are working on new chemical compounds that may, in turn, result in new products.

than they did just a few years ago. Most have drive-through windows, moved soft-drink dispensers out to the restaurant floor so that customers can get their own drinks, and installed self-ordering kiosks. Each of these moves is an attempt to increase the speed with which customers can be served, and thus to increase productivity.

Increasing Employee Involvement The other major thrust in productivity enhancement has been toward employee involvement. We noted earlier that participation can enhance quality. So, too, can it boost productivity. Examples of this involvement are an individual worker's being given a bigger voice in how she does her job, a formal agreement of cooperation between management and labor, and total involvement throughout the organization. GE eliminated most of the supervisors at its one new circuit breaker plant and put control in the hands of workers.

Another method popular in the United States is increasing the flexibility of an organization's workforce by training employees to perform a number of different jobs. Such cross-training allows the firm to function with fewer workers because workers can be transferred easily to areas where they are most needed. For example, at one Nucor Steel plant, 417 of 480 employees learned at least two skills under a similar program.

Rewards are essential to making employee involvement work. Firms must reward people for learning new skills and using them proficiently. At Nucor, for example, workers who master a new skill are assigned for five days to a job requiring them to use that skill. If they perform with no defects, they are moved to a higher pay grade, and then they move back and forth between jobs as they are needed. If there is a performance problem, they receive more training and practice. This approach is fairly new, but preliminary indicators suggest that it can increase productivity significantly. Many unions, however, resist such programs because they threaten job security and reduce a person's identification with one skill or craft.

Manager's Checklist

☐ Managers should understand the meaning of productivity and know the different levels at which it can be assessed.

☐ You should also be familiar with the basic methods that can improve productivity.

SUMMARY OF LEARNING OUTCOMES AND KEY POINTS

15-1. Describe the nature of operations management.

- Operations management is the set of managerial activities that organizations use in creating their products and services.
- Operations management is important to both manufacturing and service organizations.
- It plays an important role in an organization's strategy.

15-2. Discuss the components involved in designing effective operations systems.

- The starting point in using operations management is designing appropriate operations systems.
- Key decisions that must be made as part of operations systems design relate to product and service mix, capacity, and facilities.

15-3. Discuss organizational technologies and their role in operations management.

- Technology also plays an important role in quality.
- Automation is especially important today.
- Numerous computer-aided manufacturing techniques are widely practiced.
- Robotics is also a growing area.
- Technology is as relevant to service organizations as to manufacturing organizations.

15-4. Identify the components involved in implementing operations systems through supply chain management.

- After an operations system has been designed and put in place, it must then be implemented.
- Major areas of interest during the use of operations systems are purchasing and inventory management.
- Supply chain management is a comprehensive view of managing all of these activities in a more efficient manner.

15-5. Explain the meaning and importance of managing quality and total quality management.

- Quality is a major consideration for all managers today.
- Quality is important because it affects competition, productivity, and costs.
- Total quality management is a comprehensive, organization-wide effort to enhance quality through a variety of avenues.

15-6. Explain the meaning and importance of managing productivity, productivity trends, and ways to improve productivity.

- Productivity is also a major concern to managers.
- Productivity is a measure of how efficiently an organization is using its resources to create products or services.
- The United States is a world leader in individual productivity, but firms still work to achieve productivity gains.

DISCUSSION QUESTIONS

Questions for Review

1. What is the relationship of operations management to overall organizational strategy? Where do productivity and quality fit into that relationship?
2. Describe three basic decisions that must be addressed in the design of operations systems. For each decision, what information do managers need to make that decision?
3. What are some approaches to facilities layout? How do they differ from one another? How are they similar?
4. What is total quality management? What are the major characteristics of TQM?

Questions for Analysis

1. Is operations management linked most closely to corporate-level, business-level, or functional strategies? Why or in what way?
2. "Automation is bad for the economy because machines will eventually replace almost all human workers, creating high unemployment and poverty." Do you agree or disagree? Explain your answer.
3. Some quality experts claim that high-quality products or services are those that are error free. Others claim that high quality exists when customers' needs are satisfied. Still others claim that high-quality products

or services must be innovative. Do you subscribe to one of these views? If not, how would you define quality? Explain how the choice of a definition of quality affects managers' behavior.

Questions for Application

1. How can a service organization use techniques from operations management? Give specific examples from your college or university (a provider of educational services).

2. Think of a firm that, in your opinion, provides a high-quality service or product. What attributes of the product or service give you the perception of high quality? Do you think that everyone would agree with your judgment? Why or why not?

3. What advice would you give to the manager of a small local service business, such as a pizza parlor or dry cleaner, about improvements in quality and productivity? Would your advice differ if the small business were a manufacturing company—for example, a T-shirt printing firm? Describe any differences you would expect to see.

BUILDING EFFECTIVE COMMUNICATION SKILLS

Exercise Overview

Communication skills refer not only to the ability to convey information and ideas to others but to handle information and ideas received from them. This exercise shows how you can use your communication skills in addressing issues of quality.

Exercise Background

You're the customer-service manager of a large auto parts distributor. The general manager of a large auto dealer, one of your best customers, has sent the following letter, and it's your job to write a letter in response.

Dear Customer Service Manager:

On the first of last month, ABC Autos submitted a purchase order to your firm. Attached to this letter is a copy of the order. Unfortunately, the parts shipment that we received from you did not contain every item on the order. Furthermore, that fact was not noted on the packing slip that accompanied your shipment, and ABC was charged for the full amount of the order. To resolve the problem, please send the missing items immediately. If you are unable to do so by the end of the week, please cancel the remaining items and refund the overpayment. In the future, if you ship a

partial order, please notify us at that time and do not bill for items not shipped.

I look forward to your reply and a resolution to my problem.

Sincerely,

A. N. Owner, ABC Autos
Attachment: Purchase Order 00001

Exercise Task

1. Write an answer to the customer's letter that assumes that you now have the parts available.
2. How would your answer differ if ABC Autos were not a valued customer?
3. How would your answer differ if you found out that the parts were in the original shipment but had been stolen by one of your delivery employees?
4. How would your answer differ if you found out that the owner of ABC Autos made a mistake and that the order had been filled correctly?
5. Now review your answers to the previous questions. What are the important components of an effective response to a customer quality complaint (setting the tone, expressing an apology, suggesting a solution, and so on)? How did you use these components in your various responses?

BUILDING EFFECTIVE DIAGNOSTIC SKILLS

Exercise Overview

As we noted in this chapter, the quality of a product or service is relative to price and customer expectations. This exercise is designed to show that a manager's diagnostic skills—his or her ability to visualize the most appropriate response to a situation—can be useful in positioning a product's quality relative to price and customer expectations.

Exercise Background

Think of a recent occasion when you purchased a tangible product—say, clothing, a digital device, a backpack, or professional supplies—which you subsequently came to feel was of especially high quality. Now think of another product that you regarded as being of appropriate or adequate quality, and then a third product that you judged to be of low or poor quality. (You should now have three separate products in mind.) Next, recall three parallel experiences involving purchases of services. Examples might include an airline, train, or bus trip; a restaurant meal; a haircut; or an oil change for your car. (Again, you should have three examples total.)

Finally, recall three experiences involving both products and services. Perhaps you got some information about a product that you were buying, or you returned a defective or broken product for a refund or warranty repair. Were there any instances in which there was an apparent disparity between product and service quality? Did a poor-quality product, for instance, receive surprisingly good service or a high-quality product receive mediocre service?

Exercise Task

Review your list of nine purchase experiences and then do the following:

1. Assess the extent to which the quality that you associated with each was a function of price and your expectations.
2. Could the quality of each product or service be improved without greatly affecting its price? If so, how?
3. Can high-quality customer service offset adequate or even poor product quality? Can outstanding product quality offset adequate or even poor customer service?

SKILL-BUILDING PERSONAL ASSESSMENT

Defining Quality and Productivity

Introduction: *Quality* is a complex term whose meaning has no doubt changed over time. The following assessment surveys your ideas about and approaches to quality.

Instructions: You will agree with some of the statements and disagree with others. In some cases, making a decision may be difficult, but you should force yourself to make a choice. Record your answers next to each statement according to the following rating scale:

Rating Scale

4   Strongly agree

3   Slightly agree

2   Somewhat disagree

1   Strongly disagree

1. _____ Quality refers to a product's or service's ability to fulfill its primary operating characteristics, such as providing a sharp picture for a television.
2. _____ Quality is an absolute, measurable aspect of a product or service.
3. _____ The concept of quality includes supplemental aspects of a product or service, such as the remote control for a television.
4. _____ Productivity and quality are inversely related, so that, to get one, you must sacrifice the other.
5. _____ The concept of quality refers to the extent to which a product's design and operating characteristics conform to certain set standards.
6. _____ Productivity refers to what is created relative to what it takes to create it.
7. _____ Quality means that a product will not malfunction during a specified period of time.

8. _____ Quality refers only to products; it is immeasurable for services.
9. _____ The length of time that a product or service will function is what is known as quality.
10. _____ Everyone uses exactly the same definition of quality.
11. _____ Quality refers to the ease and speed with which a product or service can be repaired.
12. _____ Being treated courteously has nothing to do with the quality of anything.
13. _____ How a product looks, feels, tastes, or smells is what is meant by quality.
14. _____ Price, not quality, is what determines the ultimate value of service.
15. _____ Quality refers to what customers think of a product or service.
16. _____ Productivity and quality cannot both increase at the same time.

Scoring: The odd-numbered items are all true; they refer to eight dimensions of quality (see Table 15.2). Those eight dimensions are performance, features, reliability, conformance, durability, serviceability, aesthetics, and perceived quality. The even-numbered statements are all false. Thus, you should have positive responses for the odd-numbered items and negative responses for the even-numbered items. If you agree strongly with all of the odd-numbered items and disagree strongly with all of the even-numbered items, your total score is zero.

Examine your responses to determine which items you responded to incorrectly. Focus on learning why the answers are what they are. Remember that the American Society for Quality Control defines quality as the totality of features and characteristics of a product or service that bear on its ability to satisfy customers' stated or implied needs.

MANAGEMENT AT WORK

Reach Out and Give Someone a Quality Touch

Marc Chardon knows that when he talks about the "flight to quality," he has to explain himself. "When I say 'flight to quality,'" he says, "I'm talking about the observable trend of donors deciding to support fewer organizations, consolidating their giving with those that mean the most to them and treat them well. . . . I see it happening everywhere," reports Chardon, who was head of Blackbaud, the leading global provider of software and services for nonprofit organizations, until he stepped down in 2013. He adds that when it comes to cultivating and keeping donors, nonprofits need to realize that "surface relationships just don't cut it."

Professional fundraiser Claire Axelrad agrees: "Don't treat your donors like gumballs," she advises nonprofit managers. "Don't stick 'em in your database to save for later." In the current environment, she warns, in which the competition for every charitable dollar is becoming increasingly fierce, they probably won't be there later. Frank Barry, Chardon's one-time colleague at Blackbaud, argues that nonprofits need to devote at least as much energy to retaining the donors they have as they do to prospecting for new donors. "Nearly three out of four new donors," he points out, "leave and *never* come back." Where do they go? "They flee to quality," says Chardon, "to the places where they feel the most connected and the most valued."

From a financial standpoint, the imperative to hold onto donors is particularly pressing. According to Adrian Sargeant, director of the Centre for Sustainable Philanthropy at England's University of Plymouth, it costs a fundraising organization five times as much to attract a new donor as it does to maintain a relationship with an existing donor. The cost of recruiting the new donor will also amount to two or three times more than the value of the donor's first donation. Sargeant's research also indicates that the typical nonprofit will lose 10–20 percent of all donors annually, but he hastens to add that "even small improvements in the level of attrition can generate significantly larger improvements in the lifetime value of the fundraising database," with a mere 10 percent improvement in attrition yielding up to a 200 percent increase in database value.

Chardon believes that "donors are just like Amazon customers, expecting service and recognition that nonprofits know who they are and how they are unique." Likewise, Sargeant is convinced that at least "some donors will consciously evaluate the service provided by a nonprofit and compare it to what could be achieved 'in return' for their donations elsewhere." Both argue that donors value certain types of relationships with the nonprofits that they patronize, and Sargeant contends that "donor satisfaction" is "the single greatest driver of loyalty." In turn, he says, donor satisfaction depends in large measure on "delivered service quality."

So what—in a practical sense—constitutes "service quality" in the mind of a donor? Not surprisingly, it all comes down to "touches"—the contacts that the nonprofit makes with the donor. And according to a 2018 survey by Abila, a provider of software and services to nonprofits, the quality of touches is more important than their quantity (i.e., frequency). Donor communications specialist Lisa Sargent confirms the argument for "rich content" in contacts in her account of the efforts mounted by an unnamed client:

> They created a terrific donor welcome pack and special new donor thank-you; send hand-signed thank-yous promptly and make them as personal as possible; publish a donor-driven, story-focused newsletter four times yearly; invite donors to engage with their organization in ways that don't always include a monetary gift; and continue to invest in a quality donor communications program [that includes] a longer newsletter [about] legacy programs, monthly giving, and major donors.

The organization's donor file, she reports, quintupled between 2008 and 2018, when it broke the 70 percent "retention barrier."

Case Questions

1. Compare and contrast the roles of operations management, quality, and productivity between for-profit and not-for-profit organizations.
2. Are manufacturing and production or service operations techniques more relevant for fund-raising organizations?
3. In what ways do fund-raising organizations address product–service mix and capacity questions?
4. Have you ever been solicited to donate money? How would you assess the nature of the request from a quality perspective?

References: Marc Chardon, "Nonprofit Trends: Flight to Quality," *Huffington Post,* www.huffingtonpost.com on June 10, 2020; Frank Barry, "One Thing Most Nonprofits Stink At (Donor Retention) and How You Can Change It in 2019," sgENGAGE, April 19, 2019, www.npengage.com on June 10, 2020; Adrian Sargeant, "Donor Retention: What Do We Know and What Can We Do About It?" *Nonprofit Quarterly,* August 15, 2013, http://nonprofitquarterly.org on June 10, 2020; William Comcowich, "How Nonprofits Can Use Data to Improve Donor Engagement," CyberAlert, April 21, 2015, www.cyberalert.com on June 10, 2020.

Out Supply-Chaining the King of Supply Chainers

1. What is the basis of Tesco's success?
2. How easy (or hard) would it be for rivals like Walmart or Carrefour to adopt Tesco's data management techniques?
3. The global recession in 2007–2009 and the 2020 COVID-19 pandemic slowed down Tesco's plans for expansion. Why might Tesco have been more harmed by these events than Walmart?
4. What measures of quality and productivity are most relevant for firms like Walmart and Tesco?
5. If Tesco's managers asked your advice on whether or not to reenter the U.S. market, what would you say?

Endnotes

Chapter 1

1 "How Netflix Got Started," *CNNMoney.com*, January 28, 2009, http://money.cnn.com, accessed on February 6, 2020; Reed Hastings, "How I Did It: Reed Hastings, Netflix," *Inc.*, December 1, 2005, www.inc.com, accessed on February 6, 2020; Sally Aaron, "Netflix Script Spells Disruption," *Harvard Business School Working Knowledge*, March 22, 2004, http://hbswk.hbs.edu, accessed on February 6, 2020; John M. Caddell, "Frontiers of Innovation—Netflix Demolishes Its Own Business Model," *PennLive.com*, February 11, 2009, http://blog.pennlive.com, accessed on February 6, 2020; "Netflix Subscriber Loss Triggers Panic Selling," *CBSNews.com*, October 24, 2011, www.cbsnews.com, accessed on February 6, 2020; Andrew Goldman, "Reed Hastings Knows He Messed Up," *New York Times*, October 20, 2011, www.nytimes.com, accessed on February 6, 2020; and Ashlee Vance, "The Man Who Ate the Internet," *Bloomberg BusinessWeek*, May 13–19, 2016, pp. 56–62.

2 Fred Luthans, "Successful vs. Effective Real Managers," *Academy of Management Executive*, May 1988, Vol. 2, No. 2, pp. 127–132. See also "The Best Performers," *BusinessWeek*, Spring 2020 Special Issue, pp. 28–34.

3 See "The Best (& Worst) Managers of the Year," *Bloomberg Businessweek*, January 13, 2020, pp. 64–72.

4 See "Executive Compensation for 50 of the Largest U.S. Companies," *USA Today*, March 28, 2016, p. 2B. See also Jim Collins, "The Ten Greatest CEOs of All Times," *Fortune*, July 21, 2003, pp. 54–68.

5 John P. Kotter, "What Effective General Managers Really Do," *Harvard Business Review*, March–April 1999, pp. 145–155. See also Peter Drucker, "What Makes an Effective Executive," *Harvard Business Review*, June 2004, pp. 58–68.

6 Carmine Gallo, "Alan Malully, Optimism and the Power of Vision," *Forbes*, April 25, 2012, www.forbes.com, accessed on April 27, 2015.

7 For a classic discussion of several of these skills, see Robert L. Katz, "The Skills of an Effective Administrator," *Harvard Business Review*, September–October 1974, pp. 90–102. For a recent perspective, see J. Brian Atwater, Vijay R. Kannan, and Alan A. Stephens, "Cultivating Systemic Thinking in the Next Generation of Business Leaders," *Academy of Management Learning and Education*, 2008, Vol. 7, No. 1, pp. 9–25. See also Ricky W. Griffin and David D. Van Fleet, *Building Management Skills* (Mason, OH: Cengage, 2013).

8 For an interesting application, see Mark Gottfredson, Steve Schaubert, and Hernan Saenz, "The New Leader's Guide to Diagnosing the Business," *Harvard Business Review*, February 2008, pp. 63–72.

9 Samantha Cole, "Etsy CEO Chad Dickerson on Having a System—Any System," *Fast Company*, June 11, 2014, www.fastcompany.com, accessed on January 3, 2020.

10 See "The Real Reasons You're Working So Hard ... and What You Can Do about It," *BusinessWeek*, October 3, 2005, pp. 60–68; Del Jones, "I'm Late, I'm Late, I'm Late," *USA Today*, November 26, 2002, pp. 1B, 2B.

11 For a thorough discussion of the importance of time management skills, see David Barry, Catherine Durnell Cramton, and Stephen J. Carroll, "Navigating the Garbage Can: How Agendas Help Managers Cope with Job Realities," *Academy of Management Executive*, May 1997, Vol. 11, No. 2, pp. 26–42.

12 Gary Hamel and C. K. Prahalad, "Competing for the Future," *Harvard Business Review*, July–August 1994, pp. 122–128; see also Joseph M. Hall and M. Eric Johnson, "When Should a Process Be Art, Not Science?" *Harvard Business Review*, March 2009, pp. 58–65.

13 Bill Saporito, "Starbucks' Big Mug," *Time*, June 25, 2012, pp. 53–54; and "Starbucks CEO Reinvents the Spiel," *USA Today*, April 25, 2013, p. 3B.

14 Terence Mitchell and Lawrence James, "Building Better Theory: Time and the Specification of When Things Happen," *Academy of Management Review*, 2001, Vol. 26, No. 4, pp. 530–547.

15 Peter F. Drucker, "The Theory of the Business," *Harvard Business Review*, September–October 1994, pp. 95–104.

16 "Why Business History?" *Audacity*, Fall 1992, pp. 7–15. See also Alan L. Wilkins and Nigel J. Bristow, "For Successful Organization Culture, Honor Your Past," *Academy of Management Executive*, August 1987, Vol. 1, No. 3, pp. 221–227.

17 Daniel Wren and Arthur Bedeian, *The Evolution of Management Thought*, 7th ed. (New York: Wiley, 2017); and Page Smith, *The Rise of Industrial America* (New York: McGraw–Hill, 1984).

18 Martha I. Finney, "Books That Changed Careers," *HR Magazine*, June 1997, pp. 141–145. See also "Leadership in Literature," *Harvard Business Review*, March 2006, pp. 47–55.

19 See Harriet Rubin, *The Princessa: Machiavelli for Women* (New York: Doubleday/Currency, 1997). See also Nanette Fondas, "Feminization Unveiled: Management Qualities in Contemporary Writings," *Academy of Management Review*, January 1997, Vol. 22, No. 1, pp. 257–282.

20 Alan M. Kantrow, ed., "Why History Matters to Managers," *Harvard Business Review*, January–February 1986, pp. 81–88.

21 Wren and Bedeian, *The Evolution of Management Thought*.

22 Wren and Bedeian, *The Evolution of Management Thought*.

23 Frederick W. Taylor, *Principles of Scientific Management* (New York: Harper & Brothers, 1911).

24 Charles D. Wrege and Amedeo G. Perroni, "Taylor's Pig-Tale: A Historical Analysis of Frederick W. Taylor's Pig-Iron Experiment," *Academy of Management Journal*, March 1974, Vol. 17, No. 1, pp. 6–27; and Charles D. Wrege and Ann Marie Stoka, "Cooke Creates a Classic: The Story behind F. W. Taylor's Principles of Scientific Management," *Academy of Management Review*, October 1978, Vol. 3, No. 4, pp. 736–749.

25 Robert Kanigel, *The One Best Way* (New York: Viking, 1997); Oliver E. Allen, "This Great Mental Revolution," *Audacity*, Summer 1996, pp. 52–61; and Jill Hough and Margaret White, "Using Stories to Create Change: The Object Lesson of Frederick Taylor's 'Pig-Tale,'" *Journal of Management*, 2001, Vol. 27, No. 5, pp. 585–601.

26 "Frederick W. Taylor Quotes," Brainy Quote, www.brainyquote.com, accessed on March 6, 2020.

27 Henri Fayol, *General and Industrial Management*, trans. J. A. Coubrough (Geneva: International Management Institute, 1930).

28 Max Weber, *Theory of Social and Economic Organizations*, trans. T. Parsons (New York: Free Press, 1947); and Richard M. Weis, "Weber on Bureaucracy: Management Consultant or Political Theorist?" *Academy of Management Review*, April 1983, Vol. 8, No. 2, pp. 242–248.

29 Joseph B. White, "The Line Starts Here," *Wall Street Journal*, January 11, 1999, pp. R1, R25.

30 Hugo Munsterberg, *Psychology and Industrial Efficiency* (Boston: Houghton Mifflin, 1913).

31 Wren, *The Evolution of Management Thought*, pp. 255–264.

[32] Elton Mayo, *The Human Problems of an Industrial Civilization* (New York: Macmillan, 1933); and Fritz J. Roethlisberger and William J. Dickson, *Management and the Worker* (Cambridge, MA: Harvard University Press, 1939).

[33] Abraham Maslow, "A Theory of Human Motivation," *Psychological Review*, July 1943, Vol. 50, No. 4, pp. 370–396.

[34] Douglas McGregor, *The Human Side of Enterprise* (New York: McGraw-Hill, 1960).

[35] Sara L. Rynes and Christine Quinn Trank, "Behavioral Science in the Business School Curriculum: Teaching in a Changing Institutional Environment," *Academy of Management Review*, 1999, Vol. 24, No. 4, pp. 808–824.

[36] For a recent review of current developments in the field of organizational behaviour, see Ricky W. Griffin, Jean Phillips, and Stan Gully, *Organizational Behavior*, 13th ed. (Cincinnati, OH: Cengage, 2020).

[37] Wren and Bedeian, *The Evolution of Management Thought*, pp. 255–264.

[38] "Math Will Rock Your World," *BusinessWeek*, January 23, 2006, pp. 54–61.

[39] "Quantitative Analysis Offers Tools to Predict Likely Terrorist Moves," *Wall Street Journal*, February 17, 2006, p. B1.

[40] For more information on systems theory in general, see Ludwig von Bertalanffy, C. G. Hempel, R. E. Bass, and H. Jonas, "General Systems Theory: A New Approach to Unity of Science," I–VI *Human Biology*, 1951, Vol. 23, pp. 302–361. For systems theory as applied to organizations, see Fremont E. Kast and James E. Rosenzweig, "General Systems Theory: Applications for Organizations and Management," *Academy of Management Journal*, December 1972, Vol. 15, No. 4, pp. 447–465. For a recent update, see Donde P. Ashmos and George P. Huber, "The Systems Paradigm in Organization Theory: Correcting the Record and Suggesting the Future," *Academy of Management Review*, October 1987, Vol. 12, No. 4, pp. 607–621.

[41] See Robert S. Kaplan and David P. Norton, "Mastering the Management System," *Harvard Business Review*, January 2008, pp. 63–72.

[42] Kathleen M. Eisenhardt and D. Charles Galunic, "Coevolving—At Last, a Way to Make Synergies Work," *Harvard Business Review*, January–February 2000, pp. 91–103.

[43] Fremont E. Kast and James E. Rosenzweig, *Contingency Views of Organization and Management* (Chicago: Science Research Associates, 1973).

[44] "The BusinessWeek Best-Seller List," *BusinessWeek*, November 4, 2002, p. 26.

[45] See Phanish Puranam and Bart S. Vanneste, "Trust and Governance: Untangling a Tangled Web," *Academy of Management Review*, January 2009, Vol. 34, No. 1, pp. 11–31.

[46] "The Way We'll Work," *Time*, May 25, 2009, pp. 39–51.

[47] Patricia L. Nemetz and Sandra L. Christensen, "The Challenge of Cultural Diversity: Harnessing a Diversity of Views to Understand Multiculturalism," *Academy of Management Review*, 1996, Vol. 21, No. 2, pp. 434–462; and Frances J. Milliken and Luis L. Martins, "Searching for Common Threads: Understanding the Multiple Effects of Diversity in Organizational Groups," *Academy of Management Review*, 1996, Vol. 21, No. 2, pp. 402–433.

[48] Anne Fisher, "When Gen X Runs the Show," *Time*, May 25, 2009, p. 48.

[49] Craig L. Pearce and Charles P. Osmond, "Metaphors for Change: The ALPS Model of Change Management," *Organizational Dynamics*, Winter 1996, Vol. 24, No. 3, pp. 23–35.

[50] Steinway & Sons, "The Steinway Restoration Center," www.steinway.com, accessed on February 6, 2020; WGBH (Boston), "Note by Note: The Making of Steinway L1037," www.wgbh.org, accessed on February 6, 2020; Maya Roney, "Steinway: Worth Much More than a Song," *BusinessWeek*, www.businessweek.com, accessed on February 6, 2020; James Barron, "88 Keys, Many Languages, One Proud Name," *New York Times*, www.nytimes.com, accessed on February 6, 2020; Michael Lenehen, "K 2571: The Making of a Steinway Grand," *Atlantic Monthly*, August 1982, www.sherwinbeach.com, accessed on February 6, 2020; and Rick Rogers, "Steinway Builds a Legacy with Distinctive Pianos," *Daily Oklahoman* (Oklahoma City), www.oklahoman.com, accessed on February 6, 2020.

Chapter 2

[1] "Boeing: Corporate Rap Sheet," corp-research.org/boeing on February 25, 2020; "Regulators Issue Another Safety Fix for Boeing's Troubled 737 Max Plane," NPR, February 26, 2020; "Boeing," "Boeing 737," en.wikipedia.org on February 26, 2020; "Boeing Employee Said the 737 MAX 'is Designed by Clowns' and 'Supervised by Monkeys'," MarketWatch, January 11, 2020, marketwatch.com on February 26, 2020.

[2] See Jay B. Barney and William G. Ouchi, eds., *Organizational Economics* (San Francisco: Jossey-Bass, 1986), for a detailed analysis of linkages between economics and organizations.

[3] *Fortune*, March 16, 2009, p. 111.

[4] See, for example, Elizabeth Williamson, "Political Pendulum Swings toward Stricter Regulation," *Wall Street Journal*, March 24, 2008, pp. A1, A11; see also "Changing Safety Rules Perplex and Polarize," *USA Today*, February 5, 2016, pp. 1B, 2B; and Nina Easton and Telis Demos, "The Business Guide to Congress," *Fortune*, May 11, 2016, pp. 72–75.

[5] For example, see Susanne G. Scott and Vicki R. Lane, "A Stakeholder Approach to Organizational Identity," *Academy of Management Review*, 2000, Vol. 25, No. 1, pp. 43–62.

[6] Richard N. Osborn and John Hagedoorn, "The Institutionalization and Evolutionary Dynamics of Interorganizational Alliances and Networks," *Academy of Management Journal*, April 1997, Vol. 40, No. 2, pp. 261–278. See also Bernard Wysocki, "More Companies Cut Risk by Collaborating with Their 'Enemies'," *Wall Street Journal*, January 31, 2016, pp. A1, A10.

[7] "The Wild New Workforce," *BusinessWeek*, December 6, 2015, pp. 38–44.

[8] "Temporary Workers Getting Short Shrift," *USA Today*, April 11, 2014, pp. 1B, 2B.

[9] See Norman Barry, *Business Ethics* (West Lafayette, IN: Purdue University Press, 1999).

[10] Thomas Donaldson and Thomas W. Dunfee, "Toward a Unified Conception of Business Ethics: An Integrative Social Contracts Theory," *Academy of Management Review*, Vol. 19, No. 2, 1994, pp. 252–284.

[11] Suren Rajakarier, "My Top 10 Good Governance Quotes," January 27, 2013, https://surenrajdotcom.wordpress.com/2013/01/27/my-top-10-good-governance-quotes/ on March 20, 2020.

[12] Kevin McCoy, "Chains' Ties Run Deep on Pharmacy Boards," *USA Today*, December 30, 2008, usatoday.com on January 18, 2020.

[13] "Diamond Foods Restating Profits after an Audit," *Bloomberg Businessweek*, February 13–19, 2015, p. 28.

[14] "The Lies We Tell at Work," *Bloomberg Businessweek*, February 4–February 10, 2016, pp. 71–73.

[15] William Dill, "Beyond Codes and Courses," *Selections*, Fall 2002, pp. 21–23.

[16] "How to Fix Corporate Governance," *BusinessWeek*, May 6, 2012, pp. 68–78. See also Catherine Daily, Dan Dalton, and Albert Cannella, "Corporate Governance: Decades of Dialogue and Data," *Academy of Management Review*, 2003, Vol. 28, No. 3, pp. 371–382.

[17] "A New Way of Giving," *Time*, July 24, 2000, pp. 48–51. See also Michael Porter and Mark Kramwe, "The Competitive Advantage of Corporate Philanthropy," *Harvard Business Review*, December 2002, pp. 57–66.

[18] David M. Messick and Max H. Bazerman, "Ethical Leadership and the Psychology of Decision Making," *Sloan Management Review*, Winter 1996, pp. 9–22.

19 "Walmart's Discounted Ethics," *Time*, May 7, 2014, p. 19.

20 For a classic review of the literature on whistle-blowing, see Janet P. Near and Marcia P. Miceli, "Whistle-Blowing: Myth and Reality," *Journal of Management*, 1996, Vol. 22, No. 3, pp. 507–526. See also Michael Gundlach, Scott Douglas, and Mark Martinko, "The Decision to Blow the Whistle: A Social Information Processing Framework," *Academy of Management Review*, 2003, Vol. 28, No. 1, pp. 107–123.

21 "He Blew a Whistle for 9 Years," *USA Today*, February 13, 2009, pp. 1B, 2B.

22 "SEC Announces a Whistle-Blower Overhaul Plan," *USA Today*, March 6, 2015, p. 1B.

23 "IRS Pays UBS Whistle-Blower $104 Million," *USA Today*, September 12, 2015, p. 2B.

24 "The Fortune Global 500—World's Largest Corporations," fortune.com, accessed on March 20, 2020.

25 "The Fortune Global 500 Ranked within Industries," fortune.com on March 20, 2020.

26 *Hoover's Handbook of American Business 2019*, pp. 102–103.

27 "Creating a Worldwide Yen for Japanese Beer," *Financial Times*, October 7, 2014, p. 20.

28 Kenichi Ohmae, "The Global Logic of Strategic Alliances," *Harvard Business Review*, March–April 1989, pp. 143–154.

29 "What If There Weren't Any Clocks to Watch?" *Newsweek*, June 30, 1997, p. 14.

30 Geoffrey A. Fowler, "Main Street, H.K.—Disney Localizes Mickey to Boost Its Hong Kong Theme Park," *Wall Street Journal*, January 23, 2008, pp. B1, B2.

31 Intrepid Sourcing, "Trade & Business Quotes about China," https://intrepidsourcing.com/ on March 20, 2020.

32 For an excellent discussion of the effects of NAFTA, see "In the Wake of NAFTA, a Family Firm Sees Business Go South," *Wall Street Journal*, February 23, 1999, pp. A1, A10.

33 Terrence E. Deal and Allan A. Kennedy, *Corporate Cultures: The Rights and Rituals of Corporate Life* (Reading, MA: Addison-Wesley, 1982).

34 Jay B. Barney, "Organizational Culture: Can It Be a Source of Sustained Competitive Advantage?" *Academy of Management Review*, July 1986, Vol. 11, No. 3, pp. 656–665.

35 "Netflix Founder Reed Hastings: Make as Few Decisions as Possible," Insights by Stanford Business, http://www.gsb.stanford.edu on April 2, 2020.

36 For example, see Carol J. Loomis, "Sam Would Be Proud," *Fortune*, April 17, 2014, pp. 131–144.

37 *Hoover's Handbook of American Business 2015* (Austin, TX: Hoover's Business Press, 2013), pp. 268–269.

38 "Marriage at 30,000 Feet," *Bloomberg Businessweek*, February 6–12, 2015, pp. 58–63.

39 "Child Labor and Slavery in the Chocolate Industry," Food Empowerment Project, http://www.foodispower.org/slavery-chocolate on January 20, 2020; "Frequently Asked Questions," Fair Trade USA, http://fairtradeusa.org/what-is-fair-trade/faq on January 20, 2020; Rodney North, "V-Day's Dark Side," *Equal Exchange*, February 2010, www.equalexchange.com on January 20, 2020; "Cocoa's Bitter Child Labour Ties," *BBC News*, http://newsvote.bbc.co on February 1, 2020; Bill Baue, "Abolishing Child Labor on West African Cocoa Farms," *Social Funds*, www.socialfunds.com, accessed on February 1, 2020; "What Is Fair Trade?" www.transfairusa.org, accessed on February 15, 2020; Leslie Josephs, "Selling Candy with a Conscience," *Wall Street Journal*, December 25, 2010, wsj.com on February 15, 2020.

Chapter 3

1 Ricky Griffin and Michael Pustay, *International Business*, 9th ed. (Boston: Pearson Education, 2020); "LVMH" and "Bernard Arnault," Wikipedia, en.wikipedia.org on March 25, 2020; *LVMH Annual Report*, 2019.

2 See Peter J. Brews and Michelle R. Hunt, "Learning to Plan and Planning to Learn: Resolving the Planning School/Learning School Debate," *Strategic Management Journal*, 1999, Vol. 20, pp. 889–913.

3 "GM's Vision Drives Value for the Company, Communities, and Future Mobility," GM Corporate Newsroom, June 12, 2018, https://media.gm.com on April 10, 2020; Michael J. Coren, "Wall Street Is Listening to Elon Musk's 'Internal' Tesla Goals and Ignoring History," *Quartz*, October 3, 2019, https://qz.com on April 10, 2020; Elaine Low, "Could Disney Plus Reach 60 Million-90 Million Subscribers Earlier Than Expected?" *Variety*, November 19, 2019, https://variety.com on April 10, 2020.

4 Leigh Buchanan and Andrew O'Connell, "A Brief History of Decision Maker," *Harvard Business Review*, January 2006, https://hbr.org on March 15, 2020.

5 Jim Collins, "Turning Goals into Results: The Power of Catalytic Mechanisms," *Harvard Business Review*, July–August 1999, pp. 71–81.

6 Kenneth R. Thompson, Wayne A. Hochwarter, and Nicholas J. Mathys, "Stretch Targets: What Makes Them Effective?" *Academy of Management Executive*, August 1997, pp. 48–58.

7 "A Methodical Man," *Forbes*, August 11, 1997, pp. 70–72.

8 Melissa Repco, "Target Scales Back Store Remodels and Openings Amid Coronavirus Outbreak," CNBC, March 25, 2020, https://www.cnbc.com on March 24, 2020.

9 John A. Pearce II and Fred David, "Corporate Mission Statements: The Bottom Line," *Academy of Management Executive*, May 1987, p. 109.

10 Matt Mayberry, "10 Great Quotes on the Power of Goals," *Entrepreneur*, January 18, 2017, https://www.entrepreneur.com on March 25, 2020.

11 For early discussions of strategic management, see Kenneth Andrews, *The Concept of Corporate Strategy*, rev. ed. (Homewood, IL: Dow Jones–Irwin, 1980); and Igor Ansoff, *Corporate Strategy* (New York: McGraw-Hill, 1965). For more recent perspectives, see Michael E. Porter, "What Is Strategy?" *Harvard Business Review*, November–December 1996, pp. 61–78; Kathleen M. Eisenhardt, "Strategy as Strategic Decision Making," *Sloan Management Review*, Spring 1999, pp. 65–74; and Sarah Kaplan and Eric Beinhocker, "The Real Value of Strategic Planning," *Sloan Management Review*, Winter 2003, pp. 71–80.

12 "Strategic Planning Quotes," goodreads, https://www.goodreads.com on March 27, 2020.

13 *Hoover's Handbook of American Business 2019* (Austin, TX: Hoover's Business Press, 2019), pp. 33–36.

14 Jeroen De Flander, "33 Awesome Strategy Quotes," LinkedIn, https://www.linkedin.com on March 27, 2020.

15 Elizabeth Thompson, "14 Inspirational Quotes on Strategy Execution," Khorus, December 7, 2017, https://www.khorus.com/blog/14-inspirational-quotes-strategy-execution/ on March 27, 2020.

16 T. R. Holcomb, R. M. Holmes Jr., and B. L. Connelly, "Making the Most of What You Have: Managerial Ability as a Source of Resource Value Creation," *Strategic Management Journal*, 2009, Vol. 30, No. 5, pp. 457–486.

17 Jay Barney, "Firm Resources and Sustained Competitive Advantage," *Journal of Management*, June 1991, pp. 99–120. See also T. Russell Crook, David J. Ketchen Jr., James G. Combs, and Samuel Y. Todd, "Strategic Resources and Performance: A Meta-Analysis," *Strategic Management Journal*, 2008, Vol. 29, pp. 1141–1154.

18 Michael Porter, *Competitive Strategy* (New York: Free Press, 1980). See also Colin Campbell-Hunt, "What Have We Learned about Generic Competitive Strategy? A Meta-Analysis," *Strategic Management Journal*, 2000, Vol. 21, pp. 127–154. For a more recent update, see Michael E. Porter, "The Five Competitive Forces That Shape Strategy," *Harvard Business Review*, January 2008, pp. 79–90.

19 Ian C. MacMillan and Rita Gunther McGrath, "Discovering New Points of Differentiation," *Harvard Business Review*, July–August 1997, pp. 133–136.

20 "When Service Means Survival," *BusinessWeek*, March 2, 2009, pp. 26–40.

21 "It Ain't the Bellagio…" *Business Week*, June 20–26, 2011, pp. 84–85.

22 "Debbi Fields Quotes," goodreads, https://www.goodreads.com on March 27, 2020.

23 Alfred Chandler, *Strategy and Structure: Chapters in the History of the American Industrial Enterprise* (Cambridge, MA: MIT Press, 1962); Richard Rumelt, *Strategy, Structure, and Economic Performance* (Cambridge, MA: Division of Research, Graduate School of Business Administration, Harvard University, 1974); and Oliver Williamson, *Markets and Hierarchies* (New York: Free Press, 1975).

24 K. L. Stimpert and Irene M. Duhaime, "Seeing the Big Picture: The Influence of Industry, Diversification, and Business Strategy on Performance," *Academy of Management Journal*, 1997, Vol. 40, No. 3, pp. 560–583.

25 See Chandler, *Strategy and Structure*; and Yakov Amihud and Baruch Lev, "Risk Reduction as a Managerial Motive for Conglomerate Mergers," *Bell Journal of Economics*, 1981, pp. 605–617.

26 Chandler, *Strategy and Structure*; and Williamson, *Markets and Hierarchies*.

27 For a discussion of the limitations of unrelated diversification, see Jay Barney and William G. Ouchi, *Organizational Economics* (San Francisco: Jossey-Bass, 1986).

28 Asad Meah, "35 Inspirational Quotes on Strategy, https://www.awakenthegreatnesswithin.com on March 27, 2020.

29 See Barry Hedley, "A Fundamental Approach to Strategy Development," *Long Range Planning*, December 1976, pp. 2–11; and Bruce Henderson, "The Experience Curve-Reviewed: IV. The Growth Share Matrix of the Product Portfolio," *Perspectives*, 1973, No. 135, pp. 1–18.

30 Michael G. Allen, "Diagramming G.E.'s Planning for What's WATT," in *Corporate Planning: Techniques and Applications,* eds., Robert J. Allio and Malcolm W. Pennington (New York: AMACOM Books, 1979). Limits of this approach are discussed in R. A. Bettis and W. K. Hall, "The Business Portfolio Approach: Where It Falls Down in Practice," *Long Range Planning*, March 1983, pp. 95–105.

31 "Unprofitable Businesses Getting Axed More Often," *Wall Street Journal*, February 17, 2009, pp. B1–B2.

32 James Brian Quinn, Henry Mintzberg, and Robert M. James, *The Strategy Process* (Englewood Cliffs, NJ: Prentice Hall, 1988).

33 Vasudevan Ramanujam and N. Venkatraman, "Planning System Characteristics and Planning Effectiveness," *Strategic Management Journal*, 1987, Vol. 8, No. 2, pp. 453–468.

34 "Marriage at 30,000 Feet," *Bloomberg Business Week*, February 6–12, 2012, pp. 58–64.

35 K. A. Froot, D. S. Scharfstein, and J. C. Stein, "A Framework for Risk Management," *Harvard Business Review*, November–December 1994, pp. 91–102.

36 "Disney Operations Shut Down; Focus Now on When (And How) to Re-open," wdwnt.com, accessed on March 18, 2020.

37 "Business World Must be 'Watchful'," *USA Today*, January 24, 2015, p. 5T.

38 Del Jones. "Next Time," *USA Today*, October 4, 2005, pp. 1B–2B.

39 Ibid.

40 Michael Watkins and Max Bazerman, "Predictable Surprises: The Disasters You Should Have Seen Coming," *Harvard Business Review*, March 2003, pp. 72–81.

41 Google, "Corporate Information," at http://www.google.com on March 20, 2020; "The Secret to Google's Success," *BusinessWeek*, March 6, 2008, pp. 50–54; Adi Ignatius, "In Search of the Real Google," Time, February 20, 2006, http://www.time.com on March 20, 2020; "Alphabet" and "Google," Wikipedia.com on March 27, 2020.

Chapter 4

1 Arnie Weissmann, "Rolling on the Rivers," *Travel Weekly*, April 2, 2013, https://www.travelweekly.com/River-Cruising/Rolling-on-the-rivers on March 30, 2020; "Viking Cruises," Wikipedia, https://en.wikipedia.org on March 30, 2020; Gene Sloan, "Cruise Line Viking Suspends Operations Worldwide Due to Coronavirus," The Points Guy, March 12, 2020, https://thepointsguy.com/news/cruise-line-viking-suspends-operations-worldwide-due-to-coronavirus/ on March 30, 2020; Bill Bostock, "Viking Cruises Suspended Operations Worldwide Due to the Coronavirus, As Infections Ravage the Cruise Industry," *Business Insider*, March 12, 2020, https://www.businessinsider.com/viking-cruises-coronavirus-suspends-operations-industry-struggles-2020-3 on March 30, 2020.

2 Paul Nutt, "The Formulation Processes and Tactics Used in Organizational Decision Making," *Organization Science*, May 1993, pp. 226–240.

3 Richard Priem, "Executive Judgment, Organizational Congruence, and Firm Performance," *Organization Science*, August 1994, pp. 421–432. See also R. Duane Ireland and C. Chet Miller, "Decision-Making and Firm Success," *Academy of Management Executive*, 2004, Vol. 18, No. 4, pp. 8–12.

4 For a review of decision making, see E. Frank Harrison, *The Managerial Decision Making Process*, 5th ed. (Boston: Houghton Mifflin, 1999). See also Elke U. Weber and Eric J. Johnson, "Mindful Judgment and Decision Making," in *Annual Review of Psychology 2009* eds. Susan T. Fiske, Daniel L. Schacter, and Robert Sternberg (Palo Alto, CA: Annual Reviews, 2009), pp. 53–86; Gerd Gigerenzer and Wolfgang Gaissmaier, "Heuristic Decision Making," in *Annual Review of Psychology 2011* eds. Susan T. Fiske, Daniel L. Schacter, and Shelley Taylor (Palo Alto, CA: Annual Reviews, 2011), pp. 451–482.

5 H. Darr Beiser, "Fedex Chief Takes Cue from Leaders in History," *USA Today*, June 19, 2005, http://usatoday.com, accessed April 15, 2020.

6 George P. Huber, *Managerial Decision Making* (Glenview, IL: Scott, Foresman, 1980).

7 For an example, see Paul D. Collins, Lori V. Ryan, and Sharon F. Matusik, "Programmable Automation and the Locus of Decision-Making Power," *Journal of Management*, 1999, Vol. 25, pp. 29–53.

8 Huber, *Managerial Decision Making*. See also David W. Miller and Martin K. Starr, *The Structure of Human Decisions* (Englewood Cliffs, NJ: Prentice-Hall, 1976); Alvar Elbing, *Behavioral Decisions in Organizations*, 2nd ed. (Glenview, IL: Scott, Foresman, 1978).

9 Rene M. Stulz, "Six Ways Companies Mismanage Risk," *Harvard Business Review*, March 2009, pp. 86–94.

10 Natalie Kitroeff, "Disney Chief Bob Iger's Advice to Students: Don't Make Stupid Decision," *Bloomberg BusinessWeek*, October 30, 2014, http://www.bloomberg.com on April 24, 2020.

11 Eric Rosenbaum, "'The Stranded Employee' is a Coronavirus Problem the World Has Never Seen," CNBC, March 3, 2020, https://www.cnbc.com on March 31, 2020.

12 Gerard P. Hodgkinson, Nicola J. Bown, A. John Maule, Keith W. Glaister, and Alan D. Pearman, "Breaking the Frame: An Analysis of Strategic Cognition and Decision Making under Uncertainty," *Strategic Management Journal*, 1999, Vol. 20, pp. 977–985.

13 "Using Intuition in Your Business Plan," *Forbes*, September 20, 2010, accessed on April 15, 2020.

14 Glen Whyte, "Decision Failures: Why They Occur and How to Prevent Them," *Academy of Management Executive*, August 1991, pp. 23–31. See also Jerry Useem, "Decisions, Decisions," *Fortune*, June 27, 2005, pp. 55–154.

15 Quoted in *Fortune*, June 27, 2005, p. 55.

16 "Decision Making Quotes," Goodreads, https://www.goodreads.com on March 31, 2020.

17 Robert C. Litchfield, "Brainstorming Reconsidered: A Goal-Based View," *Academy of Management Review*, 2008, Vol. 33, No. 3, pp. 649–668.

18 Paul Nutt, "Expanding the Search for Alternatives During Strategic Decision-Making," *Academy of Management Executive*, 2004, Vol. 18, No. 4, pp. 13–22.

19 Champaign Williams, "These Companies Are Relocating Headquarters in Search of Young, Qualified Talent," Bisnow, February 9, 2017, https://www.bisnow.com on March 31, 2020.

20 See Paul J. H. Schoemaker and Robert E. Gunther, "The Wisdom of Deliberate Mistakes," *Harvard Business Review*, June 2006, pp. 108–115.

21 Jeffrey Pfeffer and Robert I. Sutton, *Hard Facts, Dangerous Half-Truths, and Total Nonsense: Profiting from Evidence-Based Management* (Cambridge, MA: Harvard Business School Press, 2006).

22 Jack Soll, Katherine Milkman, and John Payne, "Outsmart Your Own Biases," *Harvard Business Review*, May 2015, pp. 64–71.

23 "The Wisdom of Solomon," *Newsweek*, August 17, 1987, pp. 62–63.

24 "Making Decisions in Real Time," *Fortune*, June 26, 2000, pp. 332–334. See also Eugene Sadler-Smith and Erella Shefy, "The Intuitive Executive: Understanding and Applying 'Gut Feel' in Decision-Making," *Academy of Management Executive*, 2004, Vol. 18, No. 4, pp. 76–91; Don A. Moore and Francis J. Flynn, "The Case of Behavioral Decision Research in Organizational Behavior," in *Academy of Management Annals*, Vol. 2 eds. James P. Walsh and Arthur P. Brief (London: Routledge, 2008), pp. 399–432.

25 "Hard Choices," www.bloomberg.com, accessed on April 15, 2020.

26 Herbert A. Simon, *Administrative Behavior* (New York: Free Press, 1945). Simon's ideas have been refined and updated in Herbert A. Simon, *Administrative Behavior*, 3rd ed. (New York: Free Press, 1976), and Herbert A. Simon, "Making Management Decisions: The Role of Intuition and Emotion," *Academy of Management Executive, February* 1987, pp. 57–63.

27 Patricia Corner, Angelo Kinicki, and Barbara Keats, "Integrating Organizational and Individual Information Processing Perspectives on Choice," *Organization Science*, August 1994, pp. 294–302.

28 Kimberly D. Elsbach and Greg Elofson, "How the Packaging of Decision Explanations Affects Perceptions of Trustworthiness," *Academy of Management Journal*, 2000, Vol. 43, pp. 80–88.

29 Kenneth Brousseau, Michael Driver, Gary Hourihan, and Rikard Larsson, "The Seasoned Executive's Decision-Making Style," *Harvard Business Review*, February 2006, pp. 111–112; see also Erik Dane and Michael G. Pratt, "Exploring Intuition and Its Role in Managerial Decision Making," *Academy of Management Review*, 2007, Vol. 32, No. 1, pp. 33–54.

30 Adam Bryant, "Three Good Hires? He'll Pay More for One Who's Great," *New York Times*, March 13, 2010.

31 Walter Isaacson, "The Real Leadership Lessons of Steve Jobs," *Harvard Business Review*, April 2012, https://hbr.org on April 24, 2020.

32 Barry M. Staw and Jerry Ross, "Good Money after Bad," *Psychology Today*, February 1988, pp. 30–33; D. Ramona Bobocel and John Meyer, "Escalating Commitment to a Failing Course of Action: Separating the Roles of Choice and Justification," *Journal of Applied Psychology*, 1994, Vol. 79, pp. 360–363.

33 Peter Lattmann and Jeffrey McCracken, "Closing Time for a Rock Theme Park," *Wall Street Journal*, January 7, 2009, p. B1.

34 Gerry McNamara and Philip Bromiley, "Risk and Return in Organizational Decision Making," *Academy of Management Journal*, 1999, Vol. 42, pp. 330–338.

35 For an example, see Brian O'Reilly, "What It Takes to Start a Startup," *Fortune*, June 7, 1999, pp. 135–140.

36 Martha I. Finney, "The Catbert Dilemma—The Human Side of Tough Decisions," *HR Magazine*, February 1997, pp. 70–78.

37 See Ann E. Tenbrunsel and Kristen Smith-Crowe, "Ethical Decision Making: Where We've Been and Where We're Going," in James P. Walsh and Arthur P. Brief, eds., *The Academy of Management Annals*, Vol. 2 (London: Routledge, 2008), pp. 545–607.

38 Edwin A. Locke, David M. Schweiger, and Gary P. Latham, "Participation in Decision Making: When Should It Be Used?" *Organizational Dynamics*, Winter 1986, pp. 65–79; Nicholas Baloff and Elizabeth M. Doherty, "Potential Pitfalls in Employee Participation," *Organizational Dynamics*, Winter 1989, pp. 51–62.

39 For an extension of the nominal group method, see Kevin P. Coyne, Patricia Gorman Clifford, and Renee Dye, "Breakthrough Thinking from Inside the Box," *Harvard Business Review*, December 2007, pp. 71–80.

40 Norman P. R. Maier, "Assets and Liabilities in Group Problem Solving: The Need for an Integrative Function," in *Perspectives on Business in Organizations*, 2nd ed. eds., J. Richard Hackman, Edward E. Lawler III, and Lyman W. Porter (New York: McGraw-Hill, 1983), pp. 385–392.

41 Anthony L. Iaquinto and James W. Fredrickson, "Top Management Team Agreement about the Strategic Decision Process: A Test of Some of Its Determinants and Consequences," *Strategic Management Journal*, 1997, Vol. 18, pp. 63–75.

42 Richard A. Cosier and Charles R. Schwenk, "Agreement and Thinking Alike: Ingredients for Poor Decisions," *Academy of Management Executive*, February 1990, pp. 69–78.

43 Irving L. Janis, *Groupthink*, 2nd ed. (Boston: Houghton Mifflin, 1982).

44 Ibid.

45 Jeff Zeleny, "Is Obama Planning to Ditch His BlackBerry?" ABC News, May 21, 2014, http://abcnews.go.com on October 11, 2014; Sean Silcoff, et al., "Inside the Fall of BlackBerry: How the Smartphone Inventor Failed to Adapt," *The (Toronto) Globe and Mail*, September 27, 2013, www.theglobeandmail.com on October 13, 2014; Jeff de Cagna, "BlackBerry Breakdown: How a Smartphone Lost Its Way," *Associations Now*, August 1, 2014, http://associationsnow.com on October 9, 2014; James Surowiecki, "BlackBerry Season," *The New Yorker*, February 13, 2012, www.newyorker.com on October 8, 2014; Jay Yarrow, "All the Dumb Things RIM's CEOs Said While Apple and Android Ate Their Lunch," *Business Insider*, September 16, 2011, www.businessinsider.com on October 13, 2014; Hersh Shefrin, "Psychological Traps Snare BlackBerry Decision Makers," *Forbes*, November 7, 2013, www.forbes.com on October 9, 2014.

Chapter 5

1 "How a Turkish Immigrant Made a Billion Dollars in Eight Years Selling … Yogurt," *Bloomberg Businessweek*, January 31, 2015, pp. 60–64; *Hoover's Handbook of World Business 2019* (Austin, TX: Hoover's Business Press, 2019), pp. 450–451; "The World's 50 Most Innovative Companies in 2015," *Fast Company*, February 2015, p. 56; and "A Conversation with the 'Steve Jobs of Yogurt'," *USA Today*, usatoday.com on March 5, 2020.

2 Bro Uttal, "Inside the Deal that Made Bill Gates $350,000,000," *Fortune*, July 21, 1986, pp. 23–33.

3 Murray B. Low and Ian MacMillan, "Entrepreneurship: Past Research and Future Challenges," *Journal of Management*, June 1988, pp. 139–159.

4 NAICS Association, "Counts by Company Size," https://www.naics.com/business-lists/counts-by-company-size/ on March 1, 2020.

5 See http://www.sba.gov.

6 Small Business Administration, "Frequently Asked Questions," http://www.sba.gov/sites/default/files/advocacy/FAQ_March_2014_0.pdf on March 20, 2020.

7 "A World that's All A-Twitter," *USA Today*, May 26, 2009, pp. 1B, 2B.

8 *USA Today*, May 26, 2009, p. 1B.

9 Amar Bhide, "How Entrepreneurs Craft Strategies that Work," *Harvard Business Review*, March–April 1994, pp. 150–163.

10 *USA Today*, April 7, 2004, p. 8B.

11 *Hoover's Handbook of American Business 2019*, pp. 788–789.

12 F. M. Scherer, *Industrial Market Structure and Economic Performance*, 2nd ed. (Boston: Houghton Mifflin, 1980).

13 The importance of discovering niches is emphasized in Charles Hill and Gareth Jones, *Strategic Management: An Integrative Approach*, 12th ed. (Boston: Houghton Mifflin, 2016).

14 "A Startup's New Prescription for Eyewear," *BusinessWeek*, July 4–10, 2011, pp. 49–51.

15 D. Kirsch, B. Goldfarb, and A. Gera, "Form or Substance: The Role of Business Plans in Venture Capital Decision Making," *Strategic Management Journal*, Vol. 30, No. 5, 2009, pp. 487–516.

16 Catherine Clifford, "From Pennies to Millions: What It Felt Like to Make Money for the First Time," *Entrepreneur*, March 25, 2015, http://www.entrepreneur.com on March 20, 2020.

17 "US Venture Capital Investment Reached $130.9 Billion in 2018, Surpassing Dot-Com Era" PitchBook, January 10, 2019, https://pitchbook.com on March 20, 2020.

18 See https://www.sba.gov/offices/headquarters/oed/resources/148091.

19 James Combs, David Ketchen, Christopher Shook, and Jeremy Short, "Antecedents and Consequences of Franchising: Past Accomplishments and Future Challenges," *Journal of Management*, January 2011, pp. 99–126.

20 Lauren Covello, "Shark Tank's Barbara Corcoran: Real Winners Say 'Hit Me Again,'" *Entrepreneur*, February 5, 2015, http://www.entrepreneur.com May 16, 2015.

21 "Retail E-Commerce Sales in the United States from 2017 to 2024," Statista, January 2020, https://www.statista.com on March 28, 2020.

22 "Black Owned Businesses," BlackDemographics, https://blackdemographics.com on March 20, 2020.

23 AP wire story, January 29, 2006.

24 Norman M. Scarborough and Thomas W. Zimmerer, *Effective Small Business Management: An Entrepreneurial Approach*, 6th ed. (Upper Saddle River, NJ: Prentice Hall, 2000), pp. 412–413.

25 Andrew Keshner, "Closing Our Business to Stop the Coronavirus Violated Our Employees' Rights, Lawsuit Claims," MarketWatch, March 30, 2020, https://www.marketwatch.com on April 8, 2020.

26 See Robert A. Baron, "The Role of Affect in the Entrepreneurial Process," *Academy of Management Review*, 2008, Vol. 33, No. 2, pp. 328–340; see also Keith M. Hmieleski and Robert A. Baron, "Entrepreneurs' Optimism and New Venture Performance: A Social Cognition Perspective," *Academy of Management Journal*, 2009, Vol. 52, No. 3, pp. 540–572.

27 See https://www.cleanharbors.com/about-us.

28 Todd Woody, "Meet the Startup Making Snap-Together Office Buildings, Schools and 7-Elevens," *Forbes*, January 2, 2013, www.forbes.com on March 5, 2020; Alex Salkever, "Project Frog Seeks to Make Pre-Fab School Buildings Fab—and Green," *Daily Finance*, www.dailyfinance.com on March 5, 2020; Nathan Hurst, "The 'Componentized' School of the Future, Built in 90 Days," *Wired*, May 2, 2013, www.wired.com on March 5, 2020; Elise Craig, "Project Frog Rethinks Construction with Smart Component Buildings," Xconomy, December 17, 2013, www.xconomy.com on March 5, 2020; Annie Sciacca, "Ann Hand: CEO, Project Frog," *San Francisco Business Times*, www.bizjournals.com on March 5, 2020; Eliza Brooke, "Raising $20M, Project Frog Ramps Up Production on Its Energy Efficient Buildings," TechCrunch, November 7, 2013, http://techcrunch.com on March 5, 2020; Project Frog, "Project Frog + El Sol Science and Arts Academy of Santa Ana" [Video], *YouTube*, www.youtube.com on March 5, 2020; Joann Gonchar, "Modular Classroom Makeover," http://archrecord.construction.com on March 5, 2020.

Chapter 6

1 "Transportation Security Administration," Wikipedia, https://en.wikipedia.org on April 10, 2020; American Federation of Government Employees, "4 Reasons Why TSA Officers Quit Their Job," December 16, 2018, https://www.afge.org on April 10, 2020; https://hraccess.tsa.dhs.gov/hraccess/employees.html; Transportation Security Administration, "TSA By the Numbers," February 4, 2020, https://www.tsa.gov/sites/default/files/resources/tsabythenumbers_factsheet.pdf on April 10, 2020.

2 Ricky W. Griffin, *Task Design* (Glenview, IL: Scott Foresman, 1982).

3 Anne S. Miner, "Idiosyncratic Jobs in Formal Organizations," *Administrative Science Quarterly*, September 1987, pp. 327–351.

4 Maurice D. Kilbridge, "Reduced Costs through Job Enlargement: A Case," *Journal of Business*, 1960, Vol. 33, No. 4, pp. 357–362.

5 See fortune.com on April 10, 2020.

6 Ricky W. Griffin and Gary C. McMahan, "Motivation through Job Enrichment," in *Organizational Behavior: State of the Science*, ed. Jerald Greenberg (New York: Erlbaum, 1994), pp. 23–44.

7 "Jacks of All Trades, and Masters of All," *USA Today*, July 6, 2010, p. 1B.

8 Maurice D. Kilbridge, "Reduced Costs through Job Enlargement: A Case," *Journal of Business*, 1960, Vol. 33, No. 4, pp. 357–362.

9 Frederick Herzberg, *Work and the Nature of Man* (Cleveland, OH: World Press, 1966).

10 J. Richard Hackman and Greg R. Oldham, *Work Redesign* (Reading, MA: Addison-Wesley, 1980).

11 Richard L. Daft, *Organization Theory and Design*, 13th ed. (Cincinnati, OH: South-Western, 2017).

12 David D. Van Fleet and Arthur G. Bedeian, "A History of the Span of Management," *Academy of Management Review*, 1977, pp. 356–372.

13 James C. Worthy, "Factors Influencing Employee Morale," *Harvard Business Review*, January 1950, pp. 61–73.

14 Dan R. Dalton, William D. Todor, Michael J. Spendolini, Gordon J. Fielding, and Lyman W. Porter, "Organization Structure and Performance: A Critical Review," *Academy of Management Review*, January 1980, pp. 49–64.

15 "Cadbury Gives Its CEO More Control," *Wall Street Journal*, October 15, 2008, p. B2.

16 See Daft, *Organization Theory and Design*.

17 Carrie R. Leana, "Predictors and Consequences of Delegation," *Academy of Management Journal*, December 1986, pp. 754–774.

18 Jerry Hirsch, "Toyota Overhauls Management, Gives More Autonomy to North America," *Los Angeles Times*, March 7, 2013, p. 3B; and "Toyota Shake-Up to Speed Decisions," *USA Today*, March 7, 2013, p. 1B.

19 Guy Chazan, "Shell's New Chief Begins Wide-Ranging Shake-Up," *Wall Street Journal*, May 28, 2009, p. B4.

20 Kevin Crowston, "A Coordination Theory Approach to Organizational Process Design," *Organization Science*, March–April 1997, pp. 157–166.

21 James Thompson, *Organizations in Action* (New York: McGraw-Hill, 1967). For a recent discussion, see Bart Victor and Richard S. Blackburn, "Interdependence: An Alternative Conceptualization," *Academy of Management Review*, July 1987, pp. 486–498.

22 Jay R. Galbraith, *Designing Complex Organizations* (Reading, MA: Addison-Wesley, 1973) and *Organizational Design* (Reading, MA: Addison-Wesley, 1977).

23 Paul R. Lawrence and Jay W. Lorsch, "Differentiation and Integration in Complex Organizations," *Administrative Science Quarterly*, March 1967, pp. 1–47.

24 Max Weber, *Theory of Social and Economic Organizations*, trans. T. Parsons (New York: Free Press, 1947).

25 Paul Jarley, Jack Fiorito, and John Thomas Delany, "A Structural Contingency Approach to Bureaucracy and Democracy in U.S. National Unions," *Academy of Management Journal*, 1997, Vol. 40, No. 4, pp. 831–861.

26 For a review, see N. Anand and Richard L. Daft, "What Is the Right Organization Design?" *Organizational Dynamics*, 2007, Vol. 36, No. 4, pp. 329–344.

27 Joan Woodward, *Industrial Organization: Theory and Practice* (London: Oxford University Press, 1965).

28 Joan Woodward, *Management and Technology, Problems of Progress Industry*, Series No. 3 (London: Her Majesty's Stationery Office, 1958).

29 Tom Burns and G. M. Stalker, *The Management of Innovation* (London: Tavistock, 1961).

30 Paul R. Lawrence and Jay W. Lorsch, *Organization and Environment* (Homewood, IL: Irwin, 1967).

31 bloomberg.com on April 8, 2020.

32 Edward E. Lawler III, "Rethinking Organization Size," *Organizational Dynamics*, Autumn 1997, pp. 24–33. See also Henrich R. Greve, "A Behavioral Theory of Firm Growth: Sequential Attention to Size and Performance Goals," *Academy of Management Journal*, 2008, Vol. 51, No. 3, pp. 476–494.

33 Derek S. Pugh and David J. Hickson, *Organization Structure in Its Context: The Aston Program I* (Lexington, MA: D. C. Heath, 1976).

34 Robert H. Miles and Associates, *The Organizational Life Cycle* (San Francisco: Jossey-Bass, 1980). See also "Is Your Company Too Big?" *BusinessWeek*, March 27, 1989, pp. 84–94.

35 Oliver E. Williamson, *Markets and Hierarchies* (New York: Free Press, 1975).

36 Williamson, *Markets and Hierarchies*.

37 Michael E. Porter, "From Competitive Advantage to Corporate Strategy," *Harvard Business Review*, May–June 1987, pp. 43–59.

38 Williamson, *Markets and Hierarchies*.

39 Jay B. Barney and William G. Ouchi, eds., *Organizational Economics* (San Francisco: Jossey-Bass, 1986); Robert E. Hoskisson, "Multidivisional Structure and Performance: The Contingency of Diversification Strategy," *Academy of Management Journal*, December 1987, pp. 625–644. See also Bruce Lamont, Robert Williams, and James Hoffman, "Performance during 'M-Form' Reorganization and Recovery Time: The Effects of Prior Strategy and Implementation Speed," *Academy of Management Journal*, 1994, Vol. 37, No. 1, pp. 153–166.

40 Stanley M. Davis and Paul R. Lawrence, *Matrix* (Reading, MA: Addison-Wesley, 1977).

41 Davis and Lawrence, *Matrix*.

42 See Lawton Burns and Douglas Wholey, "Adoption and Abandonment of Matrix Management Programs: Effects of Organizational Characteristics and Interorganizational Networks," *Academy of Management Journal*, 1993, Vol. 36, No. 1, pp. 106–138.

43 See Michael Hammer and Steven Stanton, "How Process Enterprises Really Work," *Harvard Business Review*, November–December 1999, pp. 108–118.

44 Raymond E. Miles, Charles C. Snow, John A. Mathews, Grant Miles, and Henry J. Coleman, Jr., "Organizing in the Knowledge Age: Anticipating the Cellular Form," *Academy of Management Executive*, November 1997, pp. 7–24.

45 Peter Senge, *The Fifth Discipline* (New York: Free Press, 1993). See also David Lei, John W. Slocum, and Robert A. Pitts, "Designing Organizations for Competitive Advantage: The Power of Unlearning and Learning," *Organizational Dynamics*, Winter 1999, pp. 24–35.

46 Amy C. Edmondson, "The Competitive Imperative of Learning," *Harvard Business Review*, July–August 2008, pp. 60–70.

47 alshaya.com; Beth Kowitt, "The Mystery Company Importing Americana to the Mideast," *Fortune*, February 12, 2013, fortune.com on April 10, 2020; "Al-Kharafi, A-Shaya Among the Most Powerful Arabs—Business Power 500 List," *Kuwait Times*, March 6, 2013, p. 1.

Chapter 7

1 John Kotter, "Barriers to Change: The Real Reason behind the Kodak Downfall," *Forbes*, May 2, 2012, www.forbes.com on April 25, 2020; David DiSalvo, "The Fall of Kodak: A Tale of Disruptive Technology and Bad Business," *Forbes*, October 2, 2011, www.forbes.com on April 25, 2020; Bill Fischer, "There Are No 'Kodak Moments,'" *Forbes*, July 4, 2014, www.forbes.com on April 25, 2020; Julie Creswell, "Kodak's Fuzzy Future," *New York Times*, May 3, 2013, www.nytimes.com on April 25, 2020.

2 For an excellent review of this area, see Achilles A. Armenakis and Arthur G. Bedeian, "Organizational Change: A Review of Theory and Research in the 1990s," *Journal of Management*, 1999, Vol. 25, No. 3, pp. 293–315. For a more recent review, see Luis L. Martins, "Organizational Change and Development," in *Handbook of Industrial and Organizational Psychology, Vol. 3: Maintaining, Expanding, and Contracting the Organization*, ed. Sheldon Zedeck (Washington, DC: American Psychological Association, 2010), pp. 691–728.

3 Joel Cutcher-Gershenfeld, Ellen Ernst Kossek, and Heidi Sandling, "Managing Concurrent Change Initiatives," *Organizational Dynamics*, Winter 1997, pp. 21–38.

4 Michael A. Hitt, "The New Frontier: Transformation of Management for the New Millennium," *Organizational Dynamics*, Winter 2000, pp. 7–15. See also Michael Beer and Nitin Nohria, "Cracking the Code of Change," *Harvard Business Review*, May–June 2000, pp. 123–144; Clark Gilbert, "The Disruption Opportunity," *MIT Sloan Management Review*, Summer 2003, pp. 27–32.

5 See Warren Boeker, "Strategic Change: The Influence of Managerial Characteristics and Organizational Growth," *Academy of Management Journal*, 1997, Vol. 40, No. 1, pp. 152–170.

6 Rick Wartzman, "How to Change and Stay the Same," *Bloomberg Businessweek*, January 27, 2012, http://www.bloomberg.com/bw/management/how-to-change-and-stay-the-same-01272012.html on April 25, 2020.

7 Alan L. Frohman, "Igniting Organizational Change from Below: The Power of Personal Initiative," *Organizational Dynamics*, Winter 1997, pp. 39–53.

8 Nandini Rajagopalan and Gretchen M. Spreitzer, "Toward a Theory of Strategic Change: A Multi-Lens Perspective and Integrative Framework," *Academy of Management Review*, 1997, Vol. 22, No. 1, pp. 48–79.

9 Anne Fisher, "Danger Zone," *Fortune*, www.fortune.com on April 25, 2020.

10 John P. Kotter and Leonard A. Schlesinger, "Choosing Strategies for Change," *Harvard Business Review*, March–April 1979, p. 106.

11 Clayton M. Christensen and Michael Overdorf, "Meeting the Challenge of Disruptive Change," *Harvard Business Review*, March–April 2000, pp. 67–77.

12 "To Maintain Success, Managers Must Learn How to Direct Change," *Wall Street Journal*, August 12, 2002, p. B1. See also Andrew Van de Ven and Kangyong Sun, "Breakdowns in Implementing Models of Organization Change," *Academy of Management Perspectives*, August 2011, pp. 58–68.

13 See Eric Abrahamson, "Change Without Pain," *Harvard Business Review*, July–August 2000, pp. 75–85. See also Gib Akin and Ian Palmer, "Putting Metaphors to Work for Change in Organizations," *Organizational Dynamics*, Winter 2000, pp. 67–76.

14 Erik Brynjolfsson, Amy Austin Renshaw, and Marshall Van Alstyne, "The Matrix of Change," *Sloan Management Review*, Winter 1997, pp. 37–54.

15 Kurt Lewin, "Frontiers in Group Dynamics: Concept, Method, and Reality in Social Science," *Human Relations*, June 1947, pp. 5–41.

16 Michael Roberto and Lynne Levesque, "The Art of Making Change Initiatives Stick," *Sloan Management Review*, Summer 2005, pp. 53–62.

17 Christine Canabou, "Time for a Turnaround," *Fast Company*, December 31, 2002, www.fastcompany.com on April 25, 2020.

18 See Connie J. G. Gersick, "Revolutionary Change Theories: A Multilevel Exploration of the Punctuated Equilibrium Paradigm," *Academy of Management Review*, January 1991, pp. 10–36; see also John P. Kotter and Leonard A. Schlesinger, "Choosing Strategies for Change," *Harvard Business Review*, July–August 2008, pp. 120–141.

19 See Mel Fugate, Angelo J. Kinicki, and Gregory E. Prussia, "Employee Coping with Organizational Change: An Examination of Alternative Theoretical Perspectives and Models," *Personnel Psychology*, 2008, Vol. 61, pp. 1–36. See also Jeffrey D. Ford and Laurie W. Ford, "Decoding Resistance to Change," *Harvard Business Review*, April 2009, pp. 99–104.

20 See Clark Gilbert and Joseph Bower, "Disruptive Change," *Harvard Business Review*, May 2002, pp. 95–104.

21 "RJR Employees Fight Distraction amid Buy-Out Talks," *Wall Street Journal*, www.wsj.com on April 25, 2020.

22 Saffron Howden, "Flight Chaos Looms as BA Staff Vow to Strike," *Sydney Morning Herald*, December 16, 2010.

23 Arnon E. Reichers, John P. Wanous, and James T. Austin, "Understanding and Managing Cynicism about Organizational Change," *Academy of Management Executive*, February 1997, pp. 48–59.

24 For a classic discussion, see Paul R. Lawrence, "How to Deal with Resistance to Change," *Harvard Business Review*, January–February 1969, pp. 4–12, 166–176; for a more recent discussion, see Jeffrey D. Ford, Laurie W. Ford, and Angelo D'Amelio, "Resistance to Change: The Rest of the Story," *Academy of Management Review*, 2008, Vol. 33, No. 2, pp. 362–377.

25 Lester Coch and John R. P. French, Jr., "Overcoming Resistance to Change," *Human Relations*, August 1948, pp. 512–532.

26 "9 Keys to Driving Cultural Change," www.businessinsider.com on April 25, 2020.

27 Benjamin Schneider, Arthur P. Brief, and Richard A. Guzzo, "Creating a Climate and Culture for Sustainable Organizational Change," *Organizational Dynamics*, Spring 1996, pp. 7–19.

28 "Troubled GM Plans Major Tuneup," *USA Today*, www.usatoday.com on April 25, 2020.

29 Paul Bate, Raza Khan, and Annie Pye, "Towards a Culturally Sensitive Approach to Organization Structuring: Where Organization Design Meets Organization Development," *Organization Science*, March–April 2000, pp. 197–211.

30 David Kirkpatrick, "The New Player," *Fortune*, www.fortune.com on April 25, 2020.

31 Jeffrey A. Alexander, "Adaptive Change in Corporate Control Practices," *Academy of Management Journal*, March 1991, pp. 162–193.

32 Gerd Bohner and Nina Dickel, "Attitudes and Attitude Change," in *Annual Review of Psychology 2011*, eds. Susan T. Fiske, Daniel L. Schacter, and Shelley Taylor (Palo Alto, CA: Annual Reviews, 2011), pp. 391–418.

33 Thomas A. Stewart, "Reengineering— The Hot New Managing Tool," *Fortune*, August 23, 1993, pp. 41–48.

34 Peter Cohan, "How Netflix Reinvented Itself," *Forbes*, April 23, 2013, www.forbes.com on April 25, 2020.

35 Paul Nunes and Tim Breen, "Reinvent Your Business Before It's Too Late," *Harvard Business Review*, January–February 2011, pp. 80–87.

36 Richard Beckhard, *Organization Development: Strategies and Models* (Reading, MA: Addison-Wesley, 1969), p. 9.

37 W. Warner Burke, "The New Agenda for Organization Development," *Organizational Dynamics*, Summer 1997, pp. 7–20.

38 Wendell L. French and Cecil H. Bell, Jr., *Organization Development: Behavioral Science Interventions for Organization Improvement*, 2nd ed. (Englewood Cliffs, NJ: Prentice-Hall, 1978).

39 "Memo to the Team: This Needs Salt!" *Wall Street Journal*, www.wsj.com on April 25, 2020.

40 Raymond A. Noe, Michael J. Tews, and Alison McConnell Dachner, "Learner Engagement: A New Perspective for Enhancing Our Understanding of Learner Motivation and Workplace Learning," in *Academy of Management Annals 2010*, eds. James P. Walsh and Arthur P. Brief (Philadelphia: Taylor & Francis, 2010), pp. 279–316.

41 For a recent discussion on the effectiveness of various OD techniques in different organizations, see John M. Nicholas, "The Comparative Impact of Organization Development Interventions on Hard Criteria Measures," *Academy of Management Review*, October 1982, pp. 531–542.

42 Constantinos Markides, "Strategic Innovation," *Sloan Management Review*, Spring 1997, pp. 9–24. See also James Brian Quinn, "Outsourcing Innovation: The New Engine of Growth," *Sloan Management Review*, Summer 2000, pp. 12–21.

43 L. B. Mohr, "Determinants of Innovation in Organizations," *American Political Science Review*, 1969, pp. 111–126; G. A. Steiner, *The Creative Organization* (Chicago: University of Chicago Press, 1965); R. Duncan and A. Weiss, "Organizational Learning: Implications for Organizational Design," in *Research in Organizational Behavior*, Vol. 1, ed. B. M. Staw (Greenwich, CT: JAI Press, 1979), pp. 75–123; J. E. Ettlie, "Adequacy of

Stage Models for Decisions on Adoption of Innovation," *Psychological Reports*, 1980, pp. 991–995.

44 See Alan Patz, "Managing Innovation in High Technology Industries," *New Management*, September 1986, pp. 54–59.

45 See Willow A. Sheremata, "Centrifugal and Centripetal Forces in Radical New Product Development under Time Pressure," *Academy of Management Review*, 2000, Vol. 25, No. 2, pp. 389–408. See also Richard Leifer, Gina Colarelli O'Connor, and Mark Rice, "Implementing Radical Innovation in Mature Firms: The Role of Hobs," *Academy of Management Executive*, 2001, Vol. 15, No. 3, pp. 102–112.

46 See Julian Birkinshaw, Gary Hamel, and Michael J. Mol, "Management Innovation," *Academy of Management Review*, 2008, Vol. 33, No. 4, pp. 825–845.

47 See Clayton M. Christensen, Stephen P. Kaufman, and Willy C. Shih, "Innovation Killers," *Harvard Business Review*, January 2008, pp. 98–107.

48 Tom Lowery, "How to Leap from Employee to Intrapreneur (and Be the Change You Want to See," *Huffington Post*, October 22, 2013, http://www.huffingtonpost.com on April 25, 2020.

49 Dorothy Leonard and Jeffrey F. Rayport, "Spark Innovation Through Empathic Design," *Harvard Business Review*, November–December 1997, pp. 102–115.

50 "The 25 Most Innovative Companies," *Bloomberg Businessweek*, www.bloomberg.com on April 25, 2020.

51 Geoffrey Moore, "Innovating Within Established Enterprises," *Harvard Business Review*, July–August 2004, pp. 87–96. See also David A. Garvin and Lynne C. Levesque, "Meeting the Challenge of Corporate Entrepreneurship," *Harvard Business Review*, October 2006, pp. 102–112.

52 See Gifford Pinchot III, *Intrapreneuring* (New York: Harper & Row, 1985).

53 "What Is Intrapreneurship?" www.entrepreneurship.com on April 25, 2020.

54 *Hoover's Handbook of World Business 2020* (Austin: Hoover's Reference Press, 2020), pp. 27–29; "Miner Anglo to Sell Assets in Shake-Up," *Wall Street Journal*, www.wsj.com on April 25, 2020; Eric Onstad and Kate Holton, "Xstrata Seeks $68 Billion Merger with Anglo," Reuters, June 21, 2009, www.reuters.com on April 25, 2020; Martin Waller and David Robinson, "Business Big Shot: Cynthia Carroll of Anglo American," *The Times*, August 1, 2009, http://business.timesonline.co.uk on April 25, 2020; Andrew Cave, "Cynthia Carroll Digs Deep for Anglo," *The Telegraph*, August 1, 2009, www.telegraph.co.uk on April 25, 2020; Julia Werdigier, "Xstrata Ends Bid for Rival in London," *New York Times*, October 15, 2009, www.nytimes.com on April 25, 2020.

Chapter 8

1 Jon Springer, "Danny Wegman," *Supermarket News*, http://supermarketnews.com on March 5, 2017; Michael A. Prospero, "Employee Innovator: Wegmans," *Fast Company*, www.fastcompany.com on March 5, 2017; Dan Mitchell, "Wegmans Price War Against Itself," *The Big Money*, www.thebigmoney.com on March 5, 2017; "100 Best Companies to Work For," CNN, http://money.cnn.com on March 5, 2017; Business Civic Leadership Center, "Wegmans," *2015 Corporate Citizenship Awards* (Washington, DC: U.S. Chamber of Commerce, 2015), www.bclc.uschamber.com on March 5, 2017; and "In 2015, Wegmans Announces Largest Group of Employee Scholarship Recipients Yet," Press release, www.wegmans.com on March 5, 2017.

2 For a complete review of human resource management, see Angelo S. DeNisi and Ricky W. Griffin, *Human Resource Management*, 5th ed. (Boston: Cengage Learning, 2020).

3 Patrick Wright and Gary McMahan, "Strategic Human Resources Management: A Review of the Literature," *Journal of Management*, June 1992, Vol. 13, No. 3, pp. 280–319; see also Peter Cappelli, "Talent Management for the Twenty-First Century," *Harvard Business Review*, March 2008, pp. 74–84; Edward E. Lawler III, "Making Human Capital a Source of Competitive Advantage," *Organizational Dynamics*, January–March 2009, Vol. 38, No. 1, pp. 1–7.

4 Augustine Lado and Mary Wilson, "Human Resource Systems and Sustained Competitive Advantage: A Competency-Based Perspective," *Academy of Management Review*, 1994, Vol. 19, No. 4, pp. 699–727.

5 David Lepak and Scott Snell, "Examining the Human Resource Architecture: The Relationships among Human Capital, Employment, and Human Resource Configurations," *Journal of Management*, 2002, Vol. 28, No. 4, pp. 517–543. See also Wayne F. Cascio and Herman Aguinis, "Staffing Twenty-First Century Organizations," in *Academy of Management Annals*, Vol. 2, eds. James P. Walsh and Arthur P. Brief (London: Routledge, 2008), pp. 133–166.

6 http://www.shrm.org/publications/hrmagazine/, on April 25, 2020.

7 "Recent OSHA Enforcement Cases," *Industrial Safety & Hygiene News*, August 5, 2019, https://www.ishn.com on April 20, 2020.

8 "The Hidden Perils of Layoffs," *Bloomberg Businessweek*, March 2, 2009, www.bloomberg.com, April 25, 2020.

9 "An Interview with Harley Shaiken," www.usatoday.com on April 25, 2020.

10 "While Hiring at Most Firms Chills, Wal-Mart's Heats Up," *USA Today*, www.usatoday.com, April 25, 2020.

11 Peter Cappelli, "A Supply Chain Approach to Workforce Planning," *Organizational Dynamics*, January–March 2009, Vol. 38, No. 1, pp. 8–15.

12 Michelle Conlin, "The New Workforce," *Bloomberg Businessweek*, March 20, 2000, www.bloomberg.com on April 25, 2020.

13 John Beeson, "Succession Planning," *Across the Board*, February 2000, pp. 38–41.

14 Brian R. Dineen and Scott M. Soltis, "Recruitment: A Review of Research and Emerging Directions," in *Handbook of Industrial and Organizational Psychology, Vol. 2: Selecting and Developing Members for the Organization*, ed. Sheldon Zedeck (Washington, DC: American Psychological Association, 2010), pp. 43–66.

15 Robert Gatewood, Mary Gowan, and Gary Lautenschlager, "Corporate Image, Recruitment Image, and Initial Job Choice Decisions," *Academy of Management Journal*, 1993, Vol. 36, No. 2, pp. 413–427; see also Karen Holcombe Ehrhart and Jonathan Ziegert, "Why Are Individuals Attracted to Organizations?" *Journal of Management*, 2005, Vol. 31, No. 6, pp. 901–919; and Donald M. Truxillo and Talya N. Bauer, "Applicant Reactions to Organizations and Selection Systems," in *Handbook of Industrial and Organizational Psychology, Vol. 2*, pp. 379–398.

16 "Firms Cook Up New Ways to Keep Workers," *USA Today*, www.usatoday.com on April 25, 2020.

17 James A. Breaugh and Mary Starke, "Research on Employee Recruiting: So Many Studies, So Many Remaining Questions," *Journal of Management*, 2000, Vol. 26, No. 3, pp. 405–434.

18 See Paul R. Sackett and Filip Lievens, "Personnel Selection," in *Annual Review of Psychology 2008*, eds. Susan T. Fiske, Daniel L. Schacter, and Robert Sternberg (Palo Alto, CA: Annual Reviews, 2008), pp. 419–450.

19 Jeffrey Kluger, "Pumping Up Your Past," *Time*, June 10, 2002, www.time.com on April 25, 2020.

20 "Resume Falsification Statistics," April 2, 2017, www.statisticbrain.com on April 25, 2020.

21 Frank L. Schmidt and John E. Hunter, "Employment Testing: Old Theories and New Research Findings," *American Psychologist*, October 1981, Vol. 36, No. 10, pp. 1128–1137.

22 Robert Liden, Christopher Martin, and Charles Parsons, "Interviewer and Applicant Behaviors in Employment Interviews," *Academy of Management Journal*, 1993, Vol. 36, No. 2, pp. 372–386.

23 Winfred Arthur Jr. and Eric Anthony Day, "Assessment Centers," in *Handbook of Industrial and Organizational Psychology, Vol. 2*, pp. 205–236.

24 Paul R. Sackett, "Assessment Centers and Content Validity: Some Neglected Issues," *Personnel Psychology*, 1987, Vol. 40, pp. 13–25.

25 Kenneth B. Brown and Traci Sitzmann, "Training and Employee Development for Improved Performance," in *Handbook of Industrial and Organizational Psychology, Vol. 2*, pp. 469–504.

26 "30,000 Trained to Confront Shooters," *USA Today*, www.usatoday.com on April 25, 2020.

27 www.entrepreneur.com/ on April 25, 2020.

28 Renee DeRouin, Barbara Fritzsche, and Eduardo Salas, "E-Learning in Organizations," *Journal of Management*, 2005, Vol. 31, No. 6, pp. 920–940. For a recent illustration, see Fred Luthans, James B. Avey, and Jaime L. Patera, "Experimental Analysis of a Web-Based Training Intervention to Develop Positive Psychological Capital," *Academy of Management Learning and Education,* 2008, Vol. 7, No. 2, pp. 209–221.

29 "The Secret Sauce at In-N-Out Burger," *Bloomberg Businessweek*, April 10, 2009, www.bloomberg.com on April 25, 2020; Dana Mattioli, "Despite Cutbacks, Firms Invest in Developing Leaders," *Wall Street Journal*, February 9, 2009, www.wsh.com on April 25, 2020.

30 Jessica L. Wildman, Wendy L. Bedwell, Eduardo Salas, and Kimberly A. Smith-Jentsch, "Performance Measurement at Work: A Multilevel Perspective," in *Handbook of Industrial and Organizational Psychology, Vol. 1: Building and Developing the Organization*, in ed. Sheldon Zedeck (Washington, DC: American Psychological Association, 2010), pp. 303–341.

31 See Paul Levy and Jane Williams, "The Social Context of Performance Appraisal: A Review and Framework for the Future," *Journal of Management*, 2004, Vol. 30, No. 6, pp. 881–905. See also Marcus Buckingham and Ashley Goodall, "Reinventing Performance Management," *Harvard Business Review*, April 2015, pp. 40–50.

32 Di Lewis, "13 Learning and Development Quotes to Spark Inspiration," AllenComm, September 9, 2015, https://www.allencomm.com on May 18, 2020.

33 See Michael Hammer, "The 7 Deadly Sins of Performance Measurement (and How to Avoid Them)," *MIT Sloan Management Review*, Spring 2007, pp. 19–30.

34 See Angelo S. DeNisi and Avraham N. Kluger, "Feedback Effectiveness: Can 360-Degree Appraisals Be Improved?" *Academy of Management Executive*, 2000, Vol. 13, No. 1, pp. 129–139.

35 Joseph J. Martocchio, "Strategic Reward and Compensation Plans," in *Handbook of Industrial and Organizational Psychology, Vol. 1*, pp. 343–372.

36 Jaclyn Fierman, "The Perilous New World of Fair Pay," *Fortune*, June 13, 1994, www.fortune.com on April 25, 2020.

37 "To Each According to His Needs: Flexible Benefits Plans Gain Favor," *Wall Street Journal*, September 16, 1986, p. 29.

38 Paula Aven Gladych, "9 Things To Do Before Terminating a Pension Plan," October 18, 2013, www.benefitspro.com on April 25, 2020.

39 See Sherry E. Sullivan, "The Changing Nature of Careers: A Review and Research Agenda," *Journal of Management*, 1999, Vol. 25, No. 3, pp. 457–484.

40 Barbara Presley Nobel, "Reinventing Labor," *Harvard Business Review*, July–August 1993, pp. 115–125.

41 "Gawkers Staff Vote to Unionize," *USA Today*, www.usatoday.com on April 25, 2020.

42 John A. Fossum, "Labor Relations: Research and Practice in Transition," *Journal of Management*, Summer 1987, pp. 281–300.

43 Max Boisot, *Knowledge Assets* (Oxford, UK: Oxford University Press, 1998).

44 "A New Era for Knowledge Workers," www.usatoday.com on April 25, 2020.

45 "Knowledge Workers Rise to the Top of the Food Chain," www.fortune.com on April 25, 2020.

46 Elizabeth George and Carmen Kaman Ng, "Nonstandard Workers: Work Arrangements and Outcomes," in *Handbook of Industrial and Organizational Psychology, Vol. 1*, pp. 573–596.

47 "FBI Taps Retiree Experience for Temporary Jobs," *USA Today*, www.usatoday.com on April 25, 2020.

48 "Special Report on Contingent Staffing," *Workforce Management*, October 19, 2009. See also "Intuit 2020 Report: Twenty Trends That Will Shape the Next Decade," October 2010, http://http-download.intuit.com/http.intuit/CMO/intuit/futureofsmallbusiness/intuit_2020_report.pdf?_ga=1.4790131.1193111323.1407518315 on April 25, 2020.

49 Aaron Bernstein, "When Is a Temp Not a Temp?" *Bloomberg Businessweek*, December 7, 1998, www.bloomberg.com on April 25, 2020.

50 Monica Langley, "Drivers Deliver Trouble to FedEx by Seeking Employee Benefits," *Wall Street Journal*, January 7, 2005, www.wsj.com on April 25, 2020; "FedEx Wins Ruling that Contract Drivers Seeking Benefits Aren't Employees," *Bloomberg Businessweek*, www.bloomberg.com on April 25, 2020.

51 Geoff Colvin, "In the Future, Will There Be Any Work Left for People to Do?" *Fortune*, June 2, 2014, www.fortune.com on April 25, 2020; Larry, Greenemeier, "Will IBM's Watson Usher in a New Era of Cognitive Computing?" *Scientific American*, November 13, 2013, www.scientificamerican.com on April 25, 2020; Thomas H. Davenport, "Cognitive Technology—Replacing or Augmenting Knowledge Workers?" *Wall Street Journal*, June 18, 2014, www.wsj.com on April 25, 2020; "IBM's Supercomputer Watson to Help Fight Brain Cancer," BBC, March 20, 2014, www.bbc.com on April 25, 2020.

Chapter 9

1 Judith Nemes, "Dumpster Diving: From Garbage to Gold," *GreenBiz*, January 9, 2009, www.greenbiz.com on May 2, 2020; Hunter Lovins, "Employee Engagement Is Key to Sustainable Success," October 2010, www.sustainablebrands.com on May 2, 2020; Tim Mohin, "How Sustainability Is Driving Employee Engagement and the Bottom Line," *GreenBiz*, September 29, 2011, www.greenbiz.com on May 2, 2020; Suzanne Tilleman, "Is Employee Organizational Commitment Related to Firm Environmental Sustainability?" *Journal of Small Business and Entrepreneurship*, 2012, Vol. 25, No. 4, pp. 417–431.

2 Lynn McGarlane Shore and Lois Tetrick, "The Psychological Contract as an Explanatory Framework in the Employment Relationship," in *Trends in Organizational Behavior*, eds. C. L. Cooper and D. M. Rousseau (London: Wiley, 1994). See also Denise M. Rousseau, "The Individual–Organization Relationship: The Psychological Contract," in *Handbook of Industrial and Organizational Psychology, Vol. 3: Maintaining, Expanding, and Contracting the Organization*, ed. Sheldon Zedeck (Washington, DC: American Psychological Association, 2010), pp. 191–220.

3 For an illustration, see Zhen Xiong Chen, Anne Tsui, and Lifeng Zhong, "Reactions to Psychological Contract Breach: A Dual Perspective," *Journal of Organizational Behavior*, 2008, Vol. 29, pp. 527–548.

4 Elizabeth Wolfe Morrison and Sandra L. Robinson, "When Employees Feel Betrayed: A Model of How Psychological Contract Violation Develops," *Academy of Management Review*, January 1997, Vol. 22, No. 1, pp. 226–256.

5 See Arne Kalleberg, "The Mismatched Worker: When People Don't Fit Their Jobs," *Academy of Management Perspectives*, 2008, Vol. 22, No. 1, pp. 24–40.

6 Oleksandr S. Chernyshenko, Stephen Stark, and Fritz Drasgow, "Individual Differences: Their Measurement and Validity," in *Handbook of Industrial and Organizational Psychology, Vol. 2: Selecting and Developing Members for the Organization*, ed. Sheldon Zedeck (Washington, DC: American Psychological Association, 2010), pp. 117–141.

7 Lawrence Pervin, "Personality," *Annual Review of Psychology*, 1985, Vol. 36, pp. 83–114; see also Dan P. McAdams and Bradley D. Olson, "Personality Development: Continuity and Change Over the Life Course," *Annual Review of Psychology*, 2010, Vol. 61, pp. 517–542.

8 L. R. Goldberg, "An Alternative 'Description of Personality': The Big Five Factor Structure," *Journal of Personality and Social Psychology*, 1990, Vol. 59, pp. 1216–1229.

9 Michael K. Mount, Murray R. Barrick, and J. Perkins Strauss, "Validity of Observer Ratings of the Big Five Personality Factors," *Journal of Applied Psychology*, 1994, Vol. 79, No. 2, pp. 272–280; Timothy A. Judge, Joseph J. Martocchio, and Carl J. Thoreson, "Five-Factor Model of Personality and Employee Absence," *Journal of Applied Psychology*, 1997, Vol. 82, No. 5, pp. 745–755.

10 For an extension of the Big Five framework, see Robert Renn, David Allen, and Tobias Huning, "Empirical Examination of the Individual-Level Personality-Based Theory of Self-Management Failure," *Journal of Organizational Behavior*, January 2011, pp. 25–43.

11 J. B. Rotter, "Generalized Expectancies for Internal vs. External Control of Reinforcement," *Psychological Monographs*, 1966, Vol. 80, pp. 1–28. See also Simon S. K. Lam and John Schaubroeck, "The Role of Locus of Control in Reactions to Being Promoted and to Being Passed Over: A Quasi Experiment," *Academy of Management Journal*, 2000, Vol. 43, No. 1, pp. 66–78.

12 Marilyn E. Gist and Terence R. Mitchell, "Self-Efficacy: A Theoretical Analysis of Its Determinants and Malleability," *Academy of Management Review*, April 1992, Vol. 17, No. 2, pp. 183–211.

13 T. W. Adorno, E. Frenkel-Brunswick, D. J. Levinson, and R. N. Sanford, *The Authoritarian Personality* (New York: Harper & Row, 1950).

14 Susan Berfield, "Dov Charney's Sleazy Struggle for Control of American Apparel," *Bloomberg Businessweek*, July 10, 2014, www.bloomberg.com on April 15, 2020.

15 Jon L. Pierce, Donald G. Gardner, and Larry L. Cummings, "Organization-Based Self-Esteem: Construct Definition, Measurement, and Validation," *Academy of Management Journal*, 1989, Vol. 32, pp. 622–648.

16 Michael Harris Bond and Peter B. Smith, "Cross-Cultural Social and Organizational Psychology," *Annual Review of Psychology*, 1996, Vol. 47, pp. 205–235.

17 See Daniel Goleman, *Emotional Intelligence: Why It Can Matter More Than IQ* (New York: Bantam, 1995).

18 Daniel Goleman, "Leadership That Gets Results," *Harvard Business Review*, March–April 2000, pp. 78–90. See also Kenneth Law, Chi-Sum Wong, and Lynda Song, "The Construct and Criterion Validity of Emotional Intelligence and Its Potential Utility for Management Studies," *Journal of Applied Psychology*, 2004, Vol. 87, No. 3, pp. 483–496; Joseph C. Rode, Christine H. Mooney, Marne L. Arthaud-Day, Janet P. Near, Timothy T. Baldwin, Robert S. Rubin, and William H. Bommer, "Emotional Intelligence and Individual Performance: Evidence of Direct and Indirect Effects," *Journal of Organizational Behavior*, 2007, Vol. 28, pp. 399–421; and John D. Mayer, Richard D. Roberts, and Sigal G. Barsade, "Human Abilities: Emotional Intelligence," *Annual Review of Psychology*, 2008, Vol. 59, pp. 507–536.

19 For a recent review, see Gerd Bohner and Nina Dickel, "Attitudes and Attitude Change," *Annual Review of Psychology*, 2011, Vol. 62, pp. 391–418.

20 Leon Festinger, *A Theory of Cognitive Dissonance* (Palo Alto, CA: Stanford University Press, 1957).

21 See Peter Cappelli and John J. Clancy, "Is Loyalty Really Dead?" *Across the Board*, June 1999, Vol. 36, pp. 14–19.

22 Patricia C. Smith, L. M. Kendall, and Charles Hulin, *The Measurement of Satisfaction in Work and Behavior* (Chicago: Rand-McNally, 1969). See also Steven Currall, Annette Towler, Tomothy Judge, and Laura Kohn, "Pay Satisfaction and Organizational Outcomes," *Personnel Psychology*, 2005, Vol. 58, pp. 613–640.

23 Sue Shellenbarger, "Companies Are Finding Real Payoffs in Aiding Employee Satisfaction," *Wall Street Journal*, October 11, 2000, www.wsj.com on April 15, 2020.

24 Richard M. Steers, "Antecedents and Outcomes of Organizational Commitment," *Administrative Science Quarterly*, 1977, Vol. 22, pp. 46–56.

25 See Timothy R. Clark, "Engaging the Disengaged," www.shrm.com on April 15, 2020.

26 Omar N. Solinger, Woody van Olffen, and Robert A. Roe, "Beyond the Three-Component Model of Organizational Commitment," *Journal of Applied Psychology*, 2008, Vol. 93, No. 1, pp. 70–83; see also Steven M. Elias, "Employee Commitment in Times of Change: Assessing the Importance of Attitudes Toward Organizational Change," *Journal of Management*, 2009, Vol. 35, No. 1, pp. 37–55.

27 For research work in this area, see Jennifer M. George and Gareth R. Jones, "The Experience of Mood and Turnover Intentions: Interactive Effects of Value Attainment, Job Satisfaction, and Positive Mood," *Journal of Applied Psychology*, 1996, Vol. 81, No. 3, pp. 318–325; Larry J. Williams, Mark B. Gavin, and Margaret Williams, "Measurement and Nonmeasurement Processes with Negative Affectivity and Employee Attitudes," *Journal of Applied Psychology*, 1996, Vol. 81, No. 1, pp. 88–101.

28 See Robert A. Baron, "The Role of Affect in the Entrepreneurial Process," *Academy of Management Review*, 2008, Vol. 33, No. 2, pp. 328–340.

29 Kathleen Sutcliffe, "What Executives Notice: Accurate Perceptions in Top Management Teams," *Academy of Management Journal*, 1994, Vol. 37, No. 5, pp. 1360–1378.

30 Richard A. Posthuma and Michael A. Campion, "Age Stereotypes in the Workplace: Common Stereotypes, Moderators, and Future Research Directions," *Journal of Management*, 2009, Vol. 35, No. 1, pp. 148–188.

31 For a classic treatment of attribution, see H. H. Kelley, *Attribution in Social Interaction* (Morristown, NJ: General Learning Press, 1971). For a recent application, see Edward C. Tomlinson and Roger C. Mayer, "The Role of Causal Attribution Dimensions in Trust Repair," *Academy of Management Review*, Vol. 34, No. 1, January 2009, pp. 85–104.

32 For an overview of the stress literature, see Frank Landy, James Campbell Quick, and Stanislav Kasl, "Work, Stress, and Well-Being," *International Journal of Stress Management*, 1994, Vol. 1, No. 1, pp. 33–73; see also Mark A. Griffin and Sharon Clarke, "Stress and Well-Being at Work," *Handbook of Industrial and Organizational Psychology, Vol. 3*, pp. 359–397.

33 Hans Selye, *The Stress of Life* (New York: McGraw-Hill, 1976).

34 M. Friedman and R. H. Rosenman, *Type A Behavior and Your Heart* (New York: Knopf, 1974).

35 "Work & Family," *Bloomberg Businessweek*, www.bloomberg.com on April 15, 2020.

36 Richard S. DeFrank, Robert Konopaske, and John M. Ivancevich, "Executive Travel Stress: Perils of the Road Warrior," *Academy of Management Executive*, 2000, Vol. 14, No. 2, pp. 58–67.

37 Steven Rogelberg, Desmond Leach, Peter Warr, and Jennifer Burnfield, "'Not Another Meeting!': Are Meeting Time Demands Related to Employee Well Being?" *Journal of Applied Psychology*, 2006, Vol. 91, No. 1, pp. 86–96.

38 "Those Doing Layoffs Can Feel the Pain," *USA Today*, www.usatoday.com on April 15, 2020.

39 Remus Ilies, Michael Johnson, Timothy Judge, and Jessica Keeney, "A Within-Individual Study of Interpersonal Conflict as a Work Stressor: Dispositional and Situational Moderators," *Journal of Organizational Behavior*, January 2011, Vol. 32, No. 1, pp. 44–64.

40 Michael R. Frone, "Are Work Stressors Related to Employee Substance Abuse?: The Importance of Temporal Context in Assessments of Alcohol and Illicit Drug Use," *Journal of Applied Psychology*, 2008, Vol. 93, No. 1, pp. 199–296.

41 "Breaking Point," *Newsweek*, www.newsweek.com on April 15, 2020. See also "Rising Job Stress Could Affect Bottom Line," *USA Today*, www.usatoday.com on April 15, 2020.

42 See Christopher M. Barnes and John R. Hollenbeck, "Sleep Deprivation and Decision-Making Teams: Burning the Midnight Oil or Playing with Fire?" *Academy of Management Review*, January 2009, Vol. 34, No. 1, pp. 56–66.

43 John M. Kelly, "Get a Grip on Stress," www.shrm.com on April 15, 2020; see also Marilyn Macik-Frey, James Campbell Quick, and Debra Nelson, "Advances in Occupational Health: From a Stressful Beginning to a Positive Future," *Journal of Management*, 2007, Vol. 33, No. 6, pp. 809–840.

44 Charlotte Fritz, Sabine Sonnentag, Paul Spector, and Jennifer McInroe, "The Weekend Matters: Relationships Between Stress Recovery and Affective Experiences," *Journal of Organizational Behavior*, November 2010, Vol. 31, No. 8, pp. 1137–1162.

45 "Nice Work if You Can Get It," *Bloomberg Businessweek*, www.bloomberg.com on April 15, 2020; see also "Wellness," *Time*, www.time.com on April 15, 2020.

46 See Richard W. Woodman, John E. Sawyer, and Ricky W. Griffin, "Toward a Theory of Organizational Creativity," *Academy of Management Review*, April 1993, pp. 293–321. See also Beth A. Hennessey and Teresa M. Amabile, "Creativity," *Annual Review of Psychology*, 2010, Vol. 61, pp. 569–598; and Jing Zhou and Christina E. Shalley, "Deepening Our Understanding of Creativity in the Workplace: A Review of Different Approaches to Creativity Research," in *Handbook of Industrial and Organizational Psychology, Vol. 1: Building and Developing the Organization*, ed. Sheldon Zedeck (Washington, DC: American Psychological Association, 2010), pp. 275–302.

47 Robert A. Guth, "In Secret Hideaway, Bill Gates Pondered Microsoft's Future," *Wall Street Journal*, March 28, 2005, www.wsj.com on April 15, 2020.

48 Christina E. Shalley, Lucy L. Gilson, and Terry C. Blum, "Matching Creativity Requirements and the Work Environment: Effects on Satisfaction and Intentions to Leave," *Academy of Management Journal*, 2000, Vol. 43, No. 2, pp. 214–223. See also Filiz Tabak, "Employee Creative Performance: What Makes It Happen?" *Academy of Management Executive*, 1997, Vol. 11, No. 1, pp. 119–122; and Giles Hirst, Daan van Knippenberg, and Jing Zhou, "A Cross-Level Perspective on Employee Creativity: Goal Orientation, Team Learning Behavior, and Individual Creativity," *Academy of Management Journal*, Vol. 52, No. 2, 2009, pp. 280–293.

49 "Real Life Imitates *Real World*," *Bloomberg Businessweek*, www.bloomberg.com on April 15, 2020.

50 "Apple's Startup Culture," *Bloomberg Businessweek*, www.bloomberg.com on April 15, 2020.

51 See Ryan D. Zimmerman, "Understanding the Impact of Personality Traits on Individuals' Turnover Decisions: A Meta-Analytic Path Model," *Personnel Psychology*, 2008, Vol. 61, pp. 309–348.

52 For recent findings regarding this behavior, see Philip M. Podsakoff, Scott B. MacKenzie, Julie Beth Paine, and Daniel G. G. Bacharah, "Organizational Citizenship Behaviors: A Critical Review of the Theoretical and Empirical Literature and Suggestions for Future Research," *Journal of Management*, 2000, Vol. 26, No. 3, pp. 513–563; see also Dennis W. Organ, Philip M. Podsakoff, and Nathan P. Podsakoff, "Expanding the Criterion Domain to Include Organizational Citizenship Behavior: Implications for Employee Selection," in *Handbook of Industrial and Organizational Psychology, Vol. 2*, pp. 281–323.

53 Dennis W. Organ, "Personality and Organizational Citizenship Behavior," *Journal of Management*, 1994, Vol. 20, No. 2, pp. 465–478; Mary Konovsky and S. Douglas Pugh, "Citizenship Behavior and Social Exchange," *Academy of Management Journal*, 1994, Vol. 37, No. 3, pp. 656–669; and Jacqueline A.-M. Coyle-Shapiro, "A Psychological Contract Perspective on Organizational Citizenship," *Journal of Organizational Behavior*, 2002, Vol. 23, pp. 927–946.

54 Ricky Griffin and Yvette Lopez, "'Bad Behavior' in Organizations: A Review and Typology for Future Research," *Journal of Management*, 2005, Vol. 31, No. 6, pp. 988–1005.

55 For an illustration, see Sandy Lim, Lilia M. Cortina, and Vicki J. Magley, "Personal and Workgroup Incivility: Impact on Work and Health Outcomes," *Journal of Applied Psychology*, 2008, Vol. 93, No. 1, pp. 95–107.

56 See Anne O'Leary-Kelly, Ricky W. Griffin, and David J. Glew, "Organization-Motivated Aggression: A Research Framework," *Academy of Management Review*, January 1996, Vol. 21, No. 1, pp. 225–253. See also Scott C. Douglas, Christian Kiewitz, Mark J. Martinko, Paul Harvey, Younhee Kim, and Jae Uk Chun, "Cognitions, Emotions, and Evaluations: An Elaboration Likelihood Model for Workplace Aggression," *Academy of Management Review*, 2008, Vol. 33, No. 2, pp. 425–451; and Laurie J. Barclay and Karl Aquino, "Workplace Aggression and Violence," in *Handbook of Industrial and Organizational Psychology, Vol. 3*, pp. 614–640.

57 Kelli B. Grant, "Americans Don't Like Their Jobs, Even with Perks," *USA Today*, www.usatoday.com on April 25, 2020; The Conference Board, "U.S. Workers Job Satisfaction Survey," www.conference-board.org on April 25, 2020; Christina Merhar, "Employee Retention—The Real Cost of Losing an Employee," Zane Benefits, www.zanebenefits.com on April 25, 2020; "New Job Satisfaction Report from The Conference Board," www.conference-board.org on April 25, 2020; scenario adapted from Danielle Lee Novack and Karen L. Housell, "Fall 2013 Job Satisfaction Case Study," *Confluence*, November 10, 2013, https://wikispaces.psu.edu on April 25, 2020.

Chapter 10

1 Leigh Buchanan, "How SAS Continues to Grow," *Inc.*, September 2011, https://www.inc.com on May 10, 2020; Mark C. Crowley, "How SAS Became The World's Best Place To Work," *Fast Company*, January 22, 2013, https://www.fastcompany.com on May 10, 2020; "SAS Again Ranks as One of *Fortune*'s Best Places to Work for Millennials," June 2018, https://www.sas.com on May 10, 2020; "About SAS," https://www.sas.com on May 10, 2020; "Our Culture," https://www.sas.com on May 10, 2020.

2 Richard M. Steers, Gregory A. Bigley, and Lyman W. Porter, *Motivation and Leadership at Work*, 6th ed. (New York: McGraw-Hill, 1996). See also Maureen L. Ambrose and Carol T. Kulik, "Old Friends, New Faces: Motivation Research in the 1990s," *Journal of Management*, 1999, Vol. 25, No. 3, pp. 231–292; and Edwin Locke and Gary Lartham, "What Should We Do about Motivation Theory?: Six Recommendations for the Twenty-First Century," *Academy of Management Review*, 2004, Vol. 29, No. 3, pp. 388–403.

3 See Nigel Nicholson, "How to Motivate Your Problem People," *Harvard Business Review*, January 2003, pp. 57–67. See also Hugo Kehr, "Integrating Implicit Motives, Explicit Motives, and Perceived Abilities: The Compensatory Model of Work Motivation and Volition," *Academy of Management Review*, 2004, Vol. 29, No. 3, pp. 479–499; and James M. Diefendorff and Megan M. Chandler, "Motivating Employees," in *Handbook of Industrial and Organizational Psychology, Vol. 3: Maintaining, Expanding, and Contracting the Organization*, ed. Sheldon Zedeck (Washington, DC: American Psychological Association, 2010), pp. 65–135.

4 See Jeffrey Pfeffer, *The Human Equation* (Cambridge, MA: Harvard Business School Press, 1998); see also Nitin Nohria, Boris Groysberg, and Linda-Eling Lee, "Employee Motivation—A Powerful New Model," *Harvard Business Review*, July–August 2008, pp. 78–89.

5 See Craig Pinder, *Work Motivation in Organizational Behavior* (Upper Saddle River, NJ: Prentice-Hall, 1998).

6 Frederick W. Taylor, *Principles of Scientific Management* (New York: Harper & Brothers, 1911).

7 Elton Mayo, *The Social Problems of an Industrial Civilization* (Cambridge, MA: Harvard University Press, 1945); Fritz J. Rothlisberger and W. J. Dickson, *Management and the Worker* (Cambridge, MA: Harvard University Press, 1939).

8 Eryn Brown, "So Rich So Young—But Are They Really Happy?" *Fortune*, September 18, 2000, www.fortune.com on May 8, 2020.

9 Arthur C. Brooks, "A Formula for Happiness," *New York Times*, December 15, 2013, http://www.nytimes.com on May 8, 2020.

10 Abraham H. Maslow, "A Theory of Human Motivation," *Psychological Review*, 1943, Vol. 50, pp. 370–396; Abraham H. Maslow, *Motivation and Personality* (New York: Harper & Row, 1954). Maslow's most recent work is Abraham H. Maslow and Richard Lowry, *Toward a Psychology of Being* (New York: Wiley, 1999).

11 "More Than a Paycheck," www.usatoday.com on May 8, 2020.

12 For a review, see Pinder, *Work Motivation in Organizational Behavior*.

13 Clayton P. Alderfer, *Existence, Relatedness, and Growth* (New York: Free Press, 1972).

14 Frederick Herzberg, Bernard Mausner, and Barbara Snyderman, *The Motivation to Work* (New York: Wiley, 1959); Frederick Herzberg, "One More Time: How Do You Motivate Employees?" *Harvard Business Review*, January–February 1987, pp. 109–120 (reprinted in *Harvard Business Review*, January 2003, pp. 87–98).

15 Robert J. House and Lawrence A. Wigdor, "Herzberg's Dual-Factor Theory of Job Satisfaction and Motivation: A Review of the Evidence and a Criticism," *Personnel Psychology*, Winter 1967, pp. 369–389; Victor H. Vroom, *Work and Motivation* (New York: Wiley, 1964). See also Pinder, *Work Motivation in Organizational Behavior*.

16 David C. McClelland, *The Achieving Society* (Princeton, NJ: Van Nostrand, 1961); David C. McClelland, *Power: The Inner Experience* (New York: Irvington, 1975).

17 "Best Friends Good for Business," *USA Today*, www.usatoday.com on May 8, 2020.

18 David McClelland and David H. Burnham, "Power Is the Great Motivator," *Harvard Business Review*, March–April 1976, pp. 100–110 (reprinted in *Harvard Business Review*, January 2003, pp. 117–127).

19 Connie Guglielmo, Ian King, and Aaron Ricadela, "HP Chief Executive Hurd Resigns after Sexual Harassment Probe," *Bloomberg Businessweek*, August 7, 2010, https://www.bloomberg.com on May 29, 2020.

20 Victor H. Vroom, *Work and Motivation* (New York: Wiley, 1964).

21 "An Interview with J. Richard Hackman," *Harvard Business Review*, May 2009, p. 101.

22 Jenna Goudreau, "Starbucks' Secret Weapon," *Fortune*, November 2, 2011, www.fortune.com on May 8, 2020.

23 Lyman W. Porter and Edward E. Lawler III, *Managerial Attitudes and Performance* (Homewood, IL: Dorsey, 1968).

24 J. Stacy Adams, "Towards an Understanding of Inequity," *Journal of Abnormal and Social Psychology*, November 1963, Vol. 67, pp. 422–436.

25 Erin White, "The Best vs. the Rest," *Wall Street Journal*, January 30, 2006, www.wsj.com on May 8, 2020.

26 Mark C. Bolino and William H. Turnley, "Old Faces, New Places: Equity Theory in Cross-Cultural Contexts," *Journal of Organizational Behavior*, 2008, Vol. 29, pp. 29–50.

27 "Raising the Bar," *BusinessWeek*, June 8, 2009, p. 48.

28 See Edwin A. Locke, "Toward a Theory of Task Performance and Incentives," *Organizational Behavior and Human Performance*, 1968, Vol. 3, pp. 157–189.

29 Gary P. Latham and J. J. Baldes, "The Practical Significance of Locke's Theory of Goal Setting," *Journal of Applied Psychology*, 1975, Vol. 60, pp. 187–191.

30 Monica Mehta, "Why Our Brains Like Short-Term Goals," *Entrepreneur*, January 3, 2013, http://www.entrepreneur.com on May 8, 2020.

31 See Yitzhak Fried and Linda Haynes Slowik, "Enriching Goal-Setting Theory with Time: An Integrated Approach," *Academy of Management Review*, 2004, Vol. 29, No. 3, pp. 404–422.

32 B. F. Skinner, *Beyond Freedom and Dignity* (New York: Knopf, 1971). See also Raymond A. Noe, Michael J. Tews, and Alison McConnell Dachner, "Learner Engagement: A New Perspective for Enhancing Our Understanding of Learner Motivation and Workplace Learning," in *Academy of Management Annals 2010*, eds. James P. Walsh and Arthur P. Brief (Philadelphia: Taylor & Francis, 2010), pp. 279–315.

33 Fred Luthans and Robert Kreitner, *Organizational Behavior Modification and Beyond: An Operant and Social Learning Approach* (Glenview, IL: Scott, Foresman, 1985).

34 Ibid.; W. Clay Hamner and Ellen P. Hamner, "Behavior Modification on the Bottom Line," *Organizational Dynamics*, Spring 1976, Vol. 4, pp. 3–21.

35 "At Emery Air Freight: Positive Reinforcement Boosts Performance," *Organizational Dynamics*, Winter 1973, Vol. 1, pp. 41–50; for an update, see Alexander D. Stajkovic and Fred Luthans, "A Meta-Analysis of the Effects of Organizational Behavior Modification on Task Performance, 1975–95," *Academy of Management Journal*, 1997, Vol. 40, No. 5, pp. 1122–1149.

36 David J. Glew, Anne M. O'Leary-Kelly, Ricky W. Griffin, and David D. Van Fleet, "Participation in Organizations: A Preview of the Issues and Proposed Framework for Future Analysis," *Journal of Management*, 1995, Vol. 21, No. 3, pp. 395–421.

37 Robert E. Quinn and Gretchen M. Spreitzer, "The Road to Empowerment: Seven Questions Every Leader Should Consider," *Organizational Dynamics*, Autumn 1997, Vol. 26, pp. 37–47.

38 Timothy Aeppel, "On Factory Floors, Top Workers Hide Know-How from Managers," *Wall Street Journal*, July 1, 2002, www.wsj.com on May 8, 2020.

39 Russ Forrester, "Empowerment: Rejuvenating a Potent Idea," *Academy of Management Executive*, 2000, Vol. 14, No. 3, pp. 67–77.

40 Baxter W. Graham, "The Business Argument for Flexibility," *HR Magazine*, www.hrmagazine.com on May 8, 2020.

41 "Motivating Across the Board," http://www.entrepreneur.com/article/232702 on May 8, 2020.

42 A. R. Cohen and H. Gadon, *Alternative Work Schedules: Integrating Individual and Organizational Needs* (Reading, MA: Addison Wesley, 1978). See also Ellen Ernst Kossek and Jesse S. Michel, "Flexible Work Schedules," in *Handbook of Industrial and Organizational Psychology, Vol. 1: Building and Developing the Organization*, ed. Sheldon Zedeck (Washington, DC: American Psychological Association, 2010), pp. 535–572.

43 Kate Lister, "Latest Work-at-Home/Telecommuting/Mobile Work/Remote Work Statistics," March 13, 2020, http://www.globalworkplaceanalytics.com on May 8, 2020.

44 Daniel Walsh, "How Telecommuting Lets Workers Mobilize for Sustainability," GreenBiz, February 17, 2011, www.GreenBiz.com on May 8, 2020.

45 John Brandon, "This is Huge: Twitter CEO Says Employees Can Work From Home 'Forever,'" *Forbes*, May 12, 2020, https://www.forbes.com on May 20, 2020.

46 Barry Gerhart, Sara L. Rynes, and Ingrid Smithey Fulmer, "Pay and Performance: Individuals, Groups, and Executives," in *Academy of Management Annals 2009*, eds. James P. Walsh and Arthur P. Brief (Philadelphia: Taylor & Francis, 2009), pp. 251–315. See also Joseph J. Martocchio, "Strategic Reward and Compensation Plans," in *Handbook of Industrial and Organizational Psychology, Vol. 1: Building and Developing the Organization*, ed. Sheldon Zedeck (Washington, DC: American Psychological Association, 2010), pp. 343–372.

47 Daniel Wren, *The Evolution of Management Theory*, 6th ed. (New York: Wiley, 2014).

48 C. Wiley, "Incentive Plan Pushes Production," *Personnel Journal*, August 1993, p. 91.

49 Eric Krell, "All for Incentives, Incentives for All," *HR Magazine*, www.hrmagazine.com on May 8, 2020.

50 "When Money Isn't Enough," *Forbes*, www.forbes.com on May 8, 2020.

51 Jacquelyn DeMatteo, Lillian Eby, and Eric Sundstrom, "Team-Based Rewards: Current Empirical Evidence and Directions for Future Research," in *Research in Organizational Behavior*, Vol. 20, eds. L. L. Cummings and Barry Staw (Greenwich, CT: JAI, 1998), pp. 141–183.

52 Theresa M. Welbourne and Luis R. Gomez-Mejia, "Gainsharing: A Critical Review and a Future Research Agenda," *Journal of Management*, 1995, Vol. 21, No. 3, pp. 559–609.

53 National Center for Employee Ownership, "A Statistical Profile of Employee Ownership," March 2010.

54 "GM CEO Marry Barra's Pay Dipped to $21.6 Million in 2019," Autoblog, April 27, 2019, https://www.autoblog.com on May 12, 2020.

55 Ibid.

56 Ibid.

57 Ibid.

58 Harry Barkema and Luis Gomez-Mejia, "Managerial Compensation and Firm Performance: A General Research Framework," *Academy of Management Journal*, 1998, Vol. 41, No. 2, pp. 135–145.

59 Rajiv D. Banker, Seok-Young Lee, Gordon Potter, and Dhinu Srinivasan, "Contextual Analysis of Performance Impacts of Outcome-Based Incentive Compensation," *Academy of Management Journal*, 1996, Vol. 39, No. 4, pp. 920–948.

60 Rob Varnon, "GE Defends CEO's Pay Package," *The Ledger*, April 11, 2011.

61 Steve Kerr, "The Best-Laid Incentive Plans," *Harvard Business Review*, January 2003, pp. 27–40.

62 "Now It's Getting Personal," *Bloomberg Businessweek*, www.bloomberg.com on May 8, 2020.

63 Julie Ray and Stephanie Kafka, "Life in College Matters for Life after College," Gallup, May 6, 2014, www.gallup.com on May 5, 2020; Allie Grasgreen, "College Grads Less Engaged in Work than Those with Less Education, Survey Finds," *Inside Higher Ed*, July 18, 2013, www.insidehighered.com on May 5, 2020: Ry Rivard, "Gallup Surveys Graduates to Gauge Whether and Why College Is Good for Well-Being," *Inside Higher Ed*, May 6, 2014, www.insidehighered.com on May 5, 2020; Scott Carlson, "A Caring Professor May Be Key in How a Graduate Thrives," *Chronicle of Higher Education*, May 6, 2014, http://chronicle.com on May 5, 2020; "How to Motivate Employees in the Workplace," www.fortunegroup.com on May 5, 2020.

Chapter 11

1 "Steve Jobs," *Wikipedia*, https://en.wikipedia.org on May 13, 2020; "Steve Wozniak," *Wikipedia*, https://en.wikipedia.org on May 13, 2020; "7 Inspirational Quotes by Steve Jobs on Leadership," Goodnet, August 26, 2014, https://www.goodnet.org on May 13, 2020; "How Does Tim Cook's Management Style Differ from Steve Jobs?" Investopedia, June 25, 2019, https://www.investopedia.com on May 16, 2020.

2 See Ronald A. Heifetz and Donald L. Laurie, "The Work of Leadership," *Harvard Business Review*, January–February 1997, pp. 124–134. See also Arthur G. Jago, "Leadership: Perspectives in Theory and Research," *Management Science*, March 1982, Vol. 28, No. 3, pp. 315–336; and "The New Leadership," *Bloomberg Businessweek*, www.bloomberg.com on May 15, 2020.

3 Gary A. Yukl, *Leadership in Organizations*, 9th ed. (Upper Saddle River, NJ: Pearson, 2018), p. 5. See also Bruce J. Avolio, Fred O. Walumbwa, and Todd J. Weber, "Leadership: Current Theories, Research, and Future Decisions," in *Annual Review of Psychology 2019*, eds. Susan T. Fiske, Daniel L. Schacter, and Robert J. Sternberg (Palo Alto, CA: Annual Reviews, 2099), pp. 421–450; and Julian Barling, Amy Christie, and Colette Hoption, "Leadership," in *Handbook of Industrial and Organizational Psychology, Vol. 1: Building and Developing the Organization*, ed. Sheldon Zedeck (Washington, DC: American Psychological Association, 2010), pp. 183–240.

4 John P. Kotter, "What Leaders Really Do," *Harvard Business Review*, May–June 1990, pp. 103–111 (reprinted in *Harvard Business Review*, December 2001, pp. 85–93). See also Daniel Goleman, "Leadership That Gets Results," *Harvard Business Review*, March–April 2000, pp. 78–88; and Keith Grints, *The Arts of Leadership* (Oxford, UK: Oxford University Press, 2000).

5 John R. P. French and Bertram Raven, "The Bases of Social Power," in *Studies in Social Power*, ed. Dorwin Cartwright (Ann Arbor: University of Michigan Press, 1959), pp. 150–167.

6 Marja Novack, "Slovenian Cyclists Stage Anti-Government Coronavirus Protest," Reuters, May 8, 2020, https://www.reuters.com on May 15, 2020.

7 Hugh D. Menzies, "The Ten Toughest Bosses," *Fortune*, April 21, 1980, www.fortune.com on May 15, 2020.

8 "Management Secrets From the Meanest Company in America," *Bloomberg Businessweek*, January 7, 2013, www.bloomberg.com on May 15, 2020.

9 Bennett J. Tepper, "Consequences of Abusive Supervision," *Academy of Management Journal*, 2000, Vol. 43, No. 2, pp. 168–190; see also Bennett J. Tepper, "Abusive Supervision in Work Organizations: Review, Synthesis, and Research Agenda," *Journal of Management*, 2007, Vol. 33, No. 3, pp. 261–289.

10 "Management Secrets From the Meanest Company in America."

11 For more information on the bases and uses of power, see Philip M. Podsakoff and Chester A. Schriesheim, "Field Studies of French and Raven's Bases of Power: Critique, Reanalysis, and Suggestions for Future Research," *Psychological Bulletin*, 1985, Vol. 97, pp. 387–411; Robert C. Benfari, Harry E. Wilkinson, and Charles D. Orth, "The Effective Use of Power," *Business Horizons*, May–June 1986, pp. 12–16; and Yukl, *Leadership in Organizations*.

12 Bernard M. Bass, *Bass & Stogdill's Handbook of Leadership*, 3rd ed. (Riverside, NJ: Free Press, 1990).

13 Shelley A. Kirkpatrick and Edwin A. Locke, "Leadership: Do Traits Matter?" *Academy of Management Executive*, May 1991, pp. 48–60. See also Robert J. Sternberg, "Managerial Intelligence: Why IQ Isn't Enough," *Journal of Management*, 1997, Vol. 23, No. 3, pp. 475–493.

14 Timothy Judge, Amy Colbert, and Remus Ilies, "Intelligence and Leadership: A Quantitative Review and Test of Theoretical Propositions," *Journal of Applied Psychology*, 2004, Vol. 89, No. 3, pp. 542–552.

15 Rensis Likert, *New Patterns of Management* (New York: McGraw-Hill, 1961); Rensis Likert, *The Human Organization* (New York: McGraw-Hill, 1967).

16 The Ohio State studies stimulated many articles, monographs, and books. A good overall reference is Ralph M. Stogdill and A. E. Coons, eds., *Leader Behavior: Its Description and Measurement* (Columbus: Bureau of Business Research, Ohio State University, 1957).

17 Edwin A. Fleishman, E. F. Harris, and H. E. Burt, *Leadership and Supervision in Industry* (Columbus: Bureau of Business Research, Ohio State University, 1955).

18 See Timothy Judge, Ronald Piccolo, and Remus Ilies, "The Forgotten One?: The Validity of Consideration and Initiating Structure in Leadership Research," *Journal of Applied Psychology*, 2004, Vol. 89, No. 1, pp. 36–51.

19 Robert R. Blake and Jane S. Mouton, *The Managerial Grid* (Houston, TX: Gulf Publishing, 1964); Robert R. Blake and Jane S. Mouton, *The Versatile Manager: A Grid Profile* (Homewood, IL: Dow Jones-Irwin, 1981).

20 Robert Tannenbaum and Warren H. Schmidt, "How to Choose a Leadership Pattern," *Harvard Business Review*, March–April 1958, pp. 95–101.

21 Fred E. Fiedler, *A Theory of Leadership Effectiveness* (New York: McGraw-Hill, 1967).

22 Chester A. Schriesheim, Bennett J. Tepper, and Linda A. Tetrault, "Least Preferred Co-Worker Score, Situational Control, and Leadership Effectiveness: A Meta-Analysis of Contingency Model Performance Predictions," *Journal of Applied Psychology*, 1994, Vol. 79, No. 4, pp. 561–573.

23 Fiedler, *A Theory of Leadership Effectiveness*; Fred E. Fiedler and M. M. Chemers, *Leadership and Effective Management* (Glenview, IL: Scott, Foresman, 1974).

24 For reviews and updates, see Lawrence H. Peters, Darrell D. Hartke, and John T. Pohlmann, "Fiedler's Contingency Theory of Leadership: An Application of the Meta-Analysis Procedures of Schmidt and Hunter," *Psychological Bulletin*, Vol. 97, pp. 274–285; and Fred E. Fiedler, "When to Lead, When to Stand Back," *Psychology Today*, September 1987, pp. 26–27.

25 Martin G. Evans, "The Effects of Supervisory Behavior on the Path-Goal Relationship," *Organizational Behavior and Human Performance*, May 1970, Vol. 5, pp. 277–298; Robert J. House and Terence R. Mitchell, "Path-Goal Theory of Leadership," *Journal of Contemporary Business*, Autumn 1974, pp. 81–98. See also Yukl, *Leadership in Organizations*.

26 See Victor H. Vroom and Philip H. Yetton, *Leadership and Decision Making* (Pittsburgh, PA: University of Pittsburgh Press, 1973); and Victor H. Vroom and Arthur G. Jago, *The New Leadership* (Englewood Cliffs, NJ: Prentice-Hall, 1988).

27 Victor Vroom, "Leadership and the Decision-Making Process," *Organizational Dynamics*, 2000, Vol. 28, No. 4, pp. 82–94.

28 Vroom and Jago, *The New Leadership*.

29 Ibid.

30 See Madeline E. Heilman, Harvey A. Hornstein, Jack H. Cage, and Judith K. Herschlag, "Reaction to Prescribed Leader Behavior as a Function of Role Perspective: The Case of the Vroom-Yetton Model," *Journal of Applied Psychology*,

February 1984, Vol. 69, pp. 50–60; R. H. George Field, "A Test of the Vroom-Yetton Normative Model of Leadership," *Journal of Applied Psychology*, February 1982, Vol. 67, No. 5, pp. 523–532.

[31] George Graen and J. F. Cashman, "A Role-Making Model of Leadership in Formal Organizations: A Developmental Approach," in *Leadership Frontiers*, eds. J. G. Hunt and L. L. Larson (Kent, OH: Kent State University Press, 1975), pp. 143–165; Fred Dansereau, George Graen, and W. J. Haga, "A Vertical Dyad Linkage Approach to Leadership Within Formal Organizations: A Longitudinal Investigation of the Role-Making Process," *Organizational Behavior and Human Performance*, 1975, *Vol.* 15, pp. 46–78.

[32] See Kathryn Sherony and Stephen Green, "Coworker Exchange: Relationships Between Coworkers, Leader-Member Exchange, and Work Attitudes," *Journal of Applied Psychology*, 2002, Vol. 87, No. 3, pp. 542–548.

[33] See Bruce J. Avolio, Fred O. Walumbwa, and Todd J. Weber, "Leadership: Current Theories, Research, and Future Directions," in *Annual Review of Psychology 2009*, eds. Susan T. Fiske, Daniel L. Schacter, and Robert Sternberg (Palo Alto, CA: Annual Reviews, 2009), pp. 421–450.

[34] Steven Kerr and John M. Jermier, "Substitutes for Leadership: Their Meaning and Measurement," *Organizational Behavior and Human Performance*, December 1978, Vol. 22, pp. 375–403.

[35] See Charles C. Manz and Henry P. Sims, Jr., "Leading Workers to Lead Themselves: The External Leadership of Self-Managing Work Teams," *Administrative Science Quarterly*, March 1987, Vol. 32, No. 1, pp. 106–129. See also "Living Without a Leader," *Fortune*, March 20, 2000, pp. 218–219.

[36] See Robert J. House, "A 1976 Theory of Charismatic Leadership," in *Leadership: The Cutting Edge*, eds. J. G. Hunt and L. L. Larson (Carbondale: Southern Illinois University Press, 1977), pp. 189–207. See also Jay A. Conger and Rabindra N. Kanungo, "Toward a Behavioral Theory of Charismatic Leadership in Organizational Settings," *Academy of Management Review*, October 1987, Vol. 12, No. 4, pp. 637–647.

[37] David A. Nadler and Michael L. Tushman, "Beyond the Charismatic Leader: Leadership and Organizational Change," *California Management Review*, Winter 1990, Vol. 32, pp. 77–97.

[38] Jane Howell and Boas Shamir, "The Role of Followers in the Charismatic Leadership Process: Relationships and Their Consequences," *Academy of Management Review*, 2005, Vol. 30, No. 1, pp. 96–112.

[39] James MacGregor Burns, *Leadership* (New York: Harper & Row, 1978).

See also Rajnandini Pillai, Chester A. Schriesheim, and Eric J. Williams, "Fairness Perceptions and Trust as Mediators for Transformational and Transactional Leadership: A Two-Sample Study," *Journal of Management*, 1999, Vol. 25, No. 6, pp. 897–933.

[40] Robert Rubin, David Munz, and William Bommer, "Leading from Within: The Effects of Emotion Recognition and Personality on Transformational Leadership Behaviors," *Academy of Management Journal*, 2005, Vol. 48, No. 5, pp. 845–858.

[41] Kenneth Labich, "The Seven Keys to Business Leadership," *Fortune*, October 24, 1998, pp. 55–61.

[42] Dusya Vera and Mary Crossan, "Strategic Leadership and Organizational Learning," *Academy of Management Review*, 2004, Vol. 29, No. 2, pp. 222–240; see also Cynthia A. Montgomery, "Putting Leadership Back into Strategy," *Harvard Business Review*, January 2008, pp. 54–63.

[43] "The Best Performing CEOs in the World," *Harvard Business Review*, January–February 2020.

[44] "Which of These 9 Grossly Overpaid CEOs Are Worth It?" Seeking Alpha, April 20, 2011, www.seekingalpha.com on May 10, 2020; "Leadership Secrets of the Great CEOs," *Bloomberg Businessweek*, www.bloomberg.com on May 10, 2020.

[45] "An Interview With Ken Chenault," www.usatoday.com on May 10, 2020.

[46] See Kurt Dirks and Donald Ferrin, "Trust in Leadership," *Journal of Applied Psychology*, 2002, Vol. 87, No. 4, pp. 611–628. See also Russell A. Eisenstat, Michael Beer, Nathanial Foote, Tobias Fredberg, and Flemming Norrgren, "The Uncompromising Leader," *Harvard Business Review*, July–August 2008, pp. 51–59.

[47] Jeffrey Pfeffer, *Power in Organizations* (Marshfield, MA: Pitman, 1981), p. 7.

[48] Gerald R. Ferris and Wayne A. Hochwarter, "Organizational Politics," in *Handbook of Industrial and Organizational Psychology, Vol. 3: Maintaining, Expanding, and Contracting the Organization*, ed. Sheldon Zedeck (Washington, DC: American Psychological Association, 2010), pp. 435–459.

[49] Victor Murray and Jeffrey Gandz, "Games Executives Play: Politics at Work," *Business Horizons*, December 1980, pp. 11–23; Jeffrey Gandz and Victor Murray, "The Experience of Workplace Politics," *Academy of Management Journal*, June 1980, Vol. 23, No. 2, pp. 237–251.

[50] Don R. Beeman and Thomas W. Sharkey, "The Use and Abuse of Corporate Power," *Business Horizons*, March–April 1987, pp. 26–30.

[51] "How Ebbers Kept the Board in His Pocket," *Bloomberg Businessweek*, www.bloomberg.com on May 10, 2020.

[52] See William L. Gardner, "Lessons in Organizational Dramaturgy: The Art of Impression Management," *Organizational Dynamics*, Vol. 21, No. 1, Summer 1992, pp. 51–63; Elizabeth Wolf Morrison and Robert J. Bies, "Impression Management in the Feedback-Seeking Process: A Literature Review and Research Agenda," *Academy of Management Review*, July 1991, Vol. 16, No. 3, pp. 522–541; Mark C. Bolino, K. Michele Kacmar, William H. Turnley, and J. Bruce Gilstrap, "A Multi-Level Review of Impression Management Motives and Behaviors," *Journal of Management*, 2008, Vol. 34, No. 6, pp. 1080–1109.

[53] See Chad Higgins, Timothy Judge, and Gerald Ferris, "Influence Tactics and Work Outcomes: A Meta-Analysis," *Journal of Organizational Behavior*, 2003, Vol. 24, pp. 89–106; and Gerald R. Ferris, Darren C. Treadway, Pamela L. Perrewe, Robyn L. Brour, Ceasar Douglas, and Sean Lux, "Political Skill in Organizations," *Journal of Management*, 2007, Vol. 33, No. 3, pp. 290–320.

[54] Murray and Gandz, "Games Executives Play."

[55] Beeman and Sharkey, "The Use and Abuse of Corporate Power."

[56] Stefanie Ann Lenway and Kathleen Rehbein, "Leaders, Followers, and Free Riders: An Empirical Test of Variation in Corporate Political Involvement," *Academy of Management Journal*, December 1991, Vol. 34, No. 4, p. 89.

[57] "Beware of Politics in Your Start-Up," www.bloomberg.com on May 10, 2020.

[58] "Plan Crash Devastates Marshall University," https://www.history.com on May 28, 2020; "#15 Brad Smith," *Forbes*, https://www.forbes.com on May 28, 2020; Jon Schumacher, "Leadership and Legacy Lessons from Former Intuit CEO Brad Smith," *Entrepreneur*, March 1, 2019, https://www.entrepreneur.com on May 28, 2020.

Chapter 12

[1] Case prepared by Dr. Brad Wesner based on professional consulting engagement.

[2] See John J. Gabarro, "The Development of Working Relationships," in *Handbook of Organizational Behavior*, ed. Jay W. Lorsch (Englewood Cliffs, NJ: Prentice-Hall, 1987), 172–179. See also "Team Efforts, Technology, Add New Reasons to Meet," *USA Today*, www.usatoday.com on May 20, 2020.

[3] Tara C. Reich and M. Sandy Hershcovis, "Interpersonal Relationships at Work," in *Handbook of Industrial and Organizational Psychology, Vol. 3: Maintaining, Expanding, and Contracting the Organization*, ed. Sheldon Zedeck (Washington, DC: American Psychological Association, 2010), 223–248.

4 Martin Kilduff and Daniel J. Brass, "Organizational Social Network Research: Core Ideas and Key Debates," in *The Academy of Management Annals 2010*, eds. James P. Walsh and Arthur P. Brief (Philadelphia: Taylor and Francis, 2010), 317–358.

5 See C. Gopinath and Thomas E. Becker, "Communication, Procedural Justice, and Employee Attitudes: Relationships under Conditions of Divestiture," *Journal of Management*, 2000, Vol. 26, No. 1, pp. 63–83.

6 Marshall Scott Poole, "Communication," in *Handbook of Industrial and Organizational Psychology, Vol. 3: Maintaining, Expanding, and Contracting the Organization*, ed. Sheldon Zedeck (Washington, DC: American Psychological Association, 2010), 249–270.

7 I. Pavlov, "Conditioned Reflexes: An Investigation of the Physiological Activity of the Cerebral Cortex," *Simply Psychology*, 1927, http://psychclassics.yorku.ca/Pavlov/lecture6.htm on May 20, 2020.

8 See Batia M. Wiesenfeld, Sumita Charan, and Raghu Garud, "Communication Patterns as Determinants of Organizational Identification in a Virtual Organization," *Organization Science*, 1999, Vol. 10, No. 6, pp. 777–790.

9 Bruce Barry and Ingrid Fulmer, "The Medium and the Message: The Adaptive Use of Communication Media in Dyadic Influence," *Academy of Management Review*, 2004, Vol. 29, No. 2, pp. 272–292.

10 Reid Buckley, "When You Have to Put It to Them," Across the Board, www.acrosstheboard.com on May 20, 2020.

11 Joanne S. Lublin, "'Did I Just Say That?!' How to Recover from Foot-in-Mouth," *Wall Street Journal*, June 18, 2002, www.wsj.com on May 20, 2020.

12 "Executives Who Dread Public Speaking Learn to Keep Their Cool in the Spotlight," *Wall Street Journal*, May 4, 1990, www.wsj.com on May 20, 2020.

13 Albert Mehrabian, *Non-Verbal Communication* (Chicago: Aldine, 1972).

14 Michael B. McCaskey, "The Hidden Messages Managers Send," *Harvard Business Review*, November 1979, www.hbr.com on May 20, 2020.

15 Suzanne Kapner, "Changing of the Guard at Wal-Mart," *Fortune*, February 18, 2009, www.fortune.com on May 20, 2020.

16 David Givens, "What Body Language Can Tell You That Words Cannot," *U.S. News & World Report*, November 19, 1984, www.usnews.com on May 20, 2020.

17 Edward J. Hall, *The Hidden Dimension* (New York: Doubleday, 1966).

18 "The Unthered Executive," http://images.forbes.com/forbesinsights/StudyPDFs/The_Untethered_Executive.pdf.

19 See "Watch What You Put in That Office Email," *Bloomberg Businessweek*, www.bloomberg.com on May 20, 2020.

20 Nicholas Varchaver, "The Perils of E-mail," *Fortune*, February 17, 2003, www.fortune.com on May 20, 2020; Charles Gasparino, "How a String of E-Mail Came to Haunt CSFB and Star Banker," *Wall Street Journal*, February 28, 2003, www.wsj.com on May 20, 2020; Susanne Craig, "How Morgan Stanley Botched a Big Case by Fumbling Emails," *Wall Street Journal*, May 16, 2005, www.wsj.com on May 20, 2020.

21 A. Vavelas, "Communication Patterns in Task-Oriented Groups," *Journal of the Acoustical Society of America*, 1950, Vol. 22, pp. 725–730; Jerry Wofford, Edwin Gerloff, and Robert Cummins, *Organizational Communication* (New York: McGraw-Hill, 1977).

22 Nelson Phillips and John Brown, "Analyzing Communications in and Around Organizations: A Critical Hermeneutic Approach," *Academy of Management Journal*, 1993, Vol. 36, No. 6, pp. 1547–1576.

23 F.C. Bartlett *Remembering: A Study in Experimental and Social Psychology* (Cambridge, UK: Cambridge University Press, 1932).

24 Mary Young and James Post, "How Leading Companies Communicate with Employees," *Organizational Dynamics*, Summer 1993, Vol. 22, pp. 31–43.

25 Kristin Byron, "Carrying Too Heavy a Load?: The Communication and Miscommunication of Emotion by Email," *Academy of Management Review*, 2008, Vol. 33, No. 2, pp. 309–327.

26 Ann Carrns, "Those Bawdy E-Mails Were Good for a Laugh-Until the Ax Fell," *Wall Street Journal*, February 4, 2000, www.wsj.com on May 20, 2020.

27 Keith Davis, "Management Communication and the Grapevine," *Harvard Business Review*, September–October 1953, pp. 43–49.

28 C. Hymowitz, "Spread the Word: Gossip Is Good," *Wall Street Journal*, October 4, 1988, www.wsj.com on May 20, 2020.

29 See David M. Schweiger and Angelo S. DeNisi, "Communication with Employees Following a Merger: A Longitudinal Field Experiment," *Academy of Management Journal*, March 1991, Vol. 34, No. 1, pp. 110–135.

30 "Job Fears Make Offices All Fears," *Wall Street Journal*, January 20, 2009, www.wsj.com on May 20, 2020.

31 Institute of Leadership and Management, "32% of People Making Inappropriate Use of Work Emails," April 20, 2013.

32 "Your Secrets Aren't Safe at the Office," *USA Today*, www.usatoday.com on May 20, 2020.

33 Nancy B. Kurland and Lisa Hope Pelled, "Passing the Word: Toward a Model of Gossip and Power in the Workplace," *Academy of Management Review*, 2000, Vol. 25, No. 2, pp. 428–438.

34 See Tom Peters and Nancy Austin, *A Passion for Excellence* (New York: Random House, 1985).

35 For a detailed discussion of improving communication effectiveness, see Courtland L. Bovee, John V. Thill, and Barbara E. Schatzman, *Business Communication Today*, 10th ed. (Upper Saddle River, NJ: Prentice Hall, 2019).

36 See Otis W. Baskin and Craig E. Aronoff, *Interpersonal Communication in Organizations* (Glenview, IL: Scott, Foresman, 1980).

37 *BusinessWeek*, December 22, 2008, p. 15.

38 See "You Have (Too Much) E-Mail," *USA Today*, www.usatoday.com on May 20, 2020.

39 Justin Fox, "The Triumph of English," *Fortune*, September 18, 2000, www.usatoday.com on May 20, 2020.

40 Joseph Allen and Bennett P. Lientz, *Effective Business Communication* (Santa Monica, CA: Goodyear, 1979).

41 See "Making Silence Your Ally," *Across the Board*, October 1999, p. 11.

42 Boyd A. Vander Houwen, "Less Talking, More Listening," *HR Magazine*, www.hrmagazine.com on May 20, 2020.

43 C. Landwehr and M. Wood, "Reconciling Credibility and Accountability: How expert Bodies Achieve Credibility Through Accountability Processes," *European Politics and Society*, 2019, Vol. 20, No. 1, pp. 66–82; K. Stapleton and O. Hargie, "Double-Bind Accountability Dilemmas: Impression Management and Accountability Strategies Used by Senior Banking Executives," *Journal of Language and Social Psychology*, 2019, Vol. 30, No. 3, pp. 266–289.

44 For a discussion of these and related issues, see Eric M. Eisenberg and Marsha G. Witten, "Reconsidering Openness in Organizational Communication," *Academy of Management Review*, July 1987, Vol. 12, No. 3, pp. 417–426.

45 For a recent illustration, see Barbara Kellerman, "When Should a Leader Apologize—And When Not?" *Harvard Business Review*, April 2006, www.hbr.com on May 20, 2020.

46 Amy Cuddy, "Your Body Language Shapes Who You Are," TEDGlobal 2012, www.ted.com on May 12, 2020; David Hochman, "Amy Cuddy Takes a Stand," *New York Times*, September 21, 2014, www.nytimes.com on May 12, 2020; Danielle Venton, "Power Postures Can Make You Feel More Powerful," *Wired*, May 15, 2012, www.wired, com on May 12, 2020; Amy Cuddy, Matthew Kohut, and John Neffinger, "Connect, Then Lead," *Harvard Business Review*, July–August 2013, https://hbr.org on May 12, 2020.

Chapter 13

1. Andy Zynga, "The Cognitive Bias Keeping Us from Innovating," *Harvard Business Review*, June 13, 2013, https://hbr.org on May 27, 2020; Andy Zynga, "Top Five Open Innovation Myths Debunked," *Wired*, May 15, 2014, http://insights.wired.com on May 27, 2020; Betsy McKay, "PepsiCo Develops 'Designer Salt' to Chip Away at Sodium Intake," *Wall Street Journal*, March 22, 2010, www.wsj.com on May 27, 2020; David Feitler, "The Case for Team Diversity Gets Even Better," *Harvard Business Review*, March 27, 2014, https://hbr.org on May 27, 2020; Elizabeth Gudrais, "Innovation at the Intersection," *Harvard Magazine*, May–June 2010, http://harvardmagazine.com on May 27, 2020; Lynda Gratton and Tamara J. Erickson, "Eight Ways to Build Collaborative Teams," *Harvard Business Review*, November 2007, https://hbr.org on May 27, 2020.

2. For a review of definitions of groups, see Ricky W. Griffin and Jean Phillips, *Organizational Behavior*, 12th ed. (Cincinnati, OH: Cengage Learning, 2012).

3. Dorwin Cartwright and Alvin Zander, eds., *Group Dynamics: Research and Theory*, 3rd ed. (New York: Harper & Row, 1968).

4. For an interesting extension of these ideas, see Willem Verbeke and Stefan Wuyts, "Moving in Social Circles—Social Circle Membership and Performance Implications," *Journal of Organizational Behavior*, 2007, Vol. 28, pp. 357–379.

5. Rob Cross, Nitin Nohria, and Andrew Parker, "Six Myths about Informal Networks—And How to Overcome Them," *Sloan Management Review*, Spring 2002, pp. 67–77.

6. Robert Schrank, Ten Thousand Working Days (Cambridge, MA: MIT Press, 1978); Bill Watson, "Counter Planning on the Shop Floor," in *Organizational Reality*, 2nd ed., eds. Peter Frost, Vance Mitchell, and Walter Nord (Glenview, IL: Scott, Foresman, 1982), pp. 286–294.

7. "After Layoffs, More Workers Band Together," *Wall Street Journal*, February 26, 2002, p. B1.

8. Bradley L. Kirkman and Benson Rosen, "Powering Up Teams," *Organizational Dynamics*, Winter 2000, pp. 48–58.

9. John Mathieu, M. Travis Maynard, Tammy Rapp, and Lucy Gibson, "Team Effectiveness 1997–2007: A Review of Recent Advancements and a Glimpse into the Future," *Journal of Management*, 2008, Vol. 34, No. 3, pp. 410–476.

10. Arvind Malhotra, Ann Majchrzak, and Benson Rosen, "Leading Virtual Teams," *Academy of Management Perspectives*, 2007, Vol. 21, No. 1, pp. 60–70.

11. "Why Teams Fail," *USA Today*, www.usatoday.com, June 16, 2016, on May 20, 2020.

12. Brian Dumaine, "The Trouble with Teams," *Fortune*, September 5, 1994, www.fortune.com on May 20, 2020. See also Susan G. Cohen and Diane E. Bailey, "What Makes Teams Work: Group Effectiveness Research from the Shop Floor to the Executive Suite," *Journal of Management*, 1997, Vol. 23, No. 3, pp. 239–290; and John Mathieu, Lucy Gilson, and Thomas Ruddy, "Empowerment and Team Effectiveness: An Empirical Test of an Integrated Model," *Journal of Applied Psychology*, 2006, Vol. 91, No. 1, pp. 97–108.

13. Marvin E. *Shaw, Group Dynamics: The Psychology of Small Group Behavior*, 4th ed. (New York: McGraw-Hill, 1985).

14. Carol Hymowitz, "How to Avoid Hiring the Prima Donnas Who Hate Teamwork," *Wall Street Journal*, www.wsj.com on May 20, 2020.

15. See Connie Gersick, "Marking Time: Predictable Transitions in Task Groups," *Academy of Management Journal*, June 1989, pp. 274–309. See also Janis A. Cannon-Bowers and Clint Bowers, "Team Development and Functioning," in *Handbook of Industrial and Organizational Psychology, Vol. 1: Building and Developing the Organization*, ed. Sheldon Zedeck (Washington, DC: American Psychological Association, 2010), pp. 597–650.

16. See Gilad Chen, "Newcomer Adaptation in Teams: Multilevel Antecedents and Outcomes," *Academy of Management Journal*, 2005, Vol. 48, No. 1, pp. 101–116.

17. For a review of other team characteristics, see Michael Campion, Gina Medsker, and A. Catherine Higgs, "Relations Between Work Group Characteristics and Effectiveness: Implications for Designing Effective Work Groups," *Personnel Psychology*, Winter 1993, Vol. 46, No. 4, pp. 823–850.

18. David Katz and Robert L. Kahn, *The Social Psychology of Organizations*, 2nd ed. (New York: Wiley, 1978), pp. 197–221. See also David M. Sluss, Rolf van Dick, and Bryant S. Thompson, "Role Theory in Organizations: A Relational Perspective," in *Handbook of Industrial and Organizational Psychology, Vol. 1: Building and Developing the Organization*, ed. Sheldon Zedeck (Washington, DC: American Psychological Association, 2010), pp. 503–534.

19. See Travis C. Tubre and Judith M. Collins, "Jackson and Schuler (1985) Revisited: A Meta-Analysis of the Relationships Between Role Ambiguity, Role Conflict, and Job Performance," *Journal of Management*, 2000, Vol. 26, No. 1, pp. 155–169.

20. Robert L. Kahn, D. M. Wolfe, R. P. Quinn, J. D. Snoek, and R. A. Rosenthal, *Organizational Stress: Studies in Role Conflict and Role Ambiguity* (New York: Wiley, 1964).

21. Daniel C. Feldman, "The Development and Enforcement of Group Norms," *Academy of Management Review*, January 1984, Vol. 9, No. 1, pp. 47–53.

22. James Wallace Bishop and K. Dow Scott, *"How Commitment Affects Team Performance,"* HR Magazine, February 1997, pp. 107–115.

23. Anne O'Leary-Kelly, Joseph Martocchio, and Dwight Frink, "A Review of the Influence of Group Goals on Group Performance," *Academy of Management Journal*, 1994, Vol. 37, No. 5, pp. 1285–1301.

24. For an interesting application of these ideas, see Anat Drach-Zahavy and Anat Freund, "Team Effectiveness Under Stress: A Structural Contingency Approach," *Journal of Organizational Behavior*, 2007, Vol. 28, pp. 423–450.

25. Philip M. Podsakoff, Michael Ahearne, and Scott B. MacKenzie, "Organizational Citizenship Behavior and the Quantity and Quality of Work Group Performance, *Journal of Applied Psychology*, 1997, Vol. 82, No. 2, pp. 262–270.

26. Suzy Wetlaufer, "Common Sense and Conflict," *Harvard Business Review*, January–February 2000, pp. 115–125.

27. Kathleen M. Eisenhardt, Jean L. Kahwajy, and L. J. Bourgeois III, "How Management Teams Can Have a Good Fight," *Harvard Business Review*, July–August 1997, pp. 77–89.

28. Thomas Bergmann and Roger Volkema, "Issues, Behavioral Responses and Consequences in Interpersonal Conflicts," *Journal of Organizational Behavior*, 1994, Vol. 15, pp. 467–471; see also Carsten K. W. De Dreu, "The Virtue and Vice of Workplace Conflict: Food for (Pessimistic) Thought," *Journal of Organizational Behavior*, 2008, Vol. 29, pp. 5–19.

29. Robin Pinkley and Gregory Northcraft, "Conflict Frames of Reference: Implications for Dispute Processes and Outcomes," *Academy of Management Journal*, 1994, Vol. 37, No. 1, pp. 193–205.

30. Michael W. Miller, "How 2 Computer Nuts Transformed Industry before Messy Breakup," *Wall Street Journal*, August 27, 1986, www.wsj.com on May 20, 2020.

31. Bryan Pietsch, "'Deeply Offensive to the Core': Amazon VP Hits Back at Former Colleague Who Quit in Protest After the Company Fired Workers Who Raised Safety Concerns," *Business Insider*, May 6, 2020, https://www.businessinsider.com on May 28, 2020.

32. Bruce Barry and Greg L. Stewart, "Composition, Process, and Performance in Self-Managed Groups: The Role of Personality," *Journal of Applied Psychology*, 1997, Vol. 82, No. 1, pp. 62–78.

33 See Patrick Nugent, "Managing Conflict: Third-Party Interventions for Managers," *Academy of Management Executive*, 2002, Vol. 16, No. 1, pp. 139–148.

34 Gerardo A. Okhuysen and Beth A. Bechky, "Coordination in Organizations: An Integrative Perspective," in *The Academy of Management Annals* 2009, eds. James P. Walsh and Arthur P. Brief (Philadelphia: Taylor and Francis, 2009), pp. 463–502.

35 See Kristin J. Behfar, Randall S. Peterson, Elizabeth A. Mannix, and William M. K. Trochim, "The Critical Role of Conflict Resolution in Teams: A Close Look at the Links Between Conflict, Conflict Management Strategies, and Team Outcomes," *Journal of Applied Psychology*, 2008, Vol. 93, No. 1, pp. 170–198.

36 "Solving Conflicts in the Workplace Without Making Losers," *Wall Street Journal*, www.wsj.com, September 5, 2019 on May 20, 2020.

37 "Teaching Business How to Cope with Workplace Conflicts," *Bloomberg Businessweek*, www.bloomberg.com, March 22, 2015 on May 20, 2020.

38 See Kimberly Wade-Benzoni, Andrew Hoffman, Leigh Thompson, Don Moore, James Gillespie, and Max Bazerman, "Barriers to Resolution in Ideologically Based Negotiations: The Role of Values and Institutions," *Academy of Management Review*, 2002, Vol. 27, No. 1, pp. 41–57.

39 J. Z. Rubin and B. R. Brown, *The Social Psychology of Bargaining and Negotiation* (New York: Academic Press, 1975).

40 J. Lewicki and J. A. Litterer, *Negotiation* (Homewood, IL: Irwin, 1985).

41 Howard Raiffa, *The Art and Science of Negotiation* (Cambridge, MA: Belknap, 1982).

42 K. H. Bazerman and M. A. Neale, *Negotiating Rationally* (New York: Free Press, 1992).

43 Beryl Nelson, "The Data on Diversity," *Communications of the ACM*, 2014, Vol. 57, No. 11, pp. 86–95, http://cacm.acm.org on May 25, 2020; Katherine W. Phillips, "How Diversity Makes Us Smarter," *Scientific American*, October 1, 2014, www.scientificamerican.com on May 25, 2020; Vivian Hunt, Dennis Layton, and Sara Prince, "Why Diversity Matters" (McKinsey & Co., Insights & Publications, January 2015), www.mckinsey.com on May 20, 2020; Peter Dizikes, "Study: Workplace Diversity Can Help the Bottom Line," *MIT News*, October 7, 2014, http://newsoffice.mit.edu on May 20, 2020; Michael Blanding, "Cultural Disharmony Undermines Workplace Creativity," Harvard Business School Working Knowledge, December 9, 2013, http://hbswk.hbs.edu on May 20, 2020; Roy Y. J. Chua, "The Costs of Ambient Social Disharmony: Indirect Intercultural Conflicts in Social Environment Undermine Creativity," *Academy of Management Journal*, 2013, Vol. 56, No. 6, pp. 1545–1577.

Chapter 14

1 Atul Gawande, "Big Med: Restaurant Chains Have Managed to Combine Quality Control, Cost Control, and Innovation. Can Health Care?" *The New Yorker*, August 13, 2012, http://www.newyorker.com on June 1, 2020; "The Cheesecake Factory," Wikipedia, https://en.wikipedia.org on June 1, 2020.

2 For a complete discussion of how FedEx uses control in its operations, see Geoffrey Colvin, "The FedEx Edge," *Fortune*, April 3, 2006, www.fortune.com on May 25, 2020.

3 Thomas A. Stewart, "Welcome to the Revolution," *Fortune*, December 13, 1993, www.fortune.com on May 25, 2020.

4 William Taylor, "Control in an Age of Chaos," *Harvard Business Review*, November–December 2014, pp. 64–70.

5 J. Lynn Lunsford, "Fastener Woes Delay Flight of First Boeing 787 Jets," *Wall Street Journal*, November 5, 2008, www.wsj.com on May 25, 2020.

6 Janet Adamy, "Starbucks Brews Up New Cost Cuts By Putting Lid on Afternoon Decaf," *Wall Street Journal*, January 28, 2009, www.wsj.com on May 25, 2020.

7 Tamar Wilner, "Cadbury Factory Cuts Energy 60%, Costs 50% with Dehumidifier," Environmental Leader, April 5, 2015, www.environmentalleader.com on July 20, 2020.

8 "An Apple a Day," *Bloomberg*, www.bloomberg.com on May 25, 2020; "More Business People Say: Let's Not Do Lunch," *USA Today*, www.usatoday.com, March 5, 2019, on May 25, 2020; David Stires, "The Breaking Point," *Fortune*, March 3, 2003, www.fortune.com on May 25, 2020.

9 Mark Kroll, Peter Wright, Leslie Toombs, and Hadley Leavell, "Form of Control: A Critical Determinant of Acquisition Performance and CEO Rewards," *Strategic Management Journal*, 2007, Vol. 18, No. 2, pp. 85–96.

10 For an example, see Donald Lange, "A Multidimensional Conceptualization of Organizational Corruption Control," *Academy of Management Review*, 2008, Vol. 33, No. 3, pp. 710–729.

11 See Karynne Turner and Mona Makhija, "The Role of Organizational Controls in Managing Knowledge," *Academy of Management Review*, 2006, Vol. 31, No. 1, pp. 197–217.

12 Sim Sitkin, Kathleen Sutcliffe, and Roger Schroeder, "Distinguishing Control from Learning in Total Quality Management: A Contingency Perspective," *Academy of Management Review*, 2012, Vol. 19, No. 3, pp. 537–564.

13 Robert Lusch and Michael Harvey, "The Case for an Off-Balance-Sheet Controller," *Sloan Management Review*, Winter 2009, pp. 101–110.

14 Edward E. Lawler III and John G. *Rhode, Information and Control in Organizations* (Pacific Palisades, CA: Goodyear, 1976).

15 Charles W. L. Hill, "Establishing a Standard: Competitive Strategy and Technological Standards in Winner-Take-All Industries," *Academy of Management Executive*, 2007, Vol. 11, No. 2, pp. 7–16.

16 "Airbus Clips Superjumbo Production," *Wall Street Journal*, November 20, 2019, www.wsj.com on May 25, 2020.

17 "Shifting Burden Helps Employers Cut Health Costs," *Wall Street Journal*, June 10, 2016, www.wsj.com on May 25, 2020. See also "Employees' Health Costs Are Heading North," *USA Today*, www.usatoday.com, April 19, 2018, on May 25, 2020.

18 Norihiko Shirouzu, "An Efficiency Guru Refits Honda to Fight Automobile Giants," *Wall Street Journal*, September 15, 1999, www.wsj.com on May 25, 2020.

19 David S. Hilzenrath, "Botched Audits: Big Four Accounting Firms Fail Many Inspections," POGO, September 5, 2019, https://www.pogo.org on July 7, 2020.

20 Floyd Norris, "Indian Accounting Firm Is Fined $7.5 Million over Fraud at Satyam," *New York Times*, April 5, 2011, www.nyt.com on May 25, 2020.

21 William G. Ouchi, "The Transmission of Control Through Organizational Hierarchy," *Academy of Management Journal*, June 1978, Vol. 21, No. 2, pp. 173–192; Richard E. Walton, "From Control to Commitment in the Workplace," *Harvard Business Review, March–April* 1985, pp. 76–84.

22 "Best Managed Companies in America," *Forbes*, www.forbes.com on May 25, 2020.

23 See Peter Lorange, Michael F. Scott Morton, and Sumantra Ghoshal, *Strategic Control* (St. Paul, MN: West, 1986). See also Joseph C. Picken and Gregory G. Dess, "Out of (Strategic) Control," *Organizational Dynamics*, Summer 1997, pp. 35–45.

24 "Kohl's Works to Refill Consumers' Bags," *USA Today*, April 8, 2015, pp. B1, B1.

25 See Hans Mjoen and Stephen Tallman, "Control and Performance in International Joint Ventures," *Organization Science*, May–June 1997, Vol. 8, No. 3, pp. 257–265.

26 Diana Robertson and Erin Anderson, "Control System and Task Environment Effects on Ethical Judgment: An Exploratory Study of Industrial Salespeople," *Organization Science*, November 1993, Vol. 4, No. 4, pp. 617–629.

27 "Workers, Surf at Your Own Risk," *Bloomberg BusinessWeek*, www.bloomberg.com on May 25, 2020.

28 "Enterprise Takes Idea of Dressed for Success to a New Extreme," *Wall Street Journal*, August 27, 2016, www.wsj.com on May 25, 2020.

29 "UBS Relaxing Dress Code, Which Set Underwear Standards," *USA Today*, www.usatoday.com, September 5, 2016, on May 25, 2020.

Chapter 15

1 "Walmart, Inc.," www.hoovers.com on June 10, 2020; "British Grocery Chain Hits America with Fresh Ideas," *USA Today*, www.usatoday.com on June 10, 2020; "Tesco: 'Walmart's Worst Nightmare,'" *Bloomberg Businessweek*, www.bloomberg.com on June 10, 2020; "Walmart, Kroger, Safeway Better Watch Out: The British Are Coming!" CNN, www.cnnmoney.com on June 10, 2020; "Fresh & Easy Files for Bankruptcy Protection," *Los Angeles Times*, www.latimes.com on June 10, 2020; "Tesco," Wikipedia, https://en.wikipedia.org/wiki/Tesco on June 10, 2020.

2 Paul M. Swamidass, "Empirical Science: New Frontier in Operations Management Research," *Academy of Management Review*, October 1991, Vol. 16, No. 4, pp. 793–814.

3 See Anil Khurana, "Managing Complex Production Processes," *Sloan Management Review*, Winter 2009, pp. 85–98.

4 "Distribution of the Workforce Across Economic Sectors in the United States from 2009 to 2019," Statista, July 2020, https://www.statista.com on July 20, 2020; "Employment by Major Industry Sector," Bureau of Labor Statistics, September 4, 2019, https://www.bls.gov on May 26, 2020.

5 "For Filling an Ignored Food Gap," Fast Company, no. 193: 128, Business Source Premier, EBSCOhost on June 10, 2020; "Jose Manuel, Founder and CEO of Algramo, Is the Venture Social Entrepreneur Contender from Chile," https://www.theventure.com/global/en/finalists/ on June 10, 2020.

6 For an example, see Robin Cooper and Regine Slagmulder, "Develop Profitable New Products with Target Costing," *Sloan Management Review*, Summer 2009, pp. 23–34.

7 Joan Woodward, *Industrial Organization: Theory and Practice* (London: Oxford University Press, 1965).

8 See "Tight Labor? Tech to the Rescue," *Bloomberg Businessweek*, September 4, 2017, www.bloomberg.com on June 9, 2020.

9 "Ford Focuses on Flexibility," *USA Today*, February 13, 2018, www.usatoday.com on June 9, 2020.

10 James Brian Quinn and Martin Neil Baily, "Information Technology: Increasing Productivity in Services," *Academy of Management Executive*, 1994, Vol. 8, No. 3, pp. 28–37.

11 See Charles J. Corbett, Joseph D. Blackburn, and Luk N. Van Wassenhove, "Partnerships to Improve Supply Chains," *Sloan Management Review*, Summer 1999, pp. 71–82; and Jeffrey K. Liker and Yen-Chun Wu, "Japanese Automakers, U.S. Suppliers, and Supply-Chain Superiority," *Sloan Management Review*, Fall 2000, pp. 81–93. See also Mark Pagell and Zhaohui Wu, "Building a More Complete Theory of Sustainable Supply Chain Management Using Case Studies of 10 Exemplars," *Journal of Supply Chain Management*, 2009, Vol. 45, No. 2, pp. 37–56.

12 J. Lynn Lunsford, "Fastener Woes to Delay Flight of First Boeing 787 Jets," *Wall Street Journal*, November 5, 2010, https://www.wsj.com on July 20, 2020.

13 See "Siemens Climbs Back," *Bloomberg Businessweek*, December 1, 2018, www.bloomberg.com on June 9, 2020.

14 See M. Bensaou, "Portfolios of Buyer-Supplier Relationships," *Sloan Management Review*, Summer 1999, pp. 35–44.

15 Peter Galuszka, "Just-in-Time Manufacturing Is Working Overtime," *BusinessWeek*, November 8, 2007, pp. 36–37.

16 Rhonda Reger, Loren Gustafson, Samuel DeMarie, and John Mullane, "Reframing the Organization: Why Implementing Total Quality Is Easier Said Than Done," *Academy of Management Review*, 1994, Vol. 19, No. 3, pp. 565–584.

17 Ross Johnson and William O. Winchell, *Management and Quality* (Milwaukee, WI: American Society for Quality Control, 1989). See also Carol Reeves and David Bednar, "Defining Quality: Alternatives and Implications," *Academy of Management Review*, 1994, Vol. 19, No. 3, pp. 419–445; and C. K. Prahalad and M. S. Krishnan, "The New Meaning of Quality in the Information Age," *Harvard Business Review*, September–October 1999, pp. 109–120.

18 "Quality Isn't Just for Widgets," *Bloomberg Businessweek*, January 25, 2014, www.bloomberg.com on June 9, 2020.

19 W. Edwards Deming, *Out of the Crisis* (Cambridge, MA: MIT Press, 1986).

20 "When Service Means Survival," *Bloomberg Businessweek*, May 28, 2016, www.bloomberg.com on June 9, 2020.

21 Joel Dreyfuss, "Victories in the Quality Crusade," *Fortune*, October 10, 1988, www.fortune.com on June 9, 2020.

22 Thomas Y. Choi and Orlando C. Behling, "Top Managers and TQM Success: One More Look After All These Years," *Academy of Management Executive*, 1997, Vol. 11, No. 1, pp. 37–48.

23 James Dean and David Bowen, "Management Theory and Total Quality: Improving Research and Practice Through Theory Development," *Academy of Management Review*, 1994, Vol. 19, No. 3, pp. 392–418.

24 See "Porsche Figures Out What Americans Want," *USA Today*, July 10, 2017, www.usatoday.com on June 9, 2020.

25 Edward E. Lawler, "Total Quality Management and Employee Involvement: Are They Compatible?" *Academy of Management Executive*, 1994, Vol. 8, No. 1, pp. 68–79.

26 Jeremy Main, "How to Steal the Best Ideas Around," *Fortune*, www.fortune.com on June 9, 2020.

27 See James Brian Quinn, "Strategic Outsourcing: Leveraging Knowledge Capabilities," *Sloan Management Review*, Summer 1999, pp. 8–22.

28 Mark Tatge, "Global Gamble," *Forbes*, April 17, 2006, www.forbes.com on June 9, 2020.

29 Thomas Robertson, "How to Reduce Market Penetration Cycle Times," *Sloan Management Review*, Fall 1993, pp. 87–96.

30 "Speed Demons," *Bloomberg Businessweek*, March 4, 2016, www.bloomberg.com on June 9, 2020.

31 "Ford Does Fast Updates," *USA Today*, September 20, 2015, www.usatoday.com on June 9, 2020.

32 Paula C. Morrow, "The Measurement of TQM Principles and Work-Related Outcomes," *Journal of Organizational Behavior*, July 1997, Vol. 18, No. 4, pp. 363–376.

33 John W. Kendrick, *Understanding Productivity: An Introduction to the Dynamics of Productivity Change* (Baltimore, MD: Johns Hopkins University Press, 1977).

34 "Study: USA Losing Competitive Edge," *USA Today*, May 15, 2014, www.usatoday.com on June 9, 2020.

35 "Why the Productivity Revolution Will Spread," *Bloomberg Businessweek*, February 28, 2017, www.bloomberg.com on June 9, 2020.

36 Michael van Biema and Bruce Greenwald, "Managing Our Way to Higher Service-Sector Productivity," *Harvard Business Review*, July–August 1997, pp. 87–98.

Name Index

Page numbers followed by "*f*" refer to figure respectively.

Organizational & Product Index

Subject Index

Page numbers followed by "*f*" and "*t*" refer to figure, and table respectively.